AUDITING
EDP
SYSTEMS

AUInTING
EDP
SYSTEMS

Second Edition

Donald A. Watne
Peter B. B. Turney

Portland State University

 Prentice-Hall International, Inc.

ISBN 0-13-052986-9

Printed in the United States of America

10 9 8 9 6 5 4 3 2 1

ISBN 0-13-052986-9

Prentice-Hall International (UK) Limited, *London*
Prentice-Hall of Australia Pty. Limited, *Sydney*
Prentice-Hall Canada Inc., *Toronto*
Prentice-Hall Hispanoamericana, S.A., *Mexico*
Prentice-Hall of India Private Limited, *New Delhi*
Prentice-Hall of Japan, Inc., *Tokyo*
Simon & Schuster Asia Pte. Ltd., *Singapore*
Editora Prentice-Hall do Brasil, Ltda., *Rio de Janeiro*
Prentice-Hall, Inc., *Englewood Cliffs, New Jersey*

CONTENTS

Preface   **xi**

PART I   INTRODUCTION

Chapter 1
Auditing and EPD   1

Historical Development of Data Processing and Its Effect on
   Auditing   3
Auditing Skills Dilemma: Auditor Versus Computer Technician   15
EDP Controls   17
   Summary   18
   Review Questions   18

PART II   COMPUTER AUDITING: A CONCEPTUAL FOUNDATION

Chapter 2
EDP Concepts   **20**

Overview of Computers   21
Overview of Business Data Processing   30
Overview of Storage Concepts   37
Overview of Input and Processing Methods   45
Data Communication Devices   51
Data Communication Concepts   55
Small Computer Systems   57
Data-Base Systems   59
Distributed Data Processing Systems   63
   Summary   67
   Review Questions   68
   Objective Questions   70
   Cases and Exercises   73

Chapter 3
Analytical Tools: Flowcharting and Decision Tables　　**75**

Flowcharting　76
Decision Logic Tables　88
Other Analytical Tools　97
　　Summary　99
　　Review Questions　99
　　Objective Questions　101
　　Cases and Exercises　102

Chapter 4
Auditing Concepts　　**106**

Auditing Concepts　107
Auditor's Assessment of Control Risk　111
Effects of EDP on the Auditor's Assessment of Control Risk　115
Substantive Testing: The Collection of Sufficient Competent
　Evidential Matter　123
Dual-Purpose Testing in Computer Auditing　125
Role of Computer Auditors and the Computer in Performing Tests of
　Controls and Substantive Tests　126
Which? Revisited—Text Taxonomy for Computer-Aided
　Techniques　132
　　Summary　132
　　Review Questions　134
　　Objective Questions　136
　　Cases and Exercises　137

PART III INTERNAL CONTROL STRUCTURE

Chapter 5
Organization Controls, Personnel Practices,
and Standard Operating Procedures　　**143**

Segregation of EDP and User Functions　145
Segregation of Functions Within the EDP Department　149
Responsibility for Control　158
Personnel Practices　161
Standard Operating Procedures　165
　　Summary　167
　　Appendix Lava Butte, Inc.: Company Description, and

Organization Controls, Personnel Practices, and Standard
Operating Procedures Questionnaire   168
Review Questions   174
Objective Questions   175
Cases and Exercises   176

Chapter 6
Systems Development and Documentation Controls   **185**

Auditor's Role in Systems Development   187
Systems Development Controls   188
Systems Documentation Standards   206
Adequate Systems Documentation Controls   212
Software Aids to Doumentation   213
   Summary   214
   Appendix   Lava Butte, Inc.: Systems Development and
      Documentation Controls Questionnaire   215
   Review Questions   218
   Objective Questions   219
   Cases and Exercises   220

Chapter 7
Hardware and Systems Software Controls   **232**

Equipment Failure as a Source of Error   235
Data Communications as a Source of Error   236
Hardware Controls   237
Systems Software Controls   247
   Summary   256
   Appendix   Lava Butte, Inc.: Hardware and Systems Software
      Controls Questionnaire   257
   Review Questions   260
   Objective Questions   260
   Cases and Exercises   262

Chapter 8
System Security Controls   **264**

Audit Significance of System Security Controls   266
Controls That Provide a Secure System   267
Controls for Detecting Failures in System Security   279
Controls for Recovery from System Security Failures   282
   Summary   289

Appendix Lava Butte, Inc.: System Security Controls
Questionnaire 290
Review Questions 291
Objective Questions 292
Cases and Exercises 293

Chapter 9
Data Capture and Batch Data Entry Controls 304

Controls Methodology 305
Audit Trail 310
Data Capture Controls 312
Batch Data Entry Controls 317
Summary 330
Appendix Lava Butte, Inc.: Data Capture and Batch Data Entry
Controls Questionnaire and Flowcharts for Weekly
Payroll System 332
Review Questions 343
Objective Questions 344
Cases and Exercises 345

Chapter 10
On-Line Entry, Processing, and Output Controls 352

On-Line Entry Controls 353
Processing Controls 357
Output Controls 367
Summary 371
Appendix Lava Butte, Inc.: Sales Order Entry and Batch Processing
of Orders and Shipments 374
Review Questions 381
Objective Questions 381
Cases and Exercises 384

PART IV AUDITING EDP SYSTEMS

Chapter 11
Auditing Computer Programs 393

Tests of Controls and Substantive Testing 394
Dual-Purpose Testing 412
Summary 413

Review Questions   413
Objective Questions   414
Cases and Exercises   415

Chapter 12
Auditing Computer Files and Data Bases   **421**

Tests of Controls and Substantive Testing   422
Dual-Purpose Testing   435
    Summary   436
    Review Questions   437
    Objective Questions   438
    Cases and Exercises   439

Chapter 13
Auditing Computer Processing: General Concepts   **445**

Integration of Parts of the Computer Processing System:
    Nonprocessing of Data   447
Integration of Types of Tests   452
    Summary   459
    Appendix   Lava Butte, Inc.: Auditing Computer Processing in a
        Complex System Environment   460
    Review Questions   474
    Objective Questions   475
    Cases and Exercises   476

Chapter 14
Auditing Computer Processing: User-Controlled Systems   **496**

Control and Audit Problems in User-Controlled Systems   497
Controls in a User-Controlled Systems Environment   500
Auditing User-Controlled Computer Systems   509
    Summary   512
    Review Questions   513
    Objective Questions   514
    Cases and Exercises   515

Chapter 15
Auditing Computer Processing: Third-Party Systems   517

Third-Party System Characteristics   518
Controls in a Third-Party System Environment   521
Auditing Third-Party Systems   528
   Summary   531
   Review Questions   532
   Objective Questions   533
   Cases and Exercises   534

Chapter 16
Auditing Computer Processing: Expert Systems   547

Basic Concepts and Terminology of Expert Systems   548
Expert Systems as a Tool of the Auditor   553
Expert Systems as a Target of the Audit   555
   Summary   560
   Review Questions   561
   Objective Questions   561
   Cases and Exercises   562

Index   565

PREFACE

The first edition of *Auditing EDP Systems* was written with one overriding objective in mind: to create a textbook that would be teachable by auditing professors and usable by auditing students and practitioners without sacrificing quality and depth. The adoption of our text by colleges in ten different countries around the world and by a Big 8 CPA firm for internal training at the national level of their EDP auditors indicates that we have been successful in our objective and that we have filled an important eduational need.

The second edition of *Auditing EDP Systems* continues to differ from the other EDP auditing materials that are available. It is a full-blown textbook with questions, cases, and exercises at the end of each chapter, and an *Instructor's Manual* with comprehensive solutions. Many other texts in this field have few, if any, problem materials and some are more suitable for reference than for teaching purposes. *Auditing EDP Systems* follows auditing methodology quite closely and uses auditing terminology wherever possible. In contrast, some other texts follow a strong systems orientation that makes them difficult for auditing professors, students, and practitioners to use. Finally, *Auditing EDP Systems* is fully consistent with current auditing standards, including the new methodology and terminology introduced by SAS No. 55, Au 319, "Consideration of the Internal Control Structure in a Financial Statement Audit." While incorporating current auditing standards, it goes far beyond these standards in depth and consideration of systems application.

Auditing EDP Systems was written primarily for auditing professors, students, and practitioners. Auditing professors with only a limited background in EDP should have no problem teaching with this text. Descriptions of EDP concepts are clear, and we avoid EDP jargon wherever possible. For the same reasons, students and practitioners with a limited background in EDP should also have no trouble with the text. We do expect, however, that students will have had at least one course in auditing and at least one in computer concepts. A knowledge of programming is not required, although some knowledge would be helpful. For students, practitioners, and teachers who feel weak in either the auditing area or the EDP area, we have provided conceptual foundation chapters in Part II of the book.

The focus of the book is on the audit of computerized accounting systems as part of the audit of the financial statements. Accordingly, the book covers the control risk assessment procedures that the auditor performs on computerized systems in meeting objectives relating to the audit of financial statements. There are references to the standards of the American Institute of Certified Public Accountants. Questions and exercises at the end of the chapters include material from the examinations given by the Institute of Internal Auditors and the American Institute of Certified Public Accountants.

The book, however, contains a wealth of material that can be used for many purposes. Internal auditors and controllers, for example, will find valuable information on management as well as accounting controls. Management information system specialists will find in-depth coverage of controls and system-testing techniques and should gain valuable insight into the way that auditors function.

Organization of the Book

This book is divided into four parts. Part I contains a single introductory chapter. This chapter provides a brief overview of computer development, software development, and the impact both of these have had on the practice of auditing.

Part II, Computer Auditing: A Conceptual Foundation, provides an overview of computers and data processing, storage concepts, input and processing methods, analytical tools such as flowcharting and decision tables, auditing standards and concepts, and computer-auditing concepts. The purpose of this part is to review basic concepts with which the auditor should be familiar.

Part III, Internal Control Structure, provides a comprehensive coverage of the auditor's assessment of control risk in EDP systems. It describes the way the auditor performs procedures to gain an understanding of the internal control structure and to test the controls. It also describes the general and application controls found in EDP systems and the methods used to assess risk for these controls.

Part IV, Auditing EDP Systems, deals with computer and other techniques available to the auditor for testing computer programs, files, and processing. The techniques appropriate for auditing programs or files are covered in Chapters 11 and 12, respectively. The auditing of computer processing is discussed in four chapters. General concepts are presented in Chapter 13. In Chapter 14 we discuss the audit of user-controlled systems. The auditing of third-party systems is the topic of Chapter 15. Expert systems can be both a tool to aid the auditor and they can be audited as a target of the audit; these subjects are covered in Chapter 16.

Using the Book

The book is organized to provide maximum flexibility to the adopter. Syllabuses can be tailored to fit quarter or semester courses, students of different backgrounds, and the particular interests of the instructor or student. There are also sufficient cases and exercises in each chapter, ranging from easy to difficult, to permit the book to be used at different levels of intensity. The *Instructor's Manual* contains sample course syllabuses to fit each of these alternatives.

The book can be used in both quarter and semester courses by changing the selection of chapters to be covered. Courses taught on a quarter basis, for example, can cover the six chapters included in Part III and the first three chapters of Part IV. Courses taught on a semester basis can cover all twelve chapters in Parts III and IV.

This book is intended mainly for fourth-year undergraduate students or for graduate students who have had one auditing course and one EDP course. A course using the book, however, can be modified to suit the students' background. Courses containing students with a weak background in auditing and computer systems should cover the conceptual foundation chapters in Part II. Courses containing students with a strong background in these areas may wish to skip Part II. We recommend at a minimum, however, that the students be required to skim these chapters. This recommendation is based on our experience at Portland State University where our students have a strong background in these areas. They take three courses in computers and two in auditing before taking computer auditing. We still assign Part II for review because most students claim they cannot remember the material or do not undertand how it fits into computer auditing. Both the professor and the student are delighted to have Part II in the book; it eliminates the need for supplementary materials or extensive research.

The book contains numerous review questions, objective questions, cases, and exercises at the end of each chapter. This problem material provides the instructor and student with opportunities ranging from review to in-depth study. The review questions are designed for independent study or class discussion. The answers to these questions test chapter comprehension. The cases and exercises provide many opportunities to apply the chapter concepts to problem situations and to test the student's analytical skills. Some of the cases in Part III are based on the Lava Butte case, which appears as an appendix in each of the six chapters in Part III. This case describes a data processing system in a medium-size company; illustrates the use of internal control questionnaires, flowcharts, and other documentation; provides a summary of the controls covered in each chapter; and serves as a rich source of material for the exercises and cases.

Acknowledgements

Writing the second edition took less time than the first, but it was still a major commitment over a long period of time. We would certainly not have been successful without the help of many individuals. Our families, friends, and colleagues have all provided invaluable support, encouragement, patience, and understanding.

We would like to thank Portland State University for providing secretarial support and release time. Kathy Grove typed the revisions to the manuscript for this edition. She did as outstanding a job on the revisions as she did on the first edition. Thank you, Kathy. Thanks are due to all the people at Prentice-Hall who helped to make the book a quality product. We want to thank Frederick L. Neumann, Richard Boland, and Jeffrey Johnson of the University of Illinois, the American Institute of Certified Public Accountants, and the Institute of Internal Auditors for permission to reproduce cases, questions, and other materials. We also want to thank Don Henry and Jeri Flom for help in developing case and other material.

Our reviewers made outstanding contributions. We are grateful to Raymond N. Johnson, Portland State University; James K. Loebbecke, University of Utah; and Frederick L. Neumann.

Donald A. Watne
Peter B. B. Turney

AUDITING
EDP
SYSTEMS

Chapter 1
AUDITING AND EDP

Learning Objectives

After completing this chapter, the reader should be able to:

1. Identify major changes that have occurred in computer hardware and how they have affected auditing.

2. Understand major changes that have occurred in computer software and how they have affected auditing.

3. Know major changes that have occurred in computer location and how they have affected auditing.

4. Identify major changes that have occurred in the way that auditors have approached the audit of the computer.

5. Understand the response the auditing profession has made to the increasing sophistication of computers and the demand for auditing skills placed on the auditor.

According to the first general standard of the ten generally accepted auditing standards (GAAS) issued by the American Institute of Certified Public Accountants (AICPA):

> The examination is to be performed by a person or persons having adequate technical training and proficiency as an auditor.[1]

In the area of electronic data processing (EDP), specific demands as to expertise have been placed on the auditor. The second standard of field-work of GAAS of the AICPA specifies a general requirement:

> A sufficient understanding of the internal control structure is to be obtained to plan the audit and to determine the nature, timing, and extent of tests to be performed.[2]

To obtain this understanding, a more specific set of requirements is set forth in the auditing interpretation on assessing control risk.[3] The auditor must:

> consider . . . the complexity and sophistication of the entity's operations and systems, including whether the method of controlling data processing is based on manual procedures independent of the computer or is highly dependent on computerized controls. As an entity's operations and systems become more complex and sophisticated, it may be necessary to devote more attention to internal control structure elements to obtain the understanding of them that is necessary to design effective substantive tests.[4]

Furthermore:

> The auditor should obtain sufficient knowledge of the accounting system to understand . . . the accounting processing involved from the initiation of a transaction to its inclusion in the financial statements, including how the computer is used to process data.[5]

These specific demands for technical expertise are a reaction of the auditing profession to the utilization of computers for the processing of accounting data. How did the profession arrive at its present state of technical expertise requirements with respect to EDP? What is the auditor

---

[1] *Statement on Auditing Standards (SAS) No. 1,* AU Sec. 150.02.

[2] Ibid.

[3] Unless otherwise stated, our use of the term *standards* refers to the *Statements on Auditing Standards.* Technically, these standards are interpretations of the generally accepted auditing standards.

[4] *SAS No. 55,* AU sec. 319.19.

[5] *SAS No. 55,* AU Sec. 319.21.

expected to know about auditing EDP systems? Are the standards to which the EDP auditor is accountable different from those that must be adhered to by other auditors?

In this chapter we discuss the impact that EDP has had on auditing. Our discussion focuses on three main topics: (1) a historical review of the development of data processing and its effect on auditing methodology; (2) the types of skills that the computer auditor must possess to conduct the audit effectively and efficiently; and (3) the EDP controls that help ensure the reliability and accuracy of processing.

This chapter emphasizes that additional demands have been placed on the auditor solely because of EDP technology. To satisfy these demands, the computer auditor must acquire an understanding of computer concepts, control techniques, and auditing methodology not needed by the auditor of manual or mechanical systems.

HISTORICAL DEVELOPMENT OF DATA PROCESSING AND ITS EFFECT ON AUDITING

As methods for the processing of accounting data have changed, auditors have been forced to change their approach to auditing. These changes in processing include changes in the hardware or equipment used in processing, in the software used to manage the tasks performed by the hardware, and in the location of the data processing equipment. Each of these changes has had a significant effect on auditing.

Changes in Hardware

Changes in hardware can be traced from manual to mechanical to EDP systems. EDP system changes include changes from the first to the second, third, and subsequent generations of computer systems; teleprocessing and real-time systems; and minicomputers and microcomputers.

Manual Systems

Manual systems are those in which source documents are posted by hand to sales, cash receipts, and other types of journals. The totals from the journals are then hand-posted to the general ledger. Reports are then manually prepared from the general ledger or a working trial balance taken from the general ledger.

With manual systems, the auditor can visually inspect the documents, journals, ledgers, and reports in the performance of testing. Transactions can readily be traced from source document to journal, to general ledger, to printed reports, and vice versa. Subsidiary ledgers can be footed and the totals can be compared with control accounts. This entire process can also be visually observed by the auditor to determine whether the proper procedures are being followed.

Mechanical Systems

Mechanical systems utilize data processing equipment such as bookkeeping machines and unit record equipment. Bookkeeping machines, for example, are used to post transactions to subsidiary ledgers, such as contracts receivable, while preparing a journal copy of the posting. They are also used to post entries to general ledgers where each account is a separate record inserted into the machine. Reports are then manually prepared from the machine-maintained records.

Unit record equipment, on the other hand, processes punched cards. All transactions, journals, and ledgers are on punched cards. To update an account, for example, an account card containing the old balance is read, the transaction card is read, and a new account card is punched with the new balance. Reports are then prepared by reading and printing the amounts on the updated account balance cards.

With mechanical systems, the auditing process becomes slightly more complex than with manual systems. With both bookkeeping and unit record equipment, the basic arithmetic operations of posting debits and credits are under machine control. Auditors must understand this machine control if they wish to determine whether these posting operations have been performed correctly.

The type of tracing and visual observation possible with manual systems can also be done with mechanical systems, but with more difficulty. With bookkeeping machines, the auditor can trace transactions to the machine-prepared journals, ledgers, and so on, to the reports, and vice versa. With unit record equipment, this tracing can still be done, but the auditor must be able to read the punched cards that constitute the transactions, journals, and ledgers. Visual observation is more difficult because of the speed with which the equipment operates. Observing the posting of ledgers on a bookkeeping machine is not too difficult, but unit record equipment operating at normal speed may process transactions too rapidly for satisfactory observation of the procedures followed. This equipment, however, can be slowed down to where each read, punch, tabulate, print, or other activity can be followed.

EDP Systems

First Generation of Computers.   The installation of EDP first-generation systems created new auditing problems and compounded the problems that had been introduced with the development of mechanical systems.

These new auditing problems resulted from the use of electronics for data processing, the internal storage of data and procedures, the ease of changing internally stored data and procedures, and the disappearance of the audit trail.

First-generation computers were characterized by vacuum tubes. These computers were enormous, and several rooms of hardware were required to handle the processing done today by units no larger than a typewriter with storage and other devices all sitting easily on top of a desk. The vacuum tubes created tremendous heat and required large air-conditioning capacity. The computers and related environmental controls were expensive.

A major auditing problem introduced by computers is the use of electronics for data processing. The difficulties encountered by the auditor in physically observing the accounting process in mechanical systems, because of the speed with which the processing takes place, become almost insurmountable with computers. Even slowing down the system, a feature available for debugging on some computers, may be of no value to the auditor because of an inability to understand the electronic pulses or read information stored on an electronic medium.

A second major problem introduced by computers is the internal storage of both data and programs. *Internal storage* is the representation of information in electronic form inside the computer. With this internalization, the auditor is no longer able to observe the processing of data to determine whether the proper procedures are being used. Furthermore, as the data disappear into the machine, the auditor loses his or her ability to trace directly from source documents through to reports or back from the reports to the source documents.

A third major problem introduced by computers is that the procedures for processing the data, the program, can be changed without the auditor's knowledge. Such changes can occur through console intervention, insertion of malicious code through a card reader or terminal, or even code that modifies itself while the program is running and then erases all trace of the modification. The procedures that the auditor believes are being performed to process data may not be used at all.

A fourth major problem introduced by computers is the partial elimination or disappearance of the audit trail. *Audit trail* can be defined as those documents, records, journals, ledgers, magnetic medium transaction and master files, and accounting reports that enable an auditor to trace a transaction from source document to summarized total in an accounting report, or vice versa. In addition to not being able to trace data through the computer as the data disappear inside, the auditor may not be able to trace around the computer. This can be caused by such factors as elimination of source documents as data are being entered directly into the system, elimination of intermediate records (e.g., transactions listings and journals) as transactions are being posted directly to master files, and elimination of reports as information is being supplied on an inquiry basis only.

Second and Third Generations of Computers. The installation of second- and third-generation computer systems has continued the plague of auditing problems introduced with first-generation computers. These advances in computer systems have resulted in a proliferation of hardware and software, which has created additional auditing problems.

Second-generation computers were characterized by transistors in place of vacuum tubes. The transistors resulted in several changes. The computers no longer created as much heat, and air-conditioning requirements were considerably reduced. The transistors were less expensive than vacuum tubes, more reliable, and faster. Because the transistors were smaller than tubes, more capacity could be squeezed into a given space. These changes significantly reduced the cost of computers.

Third-generation computers are characterized by the use of solid-state technology and integrated circuits. The changes initiated with transistors continued with the third generation. Computers became more reliable, faster, and cheaper. Their computing capacity increased considerably. Their ability to communicate with each other enabled large networks of computers to be created.

A major problem caused by the proliferation of hardware and software is the level of knowledge required. The computer-auditing specialist must study constantly to be able to operate new computers and old or new computers with new software. This knowledge is also required simply to be able to communicate with data processing personnel as new terminology emerges.

Another problem is the ability of third-generation computers to process several applications simultaneously, which is called *multiprogramming*. Such an ability, discussed in greater detail later under "Changes in Software," creates a problem for the auditor because a program and a set of files can be modified during data processing by another program. This modification may be unauthorized and may be done without the auditor's being aware of it.

Still another problem is the ability of third-generation computers to communicate with each other using teleprocessing. This facility creates a problem because changes to programs and files can be made from thousands of miles away.

Subsequent Generations of Computers. The move to fourth-generation computers did not introduce any unique problems for the EDP auditor. The focus of this generation of computers was primarily on increasing speed and storage capacity. Fourth-generation computers are character-ized by the use of large-scale and very-large-scale integrated circuits. These systems continue the trend toward smaller computers through the miniaturization provided by the new circuitry.

The fifth generation of computers is likely to provide the biggest challenge to EDP auditors of all the computer generations. The fifth gen-eration is characterized by artificial intelligence (AI). A system that is constantly learning and modifying itself, perhaps going through several iterations during just one auditing period, creates problems that are mind-boggling.

Some of these issues are addressed in the last chapter on expert sys-tems. Expert systems, however, introduce just a subset of the problems the AI auditor is likely to encounter. These problems are the subject of on-going auditing research.

Teleprocessing and Real-Time Systems

Teleprocessing is the processing of accounting data by transmitting those data over a communications channel, such as telephone lines, micro-wave, or satellite. It permits data to be submitted to a computer from a terminal in one location and to be posted to accounts on files in a second location, with the results being printed in a third location.

A major problem created by teleprocessing capabilities is the poten-tial loss of assets from unauthorized access to programs and files. Termi-nals in the basements or garages of private residences, for example, have been used in instruct computers to send cash or inventory to the terminal operator. The auditor must evaluate the ability of teleprocessing systems to resist such unauthorized access to ensure that losses have not oc-curred.

The communications capabilities of teleprocessing have facilitated the development of real-time systems where the input, processing, and output devices are separated by considerable distance. Real-time systems update account balances immediately upon entering the data into the systems. This means that *before* the auditor has finished reading and add-ing the balances in accounts receivable subsidiary ledgers with the aid of the computer, some of the balances may already have been changed. Auditing such systems can be a challenging task.

Minicomputers and Microcomputers

Another advance in hardware technology that has created problems for the auditor is the development and utilization of hundreds of thousands of minicomputers and microcomputers. Minicomputers and microcom-puters are very small computers that rival first-, second-, and even some physically large third-generation systems in computer power. The problems caused by these systems include the following:

1. The hardware often does not contain the error-checking and correcting routines built into physically larger systems. The auditor does not have the same level of assurance, therefore, that the results of processing are accurate.

2. The programs supplied with the systems for payroll, accounts receivable, and other applications may not contain the controls for error detection that the auditor has come to expect with the programs for physically larger systems.

3. Clients are sold computers and programs as though they were typewriters, with a minimal amount of instruction and on the assumption that the client will be able to make them work. Some clients are never able to get some programs to function at all and others only partially. The result can be chaos in the accounting system and loss of relevant data.

Changes in Software

Changes in hardware have been accompanied by changes in software. Some of the software changes have created problems for the auditor; others have been welcomed. These software changes have occurred in the areas of languages, applications, operating systems, and data-base management systems.

Languages

The earliest computers required that the programmer submit instructions in a format that the computer could understand directly, without any additional processing. Such programs are referred to as *machine-language* programs. These programs are difficult for humans to write and read. Consequently, languages were developed that were easier for both the programmer and the auditor to write and read. These new languages, however, created some new problems for the auditor.

The languages that followed machine-level languages are referred to an assembler and higher-level languages. The computer cannot process the instructions in these languages directly. They must first be converted into a machine language by programs called *assemblers* or *compilers*. The input to the assembler or compiler is referred to as *source code*. The output is called *object code*.

Assembler and higher-level languages make the programmer's and auditor's jobs easier because programs can be written much faster with fewer errors. If the auditor needs a program to print the names and balances in an accounts payable file, for example, it can be written in a fraction of the time required to write in machine-level language. Chances are that it will probably run on the first attempt.

Assembler and higher-level languages, however, also create problems for the auditor. A major problem is the fact that the source code listing provided to the auditor may not agree with the object code used by the computer for processing. The auditor may be satisfied that the processing is accurate based on the source code without realizing that the program does not function that way at all. The source code used to create the object code actually used by the computer may never be made available to the auditor.

Another problem created by the development of assembler and higher-level languages is that the numerous languages, with multiple versions of some of them, place extraordinary burdens on the auditor who has to understand and work with them. The computer-auditing specialist may need to understand half a dozen to a dozen languages and be familiar with different versions of each one.

Applications

Application software is a program or set of programs for performing the processing of such tasks as payroll preparation, invoicing and updating of accounts receivable, or payment and updating of accounts payable. Such programs are required for any processing that involves instructing the computer as to what to do. Initially written in machine languages, they are now almost exclusively written in higher-level languages. The increasing sophistication of these programs is the primary cause of the auditor's problems.

The earliest application programs performed relatively simple tasks, such as the printing of an invoice, the calculation of payroll and the printing of checks, and the updating of inventory records based on receipts and issues. The auditing of such programs was not always easy, but the simplicity of the tasks usually made them easy to understand and follow.

Some of the application programs running today are the antithesis of simplicity. An example is an application that, upon receipt of an order from a customer, performs the following tasks almost instantaneously:

1. Approval of order based on customer credit limits, amount currently receivable from customer, and back-order file
2. Preparation of packing notice on terminal in warehouse stating quantities of goods to be pulled for shipment and location of those items in warehouse
3. Preparation of shipping documents, packing slips, address labels, and calculation of freight and handling charges
4. Preparation of invoice ready for mailing to customer
5. Updating of perpetual inventory records

6. Preparation of purchase order to restock inventory if level has fallen below reorder point

Determining whether all of these tasks are performed accurately on a system that runs around the clock, seven days a week, switching automatically to a backup system for preventive maintenance, will challenge even the most astute computer auditor.

Operating Systems

Operating systems are programs that manage or supervise all the activities associated with a computer system. They are sometimes called *supervisors, monitors,* or *executive programs.* Operating systems, for example, supervise the movement of application programs and data into internal storage within the computer. Operating systems also schedule jobs on a priority basis, handle all input to and output from reading and writing devices, and perform such specialized functions as sorting records into a particular order.

Operating systems have relieved the application programs of many functions. Before the development of operating systems, for example, an application program written in a machine language had to be concerned with all the instructions necessary to add two numbers together. This could include selecting the specific storage locations within the computer for the two numbers and the results of the addition. Now all the application program has to do is say, "Add 'Old Quantity' to 'Quantity Received' and place result in 'New Quantity.'" The operating system takes over and supervises finding the quantities to be added, moving them to certain storage locations, performing the addition, and placing the results in another storage location.

The development and utilization of operating systems have created both benefits and problems for the auditor. The benefits are the same as those realized by programmers. The auditor's job is easier because the operating system does many of the tedious tasks that previously had to be performed manually. Problems are created, however, because individuals with access to the operating system and the knowledge to change it can modify the processing of application programs or the contents of files without changing the application program. The auditor has to be concerned, therefore, with unauthorized changes to the operating system as well as unauthorized application program changes.

Data-Base Management Systems

A *data base* is a collection of data files containing an organization's records. Examples of records are an earnings record for each employee and an accounts receivable subsidiary ledger for each customer. Examples of files are all the earnings records for all employees and all the accounts receivable subsidiary ledgers for all customers. An example of a data base would be the payroll and accounts receivable files.

A *data-base management system* (DBMS) is the software used to control input to the files, changes in the files, and abstraction of information from the files. Perhaps the major function of such a system, however, is the linking together of various files. A bank data base can be used to illustrate such a system. In responding to a request for a loan, a lending officer wants to know what relationships that customer has with the bank. With a data-base management system, the officer could enter the customer's name, social security number, or some other identifier into a terminal and request a display of all banking relationships of that customer. The identifier is used by the system to link all the customer files together and may respond with

- Checking account balance(s) from the demand deposit accounting files
- Time deposit balances from the passbook savings and certificate-of-deposit files
- Loan payable balances from the real estate loan, installment consumer loan, and commercial loan files
- Information on loans where the customer is a guarantor

Without such a system, banking personnel have to submit separate inquiries to each file that may show a customer relationship. In addition, if the customer changes his or her address and the bank does not have a DBMS, each file has to be changed. With a DBMS, only one change need be submitted.

The benefit of the DBMS in reducing redundancies in the submission of data and managing input to the files, changes in them, and output from them can be contrasted with the problem such a system creates for the auditor. The benefit is the storage area freed by eliminating redundancies which can be used for additional files. The problem is that the redundancies on which the auditor relied in the past to verify the accuracy of recorded data are eliminated. The auditor can no longer compare the contents of two files to determine whether one of them contains an error. WIth DBMS, the auditor must instead concentrate on determining the system's reliability.

Data-base management systems introduce other problems as well. One is the additional education and knowledge required of the auditor who works with such systems. Another is the difficulty of tracing transactions forward and backward through these systems.

Changes in Location: Responsibility and Site

Changes in the location of computers have also increased the complexity of auditing them. Computers were originally used in the processing primarily of accounting data. To serve this need, they were located within and under the control of the accounting department. Since then the use of computers has expanded to include a wide range of management and operational tasks. As a result, the responsibility for computers has in many companies been taken away from accounting and given to a separate information systems group. In addition, the computers are no longer located solely in the accounting department but have been moved to other sites both inside and outside the organization.

Accounting Department

The first installation of a computer in an organization often follows an earlier installation of a bookkeeping machine in an accounting department. The computer may be acquired simply to handle the ever-increasing volume of work more efficiently.

The auditor may be comfortable with the tasks performed by the computer in such a situation, even though uneasy about the computer itself, because the tasks are the familiar applications. These applications may include payroll, inventory, accounts receivable, and accounts payable. The problems encountered are those discussed earlier in conjunction with hardware and software in general.

Information Systems Group

As mentioned earlier, a locational change has paralleled the increasing sophistication of computers—the system has been moved out of the accounting department. As the marketing, production, and personnel functions demand to share the capability of EDP systems, these systems are often placed under the control of an information systems group. This group is expected to have a broader perspective on how the computer can serve these additional functions, management purposes, and operations, along with accounting.

Locating the computer in an information systems group and using it for management and operational purposes may create new problems for the auditor. At the same time, however, it may also enhance control. A major problem is that these new applications may tie in with and affect the basic accounting applications. The auditor may therefore have to extend the scope of the audit to include components of these nonaccounting applications. Another problem is that the auditor may have to travel extensively to collect evidence because the source documents no longer flow to the accounting department. They may be retained instead in the originating operating departments. The only input received by the accounting department may be an electronic or magnetic abstract of the data from the source documents. Control is enhanced through the separation of functions occurring as custody of the computer is separated from the accounting department user.

Service Bureaus and Time Sharing

Another locational change is the movement of computer facilities to or from an independent service bureau or time-sharing system. Independent service bureaus or time-sharing systems are organizations separate from the companies whose data they process. They may be used because they are cheaper than an in-house installation or because the company does not want to devote space and management energy to an in-house installation.

Time-sharing systems differ from service bureaus in the following way. Service bureaus often pick up source documents from a customer, convert them to machine-readable form, process the data, print the results, and then deliver the output back to the customer's office. Time-sharing systems receive data that have been entered on a terminal in the customer's office and transmitted via a data communication system. The data are processed and the results are transmitted back over the data communication system to be printed on the client's terminal. All of this takes place so fast that the client has the impression that he or she is the only user being served when in fact hundreds of users are being served simultaneously.

Service bureaus and time-sharing systems create various problems for the auditor. One problem may be inaccessibility to programs, files, and data processing personnel. These independent organizations are separate legal entities and often refuse admission to the auditor for testing programs and files. Another problem is the potential for changes in the data sent to the computer and output received from it. Additional testing is required to determine the likelihood of such changes and their potential effect.

Changes in Auditing

Changes in hardware, software, and location have changed the conceptual approach to auditing. An early approach consisted of essentially ignoring the computer, treating it as a black box, and auditing around it. The increasing sophistication of computers and auditors, however, has since led to computers being used in two ways: (1) as a tool of the auditor aiding in the performance of the audit, such as printing confirmation requests, and (2) as the target of the audit where data are submitted to the computer and the results are analyzed for processing reliability and accuracy of the computer program.

Auditing around the Computer

The auditors' first response to the computers was to treat them as if they were mechanical bookkeeping systems. With the bookkeeping systems, auditors had not been concerned with the internal mechanics of how the machines posted ledgers or accounts. They could readily see the old balance, add or subtract the postings as appropriate, and compare the new balance with the correct amount computed manually. The audit trail from source documents to machine-posted records was easy to follow. The machines were essentially ignored.

The first computers were also essentially ignored by the auditors. They were treated as a black box that accepted input and produced output. Auditors traced transactions to the black box and then picked up the trail on the other side by examining printouts. The auditor was *auditing around the computer.*

Auditing with the Computer

Using the computer as a tool of the auditor in performing such tasks as printing confirmations is referred to as *auditing with the computer.* Auditors utilized computers to perform these tasks as readily as their clients utilized them to process accounting data. In addition to printing confirmations, auditors put computers to work footing subsidiary ledgers on magnetic tape or disk, calculating amounts such as depreciation, comparing the contents of two files, and examining files for missing amounts such as customers' credit limits.

To facilitate using the computer as an audit tool, some firms developed generalized audit software. Such software performs the types of tasks mentioned above on the computer systems of numerous different clients. Auditing with the computer is more efficient with such software because separate programs do not have to be written for each client.

Auditing through the Computer

The sophistication of computers eventually reached the point where auditors could no longer audit around the system. They were forced to treat the computer as the target of the audit and audit "through it." *Auditing through the computer* requires that the auditor submit data to the computer for processing. The results are then analyzed for the processing reliability and accuracy of the computer program. Technological and other developments that required this approach include the following:

- On-line data entry. In some systems, customer orders are received by phone and entered directly into the system with cathode-ray tube input devices. No source documents are created. The auditor cannot trace from source documents to output. The auditor is forced to enter the system to determine the reliability and accuracy of controls and processing.
- Elimination or reduction of printouts. With on-line direct inquiry and reports prepared only on an exception basis, printouts may not be available to trace transactions. The auditor is again forced to enter the system to determine the accuracy of processing and contents of files.

- Real-time file updating. With real-time file updating, transactions are posted as soon as they occur. A printout supplied to the auditor showing the content of such files may not be accurate even for an instant. This is because by the time the printer is halfway through the file listing balances, those at the beginning may already have changed. The auditor is again forced to enter the system to perform the audit.

In addition to technological and other developments that forced the auditor to use the computer system in the performance of the audit, some auditors decided to audit through the system for the following reasons:

- An inability to locate the source documents or printouts because of the filing system used
- An apprehension that the amounts shown on the computer printouts might not agree with the balances actually contained in the computer files

AUDITING SKILLS DILEMMA: AUDITOR VERSUS COMPUTER TECHNICIAN

The increasing sophistication of computers and the demands placed on the auditor to audit them have led to an auditing skills dilemma. Should the computer auditor be required to have a knowledge of computer concepts and processing? Should the computer auditor rely on the skills of an EDP technician as a specialist, just as auditors rely on the skills of actuaries, engineers, and geologists elsewhere? The auditing profession in the United States initially resolved this dilemma by issuing a standard for auditors, *SAS No. 3*, which specified the level of knowledge required of an EDP auditor. This standard required that the auditor acquire the knowledge. Reliance was not to be placed on specialists, as done elsewhere in the audit.

The initial standard was followed by two others which superseded it and modified the philosophy upon which it was based. This modification was accomplished by *SAS No. 43*, which changed the focus of EDP controls evaluation by requiring that such evaluation be an integral part of the audit rather than addressed as a separate component.

This change in focus was reinforced by *SAS No. 55*, which incorporated EDP issues throughout a discussion of the internal control structure. These two standards continue the demand placed on the auditor by *SAS No. 3*—the auditor must have the requisite knowledge to understand the EDP system and not rely on specialists.

The resolution of one dilemma has not resolved another one, however. Should the computer auditor be taken from the ranks of auditing and trained in computer concepts and processing? Should the computer auditor be taken from the ranks of data processing and trained in auditing? Should a team approach be used?

Auditor as Data Processing Technician

The approach that most firms use consists of selecting EDP auditors from the ranks of auditors and training them in computer concepts, control techniques, and auditing. The auditor understands the audit's objective and can readily communicate with other members of the firm because of similarities in education and experience. The auditor, however, may have to devote much time and effort to mastering computer concepts and, initially at least, may experience difficulty in communicating with data processing personnel.

Data Processing Technicians as Auditors

Some firms have not been able to wait until their auditors develop EDP skills. They need those skills immediately. One approach to meet that immediate need has been to hire data processing technicians and train them in the rudiments of auditing. The EDP technicians are able to work with the computers immediately. They have no difficulty communicating with the client's EDP personnel. The supervising auditor, however, may have difficulty communicating the audit's objectives and providing general guidance to an EDP technician who lacks an understanding of what the audit is all about.

Combining the Skills of Auditor and EDP Technician

Teams of auditors and EDP technicians have been created in some firms to combine the skills of the auditors and EDP technicians. The firm is able to draw on the demonstrated skills of both sets of individuals. Such teams often develop excellent working relationships providing a high level of computer-auditing expertise. A significant drawback initially, and sometimes ongoing, is the difficulty team members have in communicating with each other.

Skills Required of the Computer Auditor: A Conceptual Foundation

Auditors trained as EDP technicians, EDP technicians trained as auditors, and teams combining the skills of both need a basic set of skills or conceptual foundation. These skills include auditing concepts and EDP concepts.

Auditing concepts that the computer auditor must understand include an appreciation of the basic objectives of the audit—an assessment of control risk and the collection of evidence to form a basis for an opinion. To accomplish these objectives, the computer auditor performs tests of controls and substantive testing.

The computer auditor must also understand such EDP concepts as the following : (1) systems concepts, which include the types of hardware and software used, the names and functions of personnel who operate computer systems, and the procedures used in such operations; (2) file structures and organization concepts, which include the ways in which data can be organized and stored on and retrieved from a computer system; and (3) techniques for depicting the flow of data through a computer system, which include systems and program flowcharts and decision tables.

Resolution of the Auditing Skills Dilemma

The external auditing profession's response to the auditing skills dilemma was to issue an auditing standard, *SAS No. 3*, which specified the level of knowledge expected of the EDP auditor. The standard also specified some of the procedures that the computer auditor should follow in performing the audit.

The assumption in issuing the standard was that the auditor is expected to acquire the necessary skills. The auditor was not expected to rely on the EDP technician as a specialist, as is the case with actuaries, engineers, and geologists. The EDP technician is not prevented from becoming an auditor, but the orientation is that the computer auditor is primarily an auditor.

EDP CONTROLS

The profession's response to the proliferation of computers and the skills of the auditor to audit them has been the issuance of the three auditing standards discussed previously. The response has also included the development of specific controls to ensure reliable and accurate data processing. The auditor examines controls in two broad categories: user controls and EDP controls.

User controls are those established by departments whose processing is performed by the computer. An example would be a payroll department that manually calculates gross payroll, determines the number of payroll checks to be prepared, and then compares the results of data processing with those totals.

EDP accounting controls consist of general controls and application controls. *General controls* include controls on the organization and operation of the EDP department, controls on the development and implementation of computer programs and changes to them, controls built into the equipment and software by the vendor to ensure processing accuracy, controls to prevent unauthorized access to equipment, and other data and procedural controls such as plans for reconstructing damaged files. *Application controls* include input controls to ensure that accurate data are submitted to the computer, processing controls to ensure that no errors are made in processing data, and output controls to ensure that the output reconciles to the input and is distributed to authorized personnel.

SUMMARY

The methods of processing accounting data have changed in three areas: hardware, software, and location. Hardware changes include moving from manual to mechanical EDP systems, changes from first- to second- and third-generation computer systems, the development of teleprocessing and real-time systems, and minicomputers and microcomputers. Software changes include the development of numerous languages, applications, operating systems, and data-base management systems. Location changes include moving the responsibility for and physical site of computers outside the accounting department.

Changes in the hardware, software, and location of computers have been accompanied by changes in conceptual approaches to auditing. The first approach of auditing around the computer has been followed by auditing with the computer and auditing through the computer.

The auditors' skill level has had to rise with the increasing sophistication of computers. A dilemma has been whether to train auditors as EDP technicians, or vice versa. The profession's response has been to require that auditors meet specific levels of skill. This is in contrast to other audit areas that rely on such specialists as actuaries, engineers, and geologists.

In addition to specifying a skill level, the profession has issued standards to be met in understanding the control structure within which computers operate. This control structure includes user controls and EDP controls. In examining EDP controls, the auditor should evaluate general controls and application controls.

REVIEW QUESTIONS

1–1. What effect did the change from manual and mechanical systems to computers have on auditing?

1–2. What is meant by first-, second-, third-, fourth-, and fifth-generation computers? What effect did each of these generations have on auditing?

1-3. What is meant by teleprocessing and how has it affected auditing?

1-4. How have minicomputers and microcomputers affected auditing?

1-5. Describe each of the following software developments or changes and discuss how they have affected auditing:

    a. Languages

    b. Applications

    c. Operating systems

    d. Data-base management systems

1-6. Why were computers moved out of the control of accounting departments in many organizations? To where were they moved? What was the effect on auditing?

1-7. What effect does the location of a computer in a service bureau of a time-sharing network have on the audit?

1-8. Describe each of the following approaches to computer auditing and give examples:

    a. Auditing around the computer

    b. Auditing with the computer

    c. Auditing through the computer

1-9. Why does training auditors as EDP technicians versus training EDP technicians as auditors present a dilemma? What was the response of the external auditing profession?

1-10. What basic skills are required of the EDP auditor?

1-11. What auditing standards have been issued to guide computer auditors? What are the essential elements of these standards?

Chapter 2
EDP CONCEPTS

Learning Objectives

After completing this chapter, the reader should be able to:

1. Describe the common types of computer equipment encountered by auditors.

2. Understand how the typical business computer operates internally.

3. Know the computer data processing steps necessary to perform the work of an accounting system.

4. Describe how data that are stored on machine-readable computer files are organized.

5. Identify the major methods of input and processing of data and know the impact these different approaches have on the auditor.

6. Specify the types of equipment likely to be found in a data communication system.

7. Describe how data are transmitted over communication lines.

8. State how minicomputers and microcomputers differ from large mainframe computers.

9. Specify the characteristics you would expect to find in data base and distributed data processing systems.

Knowledge of EDP concepts is part of the additional competence required by auditors of computerized accounting systems. Knowledge of EDP concepts enables the auditor to develop an adequate understanding of computerized accounting systems and to select and implement appropriate procedures for the audit of these systems.

The degree of competence in EDP concepts required by the auditor varies according to the type of EDP system, the role of the individual auditor, and the nature of audit procedures. The audit of a simple system, such as a small batch processing system, requires less knowledge than the audit of an advanced on-line/real-time system. Also, not every individual assigned to the audit of an EDP system need have detailed knowledge of EDP concepts, as long as other members of the audit team possess the required competence. Finally, audit procedures vary in the degree of EDP competence they require from the auditor. The observation of computer-room security procedures, for example, requires less knowledge of EDP concepts than does the review of instructions coded in a programming language.

The EDP concepts covered in this chapter provide a foundation for auditing modern computer systems. These computer systems include batch input/batch processing, on-line transaction input via data communications, batch processing in a multiprogramming environment, real-time, and data-base management.

This chapter first provides an overview of computers, business data processing, storage concepts, and input and processing methods. Special topics then follow including data communication devices, data communication concepts, small computer systems, data-base systems, and distributed data processing systems. Expert systems are discussed in Chapter 16. The purpose of this chapter is to review basic EDP concepts with which the auditor should be familiar and to discuss their implications for the auditor. A reader with a strong EDP background may find it sufficient to skim the chapter. A reader with a weak EDP background may find it helpful to supplement this chapter with a standard computer data processing text.

OVERVIEW OF COMPUTERS

This overview of computers describes the distinguishing characteristics of a computer, the two main types of computers, the major computer applications, computer equipment, and the way the computer operates.

Distinguishing Characteristics of a Computer

The auditor is likely to encounter accounting systems with varying degrees of mechanization. A mechanized system, however, is not necessarily a computer system. An electromechanical bookkeeping machine, for example, adds mechanization to accounting functions but is not a computer. A *computer* is an electronic device that stores data and instructions internally, performs tasks based on a set of instructions stored internally, and is able to modify instructions and data without human intervention.

Main Types of Computers

The auditor should be aware that there are two types of computers: digital and analog. The *digital computer* operates by counting. All quantities, whether they be numbers, letters, or symbols, are represented as discrete numbers. The *analog computer* measures continuous electrical or physical quantities such as voltage, temperature, or length.

Accounting applications are generally run on digital computers, but the auditor may still encounter analog measurement. In some systems, the auditor may find an analog computer, such as a process control computer, interfacing with the digital computer used for accounting purposes. Systems that use data communications to transmit data from remote locations will transmit the data in analog form but process the data in the computer in digital form.

Major Computer Applications

Computers can be categorized according to the three major applications: business data processing, scientific computation, and process control.

Business data processing is characterized by large volumes of input and output, but with relatively little computation required. Consequently, business computers feature powerful input and output capabilities.

Scientific computation usually requires considerable computation, but relatively little input and output. Scientific computers are, therefore, designed with powerful computational capabilities.

Process control requires the measurement of process variables such as the mix of chemicals or the thickness of plastic film. Process control is accomplished using digital or analog computers that monitor and act upon the process measurements.

Computer Equipment

The auditor's main focus is on digital computers designed to handle the heavy input and output requirements of business data processing. Business data processing computers typically include the following types of equipment.

Central Processing Unit (CPU). The CPU, or mainframe, is the heart of the computer. It has three functions: internal storage of data and instructions, computation, and maintenance of order and control of activity in the CPU. These three functions are performed by the primary storage unit, arithmetic and logic unit, and control unit, respectively.

Secondary Storage. Secondary, or auxiliary, storage provides supplementary storage for data and instructions not currently required by the CPU. When data or instructions are required for processing, they are copied from secondary to primary storage. Secondary storage permits the storage of data and instructions that far exceed the capacity of primary storage.

Secondary storage differs in the speed at which data can be transferred, the accessibility of data, and the ability to reuse storage capacity. *Punched cards,* for example, provide relatively slow transfer of data, require that data be transferred in a predetermined (sequential) order, and can be written on (punched) only once. In contrast, a *magnetic disk* provides high-speed transfer of data, allows data to be stored in sequential or random order, and can be reused many times.

Input Devices. Input devices are used to read data into primary storage from machine-readable transaction documents, from secondary storage media, or by direct entry of transaction data. Devices that read machine-readable documents include *magnetic ink character readers* that read documents such as checks, and *optical character recognition equipment* that is used extensively to read documents such as utility and phone bills. *Optical mark recognition equipment* is used in applications as varied as payroll and retail sales order entry. Devices that read data from secondary to primary storage include *magnetic tape drives* and *magnetic disk drives.* Data are entered directly into primary storage via *console* and *terminal typewriters.*

Output Devices. Output devices write data onto secondary storage (computer-readable) or onto output media readable by humans or non-computer equipment. Output devices that write data onto secondary storage include *magnetic disk* and *tape drives.* (Magnetic disk and tape drives are dual-purpose devices providing both input and output.) Devices that prepare output in a form readable by humans provide the output in hardcopy or display form. *Line printers* and *graph plotters* write output on paper. *Visual display terminals* provide visual output on a cathode-ray tube (CRT). *Computer output microfilm* (COM) devices use a photographic process to store output on rolls of microfilm. Microfilm stores large volumes of data in a small space. COM devices are expensive, however, and data cannot be read directly into the computer.

Input/Output Control Units. Input/output devices are connected to primary storage via input/output control units. These control units are specialized devices to facilitate input and output operations. Their primary functions are code conversion and buffering.

Code conversion is the translation of the code of the input medium into a form that is readable by the CPU. It also performs the reverse conversion when data are written onto an output medium.

Buffering is the temporary storage of data to compensate for differences in speed or in the timing of events between the CPU and the input/output devices. A print buffer, for example, can hold enough data to print an entire line on the line printer. While the line printer is performing the relatively slow task of printing this line, the CPU is free to perform other tasks.

Input/Output Channel. An input/output channel is a path along which input and output data are transmitted to and from primary storage. The channel also handles the transfer of data to and from the input/output device. This relieves the CPU of responsibility for data transfer to and from input/output devices, increases the number of input and output operations that can be performed simultaneously, and reduces the time the CPU must wait for data to arrive from or be sent to an input/output device.

Channels can be selector or multiplexor. *Selector channels* can only accept data from one device at a time. They are used with high-speed devices such as magnetic disk drives that are capable of utilizing the capacity of one channel. *Multiplexor channels* handle two or more devices simultaneously. They are used with slow-speed devices such as line printers and card readers.

Data Preparation Equipment. Data preparation equipment can transcribe transaction source documents into a form that is readable by an input device. Employee time cards, for example, can be manually entered on a key-to-tape device. The time data on the magnetic tape are then read into the computer by a tape drive. Other data preparation equipment includes devices for the key entry of data onto magnetic disk and for the magnetic coding of documents such as checks. Some data preparation devices provide editing and control functions in addition to coding.

Data preparation equipment is not under the direct control of the computer; it is an off-line function that prepares data for entry into the computer system. Some computer systems avoid this separate data preparation step by direct entry of the data into the computer.

Figure 2–1 shows a computer system that utilizes magnetic tape and magnetic disks as secondary storage. Data are prepared manually on an off-line key-to-tape device. The magnetic tapes are entered into primary storage via a tape drive. The tape drive has its own control unit and shares a multiplexor channel with the line printer. The disk drive is used for the

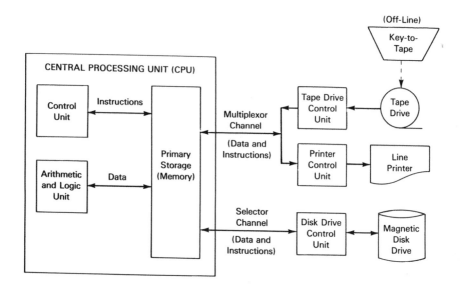

Figure 2-1. Example of Interaction of Computer Equipment

reading and writing of instructions. It is connected to primary storage via a control unit and a selector channel. Note that all data and instructions are routed through primary storage.

How the Computer Operates

In this part of the chapter we examine data representation, different methods of data coding likely to be encountered by the computer auditor, and the functioning of the CPU components.

Data Representation. Data representation in computer systems follows the binary system. The binary system is used because it is well suited to the electronic and mechanical nature of computer equipment.

The *binary system* is a number system that uses only two absolute values, 0 and 1. A 0 or 1 is known as a *binary digit* (or *bit* for short). Data are represented by strings of bits. A string may contain six, eight, or more bits. A string of six or eight bits is known as a *byte*. Large strings, such as thirty-two-bit strings, are known as *words*. The longer the string, the greater the number of data that can be represented by the string. The eight-bit byte, for example, provides $2^8 = 256$ different possible combinations of bits. Each combination can represent a different element of data. Two hundred fifty-six combinations are sufficient to represent ten numeric digits, twenty-six uppercase alphabetic characters, twenty-six lowercase alphabetic characters, and many other special characters, such as asterisks and dollar signs. As with any number system, arithmetic operations such as addition and subtraction can be performed with binary coded numbers.

The binary states of 0 and 1 are represented in computer systems by an electronic dichotomy. The CPU creates an *electronic dichotomy* by means of electrical switches that are open or closed, electrical pulses that high or low, magnetic elements with two directions of polarity, or the presence or absence of magnetic bubbles. An electronic dichotomy is signified on magnetic disks or tapes by the presence or absence of magnetic spots.

Binary Coding Methods. Although the binary representation of data is universal in digital computers, the actual method of coding differs. Knowledge of the specific coding method used in a computer is essential for proper auditor retrieval and interpretation of binary coded data. Alphanumeric data that are input to primary storage, stored in primary storage, and output from primary storage are generally coded in *character code.* Many computers convert the character code of numeric data to an *arithmetic code* for processing in the arithmetic and logic unit. The difficulty of reviewing binary coded output requires that the auditor be familiar with hexadecimal code. *Hexadecimal code* is a binary shorthand that facilitates the task of reading binary coded output. Finally, the presence of an additional bit in each byte of code will signify the presence of an error control (*parity*) bit.

The character code is the set of combinations of 0's and 1's that represents numeric, alphabetic, and special characters. To represent such a large array of alternatives, the character code requires a minimum of six bits per byte (64 alternatives). Most modern computers use an eight-bit byte that provides 256 alternatives. The six- or eight-bit byte is usually divided into the four right-hand numeric bits and the two or four left-hand zone bits. The zone bits are used in different combinations with the numeric bits to represent characters. The most common eight-bit character code is the Extended Binary Coded Decimal Interchange Code (EBCDIC). The coding of numeric and uppercase alphabetic characters using EBCDIC is shown in Table 2–1.

The six- or eight-bit byte used by the character code is larger than necessary for representing numeric data and is more difficult to manipulate arithmetically than a smaller byte. Consequently, many computers convert the character code of numeric data to an arithmetic code that is more suited to arithmetic operations. The arithmetic code uses four bits to represent the numbers from 0 to 9. It is known as *packed decimal* and refers to the ability to represent two numeric digits in one eight-bit byte.

Table 2-1. EBCDIC Code for Numeric and Uppercase Alphabetic Characters

Character	Coding		Character	Coding	
	Zone	Numeric		Zone	Numeric
A	1100	0001	S	1110	0010
B	1100	0010	T	1110	0011
C	1100	0011	U	1110	0100
D	1100	0100	V	1110	0101
E	1100	0101	W	1110	0110
F	1100	0110	X	1110	0111
G	1100	0111	Y	1110	1000
H	1100	1000	Z	1110	1001
I	1100	1001	0	1111	0000
J	1101	0001	1	1111	0001
K	1101	0010	2	1111	0010
L	1101	0011	3	1111	0011
M	1101	0100	4	1111	0100
N	1101	0101	5	1111	0101
O	1101	0110	6	1111	0110
P	1101	0111	7	1111	0111
Q	1101	1000	8	1111	1000
R	1101	1001	9	1111	1001

As an example, the number 83 is shown in both eight-bit character code (EBCDIC) and packed decimal arithmetic code (see Table 2-2).

Binary coded output is extremely difficult for the auditor to review. The multitude of 0's and 1's spread over many pages makes the output difficult to read. Errors are difficult to detect, and the review requires considerable staff time. When the binary output is numeric data in eight-bit byte character code, however, the auditor can utilize hexadecimal coding to make the review easier.

Hexadecimal code is a number system with a base of 16 that provides a shorthand representation of eight-bit byte character coded numbers. It is much easier to read than binary code. It can be used by the auditor as an intermediate step in the conversion of binary numbers to decimals. It can also be used by the auditor for the initial computer output of binary data. The relationship between hexadecimal and decimal is shown in Table 2-3. As an example of the conversion of hexadecimal to

Table 2-2. Comparison of Character and Arithmetic Codes

Code	Number	8	3
Character code (EBCDIC)		11111000	11110011
Packed decimal		1000	0011

Table 2–3. Relationship
between Hexadecimal and
Decimal

Hexadecimal	Decimal
0–9	0–9
A–F	10–15

decimal, the hexadecimal number A2F3 converts to the decimal equivalent of 41,715 as follows:

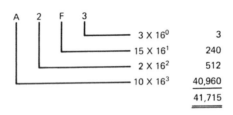

Observe that this conversion is accomplished in two steps. The first step is to convert each character in the hexadecimal number to its decimal equivalent as shown in Table 2–3. The second step is to multiply each decimal number by 16 raised to the power of its position in the hexadecimal number. The character farthest to the right, for example, is multiplied by 16^0, the second from the right by 16^1, and so on.

With the exception of a few minicomputers, the auditor will almost always encounter one more bit in a byte than is specified by the binary coding method. An eight-bit byte of character code, for example, will actually contain nine bits. The ninth bit is an error control bit known as the *parity bit.* The parity bit is checked by the computer to ensure that no data are lost or changed incorrectly during processing.

Components of the CPU. The three components of the CPU are the primary storage unit, control unit, and arithmetic and logic unit.

The *primary storage unit* holds the data and instructions currently required in processing. These data and instructions are stored in specific locations within primary storage. Each location has an *address* that identifies the physical location of the data or instructions in primary storage. When an address is specified by a program, the computer will retrieve all data or instructions stored in that location.

The *control unit* directs and coordinates the entire computer system. The control unit communicates with input and output devices in order to facilitate the transfer of data and instructions to and from primary storage, keeps track of the next instruction to be executed, and interprets the instructions of a program in primary storage. It also controls the actions of the arithmetic and logic unit, and it directs the transfer of data between primary storage and the arithmetic and logic unit. These tasks are accomplished in the following manner:

1.   The control unit accesses an input device. It directs the transfer of data and programs from the input device to primary storage.

2.   The control unit obtains the address of the next instruction to be executed from an instruction counter within the control unit.

3.   The control unit decodes this address and "fetches" the instruction from its location in primary storage. *Fetching* is the reading of the instruction in primary storage and copying it to an instruction register in the control unit. An instruction register is a temporary storage area within the control unit where a single instruction is stored.

4.   The instruction is decoded into the operation code and the operand. The *operation code* specifies what task is to be performed. The *operand* defines what is to be used in performing the task, such as a register or location in primary storage. This is illustrated by the following instruction:

A	15	45	95

The letter A is the operation code signifying the operation of addition. The numbers 15, 45, and 95 are the operands to be used in the addition. The numbers 15 and 45 are the addresses of registers containing the data to be added. The number 95 is the address of the register where the result of the addition is to be stored.

5.   The data in locations 15 and 45 are read, the operation (addition) is performed, and the result is placed in register 95. The result can then be moved to primary storage.

6.   The control unit resets the counter to the address of the next instruction and repeats cycle 2 through cycle 5 until all instructions in the program have been executed.

7.   Upon completion of the program, the control unit initiates the transfer of the results from primary storage to an output device.

The *arithmetic and logic unit* performs arithmetic computations and logical operations. Arithmetic computations include addition, subtraction, multiplication, and division. A problem in computer arithmetic consists of keeping track of the position of the decimal point; this can be done by the programmer or by the computer. Logical operations involve the comparison of conditional statements, and the branching of instructions according to the results of the comparison.

This logical process can be illustrated by a comparison that is often used as a control in payroll systems. The gross amount of each individual's pay is compared with a predetermined limit. If the amount is less than the limit, normal processing continues. If the amount is greater than the limit, the payroll record is instead processed by separate error-handling instructions (see Figure 2–2.)

OVERVIEW OF BUSINESS DATA PROCESSING

This overview of business data processing focuses on some key terms and attempts to create a basic understanding of how business data processing systems work. It also describes the elements of a data processing system, the programming languages and terminology, and the functions performed in a business data processing system.

Elements of a Data Processing System

A data processing system consists of hardware, systems software, application software, procedures, and personnel. Each of these elements is important to the auditor.

Hardware. The term *hardware* collectively describes all the equipment necessary to perform the functions of a data processing system. It includes all the computer equipment that was described earlier in the chapter. The auditor should become familiar with the hardware in a data processing system. Each individual piece of hardware has its own operating characteristics and control requirements.

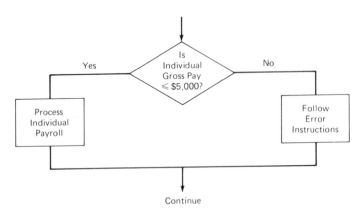

Figure 2–2. Conditional Branching in Payroll System

Systems Software. Systems software is a set of programs (instructions) that coordinates and controls the use of the hardware and supports the execution of user programs. *Systems software* is a collective term that covers the operating system, utilities, compilers, assemblers, and database management systems.

The operating system performs the tasks of coordinating and controlling the use of the CPU, secondary storage, channels, and input/output devices by the system users. The task of coordination includes the scheduling of processing; assigning the use of equipment to different users; monitoring and synchronizing processing; and facilitating the storing, accessing, and decoding of data and instructions. The task of control includes the handling of errors and the protection of programs and data from unauthorized use or destruction.

Utilities, compilers, and assemblers support the execution of user programs. Utilities relieve user programs of standard input/output tasks such as the sorting and merging of data. Compilers and assemblers convert the instructions in user programs to a form more suitable for processing by the computer.

Application Software. Application software, or user programs, consists of programs designed to solve specific data processing needs such as payroll or accounts payable processing. The programs for a particular system such as payroll contain the instructions required to perform the tasks of payroll processing. These tasks include calculations of withholding of taxes and social security and determinations of net pay and year-to-date pay. The auditor is interested not only in *how* the application software performs these tasks but also in *what* controls over these tasks may be included in the software.

Procedures. Despite the automatic functions of the hardware and software, the effective operation of the computer still requires that proper procedures be performed by operating personnel. These procedures cover the preparation of data, the operation of the computer, control over the quality of output, the resolution of errors and equipment malfunctions, and the distribution of output. The use of file control standards to ensure the proper handling of files is an example of such a procedure. Proper procedures can help assure the auditor that processing is accurate and that data, programs, and output are protected from unauthorized use, destruction, or disclosure.

Personnel. The proper functioning of a computer data processing system requires personnel with sufficient training and experience to handle the many specialized tasks. The auditor should be familiar with the titles and job responsibilities of such positions as systems analyst, systems programmer, application programmer, computer operator, and librarian. The computer operator, for example, is responsible for operating the computer according to standard procedures.

Programming Languages, Software, and Documentation

Programming languages are designed to ease the problem of communication between individuals and computers. The computer performs data processing tasks that are specified by instructions in the application programs. These instructions direct the control unit of the CPU to undertake such tasks as reading data into primary storage, performing arithmetic operations on data, and executing instructions on the basis of conditional logic. In order for the control unit to execute these instructions, they must be in binary character code. You can imagine, however, how difficult it is for people to write instructions in series of 0's and 1's. Programming languages and related software permit the writing of instructions in a form that is easily understood by humans but can readily be translated into computer code. Programming languages are universal, so it is essential that the auditor be familiar with the common programming languages and related software and documentation.

Programming languages can be *machine level, assembly level,* or *higher level.* Machine-level languages are written in combinations of 0's and 1's. Programming in a machine language is time-consuming, subject to error, and dependent on the characteristics of the CPU. Assembly-level languages are machine oriented but use symbols rather than binary code to ease the programmer's job. Higher-level languages are written to solve particular problems or procedures. They permit the programmer to focus on the problem or procedure rather than on the characteristics of the CPU.

Higher-level languages frequently encountered by the auditor include *CO*mmon *B*usiness *O*riented *L*anguage (COBOL), *FOR*mula *TRAN*slator (FORTRAN), *P*rogramming *L*anguage *1* (PL/1), *R*eport *P*rogram *G*enerator (RPG), and *B*eginners' *A*ll-purpose *S*ymbolic *I*nstruction *C*ode (BASIC). COBOL is the most frequently used programming language in business data processing. It was specifically created to handle the heavy input, output, and file requirements of business data processing. FORTRAN was designed for quantitative analysis and mathematical computations typical of scientific applications. It is used less frequently for business data processing. PL/1 is a multipurpose language designed to handle both business data processing and mathematical computations. RPG is a problem-oriented language designed to produce business reports. BASIC is an easy-to-use language that has found many scientific and business applications.

The auditor should be familiar with the following software and documentation associated with higher-level languages:

- A *source program* is a sequence of instructions written in an assembly or high-level language to solve a specific problem or to perform a particular procedure.
- A *compiler program* translates a higher-level language source program into a machine-language program. Compilation is a necessary intermediate processing step because the control unit of the CPU does not understand source code.
- An *assembler program* translates assembly-language source programs into a machine-language program.
- An *object program* is the machine-language program created by compilation or assembly of a source program.
- A *macro* instruction is a single assembly-level instruction that represents a set of several machine-language instructions. A programmer who specifies a single macro instruction avoids the need to code each individual instruction in the set. This capability increases the programming's efficiency. It is used to perform commonly required tasks such as input/output and blocking and formatting records.
- A *subroutine program* is one that is referenced by another program. It is used for repetitive operations such as arithmetic calculations or error checking. It simplifies the programming task by avoiding the need to write out the subroutine program in full each time the operation is performed.
- A *program listing* is a printed list of the instructions in a source or object program. It is an essential part of the documentation that is maintained in a business data processing system and an invaluable source of information to the auditor.

Functions in a Data Processing System

The elements of a data processing system—hardware, software, procedures, and personnel—all work together to perform the functions of a data processing system. These functions are the tasks related to the input, processing, and output of data. All of these tasks provide opportunities for control in accounting systems (see the flowchart in Figure 2–3).

Input Function.   The input function consists of data capture, data preparation (in batch systems only), and data entry. For the control of errors, it is the most important point in the processing cycle. Quality input is essential for reliable processing and output.

Data capture is a manual step that involves preparation of the source or original transaction documents. Examples of source documents are sales orders, credit memoranda, materials requisitions, and other documents that record the details of transactions. In some on-line systems, data capture is combined with data entry by direct keying of a transaction

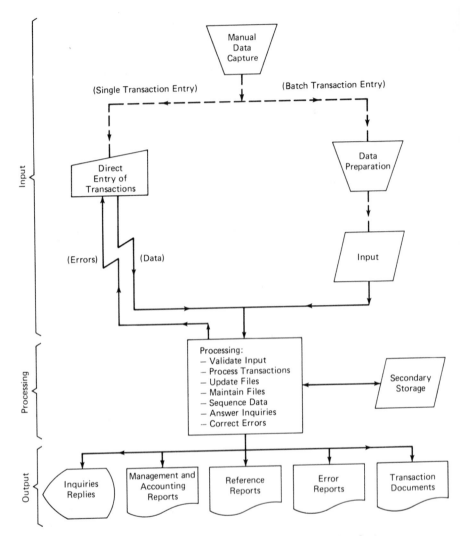

Figure 2–3. Functions in a Business Data Processing System

into a terminal without the preparation of a source document. In some advanced computer systems, such a point-of-sales (POS) systems, data capture is an automatic machine function that eliminates the preparing of source documents or keying into a terminal.

Batch data preparation is an off-line process that assembles, prepares, and controls a batch of one type of transaction prior to entry into the computer. The assembly of transactions involves the accumulation of the transactions for a period such as a day or week into a batch for purposes of computer entry and processing. The accumulation of all vendor invoices for a week is an example of such a batch. In some systems, transaction assembly includes the sequencing of transactions into master-file order. In other systems, sequencing is performed during computer processing.

Transaction preparation includes conversion and coding. *Data conversion* is the transcribing of data on the source documents to a machine-readable form. Time clock imprintings in a alphanumeric form on employee time cards, for example, may be punched in machine-readable Hollerith code on punched cards. *Data coding* is the addition of a symbol to each transaction (a transaction code) that identifies the transaction type, such as a purchase or a sale. It also includes a record key that permits the transaction to be matched with the related master-file record during subsequent processing. An example of coding that includes a record key is the use of vendor account numbers to identify transaction and master-file records in an accounts payable system.

The reliability of the transactions in the batch is ensured during data preparation by data validation tests and other controls, such as control totals. Data validation tests include the use of logic tests to check the validity of transaction codes. Control totals are used to detect error, loss, or nonprocessing of data items.

Data entry is the entry into the computer of the transaction data on the source documents. Data entry is by input of batches of transactions or by direct entry of single transactions. *Batch input* is accomplished by machine reading of data using input equipment. Data on magnetic tape, for example, are read into the computer by a tape drive. *Direct entry* is the entry of individual transactions into the computer via an on-line terminal. Direct entry avoids the intermediate off-line data preparation task required for batch input. This increases efficiency in some systems but may eliminate the possibility of establishing batch controls prior to entry. Error control is accomplished, however, by data validation at the time of direct entry and by use of batch controls subsequent to data entry.

Processing Function. Computer processing can include several tasks. Tasks of particular interest to the auditor are data validation, calculation, comparison, summarization, file updating, file maintenance, sequencing, inquiry, and error correction.

Data validation by the computer is the testing of data for errors at the time they enter the computer or upon the commencement of processing. Data validation includes determininng whether records are in the proper sequence and whether data are properly coded and classified.

Calculation is the performance of arithmetic operations on data. An example is the multiplication of hours worked by an hourly rate.

Comparison is the examination of data values using logical testing to determine appropriate courses of action. A comparison between a credit sale amount and a customer's credit limit, for example, will result in a rejection of the transaction if the amount exceeds the credit limit.

Summarization is the addition or netting of similar or related data items to produce a summary or net amount. The gross earnings of each individual employee, for example, may be summarized to total gross earnings for the company or department. The results of summarization are used for report purposes and as controls over the accuracy and completeness of processing.

File updating is the modification of the contents of data files to reflect the results of calculations and comparisons in transaction processing. The payroll master file, for example, is updated with the results of earnings calculations for the payroll period.

Control over file updating is particularly important in computer systems where files are maintained on magnetic media that are *physically* changed during file update. The physical change destroys the original data that have been updated.

File maintenance is the modification of the contents of data files to reflect changes in permanent file data, table values, and factors. It also includes the addition of new records and the deletion of old records. These changes occur less frequently than file update changes but are important because of their continuing effect on transaction processing. Examples of changes in permanent file data are changes of address for customers, vendors, and employees, and different credit limits for customers. Changes in table values include adjustments to tax-withholding tables to reflect new tax regulations. Changes in factors include the use of a new interest rate in a lease capitalization program. Additions and deletions of records include changes to reflect new and retiring employees.

Sequencing of transactions is the sorting of transactions into a specified order for processing or output. Sequencing of transactions is required if the transaction file is not sorted into master-file sequence during batch data preparation or prior to direct entry. It may also be necessary to prepare a file for output in a sequence other than the sequence of the master file.

Inquiry is the display or printing of file data in response to a request for information. An inquiry does not result in modification of the file's contents. A salesperson, for example, may inquire about a customer's credit status prior to closing a credit sale. The information is displayed to this salesperson, but no change is made in the file.

Error correction is the correction of rejected transactions, and modification of the file's contents to eliminate the effect of transaction and processing errors. Error corrections are often complex and run the risk of generating further errors if not handled with care.

Output Function.   The output of a data processing system may be updated data files in secondary storage, visual display, or hardcopy output.

Updated data files in secondary storage represent ledgers. Visual display output is the transitory representation of file data on the screen of a CRT terminal. Hardcopy output is printed output that comes in a variety of forms and serves a variety of purposes. These forms include management and accounting reports, reference reports, error reports, and transaction documents.

Management and accounting reports are designed to provide information to management and accounting. They are either periodic reports or exception reports. *Periodic reports* are scheduled and designed in advance. Their timing usually depends on the processing cycle. Examples are financial statements, accounts receivable aging reports, and reports of sales by product type, territory, or department. *Exception reports* are special-purpose reports produced upon request or in response to certain prespecified conditions. An example is the printing of all customer accounts over forty-five days old at the request of the credit department. Because of the need for accuracy and confidentiality in both periodic reports and exception reports, it is important that report quality and availability be carefully controlled.

Reference reports are documents that provide a permanent record of account balances and transactions for each processing cycle.[1] They provide management and auditors with a "trail" of processing activity and results. Reference reports include trial balances, journals, and other transaction listings.

Error reports provide a listing of all known erroneous transactions for each processing cycle. Error reports are used to determine the need for correction and to ensure that all erroneous transactions are corrected.

Transaction documents are functional items required for company transactions. They include checks for paying employees and suppliers, invoices for customers, and purchase orders for the purchasing department. These documents often represent company assets or provide control over company assets. They should, therefore, be carefully controlled.

OVERVIEW OF STORAGE CONCEPTS

The computer cannot process data or update files unless data are structured and organized in some logical manner. In this section we discuss data structures, record organization, file organization, and the storage characteristics of specific file media. Knowledge of these storage concepts facilitates the audit of permanent and transaction accounting records that are stored in machine-readable form in computer systems.

---

[1]Some companies copy reference reports onto microfilm. In these companies, the microfilm will be the permanent record of reference data.

Data Structures

The term *data* is used to identify any set of characters. Data in a computer system are structured so that they represent important input and can easily be retrieved from storage for processing or output. There are four basic data structures: field, record, file, and data base. The relationship between these structures is shown in Figure 2–4 and can be described as follows:

- A *field* is a set of characters that represents a particular data characteristic or attribute. Data fields for an employee, for example, could include the attributes of name, social security number, address, and gross pay. The actual amount or other content of a field is known as the *data value*. Gross pay of $2,000, for example, would be the data value of the gross pay field.
- A *record* is a collection of data fields that relate to a specific data object. Data objects in accounting include an employee, a customer, or an account. The record for each of these objects will include all pertinent data. The record for an individual customer in accounts receivable, for example, will contain fields for name, address, credit rating, account balance, and the date when the balance is due.

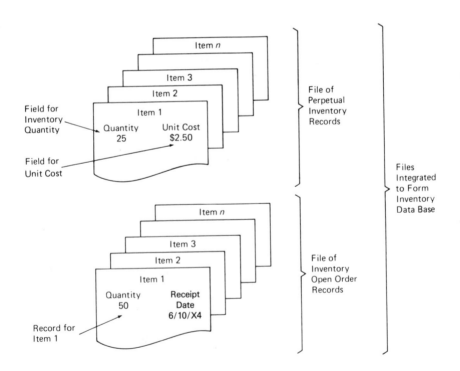

Figure 2–4.   Relationship between Field, Record, File, and Data Base for Inventory

- A *file* is a group of records of a particular type. All individual customer records, for example, constitute the accounts receivable file. Files that contain records of the balances of individual accounts are known as *master files*. Transaction data records are stored in transaction or detail files.
- A *data base* is a set of master files that is integrated to reduce data redundancy and may be used by several application programs.

Record Organization

Records vary considerably in the way they are organized. The auditor is likely to encounter the following organizational alternatives:

- The record can be identified by one or more keys. A *key* is a field within the record that serves to identify the record in the file. A customer record, for example, might be identified by the customer number. It might also be identified by salesperson or sales territory.
- A record may contain all relevant fields, or it may be divided into master and trailer records. The master record might contain vendor number, name, address, and outstanding balance, for example, while trailer records might contain the details of open vendor invoices.
- The logical content of a record will not always be identical with the physical record. The logical record may share a unit of physical record (such as a punched card) with other logical records. Two sales transactions (the logical records), for example, may be stored on one punched card (the physical record). Alternatively, one logical record may be found on two or more physical records. One sales transaction (the logical record), for example, may be stored on two punched cards (the physical records).
- The length of a field or the number of fields in a record can be fixed or variable. Variable-length fields and records accommodate variations in field and record size without waste of space. Variable length, however, requires a marker to signify the end of a field or record.

File Organization

Records are organized within a file to serve the twin objectives of (1) locating a record for processing or output and (2) facilitating file creation. The actual method of organizing files, however, varies considerably from company to company and from application to application.

File organization methods vary in their cost, suitability to different storage media, ability to locate records, method of file update, and suitability to different types of user applications. There are four principal file organization methods: sequential, direct, indexed sequential, and list organization.

Sequential. Sequential organization arranges records in sequence based on a primary key. The primary key is one field in each record. An accounts payable file, for example, may be sequenced according to the vendor number field. Sequential organization has the following characteristics:

- Sequential storage is low cost where the storage medium is magnetic tape or punched cards (although any storage medium may be used).
- Location of an individual record in sequentially organized files requires that all records in the file preceding the record desired must be read. This is because sequential files are in the same physical and logical order, and the computer does not keep track of the physical location of individual records. Sequential files also store complete records, the master and all detail records, in one physical location.
- The updating of a sequential file requires that the transaction file be sorted in the same order as the master file before processing.
- Sequential organization is best suited for user applications that may be processed periodically, using batches of transactions, and do not require frequent retrieval of individual records. Periodic processing would be satisfactory in an accounts payable system where vendor balances are paid monthly. Periodic processing would not be satisfactory, however, in an inventory control system where current inventory status must be available at all times. Retrieval of individual records for inquiry purposes is time-consuming and inefficient in sequential files. If retrieval of individual records is a frequent demand, sequential organization should not be used.

Direct. Direct (or random) organization physically stores records wherever it is convenient for easy storage and retrieval. Records are not stored in logical or physical sequential order. Direct file organization has the following characteristics:

- The cost of direct storage is usually higher than that of sequential storage because it requires expensive storage media such as magnetic disk. Magnetic tape and punched cards cannot be used for direct file organization.
- Records are not located in logical or physical order, so it is necessary to provide a method of determining the record's location or storage address. The use of an addressing method permits the easy processing or retrieval of individual records. It may, however, require additional storage for the address and additional processing time to locate the address. The most common methods of record addressing are randomizing and indexing. *Randomizing* is the application of some arithmetic procedure to the content of a record field to produce the address. Randomizing enables records to be scattered at random locations on a disk pack and reduces the time required to locate or access a record. The *indexing* method maintains a table of data records which includes the address of each record in direct storage. Indexing is most efficient when additions or deletions of records are infrequent, because such changes require that the index be updated.
- Update of a direct file requires the determination of the address, and then location of the record in the file. Transactions can be updated individually

and need not be sorted prior to the file update. It may also be possible to update several files concurrently from one transaction. The disadvantages of direct file update include the destruction of old master-file data when new data are written into a record. It is also more difficult to provide backup copies of direct files. It may also be necessary to reorganize a direct file to a sequential order for report preparation.

- Direct file organization is particularly suited for user applications that require frequent updating and frequent retrieval of individual records.

Indexed Sequential. Indexed sequential is sequential file organization combined with an index to provide direct processing or retrieval of individual records.

- Indexed sequential may be costlier than sequential or direct. It requires extra storage in the file, extra storage for the index, and extra processing time to use the index and reorganize the file. It requires the use of expensive direct-access storage media.
- Records in an indexed sequential file are stored sequentially according to a key field. An index is used to record the storage address of each record. The record is identified in the index by the key field, or by some other field. Some systems use multiple indexes based on several fields. The index provides direct access only on the basis of the index key field or fields. The search for records based on nonindexed fields must be done sequentially.
- Direct update of individual records based on an indexed key requires a search through the index to find the storage address. The given address can be the individual record or a grouping of records known as a *block*. Where there is a block of records at the address, the block must be read sequentially until the record is found. When updating requires the insertion of a new record, it is either inserted in a space in the file or located elsewhere as indicated by a pointer in the file at the given storage address.
- Indexed sequential organization is particularly suited for applications that are processed efficiently using sequential organization but require frequent retrieval of individual records based on one or more keys. The inventory master file, for example, should be updated sequentially when the volume of receipts and shipments is heavy. Sales and inventory control, however, need direct access to individual inventory records to determine item availability, order size, expected order receipt date, and other data.

List Organization. The list organization uses pointers to separate the physical from the logical order of the file. The logical order of the file is sequential, but the physical organization is direct. Each record contains a pointer to the physical storage address of the next logical record.

- List organization can be simple, inverted, or ring. The simple list logically strings records together by the sequence of the primary key field. Inverted lists link records logically by the content of some or all of the fields in addition to the key field. Inverted lists provide, in essence, several sequential organizations for a file. Ring structures use pointers to logically preceding and succeeding records to speed record retrieval and to reduce storage space required.

- The list organization reduces record redundancy in files by eliminating the need to repeat records more than once. It also reduces processing time by eliminating the need to sort to a sequential organization other than that based on the key field. It also speeds retrieval of a record when retrieval is based on a key other than the key field.
- The list organization is well suited to applications that require processing or retrieval based on several characteristics. In an accounts receivable system, for example, customer accounts may be sequenced by customer number for regular processing. The preparation of a list of overdue accounts, however, would require a list keyed on the due-date field.

File Storage Media

The two file storage media most likely to be encountered by the auditor are magnetic tape and magnetic disk. Each medium has its own particular storage characteristics and in some cases can be used in different ways to store data. Auditing data files requires that the auditor understand these differences.

Magnetic Tape.   Magnetic tape is a very common input/output and file storage medium. The storage characteristics of magnetic tape vary from one application to another and require special controls to protect tapes from inadvertent erasure.

Magnetic tape represents data by means of positive and negative magnetization. The areas of magnetization on the surface of the tape are equivalent to holes in a punched card. A vertical frame on a magnetic tape is equivalent to a column on a punched card and represents a character byte. The horizontal tracks on a magnetic tape, like the rows on a punched card, provide locations for magnetization for each frame. Different combinations of direction of magnetization in the tracks for each frame represent different character bytes.

Tapes vary according to the number of frames and tracks, and in the number of records that can be packed onto one tape. The number of frames or bytes on a tape is a function of tape density. *Tape density* is defined as the number of bytes on one inch of tape. Common tape densities vary from 200 to over 6,000 bytes per inch. The number of tracks on a tape is usually either seven or nine. This corresponds to a six- or eight-bit character byte plus a parity bit. Figure 2–5 illustrates a nine-track tape with EBCDIC character coding.

The number of records that can be packed on a tape is a function of the length of the records, the interrecord gap, and blocking. Records can be of any length subject to the number of bytes of primary storage avail-

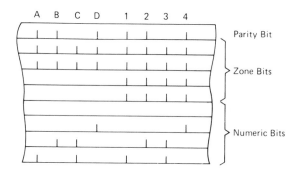

Figure 2–5. Nine-Track Magnetic Tape Using EBCDIC Code and Parity Bit

able to assemble the record. Records of 300, 500, 800, or 1,000 characters are not uncommon.

The interrecord gap is a blank space on the tape between records. The gap signifies the end of a record to the computer. The size of the gap is the space required to halt and restart the tape, and to allow the tape to come up to speed. Interrecord gaps of three-quarters of an inch are common. This means that most of a tape will be blank if records are short.

This problem is solved by blocking records. *Blocking* is the grouping of two or more records with an interrecord gap at the end of the block only. This increases the usable portion of the tape. Blocks must be small enough, however, to fit into the available space in primary storage because an entire block of records is brought into primary storage each time the tape is read. This also increases the time required to find a specific record because the computer must read the entire block to locate one record. Notice in Figure 2–6 how much less tape is required for records 1 through 5 when the records are blocked. Notice also, however, that the reading of record 4 on the blocked tape requires all five records in the block to be read into primary storage.

It is advisable to use controls to prevent the inadvertent erasure of data on magnetic tape. This is because the writing of new data on a tape destroys the old data on the tape. Controls that are used include tape marks, file labels, and file protection rings. *Tape marks* are physical markings at the beginning and end of the usable portion of the tape. They are read by photoelectric cells that determine the earliest and latest points on the tape for recording data. *File labels* may be external or internal. External labels are attached to the tape reel or container and are visible to the computer operator. They provide visual confirmation of the contents of the file. Internal labels at the beginning of the tape (header labels) or at the end (trailer labels) provide information to the computer on the identification and status of the file. The header label, for example, includes the file retention date before which the file should not be writ-

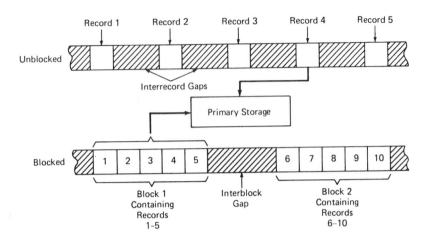

Figure 2–6. The Reading of Blocked and Unblocked Logical Records on Magnetic Tape

ten on with new data. The *file protection ring* is a plastic ring inserted into a tape reel to permit mounting on the tape drive as an output tape.

Magnetic Disk. The magnetic disk is similar to magnetic tape in its representation of data bits by magnetization. Magnetic disks differ from tapes, however, in their technology, identification of storage addresses, and operating environment.

A *magnetic disk* is a hard or soft platter with magnetic coating on both sides. Hard disks usually come in stacks of several disks called a *disk pack*. Their diameter ranges from eight inches to three feet, with fourteen inches the most common size. The number of disks in a pack can vary from five to one hundred. The top surface of the top disk in a pack and the bottom surface of the bottom disk are not used for recording. Thus, a pack with ten disks will have eighteen recording surfaces. Soft disks, also called floppies or diskettes, come as a single platter and typically have a diameter of 5 1/4 or 3 1/2 inches. Soft disks are commonly used in minicomputer and microcomputer systems.

Data are written onto or retrieved from a recording surface by means of a read/write head. The read/write head can move from surface to surface or be fixed. If the read/write head is fixed, it is necessary to have one head per recording surface. The read/write heads are attached to an access mechanism that moves the head to the location of the data on the disk.

Each recording surface is covered with concentric circles called *tracks*. Data are stored on the tracks by magnetization. Tracks are organized into vertical *cylinders* within a pack. The number 1 track on each recording surface, for example, constitutes a cylinder. The access mechanism moves all the read/write heads simultaneously from one location to

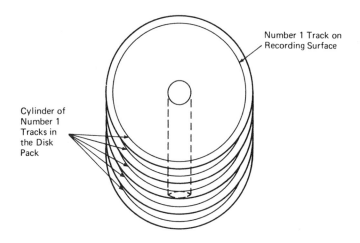

Number 1 Track on
Recording Surface

Cylinder of
Number 1
Tracks in
the Disk
Pack

Figure 2–7.   Relationship between Tracks and Cylinders on Magnetic
Disks

another so that one cylinder of tracks is available at any time. This allows records to be stored vertically through each cylinder of the pack. The relationship between cylinders and tracks is shown in Figure 2–7.

The location of data on disk is by reference to a storage address. The storage address is identified by the disk surface number and the track number. Some disk systems also address blocks of records within a track. The computer obtains a disk address by randomizing or from an index, as described earlier in the chapter.

Magnetic disk provides an operating environment that differs considerably from that of tape. Disk files can be direct, sequential, indexed sequential, or list organization, whereas tapes can only be sequential. Direct organization permits rapid update of records during processing, as well as rapid retrieval of data for inquiry or printing. It is also possible to update several disk files concurrently from one transaction.

On the negative side, disk storage is five to twenty times as expensive as tape storage per character stored. Disk storage also requires more-complicated software. Direct-access disk files may pose security hazards. Finally, disk storage is not necessary for many accounting applications that may quite satisfactorily use sequential tape files.

OVERVIEW OF INPUT
AND PROCESSING METHODS

Data processing systems vary according to the method of transaction input and processing. *Transaction input* can utilize either the immediate entry of individual transactions into the computer (on-line) or the periodic entry of accumulated batches of transactions. *Transaction processing* can provide either the immediate processing of individual transactions (real-time) or the periodic processing of accumulated batches of transactions. These different input and processing methods provide alternative ways of designing computer systems to accomplish different kinds of tasks. Together they provide three alternative system designs: batch input/batch processing, on-line input/batch processing, and on-line input/real-time processing.

Batch Input/Batch Processing

Batch input/batch processing systems accumulate transactions for periodic input and processing. They are well suited to certain types of application and conducive to good accounting control.

Batch input/batch processing systems vary in the type and number of processing steps involved. A typical system, however, will include some or all of the following steps:

- Source documents such as time cards, work orders, and vendor invoices are accumulated over a processing interval. The processing interval or period usually varies from a day to a month.
- The accumulated batch of source documents is converted to machine-readable form. The data conversion can be done in a number of different ways, including documents that are read by magnetic or optical character readers and keying directly onto magnetic disk or tape.
- Input validation is performed when the transaction file is first read into the computer.
- The transaction file can be converted to a different file medium prior to processing. Magnetic tape records, for example, can be written onto magnetic disk.
- The transaction file is sorted by the primary key in each master-file record. In some systems, sorting can be done off-line during data preparation. In both cases, sorting is necessary for sequential processing of the transaction file. A few systems process in the order of the unsorted transaction file and omit the sorting step.
- The master file is updated. A master-file record is read, the next transaction is read, and if they match, the master-file record is updated. All transactions relating to a master-file record are processed before the next record in the master file is read. The last step in the cycle is the printing of output. Output may include reports such as journals or the general ledger, transaction documents such as checks, and control information on the transaction and master files.

Figure 2–8 diagrams a system that follows these six steps.

Batch input/batch processing is most suitable for applications that have a large volume of similar transactions where files are processed se-

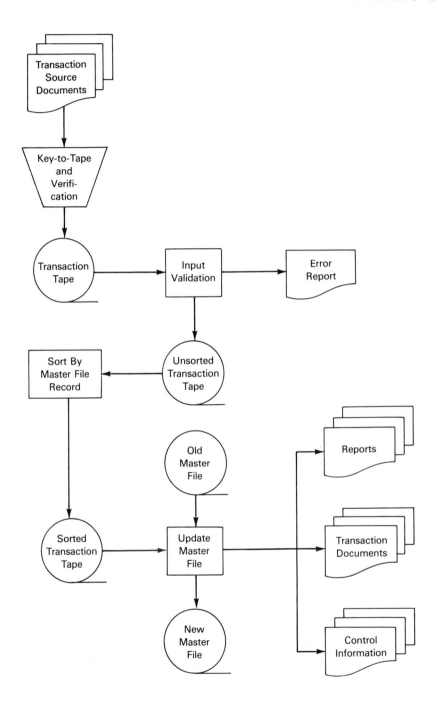

Figure 2–8. Typical Batch Input/Batch Processing System

quentially, and where periodic processing is satisfactory. Large volumes of similar transactions can be prepared for input efficiently on a batch basis. Batch update of sequential file ensures a sufficiently high level of file activity to justify processing the entire file. Periodic batch processing is satisfactory in systems that do not require output on a fast turnaround basis.

Applications that meet these criteria will be processed most efficiently using the batch approach. The cost of data preparation per transaction will be low, and it will be possible to use low-cost sequential storage such as magnetic tape. For these reasons, many accounting applications use the batch approach.

Applications that do not meet these criteria, however, should use more-advanced processing methods. It may be important, for example, to provide immediate checking of file status and rapid master-file update. In an accounts receivable system, it may be necessary to provide immediate inquiry response to the sales department on a customer's credit status. Frequent updating of customer account balances may be necessary to ensure that credit limits have not been exceeded.

Batch input/batch processing systems are usually easy to audit and are conducive to good controls. The large number of individual processing steps provides the auditor with numerous checkpoints and adequate documentation. Also, the retrieval of records for audit from sequentially organized master files is fairly straightforward. Control in batch systems is enhanced by the use of batch control totals, and by the capability for file reconstruction from the documents and files that are byproducts of the system.

On-Line Input/Batch Processing

Some newer computer systems have retained periodic batch processing but provide immediate terminal entry of individual transactions into the computer. These systems provide immediate validation of transactions coupled with periodic file update, permit inquiry of master-file contents, require new technology and controls, and provide data processing advantages over purely batch systems.

On-line terminal input permits immediate validation of individual transactions (see Figure 2–9). Validation is provided by the main computer or, in some cases, by a microcomputer within the terminal itself. A terminal with a microcomputer is known as an *intelligent terminal.* When an invalid transaction is detected, an error message is printed or displayed at the terminal. The terminal operator must respond to the error message and make the correction before the transaction will be accepted.

The actual update of the master file does not take place at the time

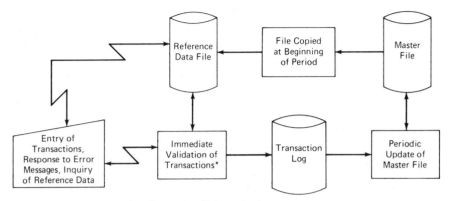

*Some systems also update the reference data file immediately.

Figure 2-9.   On-Line Input/Batch Processing System

of on-line entry. The validated transaction is stored on a transaction file known as the *transaction log*. The transaction log accumulates the trans-action for a given period, at which time all the transactions in the log are processed against the master file. In some systems, for example, the transactions are accumulated for a day and processed at night after that day's business is finished.

Systems with on-line input usually provide file inquiry capabilities. At the end of the master-file update, the reference data in the file are copied onto a separate file called the *reference data file*. This file is some-times called the *memo file*. The inquiries from a terminal user are an-swered using the contents of this file. The contents of the file are not updated by the current period's transaction log. Some systems overcome this disadvantage by updating the reference data file on an immediate individual transaction basis, but not updating the master file until the next batch of transactions is processed.

On-line input/batch processing systems use advanced technology, including multiprogramming and data communication, and create a new environment for the auditor:

• *Multiprogramming* is the concurrent execution of two or more programs in the CPU. Because the CPU can only execute one instruction at a time, this is accomplished by the CPU switching its attention from one program to another. Switching is done so fast that the computer seems to be executing programs simultaneously. In an on-line/batch processing system, for exam-ple, multiprogramming could permit terminal entry and inquiry concur-rently with batch processing. This capability can be used to advantage in accounting systems. In an open-item accounts receivable system, for exam-ple, a terminal operator can use inquiry to match a customer's check with the outstanding invoices listed in his or her customer record in the data reference file. The operator can then use this information to code the check properly to the customer's account. Meanwhile the computer may be updating the accounts receivable master file with the customer receipts in the preceding day's transaction log.

- *Data communication* is the transmission of data between two remote points. Data are usually carried over the communication links of communication companies. Data transmission is usually in analog form in contrast to the digital form of computer data. Data transmitted from a computer to a terminal or vice versa must be translated into analog form upon transmission (modulation) and back to digital form upon receipt (demodulation). A hardware device that performs this translation is called a *modem*. Data communication provides new flexibility in the design of accounting systems; data entry may be centralized or handled in remote locations using data communication. Many companies have found that the decentralized alternative provides economy and processing timeliness.
- On-line inquiry, multiprogramming, and data communication create a whole new environment for the auditor. On-line inquiry creates a problem of data security; only authorized users should be able to interrogate file data. Multiprogramming provides concurrent use of programs and data files. This poses the risk that programs and data may be altered without authority by other programs in the system. Data communication creates new opportunities for data loss and manipulation. These new risks require additional controls and a different audit approach.

On-line input/batch processing systems have some advantages over purely batch systems and are increasingly being used for accounting applications. On-line transaction validation is a powerful error prevention procedure. The elimination of the separate data preparation step can yield efficiencies in data input. The method retains the relatively uncomplicated batch processing method and its associated controls. Multiprogramming permits concurrent on-line inquiry and batch processing. Data communication permits decentralized data input from branches and other remote locations.

As a result of these advantages, on-line input is increasingly being used for accounting applications that have traditionally used batch input. The continued fall in hardware prices has made on-line input more cost competitive with batch input and has accelerated the trend away from batch input.

On-Line Input/Real-Time Processing

The most complex processing method involves on-line input and the immediate (or real-time) processing of transactions. Real-time processing updates the master file at the time that the transaction is entered into the terminal. It ensures that the master files are always completely up to date. A real-time inventory master file, for example, will include item counts adjusted for the latest receipt and requisition. Real-time processing, however, eliminates the use of batch controls prior to processing.

DATA COMMUNICATION DEVICES

Systems that incorporate data communication utilize a variety of devices to connect remote input/output devices to a central computer. These devices are remote terminals, modems, communication channels, multiplexors and concentrators, and communication control units.

Remote Terminals

Data communication systems use terminals for the input of data and receipt of output at remote locations. There are many types of remote terminals, but they all interface with the computer in basically the same way. Each terminal communicates with a central computer via a communication system. Communication of data is initiated either by the terminal or by a program in primary storage of the central computer. Data can be entered or captured at the terminal and transmitted to the central computer. Transmission is direct to the central computer without intermediate steps such as storage on magnetic tape. Data can also be transmitted from the central computer to the terminal to control the input of data, or to provide output at the remote location. The many types of remote terminals include display terminals, point-of-sale terminals, touch-tone devices, keyboard/printers, and data collection terminals.

Display Terminals.   Display terminals provide visual representation of data. Data are entered via a keyboard and displayed on a cathode-ray tube (CRT) screen. They are particularly useful in systems that require remote data entry and response to inquiries. They do not provide a permanent record of what is shown on the screen but are quieter and can display output more quickly than printers. There are different types of display terminals to meet different system requirements, such as data entry terminals, multipurpose terminals, intelligent terminals, and computer graphics terminals.

Data entry terminals are limited function devices for the entry of transaction data. Data are entered via a keyboard and are displayed on the terminal's screen. The screen display provides the terminal operator with visual confirmation of the input data. The data can be validated by a program in the central computer prior to processing or storage on disk. This approach can provide significant gains in timeliness, efficiency, and data reliability over equivalent off-line procedures.

Multipurpose terminals are similar to data entry terminals but also permit interactive computing and display of reports on the terminal's screen. *Interactive computing* is the use of dialogue between the terminal user and the central computer to facilitate the use and writing of programs. A terminal user, for example, may ask the computer to list files, guide the entry of data, review the correctness of program code, or explain error messages. Multipurpose terminals are also used to display reports not needed in hard-copy form. If the reports are too long for the size of screen, the reports can be displayed one page at a time.

Intelligent terminals are advanced terminals that can be programmed and are able to store data internally. Each intelligent terminal contains a microprocessor with control and logic capabilities and limited internal storage, which together are equivalent to a miniature CPU. The logic and storage capabilities enable the intelligent terminal to perform tasks independently of the central computer. This terminal is particularly useful for the formatting and editing of input data prior to transmission of the data to the central computer.

Computer graphics terminals display drawings as well as characters on the screen. The terminal user creates or alters the drawings by means of a special device such as a light pen or a mouse. Graphics terminals are used to display complex drawings such as engineering design prototypes or graphs and charts of business data. This latter use is of considerable value to the auditor in performing analytical review and other auditing procedures.

Point-of-Sale Terminals. Point-of-sale (POS) terminals are special-purpose terminals found in retail stores, supermarkets, and fast-food restaurants. They combine cash register functions with special-purpose functions such as credit authorization, sales analysis, inventory update, automatic calculations such as sales tax, and local reports on inventory or sales. A typical POS terminal has a keyboard for data entry, a display panel for the price, a cash drawer, and a printer for providing receipts and reports. Some POS devices have a reader for capturing the Universal Product Code (UPC) stamped on merchandise. POS terminals are usually connected to a central computer either directly or via an in-store mini-computer. This arrangement allows the credit authorization, sales recording, and inventory update to be performed automatically at the time of sale.

Touch-Tone Devices. Touch-tone devices are remote data entry devices that are used with ordinary telephone lines. Data entry can be via the buttons on a touch-tone phone or via a keyboard on a separate device. Some touch-tone devices have special readers for items such as credit cards. Applications include authorization of credit card sales, telephone bill paying for customers of financial institutions, and telephone reporting of customer account balances. In the last two examples, the central computer replies in voice form using a limited vocabulary.

Keyboard/Printers.   Keyboard/printers are terminals for keyboard data entry and hard-copy printed output. They are used on a stand-alone basis or in combination with other terminals. They communicate with the central computer on a character-by-character basis or on a line-by-line basis. A stand-alone keyboard/printer can be installed on a permanent basis to function as a small-scale remote printer. Alternatively, it can be a portable unit that can provide data entry and printing capabilities wherever there is a standard telephone. Simple keyboard/printers transmit and receive data on a character-by-character basis. More-sophisticated devices have built-in storage to permit the assembly of an entire line of characters prior to transmission or printing. Line-by-line assembly of data permits more efficient use of the data communication system.

Data Collection Terminals.   Data collection terminals are specialized and limited function devices for the capture of data in a factory or warehouse. Specialized functions include the recording of employee time and job data, and the recording of inventory transactions such as receipts, releases, and physical relocation. Each data collection terminal is a one-way communication device for the entry of a specific type of data.

Modems

Modems are devices that perform the modulation and demodulation required to connect a computer system to a data communication system. *Modulation* is the translation of binary data from the digital form used in a computer system to the analog form used in data communication. *Demodulation* is the translation of data from analog form back to digital form. A modem must be located anywhere a hardware device interfaces with the communication system. In Figure 2–10, for example, there is a modem to translate signals transmitted to or from a remote terminal, and a second modem to perform the same function for the central computer.

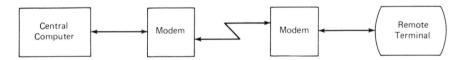

Figure 2–10.   Modems

The auditor may encounter two different types of modem—the data set and the acoustic coupler:

- A *data set* is usually connected directly to the hardware device. It not only modulates or demodulates the signal but also acts as a transmitter or receiver. There are different types of data sets to match different types and speeds of communication lines. For example, some data sets are programmable for use with multiple terminals and complex networks.
- An *acoustic coupler* is a modem that is used in connection with a standard telephone. The acoustic coupler is connected to a hardware device, and a standard telephone headset is placed on the acoustic coupler. The acoustic coupler modulates the signal from the hardware device. The resulting audible signal is picked up by the mouthpiece of the telephone headset and transmitted along a standard telephone line. The signal is received by a modem and demodulated prior to input to a hardware device. An advantage of using an acoustic coupler is that it permits the entry of data to a computer from any remote location that has a telephone.

Communication Channels

Communication channels are the means of transmitting data from one location to another. They include telegraph lines, telephone lines, coaxial cables, microwave transmission, satellite communications, and fiber optics. These channels can be provided by a common carrier such as AT&T or by an independent company. Communication channels vary in their *baud rate*. The baud rate is the number of bits transmitted per second. A channel's baud rate can be low, medium, or high.

Low-speed channels transmit data at low frequency with a baud rate ranging from 45 to 90 bits per second. A telegraph line is an example of a low-speed channel.

Medium-speed, or voice-grade, channels transmit data at baud rates ranging from 300 to 9,600 bits per second. The wide range of speed permits ordinary telephone lines, for example, to handle anything from a portable terminal to a high-speed printer.

High-speed, or broad-band, channels transmit data at baud rates ranging from 10,000 to 230,000 bits per second. High-speed channels, such as microwave, fiber optics, or satellite transmissions, are normally used for computer-to-computer communication. They are also used to transmit messages from many terminals simultaneously.

Multiplexors and Concentrators

Multiplexors and concentrators enable several terminals to use a single communication channel. Multiplexors accomplish this by combining data from several terminals and transmitting them as a single stream.

The data are combined either by assigning the data from each terminal to a separate frequency (frequency-division multiplexing) or by assigning the data to a unique time slot (time-division multiplexing).

Concentrators accomplish the same objective by assigning channel time. In some systems, concentrators are referred to as *selector channels*. A concentrator, for example, can be attached to several terminals and one communication channel. The concentrator polls the terminals to locate one that is ready to transmit. The concentrator then assigns the channel to the waiting terminal for its exclusive use. If a second terminal wishes to use the channel, it must wait until the channel is free. When the channel is free, the concentrator assigns it to the second terminal. This system works well when channel capacity exceeds the terminals' requirements and waiting time is reasonable.

Communication Control Units

The communication control unit (CCU) is a device that can programmed to relieve the central computer of many of the management, housekeeping, and control tasks associated with a data communication system. The CCU is useful in data communication systems where large amounts of data, multiple terminals, and complex communication patterns place an excessive burden on central computer time and storage. A basic function of the CCU is the assembly of data bits into characters or messages. Other functions include message switching, data validation, maintenance of an audit trail, and automatic error detection and correction.

DATA COMMUNICATION CONCEPTS

Data communication systems are designed with transmission speed and capacity that meet the timeliness and volume needs of the system users. System speed and capacity are determined by the choice of equipment and channels, modulation technique, transmission mode, and transmission direction.

Modulation

Modulation is the conversion of data from digital to analog form. The representation of data in analog form, however, can be accomplished by varying any one of three characteristics of the analog wave form: frequency, amplitude, and phase.

Data transmitted in analog form are represented by an electrical signal that has three characteristics: the strength of the signal (its amplitude), the length of time to complete one wave of the signal (its phase), and the number of times a wave is repeated within a specified time period (its frequency). These characteristics are shown in Figure 2–11.

A change in any one of these characteristics indicates a change in binary state. Systems that use low-speed transmission generally use a change in frequency to represent the two states. A change in amplitude, however, is more suitable for medium-speed transmission. A change in phase is used in systems that require high transmission speeds.

Transmission Mode

The systems designer can choose either of two modes of transmission: asynchronous and synchronous. Data transmitted in *asynchronous* mode are sent one character at a time. Each character is identified by start and stop bits attached to the beginning and end of the character, respectively. This method is quite slow and is suitable for transmission speeds of up to 2,000 bits per second. It is acceptable, however, for many applications, such as systems with nonintelligent terminals that transmit one character at a time.

Data transmitted in *synchronous* mode are transmitted without start/stop bits. The receipt of a character is identified instead by the interval of time for transmission. This method permits transmission speeds in excess of 2,000 bits per second. It is required, for example, when a computer or intelligent terminal transmits large amounts of data at one time.

Transmission Direction

A communication channel can be designed to handle one direction, alternate direction, or simultaneous two-way transmission, depending on the requirements of the system. These three alternatives are known as simplex, half-duplex, and full-duplex, respectively.

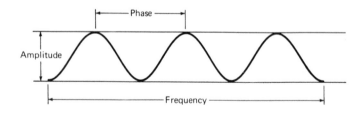

Figure 2–11.   Characteristics of an Analog Signal

A *simplex channel* can transmit in only one direction. It is rarely used in data communication because few applications communicate in only one direction. Even terminals that function only as input devices, for example, usually require that acknowledgments, data validations, and other tasks be performed by the computer.

A *half-duplex channel* can transmit in either direction, but in only one direction at a time. A device attached to a half-duplex channel cannot transmit when data are being received. It must wait until the message is finished and the channel has reversed its direction. This waiting time and direction reversal time limit the usefulness of the half-duplex channel to low- and medium-speed transmission systems.

A *full-duplex channel* can transmit in either direction simultaneously. It is suitable, therefore, for systems requiring high transmission speeds, such as computer-to-computer communication systems.

SMALL COMPUTER SYSTEMS

The advent of small computer systems has had a major impact on the auditor. In this section we define minicomputers and microcomputers and examine the hardware and software characteristics that affect the control and audit of these systems.

Minicomputers

A minicomputer is a computer in the fullest sense of the word. It typically differs from a larger computer, however, in capacity, speed, flexibility, and price. A minicomputer usually has less storage capacity than a larger computer. A minicomputer typically operates at slower processing speeds, although advances in hardware technology have reduced this difference. The user of a minicomputer has more flexibility in its operation because it can function without air conditioning and can be run on 115 volts. The price of a minicomputer is typically lower than that of a larger computer, although the price ranges overlap.

Minicomputers are used as stand-alone systems or as part of a larger system. Stand-alone minicomputers are used to perform a whole range of general-purpose applications, such as accounting, as well as special-purpose applications in science and engineering. Stand-alone minicomputers are frequently used by small and medium-size businesses for accounting applications. Minicomputers are also used as components of large data communication systems for remote processing, storage, and input/output.

Microcomputers

Like the minicomputer, the microcomputer has all the attributes of a computer. It is smaller than the minicomputer, however, and is generally slower, has less storage, and is less expensive.

Microcomputers are used as small computers or are incorporated into consumer or commercial products. Microcomputers are sold by computer stores or by mail order. They have a variety of applications and are particularly valuable for small companies that are just beginning to use the computer in their business. Microcomputers are also used as integral parts of calculators, automobile engines, robots, and many other products.

Hardware and Software Characteristics of Small Systems

The hardware and software in small computer systems differ from those in larger systems in certain respects. These differences affect the control and audit of small computer systems. A description of the major differences follows.

1. *Size.* Small-system hardware can easily be transported and exchanged with similar components. This is a particular problem with microcomputers where the computer operator may be a hobbyist with the same system at home. The computer operator may be able to remove hardware components and modify them at home.

2. *Ease of operability.* Small systems do not require a special environment. They can be operated just about anywhere. As a result, they are often located in user departments rather than in data processing departments.

3. *Nonstandardization.* Small computers are nonstandard in the sense that there are many different types of systems with different internal architecture and different software. Although this is also true for large systems, it is much more of a problem with small computer systems. Typically, a small computer from one vendor cannot communicate with or process the programs of a system from a different vendor. There are, for example, literally hundreds of different versions of BASIC used on small computers. This nonstandardization makes it virtually impossible for an auditor to be familiar with and have workable audit software for all these systems.

4. *Diskettes.* Small systems often use diskettes for secondary storage in addition to the regular hard disks and magnetic tape. Diskettes are also called floppy disks or flexible disks because they are made of soft flexible material. They are usually 5 1/4 or 3 1/2 inches in diameter, making them easily removable without detection. Unlike hard disks, diskettes have a limited life because the disk head actually touches the diskette. As a result, a diskette has an operating life of forty hours or so before it fails to read or write properly.

5. *Interpreters.* Many small computers use a programming language, such as BASIC, that is run with an interpreter rather than with the compiler that is more common in larger systems. In systems using compilers, the entire source program is compiled to produce an object program that contains the executable machine-language instructions. This object program is used for processing, while the source program may be left securely in the program library. In contrast, an interpreter reads the source program one statement at a time, generates the machine-language code for that statement only, and causes the execution of the statement. The interpreter then moves on to the next source program statement. The interpreter does not generate an object program. This means that the source program must always be used for processing. This is a disadvantage from the auditor's standpoint because source code is much more easily modifiable than object code.

6. *Menus.* Small computers typically use menus to communicate system, program, and transaction options to the terminal operator. A *menu* is a listing of available items displayed on the screen of the terminal. A menu listing system options may include available applications such as sales and receivables, and system utilities such as file maintenance. If the operator selects one of these options, a second-level menu may display available program options. If the operator has selected sales and receivables, for example, the menu may now offer a choice of order entry, sales transactions, payments on accounts, and other programs. A choice of a program may in turn generate a third-level menu of available transaction options. The selection of the sales transaction program, for example, may offer a menu of transaction options such as sales, merchandise returns, and sales allowances. Menus make system access a lot simpler for the user. They pose some danger of unauthorized access to the system, however, unless the access to menus is carefully controlled.

DATA-BASE SYSTEMS

The auditor of an advanced system is likely to encounter a *data base,* a *data-base management system* (DBMS), and a *data-base administrator.* The auditor should understand these terms, be aware of the benefits to management and users of such systems, and be familiar with the means of organizing and referencing data within the data base.

Data Base

A data base is a set of interrelated master files that are integrated to reduce data redundancy, and it is used by several application programs. The data in the data base are independent of the application programs. This contrasts with the traditional approach where each separate application program requires a separate file. The name and number of an employee, for example, may appear only once in a data base. These common data elements are linked to related data such as payroll data, personnel data, and job-cost data by means of pointers or other techniques. In contrast, a system with separate files for payroll, personnel, and work-in-process would repeat the name and number of the employee in each file.

Data-Base Management System

A data base requires software known as the data-base management system (DBMS). Application programs interface with the data base via the DBMS. The DBMS handles the storage, retrieval, updating, and maintenance of data in the data base. DBMS software includes the following:

- A *data description lanuage* (DDL) is used to create or change the data base. It defines the physical characteristics of the data, such as alphabetic or numeric, and describes the relationships between data elements and between data elements and the application programs.
- A *data manipulation language* (DML) lists the instructions, such as DELETE or FIND, used by application programs to access the data base.
- A *query language* permits access to the data base without requiring the writing of a specific program. It has many uses, including inquiry by the auditor.
- *Utilities* perform a variety of control and management functions. They include programs that generate accounting and usage statistics, and programs that copy the data base onto a tape or disk for backup purposes.

Data-Base Administrator

Large systems with a DBMS have a data-base administrator. This administrator is in charge of developing the data base and managing its use. The administrator is also responsible for designing security controls to guard against unauthorized access to the data base.

Impact of Data-Base Systems

Data-base systems provide significant operational and control advantages over traditional systems. They also pose problems that do not exist in traditional systems. These advantages and disadvantages are as follows:

- Data-base systems reduce storage requirements by reducing data redundancy.
- Data-base systems reduce the time required for file update and maintenance.
- Data in a data base are physically independent of the application programs. Accordingly, the application programmer need pay no attention to the physical structure of the file.
- Access to data is faster and easier in data-base systems. It is faster because the time lag between entry of a transaction and update of the files is reduced. Access is easier because all data are in one place and are well defined, organized, and identified.
- Data are more consistent in a data base. There are fewer instances of data elements being stored in different places with different values.
- The likelihood that data are correct is improved by the use of common edit and validation routines. These routines are typically efficient and thorough. They are also used by all application programs using the data base. Their use is not dependent on their inclusion in an individual application program.
- Control over access to the data may be better because all the data are stored in a central location.
- It is easier to set and enforce documentation standards for one data base than it is for multiple files.
- A major disadvantage of data-base systems is that they are very complex. Accordingly, it may be difficult to achieve some of the advantages listed above.
- The impact of errors may be greater in a data base. One error, for example, may create a chain of errors throughout the data base.
- Privacy of data may be a problem where multiple users have access to a common data base.
- The reconstruction of data records may be more difficult because of the elimination of redundancy from the data base.

Organizing and Referencing the Data Base

The task of organizing and referencing the data is a complex one. It requires a data dictionary, data schemata, logical data structures, and record addressing methods.

Data Dictionary

The data dictionary is a centralized inventory of the data elements stored in the data base. It is used to organize the data when the data base is created. It is also used to maintain the data base and keep track of the location of each data element within the data base. It accomplishes these tasks by maintaining a record of data on each element of data in the data base. This record might contain, for example, the source document from which the data element came, the programs that use it, and the names of all reports that are affected by it.

The data dictionary is usually maintained by software that generates a number of useful reports and performs important control functions. The software for the data dictionary either is a separate program or is built into the DBMS software. Reports generated by the software are useful to a number of people, including system designers, users, and auditors. These reports contain lists of all programs in which a data element is used, and a list of all data elements used by a particular user. The control functions performed by the software include enforcing the data definition standards, controlling access to the data base, and generating usage reports.

Data Schemata

A data schema (plural: *schemata*) specifies a logical relationship between two elements of data that are stored in the data base. In a schema, for example, a record in a vendor file will point to a record in the vendor open invoice file. The schemata are defined by the data definition language and are not included in the application programs.

The data schemata are important to the auditor. Not only do they provide a logical road map to the data base, they also define the data elements that serve as keys for retrieval of data from the file. If the field containing the inventory location code is used as a key, for example, it is easy for the auditor to extract all inventory items that are stored in a particular location.

Logical Data Structures

The logical arrangement of data within a data base is accomplished in three alternative ways: the flat file structure; a tree structure, or hierarchical data base; and a network structure.

In a *flat file structure*, every record is identical. Every record has the same number of fields, and each field is the same size and contains the same attributes. This is a traditional form of data structure for accounting files stored on sequential file media. It is required when data are stored on magnetic tapes. It is a relatively unsophisticated logical data structure but is sometimes found in data bases in combination with network structures.

In a *tree structure*, the records are logically organized in a hierarchical form. Figure 2–12 illustrates a three-level tree structure comprising customer, invoice, and line-item records. Data are retrieved from a tree structure data base by following the paths of the hierarchy that lead to the data requested. A request for the sales of a particular part to a particular customer would require a descent through the hierarchy in Figure 2–12 to read the relevant line-item records.

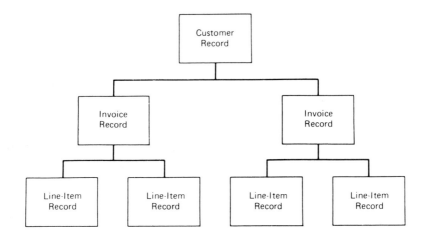

Figure 2–12. Three-Level Tree Structure

In a *network structure,* the individual files in the data base are linked together. An individual file is established for each major element (record) of data. Related records are linked together by pointers. A *pointer* is a disk address where a related record in a different file is stored. A customer record, for example, will point toward a related invoice record in the invoice file, which in turn will point toward a related line-item record in the line-item file. An individual line-item record may also point backward to the invoice record, which in turn will point back to the customer record.

Record Addressing Methods

The use of a logical data structure within a data base requires a record addressing method to enable the physical location of a record to be identified. Record addressing methods include indexed sequential, direct addressing, and lists.

DISTRIBUTED DATA PROCESSING SYSTEMS

Distributed data processing is a method of organizing and coordinating data processing. It places selective data entry, processing, and storage capabilities in the hands of the users. These users can be determined by the organization structure of the company or by their geographic allocation. Each user has a mainframe computer, minicomputer, or processing terminal to support his or her own data processing requirements. These processing systems are linked together in a network by data communications to provide central coordination and control. The term *distributed data processing* covers a variety of different types of systems. Distributed systems differ in the structure of the communications network. They also differ in the way data processing tasks are distributed around the network. A distributed data processing system covering a small geographical area is referred to as a *local area network* (LAN), whereas such a system covering a large geographical area is referred to as a *wide area network* (WAN). All of these systems, however, have had a major impact on management, EDP, and the auditors of the companies that have adopted them.

Distributed Networks

A distributed network is the interconnection of computer systems via a data communication system. A network permits one computer system to communicate with many other computer systems in the network. A network can be arranged in many alternative configurations. These configurations range from a star pattern at one extreme to a ring pattern at the other. In between these configurations are many alternative hybrid configurations.

Star Networks

In a star network, each of several satellite computer systems is linked directly to a central computer (see Figure 2–13). The central computer acts as a network-switching center. It receives transactions, analyzes them, determines the route by which they should be sent, and transmits them at properly determined times to the satellite computer.

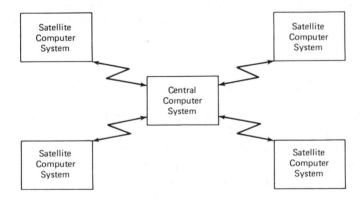

Figure 2–13. Star Network

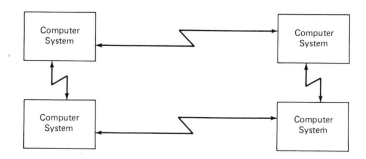

Figure 2–14.   Ring Network

Ring Networks

In a ring network, the computer system forms a circular pattern similar to that in Figure 2–14. Each computer in the ring performs its own communications activities. Communication flows around the ring unless the ring is fully interconnected, as in Figure 2–15.

Hybrid Networks

Hybrid networks contain elements of star and ring configurations. Several large computers, for example, can be connected to each other in a ring configuration, whereas each large computer can be the center of its own star configuration.

Distribution of Processing Functions

Distributed data processing systems vary in the degree to which data processing functions are distributed. One or more of the functions of data entry, processing, and storage may be distributed.

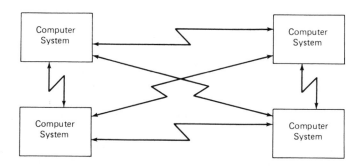

Figure 2–15.   Fully Interconnected Ring Network

Distributed Data Entry

Data entry can be performed locally using a minicomputer or intelligent terminal with secondary storage. Data can be edited locally and stored on diskettes, disk, or tape prior to transmission to a central computer system.

Distributed Processing

Processing tasks can be distributed around the network on a decentralized or centralized basis. *Decentralized distribution* gives each location similar processing tasks to perform. A wholesale distributor with warehouses in several geographical locations, for example, can perform sales order entry, accounts receivable, and inventory update on a minicomputer located in each warehouse.

Centralized distribution assigns a particular processing task to the location that is best suited to perform that task. A local minicomputer, for example, can be used to perform all fixed-asset accounting for the network. All other locations in the network will transmit data on additions, deletions, and other fixed-asset transactions to this minicomputer.

Distributed Storage

Distributed processing varies in the degree of distribution of the data base. At one extreme, the data relevant to each processing center are copied from the central data base onto secondary storage attached to the local minicomputer. Inventory and receivables files, for example, may be required locally for inventory availability and credit checks to support a sales order entry system. At the other extreme, the data base can be partitioned among the processing centers. Each processing center, for example, may perform its own payroll and maintain and update its own payroll files. These files are unique to each processing center and are not replicated on a central data base.

Impact of Distributed Processing Systems

Distributed data processing is used extensively by banks, insurance companies, hotels, hospitals, airlines, and other institutions with large data requirements and has proved to be an effective and efficient means of meeting their data processing requirements. In these institutions, distributed data processing is used for sales order entry, inventory, and other applications. At the same time, however, it has had a major impact on the control and audit of data processing systems. Some of the major changes are as follows:

- Control over access to programs may be more difficult to enforce because of the large number of locations.
- There is often decreased specialization and separation of duties because local processing centers are usually small and are controlled by the user.
- Local processing centers may not have automatic transaction logging and audit trail capabilities. This is because many of the small computers have limited processing and input/output capabilities. In particular, most transaction logs require magnetic tape, and tape is not used in many small systems.
- It may be easier to enforce common programming standards and to maintain common software in a distributed system than in a decentralized system. In a decentralized system, each locality is completely independent and may develop its own software capabilities.
- Distribution of the data base may improve security and privacy by significantly reducing the amount of data stored at any one location.

SUMMARY

The EDP auditor should be familiar with the different types of computer equipment that are available and should understand how this equipment operates. Most computers encountered by the auditor will be business-oriented digital systems. These systems may include a CPU, secondary storage, input devices, output devices, input/output control units and channels, and data preparation equipment. Digital computers represent data in binary code. Binary coding methods include character code, binary coded decimal, and hexadecimal.

Business data processing is accomplished by the interaction of the computer equipment (hardware), systems software, application software, procedures, and personnel. Application software is written in machine-level, assembly-level, or higher-level language. Most common languages for business applications are higher-level languages such as COBOL, FORTRAN, PL/1, and BASIC. Most business applications require input, processing, and output functions.

Retrieval of accounting data from computer storage requires that the auditor understand storage concepts. Data are structured by field, record, file, and data base. Alternative designs for data records include single versus master and trailer records and the use of fixed- versus variable-length fields. File organization can be sequential, direct, indexed sequential, or list. The most commonly encountered file storage media are magnetic tape and magnetic disk.

Data processing systems vary according to the methods of data input and processing. The most common installed system is the batch input/batch processing system. Many new systems, however, are using on-line input/real-time processing for accounting applications. These alternative systems require different types of controls and different audit approaches.

Data communication devices can be found in many advanced EDP systems. These devices include remote terminals, modems, communication channels, multiplexors and concentrators, and communication control units. Methods of data communication include modulation techniques, transmission modes, and transmission direction alternatives.

Small computer systems are creating a new challenge for the auditor. These small computer systems include minicomputers as well as microcomputers. The challenge involved is the result of such features as interpreter programs, menus, diskettes, and nonstandardization of hardware and software.

Data-base systems combine master files in one integrated file under the command of software known as a data-base management system. Data-base systems are managed by a data-base administrator.

Distributed data processing systems place processing power in the hands of the user while retaining central control and coordination. These systems differ in both structure and the way data processing tasks are distributed.

REVIEW QUESTIONS

2-1. When is the auditor likely to encounter data in analog form?

2-2. What seven types of equipment are often found in business-oriented computers?

2-3. Differentiate between primary and secondary storage.

2-4. What is the purpose of input/output control units and channels?

2-5. Define binary system, bit, and byte.

2-6. Why do many computers code data in both character code and arithmetic code?

2-7. What is the value of hexadecimal code to the auditor?

2-8. Define the EDP hardware concept of address as it is used in primary storage.

2-9. Describe the sequence of events followed by the control unit as it initiates and directs the processing of data.

2-10. What is a logical operation?

2-11. Name all the elements that together make a data processing system work.

2-12. Contrast machine-level, assembly-level, and high-level programming languages.

2-13. What major batch and on-line higher-level languages are most likely to be encountered by the auditor?

2-14. Differentiate between a source program and an object program.

2-15. Under what circumstances is data entry not preceded by data preparation?

2-16. Describe the nine processing tasks.

2-17. What is the relationship between field, record, file, and data base?

2-18. What is a record key? Is there only one record key?

2-19. What kinds of applications are best suited to sequential file organizations?

2-20. Is it fair to say that direct file organization is an unnecessary extravagance for accounting applications?

2-21. Contrast indexed sequential and list organization.

2-22. What is the purpose of blocking records on magnetic tape?

2-23. What controls are used to prevent inadvertent erasure of data on magnetic tape?

2-24. How are data on a magnetic disk located?

2-25. What are the advantages and disadvantages of batch input/batch processing?

2-26. Describe the function of the reference file and transaction log in an on-line input/batch processing system.

2-27. What advantages can multiprogramming and data communication provide for accounting systems? What problems do they create?

2-28. Define on-line real-time systems.

2-29. Describe the functions of each of the following terminals:
   a. Data entry terminals
   b. Multipurpose terminals
   c. Intelligent terminals
   d. Computer graphics terminals
   e. Point-of-sale terminals
   f. Touch-tone devices
   g. Keyboard/printers
   h. Data collection terminals

2-30. What is a modem? Where in a data communication system are you likely to find modems?

2-31. Medium- and high-speed channels are used most frequently for data processing applications. For each of these channel speeds, give examples of channel types and the data processing devices they can handle.

2-32. Differentiate between a multiplexor and a concentrator.

2-33. What are the functions of a communication control unit?

2-34. Data are transmitted in analog form. How is the analog form varied to represent different elements of data?

2-35. Contrast asynchronous and synchronous transmission. For each of these transmission modes, give examples of systems for which it would be suitable.

2-36. Differentiate between simplex, half-duplex, and full-duplex transmission.

2-37. Contrast minicomputers, microcomputers, and large mainframe computers.

2-38. Describe diskettes, menus, and interpreters.

2-39. Data-base systems have a data base, a data-base management system, and a data-base administrator. Define each of these terms.

2-40. Explain the function of each of the following four elements of a data-base management system:
   a. Data description language
   b. Data manipulation language
   c. Query language
   d. Utilities

2-41. The presence of a data-base system has a major impact on the auditor. Describe five characteristics of data-base systems that affect the control and audit of these systems.

2-42. The task of organizing and referencing data in a data base is a complex task. Describe the role of each of the following in completing this task:
   a. Data dictionary
   b. Data schemata
   c. Logical data structures
   d. Record addressing methods

2-43. What is distributed data processing?

2-44. Define the term distributed network. What are the main types of distributed network?

2-45. Distributed systems vary in the degree to which data processing functions are distributed. Describe what functions are distributed for each of the following:
   a. Distributed data entry
   b. Distributed processing
   c. Distributed storage

2-46. Distributed data processing systems have had a major impact on the control of data processing systems. Describe three major changes resulting from this impact on data processing systems.

OBJECTIVE QUESTIONS

2-47. An EDP batch processing system for file updating would
   a. Process transactions in the order in which they occur
   b. Be useful for an airline reservation system
   c. Normally require disk storage for the master file
   d. All of the above
   e. None of the above (*IIA*)

2-48. A macro instruction in a computer program
   a. Causes processing to stop
   b. Causes looping to occur

    c. Represents a number of output operations built into the computer by the manufacturer

    d. Is a single instruction which can initiate several machine operations

    e. None of the above (*IIA*)

2–49. A binary numbering system
    a. Is the basis of digital computer logic
    b. Uses only the symbols 0 and 1
    c. Expresses expansion in powers of 2
    d. Is convertible to hexadecimal notation
    e. All of the above (*IIA*)

2–50. A block of records on magnetic tape is most likely to be
    a. Randomly accessed
    b. Separated from other blocks of records by a "gap"
    c. Limited to 80 characters of data
    d. Created from magnetic disk input
    e. All of the above (*IIA*)

2–51. An auditor should be familiar with a client's electronic data processing hardware and software. An important element of the client's software is the application program. Another element of software is the
    a. Cathode-ray tube (CRT)
    b. Central processing unit (CPU)
    c. Magnetic tape drive
    d. Compiler (*AICPA adapted*)

2–52. The machine-language program that results when an assembly- or higher-level-language program is translated is called a(n)
    a. Processor program
    b. Object program
    c. Source program
    d. Wired program (*AICPA adapted*)

2–53. An electronic data processing technique that collects data into groups to permit convenient and efficient processing is known as
    a. Direct processing
    b. Multiprogramming
    c. Batch processing
    d. Real-time processing (*AICPA adapted*)

2–54. A group of related records in a data processing system is a
    a. Character
    b. Field
    c. Cluster
    d. File (*AICPA*)

2–55. In a real-time computer application
    a. The system provides immediate response to the user
    b. Records may be updated immediately as transactions occur
    c. Remote terminals are usually an integral part of the system
    d. Response time may be virtually instantaneous
    e. All of the above (*IIA*)

2–56. The objectives in the development of an EDP data-base management system include
  a. Reduction in the amount of stored data to meet an organization's needs
  b. Improvement of flexibility in the creation of logical records
  c. Elimination of reports that contain similar information
  d. Reduction in the amount of hardware required
  e. Both a and b above (*IIA*)

2–57. The real-time feature normally would be *least* useful when applied to accounting for a firm's
  a. Bank account
  b. Property and depreciation
  c. Customer accounts receivable
  d. Merchandise inventory (*AICPA*)

2–58. An interpreter language
  a. Compiles an entire source program and produces an object program
  b. Displays available system options on the screen for the convenience of the terminal user
  c. Provides the interface between the application programs and the data base
  d. Generates machine-language code for one program statement at a time
  e. None of the above

2–59. A distributed ring network
  a. Is several computer systems interconnected in a circular pattern
  b. Is one computer and several data entry terminals interconnected in a circular pattern
  c. Is several satellite computer systems connected to a central computer system
  d. Protects magnetic tape from accidental erasure

2–60. Intelligent terminals
  a. Are programmable
  b. Contain microprocessors
  c. Have limited storage capacity
  d. Are useful for formatting and editing input data prior to transmission
  e. All of the above

2–61. Which of the following best describes a distributed processing system?
  a. A number of independent computers at one location which users can operate through telephone lines
  b. One large-scale computer with a processing line to users
  c. A number of independent computers geographically disbursed
  d. A number of geographically disbursed computers interconnected by communications lines
  e. None of the above (*IIA*)

2–62. Which of the following is an auditor certain to encounter in the audit of a distributed data processing system?
  a. A distributed data-base management system

b. A large-scale central computer
c. Telecommunications
d. A data-definition language
e. None of the above (*IAA adapted*)

CASES AND EXERCISES

2–63. **a.** Contrast the principal characteristic of an "assembly" computer programming language with that of a "higher-level" computer programming language.
b. Name and describe two higher-level batch-oriented computer programming languages. (*IIA adapted*)

2–64. Executive management of Continental Incorporated, a rapidly expanding manufacturing company, has been reviewing a proposal prepared by the manager of the Data Processing Department to update the computer equipment now in use. The present equipment includes a central processing unit, tape drives, card punch, card reader, card sorter, and a printer. The data processing manager suggests that new equipment be acquired to provide an on-line input/batch processing system with immediate reference file update. The new system will be used for inventory stock control and more efficient operation.

Required:
a. Briefly describe the function of each item now in use.
b. Identify two types of equipment not mentioned above that would be required for the proposed on-line input/batch processing system. (*IIA adapted*)

2–65. Should sequential, indexed sequential, or direct-access file organization be used for the following applications?
a. Accounts receivable
b. Inventory
c. Payroll
d. Accounts payable

2–66. Convert the following hexadecimal numbers to their decimal equivalent:
a. B3C5
b. 6DA2
c. 93E1
d. FB56

2–67. Second Bank, Inc., has four automatic teller terminals located in downtown Portland. A bank customer inserts a special card into the machine, enters a special identification code, and depresses keys to signify the amount and type of transaction being entered. The data are transmitted immediately via voice-grade lines to a local multiplexor. The data are then transmitted via satellite to the bank's data center in Salt Lake City where the transaction is processed on an on-line real-time basis. The authority to pay cash or confirm deposits or transfers is transmitted back to the terminal. The bank customer receives cash or other confirmation from the terminal within a few seconds of data entry.

Required: Prepare a systems flowchart identifying the data processing and communications devices necessary to make such a system work.

Chapter 3
ANALYTICAL TOOLS: FLOWCHARTING AND DECISION TABLES

Learning Objectives

After completing this chapter, the reader should be able to:

1. Describe a systems flowchart and state how it is used by the computer auditor.

2. Describe a program flowchart and state how it is used by the computer auditor.

3. Describe a decision logic table and state how it is used by the computer auditor.

4. Describe a layout chart and state how it is used by the computer auditor.

5. Describe a grid chart and state how it is used by the computer auditor.

The maze through which the computer auditor must typically follow a document through the accounting system, or its processing within the logic of a computer program, can be horrendously complex. The complexity can often be attributed to systems that interweave the manual, mechanical, and computer processing of data within the same accounting application. The auditing task is easier and more efficient when analytical tools are used to guide the auditor through the processing labyrinth.

In this chapter we discuss the kinds of analytical tools that are useful in understanding the intricacies of a system for processing accounting data. Our discussion focuses on (1) flowcharting, which includes a review of general concepts, systems flowcharting, and program flowcharting; (2) decision logic tables; and (3) layout charts and grid charts.

FLOWCHARTING

Flowcharting has become an important part of the documentation of the audit process despite some disadvantages. Flowcharts are used to document both the accounting system in general and specific computer programs. System and program flowcharts that are understandable and accurate can be useful to the auditor. Understandability and ease of construction are enhanced by the use of flowcharting conventions. Accuracy is ensured by the use of flowchart testing.

Computer auditors need to understand flowcharting for several reasons. They must be able to prepare flowcharts as part of the documentation for the audit process. They must be able to analyze flowcharts prepared by others. And, finally, the flowchart provides a tool for communication about systems and programs.

Flowcharting's advantages generally outweigh its disadvantages. There are three major advantages. First, a graphic presentation of a system or a series of sequential processes is easier to understand than a verbal description. Second, a flowchart shows the steps required and the flow of documents from person to person in carrying out the functions depicted in an accounting system, or the flow of data within a computer program, thus minimizing a tendency to overlook controls existing between functions or between departments or within a computer program. Third, a flowchart avoids a detailed study of written descriptions and procedures without sacrificing the auditor's ability to appraise the effectiveness of internal controls under review. There are two major disadvantages to flowcharts. First, a flowchart is a unique medium requiring specific expertise. This disadvantage can be overcome, however, by study and practice. Second, the preparation of a flowchart requires a significant amount of time. This time requirement, however, is somewhat offset by the contribution the flowchart makes to a better evaluation of the accounting process.

The two main types of flowcharts are the *program flowchart* and the *systems flowchart*. Other systems flowcharts that may be encountered by the computer auditor are the *document flowchart* and the *audit, or internal control, flowchart*. Examples of these flowcharts are given in the following sections. In brief, a *program flowchart* shows the detailed steps and logic of a computer program. A *systems flowchart* depicts the broad flow of work through the organization; it stresses the flow of data. A *document flowchart* is a graphic presentation of the flow of documents from one department to another showing the source, flow, and final disposition of various copies of all documents. An *audit, or internal control, flowchart* is a combination of the systems and document flowcharts. It is often called a systems flowchart by auditors. This combination flowchart shows document flows through departments, which is of significance to the auditor in analyzing the separation of functions for internal control purposes. This flowchart also shows the processing steps that the documents go through, including the highlighting of internal control procedures.

The construction and interpretation of flowcharts is facilitated by the adoption of various conventions. A *convention* is a general usage or custom, or an accepted or prescribed practice. Some conventions pertain to flowcharting in general, and others are of importance primarily to auditors. Examples of these conventions are given in the following sections.

The general conventions include information flow and symbols. Information flow is from left to right, top to bottom. The standard set of symbols includes some that are applicable to both systems and program flowcharts, such as the process symbol, while others are primarily applicable to programming, such as the decision symbol. Symbols for both systems and program flowcharting appear in the following sections.

Auditor conventions include the audit trail and flowchart organization. Flowcharts prepared by auditors show the audit trail for two reasons. First, the auditor must be able to trace source documents or input through the system to computer printouts or files, and vice versa. Second, the auditor must identify the internal controls in the system. Flowchart organization can be an issue in flowcharts prepared by auditors because the auditor highlights processing decisions and areas of responsibility for subsequent analysis of internal controls.

Testing a creative document like a flowchart can be a difficult task but is necessary to ensure accuracy. The testing of systems flowcharts is often easier than the testing of program flowcharts. Systems flowcharts can be tested by following an example of every document in the flowchart through the accounting system. Program flowcharts can be tested by following the program logic through the computer program. (The testing of systems and program flowcharts is discussed later in this chapter.)

Systems Flowcharting

Computer auditors utilize systems (audit) flowcharts to portray the broad flow of documents and data graphically through an entire accounting system. The general conventions pertaining to flowcharting are observed in systems flowcharting, plus some additional ones. Systems flowcharts are tested for accuracy by following documents through them.

In depicting the broad flow of documents and data through an entire accounting system application, computer auditors utilize systems flowcharts to emphasize *what* processing is done in the system, rather than *how* it is done. The systems flowchart will show what documents are originated within the system and where they end up, but any processing performed on them will usually be described in general terms instead of detailed descriptions of every calculation or operation performed. In Figure 3–1, for example, "Prepare Payroll" in the EDP department section of the flowchart summarizes the numerous calculations and other activities required to prepare payroll checks. In emphasizing what processing is done in the system, the auditor will highlight input into it, output from it, functional responsibility for what is done, and internal control procedures performed to ensure the accuracy of processing results.

Conventions

Conventions pertaining to flowcharting in general, and additional conventions adopted by auditors, aid the systems flowchart preparer in highlighting systems input and output, functional responsibilities, and internal control procedures.

The auditor shows input into the accounting system and output from it on a systems flowchart by using various symbols. The most important of these symbols are shown in Figure 3–2. All input and output can be depicted with just one symbol, the parallelogram. This is referred to as the basic input/output symbol. The specialized symbols, however, such as the document or magnetic tape, more effectively portray what medium is actually being used. These specialized symbols highlight for the auditor the input and output for the system.

In preparing and analyzing systems flowcharts, the computer auditor may not be concerned about *how* a process is performed in the system, but he or she is concerned about *who* is doing it. The highlighting of functional responsibilities is important in determining whether there is appropriate segregation of functions to deter fraud and embezzlement.

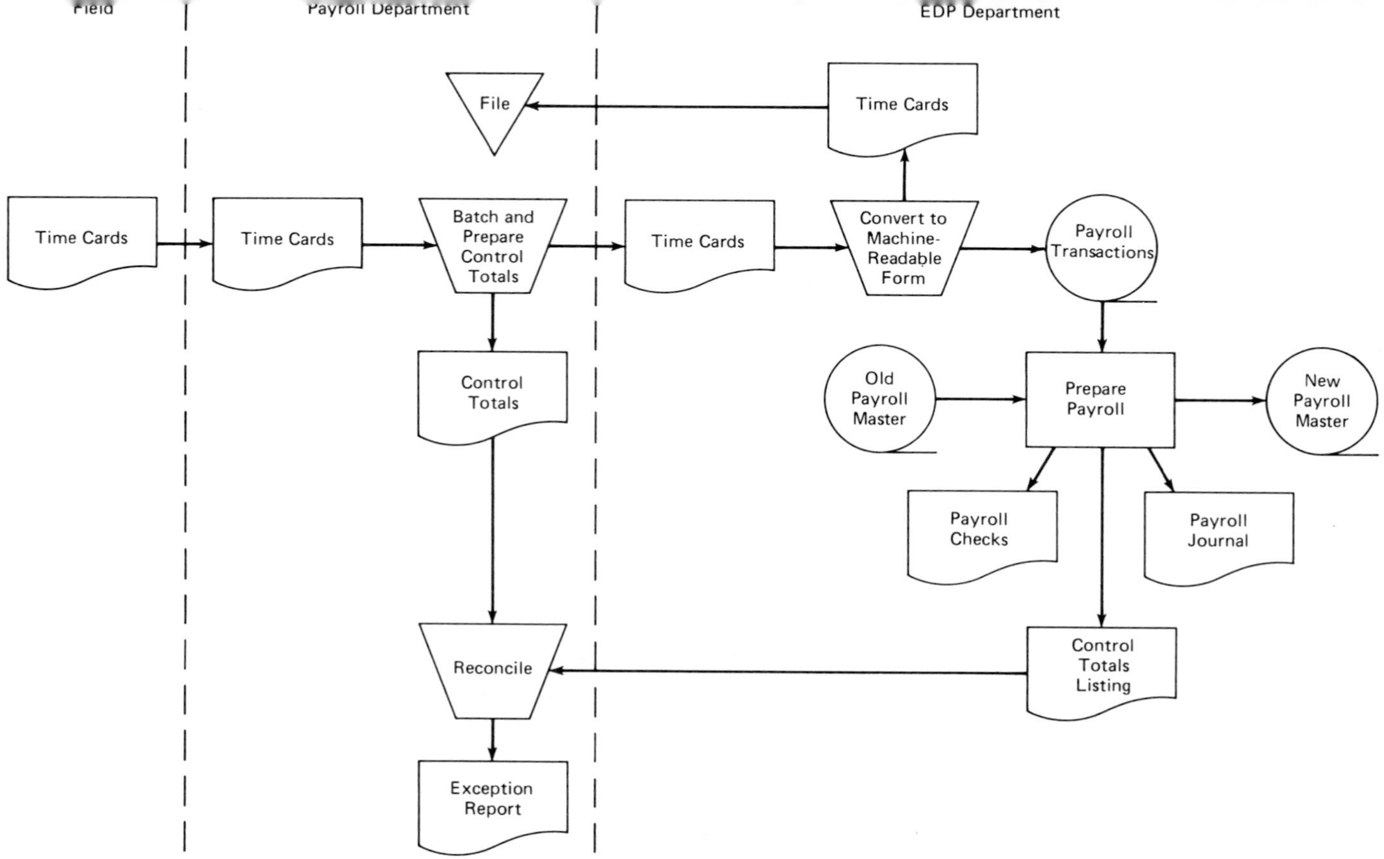

Field

Payroll Department

EDP Department

Time Cards → Time Cards → Batch and Prepare Control Totals

File ← Time Cards

Batch and Prepare Control Totals → Control Totals → Reconcile → Exception Report

Time Cards → Convert to Machine-Readable Form → Payroll Transactions → Prepare Payroll

Old Payroll Master → Prepare Payroll

Prepare Payroll → New Payroll Master

Prepare Payroll → Payroll Journal

Prepare Payroll → Payroll Checks

Prepare Payroll → Control Totals Listing → Reconcile

Figure 3–1. Simplified Systems Flowchart for Payroll

79

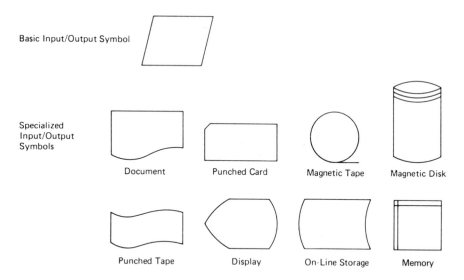

Basic Input/Output Symbol

Specialized
Input/Output
Symbols

Document   Punched Card   Magnetic Tape   Magnetic Disk

Punched Tape   Display   On-Line Storage   Memory

Figure 3-2.   Input/Output Symbols for Systems Flowcharting

To aid in highlighting the functional responsibility aspects of processing performed in the system, the basic process symbol, a rectangle, is often replaced by more-specialized process symbols. The auditor is typically concerned about *who* is performing *what* manual procedures, highlighted by the trapezoid. Other specialized symbols highlight other types of processing (see Figure 3–3).

To complete the flowchart, the computer auditor must be familiar with additional symbols. A *terminal symbol* is sometimes used to indicate the beginning or ending of a process. The *on-page* and *off-page con-*

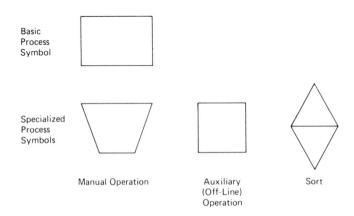

Basic
Process
Symbol

Specialized
Process
Symbols

Manual Operation   Auxiliary
(Off-Line)
Operation   Sort

Figure 3-3.   Process Symbols for Systems Flowcharting

nectors provide for a smooth flow in depicting processing and help eliminate unnecessary lines or keep a flowchart from having a cluttered look. The *annotation symbol* provides a structured means of supplying additional information about any aspect of the process. The *off-line storage symbol* identifies the point where information is stored and therefore indicates where in the processing cycle it can be retrieved for audit purposes (see Figure 3–4).

The highlighting of internal control procedures in the systems flowchart includes specifying two things: (1) those controls that have been incorporated into the system to ensure the accuracy of processing results, and (2) those components of the audit trail that allow the auditor to trace the flow of documents and data forward and backward through the processing cycle. The specification of controls includes indicating those points in the processing cycle where document counts and financial totals are created and reconciled. Highlighting the audit trail includes indicating how an amount from a source document can be followed from its initial conversion to machine-readable form, to a transaction listing, to a master file, and finally to a printout. The simplified systems flowchart for payroll in Figure 3–1, for example, shows how the time cards move from the field to the payroll department, to the EDP department, and finally back to the payroll department where they are filed. The control totals prepared in the payroll department, such as the number of time cards to be processed and perhaps the gross payroll, are then compared with the control listing prepared by the computer.

Testing

A systems flowchart is not complete until it has been tested for accuracy. Accuracy in a systems flowchart means that all significant documents and processes are shown, and that the flow of information is actually as depicted. To test for accuracy, the auditor should follow an example of

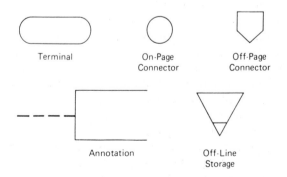

Figure 3–4. Additional Symbols for Systems Flowcharting

every document shown in the flowchart through the accounting system. The auditor should look for omissions—documents not on the flowchart—and errors in information flow. Terms that the auditor may encounter and are sometimes used to define testing a systems flowchart include *cradle-to-grave test, sample of one,* and *walkthrough.*

Program Flowcharting

Computer auditors utilize program flowcharts to portray the processing of accounting data graphically within the computer. The general conventions pertaining to flowcharting are also observed in program flowcharting, but numerous additional conventions pertain solely to program flowcharting. Program flowcharts are tested by following the program logic, a task much more difficult than testing a systems flowchart because of the incredible number of logic paths incorporated into most computer programs.

Program flowcharts, also called *block* or *logic diagrams,* show the detailed steps and processing logic of a computer program. The auditor's analysis of the detailed steps and processing logic of a computer program is similar to his or her analysis of activities performed in a manual system. In both systems, the auditor's concern is that the accounting data be processed correctly by the computer and that the errors be detected and corrected. The program flowchart is a graphic means of depicting *how* this is done.

Conventions

In depicting *how* data are processed by the computer and *how* errors are detected and corrected, the auditor follows flowcharting conventions. There are general conventions that apply to all audit flowcharts. There are also additional conventions pertaining solely to program flowcharting.

General conventions for program flowcharting include the flow of information and a standard set of symbols. Information in the flowchart flows from left to right and from top to bottom. The set of symbols for program flowcharting is much simpler than that for systems flowcharting because (1) a computer program processes one record at a time in a specific accounting application, and (2) a segment of a program typically operates in only one field of that record. For example, in showing the processing of the dollar amount of a payment received on an accounts receivable transaction record, the only input/output symbol used may be the basic parallelogram. Processing of data within the program can be depicted with only two symbols—the basic processing symbol of the rectangle and the diamond symbol—to define the alternative logic paths of decisions. The annotation symbol can be used to provide additional pro-

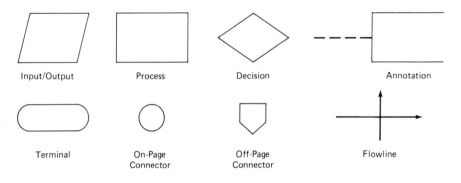

Figure 3–5. Basic Set of Symbols for Program Flowcharting

cessing information. The basic set is complete with the addition of the terminal symbol to show the beginning and end of processing, connector symbols, and flow lines (see Figure 3–5). A simplified program flowchart is shown in Figure 3–6.

In addition to the general conventions, auditors frequently utilize a convention in program flowcharting that pertains to the organization of the flowchart. The basic program flowchart shown in Figure 3–6 portrays only the logic of the program in a rather straightforward fashion. The auditor organizes the logic flow of the program to highlight several aspects of processing to facilitate the analysis of controls ensuring its accuracy. In either preparing or examining the flowchart, the auditor will search for and attempt to highlight components defining processing flow, processing analysis, and the audit trail. Figure 3–7 demonstrates the organizational approach used by auditors.

In the processing flow component, the auditor will pay particular attention to the extent of the editing of input data, the mainstream processing of the data, and the output from the program, including error handling. In Figure 3–7 all input editing is highlighted by placing it under the heading "Edit Input Data." Depending on the extent of the editing, an entire page or several pages of flowcharting may be devoted to it with appropriate page headings. A separate section in Figure 3–7, the column headed "Mainstream Processing," highlights for the auditor the mathematical computations used to calculate the payroll. The next column, "Program Output," highlights the output produced by the program. As with editing, a page or several pages may be devoted to depicting the processing and output with appropriate page headings. Error handling will be shown throughout the flowchart. In Figure 3–7 the convention adopted was to show all errors as right exits from the decision or diamond symbols. Furthermore, for the sake of simplicity, these errors are shown as EDP department errors. The input errors, in particular, are more likely to be caused by the users rather than EDP.

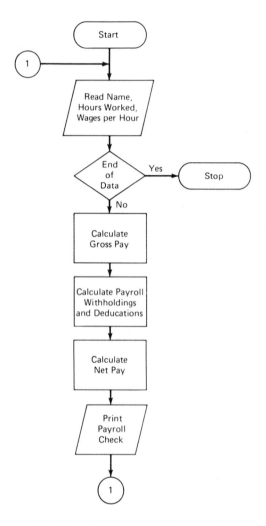

Figure 3–6. Simplified Program Flowchart for Payroll

To test processing results in the processing analysis component, the auditor will note the existence of code segments of the program to ascertain that some reasonableness limit has not been exceeded. For example, in Figure 3–7 the processing is analyzed to ascertain that no employee receives a check in excess of $3,500, an amount that would be exceeded only in the case of some error. A second reasonableness test performed on the processing is to determine whether net pay plus deductions adds to gross pay.

In the audit trail component, the concern is that data can be traced backward and forward through the program and that control totals exist to detect the loss, addition, or change in data. In the simplified example

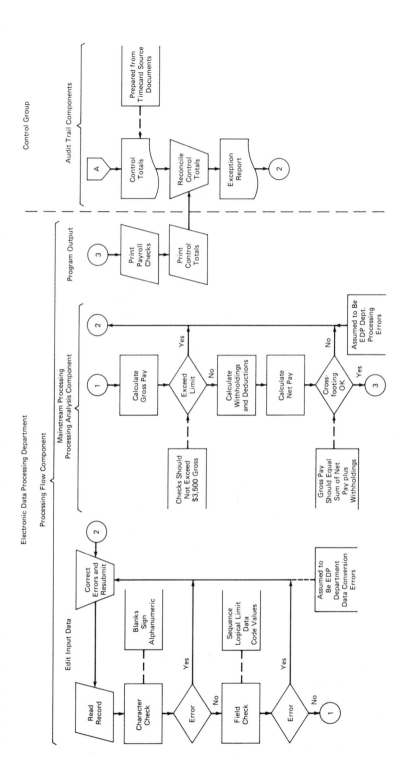

Figure 3-7. Payroll Program Flowchart Demonstrating Processing Flow and Processing Analysis

85

in Figure 3–7, we can envision tracing the information on the input record through the editing and calculation processes to a printed payroll check. The control totals, as shown in Figure 3–1, would typically be generated by the payroll department. That department, or a separate unit, would then perform the comparison shown under "Control Group" in Figure 3–7.

For purposes of analyzing the organization of the program flowchart, we have broken it into several components that receive the computer auditor's specific attention. When prepared by auditors, these organizational conventions can be followed. These components are typically intermingled in program flowcharts prepared by others. The auditor's task is to determine whether they are there and to what extent.

An additional convention that computer auditors encounter in the preparation, analysis, or discussion about program flowcharts consists of concepts for organizing the logic of a computer program into basic programming patterns. The auditors' task is easier if they can detect basic patterns used in programming. With such detection the auditors can anticipate the flow of processing and thereby follow it more easily. They can better understand what is going on than they could if every symbol encountered required reflection on what was happening. Pattern recognition can provide the auditors with an overview of the forest and prevent their becoming lost in the trees of symbols.

Figure 3–8 shows four basic programming patterns: (1) a simple sequence pattern, (2) a loop pattern, (3) a selection pattern, and (4) a branch or link pattern. Detecting a simple sequence, the auditor would not anticipate any interruption in processing flow. With a loop pattern, the auditor would anticipate the repetition of an operation until some condition was satisfied and he or she would then jump to another part of the program. A selection pattern means that either one of two paths will be followed. Recognizing a branch or link pattern, the auditor would anticipate the flow of processing to continue uninterrupted or jump to another part of the program, depending on what condition was satisfied. In each case, by being able to recognize the programming pattern, the computer auditor is better able to follow the processing flow and analyze its results.

A final convention that computer auditors encounter consists of concepts for the actual construction of the flowchart. These include the concept of contrasting the flowchart with both the narrative description of how the computer program is supposed to operate and how it actually functions and the concept of automatic flowcharting.

This concept of contrasting, however, usually results in an exercise in frustration for the auditor. If the auditor is constructing the flowchart, the program will already have been written, and the auditor will usually find that the narrative description and actual program do not agree with each other. Even worse, if the auditor is reviewing a previously prepared

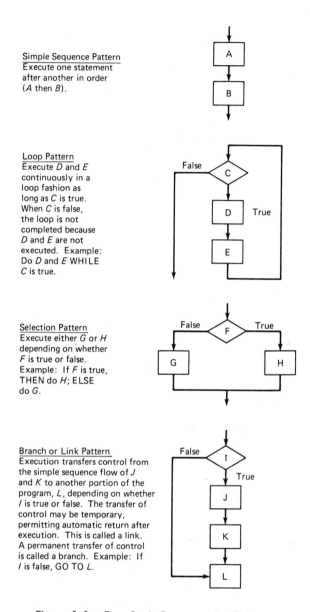

Simple Sequence Pattern
Execute one statement
after another in order
(A then B).

Loop Pattern
Execute D and E
continuously in a
loop fashion as
long as C is true.
When C is false,
the loop is not
completed because
D and E are not
executed. Example:
Do D and E WHILE
C is true.

Selection Pattern
Execute either G or H
depending on whether
F is true or false.
Example: If F is true,
THEN do H; ELSE
do G.

Branch or Link Pattern
Execution transfers control from
the simple sequence flow of J
and K to another portion of the
program, L, depending on whether
I is true or false. The transfer of
control may be temporary,
permitting automatic return after
execution. This is called a link.
A permanent transfer of control
is called a branch. Example: If
I is false, GO TO L.

Figure 3–8. Four Basic Programming Patterns

flowchart, he or she will typically find that the flowchart does not agree
with the narrative description and the program does not function according to either the narrative or the flowchart. The differences should be
brought to the client's attention and documented in the working papers,
but only rarely will they have a material influence on internal control

effectiveness or financial statement presentation. The auditor's primary concern is with the computer program and the actual processing that is being performed. Although the concept of contrasting described above should be undertaken to determine whether significant problems exist, the flowchart should agree with the actual processing performed by the computer.

Another concept that the auditor is likely to encounter in flowchart construction is automatic flowcharting. To relieve the tediousness and cost of manually preparing program flowcharts, computer vendors and some software companies have developed computer programs that will automatically generate flowcharts. These programs create flowcharts by analyzing the source code, such as a copy of the program in COBOL or FORTRAN language. If the auditor can ascertain that the source code analyzed is for the program actually used in processing the accounting data, he or she can at least be confident that the computer-prepared flowchart is a true representation of how the program operates.

Testing

A program flowchart is not complete until it has been tested. The objective of testing is to verify that the graphic presentation of the program is a true portrayal of how the program actually functions. For simple programs, desk checking may be appropriate; for complex programs, more-elaborate techniques may be required.

Desk checking program code means that the auditor compares a source-code copy of the program, such as in FORTRAN or COBOL language, with the flowchart. This line-by-line comparison of the program with the flowchart can be tedious. If the program is not a simple one, it is easy to lose track of what is going on.

Techniques available for testing the flowcharts of complex programs concentrate on an analysis of how those programs actually function. Once the auditor understands how the program processes accounting data, he or she is then in a position to determine whether the flowchart documentation is an accurate graphic representation of that processing. Examples of techniques that can aid the auditor in following the program logic in order to make a comparison with the flowchart include decision logic tables and processing real or simulated data through the program or a copy of it. Decision logic tables are discussed in the following section.

DECISION LOGIC TABLES

Although the inclusion of decision logic tables (DLT) in the documentation of the audit process is not as common as the inclusion of flowcharts, these tables are a graphic means of presenting the logic of a computer program or any other decision process. The decision logic table is divided into four parts. Several conventions pertain to the preparation and use of DLTs. Although testing is necessary to ensure the accuracy of the DLT, these tables are usually prepared by the auditor as a tool for testing something else—the computer program.

The reasons why the computer auditor needs to understand decision logic tables are the same as the reasons why he or she needs to understand flowcharting. The auditor must be able to prepare them as part of the audit documentation process in the analysis of computer programs. And the auditor must be able not only to analyze DLTs prepared by others, but also communicate with others about computer programs analyzed using a DLT.

Although the use of DLTs as documentation in the audit process is not as widespread as that of flowcharts, they have several advantages: (1) DLTs are compact and easily understood, making them an effective means of communication between the auditor and others, (2) DLTs provide a systematic approach for completely and accurately analyzing the processing logic of a computer program; and (3) it is easy to generate test data for a computer program using a DLT. A major reason why DLTs have not been adopted to the same extent as flowcharts is that auditors have not been trained to use them. Most general texts in auditing, for example, discuss flowcharts but not DLTs.

The logic of a computer program or any other decision process can be analyzed and graphically portrayed with a DLT. Different combinations of decisions that result in different combinations of processing calculations or functions are shown in tabular form in the DLT. The list of decisions is referred to as a set of *conditions*. The list of processing calculations or functions is referred to as a set of *actions*. The different combinations of conditions and resulting actions are referred to as *decision rules*, or simply *rules*. A DLT for the calculation of automobile insurance premiums is shown in Table 3–1. Decision rule 3 in this table says that for a male driver, age 25 or under, who has had an accident in the last five years, the insurance premium consists of a basic premium plus a high-risk premium adjustment with no good-driver adjustment.

Parts of Table

As shown in Table 3–2, the DLT is divided into four parts: condition stub, action stub, condition entries, and action entries.

In the *condition stub*, we list the decisions to be made. If we are preparing the DLT by reference to a flowchart, we will list a condition for each decision symbol (diamond) encountered in the flowchart (see Figure 3–9). The question to be answered yes or no is written inside the decision symbol on the flowchart and is the same question we list in the

Table 3–1. Decision Logic Table for Automobile Insurance Premiums

			Decisions Rules							
	Insurance Premiums		*1*	*2*	*3*	*4*	*5*	*6*	*7*	*8*
Conditions	Is driver a male?		Y	Y	Y	Y	N	N	N	N
	Is driver over 25?		Y	Y	N	N	Y	Y	N	N
	Has driver had accident in last 5 years?		Y	N	Y	N	Y	N	Y	N
Actions	Calculate basic premium		X	X	X	X	X	X	X	X
	Calculate high-risk premium adjustment				X	X				
	Calculated good-driver premium adjustment			X		X		X		X
	Write premium notice		X	X	X	X	X	X	X	X

condition stub. If we are preparing the DLT by reference to a program listing, we will list a condition for each *"IF"* statement in the program, as shown in Figure 3–10. The question that can be answered as yes or no following the *IF* statement is the question we list in the condition stub.

After completing the condition stub, we prepare the *action stub.* In the action stub, we list the processing calculations or functions. If we are preparing the DLT by reference to a flowchart, we will list an action for each process symbol (rectangle) encountered in the flowchart (see Figure 3–9). The calculation or function, such as "Write Invoice," written inside the process symbol is the same calculation or function that we list in the action stub. If we are preparing the DLT by reference to a program listing, we will list as actions those calculations or functions that conclude the *IF* statement as shown in Figure 3–10.

Once we have listed the conditions and actions in the condition

Table 3–2. General Form of the Decision
Logic Table

		Decision Rules				
Heading		*1*	*2*	*3*	*4*	*5*
Condition stub		CONDITION ENTRIES				
Action stub		ACTION ENTRIES				

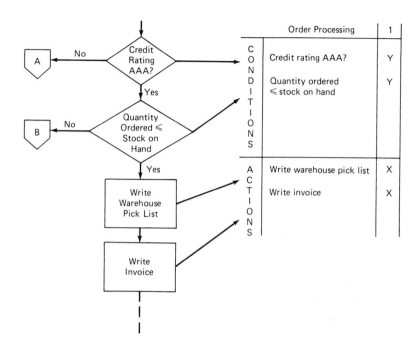

Figure 3–9. Example of DLT Prepared from Program Flowchart

stub and action stub, respectively, we complete the table by yes or no (Y or N) responses in the *condition entries* part to questions listed in the condition stub. For each combination of yes or no condition entries, we then indicate with X's in the *action entires* part those combinations of calculations or functions performed corresponding to the set of conditions specified. The set of conditions in conjunction with the set of actions constitutes a rule, often referred to as a *decision rule.* For example,

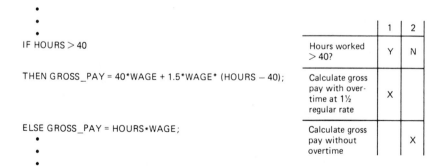

Figure 3–10.   Example of DLT Prepared from PL/1 Program Listing

decision rule 1 in Figure 3–10 indicates that employees working more than forty hours receive overtime pay at one and one-half times their regular rate for hours in excess of 40.

Conventions

Numerous conventions exist regarding the preparation and use of DLTs. The two conventions most important to the computer auditor are a technique for the systematic development of a DLT and the elimination of redundant decision rules.

The technique for the systematic development of the DLT assists the auditor in completing two tasks that seem to cause the most difficulty: (1) determining whether all possible combinations of conditions have been accounted for and whether the correct number of decision rules is specified, and (2) completing the yes or no responses in the "Condition Entries" part rapidly and without overlooking any combination.

The auditor determines whether all possible combinations of conditions have been accounted for and whether the correct number of decision rules is specified by using the formula

$$DR = 2^n$$

where DR is the number of decision rules and n is the number of conditions listed in the condition stub. For example, if there are three conditions, as in Table 3–1, there are eight possible combinations of these conditions and, therefore, eight decision rules ($8 = 2^3$). Once the auditor has listed all the conditions, he or she can determine how many combinations of conditions, or decision rules, are necessary and can provide a vertical column for each of them. The next step is to develop these combinations of conditions without overlooking possible combinations and without creating duplicate combinations.

The auditor completes the yes or no responses specifying the combinations of conditions, without overlooking or creating duplicate combinations, by following an algorithm. The algorithm specifies that the auditor start with the *last* condition in the condition stub and alternate yes or no responses for it in the condition entries. For the *next-to-the-last* condition in the condition stub, the auditor alternates two yes responses and two no responses for it in the condition entries. Moving backward up the list of conditions, the auditor then alternates four yes with four no responses, then eight yes with eight no responses, and then continues to double the number (16, 32, 64, etc.) until the list of conditions is exhausted. Following this algorithm, all possible combinations of conditions will be specified, none will be overlooked, and none will be duplicated. As an example, the reader should apply this algorithm to the DLT in Table 3–1.

Another convention important to auditors regarding the preparation and use of DLTs is the elimination of redundant decision rules and the testing of completeness of the remaining rules. By eliminating redundancies, the auditor will be able to test all the logic paths in a computer program with a smaller set of test data than would be necessary if the redundancies were not removed. A table with the redundancies removed is referred to as a *compacted DLT;* one without the redundancies removed is referred to as an *expanded DLT.* Because the decision rules of the compacted table must still represent all combinations of the expanded table, the auditor should check for completeness by following a standard formula.

Redundancy can be eliminated by use of the following convention. Two decision rules of the expanded table can be combined into one decision rule of the compacted table if two prerequisites are satisfied. First, for the two decision rules in question, all the conditions except one must have the same yes and no condition entries. Second, the actions for both decision rules must be the same. If the two prerequisites are satisfied, the two decision rules of the expanded table are combined into one in the compacted table, and the condition entry of yes and no is replaced by a dash. The dash means that the condition does not affect the actions to be taken.

The expanded decision table for automobile insurance premiums, Table 3–1, will be used to show how we derive a compacted table. Decision rules 1 and 5 have the same condition entries except for the first one, and they have the same actions. They can be combined as shown in Figure 3–11. We replace the entries of Y and N for the first condition with a dash (–). The dash means that the condition does not affect the actions to be taken. We can combine decision rules 2 and 6 in the same manner. Alternatively, we could have combined decision rules 5 and 7 and decision rules 6 and 8 had we chosen to do so. The compacted decision table is shown in Table 3–3.

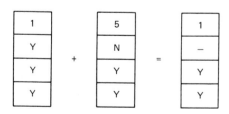

Figure 3–11. Combining Decision Rules with Y and N Responses

Table 3-3. Example of Eliminating Redundancies in Decision Rules

	1	2	3	4	5	6	7	8	*New Rule 1*
Is driver a male?	Y	Y	Y	Y	N	N	N	N	Expanded
Is driver over 25?	Y	Y	N	N	Y	Y	N	N	
Accident in last 5 years?	Y	N	Y	N	Y	N	Y	N	Decision
Calculate basic premium	X	X	X	X	X	X	X	X	Logic
Calculate high-risk premium adjustment			X	X					Table
Calculate good-driver premium adjustment		X		X		X		X	
Write premium notice	X	X	X	X	X	X	X	X	

New Rule 2

	1	2	3	4	5	6	
Is driver a male?	–	–	Y	Y	N	N	Compacted
Is driver over 25?	Y	Y	N	N	N	N	
Accident in last 5 years?	Y	N	Y	N	Y	N	Decision
Calculate basic premium	X	X	X	X	X	X	Logic
Calculate high-risk premium adjustment			X	X			Table
Calculate good-driver premium adjustment		X		X		X	
Write premium notice	X	X	X	X	X	X	

The auditor determines whether the decision rules of the compacted table still represent all combinations of the expanded table by using the formula

$$DR = \sum_{i=1}^{n} 2_i^m$$

where DR is the total number of decision rules to be accounted for in the expanded table, n is the number of decision rules in the compacted table, and m is the number of dashes shown for the ith decision rule. See Figure 3-12 for an example of this calculation.

Testing

Upon completion of the DLT, there are two aspects of testing involved: (1) testing the DLT itself to ascertain that it is complete and accurate, and (2) using the DLT as a means of testing something else.

Step 1

Number of decision rules to be accounted for, using the example in Table 3–3:

$$DR = 2^n$$
$$DR = 2^3$$
$$DR = 8$$

Step 2

Number of decision rules accounted for in compacted Table 3–3:

Decision Rule ($i = 1$ to 6)	Number of Dashes (m)	Calculation (2^m)
1	1	$2^1 = 2$
2	1	$2^1 = 2$
3	0	$2^0 = 1$
4	0	$2^0 = 1$
5	0	$2^0 = 1$
6	0	$2^0 = 1$

$$DR = 8 = \sum_{i=1}^{n} 2_i^m$$

Step 3

Ascertain that answer from Step 1 agrees with answer from Step 2.

Figure 3–12.   Determining That All Decision Rules Are Accounted For

Testing the DLT itself to ascertain that it is complete and accurate is usually *not* undertaken by the auditor as an end in itself. To test the DLT, the auditor has to compare it with something, either a flowchart of the program or the program itself. Because the auditor is usually also concerned with testing the flowchart and the program, testing of the DLT often ends up as a byproduct of testing the latter. Whether as an end in itself, or as a means to an end, the process is the same. This process is discussed below.

The auditor typically prepares the DLT as a means of testing something else, usually the computer program but sometimes a flowchart of the program. In testing the computer program, the DLT is an effective means of generating test data. In testing a flowchart, it is an aid in untangling what can sometimes be a complicated maze of programming logic depicted in the flowchart.

The DLT is an effective means of generating test data in testing a computer program because each decision rule can be used to create a test data record. For each decision rule, the computer auditor prepares a record that satisfies all the conditions specified. When that record is processed by the computer program, all the actions specified for that decision rule should be undertaken. The auditor then compares the results of computer processing with the calculations or functions specified in the DLT for that decision rule.

The information needed by an auditor in generating test data from a DLT in order to test a computer program is summarized on a control worksheet. An example of such a control worksheet is shown in Table 3–4. The information is based on the compacted DLT in Table 3–3. Each test record satisfies the conditions specified for the decision rule of the same number. Actions to be taken for that decision rule are summarized

Table 3–4. Control Worksheet Showing Test Data Input and Anticipated Processing Results (Based on Table 3–3)

Computer Transaction Record (Decision Rule)	Male? 1 = Y, 0 = N	Age	Accident Past 5 Years? 1 = Y, 0 = N	Processing	Premium Notice Amount†
1	1*	35	1	Basic premium, write premium notice	$500
2	0*	26	0	Basic premium, good-driver adjustment, write premium notice	450
3	1	23	1	Basic premium, high-risk adjustment, write premium notice	800
4	1	19	0	Basic premium, high-risk adjustment, good-driver adjust-ment, write premium notice	720
5	0	25	1	Basic premium, write premium notice	500
6	0	21	0	Basic premium, good-driver adjustment, write premium notice	450

*Even though processing is the same whether the driver is male or female as indicated by a dash in Table 3–3, the computer program needs some arbitrarily assigned value in order to operate.

†The premium notice amounts are assumed for illustrative purposes in this example.

in the column labeled "Processing." The last column shows the dollar amount of premium that the computer program should calculate. For the control worksheet, the auditor calculates the amount manually and compares that amount with the computer-calculated premium.

The formulas for determining whether all possible combinations of logic paths have been accounted for can be used in testing a flowchart with a DLT. By counting the number of decision symbols in the program, also known as *conditions*, the auditor can calculate the number of logic paths, also known as *decision rules*, that exist for that program. Once the auditor has accounted for each path, he or she can use the DLT to compare each path on the flowchart, decision rule by decision rule, to trace through all combinations of conditions and actions.

OTHER ANALYTICAL TOOLS

Two other analytical tools are *layout charts* and *grid charts*. In both cases the computer auditor must understand them in order to prepare them, use them, and discuss them with others.

Layout Charts

A layout chart is perhaps one of the simplest, yet most important, analytical tools used by the computer auditor. It merely shows the contents of a computer record. Without it, the auditor may not even be able to audit the computer records.

The layout charts normally used by computer auditors are those for tape and disk records. The layout charts for tape and disk records will show the length of the record (because it can vary), as well as the composition of the record by fields. An example of a tape layout is shown in Figure 3–13. A disk layout is similar.

The auditor may not be able to audit the computer records without referring to the layout chart because without it he or she may have no idea of where to find anything in the record. One of the first sets of documents requested by the computer auditor in starting an audit, therefore, is the set of layout charts.

Grid Charts

Grid charts can be useful to the computer auditor, although they are rarely as valuable as the tools discussed previously. Grid charts depict the interrelationships of sets of data records and can help the auditor locate the same information in different records or files for cross-checking.

Application: _Inventory_

Date: _August 12, 19X4_

Prepared by: _P. B. B. Turney_

Record: _Master File_

Reviewed by: _D. A. Watne_

Field Name	Part Number	Quantity on Hand	Quantity on Order	Unit Cost	Minimum Order Point	Lead Time	
Characteristics*	9	9	9	999999V99	9	9	
Relative Position	1-12	13-22	23-32	41-48	49-56	57-59	

*Alphabetic or Blank	A
Alphanumeric	X
Numeric	9
Assumed Decimal Point	V

Figure 3–13.   Tape Layout

The interrelationships of sets of data or records are shown on grid charts in tabular form. A grid chart may indicate, in a very simple illustration, that employee pay rates appear in both a payroll transactions file and a master file (see Table 3–5). The auditor will often compare these fields in the two files to see if the pay rates agree. The more complex the application, and the more redundant the information in various files, the more valuable the grid charts.

Table 3–5.   Grid Chart

Data Item \ Programs	Payroll Transaction File	Payroll Master File
Employee Number	✔	✔
Employee Name		✔
Employee Pay Rate	✔	✔
Social Security Number		✔
Etc.		

SUMMARY

Systems and program flowcharts are used by the computer auditor to depict visually the flow of information through an accounting system. Systems flowcharts graphically portray the broad flow of documents and data, whereas program flowcharts show the detailed processing logic of a computer program.

Numerous conventions exist for the preparation and use of systems and program flowcharts. These conventions include the flow of information and standardized symbols.

Testing is important to ascertain the accuracy of systems and program flowcharts. Systems flowcharts can be tested by following an example of every document depicted in the flowchart. Program flowcharts can be tested by following the program logic in a program listing or by processing real or simulated data through the program or a copy of it. Decision logic tables are a tabular means of analyzing and graphically showing the logic of a computer program. Different combinations of decisions that lead to different combinations of actions are referred to as decision rules.

Conventions exist in the preparation and use of decision logic tables and can help the auditor systematically develop the DLT to determine whether it is complete after all redundancies have been removed. Determining whether an expanded or a compacted DLT is complete involves using formulas to compare the number of decision rules with the number that should exist based on the conditions specified.

The testing of decision logic tables is usually done in conjunction with the testing of a program flowchart or a computer program. Computer programs can effectively be tested using a DLT because each decision rule of the table can be used to create a test data record.

Layout charts are important to the computer auditor because they graphically show the information contained in a computer record.

Grid charts may help the auditor by indicating where the same information can be found in two or more records.

REVIEW QUESTIONS

3–1. Define *flowchart.*

3–2. What are the advantages and disadvantages of flowcharting?

3–3. What are the two main types of flowcharts? Describe them. How are they used by auditors?

3–4. What is a document flowchart?

3–5. What is an audit, or internal control, flowchart?

3-6. What is a convention as it pertains to flowcharting, decision tables, and other analytical tools?

3-7. What are the general conventions and auditor conventions as they pertain to flowcharting in general?

3-8. Discuss the main concepts for testing systems flowcharts and program flowcharts.

3-9. What four basic symbols can be used to prepare any systems or program flowchart?

3-10. How does the auditor depict functional responsibility in a systems flowchart?

3-11. How are internal control procedures shown in a systems flowchart?

3-12. Draw and explain the use of the following symbols:

Input/Output	Process
Document	Decision
Magnetic tape	Manual operation
Magnetic disk	Auxiliary operation
Punched tape	Terminal
On-line storage	Flow line
Memory	On-page connector
Display	Off-page connector
Punched card	

3-13. How are systems flowcharts tested and what are the terms associated with such testing?

3-14. What are other terms for *program flowchart?*

3-15. In organizing the program flowchart, what is meant by the components defining processing flow, processing analysis, and the audit trail?

3-16. What basic patterns are used in programming? Flowchart them. Of what significance are they to the auditor?

3-17. Describe automatic flowcharting.

3-18. Describe how program flowcharts can be tested.

3-19. What is a decision logic table?

3-20. Describe the parts of a decision logic table. How does the auditor prepare them?

3-21. What is the formula for calculating the number of decision rules in a DLT? How does the auditor use the formula?

3-22. What is the technique for systematically completing the action entries?

3-23. What is meant by an expanded DLT? A compacted one?

3-24. What conditions must be satisfied to eliminate redundant decision rules?

3-25. What is the formula for determining that the decision rules of the compacted table represent all combinations of the expanded table? How does the auditor use the formula?

3-26. How can the auditor test the DLT? How does the auditor use a DLT to test a flowchart? A computer program?

3-27. What is a layout chart? How does the auditor use it?

3-28. What is a grid chart? How does the auditor use it?

OBJECTIVE QUESTIONS

3-29. One reason why an auditor uses a flowchart is to aid in the
  a. Evaluation of a series of sequential processes
  b. Study of the system of responsibility accounting
  c. Performance of important, required, dual-purpose tests
  d. Understanding of a client's organizational structure *(AICPA)*

3-30. The normal sequence of documents in operations on a well-prepared systems flowchart is
  a. Top to bottom and left to right
  b. Bottom to top and left to right
  c. Top to bottom and right to left
  d. Bottom to top and right to left *(AICPA)*

3-31. When preparing a record of a client's internal control structure, the independent auditor sometimes uses a systems flowchart, which can best be described as a
  a. Pictorial presentation of the flow of instructions in a client's internal computer system
  b. Diagram which clearly indicates an organization's internal reporting structure
  c. Graphic illustration of the flow of operations which is used to replace the auditor's internal control questionnaire
  d. Symbolic representation of a system or series of sequential processes *(AICPA)*

3-32. One important reason why a CPA, during the course of an audit engagement, prepares systems flowcharts is to
  a. Reduce the need for inquiries of client personnel concerning the operations of the internal control structure
  b. Depict the organizational structure and document flow in a single chart for review and reference purposes
  c. Assemble the internal control findings into a comprehensible format suitable for analysis
  d. Prepare documentation that would be useful in the event of a future consulting engagement *(AICPA)*

3-33. In connection with the assessment of control risk, an auditor encounters the following flowcharting symbols:

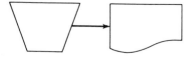

The auditor would conclude that
a. A document has been generated by a manual operation
b. A master file has been created by a computer operation
c. A document has been generated by a computer operation
d. A master file has been created by a manual operation (AICPA)

CASES AND EXERCISES

3-34. You are auditing the Alaska branch of Far Distributing Company. This branch has substantial annual sales which are billed and collected locally. As a part of your audit you find that the procedures for handling cash receipts are as follows:

Cash collections on over-the-counter sales and COD sales are received from the customer or delivery service by the cashier. Upon receipt of cash the cashier stamps the sales ticket "paid" and files a copy for future reference. The only record of COD sales is a copy of the sales ticket which is given to the cashier to hold until the cash is received from the delivery service.

Mail is opened by the secretary to the credit manager, and remittances are given to the credit manager for his review. The credit manager then places the remittances in a tray on the cashier's desk. At the daily deposit cutoff time the cashier delivers the checks and cash on hand to the assistant credit manager who prepares remittance lists and makes up the bank deposit which he also takes to the bank. The assistant credit manager also posts remittances to the accounts receivable ledger cards and verifies the cash discounts allowable.

You also ascertain that the credit manager obtains approval from the executive office of Far Distributing Company, located in Chicago, to write off uncollectible accounts, and that he has retained in his custody as of the end of the fiscal year some remittances that were received on various days during the last month.

Prepare a systems flowchart for the cash receipts function. The flowchart should show functional responsibilities. (AICPA adapted)

3-35. Charting, Inc., a new audit client of yours, processes its sales and cash receipts documents in the following manner:

a. *Cash receipts.* The mail is opened each morning by a mail clerk in the sales department. The mail clerk prepares a remittance advice (showing customer and amount paid) if one is not received. The checks and remittance advices are then forwarded to the sales department supervisor, who reviews each check and forwards the checks and remittance advices to the accounting department supervisor. The accounting department supervisor, who also functions as the credit manager, reviews all checks for payments of past-due accounts and then forwards the checks and remittance advices to the accounts receivable clerk, who arranges the advices in alphabetical order. The remittance advices are posted directly to the accounts receivable ledger cards. The checks are endorsed by stamp and totaled. The total is posted to the cash receipts journal. The remittance advices are filed chronologically.

After receiving the cash from the preceding day's cash sales, the accounts receivable clerk prepares the daily deposit slip in triplicate. The third copy of the deposit slip is filed by date, and the second copy and the original accompany the bank deposit.

b. *Sales.* Salesclerks prepare the sales invoices in triplicate. The original and the second copy are presented to the cashier. The third copy is retained by the salesclerk in the sales book. When the sale is for cash, the customer pays the salesclerk, who presents the money to the cashier with the invoice copies.

A credit sale is approved by the cashier from an approved credit list after the salesclerk prepares the three-part invoice. After receiving the cash or approved invoice, the cashier validates the original copy of the sales invoice and gives it to the customer. At the end of each day the cashier recaps the sales and cash received and forwards the cash and the second copy of all sales invoices to the accounts receivable clerk. The accounts receivable clerk balances the cash received with cash sales invoices and prepares a daily sales summary. The credit sales invoices are posted to the accounts receivable ledger, and then all invoices are sent to the inventory control clerk in the sales department for posting to the inventory control catalog. After posting, the inventory control clerk files all invoices numerically. The accounts receivable clerk posts the daily sales summary to the cash receipts journal and sales journal and files the sales summaries by date.

The cash from cash sales is combined with the cash received on account, and this constitutes the daily bank deposit.

c. *Bank deposits.* The bank validates the deposit slip and returns the second copy to the accounting department where it is filed by date by the accounts receivable clerk.

Monthly bank statements are reconciled promptly by the accounting department supervisor and filed by date.

Prepare a systems flowchart for the sales and cash receipts function. The flowchart should show functional responsibilities. (*AICPA adapted*)

3–36. During the audit of Viking Sportwear, Inc., you came across a chart labeled "Hierarchy of Modules for Inventory Update Application," shown in Figure 1. Your audit manager has asked you to prepare a program flowchart of the information depicted on the hierarchical chart.

3–37. The DLT for a program to calculate automobile insurance premiums is shown in Table 3–1. Prepare a program flowchart based on the DLT.

3–38. A flowchart for a payroll program is shown in Figure 3–7. Prepare a decision logic table for the payroll program based only on the four *major* types of tests performed by the program:

1. Character checks (ignore the separate tests for blanks, etc.)
2. Field checks (ignore the separate tests for sequence, etc.)

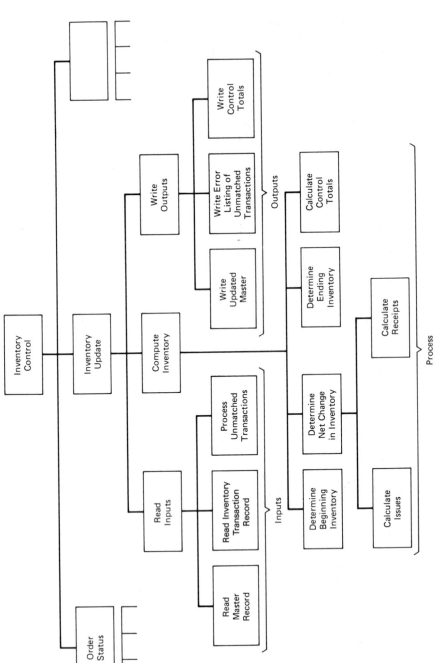

Figure 1. Viking Sportswear, Inc.: Hierarchy of Modules for Inventory

104

3. Limit test
4. Cross-footing test.

Is your DLT complete? Demonstrate how you know that it is complete.

3–39. The following program segment is written in ENGLISH, a soon-to-be-developed programming language.

SUBROUTINE-ADMIT.

IF (GPA IS GREATER THAN 3.5 OR GMAT-SCORE IS GREATER THAN 550) AND APPLICANT HAS BA-FROM-ACCREDITED-UNIVERSITY SEND ADMISSION-LETTER, OTHERWISE EXECUTE NEXT SENTENCE. READ APPLICANT-RECORD-FILE. GO TO SUBROUTINE-ADMIT.

Required:

a. Prepare a flowchart illustrating the logic of the program segment.
b. Prepare a decision logic table (DLT) showing the logic of the program segment.

Chapter 4
AUDITING CONCEPTS

Learning Objectives

After completing this chapter, the reader should be able to:

1. Describe an internal control structure and the process for auditing it.

2. Understand how the auditor's assessment of control risk is affected by EDP.

3. Know how substantive testing relates to the assessment of control risk and the role the computer plays in such testing.

4. Specify the similarities and differences between the auditing of data processed by manual or mechanical systems and data processed by computer systems.

5. State the impact EDP has on auditing procedures.

6. Understand how the scope of and approach to tests of controls change in computer auditing.

7. Understand how the scope of and approach to substantive testing change in computer auditing.

8. Describe the role that computer testing plays in performing tests of controls.

9. Describe the role that computer testing plays in performing substantive tests.

The computer auditor not only must be familiar with the basic concepts of auditing but must also understand the additional concepts applicable to auditing EDP systems. Auditing's basic concepts do not change simply because we move from a manual to a mechanical to a computer system for processing accounting data. The computer auditor, however, has the burden of mastering additional concepts applicable solely to EDP processing of accounting data. The concept of segregation of accounting functions, for example, is applicable in manual, mechanical, and computer processing. In computer processing, however, application of the concept is more complicated than in a manual system. The computer auditor is concerned with appropriate segregation of personnel within the accounting department using a computer for processing data, within the EDP department itself, and between the EDP department and the user departments.

In this chapter we review both manual and computerized audit procedures and techniques, along with the auditing objectives on which they are based and which guide the computer auditor. This review provides a foundation for all the chapters that follow.

This chapter comprises six major conceptual issues: (1) auditing concepts relevant to the computer auditor, (2) the auditor's assessment of control risk in general, (3) the specific effects EDP has on such an assessment, (4) the collection of sufficient competent evidential matter, (5) dual-purpose testing, and (6) the role that the computer auditors and the computer play in performing tests of controls and substantive tests. The chapter concludes with a description of the conceptual framework used to organize the material in the book.

The emphasis of this chapter is on the changes induced by the EDP system compared with a manual or mechanical system. These changes include those pertaining to internal control structure policies and procedures, the audit trail, and audit program procedures. Our intention is to provide a general review of computer auditing—a description of the forest in general as an aid in *not* becoming lost in the trees of auditing concepts, standards, and procedures.

AUDITING CONCEPTS

Auditing concepts provide overall guidance in performing the audit process. It is important that the computer auditor understand this process and the concepts that underlie it. In performing this process, the auditor obtains an understanding of the internal control structure and undertakes both an assessment of control risk and substantive testing. This process is performed in manual and computerized systems, but becomes more complex when auditing a computerized system.

The Auditing Process

The American Accounting Association (AAA) definition of auditing is broadly applicable to several types of auditing, including external auditing, internal auditing, and computer auditing:

> Auditing is a systematic process of objectively obtaining and evaluating evidence regarding assertions about economic actions and events to ascertain the degree of correspondence between those assertions and established criteria and communicating the results to interested users.[1]

Several concepts contained in this definition are discussed below as they pertain to computer auditing.

Systematic Process.   "Systematic process" means that auditing is structured as a dynamic activity in a logical manner. A systematic approach is used in the audit of all types of systems, but it is particularly important in auditing computerized systems.

A systematic approach is difficult in a computerized system where the computer auditor cannot visually ascertain the processing being performed or the content of files. Consequently, a haphazard, unplanned, unstructured approach to computer auditing may result in bypassing important segments of processing or the related files.

Obtaining and Evaluating Evidence.   In "obtaining and evaluating evidence regarding assertions about economic actions and events," the computer auditor is concerned about assertions relating to both the reliability of the control structure and the content of files produced by computer processing. Evidence will be collected through tests of controls to determine whether the control structure is functioning as prescribed and through substantive testing to determine whether the contents of the computer files properly reflect the firm's transactions.

Ascertain Correspondence between Assertions and Established Criteria.   The process used "to ascertain the degree of correspondence between those assertions and established criteria" in computer auditing is similar to that used in auditing manual or mechanical systems but is somewhat more complex. The process is similar because with all three systems, "the degree of correspondence" requires a subjective judgment on the auditor's part as to what constitutes a material noncompliance in the control structure or a material error in account balances. The process

---

[1]AAA Committe on Basic Auditing Concepts, "A Statement of Basic Auditing Concepts," *Accounting Review,* supplement to Vol. 47, 1972.

is more complex in computer auditing because the control structure is more sophisticated, and because it is difficult to ascertain whether the computer programs and files provided to the auditor are those actually used or bogus copies not actually used in processing.

Communicating Results. The computer auditor, like all auditors, is responsible for "communicating the results to interested users." Interested users in this case will include other members of the audit team, who must integrate the computer auditor's findings with other aspects of the audit, and the client. In both cases, the communications process is complicated by EDP terminology not encountered elsewhere and the complexity of the integration process itself. The integration process is complex because the evaluation of EDP system control structure reliability and computer-maintained account balances must be combined with the evaluation of overall control structure reliability and manually or mechanically maintained account balances.

Understanding the Internal Control Structure, Assessing Control Risk, and Substantive Testing

As part of the systematic process referred to above, the auditor obtains an understanding of the internal control structure. This understanding is necessary to plan the audit. The objectives of this understanding are to (1) identify the types of potential misstatements that could occur, (2) consider the factors that affect the risk of material misstatements, and (3) design substantive tests. To have the knowledge sufficient to plan the audit requires that the auditor understand each of the three elements of the internal control structure: the control environment, the accounting system, and the control procedures. This portion of the process is concluded by documenting the understanding.

Another phase of the systematic process is the assessment of control risk. Assessing control risk is the process of evaluating the effectiveness of internal control structure policies and procedures in preventing or detecting material misstatements in the financial statements. In making that assessment, the auditor may perform tests of controls. Where the auditor encounters strengths in the control structure, he or she will perform tests of controls to determine whether the system is actually performing as it should. If the anticipated strengths of the control structure are functioning as designed, the auditor may be able to reduce the extent of subsequent audit procedures. Where the auditor encounters weaknesses in the system, or the perceived strengths are not there, or the auditor elects not to rely on the strengths that do exist, he or she will have to increase the extent of subsequent audit procedures.

After completing that part of the systematic process referred to as the "assessment of control risk," the auditor moves on to the phase referred to as either "subsequent audit procedures" or "substantive tests." Substantive tests include both (1) tests of balances and (2) analytical procedures applied to financial information. In performing tests the computer auditor will have to determine whether the computer program is properly processing transactions. In testing the account balances, the computer auditor will have to examine the contents of both master files and transaction files resulting from computer processing. The second type of substantive test, analytical procedures applied to financial information, can be performed much more efficiently with the computer. The computer can be used to perform these procedures, typically involving ratio and trend analysis, by calculating percentage and statistical information in greater volume and much faster than could be done by hand.

Effect of Computer on the Audit Process

Computer auditing is both similar to and different from the auditing of manual and mechanical systems. The process of auditing manual, mechanical, and computer systems is similar because the auditor obtains an understanding of the internal control structure; assesses control risk; and performs tests of controls, substantive tests, and dual-purpose tests in all three types of systems. Although the conceptual approach with all three systems is to first perform tests of controls followed by substantive tests based on the results of the former, in practice the auditor often combines these tests into dual-purpose tests. For example, a test to ascertain whether a particular processing control is functioning as prescribed in testing application controls may also have as its objective the determination of whether the computations leading to a particular account balance have been performed correctly as part of the substantive testing procedures.

Differences between computer auditing and auditing other types of systems arise because of additional techniques and procedures that apply to the performance of a computer audit. The auditor has to consider utilizing computerized techniques in addition to manual procedures. Manual procedures will normally be used to obtain an overall understanding of the control structure, whereas a mixture of manual and computerized procedures can be applied in tests of controls and substantive testing.

Overall Understanding.   Manual procedures are used to obtain an overall understanding of the control structure as the computer auditor determines *what* controls have been prescribed. The procedures to make this determination include discussions with client personnel and reference to procedure manuals, job descriptions, flowcharts, decision tables, and other documentation. These manual procedures are applicable to manual, mechanical, and computer systems. In computer systems, however, the auditor uses them to search for controls not found in a manual or mechanical system. An example of a control unique to computer systems is systems documentation indicating the procedures for authorizing transactions and approving systems changes.

Assessing Control Risk and Tests of Controls.   The computer auditor uses a mixture of manual and computerized procedures to determine *how* the controls selected for testing are functioning. Except for their EDP orientation, the manual procedures are similar to those used in other types of systems. The computerized techniques are unique to computer auditing.

Even with a computer system, manual procedures are still performed. To determine whether the control known as segregation of functions is being adhered to, for example, the auditor must physically observe personnel to ascertain that the prescribed functions are indeed segregated.

A test to determine whether the controls built into a computer program are functioning properly, however, requires that the auditor will normally utilize a computerized technique. For example, the auditor may run test data through a program to determine whether invalid transactions are being rejected as prescribed.

Substantive Testing.   The computer auditor will also use a combination of manual and computerized procedures for substantive testing. The manual procedures are similar to those used to obtain an understanding of and test other types of systems, whereas the computerized techniques are unique to computer auditing.

In the direct tests of account balances for accounts receivable, for example, both manual and computerized techniques can be used. Accounts receivable confirmations returned by debtors with exceptions noted on them are manually resolved by the auditor. The confirmations themselves, however, may have been printed by audit software that determined the sampling technique to be used, selected the sample, and then printed the forms ready for mailing.

AUDITOR'S ASSESSMENT OF CONTROL RISK

Because the assessment of control risk in computerized systems is based on control principles applicable to all systems, the computer auditor must proceed from the foundation of these basic principles. These principles relate to the purpose of the assessment of control risk and include definitions and basic concepts, procedures for understanding control risk, and the relationship of control risk assessment to other auditing procedures.[2]

Purpose of Control Risk Assessment

The purpose to the assessment of control risk is to evaluate the effectiveness of an entity's internal control structure policies in preventing or detecting material misstatements in the financial statements. Control risk is assessed in terms of the financial statement assertions of existence or occurrence, completeness, rights and obligations, valuation or allocation, and presentation and disclosure.

Definitions and Basic Concepts of the Control Structure

Numerous definitions and basic concepts related to control are encountered in the assessment of control risk in all systems for processing accounting data. These include a definition of control risk and the control structure and basic concepts relating to control structure elements.

Control Risk Defined. *Control risk* can be defined very simply as the likelihood that misstatements in accounting data will not be prevented or detected and corrected. Misstatements can include both unintentional errors as well as fraud or embezzlement. A more comprehensive definition of control risk is that it is the risk that misstatements that could occur in an account balance or class of transactions and that could be material, when aggregated with misstatements in other balances or classes, will not be prevented or detected and corrected on a timely basis by an entity's control structure.

Control Structure. The *control structure* can be defined as those policies and procedures established by the entity to provide reasonable assurance that its established objectives will be achieved. Out of the wide variety of objectives and related policies and procedures encompassed by the control structure, there are three elements of that structure of interest to the auditor of account balances and transactions that affect the financial statements. These three elements are the control environment, the accounting system, and the control procedures.

---

[2]This section is based on *SAS No. 55*, Au Sec. 319.

Basic Concepts of the Control Structure Elements. The control environment, the accounting system, and control procedures have been identified as the three elements of the control structure most effective in preventing or detecting and correcting material misstatements.

The *control environment* represents the collective effect of various factors on establishing, enhancing, or mitigating the effectiveness of specific policies and procedures. Such factors include:

- Management's philosophy and operating style.
- The entity's organizational structure.
- The functioning of the board of directors and its committees, particularly the audit committee.
- Methods of assigning authority and responsibility.
- Management's control methods for monitoring and following up on performance, including internal auditing.
- Personnel policies and practices.
- Various external influences that affect an entity's operations and practices, such as examinations by bank regulatory agencies.

The control environment reflects the overall attitude, awareness, and actions of the board of directors, management, owners, and others concerning the importance of control and its emphasis in the entity.

The *accounting system* consists of the methods and records established to identify, assemble, analyze, classify, record, and report an entity's transactions and to maintain accountability for the related assets and liabilities. An effective accounting system includes an ability to:

- Identify and record all valid transactions.
- Describe, on a timely basis, the transactions in sufficient detail to permit proper classification of transactions for financial reporting.
- Measure the value of transactions in a manner that permits recording their proper monetary value in the financial statements.
- Determine the time period in which transactions occurred to permit recording of transactions in the proper accounting period.
- Present properly the transactions and related disclosures in the financial statements.

The *control procedures* are those policies and procedures, in addition to the control environment and accounting system, that management has established to provide reasonable assurance that specific entity objectives will be achieved. These procedures include provision for

- Proper authorization of transactions and activities
- Segregation of duties
- Design and use of adequate documents and records
- Adequate safeguards over access to and use of assets and records

- Independent checks on performance and proper valuation of recorded amounts

Understanding the Control Structure

The auditor must obtain an understanding of the control structure sufficient to plan an examination of the account balances and transactions. Issues to be addressed by the auditor in planning the examination include

- The types of misstatements that could occur
- The risk that such misstatements may occur
- The factors that influence the design of substantive tests
- An assessment of inherent risk
- Materiality
- Complexity and sophistication of the entity's operations and systems

In order to obtain an understanding of the control structure, the auditor needs to obtain information about

- The classes of transactions in the entity's operations that are significant to the financial statements
- How the transactions are initiated
- The accounting records, supporting documents, machine-readable information, and specific accounts in the financial statements involved in the processing and reporting of transactions
- The accounting processing involved from the initiation of a transaction to its inclusion in the financial statements, including how the computer is used to process data
- The financial reporting process used to prepare the entity's financial statements, including significant accounting estimates and disclosures

Relationship of Control Risk Assessment to Other Auditing Procedures

Activities performed by the auditor to obtain an understanding of the control structure provide a basis for a preliminary assessment of the level of control risk. The assessment is considered preliminary because several options are available to the auditor which may lead to subsequent modification of the preliminary assessment.

The auditor's assessment of control risk will determine the audit strategy as to the allocation of time between additional control evaluation procedures and substantive tests. The lower the assessment of control risk the auditor can place on the control structure, the less substantive testing the auditor has to do, and vice versa.

One important issue to be resolved in making that allocation is the efficiency of the audit. The efficiency of the audit will be enhanced if the decrease in audit effort associated with reduced substantive testing is greater than the increase in audit effort associated with extending control risk assessment procedures to support a lower assessment of control risk. The auditor may reach several different conclusions at this point:

- The control structure is weak; additional audit effort in the control structure area is inappropriate; control risk is high; and significant substantive testing will be necessary.
- The control structure seems to be strong; the efficiency of the audit might be improved if control risk can be assessed at a low level allowing reliance on the control structure

  —Tests of those controls might demonstrate that they are functioning properly and that substantive testing can therefore be reduced.
  —Tests of those controls might demonstrate that they are not functioning properly and that substantive testing cannot therefore be reduced.

- The control structure seems to be strong, but the efficiency of the audit would probably not be improved through tests of controls because the reduction in substantive testing would not be sufficient to offset the additional risk assessment procedures.

EFFECTS OF EDP ON THE AUDITOR'S ASSESSMENT OF CONTROL RISK

In addition to the general requirements to be met in the assessment of control risk applicable to all systems for processing accounting data, the EDP auditor is required to evaluate numerous controls relating specifically to computer processing. These additional controls, called general and application controls, are necessary because of the effects of EDP. In this section we will discuss the effects of EDP on controls and the audit trail, the general and application controls that have been defined for EDP systems, the assessment of control risk, and tests of controls.

Effects of EDP on Accounting Control

EDP has numerous effects on the system for processing accounting data. EDP induces changes in the accounting system. These changes affect the characteristics of control. Changes in the accounting system and the characteristics of control affect the audit trail.

The introduction of a computer into an accounting system induces numerous changes in that system. The following are examples of some of these EDP-induced changes:

- Activities previously decentralized and performed by several clerks may be centralized into one computer program, eliminating the internal control previously available through segregation of functions. For example, a payroll program may handle the activities of several payroll clerks previously required to calculate gross pay based on hours and pay rate, calculate withholdings and other deductions, write the payroll checks, post the payroll to employees' earnings records and the payroll journal, and verify all of these activities. The cross-checks of the manual system may not be built into the computer program.
- Lack of documentation is a significant problem in many computer installations. Without adequate documentation, the audit trail may disappear and the auditor may find it difficult, if not impossible, to follow the processing in a particular application area.
- The storage of processing procedures or programs and the data to be processed on machine-readable files means that the auditor must rely on both a computer and a program to reveal those processing steps and related data.
- Although numerous organizations have found that the total number of employees increases with the installation of a computer, there is typically a decrease in human involvement in the actual processing of accounting data. This decrease in human involvement eliminates most of the visual checking performed during processing in manual systems to detect errors.
- In place of the pattern of random errors typically encountered in manual systems, with computer processing we must be content with systematic errors caused by similar transactions encountering the same program or system flaw.
- The EDP department is staffed by personnel with specialized knowledge that the auditor must acquire to audit effectively the processing performed by them.
- Because many of the accounting controls relied on by the auditor must be built into the computer program, the EDP auditor must frequently become involved in the early stages of systems design.
- The changes induced by the computer just described affect the EDP and related departments of all sizes, but the problems and difficulties encountered by the EDP auditor often vary inversely with the size of the computer installation. For example, segregation of functions is more difficult to achieve in smaller installations where lack of specialized personnel often results in a reduction in the quality of documentation, programming, and operating procedures.

The control structure elements should be reexamined by the auditor upon the introduction of a computer system to determine whether the objectives of these elements are being met. In the control procedure called segregation-of-functions, for example, functions previously desegregated in a manual system may be combined into one computer program. An individual having access to this program and related data files may be able to make undetected changes in the program and files as part of an embezzlement scheme.

Another control procedure that may cause problems for the computer auditor is the requirement that transactions be executed only as authorized. Because many computer systems are programmed to execute transactions automatically, such as dispersing checks to vendors on previously scheduled payment dates, the computer may be programmed as part of a fraud to generate unauthorized checks.

The control requiring proper recording of transactions may be adversely affected by the introduction of a computer into the accounting system. Flaws in programming logic may cause transactions to be incorrectly recorded or omitted entirely, whereas the same transaction may be questioned in a manual system.

The control restricting access to assets may easily be circumvented in a computer system. This could happen, for example, if the data processing personnel are able to instruct the computer to issue shipping instructions for inventory without detection.

Periodic comparison of what the accounting records show with the physical assets that they represent may be circumvented as a control if the computer is used to make these comparisons. This could occur through overstating physical counts, inserting fictitious physical counts, or suppressing the printout of differences.

Audit Trail in an EDP System

Audit trail can be defined as those records that enable a transaction to be traced from its source forward to a summarized total in a financial statement or other document or to provide for tracing an amount in a summarized total back through the records to its source. These records include the source documents; the journals of original entry; the ledgers, worksheets, and other records in a manual system; and the magnetic tapes and disks, and printouts in a computer system.

Although the audit trail is primarily used by the auditor when he or she traces transactions through the systems in performing both compliance and substantive tests, it also serves management in the normal operation of the business. The audit trail is an aid to management in responding to questions from employees, customers, vendors, and government agencies as to the status of payments, shipments, and so forth.

An EDP system can affect the audit trail in the following ways:

1. Source documents, once transcribed onto a machine-readable input medium, may be filed in a manner that makes subsequent access difficult. For example, a company had a manual system where all time cards were sent to a centralized location for payroll processing. The company converted to an on-line computer where data were entered into the computer via remote terminals. The time cards were then filed in twenty-two decentralized locations.

2. In some systems, traditional source documents may be eliminated by the use of direct input devices. For example, a salesperson might enter an order through a cathode-ray tube terminal rather than complete a sales order.

3. Ledger summaries may be replaced by master files that do not show the amounts leading up to the summarized values.

4. The data processing cycle does not necessarily provide a transaction listing or journal. To provide such a listing may require a specific action at a recognizable cost.

5. It is sometimes unnecessary to prepare frequent printed output of historical records. Files can be maintained on computer media and reports prepared only for exceptions.

6. Files maintained on a magnetic medium cannot be read except by use of the computer and a computer program. For example, an inventory file maintained on magnetic tape requires the use of a computer and a program to print out or analyze its contents.

7. Sequence of records and processing activities is difficult to observe because much of the data and many of the activities are contained within the computer system.[3]

General and Application Controls

Additional accounting controls, beyond those necessary for a manual or mechanical system, have been specified when a computer is used to process accounting data. In a sense, these additional controls are a response to the effects of EDP on the accounting system. These controls are referred to as general and application controls. *General controls* are defined as having pervasive effects, which means that if they are weak or absent, they may negate the effects of the application controls. For this reason, the auditor will examine application controls only if control risk for general controls is assessed at a low level. *Application controls* are defined as those relating to the specific tasks performed by the computer, such as a payroll application and inventory application.

General and application controls are discussed in depth in the next section of this book. The six chapters devoted to them are as follows:

---

[3]Adapted from Gordon B. Davis, Donald L. Adams, and Carol A. Schaller, *Auditing and EDP,* Second Edition (New York: American Institute of Certified Public Accountants, 1983), pp. 186–192.

General Controls

- Organization controls, personnel practices, and standard operating procedures (Chapter 6)
- Systems development and documentation controls (Chapter 7)
- Hardware and systems software controls (Chapter 8)
- Systems security controls (Chapter 9)

Application Controls

- Data capture and batch data entry controls (Chapter 10)
- On-line entry, processing, and output controls (Chapter 11)

Assessing Control Risk

The auditor's assessment of control risk is affected by the impact of EDP on controls and the audit trail, as well as the general and application controls specified as additional controls to respond to these EDP effects. Although the general approach to the assessment of control risk when EDP is involved is the same as that for a manual or mechanical system, the analysis of the interrelationships of the computer and the users and other aspects of the accounting system can become quite complex.

The general approach to the assessment of control risk includes understanding the control structure, assessing control risk, testing controls, and determining audit strategy. In performing these procedures, the auditor must assess accounting control beyond the computer. The computer audit is unique in that it is *not* restricted solely to EDP activities.

The computer auditor is required to assess controls in two areas beyond the computer. First, the auditor must assess controls in all significant applications performed by intertwined manual, mechanical, and EDP systems. For example, a sales and collection system may start out with manual preparation of sales orders, continue with mechanical preparation of invoices on a bookkeeping machine that produces a cassette tape as a byproduct, and conclude with the cassette tape's being used to update a computer-maintained accounts receivable master file. The evaluation of control must include the manual and mechanical portions of the system as a component of the EDP assessment. Second, the computer auditor must assess the controls between the EDP department and the user departments. This assessment will include an evaluation of EDP controls, user controls, and a combination of both.

EDP controls refer to controls maintained by EDP personnel or the computer itself on input, processing, and output. *User controls* refer to controls maintained by the user department. The same control could be an EDP control, user control, or both. This interrelationship is illustrated

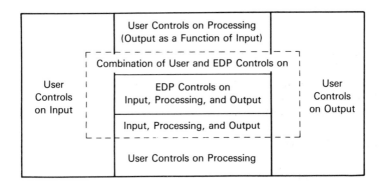

Figure 4-1. Control Subsystems

in Figure 4-1. For example, a record of the number of payroll transactions to be processed could be maintained by the user department and EDP personnel and entered into the computer for internal verification. The auditor's task is to determine to what extent control risk in the system is reduced by EDP or user controls, or a combination of both of them.

The process followed by the computer auditor in assessing control risk is illustrated in Figure 4-2. The understanding phase of the assessment is performed to gather information and to assess the effectiveness of control within EDP in relation to the entire system of accounting control. As a result of this assessment, the auditor must determine the extent of the procedures for assessing controls.

The preliminary determination of EDP control risk is the basis for deciding what further action to take. The auditor has three major alternative courses of action. First, the auditor may conclude that EDP control risk is sufficiently low to serve as a basis for restricting the extent of the substantive tests. The auditor would then complete his or her assessment of these controls, perform the related tests of controls, and design the substantive tests based on the results of the assessment of the controls.

Second, the auditor may conclude that control risk is high because the EDP controls are weak. The auditor may reach this conclusion either during assessment at the end of the preliminary phase or during assessment at completion of the entire assessment phase. Because the auditor decided that EDP controls were weak, he or she would not perform tests on them but would instead accomplish the audit objectives by other means, such as substantive testing.

Third, the auditor may decide not to pursue a reduction in the preliminary assessment of control risk even though EDP controls are strong because the additional work required is not cost effective. For example, the audit effort required to complete the assessment and tests of controls may exceed the reduction in effort in substantive testing that could be achieved.

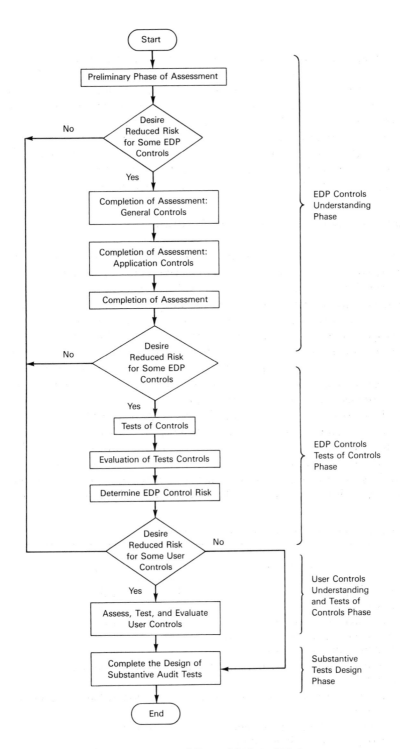

Figure 4–2. Assessment of Control Risk in EDP Systems

Independently of any determination made regarding EDP control risk, the auditor will also assess user controls and the interrelationship between the user controls and the EDP controls for each application. There are several reasons why the auditor may decide to focus on user controls. First, the auditor may conclude that focusing on them is more cost effective than focusing on the EDP controls. Second, the auditor may focus on them after concluding that the EDP controls are weak. Third, the auditor may conclude that a mixture of user and EDP controls is the best approach for determining the system's overall control risk.

Controls Testing in Computer Auditing

Controls testing in computer auditing is similar to testing with a manual or mechanical system because the objective is to determine whether the prescribed controls are functioning as designed. The testing is different when a computer is involved, however, because of the specific procedures necessary to test the controls found in EDP systems—general systems controls and specific application controls. These additional controls expand the role of testing substantially by requiring the performance of numerous manual and computerized procedures. As discussed previously, the auditor will examine application controls only if control risk for general controls is assessed at a low level.

In testing the general controls, the auditor relies most heavily on manual procedures. For example, manual procedures are appropriate for testing controls 1, 2, and 5 in Table 4–1. The auditor can physically observe the segregation of functions (control 1), manually review a log for recording approvals to system changes (control 2), or determine the extent to which internal auditors have reviewed and evaluated the EDP ac-

Table 4–1. General Controls and Audit Procedures

General Controls	Audit Procedures
1. Plan of organization and operation of EDP activity	1. Manual
2. Procedures for documenting, reviewing, testing, and approving systems or programs and changes thereto	2. Manual
3. Controls built into the equipment by the manufacturer	3. Computerized
4. Controls over access to equipment and data files	4. Manual and computerized
5. Other data and procedural controls affecting overall EDP operations	5. Manual

tivity (control 5). Testing control 3, on the other hand, normally requires a computerized technique. The auditor has to use the computer, for example, to determine whether the system will write on a tape file missing a file protection ring. Testing controls over access to equipment and data files, control 4, may require both manual and computerized procedures. For example, determining whether personnel are physically restricted from access to equipment can be done manually, whereas testing passwords restricting access to files requires the use of a computer. (Numerous tests applicable to all of these controls are discussed in depth in subsequent chapters.)

In contrast to the general controls, testing of the application controls relies most heavily on computerized techniques. A computerized technique is used, for example, to test an application control to ensure that numeric input is in fact numeric. A computerized technique is also used to test the proper functioning of a control that prevents individual payroll checks from exceeding a specified limit. Some application controls, however, may require manual tests to ensure that they are functioning properly. Controls that ensure that output is distributed to authorized individuals, for example, are tested manually.

SUBSTANTIVE TESTING: THE COLLECTION OF SUFFICIENT COMPETENT EVIDENTIAL MATTER

After the assessment of control risk, the auditor collects sufficient competent evidential matter in order to render an opinion on the financial statements. The collection of this evidence is defined as *substantive testing*. The purpose of substantive testing in computer auditing is the same as for the auditing of manual and mechanical systems. Substantive testing also has the same two components as for the auditing of these other systems.

The purpose of substantive testing is to detect whether there are material monetary errors in account balances. The auditor focuses on several objectives in this search for material monetary errors. Are the recorded amounts valid and supported by adequate documentation? Have the recorded amounts been properly authorized? Have all the transactions that occurred and should have been recorded, been in fact recorded? Have the recorded transactions been classified in the correct accounts? Have the transactions been recorded in the proper time period? Have the transactions been recorded for the proper amount?

Substantive testing has two components that are relevant whether a manual, mechanical, or computer system processes the accounting data: (1) tests of balances and (2) analytical procedures applied to financial information.

Tests of Details of Transactions and Balances. The scope of and approach to testing the details of transactions and balances will differ depending on the sophistication of the system. If the computer is simply used as a giant electronic bookkeeping machine, performing exactly the same type of processing as a manual or mechanical device, the substantive testing may be no different from that used with these other systems. For example, the computer may use the same format to prepare and print the journals, subsidiary ledgers, and general ledger postings found in a manual system. In this situation, the auditor may have no difficulty in tracing source documents to the entries in these journals and ledgers, or vice versa. Manual procedures, utilizing the same tick marks, may be appropriate.

If the computer is used in a more sophisticated manner, however, the substantive testing may be vastly different. A more sophisticated computer system, for example, may be programmed to authorize sales transactions automatically within certain limits, or even execute transactions by issuing checks to vendors on appropriate due dates. There may, however, be no journals. The subsidiary ledgers may exist only on a magnetic tape or disk. The general ledger may also contain only current balances with no details on debits or credits that lead to that balance. The substantive testing in this situation is different in the sense that the computer can no longer be ignored. The computer auditor must utilize a computer and program(s) to obtain, at a minimum, the balances of the subsidiary and general ledger accounts.

The substantive testing in computer auditing becomes even more complex when the auditor wants something other than just account balances. Examples of additional testing include tracing transactions and processing through the computer system or examining the contents of files on a magnetic medium. For such testing, the auditor may rely heavily on a computer and sophisticated audit software.

Analytical Procedures. The role of substantive testing pertaining to analytical procedures in computer auditing is not significantly different from that in a manual or mechanical system. Analytical procedures are performed to detect unusual relationships among financial data or information. Such relationships may result from errors or irregularities in the processing of accounting data. Procedures performed to detect these relationships include ratio and trend analysis. Although the computer may be used to perform such tests, such use is not normally a significant issue in computer auditing.

A major aspect of analytical procedures consists of comparing sets of financial information, such as (1) this year's statement amounts with last year's or those of other prior periods; (2) this year's actual results with the budgeted or forecasted results; and (3) the client's financial statement ratios, such as working capital or net income as a percentage of revenue, with industry averages.

Even with a fully computerized and relatively sophisticated system, many of these comparisons and related calculations can be performed at low cost: comparisons may be performed manually, with a pocket calculator, or with an electronic spreadsheet program on a microcomputer. Although very detailed analyses, such as comparing sales, costs, and expenses for several product lines, may sometimes be performed using a computer and details contained in magnetic files, it is typically not cost effective to do so.

Other analytical procedures, such as determining the relationship between financial information and pertinent nonfinancial information, may have to be performed manually or with a pocket calculator because the information is not contained in the computer data base. The square feet of selling space by department or branch used in performing reasonableness tests on sales, for example, may not be stored in the computer system.

DUAL-PURPOSE TESTING
IN COMPUTER AUDITING

Although the auditing standards suggest a very structured approach, stating that the auditor first perform controls testing and then perform substantive testing based on the results of the controls testing, these same standards recognize that both types of tests are often performed concurrently. We use the term *dual-purpose testing* when both types of tests are performed at the same time. This concept is just as applicable in computer auditing as it is in auditing a manual or mechanical system.

Both tests of controls and substantive testing are often performed concurrently to make more efficient use of the auditor's time. This gain is efficiency can result from the use of manual and computerized audit procedures. This is illustrated by the audit of sales invoices. In the manual audit of sales invoices, for example, the auditor may perform two procedures—a controls test and a substantive test—when he or she examines each invoice selected for testing. First, the auditor may look for the initials of the clerk responsible for checking each invoice for clerical accuracy, proper classification in the sales journal, and consistency with the supporting documentation. Looking for the accounting clerk's initials to ascertain that the verification was done as part of the client's internal control system is a controls test. Second, the substantive test is performed when the auditor also examines the invoice for clerical accuracy, proper classification in the sales journal, and consistency with the supporting documentation. It would be inefficient to go through the invoices to look for initials and then go through them again to verify the clerk's work.

Dual-purpose tests are also applicable in the computerized testing of sales invoices. A computer program may contain a reasonableness test to detect invoices of over $10,000. Such an invoice may be possible only as a result of some error in entering prices or quantities. In the test data submitted for processing, we may include records to ascertain if the reasonableness test is functioning, a controls test, and also to verify extensions of price times quantity by the computer, a substantive test.

ROLE OF COMPUTER AUDITORS
AND THE COMPUTER IN PERFORMING TESTS
OF CONTROLS AND SUBSTANTIVE TESTS

In contrast to the preceding section, in which we described how tests of controls and substantive testing can change when a computer is involved, we now reverse our approach and describe how the auditor incorporates the computer into certain procedures when performing these tests. This discussion is divided into three major issues. First, who is the auditor who is performing these tests? Second, what techniques are available to the auditor in this testing? Third, how are the techniques utilized? How the techniques are utilized is further subdivided into: Why is the computer used or not used in performing the audit? When in the processing cycle is the audit performed? Where in the cycle are the techniques utilized? and Which parts of the computer system are audited? Each of these issues will be discussed by responding to the questions *who, what, why, when, where,* and *which.*

Who?—Who Performs the Computer-Auditing Tasks?

The computer auditors are members of the same groups that perform other auditing tasks—the external auditors, the internal auditors, and the hybrids performing both functions, such as the General Accounting Office (GAO) auditors. The procedures performed in computer auditing are used by all three types of auditors. In addition to the auditing procedures discussed, however, internal auditors, GAO auditors, and CPAs performing management services work may have other interests. For example, these other interests may include performance measurement procedures such as determining how *efficiently* the computer is being utilized.

The external auditors restrict their testing to controls and substantive tests. Internal auditors and GAO auditors also perform these same types of tests on behalf of their client, their employer. They may not refer to them as tests of controls and substantive tests, but they *are* concerned about testing the effectiveness of internal control and performing direct tests of account balances. Whatever the name given to them, the computer plays a role in performing tests on the EDP processing of accounting data for all types of auditor.

What?—What Computer-Auditing Techniques Are Available?

There are dozens of techniques available to the computer auditor. Selecting a technique appropriate to the auditing task at hand, however, can be difficult. The rest of this chapter concerns factors the auditor should consider in selecting an appropriate technique. The discussion of techniques available to the auditor is deferred until later in the book after other prerequisite information has been covered.

How Are Computer-Auditing Techniques Utilized?— Why, When, Where, and Which?

Various classification schemes, or taxonomies, can be used to organize the numerous computer-auditing techniques. These taxonomies can help the computer auditor understand which technique may be appropriate for a given situation. They are discussed here under the headings *why, when, where,* and *which. Why* refers to why the auditor may or may not use the computer in performing the audit. *When* refers to when in the processing cycle the computer auditor applies his or her techniques. *Where* refers to where in the processing cycle the techniques are utilized. *Which* refers to which parts of the computer system are audited.

Why?—Auditing around, through, or with the Computer?

The auditor may or may not use the computer in performing the audit. In deciding whether to use the computer, the auditor is faced with the choices of auditing around the computer, auditing through the computer, or auditing with the computer. Why the auditor selects a particular approach or combination of approaches depends on numerous factors in each audit situation.

Auditing around the computer is performed by examining and reconciling the input to the computer with the output from it. This reconciliation can be easy or difficult. The accounts receivable control total that is calculated after updating, for example, can easily be reconciled in many systems to the beginning balance plus sales on account and other debits less payments on account and other credits. In auditing around the computer in a payroll application, however, the auditor may have difficulty ascertaining that net pay is correct without manually reviewing numerous computations for various types of withholdings.

The concept of auditing around the computer means that the auditor bypasses the computer. Such an approach may be acceptable in some situations but unacceptable in others. It may be acceptable if the computer is simply functioning as a giant bookkeeping machine, as described previously, where the reconciliation of input to output is relatively easy. It is unacceptable if the relationship between the output and the input cannot be properly understood without examining the intervening computer processing. This is the case, for example, when there is no visible audit trail. Auditing around the computer is inexcusable if the sole reason is the auditor's lack of understanding of the computer system. And an auditor who lacks technical competence in EDP systems may be violating professional standards.

Auditing through the computer means that the computer and its programs are treated as the "target" of the audit. *Target* means that the auditor focuses on the computer and its programs directly as contrasted with examining the results of processing, such as printouts or files. In auditing through the computer, the intent of the auditor is to perform compliance and substantive tests on the computer and its software, both operating system software and application program software. For example, the auditor may perform a controls test to determine whether the operating system is creating the header and trailer labels on magnetic tape correctly. Alternatively, the auditor may perform substantive tests to determine whether payroll calculations are correct.

Auditing with the computer means that the computer and its programs are treated as a tool of the auditor. In auditing with the computer, the intent of the auditor is to perform controls and substantive tests using the computer and its programs as if they were an assistant or junior accountant. The auditor may use the computer, for example, to scan accounts receivable records on magnetic tape to test whether each record contains the proper credit limit information. Alternatively, the auditor may use the computer to prepare confirmation requests in substantive testing of accounts receivable.

In the preceding discussion, the concepts of auditing with, through, and around the computer are reviewed separately, but they are often used in combination. For example, a payroll program may be tested directly by processing data through it (auditing through the computer), and indirectly by using another program to examine the content of files created by the payroll program (auditing with the computer).

Whether the auditor audits with, through, or around the computer, or utilizes a combination of these approaches, is a function of many things. Among these are the effectiveness of a particular approach, the costs to be incurred and the benefits to be realized, the accessibility to equipment and programs, the availability of the audit trail and related documentation, and the auditor's technical competence.

Determining the relative effectiveness of a particular approach can be a complex decision. Numerous conditions have to exist, for example, in order to be able to audit around the computer. Auditing around the computer may not be effective if one of these conditions, such as the audit trail, does not exist.

Whether the benefits equal or exceed the costs is an important criterion in determining whether the auditor audits around, through, or with the computer. In some circumstances, for example, it may be more efficient to have a junior accountant select, prepare, and mail accounts receivable confirmation requests. This may occur if the auditor has no generalized audit software for the specific computer system used by a client and it would be too expensive to develop the software for that one situation.

The auditor's access to computer equipment and programs may determine whether the auditor audits around, through, or with the computer. The client may have a one-of-a-kind system from a small vendor, for example, that the client operates around the clock except for maintenance downtime. The auditor may be forced to audit around the computer to prevent drastic disruption of the client's operations. The availability of an audit trail and related documentation is another important factor in determining whether to audit around, through, or with the computer. For example, the auditor may be forced to audit through the computer if all input is through visual display terminals and there are no source documents for manual review.

The auditor's technical competence may be the least justifiable reason for determining whether to audit around, through, or with the computer. Unfortunately, it is often the primary factor. Auditors who do not understand computers and their operation are forced to audit around them. Although the auditors may erroneously believe that the client's sophisticated computer system is simply a giant version of the bookkeeping machine they have been auditing in a similar fashion for many years, the very nature of computer systems creates exposures that did not exist before. For example, programmers can easily suppress the printing of information or print erroneous information. Such suppression can completely circumvent the auditor procedures utilized. In such a situation, the auditor's use of the around-the-computer approach, adopted inappropriately because of a lack of technical competence, may fail to detect material errors and irregularities.

When—Auditing Concurrently
with or after Processing

Another issue to be resolved by the computer auditor is *When* the procedures will be performed. Techniques that are now available enable the auditor to perform auditing procedures on an application (1) concurrently with processing, that is, while the computer is processing the application; or (2) after the computer has completed its processing. The auditor must primarily consider one factor, system sophistication, to determine which approach will be used.

Auditing *concurrently with processing* means that information is made available to the auditor while a program is running so that appropriate audit procedures can be performed. For example, in determining the propriety of sales, the auditor may have a computer terminal that is located next to his or her desk and prints out sales order information for every transaction over a certain dollar amount, for a specific product or service, or from a specific territory or customer. To perform an audit concurrently with processing, the auditor has two choices: to determine in advance what information is necessary so that a means of obtaining it can be built into the system, or to have a means for querying the system. The auditor may query the system as to the contents of a particular field in a file or the status of a program processing step or series of steps.

Auditing *after processing* means that the audit procedures are performed after a computer program is finished. For example, the auditor may use a utility program to print the customer names and balances of all accounts receivable subsidiary ledgers maintained on magnetic tape.

Whether the auditor performs the procedures concurrently with processing or after processing is primarily determined by the sophistication of the system. In some systems, such as on-line real-time systems where files are updated at the time of transaction input, the auditor may be unable to reconstruct the previous contents of the file. The auditor's only recourse may be to monitor file activity as it occurs. In systems where batch processing is performed, however, most audit procedures can be applied after the processing is complete. But even with a relatively unsophisticated system, the auditor should perform some procedures while a program is running. The auditor should, for example, observe and test the handling of errors while an actual program is running.

Where?—Auditing the Phases
or Results of Processing

The auditor must also determine *where* in the processing cycle the auditing techniques are to be performed. The auditor can apply his or her techniques to either the phases of processing or the results. The audit of phases or results is determined by the objectives of the audit procedures.

Auditing the *phases* of processing refers primarily to the assessment of control risk. Included in this assessment is the evaluation of general and application controls.

Auditing the *results* of processing refers primarily to the collection of evidential matter. The emphasis in this aspect of the audit is on direct tests of account balances.

The performance of audit procedures on the phases of processing or the results of processing is determined by the objectives to be satisfied. If the objective is controls testing, most of the auditor's efforts will be directed toward the phases of processing. If the objective is substantive testing, most of the auditor's efforts will be directed toward the results of processing.

Which?—Auditing Programs, Files, or Systems

The auditor must also determine *which* parts of the system are to be audited. Computer-auditing techniques can be applied to computer programs, files, or the entire system—it depends on the audit objectives and the audit trail.

Auditing computer programs can involve both controls testing and substantive testing. Controls testing involves testing programs for controls. Techniques for auditing programs are primarily oriented toward controls testing. Substantive testing involves ascertaining the accuracy with which a computer program processes the transactions.

Auditing computer files can also involve both controls testing and substantive testing. Files can be tested for evidence of compliance with controls or the accuracy of the data they contain. Techniques for auditing files are primarily oriented toward substantive testing of the balances in those files.

Auditing computer systems involves performing controls and substantive tests on the system as an integrated unit. Integration can refer to several things: combining the separate testing of programs and files into an overall evaluation; combining the testing of programs and files into a single test; using a mixture of techniques to accomplish the controls and substantive testing objectives and combining the results into an overall evaluation of the entire system or a specific application; and treating the computer system with its programs and files as a single unit that receives input, produces output, and can be audited around by examining the input and output.

The performance of audit procedures on individual programs and files or on the entire system as an integrated unit is determined by the audit objectives and the nature of the audit trail. To test the functioning of input controls, for example, the auditor can perform tests on a specific program. To test the accuracy of processing, the auditor can perform substantive tests on a specific file. The system may be controls tested as an integrated unit by processing test data through it and examining errors rejected by the program and the contents of files for evidence of controls such as credit limits.

The nature of the audit trail will also determine the procedures performed. With an audit trail, the auditor may decide to trace selected transactions through the entire computer system. Without the trail, the auditor may decide to perform extensive substantive tests on the computer files.

WHICH? REVISITED—TEXT TAXONOMY FOR COMPUTER-AIDED TECHNIQUES

All the taxonomies for computer-auditing techniques discussed have merit because they can aid the auditor in selecting a specific technique for a particular audit situation and in understanding why, when, or where a particular technique should be utilized on which part of the system. The auditor must understand all of them in order to make those determinations and to communicate with other practitioners who may use the terminology.

The taxonomy used in this text, however, organizes computer-auditing techniques according to those used for programs, for files, and for systems. We believe that there are several advantages to this approach. A significant advantage is that this organization closely parallels the auditor's major objectives in terms of controls testing programs and substantive testing files while recognizing dual-purpose testing. For example, although the auditing of programs is associated with controls testing, the auditor may simultaneously perform substantive tests as he or she examines the programmed arithmetic producing account balances.

Another significant advantage is that this organization closely parallels the physical objects—the programs or files—with which the auditor must work. We can discuss the audit's objectives somewhat abstractly, but the work is done on the programs and files.

A final advantage is that most of the techniques that have been developed work with the physical objects of the program or file. As in auditing manual systems, the techniques are developed and applied to physical objects.

SUMMARY

Auditing concepts pertaining to the assessment of control risk and related controls testing and the substantive testing related to the collection of sufficient competent evidential matter necessary to render an opinion are as relevant to computer auditing as to the auditing of manual and mechanical systems. Computer auditing is both similar to and different from the auditing of these systems. The process is similar in that controls and substantive tests are still performed, whereas the differences arise from additional procedures unique to computer auditing.

Computer auditing includes the application of both manual techniques and computerized techniques in performing controls and substantive testing. The procedures used to accomplish the audit's objectives change while the audit objectives do not. The procedural changes occur both in the assessment of control risk where controls testing is performed and in the collection of evidence where substantive testing is performed.

The concepts and procedures involved in the auditor's assessment of control risk for manual and mechanical systems are also applicable when the processing is done by a computer. The purpose of the control assessment is still to determine the extent to which the auditor can rely on the controls for restricting subsequent auditor procedures and to plan those subsequent audit procedures. The elements of the control structure—control environment, accounting systems, and control procedures—are applicable to all systems for the processing of accounting data. Procedures to obtain an understanding of the control structure are followed by an assessment of control risk when the auditor determines the extent to which he or she can rely on controls in designing subsequent audit procedures.

The introduction of EDP into the processing of accounting data has effects on controls and the audit trail. EDP induces numerous changes in the processing cycle. As a result of these changes, the auditor must evaluate the effects on the elements of the control structure. The auditor must also be aware of how EDP may change the audit trail. Additional controls that have been specified in response to the effects of EDP on the processing of accounting data include general and application controls. In reviewing the system of control, performing tests of controls, and assessing control risk, the auditor must analyze the effectiveness of user controls, EDP controls, and their interrelationships in determining the extent to which he or she will be able to rely on the control structure.

Substantive testing to collect sufficient competent evidential matter to render an opinion on the financial statement follows the assessment of control risk. The computer can be used in this aspect of the audit to perform analytical procedures and direct tests of account balances. In performing direct tests of account balances, the computer can be utilized for dual-purpose testing in conjunction with controls tests or independently in direct tests of account balances by examining the files resulting from computer processing.

The scope of and approach to tests of controls and substantive testing change when a computer is involved. The major change occurs in controls testing because of the need to test the additional controls found in a computer system. The scope of and approach to substantive testing change because the auditor may be forced to rely on the computer to obtain account balances. Combining tests of controls and substantive tests into dual-purpose tests is just as applicable in computer auditing as it is in auditing manual or mechanical systems.

Computer auditors, the computer, and computer testing can play major roles in controls and substantive testing. These roles can be analyzed by asking the following questions:

- Who performs the computer auditing?
- What computer-auditing techniques are available?
- Why is the computer used or not used in performing the audit?
- When in the processing cycle is the audit performed?
- Where in the processing cycle are the techniques utilized?
- Which parts of the system are audited?

The computer auditors are members of the same groups that perform other auditing tasks: the external auditors, the internal auditors, and the hybrids performing both functions, such as the GAO auditors.

Many techniques are available to the computer auditor. A significant task is selecting a technique appropriate to the auditing task at hand. To aid the auditor in understanding which technique may be appropriate, alternative schemes for categorizing them, or computer-auditing taxonomies, have been proposed.

Four taxonomies were discussed in the context of *why, when, where,* and *which. Why* refers to auditing around, through, and with the computer. *When* refers to auditing concurrently with and after processing. *Where* refers to auditing the phases and results of processing. *Which* refers to which parts of the computer system are audited.

The organization of computer-auditing techniques in this text is in terms of programs, files, and systems. Advantages include a close approximation of this taxonomy to the auditor's objectives, to the physical objects to which the auditor applies the procedures, and to the types of techniques that have been developed to aid the auditor.

REVIEW QUESTIONS

4–1. What are the major phases of the audit and how do they relate to each other?

4–2. How does the introduction of a computer affect the auditor's objectives, processes, and procedures?

4–3. Why is a mixture of manual and computerized techniques utilized in computer auditing?

4-4. Where in the audit is the auditor most likely to use manual procedures? Computerized techniques?

4-5. What impact does EDP have on manual procedures in the assessment of control risk?

4-6. What manual-auditing procedures in the assessment of control risk will probably not change when a computer is installed?

4-7. What impact does EDP have on manual-auditing procedures in the collection of evidence?

4-8. What manual-auditing procedures in the collection of evidence will probably not change when a computer is installed?

4-9. What is the purpose of the auditor's assessment of control risk?

4-10. What is the internal control structure?

4-11. The internal control structure contains the elements of control environment, accounting systems, and control procedures. Describe these three elements and discuss the components of each.

4-12. What is meant by "understanding" the control structure?

4-13. What is meant by "assessing" control risk?

4-14. What is the relationship between the assessment of control risk and other auditing procedures?

4-15. What are some of the changes induced by EDP in the accounting system?

4-16. What are some of the effects that EDP may have on the elements of the internal control structure?

4-17. What is the audit trail and what effects might EDP have on it?

4-18. What is the main purpose of the general controls and what are they?

4-19. What is the main purpose of the application controls and what are they?

4-20. Distinguish between user controls and EDP controls.

4-21. Under what circumstances will the auditor probably focus on user controls? EDP controls? A combination of both?

4-22. What is the purpose of substantive testing? What are the objectives of substantive testing?

4-23. What are the two types of substantive testing?

4-24. What role does the computer play in substantive testing?

4-25. Why does the auditor rely most heavily on manual procedures when control testing the general controls?

4-26. Why does the auditor rely most heavily on computerized techniques when control testing application controls?

4-27. Under what circumstances is the utilization of a computer for processing accounting data likely to have no effect on substantive testing procedures?

4-28. Under what circumstances is the utilization of a computer for processing accounting data likely to have the most significant effect on changing substantive testing procedures?

4-29. How do analytical procedures, performed as part of substantive testing, change when a computer processes the accounting data?

4-30. What effect, if any, does the computer have on dual-purpose testing as contrasted with a manual system?

4-31. Who are the computer auditors and what are their primary concerns in performing computer audits?

4-32. What is meant by auditing *around, through,* and *with* the computer? Why is the auditor likely to select each of these three techniques?

4-33. What is meant by auditing concurrently with and after processing? Why is the auditor likely to select either of these approaches?

4-34. What is meant by auditing the phases and results of processing? Why is the auditor likely to select either of these approaches?

4-35. What is meant by auditing programs, files, and systems? Why is the auditor likely to apply his or her techniques to a specific part of the system or to the system as a whole?

OBJECTIVE QUESTIONS

4-36. Audit programs are modified to suit the circumstances on particular engagements. A complete audit program for an engagement generally should be developed
  a. Prior to beginning the actual audit work
  b. After the auditor has completed an assessment of control risk
  c. After reviewing the client's accounting records and procedures
  d. When the audit engagement letter is prepared (AICPA)

4-37. The primary purpose of tests of controls is to provide reasonable assurance that
  a. The control procedures are adequately designed to assure employee compliance therewith
  b. The control environment procedures are being applied as prescribed
  c. The accounting system procedures are being applied as prescribed
  d. The control structure is being applied as prescribed (AICPA)

4-38. Which of the following best describes a fundamental weakness often associated with electronic data processing systems?
  a. Electronic data processing equipment is more subject to systems error than manual processing is subject to human error.
  b. Electronic data processing equipment processes and records similar transactions in a similar manner.
  c. Electronic data processing procedures for detection of invalid and unusual transactions are less effective than manual control procedures.
  d. Functions that would normally be separated in a manual system are combined in the electronic data processing system. (AICPA)

4-39. An auditor is reviewing an audit program for an upcoming audit for a client who has just installed a computer system. The best response for the effect the computer will have on the audit is that

    a. The manual procedures to satisfy the control risk assessment objective will not change

    b. The manual procedures to satisfy the collection-of-evidence objective will not change

    c. The audit's objectives will not change

    d. Computerized techniques will be required to perform tests of controls and substantive testing

4–40. Auditing through the computer is most closely related to

    a. Auditing the results of processing

    b. Auditing the phases of processing

    c. Auditing after processing

    d. Auditing concurrently with processing

4–41. Auditing around the computer may be appropriate when

    a. The auditor does not have the technical competence to audit through the computer

    b. The detail for all transaction input, processing of accounts or ledgers, and output is available in printed form

    c. The auditor's primary objective is testing the processing control component of application controls

    d. The computer is to be used to prepare accounts receivable confirmation request forms

4–42. Auditing concurrently with processing is most likely to be used in a system with

    a. Batch input and processing, on-line files

    b. On-line input, batch processing, on-line files

    c. Batch input and processing, off-line files

    d. On-line input and real-time processing

4–43. The objective of controls testing is most closely associated with which of the following techniques?

    a. Auditing the phases of processing

    b. Auditing with the computer

    c. Auditing computer files

    d. Auditing the results of processing

CASES AND EXERCISES

4–44. You are reviewing audit work papers containing a narrative description of Tenney Corporation's factory payroll system. A portion of that narrative is as follows:

Factory employees punch time clock cards each day when entering or leaving the shop. At the end of each week the time-keeping department collects the time cards and prepares duplicate batch-control slips by department showing total hours and number of employees. The time cards and original batch-control slips are sent to the payroll accounting section. The second copy of the batch-control slips are filed by date.

In the payroll accounting section, payroll transaction records are created from the information on the time cards. These records are created on a cassette tape with a key-to-tape data entry device. A batch total record for each batch is created from the batch-control slip. The batch total records are recorded on the cassette tapes as the first record for each batch of payroll transactions. The time cards and batch-control slips are then filed by batch for possible reference. The cassette tapes containing the payroll transactions and batch totals are sent to data processing where they are sorted by employee number within batch. Each batch is edited by a computer program which checks the validity of employee number against a master employee tape file and the total hours and number of employees against the batch total records. A detail printout by batch and employee number is produced which indicates batches that do not balance and invalid employee numbers. This printout is returned to payroll accounting to resolve all differences.

In searching for documentation you found a flowchart of the payroll system which included all appropriate symbols (American National Standards Institute, Inc.) but was only partially labeled. The portion of this flowchart described by the above narrative is shown in Figure 1.

Required:
a. Number your answer 1 through 16. Next to the corresponding number of your answer, supply the appropriate labeling (document name, process description, or file order) applicable to each numbered symbol on the flowchart.
b. Using the format shown below, analyze the strengths and weaknesses in controls for the factory payroll system.

Strengths	*Weaknesses*

4–45. Auditors must adequately plan their work. Discuss what factors auditors should consider in *timing* their assessment of control risk for both general and application controls.

4–46. The auditor's assessment of control risk has both primary and secondary objectives. Describe the primary objectives. Discuss the secondary objectives and describe how their relationship to the primary objectives appears to be evolving.

4–47. The basic concept of control that recognizes that the cost of control should not exceed the benefits expected to be derived is known as *reasonable assurance*. Discuss the relationship of this concept to the factors the

Tenney Corporation
Flowchart of Factory Payroll System

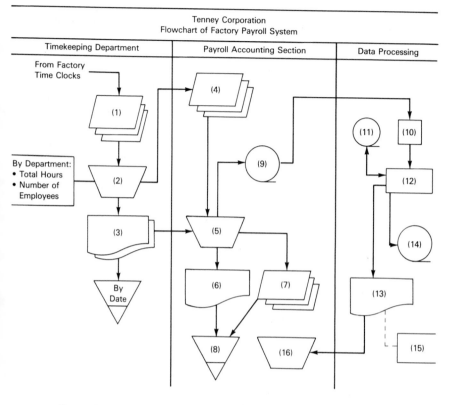

Timekeeping Department	Payroll Accounting Section	Data Processing

Figure 1.   Tenney Corporation Payroll System (*AICPA adapted*)

auditor must consider in deciding whether to audit around, through, or with the computer.

4-48. Under certain circumstances, the auditor may elect to focus on user controls instead of EDP controls. Discuss in general the type of information the auditor would expect the user to have if he or she were to do this.

4-49. The auditor may elect not to pursue a reduction in control risk for some EDP controls at the end of the preliminary assessment phase and again at the end of the completion assessment phase and instead accomplish the audit objectives by other means. Does this mean that from the *client's* standpoint the cost/benefit test for EDP controls fails and that the client should dismantle the EDP accounting control system? Discuss.

4-50. The computer can be programmed to execute transactions automatically, such as preparing checks to vendors on due dates or reordering inventory when quantities drop to some level. In the auditor's assessment of control risk, to which general and application controls will attention probably be directed and why?

4-51. Describe what is meant by *random error* in a manual system and *systematic error* in an EDP system, give examples of each, and discuss how the auditor is likely to detect each.

4-52. Meyers Pharmaceutical Company, a drug manufacturer, has the following system for billing and recording accounts receivable:

1. An incoming customer's purchase order is received in the order department by a clerk who prepares a prenumbered Company sales order form in which is inserted the pertinent information, such as the customer's name and address, customer's account number, and quantity and items ordered. After the sales order form has been prepared, the customer's purchase order is stapled to it.

2. The sales order form is then passed to the credit department for credit approval. Rough approximations of the billing values of the orders are made in the credit department for those accounts on which credit limitations are imposed. After investigation, approval of credit is noted on the form.

3. Next the sales order form is passed to the billing department where a clerk types the customer's invoice on a billing machine that cross-multiples the number of items and the unit price, then adds the automatically extended amounts for the total amount of the invoice. The billing clerk determines the unit prices for the items from a list of billing prices.

   The billing machine has registers that automatically accumulate daily totals of customer account numbers and invoice amounts to provide "hash" totals and control amounts. These totals, which are inserted in a daily record book, serve as predetermined batch totals for verification of computer inputs.

   The billing is done on prenumbered, continuous, carbon-interleaved forms having the following designations:
   a. "Customer's copy."
   b. "Sales department copy," for information purposes.
   c. "File copy."
   d. "Shipping department copy," which serves as a shipping order. Bills of lading are also prepared as carbon-copy byproducts of the invoicing procedure.

4. The shipping department copy of the invoice and the bills of lading are then sent to the shipping department. After the order has been shipped, copies of the bill of lading are returned to the billing department. The shipping department copy of the invoice is filed in the shipping department.

5. In the billing department one copy of the bill of lading is attached to the customer's copy of the invoice and both are mailed to the customer. The other copy of the bill of lading, together with the sales order form, is then stapled to the invoice file copy and filed in invoice numerical order.

6. A key-to-tape data entry device is connected to the billing machine so that cassette tapes are created during the preparation of the in-

voices. The invoice records on the cassette tapes then become the means by which the sales data are transmitted to a computer for preparation of the sales journal accounts receivable subsidiary ledger and perpetual inventory records.

The cassette tapes are fed to the computer in batches. One day's accumulation of tapes comprises a batch. After the tapes have been processed by computer, they are placed in files and held for about two years.

Required

a. Flowchart the billing system as a means of understanding the system.

b. Determine the weaknesses and recommended improvements in the system organizing your answer as follows:

Weakness(es)	*Recommended Improvement(s)*

c. Specify the strengths in the system and describe the audit procedures you would perform in testing these strengths, organizing your answer as follows:

Strengths	*Tests of Controls*

(AICPA adapted)

4-53. Discuss what the auditor needs in terms of data, programs, files, and so forth, in order to perform a computer audit utilizing each of the following approaches: (a) auditing around the computer, (b) auditing through the computer, (c) auditing with the computer, (d) auditing concurrently with processing, (e) auditing after processing, (f) auditing the phases of processing, (g) auditing the results of processing, (h) auditing programs, (i) auditing files, and (j) auditing systems.

4-54. Two auditors were discussing the best approach to use in conducting a computer audit. One of them, who understood the taxonomy of auditing around, through, and with the computer, believed that the best approach to testing application controls was to audit through the computer. The other, who understood the taxonomy of auditing the phases and results of processing, believed that the best approach for the testing was to audit the phases of processing.

a. Discuss the conclusions these auditors probably made after obtaining an understanding of the control structure.

b. Discuss the assumptions these auditors have made about the computer system and the best means of testing it in order to propose the approaches suggested.

c. Discuss the similarities and differences of the two proposed approaches.

4-55. The role of tests of controls and substantive testing is subject to change when a computer is installed to process accounting data.

a. Discuss the type of computer system likely to result in the least significant changes. Explain why.

b. Discuss the type of computer system likely to result in the most significant changes. Explain why.

4-56. The computer can play a signficant role in performing tests of controls and substantive tests.

a. Discuss the circumstances under which the computer's role in performing tests of controls and substantive tests is likely to be significant. Explain why.

b. Discuss the circumstances under which the computer's role in performing tests of controls and substantive tests is likely to be insignificant. Explain why.

4-57. Some computer auditors believe that there are only two choices to be made regarding whether to use the computer in the performance of the audit: You either bypass the computer and audit *around* it or attack it directly and audit *through* it. The concept of auditing *with* the computer is not considered a separate approach. State whether you believe there are either these two or these three approaches to using the computer and explain why.

4-58. Auditing around the computer may be feasible under certain conditions. Even when these conditions exist, however, some computer auditors believe that it should not be done. Ignoring these conditions or technical considerations, discuss the social, political, and legal implications of auditing around the computer.

Chapter 5

ORGANIZATION CONTROLS, PERSONNEL PRACTICES, AND STANDARD OPERATING PROCEDURES

Learning Objectives

After completing this chapter, the reader should be able to:

1. Determine how weaknesses in organization, personnel, and operations controls affect the audit examination.

2. Understand the effect of EDP on the separation of functions in transaction functioning.

3. Determine which functions should be segregated within the EDP department.

4. Identify who is responsible for internal control in computerized systems.

5. Understand how personnel practices and standard operating procedures affect internal control in EDP.

The use of the computer in data processing systems frequently eliminates the basic internal control of appropriate segregation of duties. In a manual system, incompatible functions such as authority to initiate and execute a transaction, and the recording of the transaction, are assigned to different departments or to different individuals within the accounting department. In a computer system, these incompatible functions may be consolidated within the EDP department. In a computerized inventory control system, for example, the processing of transactions, and the authorization to replenish inventory, would be performed by the EDP department if the rules for replenishment of inventory were programmed into the system. As a result, the EDP staff would be in a position to divert inventory or cash to their own use if there were no alternative compensating controls.

The alternative controls that compensate for this consolidation of incompatible functions include organization controls, personnel practices, standard operating procedures, and systems development and documentation controls. *Organization controls* relate to the segregation of duties within EDP systems and with the EDP department itself. They also cover the assignment and division of responsibility for control over EDP systems. The purpose of the organization controls is to reduce the risk of error or fraud in EDP systems. Sound *personnel practices* provide control over the quality of work by ensuring that the EDP staff are competent and honest, and they provide policies that encourage the EDP staff to comply with management's policies. *Standard operating procedures* identify procedures for the operation of the computer that ensure high-quality processing and limit the opportunity for errors and unauthorized use of files, programs, and reports. *Systems development and documentation controls* are standard practices relating to the design, development, programming, maintenance, and documentation of application systems. They encourage the proper design of systems and increase the chances that systems will operate reliably when completed. The effect of sound personnel practices, standard operating procedures, and systems development and documentation controls is to ensure compliance with the organization controls.

Our discussion in this chapter focuses on (1) the segregation of EDP and user functions, (2) the segregation of functions within the EDP department, (3) responsibility for control, (4) personnel practices, and (5) standard operating procedures.

This chapter also includes an Appendix relating to the Lava Butte, Inc., case. The Lava Butte case is a continuing case on EDP and internal control that appears in Chapters 5 through 10. The Appendix to each chapter includes a completed internal control questionnaire or system narrative. There are also several cases at the end of each chapter that relate to the material in the questionnaire or system narrative. The Lava

Butte appendixes and the related cases should be used by the reader for review and consolidation of the chapter material. The background material for the case is contained in the Appendix to this chapter.

A particular emphasis in this chapter is the impact of size on organization controls. The controls that are both necessary and possible in a large EDP department are different from those in a small department. It is possible, for example, to provide much greater segregation of duties in a large department than in a small one. Such differences, and their implications, are discussed throughout the chapter.

SEGREGATION OF EDP AND USER FUNCTIONS

The appropriate segregation of functional responsibilities in a computer system requires segregation of EDP and user functions. The purpose of such a segregation of responsibilities is to maintain, as far as possible, a separation of the incompatible functions of authorizing transactions, executing transactions, recording transactions, and maintaining accountability over assets involved in the transactions. This separation is achieved by prohibiting the correction of non-EDP errors by the EDP department and, in some cases, by denying EDP the right to perform incompatible functions.

Error Detection, Correction, and Resubmission

The separation of the EDP department from the user departments makes it possible to improve internal control by dividing responsibility for the handling of errors between these departments. The EDP department is responsible for controlling the processing of data within the department. Consequently, the detection of errors during processing, the correction of errors originating within the EDP department, and control over the resubmission of transactions after correction are all the responsibility of EDP. The detection of errors during processing generally includes the entry of all data rejected during transaction processing in a manual error log, and the preparation of an error report explaining the nature of each error. Errors that originate within the EDP department, such as data entry errors, are corrected within the department. The EDP department is responsible for ensuring that all transactions rejected by the system are in fact resubmitted and reentered for processing. (These responsibilities are discussed in greater detail later in the chapter.)

The user departments are responsible for errors that originate outside the EDP department. Such errors might include the omission of transaction data or the use of incorrect transaction data, such as invalid part or product codes. The user departments are responsible for correcting these errors and resubmitting the corrected transactions to EDP for data processing. The EDP department control staff may assist the users in performing these tasks by communicating the errors and nature of the errors to the users. In no event, however, should the EDP staff attempt to correct the errors themselves.

In small companies, the EDP function may be a part of the user department, precluding the departmental separation of error-handling functions. In such cases, it is necessary to divide the error-handling duties between two or more persons in the user department. With adequate management supervision of these persons, this division of duties can partially compensate for the lack of functional separation between EDP and users.

Segregation of Incompatible Functions

A general principle of segregation of incompatible functions is to separate the four primary functions of authorizing, executing, and recording transactions, and maintaining accountability over the assets involved in the transactions. Of these four functions, EDP should only perform the recording of transactions. Many computer systems, however, also perform authorization and execution functions and provide EDP with opportunities for custody over assets. In such cases, systems design should include compensatory controls to offset the failure to segregate incompatible functions.

1. *Authorization Function.* As a general rule, the EDP department should not be permitted to authorize transactions. Some data processing systems, however, incorporate authorization functions into the instructions of the computer programs. In these systems, the authorization and recording functions are performed simultaneously by data processing when the programs are run.

The materials reordering system provides an excellent example of the impact of computerization on the authorization function. In a manual system, the inventory control department usually determines the type and quantity of inventory items to be ordered and prepares a purchase requisition to this effect. The purchase requisition is routed to the purchasing department where a purchase order is prepared. In EDP systems, however, some or all of these functions may be performed automatically by the computer system. The application programs may include instructions that identify the type and quantity of items to be ordered, print a notification list of items to be ordered, or even print the purchase orders themselves. Compensatory controls in this kind of system should include careful review and approval of notification lists or purchase orders by the purchasing department. They should also include proper assignment of responsibility for setting reorder criteria, and the review of reorder criteria in the inventory file.

2. *Execution Function.* The execution of steps in the transaction processing cycle, and changes to master files, should normally be performed outside of EDP. In many data processing systems, however, the execution of transactions is performed automatically by instructions in the computer programs.

The identification of overdue accounts in accounts receivable, for example, is a credit department function. If the credit department performs the identification, and EDP records the results of the identification, the risk of one department or person overlooking a particular account is reduced. In many data processing systems, however, the identification of overdue accounts is an automatic EDP function. The selection of overdue accounts is accomplished by automatic aging of each account.

To the extent that EDP is used to execute such steps, controls should be built into the EDP application programs to ensure that the steps are executed in conformity with specific or general authorizations. Predetermined limits and tests for overall reasonableness are examples of such controls.

3. *Accountability Function.* EDP should not have custody of, or control over, non-EDP assets. The separation of the recording function, and physical custody or control of assets involved in the transaction, provide for an independent check of records and assets. The recording of the acquisition cost of non-EDP equipment, for example, may be performed by EDP, but EDP should not have custody or control over the equipment itself.

In some cases, however, EDP will have direct or indirect access to assets. If the EDP activity includes the preparation and signing of disbursement checks, EDP personnel will have direct access to cash. In other cases, the access to assets is indirect, such as where EDP generates shipment orders authorizing the release of inventory or creates transfer orders authorizing the release of customer-owned securities. In these cases, alternative controls should be established to minimize the possibility of unauthorized access to assets by EDP personnel. These alternative controls could include control over access to EDP equipment, effective library controls, user department control totals, and other controls described in this chapter.

Tables 5–1 and 5–2 illustrate the impact of computerization on the segregation of functions in a sales transaction processing system. In Table 5–1 the transaction steps are handled by six different departments, permitting segregation of incompatible functions. In Table 5–2, however, the impact of the computer reduces the number of departments to four (in-

Table 5–1.   Sales Transaction Processing: Manual System with Segregation
of Incompatible Functions

	Department					
Transaction Step	Sales	Credit	Finished Goods Store	Shipping	Billing	Accounts Receivable
1. Preparing the sales order	X					
2. Obtaining credit approval		X				
3. Releasing the merchandise to shipping			X			
4. Preparing the bill of lading				X		
5. Shipping the merchandise				X		
6. Billing					X	
7. Entering in sales journal					X	
8. Posting customer's accounts in general ledger						X

cluding EDP). The result is that, in this particular example, the EDP department performs the incompatible functions of authorization, execution, and record keeping.

Understanding and Tests of Controls

If the auditor plans to assess a low level of control risk on the segregation of EDP and user functions, he or she should perform procedures to obtain an understanding of the internal control structure and make tests of controls that include some of the following:

1. Review organization charts for the location of the EDP function within the organization.
2. Review job descriptions of EDP and user staff involved in error handling to ascertain the proper segregation of functions.
3. Observe actual operations including preparation, scrutiny, and distribution of error listings. Note the degree of management supervision being exercised.
4. Interview EDP management and operating staff to determine the degree and effectiveness of management supervision. (This is particularly important in small organizations.)
5. Review available management reports, studies, or evaluation of the error-handling process.

Table 5–2. Sales Transaction Processing: Computerized System Showing Performance of Incompatible Functions by EDP

Transaction Step	Department			
	Sales	Finished Goods Store	Shipping	EDP Department
1. Preparing the sales order	X			
2. Obtaining credit approval				X*
3. Releasing the merchandise to shipping		X		
4. Preparing the bill of lading				X
5. Shipping the merchandise			X	
6. Billing				X
7. Entering in sales journal				X
8. Posting customer's accounts in general ledger				X

*Credit approval becomes an EDP department function when the rules for granting credit are written into the application programs. For example, a program instruction may compare the dollar amount of each sale with the customer's predetermined credit limit.

6. Prepare a systems flowchart for each transaction processing cycle and review the segregation or nonsegregation of functions.
7. Review the reconciliation of control totals maintained outside the EDP department to the totals that result from computer processing.
8. Test-check such reconciliations to ensure that the control is being performed effectively.
9. Examine available evidence, such as working papers, interdepartmental memos, and error listings to indicate that such reconciliations take place in the normal course of operations.
10. Review processing controls (such as prior approval of master-file changes), postprocessing controls (such as review of master-file status subsequent to processing), and programmed controls (such as reasonableness checks) to determine whether they provide for processing in accordance with management's authorization.
11. Test preprocessing, postprocessing, and programmed controls to ensure that the control is being performed effectively.

SEGREGATION OF FUNCTIONS WITHIN THE EDP DEPARTMENT

In the preceding section we learned about the need for the segregation of incompatible functions in transaction processing. We also learned about the tendency in computer systems to centralize these functions within

EDP. This centralization of incompatible functions in EDP would, in the absence of alternative controls, enable EDP personnel to perpetrate and conceal irregularities in the normal course of their duties. Consequently, it is important to have compensating internal controls within the EDP department that reduce the likelihood of this occurring. These compensating controls relate to the internal organization of the EDP department. In this section we discuss the assignment of responsibilities, the control function, separation of duties, separation of duties in small companies, and separation through division of knowledge.

Assignment of Responsibilities

The correct processing of transactions requires that each employee in the EDP department has clearly understood duties that are followed consistently. This division of duties is not possible if each person does not have a job title and complete position description. Although the number of titles and descriptions will vary depending on the size and complexity of the EDP operation, the following seven positions are typical of most EDP departments.

JOB TITLE	POSITION DESCRIPTION
Systems analyst	Analyzes and defines the requirements for new and existing applications, such as payroll. Designs new or improved processing systems to meet these requirements. Prepares specifications for the systems to guide programmers. Writes procedures and user instructions.
Systems programmer	Is responsible for the maintenance, improvement, and testing of operating systems; library software; and system utility programs. Coordinates the operating and control interrelationships of application and systems programs.
Application programmer	Identifies programs required by the systems design, and flowcharts the logic of these programs. Codes the logic in a programming language. Tests and debugs the programs. Prepares the program documentation.
Computer operator	Performs tasks such as operating the computer equipment. Operates the computer in accordance with standard procedures and the documentation for each application.
Librarian	Has custody of files, programs, and documentation. Checks files, programs, and documentation in and out of the library according to management policy. Catalogs all documentation. Maintains a record of all file, program, and documentation usage.

Data entry operator	Prepares data for computer processing by entry into an off-line device or by direct entry into the computer. Uses off-line device to record data in machine-readable form on magnetic tape or disk. Enters data directly into the computer via a terminal or other on-line device.
Control clerk	Establishes control over all data received by the EDP department. Reconciles control totals after processing. Reviews output and controls the distribution of output.

Some EDP departments may have additional positions that relate to their large size or to the complexity of their systems. For example, large organizations usually have a quality control manager and a security officer; and certain types of systems require a data-base administrator and a network administrator.

Quality control manager	Establishes systems design, programming, and documentation standards. Reviews documentation to ensure compliance with standards and provides approval of documentation when standards are met.
Security officer	Establishes procedures relating to access to equipment, data, programs, and other aspects of physical security. Monitors work of security force. Investigates procedures violations, reviews violation logs and statistics, and carries out spot checks and audits of physical security procedures. Issues passwords or security codes and is responsible for ensuring that they are used correctly.
Data-base administrator	Is responsible for the development and maintenance of a data-base system.
Network administrator	Is responsible for the development and management of a data communications system. Reviews error frequency and other operating statistics. Acts as coordinator between the EDP staff and the communications vendors in the resolution of problems.

EDP Department Control Function

The EDP department's plan of organization and operating procedures should provide for a separate control function within the department. This control function is responsible for monitoring the accuracy of transaction processing and ensuring that no data are lost or mishandled within the department. In a large EDP department this responsibility is assigned to a control group; in a small EDP department it is assigned to a control clerk.

The control function's duties cover the receipt and input of data, the processing of data, and the distribution of output. These duties are described in the systems and procedures manual, and in the operations documentation of each EDP application, and generally include the following:

1. Recording the control totals for data received from the users in a manual control log.
2. Tracking the progress of work through the EDP department.
3. Reviewing error listings and console error messages to ensure that all errors are logged, corrected, and reentered into the system.
4. Reviewing the console log for evidence of unauthorized activity.
5. Monitoring error frequency to determine the need for corrective action.
6. Reconciling each application's output control totals to input totals in the manual control log. This reconciliation is a test of accurate and complete processing. It is performed prior to the release of output to the user.
7. Reviewing output reports for completeness and timeliness.
8. Maintaining a distribution log showing the destination, recipient, and date of distribution for each copy of each output report. The distribution log is reconciled to a master distribution schedule.
9. Maintaining an error log and preparing an error report for periodic review by data processing management.
10. Correcting all errors that originate within the EDP department.
11. Returning all errors that originate outside EDP to the appropriate user department.

For example, in a typical EDP processing control function, a detail accounts receivable transaction file such as sales or cash receipts is processed with the accounts receivable master file to produce an updated master file. The sum of the transaction file and original master file should equal the total of the updated master file. The EDP processing control person would make the reconciliation or would review such a comparison.

Separation of Duties

The centralization of processing in the EDP department requires that duties be segregated within EDP. The segregation of duties makes it more difficult for employees to make unauthorized changes in the processing of data. This increase in internal control is particularly evident if the six functions of systems analysis, application programming, systems programming, operations, library, and control are separate and distinct.

The separation of systems analysis and application programming provides for independent checks on the design and change of systems and program specifications. Frequently, however, these two functions are combined without a significant weakening of internal control.

Of greater importance is the separation of the duties of systems analysis and application programming from systems programming. Without this separation, it would be possible for a systems programmer to make unauthorized changes in application programs or files. Systems programmers have the ability to make these changes because of their access to system utility programs and data entry devices. *System utilities* are programs that perform frequently used data-handling tasks such as sorting data, merging files, and transferring data from one input/output device to another. Some system utilities have the capability of copying files, making changes to application code without reassembling, or even making direct modifications to data in a file. The system programmers may have access to these programs to perform systems-level maintenance. They may even be assigned a terminal from which to perform the maintenance. If they had knowledge of the application programs, including file layouts, they would be in an excellent position to make unauthorized modifications to programs or data. The program changes would be difficult to detect because they could be temporary changes leaving no evidence on paper or file. Separation of application and systems responsibilities cannot eliminate this risk, but it can certainly make it more difficult for systems programmers to identify changes in application programs that would be beneficial to them.

Systems analysis, application programming, and systems programming should all be separated from operations. If programmers and systems analysts were able to run programs, they would have the opportunity to perform unauthorized modifications to programs and data files. This is a particular danger where programmers and analysts are aware of the parameters used in limit tests, and the formulas and calculations included in application programs. A programmer armed with this knowledge and with uncontrolled access to the computer could circumvent these software controls.

An independent librarian function provides additional separation between systems and programming, and operations, by making files available only to authorized personnel for use in required processing. Without adequate control over the issue of files, programmers would be able to obtain, for example, the payroll master file for unauthorized processing of their own or a fictitious payroll record.

The control group within the EDP department should be organizationally separated from operations. A separate control group provides an independent check of the output from operations.

Separation of Duties versus Size

The complete segregation of functions within the EDP department is generally possible only in large organizations. Large organizations tend to follow bureaucratic norms and are susceptible to high specialization of duties, a detailed division of labor, many and elaborate rules, and little personal interaction. Small organizations, in contrast, are characterized by open norms and have little specialization, a broad span of control, few and general rules, and extensive interaction on a personal basis.

These basic organizational principles are evident in the organization charts shown in Figures 5–1, 5–2, and 5–3. Figure 5–1 shows the organization chart for a large EDP department. Not only is there a division between systems and operations, there is also extensive specialization within each of these areas. Within the systems area, for example, there is a division between systems analysis, application programming, and systems programming. The department's large size supports such staff positions as security officer and quality control manager. In the medium-size EDP department in Figure 5–2, there is still a separation of the basic functions, but there is less specialization, and there are no separate staff positions. In the small EDP department in Figure 5–3, the systems and programming functions are combined. Systems and programming are still segregated from operations, but there is no separate control clerk, nor a separate librarian. Presumably these tasks are performed by other EDP or user staff.

These differences in organization of the EDP departments as the size varies are partly a function of internal control and partly a function of operational efficiency. In a large organization, the specialization and division of duties are conducive to good control but also promote operational efficiency. In a small EDP department with only one operator, for example, it would be uneconomical to have either a full-time librarian or a full-time control clerk. At a very minimum, however, even small departments should segregate the systems and programming function from the operations function.

This basic segregation of duties may be difficult to accomplish in small EDP departments where programmers and operators work on a part-time basis. In such cases, it is not uncommon to find operators assigned programming duties, and programmers assigned operator duties, to keep them busy. Such assignments clearly violate the segregation of functions within EDP and should be avoided even in small EDP depart-

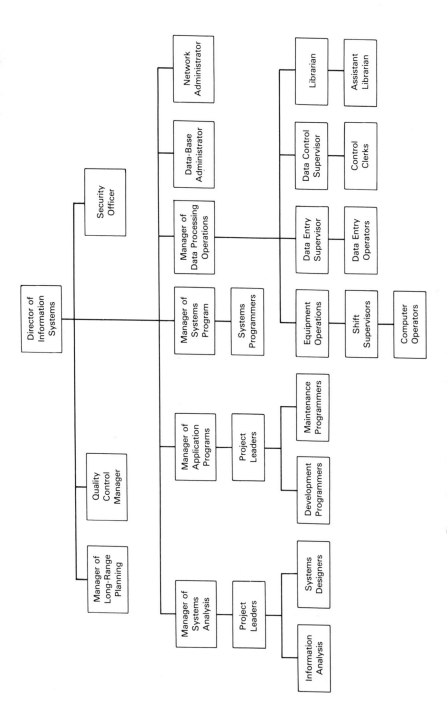

Figure 5–1. Organization Chart for a Large EDP Department

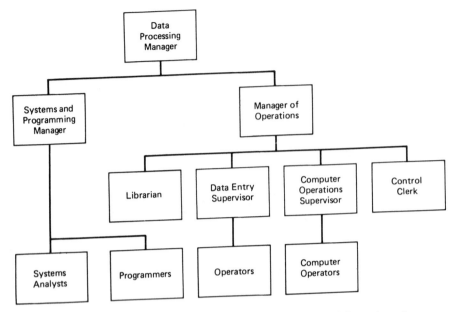

Figure 5-2.   Organization Chart for a Medium-Size EDP Department

ments. A more appropriate solution, and one that maintains the segregation of functions, is to assign part-time operators and programmers to
duties outside the EDP department.

If the EDP department's plan of organization does not provide for
the minimum segregation of systems and programming from operations,
the auditor may be unable to rely on the results produced by the system.
The auditor may have to increase substantive testing because of this control weakness.

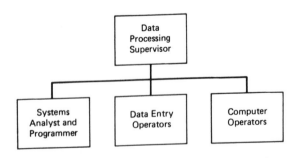

Figure 5-3.   Organization Chart for a Small EDP Department

Separation through Division of Knowledge

One important factor that may strengthen internal control in large EDP departments is the general complexity of systems. This complexity requires that a person have a thorough knowledge of the systems and operations before he or she can commit a deliberate error. An individual would have to know the authorization procedures, passwords, file protection devices, application controls, and audit procedures to be able to tamper successfully with a system. A basic principle of control in a complex system, therefore, is that no one person should have all the knowledge that is required to tamper successfully with a system. Deliberate separation of knowledge and careful control over application program documentation prevent unauthorized personnel (including systems analysts and programmers) from obtaining complete knowledge about program procedures and controls.

The principle of separation of knowledge is something that should be designed into the system. Systems should be structured on a modular basis, with the work of designing and programming the system divided between different individuals or groups. In this way, no fraud can be committed without collusion between the groups.

As an example, Figure 5–4 identifies the program modules in a payroll system: edit, sort, file maintenance, transaction processing, master-file updates, and printing of journals and reports. Each module contains three different programs, one of which is selected for a specific processing application. The dark circles and connecting lines represent the programs from each module required to process hourly payroll. An alternative combination of programs would be required for other payroll applications, such as salary payroll and executive payroll. A person would have to modify two or more of the programs in a particular payroll application to be able to execute unauthorized transactions or master-file changes and to conceal the results. This possibility would be avoided by a careful assign-

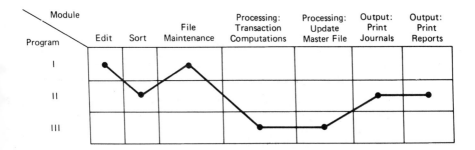

Figure 5–4. Program Modules in a Payroll System

ment of design and programming responsibilities by module within each payroll application.

Understanding and Tests of Controls

If the auditor plans to assess a low level of control risk on the segregation of functions within the EDP department, he or she should peform procedures to obtain an understanding of the internal control structure and make tests of controls that include some of the following:

1. Obtain the organization chart for EDP to determine the degree to which the incompatible functions of systems, programming, operations, control, and library are organizationally segregated.
2. Review position titles and descriptions of key EDP personnel, including systems analyst, programmer, computer operator, librarian, data entry operator, and control clerk, to ensure that no individual is assigned incompatible duties.
3. Observe EDP operations to ensure that systems analysts and programmers do not have unrestricted access to hardware, files, or programs. (See a later section in this chapter for standard operating procedures that restrict access to the hardware and reduce the risk of unauthorized operation of hardware.)
4. Observe the operation of the librarian function. Review library logs and records to ensure that usage records are maintained consistently, and that only authorized personnel are permitted to remove transaction and master files, and program documentation.
5. Review systems design documentation of large transaction processing systems to determine whether they are constructed on a modular basis, to determine whether different individuals perform systems and programming work on different modules, and to determine whether access to the documentation for each module is restricted. The purpose of these reviews is to ensure that no one programmer or analyst has access to all the information available concerning the transaction processing system.

Responsibility for Control

Responsibility for internal control in EDP systems rests with management. Indeed, EDP systems are sufficiently important to the functioning of most companies that the responsibility for control in these systems requires continuing attention from the board of directors and senior management. This responsibility should include the monitoring of new systems development, coordinating of new systems, and monitoring of changes in existing systems and programs.

Carrying out this responsibility requires the assignment of control duties to the EDP and other departments within the company. Control duties that should be assigned to the EDP department fall into two separate areas: responsibility for the design of systems, and responsibility for day-to-day operations. These responsibilities will be handled satisfactorily by EDP if they follow an appropriate plan of organization and assignment of responsibilities as described earlier in this chapter.

Outside the EDP department the responsibility may be assigned to several parties, including the board of directors, audit committee, senior corporate management, corporate financial management, operating and reporting units, internal audit department, and outside control group. The following responsibilities would normally be assumed by each of these parties:

Board of directors	A primary responsibility of the board is to ensure that the internal control structure fulfills company needs. In practice, the board delegates this responsibility to an audit committee comprised of a few directors.
Audit committee	The audit committee is likely to meet with senior corporate management, and periodically with the internal and external auditors, to discuss improvements in EDP system controls. The committee should receive reports from the internal and external auditors on the functioning of controls in existing EDP systems, as well as review the specifications of new systems.
Senior corporate management	Senior corporate management will approve overall EDP systems design, including provisions for internal control. It will also approve the delegation of authority for EDP system controls to individual departments and units.
Corporate financial management	Corporate financial management is usually responsible for control functions in corporate accounting systems and for reporting control guidelines to operating units, and it may also be responsible for determining whether control policies are implemented effectively by the operating units.
Operating and reporting units	The operating and reporting units should establish specific controls in their EDP systems in accordance with company policy.
Internal audit department	The internal audit department is used to help monitor and review the EDP internal controls structure. Typically its functions will include periodic visits to operating units and staff offices to test the effectiveness of controls in EDP systems. Reports on important EDP systems will generally be re-

Outside
control
group

viewed with corporate management, and highlights will be presented to the audit committee.

The purpose of the outside control group is to establish an independent check on the functioning of the EDP department. The responsibility of the outside control group includes the following kinds of tasks: (1) compare output control totals generated by the EDP department with user-generated totals, (2) sample output from the EDP department to determine whether the systems are functioning as designed, (3) maintain an overall knowledge of the EDP system and control all changes in systems and programs, (4) review program and data specifications before programs are written, (5) review requests for changes in program specifications, and (6) communicate all changes in system and program specifications to persons who should know about them.

As a practical matter, the independent and critical review function of the outside control group can be accomplished by one or more of the users of EDP systems. For example, the payroll department may have its own control group responsible for evaluating the payroll data produced by the computer, and the accounting department may perform the control function of maintaining totals of debits and credits to be posted to the general ledger.

Understanding and Tests of Controls

The audit examination for responsibility for EDP controls assigned outside the EDP department will be tied in with assessment of responsibility for internal controls in general. Some of the tests and procedures, however, will be EDP oriented. If an internal control questionnaire is used, it should include questions on the plan of organization for the system of internal control as it relates to the assignment of responsibility for EDP systems and operations. Questions should be addressed to each level of authority, and tests and procedures should be adopted to ensure compliance with the plan of organization. These tests and procedures should include the following:

1. Review written descriptions of responsibility for control at each level of the organization plan to ensure appropriate assignment of responsibility for control.
2. Review minutes of board of directors and audit committee to ensure that their responsibility for control in EDP systems is being carried out.

3. Review documentation for new systems for appropriate authorization by corporate management.
4. Review new EDP accounting system documentation for issuance of control guidelines by accounting to the users.
5. Review the audit program of the internal auditors to determine the completeness and adequacy of their review and test of internal control, including tests of input data and processing results.
6. Review internal auditors' working papers and reports to verify their monitoring and thorough review of internal control in EDP systems.
7. Observe the functioning of the outside control group to ensure its operational independence from EDP. This can be accomplished by reviewing program specification requests, program change requests, written control group responses, and EDP follow-up to control group recommendations.

PERSONNEL PRACTICES

Sound personnel practices are essential to both the quality of data processing and the functioning of other organization and operation controls. Generally speaking, very capable EDP staff are likely to create high-quality systems and produce high-quality output, especially when personnel practices follow sound management principles. In the absence of good personnel practices, however, the auditor may find a lack of compliance with stated policies of internal control. If staff do not follow their defined position responsibilities, for example, it will be difficult to rely on job descriptions and the separation of duties as strengths of internal control.

The assessment of competency in EDP personnel is a difficult task for the auditor. The auditor will possess EDP skills but is primarily an auditor and not an EDP specialist. Consequently, the auditor must assess the caliber of EDP personnel indirectly. Indirect evaluation will include a review of hiring and personnel evaluation practices. The auditor should also review other personnel practices related to the efficient functioning of personnel: personnel scheduling, EDP career paths, formalization of personnel practices in the systems and procedures manual, and psychological aspects of security.

Hiring and Evaluation of Personnel

The attraction and promotion of high-caliber EDP personnel can be accomplished in several ways, including hiring tests, background checks, fidelity bonds, continuing professional education, and periodic evaluation of personnel.

Individual aptitude for EDP tasks, such as systems design and programming, can vary considerably from individual to individual. *Hiring tests* are used to select those individuals most likely to succeed in an EDP environment. There are generally two approaches to such tests, depending on whether the applicant is experienced or not. Experienced applicants may be asked to flowchart a simple system or to write a short program. The elapsed time required to complete the task, and the quality of the results, will be used to evaluate the applicant's potential performance. If applicants are relatively inexperienced, they may be asked to complete an aptitude test. Standard EDP aptitude tests are widely available, particularly from equipment manufacturers, to test specific EDP skills.

Background checks of individual applicants for EDP positions will help minimize the possibility of hiring an incompetent or dishonest individual. Background checks may include requests for references or the retention of an investigating firm to research the individual's past career. Because of the concern over individual privacy in today's society, such checks should be handled with great sensitivity. To request that prospective EDP personnel demonstrate untarnished integrity, however, is not inconsistent with the requirements of such professional groups as accountants, bank and trust officers, and auditors.

Fidelity bonds should also be used to help reduce the risk of hiring dishonest EDP staff. Fidelity bonds are a form of insurance in which a bonding company agrees to reimburse an employer, within limits, for losses attributable to theft or embezzlement by bonded employees. To minimize its potential losses, the bonding company will thoroughly investigate the background of prospective employees. In addition, in the case of a defalcation, the bonding company is more likely to prosecute vigorously than the employer. The background check, and the employee's awareness of almost certain prosecutions of a defalcation, are deterents to dishonest individuals.

Continuing professional education (CPE) for EDP staff is essential if they are to maintain and enhance their skills. There are many sources of CPE for EDP staff, including courses provided by equipment manufacturers, university and college courses, self-study courses, courses presented by independent training firms, and special in-house programs. Whatever the CPE method, the purpose should be to ensure that all staff are adequately trained for their positions.

Hiring tests, background checks, and fidelity bonds are no guarantee against poor or dishonest work and are no substitute for *periodic evaluation* of EDP personnel. The evaluation should cover personnel in the systems and programming area, as well as in operations. Performance measures for systems analysts and programmers may include review of the quality of work, comparisons of the amount of work completed with standard, and evaluation of the performance of the system or program. Operating personnel can be evaluated via equipment performance standards, data entry standards, and other standards of operational control.

Personnel Scheduling

The scheduling of personnel on a regular basis, and during periods of vacation and sick leave, assists in the separation of incompatible EDP functions. Systems analysts and programmers should be assigned to specific projects, given a time budget, and asked to report periodically on progress against the budget. Equipment operators should be assigned to specific duties or specific pieces of equipment and should be obliged to report any failure to complete duties required within the allotted time period to their supervisor. Specific assignments should be made to cover vacations and sick leaves.

In large organizations, EDP management may use scheduling techniques such as bar charts or networks to assign staff on an efficient basis. Scheduling in small and medium-size EDP departments may involve less-sophisticated techniques, but the need for scheduling is just as critical as in large departments.

Rotation of Duties

The schedule for equipment operators should include rotation of operator duties and required vacations. This will prevent one person from being continuously in charge of operating one program or set of programs.

Career Paths

In EDP it is fairly common for an individual to start out as an equipment operator and progress upward to programmer and systems analyst. Ideally this should never happen, but as a practical matter its prohibition would frustrate the aspirations of many EDP staff. In some EDP departments, the EDP manager may permit and encourage an operator or data entry person to "do a little programming" so that the individual can grow professionally. Such practices clearly violate the separation of duties and provide the operator with opportunities to manipulate the system. Since the practice of transferring operators to the systems and programming section is so common, at a minimum such individuals should be removed immediately from operator duties, and restriction of access should be strictly enforced. It is less common to see a programmer transferred to operator duties, but such transfers should be avoided even temporarily to help scheduling problems. An operator with a knowledge of the application programs presents considerable risk to the system.

Formalization of Personnel Practices

Current auditing literature stresses the need for accounting and control practices to be formalized in writing in an accounting manual. In EDP the equivalent to the accounting manual is the systems and procedures manual.

In other areas of the organization, it may be preferable to stress informality, spontaneity, or participation as management styles. In EDP, however, the level of technical complexity is sufficiently high, and the separation of duties is so important, that formalization of practices is inevitable.

The use of the systems and procedures manual to formalize EDP personnel practices in writing is both an aid to management and a further assurance that the required practices are followed. Conventions of programming, documentation, operating, scheduling, and so forth, are so varied that in the absence of a systems and procedures manual, there may be confusion as to the appropriate practices to follow.

Psychological Control

Sound personnel practices go beyond the establishment and formalization of appropriate control procedures. The EDP staff should follow these procedures consistently and enthusiastically. Generating consistent and enthusiastic support of required procedures is not an easy matter, however, since controls tend to structure the work environment and reduce the speed with which a job might otherwise be accomplished. It is not surprising that control procedures often generate a negative attitude among EDP staff.

EDP management, therefore, should deliberately foster a positive attitude toward controls. Measures that might foster such an attitude include education and training of staff in control procedures, monitoring the observance of procedures, and management by example. Of particular importance is maintaining morale among the EDP staff and watching for individuals who might disregard procedures deliberately. When morale is low, and staff turnover is high, disgruntled employees may deliberately damage the system. There have been several reported examples of deliberate destruction or manipulation of files and programs. In addition, an employee who is terminated should be asked to leave the computer installation immediately. When an EDP department manager was fired, he was found two hours later in the computer room making copies of application programs.

Understanding and Tests of Controls

Audit assessment of personnel practices will require performance of procedures to obtain an understanding of the internal control structure and tests of controls that include the following:

1. Review hiring and evaluation procedures, including aptitude tests, background checks, fidelity bonds, CPE, and measures of performance, to determine their effect on the caliber of personnel.
2. Review personnel schedules to ensure that personnel are assigned to appropriate tasks and that operators are rotated periodically.
3. Observe EDP operations to ensure that systems analysts and programmers do not have unrestricted access to hardware and files.
4. Review promotion policies and recent promotions to ensure compliance with written policies, and to ensure that inter-EDP department transfers pose no threat to control.
5. Review staff turnover statistics, and frequency and form of staff firing, to ensure that the attitude of EDP personnel poses no undue risk to control.

STANDARD OPERATING PROCEDURES

In the preceding section we discussed a recommended personnel practice—the formalization of personnel practices in a sysems and procedures manual. The same principle of good management applies to each section of the EDP department. Each section should have standard procedures and conventions included in the systems and procedures manual. The standard procedures for the operations section are included here. Standard conventions for systems and programming are covered in Chapter 6.

Standard operating procedures ensure the use of uniform operating techniques, increase the likelihood of high-quality processing of accounting data, and help protect data files and programs from loss, destruction, manipulation, or unauthorized disclosure. Standard procedures include the following:

Scheduling	The operations of the computer should follow schedules. Schedules should be realistic and allow time for reruns, assembly runs, and preventive maintenance. Preventive maintenance should include periodic cleaning of tape and disk drives, printers, and other peripheral equipment, and routine inspection of tapes and disks. Schedules should be established according to priorities set by management or according to priority scheduling by the operating system.

Machine operation	Standard operating procedures are set for the computer and input/output equipment operation. They include, for example, a requirement that operators respond uniformly to console error messages. They also include standard procedures for loading programs and changing disk packs and tapes.
Machine performance	Equipment standards are set for elapsed time usage, maintenance time, expected downtime due to breakdown, and other conditions. These standards permit evaluation of equipment performance. Procedures should require periodic review of equipment maintenance and failure logs, and comparison of actual equipment performance with standard performance. Identification and correction of substandard equipment may help reduce the incidence of hardware-induced errors.
Job-run procedures	Computer operators should follow the procedures outlined in the operations documentation of each job. These procedures generally outline the sequence of programs, the use of equipment and files, and any special operator actions such as terminations and restarts.
Console logs	A console log should be prepared by the operating system. This log should list all operating system activity, maintain an equipment utilization record, and identify operator-initiated actions. This record of system activity provides an important control over unauthorized system use.
Personnel time record	Since not all individuals will be operating the equipment, each staff person in operations should maintain a personal log of his or her time. The log will show tasks performed and the elapsed time for each task.
Housekeeping	Housekeeping procedures relating to the use of supplies, storage of programs, and handling of files are used to keep the computer room tidy. They are designed to reduce the risk of loss of destruction of programs and data and to ensure that sensitive output does not fall into unauthorized hands.
File control standards	Standards for the handling of files are necessary to minimize opportunities for misuse, damage, or loss of files. Standards include file names, retention dates, reconstruction procedures, and storage location. All files should be controlled by a librarian in an area to which access is restricted.
Adequate supervision	Standard procedures should call for supervision and review of operating activities. Supervision

Emergency
and physical
security
procedures

should include periodic review and comparison of console logs, job records, and personnel time records. The EDP department should have plans and procedures to protect programs, files, and equipment from fire, theft, natural disasters such as floods, power failure, or failure of communications. Typically the emergency and physical security procedures include the duplication of files and programs and storage of the duplicates off premises. Emergency and physical security procedures should be written and included in the systems and procedures manual.

Understanding and Tests of Controls

Job-run procedures, file control standards, and emergency and physical security procedures are covered at greater length in subsequent chapters. Audit procedures to obtain an understanding of the internal control structure and tests of controls for these items will be described at that time. The audit tests described here are for the remaining items. Suggested procedures and tests are as follows:

1. Review the operations section of the systems and procedures manual to determine the adequacy and completeness of written standards.
2. Observe computer operators to determine whether they follow standard operating procedures for equipment operation.
3. Review supervisory comparisons of console logs with personnel time records to determine whether schedules and procedures are being followed by the computer operators.
4. Review comparisons of equipment failure logs and other performance measures with equipment performance standards to ensure that equipment performance is monitored appropriately.
5. Observe housekeeping procedures and the general tidiness of the computer room to ensure that programs and files are unlikely to be lost.

SUMMARY

A major problem in computerized transaction processing systems is the centralization of incompatible duties within the computer. Control is maintained by segregation of EDP and user functions, where still possible, and by segregation of incompatible functions within the EDP department.

The segregation of functions can only be achieved through appropriate assignment of responsibility for control, adequate personnel practices, and standard operating procedures. Responsibility for control rests with top management, who in turn assign control responsibility to each level of the organization, including the EDP department. Sound personnel practices increase the likelihood that sound control procedures will be followed in the EDP department. Standard operating procedures ensure high-quality processing of accounting data and help protect data files and programs.

APPENDIX

Lava Butte, Inc.: Company Description, and Organization Controls, Personnel Practices, and Standard Operating Procedures Questionnaire

Business Background

Lava Butte, Inc., is a wholesale distributor ($100 million sales) located in the high desert in central Oregon. Sales orders are taken on the telephone by salespeople in the main office. Shipments are made from the inventory

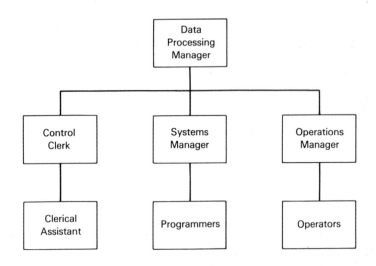

Figure A5–1. Lava Butte, Inc. EDP Department Organization Chart

maintained in a central warehouse. Lava Butte receives 400 to 500 customer orders on a typical day. It has eight thousand active customer accounts and nine thousand inventory items in the warehouse. It purchases inventory from five hundred active vendor accounts and currently has 300 employees.

Data Processing Background

1. Number of personnel (by level) within each area of the EDP department.

	Data Control	Systems and Programming	Operations and Scheduling
Managers/supervisors		1	1
Systems analysis		1	
Programmers		2	
Operators			4
Control clerks	1		
Clerical assistants	1		
Total	2	4	5

Note: Transaction entry performed by user personnel at terminals and with key-to-tape equipment located in user departments.

2. EDP organization chart (see Figure A5–1).
3. Description of the major duties and responsibilities for each key individual or section within the EDP department.

JOB TITLE	MAJOR DUTIES AND RESPONSIBILITIES
Manager	Supervises all EDP personnel. Performs long-range planning. Assists programmer/analyst 1 in developing new systems.
Systems manager	Supervises programmers. Designs new systems.
Programmer 1	Programs and implements major applications. Assists systems manager.
Programmer 2	General program maintenance. Programs and implements small applications. Assists programmer 1.
Operations manager	Supervises computer operators. Establishes processing schedule.
Operators	Operate equipment on a three-shift basis. Review run-to-run totals. Burst and decollate reports.

Control clerk	Logs in batches received. Balances reports to batch-control log. If errors are noted during processing: (a) contacts the user department, (b) makes corrections as instructed by users, and (c) reprocesses corrections. Routes reports to authorized users. Performs librarian functions.

4. Description of equipment used.

	Description	Quantity
Control processor:		
CPU	IBM 4381	1
Internal storage	16 megabytes	
Console	IBM 3205	1
External storage units:		
Magnetic tape drives	IBM 3480 (1 A22, 2 B22s)	4 transports
Magnetic disk drives	IBM 3380 (5 gigabytes) (1 AD4, 1 BD4)	2
Other	N/A	
Input/Output units:		
Line printer	IBM 4245	1
On-line terminals	IBM 3192	4
Other units	N/A	

5. Layout of computer room (see Figure A5–2).
6. List of major applications.

APPLICATION	EDP METHOD
General ledger	On-line input, batch processing
Accounts payable and cash disbursements	Batch input, batch processing
Sales, accounts receivable, and cash receipts	On-line input, batch processing
Payroll	Batch input, batch processing
Inventory	Batch input, batch processing

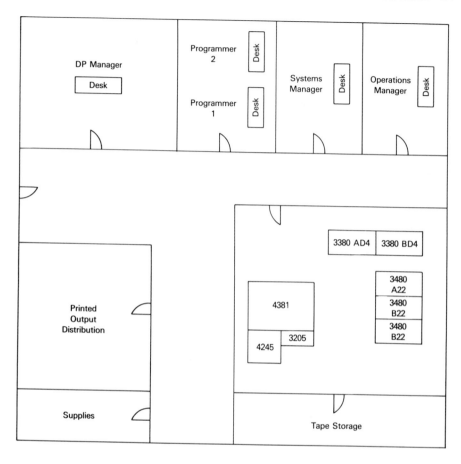

Figure A5–2.

The Questionnaire

Questionnaire
Prepared by: _____

Questionnaire
Reviewed by: _____

Date: _____

Date: _____

Name of Company _____

Location of EDP Facility _____

Organization Controls and Personnel Practices:

1. Do the company's organizational structure, its division of duties, assignments of responsibility for control, and personnel practices appear to provide for adequate supervision and segregation of functions within the EDP department and between EDP and user departments?

_____✔_____ Yes   _____ No

In assessing organization controls the auditor should consider the following:	Contributes to Possible Reduction in Control Risk		Comments
	Yes	No	
— EDP precluded from correcting user originated errors	✓		
— Separation of programming from systems analysis		✓	*Staff not large enough to permit separation*
— Separation of library function from operations and programmer/systems functions		✓	*Tapes are backup to fixed, nonremovable disks*
— Separation of programming, systems analysis, and operations functions	✓		
— Data processing control function separate from user and operations functions	✓		
— Independence of EDP department	✓		
— Division of programmer and systems analyst duties by program and system module		✓	*Systems function too small to permit adequate segregation*
— Organization plan for internal control in EDP systems		✓	*N/A*
— Board of Directors/Audit Committee responsibility for EDP system control		✓	*N/A*
— Top corporate management reviews control in new EDP Systems		✓	*N/A*
— Financial Management establishes control guidelines			*N/A*

In assessing organization controls the auditor should consider the following:	Contributes to Possible Reduction in Control Risk		Comments
	Yes	No	
− Internal auditor's program includes a review of: a. The arrangement of duties and responsibilities in the data processing department		✓	
b. Programs supplied by the data processing department which are used to prepare audit data		✓	*no internal audit department*
c. The controls of the user departments over the processing performed by the data processing department		✓	
− Outside control group performs independent review	✓		*Located in user departments*
− Hiring tests administered to applicants for employment in EDP	✓		*Aptitude tests*
− Background checks for applicants for employment in EDP	✓		*Use investigative agency*
− EDP employees are covered by Fidelity Bonds	✓		*all EDP Staff covered*
− Continuing Professional Education for EDP staff	✓		*Systems and Programming Staff only*
− Periodic evaluation of EDP staff	✓		
− Scheduling of EDP staff	✓		
− Regular rotation of duties	✓		
− Career path policies prevent transfer of staff to incompatible functions	✓		
− Personnel practices written in Systems and Procedures manual	✓		*Reviewed selected binders*
− Morale and attitude of EDP staff conducive to control	✓		

Standard Operating Procedures:

2. Are the general controls over computer operations sufficient to provide reasonable assurance as to the accuracy and completeness of processing results?

_____ ✔ _____ Yes　　　_____ No

In assessing organization controls the auditor should consider the following:	Contributes to Possible Reduction in Control Risk		Comments
	Yes	No	
— User departments initiate and originate items for processing	✔		
— Initial preparation of data is outside EDP	✔		
— Authorization to originate master-file changes is outside EDP	✔		
— Supervision of operations personnel and review of all computer activities on a periodic basis	✔		Observed operations on surprise basis on three separate days
— Restricting access to systems and program documentation	✔		Observed during surprise visit
— Adequate operating instructions	✔		Reviewed operations manuals
— Limiting operator intervention	✔		
— Scheduling computer work load	✔		
— Restricting access to computer facilities and data files	✔		Observed during surprise visits
— General housekeeping and orderly work flow in EDP facility	✔		

REVIEW QUESTIONS

5-1.　What is the purpose of the auditor's procedures to obtain an understanding of organization and operations controls?

5–2. At what stage in the audit will the auditor be concerned with organization and operations controls?

5–3. What are the consequences of absence or weakness in organization and operations controls?

5–4. How has EDP affected the segregation of functions in the transaction processing cycle? What are the audit implications of such changes?

5–5. What general deficiencies are you likely to find in EDP organization controls in a small company?

5–6. Why are position descriptions for EDP staff important for internal control?

5–7. Why should application systems and programming be separated from systems programming?

5–8. What is the purpose of the EDP department control function? Why should it be separated from operations? What duties might be assigned to a control clerk?

5–9. Large EDP application systems are often made up of several program modules. How can the complexity of such systems be a control advantage?

5–10. Why is it important to assign responsibility for internal control in EDP systems to parties outside as well as inside EDP?

5–11. How does the outside control group differ in purpose from the EDP department control function?

5–12. How might personnel practices affect other organization and operations controls?

5–13. What are the limitations of background checks?

5–14. Why should the career paths of EDP staff be of concern to the auditor?

5–15. If the morale of EDP staff is low or their attitude is negative, what effect might this have on control practices?

5–16. Why are standard operating procedures necessary?

5–17. How should an audit committee of the board of directors discharge its responsibility for internal control in EDP systems?

OBJECTIVE QUESTIONS

5–18. Daylight Corporation's organization chart provides for a controller and an EDP manager, both of whom report to the financial vice-president. Internal control would not be strengthened by

    a. Assigning the programming and operating of the computer to an independent control group which reports to the controller

    b. Providing for maintenance of input data controls by an independent control group which reports to the controller

    c. Rotating periodically among operators the assignments of individual application runs

    d. Providing for review and distribution of computer output by an independent control group which reports to the controller (*AICPA*)

5-19. An internal control that is sometimes used in connection with procedures to detect unauthorized or unexplained computer usage is
   a. Maintenance of a computer tape library
   b. Use of file controls
   c. Maintenance of a computer console log
   d. Control over program tapes (*AICPA*)

5-20. The detection and correction of errors in the processing of data should be the responsibility primarily of
   a. The data processing manager
   b. The operator
   c. The EDP department control group
   d. The independent public accountant (*AICPA*)

5-21. Which of the following employees in a company's electronic data processing department should be responsible for designing new or improved data processing procedures?
   a. Flowchart editor
   b. Programmer
   c. Systems analyst
   d. Control group supervisor (*AICPA*)

5-22. Where computers are used, the effectiveness of internal control depends, in part, upon whether the organizational structure includes any incompatible combinations. Such a combination would exist when there is no separation of the duties between
   a. Documentation librarian and manager of programming
   b. Programmer and console operator
   c. Systems analyst and programmer
   d. Processing control clerk and data entry supervisor (*AICPA*)

CASES AND EXERCISES

5-23. Two-Byte Company's EDP department has a separate control function. During the understanding phase of assessing control risk, it is determined that the control function is both initiating transactions and making corrections without involving the user department.

   Required:
   a. How does this affect your assessment of control risk?
   b. The accounts payable department maintains input totals for all transactions sent to EDP. These input totals are balanced against output control totals when the output is returned by EDP. How will this affect your judgment of internal control as it applies to accounts payable?

5-24. Your review of the EDP department's organization chart shows separation of the four functions of systems, programming, control, and operations. You attempt to verify this separation by observation and inquiry. You reach the conclusion that the separation of duties is not operational. Give reasons as to why this might be despite the separation in the organization chart.

5–25. Outline a plan for hiring EDP staff that would improve the likelihood of hiring high-caliber personnel.

5–26. In the understanding phase of assessing control risk, you have become aware that there are no written procedures to guide the computer operators. Operators generally rely on guidance from F. Baggins, the operations supervisor, if something nonroutine happens. What are the implications for your assessment of control risk?

5–27. Define the following job functions: (a) systems analyst, (b) programmer, (c) computer operator, (d) librarian, (e) data preparer, and (f) control clerk.

5–28. In completing the Internal Control Questionnaire for Lava Butte, Inc. (see the Appendix to this chapter), you receive "yes" answers to all your questions on personnel practices and procedures. What documentation would you include in the working papers to assess risk at a low level on this control?

5–29. Responses to the Internal Control Questionnaire for Lava Butte (see the Appendix to this chapter) indicate a lack of separation of the programming and systems function, and no separate librarian function. How critical are these deficiencies?

5–30. In reviewing the responses to the Internal Control Questionnaire for Lava Butte (see the Appendix to this chapter), you notice that there are "no" answers indicating the absence of an organization plan for internal control, and the lack of an internal audit department. How will these "no" answers affect your audit? If the answers to these questions had been "yes," how might they have affected your audit program?

5–31. Terwilliger, Inc., has developed several computerized accounting applications. In all cases, the application programs are vendor-supplied packages that have been modifed to fit Terwilliger's requirements. Initial modifications were made a year ago and have been operating satisfactorily ever since. The EDP department consists of six key entry operators, three computer operators, one programmer, and a data processing manager.

The programmer's job description indicates that his primary function is to maintain the existing application programs. There is not enough maintenance work, however, to represent a full-time workload. Accordingly, he is assigned to other part-time duties. These other duties include performing operator duties at month-end to help with the heavy workload and reconciling the input and output control totals for the accounting department.

The data processing manager devotes most of his time to management duties but does assist the programmer when major programming changes are required. The manager also performs operator duties at month-end and fills in during operator sick leave and vacations.

Required:
a. Comment on the control situation.
b. Is this a situation where management efficiency must necessarily conflict with internal control?

5-32. Three operators copied their employer's list of customers during a night shift. They subsequently attempted to sell the list to a competitor for a large sum of money. What organization control, personnel practices, and operating procedures might have prevented the fraud from taking place? What controls might have disclosed the fraud once it had occurred?

5-33. The internal audit department of Grot Company assigned the duty of reviewing data processing operating procedures to Mr. Reginald Perrin. Mr. Perrin reviewed the operations section of the systems and procedures manual and then paid a surprise visit to the computer room. His subsequent report included the following observations:

1. In the hallway outside the computer room are open racks of magnetic tapes. All the tapes are labeled and include such files as the Accounts Receivable Master File, Year-to-Date Payroll Master File, and Stockholder Records Master File.
2. Just inside the computer room is a box marked "Input." User department staff walk into the computer room and leave loose source documents in this box.
3. Key entry operators retrieve the input documents from the bottom of the pile for key entry into on-line terminals.
4. The computer operators routinely separate copies of the output from the carbons. It was noticed that the fourth copy of the payroll checks was discarded with the carbons—it had been thrown into the wastebasket.
5. The computer operators periodically remove the console log from the console typewriter and throw it into the wastebasket.
6. Output of reports and documents is placed on a table outside the computer room for collection by user personnel.
7. Operators routinely make programming changes to ensure smooth running of the programs.

For each observation, describe the control weakness and the audit implications of the weakness, and suggest an alternative procedure that would provide better control.

(Adapted from Paul D. Johnson, "Mark Tick's Data Center Audit," ED-PACS, June 1974, pp. 16–17.)

5-34. Equivocal Savings and Loan (ES&L)

Introduction

ES&L is a large savings and loan association located in the northwestern United States. Business is conducted through branches located in four states. These branches operate terminals that are connected via an on-line data communications system to a centralized computer department.

The data processing department is headed by a vice-president of data processing who reports directly to the senior vice-president of finance but also has a "dotted-line" relationship with all other senior vice-presidents. The purpose of the dotted-line relationships is to make data processing responsive to user needs by creating working relationships between the data processing department and the user departments.

Responsibility for Control

Responsibility for control in EDP systems is assumed by the audit committee of the board of directors. The committee carries out this responsibility through the internal audit department and user control groups. There is no control group within the EDP department. Specific responsibilities are as follows:

Audit Committee—The audit committee oversees the audit function on behalf of the board of directors. Its responsibility for EDP systems is to ensure the accuracy of records and reports, and to ensure the safety of association assets. The committee is also responsible for ensuring that adequate controls are built into new systems. It receives reports from both the external auditors and the internal auditors on control in existing EDP systems. The committee also receives reports from the internal auditors on controls built into new systems.

Internal Audit—The internal audit department has a designated EDP audit specialist. This specialist is responsible for audit of control within the EDP department, the on-line data communication system, and the EDP activities of the users, including branch offices. These audit responsibilities are coordinated via an overall audit program that integrates all EDP audit functions. The EDP audit specialist reports to the vice-president of audit, who reports directly to the audit committee and has a dotted-line relationship with the chairman of the board. The dotted-line relationship reflects a day-to-day involvement with audit matters by the chairman and demonstrates his commitment to control.

User Control Groups—The accounting department (responsible to the senior vice-president of finance) has a control group whose responsibility is to monitor data processing accuracy and completeness on a daily basis. All master-file activity is reviewed; the general ledger, branch, and customer files are balanced; and discrepancies are reviewed and resolved. The branches also have balancing responsibilities, but these are performed by line personnel.

Data Processing Department—There is no control group within the EDP department because all transactions are entered on-line from remote locations, eliminating batch control over input within the EDP department. ES&L considers it unnecessary to maintain a control group within the EDP department and assigns balancing responsibilities to the user departments.

Organization of the Data Processing Department—The EDP department is divided into three sections, with each section headed by a manager who reports to the director of data processing. In addition to the three sections, there are staff specialists who report to the director of data processing. The following describes the three sections and staff specialists:

- *Technical Support.* The technical support section is responsible for preventing and monitoring problems relating to the system hardware, system software, and communications system. The manager coordinates the activities of the section, retains responsibility for the hardware, and works closely with IBM to help resolve problems. A software specialist maintains the operating system, utilities, and other support software and coordinates with the software vendors to resolve problems. The communications analyst monitors exposure to line failure and wire tapping, diagnoses line problems, and works with the communications vendors to resolve problems.
- *Systems Development.* The systems development section is divided into four areas. The first area, application systems design, is responsible for new systems development and consists of two systems analysts and one programmer analyst. The other three areas are responsible for maintaining each of the three major areas of application systems: loans, savings, and financial accounting (general ledger and payroll). Each of these areas is staffed with a programmer analyst and two programmers. All staff in these four areas report directly to the systems development manager and to the project director for the duration of individual maintenance and development projects. The project director is a staff specialist responsible for coordinating individual projects. The systems development manager is responsible for coordinating user and EDP department project requests, approval of project maintenance and development requirements, monitoring of project progress, and review and approval of project test results.
- *Operations.* The operations manager is responsible for scheduling and monitoring the work of data entry and computer operations. The data entry function is performed by a supervisor with three data entry operators. Computer operations has a shift supervisor and an operator assigned to each of the day and night shifts. Shift supervisors review the operation of the on-line system and prepare a written report for each shift detailing problems encountered. This report is submitted daily to the operations manager. The shift supervisor also performs library duties. The operators are responsible for operating the equipment, including monitoring the computer console and responding to console messages.

Staff Specialists. There are two staff specialists whose titles and functions are as follows:

- *Project Director.* The project director is responsible for coordinating individual system maintenance and development projects. He heads project task forces that include EDP systems and user staff.
- *Documentation Director.* The documentation director is responsible for the adequacy and security of documentation. He reviews documentation for completeness and conformity with standards.

He establishes and monitors security procedures to restrict access to documentation to authorized individuals.

Required:

1. Prepare an organization chart showing the assignment of responsibility for control of EDP systems within ES&L.
2. Prepare an organization chart for the EDP department of ES&L.
3. Prepare a memo to your audit manager that presents an evaluation of the two organization charts. Make sure you not only identify individual strengths and weaknesses but provide an overall conclusion.

5-35. ROBINSON INDUSTRIES: Organization of the EDP Function

Introduction

Robinson Industries is a loosely knit conglomerate which offers centralized data processing services to its affiliated companies. To improve the attractiveness of its services, the Data Processing Department this past year introduced on-line service. Several affiliates have become or are becoming users of this service. It has resulted in a reorganization of the Data Processing Department which concerned Mat Dossey, the senior on the audit. Dick Goth, the semi-senior on the engagement, reported that the client had not prepared a new organization chart but agreed to see what he could find out. His report is as follows.

Data Processing Department Organization

The Data Processing Department now consists of twenty-five persons reporting to the President through the Director of Data Processing. In addition to these Data Processing Department employees, key committees perform important roles as do the internal and external auditors for the Company. The internal auditors now report operationally to the Board of Directors and functionally to the President.

Committees

Selected functions of key committees that are important to the management and control of the Data Processing Department are described briefly in the following:

- *Data Processing Committee*—This committee, composed of three members of the Board of Directors, meets as required to review and evaluate major changes in the data processing area and to review approval of all pricing of services offered. Their responsibilities also include a review of major agreements with hardware and software vendors.

- *Audit Committee*—In its oversight of the audit function, this committee of the Board of Directors is directly concerned with the quality of the records and reports processed by the Department and the controls employed.

- *User Groups*—These groups consist of representatives from on-line users within a specific geographical area. They meet periodically throughout the year to discuss common areas of interest, possible enhancements, and current problems related to the on-line system. The results of these group meetings are reported directly to the Data Processing Department through a User Advisory Committee.

Data Processing Department

Data Processing Department management consists of five managers who report to the Director through an assistant director. The Department management meets weekly to review the status of projects, customer service levels, and any problems. Weekly status reports are then prepared and distributed to each level of line management. Formal meetings with Robinson's President are held quarterly, or more often if required, to review future plans and past performance.

The following describes the sections within the Department under the direction of each of the five managers.

On-Line Services

- *On-Line Technical Staff*—This staff conducts all user training, conversions, and parameter definitions necessary to set up a new user. Training classes are conducted at the Data Processing Center. Conversion assistance is provided to the user prior to the initiation of on-line services. If conversion programs are required, these are defined by the On-Line Services Section to the On-Line Analyst Programmers for program preparation. During the first month after conversion of a new user, calls are directed to On-Line Services; thereafter, user calls are directed to the User Liaison Section.
- *Applications Coordinator*—This person is responsible for coordinating the approval of user and Data Processing Department project requests, assisting in the requirements definition of a systems maintenance project, monitoring ongoing projects, and approving project test results.

Operations

- *Data Communications Coordinator*—This person monitors all service levels and response time related to the communications network and terminals. The Coordinator receives all user calls regarding communications problems. The Coordinator logs all calls, identifies the nature of the problem, and reports the status of the problems until they are corrected.
- *Computer Operators*—This section consists of operators, supervisors, and librarians who execute, review, and service the daily computer production runs, special computer runs, and program compilations and tests. The operations are scheduled on a twenty-four-hour basis for six days a week. Shift supervisors review all on-line operations and prepare written documentation of each problem encountered.
- *Scheduler*—This person is responsible for setting up the computer job runs and adjusting them for on-time special requests.

- *User Liaison*—This staff consists of four persons who receive, log, and report all questions or potential problems, other than communications problems, by on-line users. User input is obtained through telephone calls, letters, and on-line messages over the communications network and notes from user committee meetings.
- *On-Line Reports Control*—This staff is responsible for the distribution of all hard-copy output to all users. Microfiche are sent directly to users from the outside processing vendor. Logs are maintained where appropriate to control distribution and to reconcile items such as check numbers and dividend totals.

Systems and Programming

- *On-Line Analyst Programmers*—This staff is responsible for all of the applications and system software programming required for the On-Line System. Systems analysis and programming consists primarily of maintenance to existing computer programs, correction of problems, and enhancements to the current applications.
- *In-House Analyst Programmer*—This staff is responsible for all applications and system software programming not on-line.

Research and Development

- This staff evaluates and conducts preliminary investigations into new applications such as electronic funds transfers.

Marketing

- This staff responds to requests for information regarding the services provided by the Data Processing Department. Once a user signs an On-Line Service Agreement as a new user, that member is turned over to On-Line Services for training and conversion.

Question:

Based on Dick Goth's report above, prepare an organization chart of the Data Processing Department and of its relationships to the rest of the organization affecting it.

(Prepared by Frederick Neumann, Richard Boland, and Jeffrey Johnson, with funding from the Touche Ross Foundation. Used and adapted with permission of the authors.)

5–36. The head teller at the Union Dime Savings Bank in New York took advantage of an error-correction routine built into the computer system to embezzle $1.5 million over a period of three years. The head teller was responsible for training new tellers in the operation of the bank's on-line system. Because these trainees made numerous errors, the head teller explained his entries to several accounts each day using the error-correction routine as necessary to correct the errors of these trainees. Toward the end of the embezzlement period he was making upwards of fifty supervisory corrections per day to support a $30,000-per-day gambling addiction. The following controls were prescribed for the system:

a. A daily review of all supervisory transactions was made by a control clerk at the center. Although the control clerk had been told to look for an unusual volume of corrections, such a condition for this branch did not cause alarm because the condition had existed since the first day the clerk performed the review.

b. A report of all supervisory corrections sent to the branch manager each day was ignored by that individual because he did not understand the purpose of the report.

c. The head teller was required to take a vacation each year, but problems that arose during his absence because of the defalcation were saved for him to resolve upon his return.

d. Exceptions turned up by the auditors when they confirmed account balances were taken to the head teller for resolution. Blaming the errors on recently hired tellers, he would correct the misposting with the error-correction routine.

Required:

a. Discuss the relevance of the controls that were prescribed.

b. Describe the procedures to obtain an understanding of the internal control structure and tests of controls that might have detected the fraud.

Chapter 6
SYSTEMS DEVELOPMENT AND DOCUMENTATION CONTROLS

Learning Objectives

After completing this chapter, the reader should be able to:

1. Understand the importance of systems development and documentation controls.

2. Examine the relationship between sytems development and documentation controls and application controls.

3. Appreciate the impact of a weakness in systems development and documentation controls on the audit program.

4. Understand how adequate documentation of significant accounting applications assists in the performance of an audit.

New applications systems are sometimes developed haphazardly without adequate systems development procedures and documentation, and this may create problems for the auditor. In some cases, the systems designer may write unacceptable accounting policies into the system or generate a system that is susceptible to inaccurate or incomplete record keeping. In other cases, the ability to commit fraud may be designed into the system accidentally or deliberately during the development of the application. In extreme cases, such deficiencies could result in temporary, or even permanent, business interruption. An industrial products company, for example, developed a new consumer product. The success of the new product changed the business from one that served a few industrial users to one with many thousands of retail outlets. The company's accounts receivable system, however, proved inadequate to support this change. The resulting difficulty in collecting receivables led directly to the company's bankruptcy only three years after the successful introduction of the product.

The risk of such exposure can be reduced if systems development and documentation controls are in place. These controls encourage the proper design and documentation of EDP applications, and they increase the chances that an application will operate reliably when completed. Systems reliability is enhanced by the avoidance or disclosure of the following kinds of problems:

1. Implementation of systems that do not have adequate application controls
2. Development of systems that either do not meet management objectives or do not operate in accordance with original specifications
3. Implementation of systems that have not been adequately tested
4. Implementation of systems that are susceptible to unauthorized modification

The auditability of the system is enhanced by the use of (1) standard practices and procedures in systems development, which not only make it easier for the auditor to review the systems development process but simplify the subsequent review of the EDP application; and (2) adequate documentation, which provides an audit trail of the process of development and maintenance, as well as complete documentation of each application system.

While reading this chapter, you should be careful not to confuse the general controls of systems development and documentation with the application controls of an individual application system. The purpose of systems development and documentation controls is to create an environment that assures the auditor that effective application controls are included in all new systems, and that the integrity of these application controls will be preserved after the system has been implemented. The existence of effective application controls may be evidence of compliance with systems development and documentation controls. Our concern at this stage of the audit, however, is not with the application controls themselves, but with the process by which they are created and maintained.

This chapter focuses on systems development and documentation controls in the audit of EDP systems. It describes (1) the auditor's role in systems development; (2) systems development controls, including systems development methodology and related management practices such as system testing and conversion control; (3) systems documentation standards; (4) adequate systems documentation controls; and (5) software aids to documentation.

AUDITOR'S ROLE IN SYSTEMS DEVELOPMENT

From an audit standpoint, the development and documentation of a system is an important time in which to emphasize control. It makes sense to build application controls in *before* a system becomes operational, so that the system will be reliable from the very outset. It is certainly easier and less costly to do it right the first time than to go back and add the application controls later. Actually, it may not be feasible to add application controls later because of the major system revisions often required. Some large companies, therefore, include the internal auditors on each systems development task force. The participation of the internal auditors often represents their heaviest involvement in the audit of EDP systems. One Fortune 500 company located in the northwestern United States, for example, dedicates its entire EDP audit staff to involvement in systems development to the exclusion of tests of controls and substantive testing.

Although most companies do not actually involve their internal auditors in systems development, there is general agreement that such involvement would help ensure that systems work properly and include adequate application controls. There is less agreement, however, as to the role the independent auditors should play in the systems development process. Should the independent auditors merely review the systems development process and the application controls of the system that result, or should they actively involve themselves in the systems design process?

One school of thought—those who favor a role of limited review for the independent auditors—holds that involvement in the development and testing of systems that will ultimately be reviewed by the auditors will inevitably lead to a loss of independence. They also feel that involvement in the design and testing of systems *not yet* operational is too remote from the financial statements to be a cost-effective use of auditor time.

The other school of thought holds that the auditors are experts in internal control and should contribute their knowledge to the design and testing of a reliable system. They believe that there is no better time to make recommendations for improvements in internal control than during the development and testing stages and that the cost of making recommendations for improvements in application controls *after* a system is operational may be very high. Also, the Foreign Corrupt Practices Act of 1977 implies that every effort should be made to spot control deficiencies *before* a system is operational. In addition, this school holds that the independence issue is somewhat of a red herring. It can be solved by assigning different audit or consulting staff to the systems development and testing work, and by limiting their involvement to the design and testing of controls (and thereby avoiding association with the implementation and operation of the system).

The choice between the two views is not just a choice in the timing of the auditor's review. In the ex-post review the auditor's role is passive, even though their review may lead to control improvements. When the auditors are actively involved, they themselves become a general control contributing to the reliable operation of systems. This contribution will be particularly significant when a company does not have an internal audit department. Accordingly, we include auditor involvement in the design and testing of controls as a recommended systems development control. We also describe the ex-post reviews and tests of systems development controls that would be performed by the independent auditor subsequent to the completion of the design of a system.

SYSTEMS DEVELOPMENT CONTROLS

Systems development controls start with written standard procedures for the planning, development, and implementation of systems. These written standard procedures represent a generalized process of systems design that increases the ability to review and evaluate controls both on an ongoing basis throughout the systems development process and subsequent to the completion of the systems design. This is particularly true where management follows sound project management practices, requires standard programming conventions and procedures, encourages participation in the development process by interested parties, requires review and approval of the system, tests the system, provides final approval, maintains control over conversion, and institutes a postimplementation review. After completion of the system, management continues to emphasize its concern over system quality by maintaining control over program changes. All of these controls apply to in-house application development. With the exception of systems development methodology and project management, the same controls apply to the adaptation of third-party packaged software.

Systems Development Methodology

In the early days of computers, the development of application systems was generally considered a technical process centered on the programming function. Emphasis was placed on programming tasks such as flow-charting or coding rather than on the management of the systems development process. This emphasis changed in the middle 1960's when it was recognized that project control techniques used elsewhere in industry could successfully be applied to EDP systems development.

Systems development methodology requires that the development process be broken down into a series of small tasks. Each of these tasks represents a definable step toward the completion of the overall project. The completion of each step provides an opportunity to review progress toward the systems development objective and to ensure that the quality of the system is satisfactory and that controls are being included and designed as intended.

The steps involved in the systems development process encompass three broad areas: system planning, system development, and system implementation. The amount of work required in each of these areas will vary depending on the scope and nature of the system development project. The following list of tasks, however, is representative of the typical system development project.

TASK	DESCRIPTION
System planning	The purpose of system planning is to establish the objectives of the project; determine its scope; review its technical, operational, and economic feasiblity; and evaluate system control requirements.
System development:	
—User specifications	The user specifications are a statement of solutions to specific business problems of the user. Typically the systems analyst flowcharts the existing system in order to understand fully the existing solutions and then flowcharts a new system that incorporates changes and improvements in the way user problems are solved.
—Technical specifications	The user specifications are translated into technical solutions to such problems as how to structure the data files.
—Audit specifications	The planning of audit specifications involves the definition of both required ap-

plication controls and special system audit features. Application controls may include, for example, limit and reasonableness tests, sequence tests, and the use of control figures. A typical audit feature is the use of special audit files for collecting sample transactions.

—Implementation planning

Implementation planning serves to identify remaining tasks and to assign responsibilities to EDP and user personnel.

—Programming

Programming is a technical activity designed to prepare computer programs that follow the defined technical specifications and procedures. This step includes preparing program logic, coding, and testing programs.

—User procedures and training

At this stage, user personnel are trained to operate the system. Important outputs include user procedures manuals and job descriptions.

—System testing

System testing includes such procedures as parallel testing and string tests. Its purpose is to determine whether the system is operating in conformance with user, technical, and audit specifications. This task provides a major opportunity for the auditor to gain an appreciation of system compliance with the planned application controls and audit features.

Implementation:
—Conversion

The objective of the conversion process is to achieve a successful switch from the old equipment, files, and procedures to the new system. Conversion is an operationally complex task, and one that can pose dangers to the auditor from data loss or manipulation and from the failure to resolve discrepancies between the old system and the new system.

—Postimplementation review

After the new system is implemented and running, a postimplementation review serves to determine how well the system meets its operating and control objectives.

—Documentation

Documentation of the systems development process provides control over the prevention, detection, and correction of errors. Adequate documentation assists in the prevention of errors by establishing a disciplined work environment, and by improving communications among systems designers. The existence of an audit trail of the systems development process permits detection of errors by facilitating supervisory reviews by management, users, technical staff, and internal auditors. The audit trail also provides evidence of compliance with systems development controls. Documentation of the errors that are detected, and of their subsequent correction, serve to ensure that errors are corrected effectively. See Figure 6–1 for an example of systems development documentation.

The auditors should be familiar with the company's methodology and documentation requirements for systems development and should review the specific applications involved. In total, the systems develop-

SYSTEM TESTING LOG				
User *Fabrication Department*			Project No. *123*	
System *Payroll/Labor Distribution*		Tested by *M. Corning*		
User Representative *S.S. Boge*		Reviewed by *R. Pringle*		
			Date *6-5-X4*	

Date	Time	Program	Operator	Results
6-1	14.45	Job Card Processing	R. Poor	Overtime hours extended using straight time rate
6-3	15.28	Job Card Processing	R. Poor	Overtime hours extended correctly

Figure 6–1.   System Testing Log

ment process provides assurance that adequate controls are included in the development of new applications.

Understanding and Tests of Controls

If the auditors plan to assess control risk at a low level on the systems development process, their audit program should include one or more of the following:

1. Review the systems development standards manual to determine the existence of policy and guidelines. Evaluate the thoroughness and comprehensiveness of the standards, and be sure that the standards are updated on a regular basis.
2. Select applications from those under development and from those in operation. Review the related systems development documentation to determine whether the standards are being met.
3. Interview management, systems development, and user personnel regarding the adequacy of systems development standards.

Project Management

A systems development methodology will be of little use to the auditors if development projects are not adequately managed. The value of project management techniques in project planning and control cannot be over-estimated. *Project planning* is the process of ensuring that the project's objectives are translated into a work program. *Project control* is the process of ensuring execution of the tasks identified in the project plan.

A project plan should be designed to reflect the objectives of the systems study through guidelines, task definitions, and time schedules.

Guidelines.   Guidelines include the project's objectives, its scope, the procedures to be used in development, and the required end products.

Task Definitions.   The overall project is broken down into identifiable tasks, each of which has a measurable output that can be reviewed and evaluated. It is easier to control a project that is broken down in this manner.

Time Schedules.   Developing time schedules and estimates of time required for each task greatly facilitates subsequent management review and evaluation of work done. Figure 6–2 shows a time schedule developed in the form of a GANTT chart.

Project control ensures execution of the project by monitoring progress and by taking steps to ensure that each task is accomplished as intended. Accordingly, project control will include the assignment and supervision of work performed, the recording of work accomplished, a comparison of work performed with the project plan, the determination of discrepancies, and the initiation of corrective action where necessary.[1]

The auditors should review project management techniques to determine their adequacy. This can be accomplished by selecting one or more applications and reviewing the project planning and control documentation. This documentation should include task lists, checklists, personnel planning forms, GANTT charts or other activity schedules, and status reports.

Programming Conventions and Procedures

The quality of application systems and the ability to review system documentation are both likely to be enhanced if standard programming conventions and procedures are established and observed. Without such standards, it would be easier for programmers to misunderstand program documentation. Conventions and procedures that are generally found in systems and procedures manuals include the following:

CONVENTION	EXPLANATION
Flowcharting conventions	The use of standard forms, symbols, and conventions in flowcharts enhances the ability of users, auditors, and others to visualize program logic.
Decision table conventions	Conventions should be established for the preparation of decision tables, including abbreviations for condition and action entries to the table.
Coding conventions	The use of standard forms, abbreviations, symbols, and data and procedure names can help reduce clerical errors in coding and ease the task of audit review of program coding. An example of the use of standards is the designation of symbols to distinguish the look-alike number 0 from the letter O. Conventions may restrict the use of program terms that provide audit exposure. Restricting the use of the ALTER verb in COBOL, for example, may reduce the opportunity for unauthorized alteration of programs. Both the users and the auditors should be involved in designating forbidden coding features.

---

[1]It is of course necessary that the staff assigned to a project possess adequate skill. See Chapter 5 for a discussion of personnel practices that can influence this skill.

Division __Western__

System Project __Accounts Payable System__

DALLES INDUSTRIES INC.
ACTIVITY SCHEDULE

Development Activities	No.	Week Ending 2/3	2/10	2/17	2/24	3/3	3/10	3/17	3/24	3/31	4/7	4/14	4/21	4/28	5/5	5/12	5/19
Define requirements of new A/P system	001		├───────────────┤														
Design new A/P system	002					├───────┤											
Prepare program specifications	003						├───────────────┤									
Develop program logic	004								├───────┤								
Code A/P programs	005									├───────────────────────┤						
Perform systems test of A/P system	006															├───────┤	
Test audit specifications	007															├───────┤	
Plan conversion	008														├───────────────┤	
Write new manual procedures	009								├───────────────┤							
Plan and implement training program	010														├───────┤	
Conversion of A/P system	011																↑

Prepared by: __DAW__   Approved by: __PBB1__

Standard glossary and standard abbreviations

Some but not all terms are standard in the data processing industry. Those that are not, along with terms and abbreviations unique to a particular installation, should be carefully defined and included in a glossary for use by programmers. The prohibition of nonstandard terms and abbreviations makes it easier to review systems documentation such as flowcharts.

Standard program routines

Although each program has a different objective, it may incorporate routines that are common to many programs. These common routines may include the use of standard formats for printing, or standard algorithms for calculating a storage address on a magnetic disk. The use of standard routines reduces programming effort and simplifies the testing and audit of systems.

Standard job-control routines

Every program must be written so that it can be run on the computer for which it is intended. This means that it must be compatible with the operating system that runs the computer. This compatibility is achieved via the use of program routines that provide the interface between the application program and the operating system. These routines are called job-control programs and are usually written in a job-control language. The use of standard systems routines prepared in a standard job-control language makes it easier for the auditor to review the operation of the application programs.

Debugging

Debugging of program coding consists of the elimination of errors from that coding. Standard techniques for debugging can increase the chance that errors will be found, provide a trail of program changes, and reduce the opportunity for unauthorized program changes. Standard debugging procedures include desk checking and running the program with test data.

Auditing conventions

The programming standards manual should include a list of required controls and audit features. Examples of required controls are document totals for record counts, hash totals for identification numbers, and financial totals for dollar postings. Examples of required audit features are the tagging of transactions to trace their process through the system, and snapshots of transactions at specific points during processing. (Tagging and snapshots are covered in Chapter 11.)

Understanding and Tests of Controls

If the auditors plan to assess control risk at a low level on programming conventions and procedures as an internal control, procedures to obtain an understanding of the internal control structure and tests of controls should include the following:

1. Review the programming standards section of the systems and procedures manual to determine whether standards are reasonably comprehensive.
2. Examine the selected flowcharts, decision tables, and coding sheets to verify that standard programming conventions and procedures are being followed.

User, Accounting, and Audit Participation

Developing a new system with an adequate internal control structure, built-in audit features, and a complete audit trail will be much easier if user personnel, accounting department staff, and internal and external auditors participate in the systems development process. From the external auditor's standpoint, such participation may generate the following benefits:

- Communication between the user and EDP personnel may be improved. Because of the technical nature of systems, it is easy for communication problems to arise. The user may be able to define his or her needs, for example, but may have difficulty expressing them in terms that EDP personnel can understand. If participation by the user in the systems development process can reduce these communication difficulties, then the auditors should have greater assurance that the system will work as the user intended.
- Participation by the user represents a form of commitment and approval. The need to make this commitment will encourage user personnel to involve themselves more deeply in the systems development process. This involvement generates a greater recognition by the user personnel of their responsibility for the output of the system, and of their dependence on the quality of that output. This greater recognition should in turn ensure the inclusion of user controls in the design of the system.
- Participation by the internal and independent auditors provides an opportunity for these experts on internal control to make suggestions to the EDP systems staff regarding improvements in control. It is more efficient to incorporate these improvements into the system during the development phase, and the result should be a more reliable system.
- Participation by the internal and independent auditors provides evidence relating to compliance with systems development controls, and inclusion of required internal controls and audit features. There is no better way of

gaining knowledge of the systems development controls applied to each application than to be involved in the development process. Participation can also indicate that application controls such as control totals, and audit features such as transaction tagging, are provided for at this stage. The inclusion of audit features will improve the audit trail and make the subsequent application of computer audit techniques easier.

• The independent auditor can gain the required understanding of each significant EDP application by participating in the systems development process.

Understanding and Tests of Controls

If the auditors plan to assess control risk at a low level on participation by the user, accounting, and audit personnel, then procedures to obtain an understanding of the internal control structure and tests of controls should include one or more of the following:

1. Interview representatives of the user and accounting departments for evidence of the level of their participation in the systems development process.
2. Review appropriate documents and related approvals for evidence that the user and accounting departments have an adequate understanding of system inputs, processing procedures, controls, and system outputs.
3. Review the auditors' working papers to determine the extent of their involvement in the systems development process.

Technical, Management, User, and Auditor Review and Approval

Ongoing review of work accomplished during the systems development process, and approval at the end of each phase of the systems development process, represent strong controls over the content of the system programs and outputs. Review and approval provide an opportunity to ensure that the system has adequate controls. In addition, review and approval facilitate the monitoring and maintenance of an acceptable level of quality of output from each phase of the systems development process. Adequate review and approval is best accomplished at two levels: the technical level, which involves systems and programming supervisors; and the output level, which involves management, users, and auditors.

The *technical level* requires that systems supervisors review the work of the systems staff on an ongoing basis. In addition, the supervisors should review and approve each phase of the output before submitting it to management, users, and auditors for approval. The purpose of these reviews and approvals is to ensure that the project meets all user, technical, and audit specifications. Approval should be evidenced by the supervisor's initials and the date on each document.

The *output level* requires that management, users, and auditors review and approve the end products of systems planning and development, not including programming. The purpose is to ensure that the system meets user and audit specifications. The review takes place at the end of each phase, with approval given in time to affect work on subsequent phases. Sometimes work is delayed where approval is withheld pending revisions. This delay is worthwhile if the quality of the system is improved.

Understanding and Tests of Controls

If the auditors plan to assess control risk at a low level on technical, management, user, and auditor review and approval, they will perform procedures to obtain an understanding of the internal control structure and test controls using one or more of the following:

1. Review the section of the systems development standards manual that covers review and approval requirements.
2. Interview technical staff, management, and users to determine the process of review and approval.
3. For selected applications developed during the accounting period, review technical and output documentation for written evidence of approval by technical supervisors, management, and users.

System Testing

System testing is an important control because it is the last opportunity before implementation of the system to discover and correct problems so that controls will work as intended. Thus the purpose of system testing is

- To ensure that the system will operate in conformance with its design specifications
- To determine whether the system's operation meets user requirements
- To test all application controls so that they will work as intended
- To show that the introduction of correct input will result in correct output
- To verify that incorrect input, processing, or output will be detected

The scope of a system test encompasses all aspects of a system and should include both the manual phase and the computerized phase. Since it is a comprehensive evaluation, the test will cover the programs, computer operations, user activities, and control group functions.

System testing is a joint effort of the users, internal and independent auditors, and systems personnel. The systems personnel will generally be responsible for performing tests, including the writing of test programs. User and auditor involvement, however, provides additional opportunity for these interested parties to review the controls' effectiveness.

Systems testing can take place on five different levels: program tests, string tests, system tests, pilot tests, and parallel tests.

Program tests are designed to test the processing logic of the programs, that is, to gain an understanding of how the program works, and to test the validity of its logic. Gaining this understanding is difficult because of the range of logic that exists in most programs, and because of the time and effort required. As a result, program tests are usually applied on a modular or program-by-program basis to facilitate the review process. It is easier to prepare a flowchart or decision logic table for an individual program or module than for several interrelated programs. In addition, the time and effort required to unravel the program logic can be reduced by the use of software aids. These software aids include programs that provide logic analysis and generate flowcharts automatically.

String tests are also tests applied to programs, but instead of being applied to a single program, they are applied to a string of logically related programs. The purpose of string tests is to ensure that data are correctly transferred from one program to another in the string. For example, a payroll program for computing executive salaries should use valid output from an executive bonus program.

Systems tests are those that apply to all programs within an application. In a system test of a payroll system, for example, all payroll programs would be tested at the same time. The purpose is to ensure that the programs all work correctly when they interface with each other. This is accomplished by introducing simulated valid and invalid transactions into the system and observing the results. An example of a system test of an invalid transaction would be the introduction of time data for a nonexistent employee into the payroll system. If the system is working correctly, the incorrect input will be rejected.

Pilot tests involve the processing of an actual period's transactions on an after-the-fact basis. The results of the processing are compared with the results of the existing system. The purpose is to reconcile the results of the new and old systems, and to detect and correct any differences. This reconciliation will be useful if the period chosen is representative of normal processing.

Parallel tests are a typical method of ensuring that the system is processing input correctly. This is where the old and new systems are run in parallel, with subsequent comparison of the output from both systems. If both systems are working correctly, the results will be the same. This is a valuable method of detecting system errors and is essential for complex systems. It is an expensive method, however, requiring additional personnel and equipment resources.

Understanding and Tests of Controls

If the auditors plan to assess risk at a low level on the control of system testing, they will need to review new systems that were developed and implemented during the accounting period, as well as the written standards for system testing. Procedures to obtain an understanding of the internal control structure and tests of controls of the standards and of one or more of the new systems should include the following:

1. Review standards for system testing for comprehensiveness.
2. Interview internal audit and user staff to determine the extent of their involvement in testing.
3. Review test data and the resulting output for selected new systems to determine whether testing is reasonably comprehensive.
4. Review the results of program and string tests, including flowcharts and logic analyses, to ensure that such tests are thorough and comprehensive.
5. Review the results of system tests of valid and invalid transactions to ensure that the system as a whole is being tested adequately.
6. Review the procedures for reconciling output produced during pilot and parallel testing.
7. Examine programs used to compare output files in pilot and parallel tests.
8. Examine reconciliations for selected tests to determine whether discrepancies were corrected by systems personnel.

Final Approval

Final approval from management, users, and EDP personnel is necessary before the system is implemented and put in operation. This control provides an opportunity to examine the final test results, make a final judgment on the quality of application controls, consider changes from the original systems design specifications, ensure that all errors are corrected, and approve planned procedures for system implementation and operation.

Understanding and Tests of Controls

If the auditors plan to assess risk at a low level on final approval as a general control, they should perform either or both of the following:

1. Review evidence of the approval of new applications by management, users, and EDP personnel. Evidence may include signatures on system documentation, minutes of meetings, letters or reports demonstrating approval.
2. Interview management, user, and EDP personnel involved in the final approval process, inquiring about their understanding of the system and their satisfaction with its specifications.

Conversion Control

Control over the conversion process is necessary because numerous errors can result when master and transaction files are converted to the new system. These errors can result when field data within a record are inadvertently changed or lost, or when entire records are omitted.

Control procedures that can detect or prevent these errors include the following:

- File conversion approval should be given before the conversion process begins. This approval is used to ensure that the files being converted are fully controlled.
- The original and new files can be reconciled by record counts, hash totals, and amount totals. (See Chapter 9 for a discussion of these controls.)
- Selected portions of records from the original files can be compared with the new files to ensure that there are no discrepancies.
- Confirmation requests can be sent to third parties, such as customers and suppliers, asking them to confirm the data on the files as they relate to them.
- Discrepancy reports can be used to detect inconsistencies and correct them. Figure 6–3 illustrates the use of a discrepancy report during conversion of an accounts payable disbursements system.
- Operational approval should be obtained from the users after they have used the system a few times. Approval indicates their satisfaction with the way the system is operating.

Understanding and Tests of Controls

If the auditors plan to assess risk at a low level on conversion control as a general control, they should perform the following:

1. Review plans for controlling the conversion from one system to another to determine whether they are sufficient to ensure that data on the new files are accurate and complete.
2. Examine documentation for evidence of file conversion approval.
3. Evaluate the procedures used to reconcile the original and new files.
4. Review or observe the use of record comparisons and confirmation requests.
5. Examine discrepancy reports for evidence of appropriate correction of errors.
6. Test the conversion by tracing record data from the original files to the new files, and also from the new files to the original files.

Postimplementation Review

The postimplementation review is conducted by users, EDP personnel, and internal audit personnel several months after implementation of the system. The purpose of the review is to determine whether the system is

---

DISCREPANCY REPORT

User _A/P_

Number _82-15_

System _A/P Disbursements_

Reviewed by _PBBT_

User Representative _RS_

Date _8-31-X4_

Problem Description: _Number of records loaded on file did not agree with document count from A/P._

_RS_ — User Representative

_8-25-X4_ — Date

Problem Diagnosis: _Old file was loaded which did not include most recent changes._

_DH_ — EDP Representative

_8-26-X4_ — Date

Problem Solution: _Run maintenance program to update file with recent changes; reload updated file._

_DH_ — EDP Representative

_8-28-X4_ — Date

Approval of Problem Disposition:

PBBT — User Representative

_8-31-X4_ — Date

Figure 6-3. Example of Use of Discrepancy Report during Conversion

operating as intended, and to evaluate the effectiveness of the entire process of developing the system.

The significance of the postimplementation review to the auditors is that it provides feedback to users and EDP personnel on the development and operation of the system. This feedback indicates that controls are either working as intended or need improvement. It also provides an opportunity to make adjustments to the systems development standards to the benefit of systems that may be developed in the future. The postimplementation review should not be relied on, however, to reveal major problems. Such problems should have been discovered and corrected by this time.

Understanding and Tests of Controls

If the auditors plan to assess risk at a low level on the general control of postimplementation review, the procedures to obtain an understanding of the internal control structure and tests of controls should include the following:

1. Review internal audit working papers for conclusions on the operation of system controls, and on the effectiveness of the systems development process.
2. Interview systems development staff, users, and management to determine their views on the effectiveness of controls in the system.
3. Review the final report of the postimplementation review committee.

Program Change Controls

Strong systems development controls provide assurance that systems are being developed according to management's accounting, operating, and control policies. This assurance is of little value, however, if subsequent unauthorized modifications to the programs result in the change or elimination of these policies. Without adequate control over program modifications, the integrity of a system could be destroyed.

If the auditor ascertains that program change controls are adequate and working, he or she can be confident that the program being used is the same as the one initially developed or is the same but with known modifications. In addition, the auditor can test versions of the program prior to and subsequent to the changes to ascertain that any changes are consistent with approved program change documentation. This is crucial if changes have been made to application controls during the period of reliance.

Program changes are a relatively frequent occurrence in most organizations. They result from a desire to improve systems, the need to adjust systems to changing business conditions, and the need to incorporate new operating, accounting, and control policies into the system. Such changes are often referred to as *program maintenance*. Examples of such changes include revisions of withholding tables in a payroll system to meet new federal or state tax laws, or a revision in estimates of asset lives for depreciation purposes in a fixed-asset system. Program changes that represent major systems revisions are called *enhancements* and are properly excluded from this definition. They are instead tested as full systems development projects.

The objectives of program change controls are to ensure that all changes to programs are properly approved and authorized, and to ensure that all authorized changes are completed, tested, and properly implemented. These objectives require control over the planning, development, and implementation of program changes. These program change activities are similar to those of new systems development except that the process is less complex because of the narrower scope.

Planning Program Changes.   Control over planning system changes requires proper approval authorization and documentation of program change requests:

- Program change requests should be approved by the user, by internal audit, and by data processing management. The involvement of the user and internal audit in the approval process provides a check on the usefulness and implications of the change. The approval should cover such matters as the impact of the change on system controls, on system documentation, on user and operator training procedures, and on the system's operational efficiency.
- All program change requests should be authorized after proper approval. Authorization should be given by the person or level to whom management has delegated this responsibility. This level is usually data processing management. Authorization of program changes should never be given by operating personnel because this would break the segregation of systems and operating duties. Operating personnel should be permitted to do no more than suggest possible program changes.
- The program change request should be fully documented. The documentation should include a full description of the purpose of the change and provide evidence of initiation, approval, authorization, and work performed. Figure 6–4 shows a program change form that provides this information.

Developing Program Changes.   Controls over the development of program changes should include the following:

- Development only of properly approved and authorized change requests.
- Program changes should be completed following established systems, programming, and documentation standards.
- Program changes should be restricted to systems personnel. Operating personnel should not make changes to programs—even temporary changes to facilitate the running of a program.
- The design specifications of program changes should be reviewed and approved by the user and internal audit to ensure conformity with the purpose of the original change request.
- Changes should be made to the test program and not the production program. The test program is a copy of the one authorized as the production program in the processing of data. Using the test program limits opportunities to make unauthorized changes to the production program.
- All program changes should be tested thoroughly before implementation. All the testing techniques discussed earlier are applicable here. As a minimum, however, test data should be prepared with the modified test program and compared with and reconciled to the test data prepared with the original production program.

```
                            PROGRAM CHANGE FORM

 Program Name                      Program Number

 Change initiated by  _____  Date _____
 Purpose of change:



 Approval by:
 -Data processing     _____  Date _____
 -Internal audit      _____  Date _____
 -User                _____  Date _____

 Change authorized by _____  Date _____

 Change made by       _____  Date _____
 Explanation of change:



 Approval of
   change by
 -Internal audit      _____  Date _____
 -User                _____  Date _____

 Change tested by     _____  Date _____
 Test results
   reviewed by        _____  Date _____

 Change posted to:
 -Systems documentation _____ Date _____
 -Program documentation _____ Date _____
 -Operations documentation _____ Date _____
 -User documentation    _____ Date _____

 Conversion by: _____   Date _____

 Final approval by:
 -Data processing     _____  Date _____
 -Internal audit      _____  Date _____
 -User                _____  Date _____
```

Figure 6–4.   Program Change Form

- Upon completion of testing, the program changes and test results should be reviewed and approved. Preferably this review and approval should be by a systems supervisor who is not involved in the testing or revision of the program.
- User and operating personnel should be retrained, if necessary, to handle new procedures.

Implementing Program Changes.   Controls over the implementation of program changes should include the following:

- All documentation that is affected by the change should be updated. This may include systems, program, operations, and user documentation.

- Control should be established over the conversion to the new program. This is accomplished by changing the new program to production status, copying the old program to a backup file, and deleting it from the library of production programs.
- Conversion should not be permitted before approval of the test results and completion of the changes to documentation.
- Final approval should be given by data processing management, the user, and internal audit.

Understanding and Tests of Controls

If the auditors plan to assess risk at a low level on systems change controls, they should use some of the following:

1. Interview operations and systems personnel to determine what procedures and policies govern program changes.
2. Review documentation in support of selected program changes to determine whether the procedures and policies are being followed.
3. Review documentation in support of program changes to determine whether the changes have been properly approved.
4. Examine results of tests performed on modified programs to verify that modifications were made correctly.
5. Where program changes are deemed to have significant control implications, compare the original program source coding with the modified program source coding. Any difference should be reconciled to the authorized changes. Such comparisons are valuable, though expensive, audit tests. In some cases, it may be possible to reduce the cost by use of audit software packages.
6. On a test basis, select current application programs for which there is no documentation of changes during the preceding year, and compare the code of current programs with the code of the same programs of a year ago to ensure that there have been no changes. This can be accomplished quite efficiently by use of software that computes a hash total of the binary digits of each program at the two dates. The hash total for each version of the program will be the same if there have been no changes.

SYSTEMS DOCUMENTATION STANDARDS

The AICPA's *Auditing and EDP* defines *documentation* as follows:

> Documentation consists of records, reports, work papers, and other materials that describe the system and procedures for performing a data processing task. It is a means of communicating the essential elements of the data processing system, including the logic followed by the computer programs.[2]

---

[2]Gordon B. Davis, Donald L. Adams, and Carol A. Schaller, *Auditing and EDP,* Second Edition (New York: American Institute of Certified Public Accountants, 1983), p. 59.

This documentation will typically include systems and program descriptions, flowcharts, decision logic tables, program listings, record layouts, operating instructions, control procedures, examples of input documents, and sample output reports.

As a general EDP control, documentation contributes to an environment that is conducive to control. It accomplishes this by serving the following purposes:

1. It is an integral part of the systems design and documentation process. (This purpose was discussed in detail earlier in the chapter.)
2. It provides a source of information for systems analysts and programmers who are responsible for maintaining and changing existing systems and programs.
3. It provides explanatory information necessary for supervisory reviews of proposed systems and programs.
4. It is a basis for training new personnel by providing background on existing programs.
5. It provides data necessary for responding to inquiries regarding the operation of computer programs.
6. It is a basis for communicating common information to systems analysts, programmers, and computer operators.
7. It provides computer operators with current operating instructions.
8. It helps preserve continuity when experienced personnel leave the data processing organization.
9. It is a source of information about accounting controls.

Historically, documentation standards have frequently been neglected. Such neglect may be indicative of a poorly controlled or poorly managed EDP system. In the absence of documentation standards, documentation is likely to be missing or otherwise unreliable. In addition, management, auditor, and user review and approval of systems will be difficult to perform. Also, system change control will probably be lax, audit trails inadequate, and compliance with systems and operations standards difficult to monitor.

Auditors generally depend on adequate documentation to obtain their understanding of application controls, obtain an understanding of significant EDP applications, and perform computer-assisted tests of the computer files. Adequate documentation reduces the audit time and cost required in each of these areas. During the application understanding phase, the auditors will review flowcharts, coding, and other items to gain a general comprehension of the system, identify the audit trail, determine the current status of each program and its controls, and determine the role of operations and their use in processing. In addition, audit tests of computer files using computer-assisted audit techniques are facilitated by adequate documentation—the availability of documented record formats, file layouts, and other file information makes it easier for the auditor to define the testing procedures.

Although documentation standards and terminology tend to differ from one organization to another, it is possible to specify what constitutes adequate documentation from a control standpoint. The following classifications were provided as a guide to adequate documentation by the AICPA's Computer Services Committee: (1) problem definition documentation, (2) systems documentation, (3) program documentation, (4) operations documentation, and (5) user documentation.[3]

This section discusses the purpose and content of each of the above five classifications of documentation. Although each classification has a separate purpose, there is some content overlap. There is enough different and sensitive material in each area, however, to recommend that each classification of documentation be available only to authorized personnel. The purpose of operations documentation, for example, is to guide computer operators in the running of programs. Computer operators should not, however, have access to systems, program, or user documentation. Access to systems and program documentation might enable the operator to make unauthorized program modifications. Access to user documentation might permit circumvention of user controls.

Problem Definition Documentation

Problem definition documentation is a permanent summary of the problem solved by the system. It represents the basic source of information regarding the purpose of the system. The availability of problem definition documentation permits the auditors to gain a general understanding of the system quickly and easily without the necessity of becoming involved in the details of the programs.

In organizations that utilize systems design standards, the original source of problem definition information may be a System Planning Study Report. This report covers all aspects of systems planning. The following parts should be included in the problem definition documentation:

1. A description of the reasons for implementing the system, including the background, objectives, and scope of the project
2. System specifications describing the operations performed by the system
3. Evidence of approval of both the original system and any subsequent changes in system specifications
4. Staffing charts or staffing requirements forms showing the assignment of systems development responsibilities

---

[3]AICPA, *The Auditor's Study and Evaluation of Internal Control in EDP Systems* (New York: 1977), pp. 64–65.

Systems Documentation

Systems documentation is a record of the way information flows through the system from input, onto a file medium, and then to output. This summary is useful to the auditors because it permits the tracing of the *theoretical* flow of accounting data from the original entry to the system output. From this tracing, the auditors can evaluate the adequacy of the audit trail provided by the system. The auditors can also identify data that can be generated by the system but are not currently being printed.

Typical systems documentation would include the following:

1. System flowcharts show the flow of data through the system. These flowcharts show the source and nature of system inputs and outputs; the various manual, mechanical, and computer operations that are performed on the input; and the nature and disposition of the resulting outputs.
2. Input descriptions identify the type of source documents used. This may, for example, be a description of time cards as a source of job and time data in a payroll/labor distribution system.
3. Output descriptions show each type of output generated by the system, such as payroll checks, management reports, journals, and updated files.
4. File descriptions will list individual files and describe the scope and function of each file. An earnings record master file in a payroll system, for example, may be described as a set of earnings records providing cumulative W-2 data for all fiscal-year employees.
5. Control descriptions summarize the main control features that are designed into the system, including control group functions, user functions, and application program control points.
6. Summaries of any changes that have been made in system flowcharts, input, output, file, and control descriptions, along with copies of authorization of these changes and their effective dates.

Program Documentation

Whereas the system documentation describes the working of the entire system, the program documentation focuses on detailed information regarding each program in the system. This detailed information is primarily used to maintain effective control over program changes by systems and programming personnel and to define the current status of each program.

Program documentation generally includes the following:

1. Brief narrative descriptions provide summaries of the functions of the programs.
2. Program flowcharts, decision tables, or detailed logic narrative show how the program should operate. Program switch settings that change the path of the program should be identified, with the conditions that result from

each switch setting fully described. For example, a switch setting might determine whether all account balances should be printed out, or just those with debit balances.

3. A copy of the most recent source coding may be used by the auditors in conjunction with flowcharts or decision tables to follow the detailed logic of the programs.

4. Listings of parameters used in the program, such as a tax withholding table, are necessary for a complete understanding of the program operation.

5. A list of application controls, such as control totals, identifies the controls in each program.

6. Detailed descriptions of file formats and record layouts (input, master, and output records) identify the format and location of data items on file media such as magnetic tapes and disks. Typical information includes the names of all fields within a record, field locations, and field sizes. Additional information may be provided relating to the particular file medium used. Where magnetic tape or disk is used, for example, information is provided on the size of records, the use of blocking, and internal labels.

7. A description of code values used in processing provides a set of valid codes for each program. These codes will include the codes used to identify transactions being processed, and also the codes in the files that indicate the type of general ledger account, debit or credit balance, and so forth. An example of a magnetic tape record layout with associated transaction codes in shown in Figure 6–5.

8. A record of all program changes, including test results, the authorization for the changes, and their effective date ensures that program documentation is up to date. An example of a program change form is shown in Figure 6–4.

9. The operating instructions required by the computer operators to run the program are generally a part of program documentation, as well as a separate manual provided to computer operators. The contents of this manual are described in the following section.

Operations Documentation

Operations documentation is the information provided to enable the computer operator to run the computer program. In some EDP departments, the operations documentation is known as the *systems and procedures manual,* or simply the *operations manual.* The auditor can review operations documentation to see how the program is run, and to determine whether the documentation provided the operator is limited to that required to run the program. The operator should not have access to all the systems documentation, since this might provide the operator with the opportunity to modify the program. Information that is limited to the kind necessary for running the program includes the following:

1. A brief narrative that indicates the purpose of the program. (A description of the processing logic of the program should *not* be included.)

Command Code	Customer Number, Right Justified	Customer Name	Customer Address	Credit Limit in dollars, Right Justified
1	2 – 18	19 – 38	39 – 68	69 – 75

Command Codes

A — add a customer
M — modify customer record
D — delete customer record
P — print contents of master file

Figure 6–5.   Input Command for Fixed-Length Magnetic Tape Record for Accounts Receivable File Maintenance Program

2. An input/output chart that lists all the input and output files required for processing the program, and the sequence in which they are to be used.
3. A description on input/output forms and formats, including an output distribution list, that is provided for the operator's guidance.
4. A list of setup instructions and operating system requirements. Inclusion of job command language statements necessary to execute the program permits the operator to determine whether the job has been set up properly for operation.
5. A list of all program error messages and halts. The operator is given a description of the action to be taken in response to each error message and halt condition.
6. Detailed instructions regarding recovery and restart procedures to be used in the event of hardware or software malfunctions.
7. To assist in work scheduling, a list of estimated normal and maximum run times.
8. A list of instructions to the operator in the event of an emergency.

User Documentation

User departments should be provided with a set of user instructions. These instructions will include descriptions of required input, output listings, and procedures for handling errors and controls. They are required by the user for retraining personnel when new systems are added or old systems are changed, and for training new or replacement personnel. User documentation is valuable to the auditor in understanding the user's role in the processing of information, and in evaluating the degree of control provided by the user. Typical user documentation includes the following:

1. A nontechnical description of the system, including the benefits the user may derive from it.
2. A description of the types of source documents required, such as purchase orders, with instructions for filling out the source documents as required.

3. A description of the form and purpose of each output received by the users.
4. Detailed instructions for the use of control procedures, with identification of responsibility for performance of these control procedures. Responsibility is defined by the position responsible, rather than by the individual person.
5. Procedures for correcting errors in input data or in processing that are detected by the user.
6. Instructions for handling additions, deletions, or corrections to files.
7. Procedures for cutoff of data submitted to the data processing department, including dates and times for final submission of data.
8. A checklist for review of reports for completeness and accuracy.

ADEQUATE SYSTEMS DOCUMENTATION CONTROLS

The question arises, What constitutes adequate documentation for a specific EDP application? It depends on the complexity of the EDP environment. The five classifications of documentation are adequate in a simple EDP environment. As the complexity of applications increases, however, the five-part classification gives way to a seven-part classification. The systems and program documentation of the simple system are split into four levels of documentation, as shown in Figure 6–6.

The *systems documentation* of the simple system is divided into two parts in the complex system: systems and job documentation. The systems documentation provides an overall view of the entire system. The job documentation provides a general statement of purpose and function for each "job" within the overall system. A *job* is a set of interconnected programs that perform one or more functions within the overall

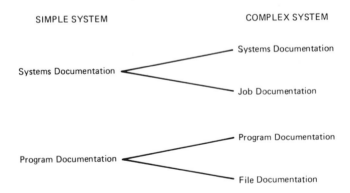

Figure 6–6. Systems and Program Documentation in Simple and Complex Systems

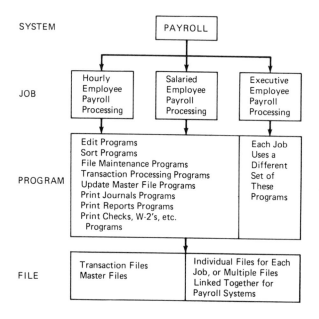

Figure 6–7. Example of Documentation Levels in Payroll System

system. Figure 6–7 illustrates the relationship between the system, the jobs, and the programs in a complex payroll system.

Program documentation in a simple system includes detailed descriptions of the files. This is appropriate where individual programs utilize their own files. In complex systems, however, there is a trend toward the use of a data base that serves several programs or jobs. In such cases, it makes more sense to prepare file documentation at the data-base level rather than the program level. Consequently, the program documentation of the simple system is split between program documentation and file documentation in the complex system. Figure 6–7 shows the relationship between files and programs and jobs in a payroll system.

SOFTWARE AIDS TO DOCUMENTATION

Review of EDP application documentation can be a time-consuming and difficult task, particularly in organizations that have inadequate documentation or documentation that is so technical or nonstandard that it is unintelligible to the auditor. A partial cure for such inadequate or unintelligible documentation may consist of using software aids.

Software aids are program packages that provide automatic preparation of standard documentation. Although these packages are designed to ease the burden of client preparation of system documentation, the auditor's awareness of the capabilities of these packages may permit him or

Table 6–1. Software Aids to Documentation

Software Aid	Purpose	Advantages
1. Flowchart packages	—Produce flowcharts from program source code	—Ensure standard flow-charts —Reflects current program status —Low-cost preparation
2. Cross-reference listings	—Provide an alphabetic list of names used in the program cross-referenced to the lines of code where they appear	—Can be used to review program logic
3. File description generators	—Prepare a description of file structure in graphic or tabular form	—Help understanding of file structure
4. Program code formatting or shorthand packages	—Convert nonstandard or shorthand source code to standard code	—Enhance readability of program source code
5. Librarian package	—Is a system for maintaining application programs —Maintains a program change log —May enforce source code standards	—Reduces burden of reviewing program change documentation —Increases control over program changes —Ensures standard program source coding

her to persuade the client to provide a more satisfactory set of system documentation.

There are five broad classifications of software aids to documentation: flowchart packages, cross-reference listings, file description generators, formatting or shorthand systems, and librarian packages. Table 6–1 summarizes the purpose and major advantages of each type.

SUMMARY

When the general controls of systems development and systems documentation are strong, the auditability of the system is enhanced, and there is greater assurance that application controls exist and are working as intended.

Systems development controls relate to the process of developing and maintaining systems. Systems development methodology is a generalized approach to systems development and maintenance. When systems development methodology is implemented along with such systems development controls as project management, system testing, conversion control, and program change control, the chances of a new application system being designed with adequate controls are greatly enhanced.

Documentation serves as a source of information to the auditors on the workings of data processing applications. Good documentation is also important to the design and implementation of a well-controlled system. Adequate application documentation in a simple system will include problem definition, systems, program, operations, and user documentation. In complex systems, there will be separate classifications for job and file documentation.

APPENDIX

Lava Butte, Inc.: Systems Development and Documentation Controls Questionnaire

1. Are the general controls over system development, program development, and change activities sufficient to ensure that applications are properly developed, implemented, and maintained?

___✓___ Yes _____ No

In assessing systems development controls, the auditor should consider the following:	Contributes to Possible Reduction in Control Risk		Comments
	Yes	No	
— Standard procedures for the development of systems	✓		*Reviewed systems procedures manual*
— Project management of application development	✓		*Interviewed systems development supervisors*
— Standard programming conventions and procedures including a. Flowcharting conventions	✓		*(See next page)*

In assessing systems development controls, the auditor should consider the following:	Contributes to Possible Reduction in Control Risk		Comments
	Yes	No	
b. Decision table conventions	✓		
c. Coding conventions	✓		
d. Standard glossary and abbreviations	✓		Reviewed Programming Standards Manual
e. Standard program routines	✓		
f. Standard job-control routines	✓		
g. Debugging	✓		
h. Auditing conventions		✓	no control or audit feature standards
— Users, accounting, and audit participation in systems development	✓		no internal audit department, but firm's consulting staff does participate
— Review and approval of systems development by technical staff		✓	Programs are not complex
— Review and approval of systems development by management users		✓	no review during systems development process
— Testing of new accounting applications before implementation include a. Involvement of users, auditors, and systems personnel	✓		Participation by our firm's consulting staff
b. Program tests	✓		
c. String tests	✓		
d. System tests	✓		
e. Pilot test	✓		
f. Parallel processing		✓	Rely on results of pilot tests
— Final approval by management, user, and EDP before implementation	✓		Reviewed approval signatures for several accounting applications

In assessing systems development controls, the auditor should consider the following:	Contributes to Possible Reduction in Control Risk		Comments
	Yes	No	
— Control over conversion to new accounting applications	✓		*Client uses file Comparisons and confirmation requests*
— Review of system by users, EDP, and internal audit subsequent to conversion		✓	*no formal post implementation review*
— Procedures for control over program changes: a. Approval, authorization, and documentation of program change requests	✓		
b. Program changes follow systems, programming, and documentation standards	✓		
c. Program changes restricted to systems personnel		✓	*Data processing manager assists systems personnel*
d. Review and approval by user and internal audit	✓		*no internal audit department*
e. Changes made to test copy of program		✓	*Changes made to production program*
f. Program change testing	✓		
g. Retraining of personnel	✓		
h. Documentation updated	✓		
i. Control over conversion		✓	*Control not possible because changes made to production program.*
j. Final approval	✓		

2. Are the general controls over all levels of documentation for EDP systems sufficient to ensure (for audit purposes) that documentation is adequate, complete, and up to date?

_____✓_____ Yes _____ No

In assessing documentation controls, the auditor should consider the following:	Contributes to Possible Reduction in Control Risk		Comments
	Yes	No	
— Formal documentation standards	✓		*Reviewed selected binders*
— Formal management review and acceptance of documentation		✓	*no formal review and acceptance*
— Documentation prepared as evidence of compliance with systems development standards	✓		*Reviewed systems documentation of selected applications*
— Separate levels of documentation for problem definition, systems programming, operations, and users	✓		*Documentation directed to appropriate levels of users*
— Separate levels of documentation for jobs and files		✓	*Programs not complex*
— Access to each level of documentation restricted to authorized individuals		✓	*Documentation stored in unlocked storage room*

REVIEW QUESTIONS

6-1. What are the consequences of treating the systems development process as a technical process rather than emphasizing good management?

6-2. Systems development methodology varies from one organization to another. What is the main characteristic of this methodology?

6-3. What is the purpose of the auditor's obtaining an understanding of systems development methodology?

6-4. What is the purpose of a project plan and what does it include?

6-5. What benefits can be derived from user, accounting, and audit participation in systems development? Should the independent auditors participate in the systems development process?

6-6. Differentiate between the technical level and the output level of review and approval.

6-7. Why are programming conventions important? What coding conventions would you hope to find in the understanding phase of assessing control risk?

6-8. What are the likely advantages of auditing a significant accounting application that has been subject to system testing?

6-9. How is the responsibility for system testing divided? Why is it divided this way?

6-10. What is the purpose of each of the five types of system tests?

6-11. Why should final approval of systems be necessary if all other controls are evident? How does the auditor determine whether final approval has been given?

6-12. What is the danger of uncontrolled conversion? How can this danger be avoided?

6-13. What assurance does an adequate postimplementation review provide the auditors?

6-14. Would a lack of system change control generally be viewed as an isolated weakness or is it likely to affect other general and application controls?

6-15. What constitutes adequate program change control?

6-16. What impact might inadequate program change controls have on the audit?

6-17. What impact does poor documentation have on systems development controls?

6-18. What difficulties might an auditor have in evaluating the adequacy of application documentation?

6-19. How can the auditors make use of systems documentation?

6-20. Is the operations documentation a carbon copy of program documentation? Justify your answer.

6-21. Why should documentation be kept current?

6-22. How might the audit program be modified in light of weaknesses in systems development and documentation controls?

6-23. To the auditor, what are the advantages of software aids?

OBJECTIVE QUESTIONS

6-24. Which of the following employees normally would be assigned the operating responsibility for designing an electronic data processing installation, including flowcharts of data processing routines?
  a. Computer programmer
  b. Data processing manager
  c. Systems analyst
  d. Internal auditor *(AICPA)*

6-25. The postimplementations review

a. Is conducted by the audit manager upon completion of the audit
b. Is an evaluation of each individual programmer and systems analyst
c. Is an alternative to final review and approval
d. Provides information on how well the system and its controls are functioning
e. All of the above

6-26. An auditor who plans to assess risk at a low level on system testing as a control might perform which of the following?
   a. Review the procedures for reconciling output produced during parallel testing
   b. Trace record data from the original files to the new files
   c. Review the programming standards section of the systems and procedures manual
   d. Review the systems development standards manual

6-27. Operations documentation should include
   a. Program flowcharts
   b. A list of transaction codes
   c. A description of programmed controls
   d. A description of required inputs and outputs

6-28. If systems development controls are judged to be weak or nonexistent
   a. The auditors may have to extend their tests of account balances
   b. Application controls are likely to be weak
   c. The auditors should consider this in their overall assessment of control risk
   d. All of the above

CASES AND EXERCISES

6-29. In completing the Internal Control Questionnaire for Lava Butte, Inc., you receive a "yes" answer to your question on project management of application development. What documentation would you include in the working papers to support a reduction in risk on this control?

6-30. Responses to the Internal Control Questionnaire for Lava Butte indicate a failure to review and approve systems developments by either technical staff or management and users. What are the implications of this deficiency? What effect might this have on the assessment of control risk? To what degree are your conclusions changed by the "yes" answer to the question on users and accounting participation in systems development?

6-31. In reviewing the Internal Questionnaire for Lava Butte, you notice that management does not review documentation. To what extent does this offset the advantage of maintaining formal documentation standards?

6-32. The responses to the Internal Control Questionnaire for Lava Butte indicate that program changes are not restricted to systems personnel. Why should program changes be restricted to systems personnel? Is the assistance given by the data processing manager a major violation of this control?

6–33. According to a response to the Internal Control Questionnaire, Lava Butte uses its production program for program change purposes. What are the implications of this? How does it affect the conversion process?

6–34. According to the Internal Control Questionnaire for Lava Butte, application documentation is stored in an unlocked storage room. What conclusions would you expect the auditor to draw from this? How might it affect the auditor's assessment of control risk?

6–35. You are completing the Internal Control Questionnaire for systems development and documentation control. In reply to a question on the use of systems development standards, the manager of EDP replies: "We are a fairly small EDP department. We can't afford to maintain a large staff of systems analysts and programmers. Accordingly we purchase our application software from a software vendor and make modifications ourselves to make the programs work for us. Consequently systems development standards and documentation are irrelevant for our organization." Comment.

6–36. An important systems development control is internal audit participation in the systems development process. Describe the appropriate responsibilities of the internal auditor who participates in each of the following steps of the systems development process: system planning, user specifications, technical specifications, audit specifications, implementation planning, programming, user procedure and training, system testing, conversion, postimplementation review, and documentation.

6–37. A programmer altered the bank's program for demand deposit accounting, instructing the computer to ignore overdrafts in his own checking account. The fraud was discovered when the system was down and overdrafts had to be processed manually. Assuming the programmer had no access to the computer room, what general controls would have prevented this fraud?

6–38. A manufacturing company converted its inventory control system from a manual system to a computerized system. It was later discovered that the new system was overstating inventory by $500,000 as a result of misclassifying certain parts. How might this problem have been prevented at the time of conversion? Could the problem have been discovered earlier by other controls? What is the best way to avoid such problems in the first place?

6–39. Some large publicly held companies have established a "zero comments" objective for reviews of significant EDP applications by the internal audit staff. How might systems development and documentation controls aid in such an objective? Is such an objective possible?

6–40. Tiklonix auditors are performing a review of Tiklonix system change controls as part of their overall review of general controls. Tiklonix is a major electronics manufacturer with worldwide operations. Its data processing center is located in the northwestern United States. It has a large systems and programming staff who handle most of the systems development and maintenance work. Small development and maintenance projects are occasionally completed under contract with a Seattle software company.

The following extract from the auditors' working papers is a memo summarizing an interview with Bill Slow, Tiklonix's data processing manager:

Mr. Slow explained that program change requests were initiated by either the operations staff or the systems staff depending on the nature of the change. All change requests were discussed in Mr. Slow's office with the initiating staff prior to his oral approval. Mr. Slow indicated that he encouraged systems personnel to visit with him from time to time to discuss progress on the project. He explained that he used his long and varied experience in the systems area to evaluate the work performed and to make suggestions for improvement. He expressed his complete faith in his systems personnel. He felt that if he controlled their activities too carefully he would stifle their creativity.

Upon completion of the design specifications, they were reviewed by Mr. Slow. It was rarely necessary for him to suggest changes before granting his approval. One evening a week was set aside in the computer room for program debugging and testing purposes.

The programmers stayed late that evening so they could load the programs themselves. In order to speed up the coding, debugging, and testing process, the programmers worked with the production program. As a safeguard, however, testing was performed on copies of the files. The original files were locked carefully in the file storage room.

When the program changes were tested to the satisfaction of the programmers, the test results were reviewed by Mr. Slow. If he approved of the test results, he personally took care of all necessary communications and documentation. This involved preparing a short narrative description of the change (usually no longer than a paragraph). A copy of the narrative was sent to the internal audit department and to the user. Another copy was filed with the systems documentation. Only when this was complete did he instruct operations to resume normal production.

Evaluate the system change controls for Tiklonix. Include a discussion of strengths and weaknesses as well as an overall conclusion.

6–41.   In late March a programmer made a minor change in the program that was used to update the New York City Welfare Department's master file. Because the revision was "trivial," the program was not tested. In the ensuing months welfare recipients died, moved away, or lost their eligibility to receive further payments. Delete transactions were prepared in each case and processed as part of the normal master-file update.

The update program received both batch and on-line updates. Because of the program change, however, it no longer was able to handle batch transactions. The "trivial" change caused the update program to ignore batch-entered deletions to the master file, so closed cases remained open.

During April, May, and June, the printers on the system kept spewing out checks. After they were burst and stuffed into envelopes, they went winging on their way to dead men and women, people who were long gone from the city, and those no longer entitled to receive payments. Finally, field workers started to report payments on closed cases. By this time, $7,500,000 had been disbursed to people who should have been deleted from the files.

Now, it is possible to go back and find which checks should not have been written. Getting the money back is another question. Most of the checks are in low three figures. It costs abut $150 to file the legal papers to bring suit for recovery of the funds. Collecting the $7,500,000 might end up costing $7,500,000 . . . Oh well, it wasn't real money! It came out of the taxpayers' pockets

What system development controls would have prevented this loss of assets?

(*Reprinted from Donald L. Adams, "We Didn't Test the System, but, How Much Could We Lose? Would You Believe $7,500,000!!!" EDPACS, Vol. II, No. 2, August 1974.*)

6–42. RAYO CORPORATION: Program Change Controls

Mike Kess, a senior auditor for the regional accounting firm Sanders and McDonald, was assigned to audit the Rayo Corporation. He was to obtain an understanding of the general controls over systems and programming. He had already identified the current applications and the equipment used in the data processing system, and is about to start on system maintenance.

Mike contacted Jim Stram, the manager of systems and programming in the EDP department. A summary of their conversion is presented below.

Mike	How are system maintenance projects initiated and developed?
Jim:	All potential projects are sent to a member of my staff called an Applications Coordinator, for analysis. We do all our systems and programming work in-house. If a programming change is required for a project, the Applications Coordinator prepares a revision request form. These revision request forms must be approved by both the Manager of Operations and myself. The Director of Data Processing and the Internal Auditor receive copies of each revision request form for information purposes.
Mike:	How does the Applications Coordinator keep track of the revision request form and any change that might be made to it?
Jim:	The revision request forms are numbered in different series depending on the nature of the change requested. The Applications Coordinator assigns the next number in the sequence and records in a master log

each request he prepares. Changes in revision requests, from whatever source, are prepared on request forms just as initial requests are. Each change request is given the same basic number with a suffix indicating it is an amendment, and there is a place for recording amendments in the master log.

Mike: What is the distribution of an approved request form?

Jim: It goes to one of my systems supervisors for design, programming, and testing. The primary effort is usually performed by a programmer who has responsibility over the area of the application or the specific programs to be changed.

Mike: But how are projects controlled?

Jim: At the beginning of each programming project, an estimated start and completion date are assigned and entered on the request form and the master log. The system supervisor keeps on top of the projects assigned to him, and the Applications Coordinator also monitors the open requests. The system supervisor files a written status report with the Applications Coordinator twice a month, and he briefs me on any problems. However, I'm usually aware of any difficulties long before then.

During the programming and testing phase, I think we have good control over the project. None of the compilations made during this phase changes any production source code for the existing computer programs. Also, all test object programs are identified by a strictly enforced naming convention that clearly distinguishes them from production programs. So far this has been successful in inhibiting their use in production processing. If a programmer has specific questions or problems on a project, his systems supervisor is generally available to give advice.

Mike: Are there written guidelines to direct this activity? If so, how detailed are they?

Jim: Only informal procedures exist to provide any uniformity to the programs and the coding changes which are made to a program. But, formal standards do exist which define what documentation should be present for a system and for the programs within a system. These apply to program changes as well, and again are strictly enforced. There is a periodic management review to see we comply. We just had one about a month ago and got a clean bill of health.

Mike: Are adequate tests and reviews made of changes before they are implemented?

Jim: The Applications Coordinator, the systems supervisor, and the individual programmer informally discuss the necessary tests for a specific project. Sometimes I get involved too, but our guidelines are pretty good in this area and provide a fairly thorough approach to test design. After the tests have been completed to the systems supervisor's satisfaction, the Applications Coordinator reviews and approves the test results. This must be done on all revision requests before they are implemented into production. I usually review the programmer's work to see that all authorized changes are made correctly and are adequately tested and documented.

Mike: How does implementation take place and what controls are exercised over it?

Jim: After the test results for a revision request have been approved by the Applications Coordinator, it is the responsibility of the programmer to implement the changes into production. In order for a programmer to put a program change into production, he must update the source code of the production program version. The programmer is required to provide program name and compile date information for all changed programs to his system supervisor. The programmer also has the responsibility of updating the systems and programming documentation. His system supervisor is supposed to review this and certify completion to the Applications Coordinator who then completes the log entry.

Mike: Are postimplementation reviews undertaken on system maintenance projects?

Jim: Once the project is implemented the Applications Coordinator reviews the output from the first production runs of the changed program. He also questions users to see if any problem areas can be identified.

A documented audit trail is provided by a completed project file that is maintained by the Applications Coordinator for each request number. This file contains all the required documentation, including test results. A copy of the final summary goes to the department which originally submitted the request. A table in the computer is updated to provide listings of the most current compile dates for each set of production object code within the system. Before any program is implemented it is checked against this table.

Mike: Well, that seems to be it. I think I have all that I need for now, but I'll probably be back to take a look at the files and records. I may have more questions for you then. Thanks very much for your time and thoughtful answers. I really appreciate your help.

Jim: That's quite all right. If I can be of any more help, just let me know.

Questions:

Keeping in mind that this is part of the understanding phase of assessing control risk, are there any additional questions you would have asked of Jim if you had been in Mike's place?

Make a list of weaknesses that you feel should be considered in the preliminary assessment of control risk in this area.

(*Prepared by Frederick Neumann, Richard Boland, and Jeffrey Johnson, with funding from the Touche Ross Foundation. Used and adapted with permission of the authors.*)

6-43. BANK HOLDING CORPORATION: System Maintenance and Development Controls

Introduction

Early this year, Bank Holding Corporation (BHC) of Cleveland, Ohio acquired its twenty-fifth affiliate by purchasing the stock of the First National Bank of Lordstown. Since the late 1960's, BHC has been expanding its assets and geographic area through the acquisition of small independent banks in several counties. The holding company's assets have increased from $1.2 billion in 1969 to $5.3 billion today, and continued growth, by acquisition, is forecasted. Local banks are allowed to manage themselves as long as operating results are satisfactory to the management of the holding company. Consequently, top management of BHC rarely get involved with the internal operations of the affiliates, except at the policy level.

One such policy was to implement on-line processing for all subsidiary banks and their branches. The on-line system was centralized at the BHC computer center just outside Cleveland. Previously, each subsidiary had performed its own data processing. They had developed a variety of different systems, ranging from manual processing to small computer operations in a batch mode. When the on-line system was instituted by the BHC data center, the affiliates ceased processing their own data except for minor applications.

BHC's centralized Data Center consists of two large CPUs, twenty-eight disk drives, twenty-two tape drives, and related peripheral equipment. It currently provides the branches with all the data processing required for following applications:

- Demand Deposit (checking)
- Passbook Savings
- Certificates of Deposit
- Commercial Loans
- Personal and Auto Loans
- General Ledger

The major components of the BHC on-line system are:

- The main computers, which accept data, apply prescribed processing to the data, and output the results. The computer hardware consists of two communication-oriented computers. Each central processor contains several million characters of main memory.
- The on-line files, which provide direct access to the large store of information necessary for processing daily transactions. An average of 50,000 on-line transactions are processed daily.
- The terminals, which are attached to the communication network. There are 170 terminals at the 25 subsidiaries and their branch locations. The terminals, manufactured by NCR, are application-oriented with self-contained logic and memory.

- The communication network, which links the remote terminals to the computer. The communication network is composed of eighteen dedicated lines leased from the telephone company.
- The software, which is the collection of computer programs and program segments or subroutines that enable the system to logically process entered transactions against stored data.

The four major objectives of the centralized Data Center are to provide and maintain for all affiliates:

1. Computer services to strengthen the financial security of affiliates
2. Computer services to assist in the decision-making processes of affiliate management
3. Computer services to improve the efficiency of the day-to-day operations of affiliates
4. Research and development programs to improve existing systems and innovate new services for the affiliates

Operation Committee Request

At the annual meeting of the corporate-wide operations committee in February, the vice-presidents of operations from several affiliate banks voiced a growing concern over the centralized data center concept. They were concerned about the cost and competitive disadvantage of an interruption in business activity that might be caused by the loss of data or the ability to process it. The centralized processing made them especially sensitive as they no longer had control over their own data. Even short processing interruptions could have negative effects on customer good will and any extended period of downtime could severely hamper the business activity of affiliates. As a result of these concerns, the operations committee sent a request to the BHC internal audit staff to perform an internal control review of the Data Center.

The request for a review of the Data Center went to the newly appointed head of BHC's internal audit department, Ms. Margaret Johnson. Ms. Johnson, in light of the importance of this review, chose to undertake the project herself. She discovered that the internal audit department had not performed such a review before, and decided to begin with systems maintenance and development activities.

The committee felt that it was important for changes to the processing and reporting capabilities of the system to be made on a timely basis and that they be implemented as intended. They wondered if changes to the computer system were effectively managed and controlled. Ms. Johnson sensed that the operating vice-presidents had little faith in the system maintenance and development activities in particular and shared reservations about the quality of the center's management in general. She felt the report on her first study probably has not helped to improve this.

Ms. Johnson found that the Data Center considered system development to include all activities and standards for planning, designing, programming, and testing new systems. System maintenance, on the other hand, included project initiation, programming, and testing of any change to an existing system or program. She inquired of Michael Heckman, head of Data Center operations, about the initiation of development and maintenance projects. He explained that until a few years ago subsidiary banks initiated most of the changes and a corporate-wide steering committee reviewed them. This steering committe provided direction to the overall data processing and system development effort by resolving conflicts and giving guidance for the orderly evolution of data processing services. It had not met in over two years, however. Currently all maintenance and development activities were either initiated by one of the subsidiaries of BHC or by Mr. Heckman himself. "Since I am most familiar with the real strengths and weaknesses of the system, however, I probably initiate 90 percent of all projects," he said.

Ms. Johnson could not find any formal documentation or standard procedures for identifying, defining, and evaluating projects, or for determining priorities, defining schedules, assigning responsibilities, or allocating resources by a cost/benefit analysis. As a consequence, she questioned Mr. Heckman further on how he went about initiating a change in the system. "Well, I constantly monitor systems looking for trouble areas and ways to improve them," he replied. He pointed out that a software program produces certain reports such as:

- Work Flow Language Log
- CPU Usage Per Application
- Files Accessed/Changes Made
- Downtime Log
- System Log

"These reports review all activity on the computer and monitor the processing and recording, and any abnormal use or improper run procedures. But to tell you the truth, these reports were developed by a very technical software expert and I really do not use them. They are too lengthy and hard to understand. Besides, by listening to my operators and generally being aware of day-to-day problems, I get a very good intuitive feel for what needs to be done. You know, even though this is a very sophisticated operation, technically, managing its development and maintenance is really an art, not a science."

Ms. Johnson found out that not all system development and maintenance activities were performed in-house. Due to the rapid growth of BHC the Data Center has been unable to implement all changes by itself. Some system changes were contracted out to a programming company. These findings led her to expand her scope and review a system change conducted by the programming company as well as one conducted by the in-house group. Since one project was currently being performed by the programming company she decided to investigate that immediately. Mr. Heckman said, "I am very satisfied with the work they do. Once we give them the system specifications they do everything from coding to running system tests with historical data."

The programming company was currently involved with updating the banks' interest system. The documentation of these programs is minimal, runs are slow and cumbersome, and programmers at the Data Center understand only COBOL. The programming company was recoding the present interest system in COBOL. Ms. Johnson was informed that the system was just being recoded and no attention was being given to basic system redesign because of the time and cost involved. "First things first," said Mr. Heckman.

Ms. Johnson then decided to investigate the in-house procedures for system development and maintenance. She saw that all requests for system changes were reviewed by Heckman and at least one technical support person to see if the change was economically feasible. The system change request was then sent to the systems and programming group. It was their responsibility to actually define system specifications, and to program and test the system changes. Once a manager in the system and programming group decided what existing programs needed to be altered, the change was assigned to a programmer. Whenever possible, the programmer assigned had had prior responsibility over the area of the application or the specific programs to be changed. The programmer was then totally responsible for performing the necessary maintenance to the production program files and the related job-control language. The programmer also tested the finished programs with historical data, on the operating equipment, to see if the system change was working properly.

By talking to a programmer, Ms. Johnson discovered the maintenance of the present system was very difficult because of a lack of flow-charts and program listings. The programmer also pointed out that very few new system development and maintenance projects were well documented because of the severe time limitation put on the Data Center personnel.

After a system change has been completed by a programmer, a supervisor in the Data Center briefly reviews the test results and change is implemented. The only interaction with the subsidiary bank users occurred when the change was originally initiated and later when the change was finally implemented. Once each year the internal audit group usually reviewed the changes that affected each branch.

In concluding her investigation, Ms. Johnson felt that there was a lack of involvement by users and internal auditors in the system life cycle. Because of this she wrote a memo to the operating vice-presidents of the subsidiaries and pointed out where she felt involvement was necessary.

MEMO

To: Operating Vice-Presidents of Subsidiary Banks
From: Margaret Johnson, Head of Internal Auditing

As BHC continues to implement more extensive and sophisticated computer systems, the internal audit department needs to become an active participant in the design and testing of any new applications and in the maintenance of existing systems. The internal audit department's primary objective will be to assure management that newly implemented, as well as established, computer applications include sound and reliable control features.

I feel that the following guidelines set forth the minimum level of audit and user involvement necessary for implementing new applications and maintaining existing systems. The internal auditor needs to be involved in the critical phases of the system life cycle as follows:

System Life Cycle (Development Life Cycle)

System Planning

In this phase, the project's scope, objectives, costs, benefits, technical and economic feasibility are defined and determined. The internal auditors should be involved in this phase so they can anticipate future systems developments which may require them to gain the necessary knowledge to deal with any new technical concepts that are planned.

User Specification

This is the most important phase because basic functional concepts of the new system are defined from the user's perspective. In this phase, the auditor should define the controls by which the system can be monitored and regulated. The auditor should review the potential exposures and related controls. Internal auditing may also be a user of a new system.

Technical Specifications

Within this phase, the system analyst translates the user specifications into technical concepts at the level necessary to communicate with programmers. With appropriate technical knowledge and computer experience, the auditor can review this phase to ascertain if a reasonable translation has been made with adequate provision for any technical constraints.

Implementation Planning

This phase involves even closer coordination between the user and the EDP department in preparation for conversion. The auditor should be vitally interested in the controls planned over the conversion process, for problems in implementation can be costly.

Programming

The conversion of the technical specifications defined by the system analyst to computer operating instructions is completed in this phase.

User Procedures and Training
This phase includes the preparation of procedures for the conversion to, and the operation of, the new system. Auditors should check to see if the user has adequate procedure manuals and related job descriptions which serve to increase user awareness and control over the system.

System Test
The system test is an acceptance test conducted by the systems group and the user. Internal audit participation is essential, for it is the last line of defense before implementation. Tests performed should be recorded and test checks retained with their results to indicate the adequacy and success of the testing. User approvals should be the last step of this phase.

Conversion
This is the phase in which the conversion of data, equipment, procedures, and personnel to the new system takes place. It should occur in a carefully planned and controlled environment. The auditor should be concerned about file integrity and the consistency of data affecting accounting reports.

Postimplementation
A review should be made by the auditor sometime after implementation to assure that all areas of the system are operating as intended.

Questions:

- Why is it important to control systems development and systems maintenance? What are some possible consequences if control over these processes is lacking?
- Evaluate Ms. Johnson's report on the system life cycle. Do you agree with her characterization of the role of the internal auditor? What changes would you suggest?
- What weaknesses are there in the existing system?

(Prepared by Frederick Neumann, Richard Boland, and Jeffrey Johnson, with funding from the Touche Ross Foundation. Used and adapted with permission of the authors.)

Chapter 7
HARDWARE AND SYSTEMS SOFTWARE CONTROLS

Learning Objectives

After completing this chapter, the reader should be able to:

1. Understand how hardware and software controls affect system reliability and accuracy.

2. Determine the factors that serve to reduce the effectiveness of hardware and systems software controls.

3. Understand how data processing equipment and data communications networks contribute to system error.

4. Appreciate how the effectiveness of hardware and systems software controls are affected by weakness in other general controls.

5. Appreciate the relationship between system complexity and control objectives.

Some data processing specialists believe that it is unnecessary to devote much attention to hardware and systems software controls. Modern computers are designed to be very reliable, and most of them have built-in hardware controls. Software technology has advanced to the point where systems software is extremely effective both in managing the system and in providing control. As a result, the auditor should encounter effective hardware and systems software controls. In actual practice, however, several factors can reduce their effectiveness. In addition, the risk to the auditor of weakness in these controls is considerable because of their pervasive influence on system reliability. Consequently, it is essential that the auditor evaluate the impact of hardware and systems software on system reliability.

Following are some of the factors that can reduce the effectiveness of hardware and systems software control:

1. Some hardware vendors fail to specify a full complement of controls in their hardware and software. Some minicomputer vendors, for example, do not include the redundant character check (parity bit) as a standard feature.

2. Not all systems software is equally reliable; it depends partly on the source of the software. There are three sources of systems software: hardware vendors who make a whole range of systems software for use with their equipment, independent software companies, and a company's own systems staff. The reliability of systems software is likely to vary depending on the source used and the quality of the vendor or staff used.

3. A company may not acquire or use all the available systems software. Systems software is modular by design, so that each installation may pick the modules most useful to it and omit others. Control modules, however, may be the ones omitted. A module that monitors terminal passwords, for example, could be omitted in an on-line system. As a result, unauthorized access to programs and data would be easier.

4. Hardware and systems software controls may be available in the installation but may not be utilized by the application programs. A hardware error may be detected by the hardware or software, for example, but may require that the application program check for the error conditions. If the application program does not make this check, processing will continue with the error uncorrected.

5. The systems software may be quite reliable initially, but controls may be rendered ineffective by subsequent changes. Systems software, like application software, is susceptible to changes that render controls ineffective.

6. Systems software can be a powerful source of control, but it can also be a powerful tool for manipulation if subject to unauthorized use. For example, some systems software utility programs can circumvent controls. These utilities can be used to modify other programs or data—with no trace left of the modification! IBM's SUPERZAP is an example of such a utility.

7. Effective hardware and systems software controls may be rendered ineffective by poor organization and operation controls. The failure to perform routine hardware maintenance, for example, may drastically reduce hardware reliability. Systems software controls may be rendered inoperative by uncontrolled access to the programs and by lack of control and documentation of changes to the programs.

Ineffective hardware and systems software controls pose considerable risk to the auditor because of their influence on system reliability. This influence is a result of the interrelationship between the application programs and the computer hardware and systems software. As part of this interrelationship, both application programs and the hardware and systems software act together to ensure system reliability. Each application program has its own specific controls to contribute to its own processing reliability. The hardware and systems software controls are general controls that affect the reliability of each individual application, creating an environment conducive to reliable error-free processing. Nonexistent or ineffective hardware or systems software controls, however, may create an error-prone environment that mitigates the effectiveness of individual application controls. Consequently, the auditor should obtain an understanding of and test for the existence and effectiveness of hardware and systems software controls. The auditor should also review processing results for evidence of errors induced by hardware problems or software deficiencies.

Hardware and systems software controls are controls provided by the manufacturer of the hardware and by the software vendor and utilized by the EDP system and its applications. They provide reasonable assurance that the reliability of processing will not be affected by errors resulting from equipment failure, and from system problems such as the improper handling of errors and the failure to protect files and programs from unauthorized access.

Hardware and systems software controls are discussed together in this chapter because of their common objective, and because modern technology is blurring the distinction between the two types of control. The common objective of hardware and systems software controls is to create an operating environment that is conducive to reliable input, processing, and output. In modern computers, there is a degree of interchangeability between the two types of controls. Error handling, for example, can be accomplished by computer circuitry or by the operating system software. As long as controls exist and are operating effectively, it makes no difference to the auditor whether they are hardware or software controls.

In this chapter we discuss (1) the role of data processing equipment and data communications in causing error, (2) hardware controls, and (3) software controls. The Appendix contains an internal controls questionnaire on hardware and systems software controls for Lava Butte, Inc.

EQUIPMENT FAILURE AS A SOURCE OF ERROR

Errors may occur because of a failure in an electronic element or in a mechanical part of the computer equipment. The failure of an electronic element such as a semiconductor, diode, or transistor may affect the electrical pulses used in the processing of data, the storage of data in memory, and the communication of data between different pieces of equipment in the computer system. If the failure leads to a change in the timing, strength, shape, or frequency of the pulses, the result could be an invalid operation with the data, storage or transmission of invalid data, or the modification or destruction of data or program instructions. For example, data may be transmitted along a channel from memory to a printer. The data may be modified during the transmission as a result of a failure in an electronic element. In the absence of a control, the printer would print the invalid data.

The failure of a mechanical part is a hazard of the operation of peripheral input/output and storage devices. Such a failure can result in an error in reading data during an input operation, in an error in writing data onto storage, or in an error in the printing of data. There are three general causes of mechanical failure:

1. Defective media, such as defective magnetic tape caused by imperfections in the coating
2. Problems with the movement, speed, or timing of a transport mechanism, such as a movable arm in a disk storage device
3. A fault in a read/write mechanism, such as the reading head in a magnetic tape drive

A mechanical failure is also related to the specific peripheral device. The mechanical problems associated with a printer, for example, are different from those associated with a disk drive. Table 7–1 summarizes the major causes of failure, and their related errors, for each of the most common peripheral hardware devices. The table does not cover errors resulting from failure of electronic components that may also cause errors in the operation of these devices. Nor does it describe the differences in the design of these devices, differences that may affect the mechanical

Table 7–1. Mechanical Problems in Common Hardware Devices

Hardware Device	Description	Cause of Mechanical Failure	Possible Error
Printer	Output device that prepares printed output—may be impact or nonimpact	1. Timing failure 2. Malfunction of specific device 3. Poor-quality paper	Print incorrect or incomplete set of characters
Magnetic tape drive	Peripheral storage device that uses magnetic tape as storage medium	1. Malfunction of read/write head 2. Malfunction of tape drive 3. Imperfections in the tape	1. Incorrect reading or writing 2. Loss of data
Disk drive	Peripheral on-line storage device that uses magnetic disks as storage medium	1. Head crash (debris on the disk surface causes head to touch surface of disk) 2. Head bounce (head fails to maintain proper position above disk surface)	1. Incorrect reading or writing 2. Loss of data

operation of the device. The printer, for example, may be of the impact type utilizing a rotating drum or wheel, or a horizontally moving train, chain, belt, bar, or wire matrix. Alternatively, the printer may be nonimpact, using electrothermal or electrostatic means of creating an image.

DATA COMMUNICATIONS AS A SOURCE OF ERROR

In the preceding section we learned that a failure in an electronic element of the computer may cause an error by affecting the frequency, timing, strength, or shape of an electrical pulse. Another source of change in the electrical pulse is the use of data communications facilities to move data from one location to another. In data communications, data are transmitted in the form of an electrical signal. An inadvertent change in this signal will result in the data received being in some way different from the data sent. The electrical signal may be changed by failure of a mechanical component of the data communication network, or by a problem related to the characteristics of data communications. Of these two sources of error, the latter is by far the more important. Data communications is the one area where the auditor should expect errors to be frequent (making detection and correction essential).

Errors related to the communication of data, rather than to a mechanical failure, are due to noise, fading, or distortion. *Noise* is electrical interference with the signal. It may be background noise or impulse noise, and it may be random or cyclical. Background noise usually has little effect on the transmission of the signal. Impulse noise, such as that caused by a sudden surge in the voltage, is more likely to mask or distort the signal. As long as the noise occurs randomly, it is usually easy to detect an error. Cyclical noise, however, such as a voltage oscillation where a peak is followed by a dip, can create compensating errors that are difficult to detect.

Fading of a signal is a decline in its strength. Fading occurs when the signal is transmitted by microwaves. Under certain weather conditions, the signal picked up by the receiving unit can be quite weak. A weak signal is more susceptible to noise and error.

Distortion of a signal results from a lack of synchronization between the time the data are sent and the time they are received. Lack of synchronization occurs when the signal travels several paths with different delays on each path. This will result in distortion when there is overlapping in the receipt of the different paths of the signal.

HARDWARE CONTROLS

In this section we discuss hardware controls by type of control: redundant character check, duplicate process check, echo check, equipment check, validity check, and operational controls (media controls, equipment failure logs and reports, environmental controls, power protection, formal recovery procedures, operation procedures, and preventive maintenance). Some of these controls can be found on two or more types of equipment, and therefore this section includes a controls and equipment cross-reference. The section ends with a summary of the procedures to obtain an understanding of the internal control structure and tests of controls.

Redundant Character Check

The redundant character check is a bit, two bits, or a set of bits attached to a data character, word, or block of data for the purpose of detecting errors. This method of error detection utilizes the principle of redundancy. The extra bits are derived from the relevant data and, therefore, bear a logical relationship to the data. This logical relationship is a control relationship only and has no modifying effect on the data. If the data are moved, or some operation is performed on the data, the extra bits will remain attached to the data. Error detection is accomplished by the computer's recalculating the redundant character check using the same logical relationship. If there has been no electronic or transmission error, the recalculation and the original should be the same. A difference between the two calculations would indicate that data have been lost or changed during the operation.

The redundant character check is a valuable control, but it is not foolproof. It is designed to detect electronic and transmission-caused errors, but not to detect otherwise invalid data. Also, its reliability in error detection is a function of the degree of built-in redundancy. Of the three types of redundant character checks, the single parity bit has the least redundancy, followed by the double parity bit and the error correction code.

The single parity bit is the creation of an additional bit for each character processed. The computer stores data in binary code, with each character of the data represented commonly by six, seven, or eight bits. Depending on the character in question, the six, seven, or eight bits will be the collection and sequence of 0's and 1's that represent that character. The computer counts the number of 1 bits in each character to determine whether the count is odd or even. In an odd parity bit check, the computer will add a parity bit of 0 if the count is odd and a 1 if the count is even. The objective is to create an odd count of bits for each character. The even parity bit check adds a 0 or 1 bit to achieve an even count. The idea of the single parity bit is that a loss, change, or addition to the data during an operation or move may destroy parity and signal an error. Examples of the successful use of the single odd parity bit are given in the first three lines of Table 7–2.

Table 7–2. Odd Parity Check Using Eight-Bit Extended Binary Coded Decimal Interchange Code (EBCDIC)

Odd Parity Bit	Data								Character
1	1	1	1	1	0	1	0	1	Digit 5 (valid)
0	1	1	1	0	0	0	1	1	Letter T (valid)
0	1	1	0	0	0	0	1	1	Letter T (invalid)—one digit lost; error detected
0	1	0	0	0	0	0	1	1	Letter T (invalid)—two digits lost; error not detected

The single parity bit has limited redundancy and therefore limited ability to detect errors. The single parity bit will fail to detect an error when two errors occur in the same operation. The first error will destroy parity, but the second error will compensate for the original change in parity leaving a net no change in parity. An example of compensating errors is given in the last line of Table 7–2. As a result of its limited redundancy, this control is used where the equipment is reliable, and few errors are likely. It is generally used in the CPU, in disk storage, and to test data moved along a channel to a print buffer in preparation for printing.

The double parity bit follows the same principle as the single parity bit but uses a second parity bit to gain additional redundancy. The single parity bit that is attached to each character is called the *vertical parity bit*. A second parity bit, the *horizontal* or *longitudinal parity bit*, is attached to all the equivalent bits in the data element. The equivalent bits are simply the row of bits in each of the bit positions. Table 7–3 shows a double parity bit where three characters constitute the data element.

The double parity bit is generally used as a control for magnetic tape, and for data communications. It is also used in the CPU and memory of some scientific computers. The double parity bit is used for magnetic tape because the cost of tape is low, and therefore the cost of the additional space required by the second parity bit is minimal. In Table 7–

Table 7–3. Even Double Parity Bit Using Eight-Bit Extended Binary Coded Decimal Interchange Code (EBCDIC)

	Data Character 1	Data Character 2	Data Character 3	Longitudinal Parity Bit
Bit position 1	1	1	1	1
Bit position 2	1	1	1	1
Bit position 3	1	1	1	1
Bit position 4	1	1	1	1
Bit position 5	0	0	0	0
Bit position 6	0	0	0	0
Bit position 7	0	1	1	0
Bit position 8	1	0	1	0
Vertical parity bit	1	1	0	0

↑
End of block of data on tape.

3 the vertical data characters represent frames on a magnetic tape. There are nine (horizontal) channels on the tape for each frame in Table 7–3; the first through the eighth for the data, and the ninth for the parity bit. A longitudinal parity bit is added to each channel at the end of the block. The double parity bit is also used in data communications where the extra redundancy is useful in detecting the large number of errors occurring during transmission. In data communications, the longitudinal parity bit may be attached to a message segment, a message, or a block of messages. The use of the double parity bit in scientific computers is a function of demands for accuracy and of the difficulty in establishing adequate application controls in scientific applications.

One advantage of the double parity bit is that an error is defined in two dimensions: vertical and horizontal. This allows the precise bit that is causing the error to be detected, thus permitting automatic correction of the error.

The error correction code follows the same principle as the longitudinal parity bit but is better able to detect and, therefore, correct errors. This error detection and correction capability is accomplished by creating a group of bits that is mathematically derived from the data. The correction code is then attached to the set of data bits from which it is derived. The smaller the set of data bits to which the code is attached, the greater the ability of the code to detect and correct errors. The code is used extensively on magnetic tape and in data communications for the same reasons as the double parity bit. An example of an error correction code is one derived using the properties of divisions of polynomials. A message transmitted with a polynomial code should be exactly divisible by the generating polynomial. If the message received is not exactly divisible, then an error has occurred.

Duplicate Process Check

The duplicate process check utilizes the principle of duplicate or complementary operation to detect and correct errors. In this control, an operation is performed twice. The results of the two operations are compared, and any difference between them will indicate a hardware-induced error. If the second operation is a repeat of the first, it is a duplicate operation. The duplicate operation may be performed on independent components or on the same component. Alternatively, the second operation may be complementary to the first, such as where a read is performed after a write to check what was written.

The duplicate operation is used in some older-model magnetic tape drives and in the arithmetic logic unit of the CPU. Some of these older magnetic tape drives have *dual read*. In dual read the records are read twice, and the results of the two reads are compared. In some cases, the records are read by two independent read stations; in other cases, they are read twice by the same read station. A *dual operation* is sometimes used in the arithmetic logic unit of the CPU. Calculations are carried out twice either by the same circuitry or by duplicate circuitry. The results of the two calculations are then compared.

The complementary operation is also used in older-model magnetic tape drives. The complementary operation in a magnetic tape drive is the *read after write*. Data are written onto the tape and are immediately read and compared with what should have been written. The auditor will only find this control and the two-head dual read on older tape drives that have a two-gap head to perform the two operations. More recent tape drives have a single head and rely on other controls such as an equipment check to ensure that recording is taking place.

Echo Check

The purpose of the echo check is to ensure that commands sent to peripheral or remote equipment are obeyed and that data are received correctly. The computer checks to ensure that its commands are obeyed by requiring that printers and other equipment return a signal verifying that the command has been received and complied with. For example, the CPU transmits a command to a printer to commence operation, and the printer transmits a message back to the CPU that it has been activated as instructed. The same technique is used in data communications to ensure that data are received correctly. Data are retransmitted by the receiving computer back to the sending terminal. The terminal then compares the echo with the original data for possible transmission errors.

Equipment Check

Equipment checks are controls built into the circuitry of the computer to check the circuitry or equipment to ensure that it is functioning properly and, where necessary, to provide automatic error correction. These two functions are known as *automatic error diagnosis* and *automatic retry.*

Automatic error diagnosis is utilized by several hardware components. The CPU has circuitry to diagnose parity errors in the CPU and storage. The CPU may also have self-diagnostic capabilities to identify defective circuitry or memory. In some instances, the CPU may be able to route operations and storage around the defective components. Automatic error diagnosis is also used to identify faulty magnetic tape read/write heads. The CPU checks the read/write head during reading or writing to ensure that current is flowing through the head. With a positive check, it is assumed that reading or writing is taking place. The CPU also monitors the printer's operation to ensure correct print synchronization. Here the CPU checks the printer's timing to ensure that the image is created when the print device is in the right position. Data communication facilities may have automatic line and equipment diagnosis. This automatic diagnostic equipment may be part of the communications equipment rather than the CPU.

Automatic retry provides automatic error correction in several situations. It is particularly valuable in the CPU, which is subject to transient error. Transient errors, such as parity errors, may occur because of temporary conditions such as static electricity or random variations in switching times. Since it is likely that such a condition will have disappeared of its own accord, a simple repeat or retry will eliminate the error. Automatic retry is also used with magnetic tape. Imperfections on the surface of the magnetic tape that interfere with reading or writing can be dislodged by backspacing the tape and trying again. Disk drives use automatic retry to facilitate successful read/write operations. The original read/write may fail because the data are slightly offset from the designated recording track. The read/write operation will be repeated several times at different offset locations until the data are located or until it is clear that some other problem is at fault. Automatic retry is utilized in data communications by retransmission of erroneous messages. Retransmission is used in conjunction with an error-detection device and involves the retransmission of a character, word, record, or batch of records.

Validity Check

The purpose of the validity check is to ensure that actions taken by the computer are valid actions. A *valid action* is one that conforms to a set of actions that are considered to be correct. The validity check compares each action with the set of valid actions to ensure that it is indeed valid. The determination of the validity of an action is something a redundant character check is unable to perform. In conjunction with the redundant character check, however, it provides considerable assurance that processing and transfer of data will be reliable and accurate. A limitation of the validity check is that it will not detect an error when a valid character is recorded improperly in place of another during input of data. There are three types of validity check: operation validity, character validity, and address validity.

Operation validity is a validity check of operation codes within the CPU. Each computer system has a recognizable instruction set with a designated code for each instruction, such as addition, subtraction, multiplication, and division. The operation validity check will signal an error condition if a program attempts to process an invalid instruction.

A *character,* or *field, validity* check compares data characters or fields that are written or read with a set of all valid characters or fields of characters. It is a particularly useful technique with peripheral devices such as a printer. A printer, for example, may be limited to a certain number of characters. If there are 64 characters on a print drum or chain, for example, the character validity check would accept data containing any of the 64 characters as valid but would reject data representing other invalid characters.

Address validity is a check of storage locations in memory or in a peripheral device. Memory has only certain addresses that can be accessed as storage addresses. The address validity check compares the memory address requested with the list of valid addresses to detect an invalid request. Some systems are capable of assigning whole sections of memory for prescribed operations or programs. These assigned sections of memory can be protected by a hardware address validity check. This control is also known as *boundary* or *storage protection.* Address checks are also used on disk drives. The hardware compares the address on a disk pack requested in a write instruction with a set of valid disk storage locations.

Operational Controls

The above hardware controls are extremely effective in an environment where the computer is reliable and where appropriate action is taken by operators or programs to ensure that error conditions are handled correctly. The auditor should therefore review the operational procedures in data processing that affect reliability and error handling. These operational procedures include media controls, equipment failure logs and reports, environmental controls, power protection, formal recovery procedures, error checks by operators and application programs, and preventive and corrective maintenance.

Media Controls.   The reliability of peripheral devices will be greater if the storage media are of high quality. Errors may result from worn or defective media. Magnetic tape is susceptible to wear. A careful periodic review of tape quality, however, can minimize problems associated with wear. The tape can be cleaned, worn sections can be cut out, or defective sections can be marked so that they will be skipped. Dented or warped disk packs should be removed from service. Defective tracks on disk packs can be marked so that they may be skipped.

Equipment Failure Logs and Reports.   Hardware is generally reliable, but specific components or devices may give persistent problems. Equipment failure logs provide data on the frequency and type of equipment problems. The log can be prepared manually or can be an automatic log prepared by the hardware or systems software. The data in the logs can be used to pinpoint problems that require corrective action. This is done by preparing equipment reliability reports from the logs. These reports should be reviewed by management on a regular basis.

Environmental Controls. Controls over the hardware environment are designed to counteract the problems caused by dust, temperature, and humidity. Dust particles can attach to the surface of magnetic tapes and disks and interfere with reading or writing. High temperatures can cause plastic components to deform. High humidity can cause condensation on electrical components and hasten their deterioration. Low humidity can create static electricity, causing dust to be attracted to magnetic surfaces. These problems can be controlled by climate control of temperature, humidity, and air quality.

Power Protection. Hardware-induced errors can result from fluctuations or interruptions in the power supply. Fluctuations in the voltage, amperage, or cycles occur frequently. Small fluctuations can be tolerated, but fluctuations of 10 percent or more can cause errors in processing or cause the equipment to shut down. Momentary fluctuations can be isolated from the hardware by use of a surge suppressor. The best surge suppressors protect against all three conditions. Sustained increases or decreases usually require shutting down the equipment. Shutdown can occur automatically through the use of circuit breakers.

Interruptions of the power supply are less likely to cause errors, but only if the system can be shut down without destroying data that are in memory. This can be accomplished if the system can shut down smoothly by the use of standby storage batteries. These batteries may only permit the system to run for a few minutes, but this may be long enough to copy the contents of memory onto a nonvolatile storage medium such as tape or disk. Standby generators permit the system to operate indefinitely, but this is an expensive solution.

Formal Recovery Procedures. Recovery procedures are essential if errors are to be avoided following interruption of hardware operation. The auditor should look for a formal recovery plan that documents the activities and responsibilities of recovery. This recovery plan should cover all aspects of recovery, the most important of which is *data recovery*. The plan for data recovery should spell out the sources of recovery data and the methods of recovery. All data reconstruction should be adequately reviewed and approved. (Recovery procedures are covered in Chapter 8.)

Operation and Application Program Error Checks. One of the equipment checks discussed above was the automatic retry, or correction of an error. Not all computers, however, have these error correction routines built into the hardware. Instead the hardware simply sets an error code that must be checked either by the computer operator or by the application programs. In the first case, the error condition will be displayed on the computer console, requiring the operator to take appropriate corrective measures. In the second case, the error code must be interrogated by an instruction in the application program. For the hardware controls to work correctly, the operator would have to follow standard procedures for handling errors, and the application programs would have to contain the required instruction for interrogation.

Preventive and Corrective Maintenance. With the exception of data communications, hardware is reliable and errors are infrequent. Reliability may deteriorate, however, in the absence of regular preventive maintenance and field replacement of troublesome parts. Regular preventive maintenance serves to identify and replace marginal electrical parts and mechanical components. It also permits cycle replacement of parts that wear out. Certain parts or components may be unreliable because of faulty or inferior design. These parts should be exchanged for improved ones in the computer vendor's field replacement program. All maintenance should be adequately supervised, and the results should be included in the equipment failure reports.

Controls and Equipment Cross-Reference

The discussion of hardware controls has been by type of control, with examples given of applications of each control or specific hardware components. Some of the controls can only be used on one type of equipment; others can be used on various types. Table 7–4 provides a control/equipment cross-reference for the most common applications of hardware controls.

Understanding and Tests of Controls

If the auditors plan to assess risk at a low level on the utilization of hardware controls as a general control, they should employ the following procedures to obtain an understanding of the internal control structure and tests of controls:

1. Inquire regarding the make, model, size, and number of computer and peripheral hardware devices.

Table 7-4. Hardware Controls and Equipment Cross-Reference for Controls Generally Found in Business Application Computer Systems

Hardware Control \\ Equipment	CPU	Memory	Magnetic Tape Drive	Disk Drive	Printer	Data Communications
Redundant Character Check						
1. Single parity bit	X	X			X	
2. Double parity bit			X	X		X
3. Error correction code			X	X		X
Duplicate Process Check						
1. Dual read			X			
2. Read after write			X			
3. Dual operation	X					
Echo Check			X	X	X	X
Equipment Check						
1. Automatic error Diagnosis	X	X	X	X	X	X
2. Automatic retry	X	X	X	X		X
Validity Check						
1. Operation validity	X					
2. Character or field validity					X	
3. Address validity		X			X	

2. Review vendor literature or other documentation to determine what hardware controls are available.
3. Inquire of management and data processing personnel regarding the available controls that are utilized.
4. If certain controls are not utilized, discuss with management to determine whether there are any resulting weaknesses in internal control.
5. Utilize technical assistance to help evaluate the effectiveness of hardware controls.
6. Review error logs to determine the frequency of hardware-induced errors.
7. Review equipment failure logs, downtime reports, maintenance reports, and other operating statistics to determine the reliability of the hardware.

8. Inquire regarding measures to protect against power fluctuation and interruption.
9. Review operations documentation to determine the adequacy of operator error-handling procedures, media controls, and recovery procedures.
10. Observe the operation of the hardware to confirm the use of prescribed controls and operating procedures.
11. Review temperature and humidity logs to ensure that environmental standards are met.
12. Review the hardware maintenance contract equipment failure reports and maintenance reports to determine whether regular preventive and corrective maintenance is specified.

SYSTEMS SOFTWARE CONTROLS

Systems software is a set of program routines that perform system-level functions of management, applications program support, and control. Systems software is systems level because it performs tasks that are common to many applications, in contrast to application software that is specific to one application. Systems software covers operating systems, utilities, compilers and assemblers, and data-base management systems.

The management function is performed by the operating system and includes both the control of all operations within the computer and the allocation of the resources of the computer system among the application programs. As operations controller, the operating system guides the application programs through the system. It initiates such events as the translating of source code to object code, the accessing of data required by the program, and the routing of output to an output device such as a printer or terminal. The management of computer resources involves the allocation of CPU time, memory, software, and input/output devices among the various application programs. Accordingly, the operating system performs such tasks as the scheduling of processing and the synchronizing of processing activities.

The support function is provided by utilities, compilers and assemblers, and data-base management systems. *Utilities* are programs that either perform commonly encountered input/output functions or provide special service functions for computer operations. Examples of the former type of utility include programs for sorting data, merging files, or copying files. Service utilities include programs to flowchart software, edit software, test new systems, and provide control analyses for management. *Compilers* and *assemblers* are automatic language translators that convert source code written by programmers in FORTRAN, COBOL, or similar language into machine language for computer processing. *Data-base management systems* are programs for handling integrated files.

The control function is performed by the operating systems and by some utilities. This section groups the controls into five areas: handling errors, program protection, file protection, security protection, and self-protection. Our discussion covers both the specific controls built into the software and the operational controls required to ensure that the systems software functions as intended and is not subverted in some way to unauthorized use. A controls and systems complexity cross-reference relates the need for controls to the complexity of the computer system. The section ends with a summary of procedures to obtain an understanding of the internal control structure and tests of controls.

Handling Errors

The operating system provides detective and corrective capabilities for processing errors caused by hardware and software problems. This capability is shared with the hardware. The division of responsibility for handling errors between the hardware and the software will depend on the specific operating system and hardware. Typical operating systems error-handling abilities, however, include the following.

Read or Write Error Routines. The operating system reacts to a read or write error in several different ways. The particular reaction of the operating system will depend on the type of read or write error. If the error is an unsuccessful read by a storage device such as a magnetic tape drive, the operating system will attempt to reread the record ("automatic retry"). If this second read is unsuccessful, the system will respond according to the seriousness of the error. Where the problem is with a specific record, the problem record may be written onto an error file. In the case of a faulty medium such as damaged tape, the system will interrupt the processing of the program until the operator has investigated and corrected the problem. The operating system will store all data necessary for a successful restart of processing once the problem is resolved. A serious error, such as an attempt by an application program to access an unauthorized section of memory, could cause a halt in processing.

Record Length Checks. Some operating systems check to ensure that data read into the computer from magnetic tape or disk are of the correct length. This check prevents such errors as blocks of records being too long for the memory buffer storage area.

Storage Device Checks. An error condition will be signaled when an application program attempts to use a storage device that is not operational.

Program Protection

The purpose of program protection is to prevent application programs from interfering with each other during processing and to ensure that there are no errors in the referencing of subroutines in the program library, and no unauthorized changes made to application programs. The following controls provide program protection.

Boundary Protection. The operating system can partition the memory into sections. Each application program or set of programs will be assigned a particular memory partition. This means that several programs can be processed simultaneously in a multiprogramming environment without interfering with each other. The operating system monitors the partitions to ensure that no program coding or data are moved into the wrong partition.

Control over External References. Rather than include all necessary instructions in an application program, many programs simply reference other programs, or subroutines, that may be available in the program library. A program for calculating capitalized lease values, for example, might reference a present-value subroutine. When a program makes a reference to a subroutine, it is the operating system that calls the subroutine in from the library and makes it available to the program. This process is known as *linkage editing.* Linkage editing poses two risks to the auditor: the fraudulent use of subroutines and the fraudulent suppression of subroutines that should be used. In the first case, an application program might use a job-control statement requesting the use of an unauthorized subroutine that performs an illegal task. In the second case, the program might use a job-control statement that suppresses the use of a required subroutine. The suppressed subroutine could be, for example, a control procedure or audit function.

These risks can be controlled in the following ways:

- An error message is displayed or other action taken when reference is made to an unauthorized subroutine, or when an external reference is unresolved.
- The operating system can maintain a log of library program usage.
- The linkage editor of the operating system can maintain a processing history of each program, including a list of control statements used. This represents control information that can be reviewed for the use of "dangerous" job-control statements.

Library Program Software. Control over application program libraries is provided by the operating system or by separate library program software. The *operating system* usually includes basic library functions such as setting up and maintaining program libraries, creating and maintaining library directories to locate programs, and controlling external references. *Library program software* provides additional controls over the use and change of programs. These controls may include the restriction of access to use and change of programs, the generation of control reports, and the maintenance of control information. In some cases, the library program software includes all of these controls; in other cases, the controls are not available from a particular vendor or on a particular computer. Even if the controls are available, the purchaser of the software may choose not to implement one or more of the control features. Consequently, the auditor should review the library controls that are available and identify the control options that have been implemented.

Library program software can prevent unauthorized changes to software by restricting access to the application programs as well as to the library software itself. Restriction of access to application programs stems from the use of passwords or the encryption of programs in storage. *Passwords* restrict access to programs to authorized individuals, departments, or terminals. *Encryption* is a method of secret coding that prevents understanding of the program without a necessary key.

Restriction of access to the library program software is accomplished by the use of passwords. The passwords limit a programmer's use of the library software to those commands that are necessary to make the authorized changes. A programmer may be assigned a password, for example, that permits him or her to make changes only to programs with a "test" status.

Library program software helps detect unauthorized program changes by the preparation of management control reports. These control reports show what the programmer has changed and how the program has been changed. They facilitate review of authorized changes made and provide assurance that unauthorized changes have not been performed. Examples of library software control reports include a program listing, a source statement change summary, a source code listing, and a program listing by programmer.

The *Program Listing* report identifies the version of each program used in production. It lists the program run date, the date last copied, and the date last changed. This report can be reviewed to ensure that the current authorized version of each program is used.

The *Source Statement Change Summary* identifies the changes made during the most recent time period. The report itemizes all the source statements that have been added, changed, copied, or deleted. It provides a description of the change, including the new and old source statement.

The *Source Code Listing* identifies all the source statements in each program. Attached to each source statement is the date it was created or last changed or copied. A count of source statements for each program provides a quick check for additions or deletions of statements.

A *Program Listing by Programmer* identifies all the programs assigned to a specific programmer. The report lists the current status of the program, and dates of changes or other programmer activity. Review of the report provides a useful control over the programmer's work.

Control over System Modification Programs.   Certain utility programs can be used to suppress or modify application program coding. The use of these programs must be carefully controlled. A good example of a utility of this kind is IBM's SUPERZAP. This program is capable of making unauthorized modifications of programs or data without leaving a trace. Control over utility programs should include the following:

- Identify high-risk utilities.
- Place high-risk utilities in a restricted library.
- Use passwrod protection for the restricted library.
- The operating system or librarian should maintain a record of all usage of the restricted utilities, including information on the person who authorized its use, and the reason for its use.
- Exercise close supervision of computer operators.
- Review the output produced by the utility programs.

File Protection

The purpose of file protection is to prevent the unauthorized use or modification of data. File protection applies to data stored in memory and in peripheral storage devices. Controls that protect the files include the following.

Checking Internal File Labels.   The operating system can check internal file labels to prevent the processing of a wrong file, prevent premature data destruction, prevent unauthorized access and use, and ensure that all data are processed.[1] A wrong file could be processed if the librarian or operator error causes the wrong file to be mounted. Processing will be prevented, however, where the operating system compares the identifying information in the file's header label with the program reference. Header label information will include the file number, name, creation data, owner, and password. If the header label also includes the file retention date—the earliest date for file update or destruction—the operating

---

[1]Checking of internal file labels can be performed by the operating system or by individual application programs.

system can check to ensure that data are not being prematurely modified or destroyed. The header label may also include information on who is authorized to use the file, and how each user may use the file. Some users may be able to read and update the file, others may only be able to read the file. The file trailer label is used to ensure that all data in the file are processed. The operating system may check trailer information including the block count, record count, and end-of-file or end-of-reel code.

Storage Protection.   Data that are moved into memory are protected from inadvertent overwriting or modification by storage assignment and boundary protection. (See discussion under "Program Protection.")

Memory Clear.   The operating system can automatically clear memory of data after processing is complete. This removes the risk of sensitive data being available for subsequent access by other programs.

Address Compare.   The operating system can compare a data address in memory with the address in memory that is referenced by a peripheral device such as a disk. If the addresses are not identical, an error condition occurs.

Security Protection

A potential source of error in a computer system is the use of the system by an unauthorized party. Systems software plays a major role in controlling this error by either preventing or detecting unauthorized system penetration. The following controls provide this capability.

Maintenance of Logs and Activity Information.   The operating system can create a log of system users and provide a record of system activity. The activity information permits verification that all use of files and programs is authorized, and it also permits detection of attempts at unauthorized access of the system, files, or programs.

Log and Activity Analysis Utilities.   Utility programs that are available to management and the auditors can be used to analyze log and activity data to detect unauthorized usage or changes to files or programs.

Password Monitoring.   Some systems use passwords to control access to the system. The operating system can process each password to ensure that access to the computer system, programs, and files is authorized.

Self-Protection

Systems software can be a powerful source of control. The same capabilities that increase control, however, can also be used to defeat control. The very power of the software, and its pervasive influence, make the system very vulnerable to unauthorized use and modification of the software. Self-protection, therefore, is a crucial element of systems software control. The following controls will help protect the systems software.

Control over Installation and Changes.   The acquisition or modification of systems software should be subject to the same systems development and documentation controls that apply to application programs. Controls that are of particular importance include participation in the acquisition, development, and modification of systems software by internal audit; testing of the systems software prior to implementation; and management and EDP review and approval during and upon completion of the development process.

Segregation of Duties.   The risk of unauthorized modification can be reduced by restricting the number of staff who can make changes to systems software and removing them from the responsibilities for application systems operations, the EDP control function, and the library. The dedication of staff to systems software makes it difficult for them to gain a knowledge of the business. Without such knowledge, any tampering with the operating system would probably be caught by application program controls.

Log of Systems Software Changes.   The log and activity information generated by the operating system provides a listing of modifications to the systems software.

Utility Scan.   Some utility programs can scan the operating system for unauthorized changes. These utility programs maintain a hash count of the binary digits in the operating system programs. Any change in the hash count will signal a change in the operating system.

Control over System Modification Program.   Utilities such as SUPER-ZAP are just as dangerous in their ability to modify the operating system without trace as they are with application programs. (See discussion under "Program Protection.")

Privileged Mode.   Some computer systems have two classes of instruction: privileged and nonprivileged. *Privileged instructions* are those used exclusively by the operating system. *Nonprivileged instructions* can be used by either the operating system or the application programs. Without the privileged instructions, application programs cannot perform sensitive operating system tasks. The operating system should always operate in privileged mode to restrict its use to authorized purposes and to limit the possibility of unauthorized modification of operating system functions. An example of what should be a privileged operation is error handling relating to input/output devices and processing. If error handling were a nonprivileged operation, it might be possible for an application program to modify or suppress the operating system's response to an error condition.

Hardwiring. The ultimate solution to the risk of modification of software is to encode the software logic in hardware. This encoding is known as *hardwiring*. Hardwiring has the effect of representing logic in a form that cannot be modified by programming. Modification can only be accomplished by removal and replacement of the hardwiring.

Controls and System Complexity Cross-Reference

Not all computer systems require a full complement of systems software controls. The required controls are a function of the technological complexity of the particular computer system. Systems software plays a limited role in a simple batch input, batch processing, and off-line file environment. In this environment, the control objective of the systems software is limited to detection and correction of errors. As the complexity of the system increases, however, the control objective of the systems software expands. Each incremental increase in system complexity is matched by an additional (and cumulative) control objective. Each additional control objective requires an additional array of controls. This relationship between system complexity, control objective, and system software controls is summarized in Table 7–5.

Understanding and Tests of Controls

An understanding of systems software should be an important part of the auditor's assessment of control risk because of its pervasive influence on system reliability and accuracy. If the auditors do plan to assess a low level of risk on systems software controls as a general control, they should include the following kinds of procedures to obtain an understanding of the internal control structure and tests of controls in their examination:

1. Inquire of management regarding the extent and source of systems software, including operating systems and utilities.

Table 7-5. System Software Controls and System Complexity Cross-Reference

System Complexity	Additional (Cumulative) Control Objective	System Software Controls				
		Handling Errors	Self-Protection	File Protection	Program Protection	Security Protection
Batch input and processing, off-line files	Detection and correction of input/output and processing errors	X				
Batch input and processing, on-line files	Operating system must protect itself and files from programs	X	X	X		
Batch input and processing, on-line files, multi-programming	Keep programs from interfering with each other	X	X	X	X	
On-line input, batch processing, on-line files, multiprogramming	Protect against unauthorized terminal use	X	X	X	X	X
On-line input, on-line files, real-time processing	None	X	X	X	X	X

255

2. Review literature on vendor software, and in-house documentation for additions and changes performed by systems personnel, for controls that are available.
3. Inquire of management regarding the software controls actually used.
4. If certain controls are not used, discuss with management the impact of nonuse of internal controls.
5. Review the list of controls that are utilized to determine whether they match the control objective appropriate for the type and complexity of computer system.
6. Inquire regarding the adequacy of authorization and control over the implementation of, and changes to, systems software.
7. Inquire regarding the segregation of duties of system software development and maintenance personnel.
8. Review documentation to ensure that procedures for control over changes to systems software, including segregation of duties, are being followed.
9. Review the results of preimplementation testing of systems software.
10. Inquire regarding controls over the use of system modification utilities.
11. Review computer utilization logs and activity reports for unauthorized usage and changes to systems software.
12. Utilize technical help to evaluate the effectiveness of systems software controls.

SUMMARY

Various standards are involved in the general controls relating to the use and operation of equipment and systems software. Where this control is effective, the computer system creates an operating environment that is reliable and accurate. The auditors, therefore, can be reasonably certain that the computer system will not be a cause of inaccurate application processing.

Hardware controls are controls provided by the manufacturer of the hardware and include redundant character checks, duplicate process checks, equipment checks, and validity checks. *Systems software controls* are controls built into system-level programs, such as the operating system and system utilities. Systems software controls provide error-handling capabilities, protect application programs during processing, protect data files from unauthorized use or modification, restrict unauthorized use of the system, and protect the systems software itself from unauthorized use of modification.

The auditor should understand and test the existence and effectiveness of hardware and systems software controls. The existence of these controls depends not only on their availability but also on whether a data processing department chooses to implement the available controls. The effectiveness of these controls is influenced by the use of proper procedures such as regular routine maintenance, and operator and application program response to error conditions.

APPENDIX

Lava Butte, Inc.: Hardware and Systems Software Controls Questionnaire

Are the general controls over hardware and systems software sufficient to ensure that errors are detected, and that programs, files, equipment, and systems software are used only as authorized?

Yes _____ No _____✔_____

In assessing hardware and systems software controls, the auditor should consider the following:	Contributes to Possible Reduction in Control Risk		Comments
	Yes	No	
—The utilization of automatic hardware error detection and correction:			
a. Redundant character check	✓		Reviewed vendor literature and installation systems documentation
b. Duplicate process check	✓		
c. Echo check	✓		
d. Equipment check	✓		
e. Validity check	✓		
—Operational controls to ensure the effectiveness of hardware controls:			
a. Controls over storage and output media	✓		Tape quality reviewed on a regular basis. Equipment failure log completed, but no report and no review.
b. Equipment failure logs and reports		✓	

In assessing hardware and systems software controls, the auditor should consider the following:	Contributes to Possible Reduction in Control Risk		Comments
	Yes	No	
c. Environmental controls	✓		*Temperature and humidity logs reviewed daily by operations manager. Has alternator regulator, but no provision for power interruptions. Recovery is informal and spontaneous.*
d. Power protection	✓		
e. Formal recovery procedure		✓	
f. Operator procedures	✓		
g. Program interrogation	*see Comment*	*	
h. Preventive maintenance	✓		
i. Field replacement of defective parts	✓		** Inventory programs fail to interrogate error conditions.*
— The operating system has error handling capabilities:			
a. Read or write error routines	✓		*Used for magnetic tape drive and printer*
b. Record length checks	✓		*Used for magnetic tape and disk*
c. Storage device checks	✓		*used for magnetic tape drive and disk drive*
— The operating system prevents programs from interfering with each other:			
a. Boundary protection	✓		*Reviewed vendor operating system literature and installation documentation*
b. Control over external references	✓		
c. Library program software	✓		
d. Control over system modification programs	N/A		
— The operating system protects data from unauthorized use or modification:			
a. Checks internal file labels	✓		
b. Storage protection	✓		

In assessing hardware and systems software controls, the auditor should consider the following:	Contributes to Possible Reduction in Control Risk		Comments
	Yes	No	
c. Memory clear	✓		
d. Address compare	✓		
— Protection of files, programs, and equipment from unauthorized use:			
a. Activity log	✓		Created automatically by the operating system.
b. Activity analysis		✓	Activity log is not reviewed on a regular basis.
c. Password monitoring		✓	No password required for terminal use.
— Protection of systems software from unauthorized use:			
a. Control over development and maintenance of systems software including			
— internal audit participation		✓	No internal audit department
— technical staff review and approval		✓	
— management review and approval		✓	IBM operating system is modified by Systems Manager. No review and approval of either the original operating system or modification.
— testing prior to implementation	✓		
— final approval by management, EDP, and internal audit prior to implementation		✓	
b. Segregation of systems software development and maintenance responsibilities		✓	
c. Utility for operating system scan		✓	
d. Use of privileged operation mode		✓	
e. Hardwiring		✓	

REVIEW QUESTIONS

7-1. What is the purpose of hardware and systems software controls?

7-2. What are the two types of equipment failure?

7-3. What are the causes of mechanical failure?

7-4. Describe the causes of error in the communication of data from remote locations.

7-5. Contrast the principles of redundancy and validity, as used in hardware controls.

7-6. What are the three types of redundant character check? How do they differ from each other?

7-7. Why might a parity error not be discovered by a redundant character check?

7-8. Describe the kinds of invalid actions that can be detected by a validity check. What kinds of errors will not be detected by the validity check?

7-9. What kind of a control is the dual read? How does it work?

7-10. Explain how the hardware control of automatic retry works.

7-11. What is the impact of weak operational controls on the effectiveness of hardware controls?

7-12. Explain how linkage editing creates a risk of error. How can this risk be controlled?

7-13. Why are system modification utilities so dangerous? What can be done to reduce the danger?

7-14. Explain how a header label can be used for control purposes.

7-15. Why is it important that the operating system protect itself?

7-16. What is the advantage of running the operating system in privileged mode?

7-17. What impact might weakness in hardware and systems software controls have on application controls?

OBJECTIVE QUESTIONS

7-18. In multiprogramming computer operations, several programs may be in memory at one time. The intermixing or overlapping of data is prevented by the use of
  a. Boundary protection
  b. Internal file labels
  c. Control over external references
  d. Address validity checks

7-19. A magnetic tape header label is used to warn the operator that
  a. The next processing step is about to begin
  b. A wrong input tape has been mounted

    c. An incorrect number of records have been processed

    d. A different type of input or output device must be used (*AICPA*)

7–20. If a trailer label is used on a magnetic tape file, it is the last record and summarizes the file. Which of the following is information not typically found on a trailer label?

    a. Record count

    b. Identification number

    c. Control totals for one or more fields

    d. End-of-file or end-of-reel code (*AICPA*)

7–21. Automated equipment controls in an electronic data processing system are designed to detect errors arising from

    a. Operation of the electronic data processing equipment

    b. Lack of human alertness

    c. Incorrect input and output data

    d. Poor management of the electronic data processing installation (*AICPA*)

7–22. A control feature in an electronic data processing system requires the CPU to send signals to the printer to activate the print mechanism for each character. The print mechanism, just prior to printing, sends a signal back to the CPU verifying that the proper print position has been activated. This type of hardware control is referred to as

    a. Echo check

    b. Validity check

    c. Signal check

    d. Dual transmission (*AICPA adapted*)

7–23. Echo checks and dual heads are both control devices. The major advantage of dual heads over echo checks is that

    a. The cost is less

    b. They require less time

    c. They check the recorded information

    d. They check record length for overflow of data (*AICPA adapted*)

7–24. Parity checks, read-after-write checks, and duplicate circuitry are electronic data processing controls that are designed to detect

    a. Erroneous internal handling of data

    b. Lack of sufficient documentation for computer processes

    c. Invalid programming commands

    d. Unauthorized use of memory partitions (*AICPA adapted*)

7–25. System modification utilities pose a danger of unauthorized use or modification of systems and application software. This danger can be reduced by

    a. Internal file labels

    b. A utility usage log

    c. A utility scan

    d. Hardwiring

CASES AND EXERCISES

7-26. You are an internal auditor charged with the responsibility for reviewing hardware and systems software controls. You have had considerable experience in auditing EDP systems but limited technical expertise with respect to hardware and systems software. Consequently, you call in a technical specialist to assist you in completing the audit program. What are some procedures to obtain an understanding of the internal control structure and tests of controls that are likely to require the assistance of a technical specialist?

7-27. In completing the Internal Control Questionnaire for Lava Butte, Inc., you receive a "no" answer to your question on formal recovery procedures. You also discover that the hardware is protected from momentary fluctuations in voltage, amperage, or cycles, but has no facilities to protect against interruption of the power supply. What conclusions would you draw from this? How might this affect your assessment of control risk?

7-28. In reviewing the Internal Control Questionnaire for Lava Butte, you notice that the inventory programs fail to interrogate for error conditions signaled by either the hardware or the systems software. What is the likely impact, if any, on the reliability of the inventory programs?

7-29. According to the response to your Internal Control Questionnaire, Lava Butte has a computer activity log prepared automatically by the operating system. What advantage does this control provide? To what extent is this advantage offset by the failure to either review the log on a regular basis or prepare an activity analysis report?

7-30. Lava Butte, Inc., uses IBM Operating System programs. During completion of the Internal Control Questionnaire, you discover that the Operating System programs were chosen by the systems manager without the review and approval of management. Subsequent to installation, you find that the operating system has been modified several times by the systems manager. None of these modifications have been subject to management review and approval. The systems manager is responsible for both systems programs and application programs. In addition, he has recently taken accounting classes at Bend Community College. He also used to work in the inventory control department of Lava Butte before transferring to data processing several years ago. Comment.

7-31 Responses to the Internal Control Questionnaire indicate that Lava Butte does not use a utility program for scanning the operating system. In addition, it does not specify a privileged mode for the operating system. How do these omissions affect your response to Case 7-30?

7-32. Based on the responses to the Internal Control Questionnaire, Lava Butte prepares a log of equipment failure, performs regular routine maintenance, and permits IBM to make field replacements of defective parts. It does not, however, prepare an equipment failure report from the log, nor is the log reviewed by management. Comment.

7-33. Equipment checks are important hardware controls. Describe the two functions of equipment checks, and explain how they work in the CPU and with magnetic tape. Why are equipment checks useful for typical CPU or tape problems?

7–34. Hardware is usually reliable, and systems software is usually well developed and standardized. Why then does the hardware and systems software pose a danger of creating or permitting undetected errors?

7–35. How much time should the auditors allocate to obtaining an understanding of hardware and systems software controls relative to that of other general controls?

7–36. The audit senior who completed the Internal Control Questionnaire for Lava Butte gave a "no" rating to the hardware and systems software controls. This says that he is unwilling to rely on these controls as assurance of error detection and control over unauthorized use of EDP resources. Based on the responses to the questions, is this a fair evaluation? What effect might it have on the audit program?

7–37. Robin Hood and Little John were application programmers with the Nottingham Corporation. Mr. Sheriff, the data processing manager, called them into his office one day and gave them temporary assignments to perform maintenance work on the operating system. This was necessary, he said, because the systems programmer had just quit without giving notice. Mr. Sheriff gave Hood and John copies of the operating system manual to enable them to perform their new duties. The manual contained all the documentation on the system, including the list of secret passwords. One of the passwords provided was the one that overrode the normal privileged mode of the operating system and permitted changes to be made to the system programs.

Hood and John used the special password to make a scheduled change to the operating system. The documentation of the change was printed automatically as usual. The documentation did not, however, include an unauthorized insert that Hood and John had included with the change. The insert permitted Hood and John to suppress system audit trail information. In particular, it ensured that any unauthorized interference in the system would not be recorded on the console log, and it suppressed the printing of unauthorized changes to the operating system.

Hood and John used the insert to display the application files on a terminal and to make subsequently selective changes to these files. The use of computer time for these purposes was not included on the console log. Nor was there any record of the use of the terminal. Hood and John continued to make changes to the files for several months even though all passwords were changed at the end of each month. The fraud was discovered accidentally when a new systems programmer noticed some unfamiliar coding while performing routine system maintenance.

The technique used by Hood and John to penetrate the operating system is known as a "trojan horse" technique. The insert they placed in the operating system is known as a "trap door." What controls would have prevented the "trap door" from being inserted or would have reduced the time period during which it was used successfully?

Chapter 8
SYSTEM SECURITY CONTROLS

Learning Objectives

After completing this chapter, the reader should be able to:

1. Identify the security hazards that are present in a computerized system.

2. Understand the principal objective of system security controls.

3. Understand how weakness in system security controls can endanger assets and data.

4. Determine how the loss of assets and data can be minimized after a system security failure.

The reliability of accounting systems, accuracy of accounting information, and safety of corporate assets are all dependent on adequate system security controls. Weakness in system security controls can result in unauthorized processing of transactions, inaccurate reports and data records, loss of assets, loss of vital data, and disclosure of sensitive information such as trade secrets. System security controls are crucial because of the vulnerability of modern computer systems to destruction, error, and abuse.

System security is the protection of computer facilities, equipment, programs, and data from destruction by environmental hazards, by equipment, software, or human error, or by computer abuse. *Environmental hazards* include fires, floods, tornadoes, earthquakes, and other natural disasters. They generally occur infrequently but with a high cost per occurrence. *Errors* include damage to disk packs by faulty disk drives, mistakes in application programs that destroy or damage data, and operator mounting of incorrect files. Errors such as these occur frequently but usually at a low cost per incident. *Computer abuse* is the violation of a computer system to perform malicious damage, crime, or invasion of privacy. *Malicious damage* includes looting and sabotage. *Crime* includes embezzlement, industrial espionage, and the sale of commercial secrets. *Invasion of privacy* includes discovery of confidential salary information, and the review of sensitive data by a competing company. The frequency of occurrence of computer abuse is difficult to determine, and the cost per incident can vary widely.

System security controls are general controls that prevent failures in system security, detect failures in system security, and provide for recovery from failures in system security. The prevention of failures in system security is provided by limiting access to the equipment, programs, and data and by taking other steps to reduce the likelihood of security failures. Unfortunately, it would be prohibitively expensive to eliminate entirely the risk of system security failures. Good system security controls, therefore, not only include provisions for the detection of failures in security should they occur but also include procedures to minimize the impact of security failures.

In this chapter we discuss (1) the audit significance of system security controls, (2) controls that provide a secure system, (3) controls that detect failures in system security, and (4) controls for recovery from system security failures. The Appendix contains an internal controls questionnaire for Lava Butte, Inc.

AUDIT SIGNIFICANCE
OF SYSTEM SECURITY CONTROLS

There are several reasons why system security controls are important. These reasons include the impact of system security controls on other general controls, the vulnerability of computer systems to loss of assets, the impact of security failures on data reliability, the possibility of lack of compliance with legal requirements, the possibility of a loss contingency if data processing security risks are severe and uninsured, and the vulnerability of computer systems to unauthorized use.

The adequacy of many of the general controls discussed in the preceding three chapters is dependent on system security controls. The segregation of duties in the data processing department, for example, will have little effect if programmers have unrestricted access to the computer room. Hardware controls may be rendered ineffective in the absence of environmental controls over temperature and humidity. Systems software controls can be neutralized if the systems software is not secure from unauthorized use or changes.

Inadequate system security controls increase the opportunity for unauthorized changes to application programs and data files and make the system vulnerable to the loss of assets. The centralization of accounting systems within the computer makes it easy for a programmer to make changes that can result in a loss of assets. A bank programmer, for example, could insert a program instruction to "round down" all calculations of interest and to deposit the resulting difference in his or her own account. It would be easy for the programmer to remove all evidence of the program change by simply returning the program to its original condition. In effect, the programmer would have made a temporary change in the electronic representation of the program in the computer. There would be no permanent or documentary evidence of the change in the program. Anyone who is able to make such changes has effective control over company assets.

Attempts to divert company assets to unauthorized purposes may fail but may still affect data reliability. The attempt to penetrate the system may change processing logic or may create erroneous or invalid file data. Data reliability may deteriorate rapidly if these changes are not discovered promptly. The deterioration of data reliability may result in loss of assets, affect the fairness of the financial statements, affect operating efficiency, and require considerable effort to restore the system to its authorized state.

System security controls are required to ensure compliance with legal requirements and to avoid the possibility of a loss contingency. A data retention and recovery plan is necessary to meet the audit trail requirements of the Internal Revenue Service. In addition, system security controls are probably included within the scope of the 1977 Foreign and Corrupt Practices Act. Failure to provide adequate system security controls could place a company in violation of the act's requirements for an adequate system of internal control. Finally, failure to provide system security controls exposes the system to the risk of asset or data loss. If the potential loss is material and the risk is uninsured, there may be a loss contingency that requires financial statement disclosure.

Computer systems are vulnerable to unauthorized use. It is impossible to safeguard a computer system simply by restricting physical access to programs, data, and equipment. The use of on-line terminals and data communication provides opportunities for unauthorized access to a computer system by persons who need never step inside the computer room. A person with access to a remote terminal or telephone, for example, could gain access to programs or data if he or she had the necessary passwords and codes. Access to data could also be accomplished by wiretapping when data are transmitted via telephone lines. These threats can only be dealt with by the use of passwords, coding of data, system monitoring, and other system security controls.

For all of these reasons, the auditor should understand and test system security controls. Weak system security controls may make it impossible to assess control risk at a low level on application controls and may require the auditor to increase substantive testing.

CONTROLS THAT PROVIDE A SECURE SYSTEM

A major objective of system security controls is to reduce the likelihood of system security failures. In this section we discuss those controls that help accomplish this objective: security management, facilities security controls, library controls, and on-line access controls. The section ends with a summary of procedures to obtain an understanding of the internal control structure and tests of controls.

Security Management

A system's vulnerability to disaster, error, or abuse is more likely to be reduced by deliberate management planning and control of system security than by the random selection of individual controls. Planning system security ensures that the controls will provide the maximum security benefit. Management control over system security increases the likelihood that controls will work in the event of a failure in system security. Security management planning and control should include the following steps.

1. *Establish security objectives.* Management should establish the overall objectives for system security. These objectives provide the standards against which actual system security can be judged. A typical objective would be "to protect computer equipment, facilities, programs, and data from the hazards of hurricanes, tornadoes, earthquakes, fire, rising water, vandalism, riot, or war."

2. *Evaluate security risks.* Management should evaluate data processing security risks for likelihood and cost of occurrence. Some security failures, such as floods or earthquakes, will have a low probability of occurrence and a high cost per occurrence. Other security failures, such as damage to tapes or disks because of human carelessness, will occur more frequently but at a low cost per incident. Management should estimate probabilities and costs associated with each possible security failure. Computed expected values of loss can then be used as guides to the choice of system security controls. A fire in the computer center, for example, may be estimated to cause $500,000 damage. If the likelihood of a fire occurring during a given year is .008, the expected annual loss from fire is $500,000 × .008, or $4,000. This expected annual loss can then be compared with the cost of system security controls that reduce the risk of fire.

3. *Develop a security plan.* Management should develop a plan that will provide an acceptable level of security at a reasonable cost. The plan should describe all controls and identify the purpose of their inclusion in the plan. The plan should be reviewed and approved prior to implementation.

4. *Assign responsibilities.* Management should assign responsibilities for system security. The responsibilities should include implementation of the plan and monitoring of system security on an ongoing basis.

5. *Test system security.* System security controls should be tested by management to determine whether they prevent or detect security failures, or provide recovery from security failures as intended. Testing provides assurance that responsibilities are fully assigned, procedures are understood and followed, and control devices function properly.

6. *Evaluate system security.* The results of testing system security controls should be used to evaluate the effectiveness of controls in meeting system security objectives.

Facilities Security Controls

Facilities security controls are designed to protect computer buildings and equipment from physical damage. Physical damage can disrupt processing and cause damage to or loss of vital data, programs, and documentation. Controls that prevent such damage are location controls, construction controls, and access controls.

Location Controls. Whenever possible, the computer center location should be remote from environmental, technological, and social hazards. The risk of damage from earthquake and flood can be reduced by avoiding such areas as the San Andreas fault or a known flood plain. The risk of damage from accidents can be reduced by locating away from airports and heavy traffic. The risk of damage from social disruption can be reduced by avoiding decaying urban areas and highly visible locations. Although location is a major factor in reducing these hazards, some companies may have little flexibility because of prior location decisions. Their administrative offices may be located in a known earthquake area, for example, and it may not be practical to locate the computer center elsewhere.

Construction Controls. Proper construction of the computer facilities can reduce the risk of damage from security or environmental hazards. Proper construction requires physical isolation of the computer facilities, the use of construction standards, and compliance with fire and water standards.

Isolation can be accomplished by construction of a separate building for the computer center or by location in a secure part of the building. A separate building can provide three levels of security: an outer wall or perimeter, the building itself, and the innermost areas containing the equipment and files. Each level provides an opportunity to restrict unauthorized access. If it is not feasible to dedicate an entire building to the computer center, the computer facilities should be located in a secure part of a building, such as the center, the basement, or the top floor. They should also be located away from such hazards as the kitchen and heating plant.

Security risks can be reduced by adequate construction standards. The walls and doors of the computer facilities should be strong, and windows should be avoided where possible. If an interior window is provided for visitor viewing of the computer facilities, the window should contain bulletproof glass. Safes and vaults should be used for storage of files and documentation. Power and communication lines leading into the building and into the computer facilities should be adequately protected. Building design should avoid security weaknesses such as uncontrolled air-conditioning vents, storm drains, utility tunnels, and other possible sources of entry.

The risk of environmental damage can be reduced by the use of fire and water standards. Construction standards for fire include the use of fire-resistant walls, floors, ceilings, and doors. Common or exterior walls should have at least a one-hour fire rating. Vaults and safes should have two- to four-hour fire ratings. Air-conditioning and heating ducts should have fire dampers. Sprinkler or flooding systems can minimize fire damage but may create other problems. Sprinkler systems may cause water damage to equipment. This damage can be reduced by the use of sprinkler systems that automatically shut down power to computer equipment and provide time for operator intervention. A short delay would permit the operator to take alternative action or to place waterproof covers over the equipment. Carbon dioxide flooding systems avoid water damage from sprinklers, but the gas may be dangerous to data processing personnel. Halon gas fire extinguishment poses the least risk of environmental damage. It avoids water damage, and there is little danger to personnel if they are evacuated promptly.

Water damage from sprinklers or floods can be minimized by the installation of pumps and drains. Watertight floors in the computer room will help keep out water from floods or from other parts of the building.

Access Controls. Control over access to the computer facilities is necessary to prevent unauthorized access, and to enforce segregation of duties by excluding systems and programming staff from the computer room and the library. Access should be controlled at the building perimeter, upon entry to the building, and upon entry to the computer facilities. The building perimeter provides the first line of defense against unauthorized access. A wall or fence can limit access to the building. Security patrols can enforce perimeter security. Access to the building can be restricted by locked doors and windows, by electronic detectors, and by the use of guards.

Access to the computer facilities can be restricted by various security procedures and devices. Company procedures should identify those personnel that are permitted access to each area of the computer facilities. Access to the storage room, for example, should be restricted to library personnel. All persons entering or leaving the computer facilities should be required to sign a register showing their name, purpose, and duration of visit. Authorized personnel should be required to wear badges that are checked by guards to the computer facilities.

Security devices that restrict access to the computer room require a locked door and a "key" that unlocks the door to authorized personnel only. The "key" may take such forms as the following:

- Conventional keys that are issued to authorized personnel.
- Magnetic-stripe cards that have an electronically encoded key that will unlock the door when the card is entered into an access control device. The key can be encoded to restrict individual access to certain areas of the computer facilities, and to certain times of the day or week.
- Physical characteristics can be used to control access. There are devices, for example, that read hand geometry. When an individual enters an identification card, he or she activates a reader that measures the length of his or her fingers. The reading is then compared with the same characteristic on file.

If the two readings are the same, the door is unlocked. Similar systems use voiceprints, thumbprints, and other physical characteristics.

- Signature verification systems measure the time required to complete the signature and the pressure applied to the pen. If these two factors match information kept on file, then the door is unlocked.

Security can be enhanced by combining two or more of these access devices. A signature verification system, for example, could be used in combination with a magnetic-stripe card. This reduces the risk of error and the risk from lost cards.

Library Controls

Systems security controls should include library controls to restrict access to data files, computer programs, and documentation. These controls are crucial because unrestricted access to data, programs, and documentation provides access to company assets. Library controls are provided by a librarian function and by physical safeguards over file usage. They are most effective when accompanied by program change controls, library software, and on-line access controls.

Library Function.   The library function provides a physical control over file usage and quality. It should be performed by a full-time librarian. If this is not possible in a small data processing department, an individual should be assigned to part-time librarian duties. This individual's remaining time should be assigned to compatible duties such as duties outside of data processing. Companies that operate their computer more than one shift per day should assign a librarian to each shift. If this is not possible, an acceptable alternative solution consists of having the librarian check out the files required for the second shift. He or she should assign control for these files to the second-shift supervisor. All other files should remain locked in the storage room and be unavailable until the librarian's return the following morning.

The librarian's duties will vary from one installation to another but should include the following.

- *Testing and Control of Files.*   The librarian should test each tape or disk upon receipt to ensure that it is not defective. He or she should assign a serial number to each file and establish a file record. The file record should document a history of usage, the status of the file (for example, that it can be written on), the number of times it has been cleaned, and its physical location. The file record can be used to help assess the physical quality of the tape or disk.

- *Storage of Files and Documentation.* The librarian is responsible for secure storage of program and data files and documentation. Files should be clearly labeled and indexed for easy retrieval.

- *Release of Files and Documentation.* The librarian should release files and documentation according to general or specific authorization. General authorization would require the librarian to issue files for processing at specific times in the processing cycle. The general ledger, for example, would be released once a month for update. Other releases of the general ledger would require specific authorization. Confidential files, such as executive payroll, would also require specific authorization for release.

- *Log Usage of Files and Documentation.* The librarian should maintain a usage log of files and documentation. This log represents a record of material released from the library, including the times of checkout and return, the person to whom the material is released, and the purpose for which it is being used.

- *Inventory of Files and Documentation.* The librarian should take a periodic inventory of the files and documentation. This physical inventory should be compared with the file and documentation records, and any discrepancies should be resolved.

Physical File Controls. Physical controls over file usage protect files from damage during handling. They include internal header and trailer labels, external file labels, file protection rings on tapes, and read-only switches on disk drives.

- *Internal Header and Trailer Labels.* These labels can be read by the system software to ensure that the correct file is being used for processing, that files are read in their entirety, and that no records have been lost or added.

- *External Labels.* These labels provide visible confirmation to the operator that the correct file is being used. They are attached to the outside casings of files and include identifying information such as the file name and date produced.

- *Protective Rings.* Magnetic tape files can be protected against premature erasure or overwriting by the use of protection rings. A protection ring is usually plastic, about four inches in diameter, and is inserted in a recess in the tape reel. When a tape reel is mounted on the tape drive, the ring depresses a switch that permits the tape drive to write on that tape. Writing is not possible, however, when the ring is absent. The control can be remembered as "no ring, no write."

• *Read-Only Switch.*   Some disk drives have a control that is equivalent to the protection ring for tapes; it is called the read-only switch. This switch permits the operator to turn off the writing capability of the disk drive. If this is done when using a disk that should not be modified, such as a disk containing a utility program, the chances of accidental erasure are reduced. A limitation of this control is that it cannot be used either with disk drives that hold more than one file or with files that can be both read from and written on.

On-Line Access Controls

Control over physical access to the computer room may provide security in a batch system, but it is insufficient in an on-line system. On-line systems use terminals that are usually located *outside* the computer room. Restriction of access to the computer room will not, therefore, restrict access to the system.

On-line access must be restricted in some other way. Physical access to the terminals should be restricted wherever possible. In addition, terminal, program, and data use should be controlled by authorization schemes that designate authorized users and uses of the system. Identification controls should be used to ensure that only authorized users can access the system for authorized purposes. Finally, data communication lines and equipment should be controlled to restrict opportunities for unauthorized access to the system during transmission of messages between the terminals and the computer.

Physical Security of Terminals.   Access to the terminals should be restricted by terminal room access controls and by the use of physical terminal locks. Access to the terminal room should be restricted in much the same way that access is restricted to the computer room. The door to the terminal room should be locked, with entry by key, card, badge, or some other identification method. In many systems, however, this may not be possible because the terminals are organizationally and physically dispersed throughout the company. Dispersion of the terminals to isolated locations makes it difficult or impossible to establish terminal room security, especially when terminals are located in open office areas. In such situations, access should be restricted by installation of physical terminal locks. Locks restrict use of the terminals to those who possess the appropriate key.

Authorization Controls. Even if the terminals are physically secured, this may not be sufficient to restrict access to the system. On-line systems typically provide access to multiple program and data files for large numbers of users. This multiplicity of uses and users creates the possibility of unauthorized use by authorized users. Certain salespersons, for example, could be given authority to use a terminal to inquire about inventory status and to enter sales transactions. They should not, however, be given authority to change the credit limits for individual customers. If they were to have this authority, they would be able to modify management's authorized credit policy to their own advantage.

What is required in an on-line system is a formal authorization scheme devised by the management. The purpose of the authorization scheme is to restrict access to the system to authorized terminals and to users who perform only authorized activities. The authorization scheme should be implemented using one of several available procedures.

- *Authorized Terminals.* The authorization scheme should prevent illicit terminals from accessing the system and should restrict each authorized terminal to programs and data files normally used by that terminal. The computer should have a list of all terminals that are authorized to access the system. An illicit or "private" terminal will not appear on this list and should be denied access to the system.

Each authorized terminal should be restricted to programs and data files consistent with its location and physical security. A terminal located in the payroll department, for example, should be restricted to payroll-related programs and files. It should not be possible to access an accounts receivable file from the payroll terminal. A terminal located in an unsecured area should not have access to confidential data files. It should not be possible, for example, to read executive payroll records from an unsecured terminal in the payroll department.

- *Authorized Users.* The authorization scheme should identify the programs and data files that each user is permitted to access. This access should be based on a user's functional responsibility and on his or her authority to read confidential data.

Functional responsibility is determined by the user's department and by the division of duties within a department. A clerk in the payroll department, for example, should perform only payroll functions and should perform only the specific payroll functions that relate to his or her job description. The clerk who enters hourly data from time cards should not be permitted to modify hourly wage rates. The clerk whose normal responsibility consists of completing payroll tax forms should not be authorized to modify payroll records for address or deduction changes. Failure to restrict these clerks to their authorized duties could result in the performance of incompatible duties. This in turn could lead to deliberate fraud or inadvertent error due to inadequate training.

A user should not be granted authority to read files, records within files, or fields within records that contain confidential data. Determination of whether data are confidential is based on department function, employee level, and data sensitivity. The manager of the payroll department, for example, should be able to read the records of all hourly employees and nonexecutive salaried employees. He or she should not be able to read the records of executives at the vice-presidential level and above because of the sensitivity of these data.

• *Implementation of the Authorization Scheme.* The authorization scheme should be implemented by the use of one of several procedures. The procedures formalize the authorization scheme and ensure the complete cross-referencing of terminals, users, programs, and data. Procedures for implementation include authorization tables and locks on data records.

• *Authorization tables* list the programs and data that each terminal and user is permitted to use, and they identify the activities each user is authorized to perform with each program and data set. The table is checked each time a user wishes to use a program or data, or perform an activity such as modify or delete data, or ensure that the user has proper authorization.
• *Locks on data records* are controls that indicate which terminal or user may read a record or field and for what purpose. The lock may be placed in the record as a separate field, in a separate table, or in the index used for addressing the record.

Identification Controls. To be effective, the authorization scheme must be enforced. This is accomplished by a method of identifying the terminal and the user so that access can be granted based on the authorization scheme.

Terminal identification ensures that the computer is linked to an authorized terminal. Without such a check, it might be possible for a pirate terminal to pose as an authorized system terminal. In some systems, terminal identification is provided in response to a request from the computer operating system. In other systems, it is sent automatically by the terminal when it comes on-line.

User identification can be accomplished by physiology, by a special "key," or by a password. The use of *physiology* or a *special "key"* to identify a terminal user is similar to computer facilities access devices discussed earlier in the chapter. Physiological characteristics include voiceprints, handprints, and thumbprints. Special "keys" include a key to unlock the terminal, a magnetic-stripe card, or an optically encoded badge.

An inexpensive method of user identification is the *password*, which is a code that permits a user to identify his or her authority. The code may be either simple or complex. Passwords are most effective when procedures are used to reduce the chance of discovery and use of the code.

Simple passwords are stored in a password file. A password is assigned to system resources and activities. Passwords are then released to the users according to the authorization scheme. The inclusion of the password in the job-control statements required to run a program gives the user access to specific programs and files, and authority to perform specific activities such as read, modify, add, or delete data.

Security can be improved by increasing the complexity of the code. Instead of a user's being assigned one password, for example, he or she may be assigned a list of passwords. Each time this individual uses the system, he or she will pick up one password from the list and then cross it off. Once the specific password has been used, it can never be used again. Another example is the use of a question-and-answer sequence. This requires a series of responses from the computer.

Passwords are most effective when used in conjunction with procedures to reduce the likelihood of discovery or use. Following are examples of such procedures:

- Passwords should not be chosen because they are easy to remember. The names and birthdays of terminal users, for example, are easy to remember and therefore ineffective.
- Terminal users should be discouraged from disclosing their passwords to other staff. Passwords should not, for example, be pinned to bulletin boards.
- Passwords should not be printed or displayed on the terminal where they may be seen by unauthorized users. Inhibition of printing or display of the password should be an automatic function and not dependent on the action of the terminal operator.
- The password file should be protected by the operating system from access by unauthorized users. Individual password security is of little value if the password file is open to perusal by system users.
- The operating system should monitor unsuccessful attempts to use a terminal. Repeated attempts could suggest that someone is trying random or deliberate code variations in order to identify a password.
- Password security will decrease over time if the codes are not changed periodically, in response to personnel changes, or because of security leaks. Periodically may mean changing the passwords by shift, daily, weekly, or monthly, depending on the security level of the password. Passwords should be changed when a password user is moved to a new position or leaves the organization. Any knowledge or suspicion of password disclosure should require immediate change of the password.
- Passwords are most effective when used in combination with some other identification technique. A requirement that a magnetic-stripe card be used in conjunction with a password, for example, would reduce the danger to

the system of password discovery. An unauthorized user would have to steal the card as well as discover the password.

Data Communication Access Control.   Control over access to terminals may not be effective in an on-line system unless access to the data communication system is also restricted. Many on-line systems have terminals located at considerable distance from the central computer requiring connection via data communication. The data communication system is vulnerable to unauthorized access via wiretapping. Controls that reduce the danger from wiretapping include fragmentation, intermixing, and encryption.

Fragmentation is the communication of a message one fragment at a time. The central computer, for example, might only accept one byte of the message in each communication with the terminal. To obtain an entire message, a wiretapper would have to intercept all the bytes that constitute a particular message.

Intercepting a message is difficult when fragmentation is used with message intermixing. *Message intermixing* is the communication of several messages simultaneously. A major savings and loan association, for example, transmits bytes from two or three branch terminals along a single telephone line to the central computer. A wiretapper would have difficulty identifying which bytes belonged to which message from which branch terminal.

Encryption of data provides an additional level of security over data transmission. *Encryption* of data is the encoding of data to disguise their meaning. The original data can only be discovered by the person or device that knows the key that decodes the data. The encryption system can be implemented using hardware or software and can be applied in a variety of data processing situations.

The encoding of data is accomplished by the use of an algorithm. An *algorithm* is one or more operations on the data that disguise their information content. The algorithm may alter the order of the characters in the data, replace certain characters in the data with their characters from a table, change the length of the data by adding or removing characters, or otherwise confuse the information content. A standard algorithm published by the National Bureau of Standards (NBS) provides reasonable security over the transmittal of data.[1]

The decoding of encoded data is accomplished by the use of a key. This key is the exact series of operations necessary to reverse the encoding and reveal the original data. Unlike the algorithm, which may be pub-

---

[1]Federal Information Processing Standards Publication 46, *Data Encryption Standard*, January 15, 1977.

lic property, the key should be known to as few people or devices as possible. The chances of the key being discovered by an unauthorized person will be reduced if the key is changed frequently.

Encryption requires that computers and terminals possess the logic for encoding and decoding. This can be accomplished by hardware or software. The use of hardware for encryption requires the location of a hardware device at each point in the communication network that sends or receives encoded data. In the past, these hardware devices have been bulky mechanical devices known as *cryptoboxes*. The modern solution is to build the logic circuitry on a large-scale integrated (LSI) chip. The use of software avoids the need for the special hardware devices but is generally slower than hardware and consumes more computer resources. Software is also easier to modify, and unauthorized modifications are more difficult to discover. In addition, the standard algorithm of the NBS is designed for use in hardware devices rather than software.

Coding of data has many applications in controlling access to data. Encoded data can be sent between computers and terminals, and from computer to computer. These data can be used to transmit individual messages or batches of transactions. In a financial system, for example, encoded data can be transmitted between automatic cash-dispensing machines and a central bank computer. These machines generally dispense cash to customers who identify themselves properly by the use of a secret number. If the secret number were not coded, it could be intercepted by a wiretapper. Knowledge of the secret number would provide the wiretapper with direct access to the bank's cash.

Understanding and Tests of Controls

If the auditors plan to assess risk at a low level on controls that provide a secure computer system, they should include the following procedures to obtain an understanding of the internal control structure and tests of controls in their examination:

1. Inquire of management regarding the utilization of facilities, library, and on-line systems security controls.
2. Review the master security plan to determine the adequacy and completeness of system security controls.
3. Review the results of tests of system security controls and examine management's evaluation of the test results.
4. Visit the computer facilities to ensure that access controls work and that construction and location are as indicated by management.
5. Visit the library to determine whether procedures effectively restrict access to data, programs, and documentation and safeguard files during use.
6. Visit computer terminal locations to ensure that access is effectively restricted.

7. Review the authorization scheme to determine whether authorization to gain access to the system is consistent with the segregation of duties and provides for the confidentiality of sensitive data.
8. Review the methods of identifying authorized users to determine whether only authorized users are able to use the system for authorized purposes.
9. Trace selected entries in the computer utilization log to the authorization table to determine whether only authorized users are permitted access to the system for authorized purposes.
10. Review the methods of data communication access control to ensure that access by wiretapping is a remote possibility.
11. Examine the internal auditors' reports on system security controls and review their conclusions on the adequacy of controls.
12. Examine the report of the company's insurer to determine his or her recommendations on system security.

CONTROLS FOR DETECTING FAILURES IN SYSTEM SECURITY

No system is sufficiently secure to prevent all breaches of security. Controls that provide a secure system do not create absolute security; instead they reduce the likelihood of security failures. The likelihood of security failures makes it necessary, therefore, to provide a second level of defense against disaster and unauthorized access. This second level is the *detection* of failures in system security. Detection controls provide an opportunity to minimize damage or loss from the security failure, and they trigger the timely use of controls that ensure recovery from any damage or loss. Detection controls include detection devices, authentication, and system monitoring. Application controls are also important in detecting security failures.

Detection Devices

Detection devices are electronic or mechanical devices that detect fire or unauthorized access. Their purpose is to provide an opportunity for intervention to minimize damage or loss.

Fire Detection Devices.   The purpose of installing fire detection devices is to alert personnel to take action to protect equipment and files and to put out the fire. Fire detection devices are heat-sensitive or smoke-sensitive. They should be located where they can provide maximum detection capability.

Heat-sensitive devices are usually fusable links built into the water nozzles of sprinkler systems. Their connection with the sprinkler system is a disadvantage because sprinkler systems can cause water damage to computer equipment and files. Also, the temperature required to trigger most heat-sensitive devices is well above that required to cause damage to equipment and files. Electrical equipment fires are usually localized and may not be detected until considerable damage has been done. Finally, enough heat may be dissipated by the air-conditioning system to delay detection of a fire.

Smoke-sensitive devices are able to detect electrical fires much more quickly than heat-sensitive devices. The greater sensitivity of smoke detectors, however, makes them more likely to give false alarms. Generally speaking, false alarms are preferable to fire damage as long as the smoke alarm is not connected to the sprinkler system. A smoke alarm should require operators to diagnose the problem and take whatever protective or corrective measures are necessary.

Fire detection devices should be located wherever a fire may occur, or wherever a fire may be detected quickly. These locations should include each area of the computer facilities, as well as air-conditioning ducts, areas above false ceilings, and areas below raised floors.

Unauthorized Access Detection Devices.   Restricting access to authorized personnel for authorized system uses is essential to enforce segregation of duties and to limit opportunities for unauthorized system changes. Access controls do not provide absolute protection from penetration, however, and should be supplemented by controls that detect unauthorized access and trigger appropriate action. These controls include the following:

- *Microswitches* are used to detect the presence of an intruder by breaking or completing an electrical circuit. A circuit may be broken by the opening of a window or an emergency door. A circuit may be closed by someone stepping on a pressure-sensitive switch located under a mat or a floor panel.
- *Beams* can be directed across computer room entrances or other high-security areas. If an intruder breaks the beam, an alarm sounds. The beam may be light, laser, ultraviolet, or infrared.
- *Ultrasonic* and *radar detectors* are designed to detect movement within the computer facilities. They are particularly useful when the facilities are closed or in rooms that have restricted access.
- *Microphones* can detect sound in the computer facilities. Sound above a certain level may trigger an alarm, or the sound may simply be broadcast from a speaker in a control station.

Authentication

Earlier in the chapter we discussed the use of identification and authorization controls that restrict access in on-line systems to authorized users. Successful identification will permit a user to access the system for an authorized purpose. There is no assurance, however, that continued use of the system is by this same person. Consequently, many on-line systems use authentication controls to detect unauthorized usage subsequent to the initial identification. Authentication controls include the following:

- Physical observation of the terminal user can provide confirmation that the person identified by the computer is in fact the person using the terminal.
- Requests for further identification can be made periodically during use of the terminal.
- The terminal may be disconnected and called back by the computer to ensure that the terminal being used is the one originally identified.
- An authenticity check is used in some data communications systems. An *authenticity check* is a code that is included in every message transmitted. It is an effective control against wiretapping.

System Monitoring

Even the most effective detection controls will not reveal all breaches of system security as they occur. It may be possible, however, to detect breaches of security on an ex-post basis by monitoring system usage. Monitoring is particularly effective in detecting repeated attempts to breach the security system. Monitoring controls include the following:

- Cameras are often used to monitor activity in the computer facilities. The cameras may be closed-circuit television cameras or time-lapse cameras. Closed-circuit cameras are connected to a monitor that is reviewed by a security guard. The guard often has the power to change the angle of view of the camera to scan the area. Time-lapse cameras shoot a frame every minute or so, and the film is later reviewed by the security staff. Cameras should be located in strategic areas such as entrances to the computer facilities.
- The security system should monitor unsuccessful attempts to access the system. Unsuccessful attempts to use a terminal or file should be logged. Repeated attempts should result in the disconnection of the terminal.
- The operating system should log all access failures and other violations of security procedures. Reports of system usage should be prepared from the computer usage log. The reports should include charts and statistics to highlight trends in system usage. They should be reviewed daily by the security officer for security violations and unusual trends in usage. A summary report should be sent to the internal auditors monthly.

Understanding and Tests of Controls

If the auditors plan to assess risk at a low level on controls that detect failures in system security, they should include the following kinds of procedures to obtain an understanding of the internal control structure and tests of controls in their examination:

1. Inquire of management regarding the type and location of fire detection devices, and determine the procedures to be followed by the EDP staff upon sounding of the fire alarm.
2. Inquire of management regarding devices to detect unauthorized access to the computer room, and determine from management the procedures to be followed when unauthorized access is detected.
3. Visit the computer facilities to determine the existence, number, and location of detection devices.
4. Review the results of tests of system security to determine the adequacy of detection devices.
5. Inquire of management regarding devices for authenticating the use of on-line systems.
6. Review computer usage logs and examine usage reports for detection and follow-up of system security failures.

CONTROLS FOR RECOVERY FROM SYSTEM SECURITY FAILURES

A data processing system should have controls that ensure effective recovery from detected system security failures. An *effective recovery* is one that minimizes loss or damage from the immediate security failure, and from subsequent operational problems. Recovery controls include controls that minimize damage from fire, adequate insurance, failure bypass procedures, a recovery plan, and recovery procedures.

Fire Extinguishment

Damage from fire can be minimized by the careful choice and design of fire-extinguishing systems. Ideally the computer facilities should be secured by strategic placement of hand-operated and automatic extinguishers.

Hand-operated extinguishers should be provided for electrical and combustible fires and should be located where there is a clear view and easy access. Carbon dioxide extinguishers are effective with electrical fires. Soda acid extinguishers should be used for combustible materials such as paper. Extinguishers should be placed in sufficient locations to ensure ready availability. They should be clearly marked, and the path to them should be unobstructed.

Automatic extinguisher systems should be installed in all computer facilities. These systems differ in their ability to extinguish fires, in the possibility of equipment damage from the extinguishing agent, and in the risk of injury to personnel. Three types of automatic extinguisher systems are used in computer facilities:

- *Sprinkler* systems use water to extinguish the fire. They are most effective in extinguishing combustible fires. However, the water can cause serious damage to computer equipment, as well as injury to personnel from electrical shock. Sprinkler systems are more efficient when action is delayed. Delay gives the operator a chance to shut down the equipment and to install protective plastic covers. The operator can also use the delay as an opportunity to deactivate the system in the event of a false alarm.
- *Carbon dioxide* systems are most effective for electrical fires. Carbon dioxide is unlikely to damage equipment but poses considerable danger to personnel from suffocation. It is essential that the system have a built-in warning and delay to permit personnel to evacuate the area.
- *Halon gas* is an effective fire extinguisher. The level of concentration of halon required to extinguish a fire is unlikely to be hazardous as long as personnel are evacuated promptly. Fortunately, halon has a distinctive odor that provides warning of its release. Its major disadvantage is its high cost.

Insurance

Adequate insurance coverage is a necessary control but is no substitute for procedures that minimize loss by prevention of, early detection of, and recovery from security failures. These other procedures are generally cheaper than insurance, provide control over data and assets, and reduce the likelihood of business interruption. Insurance does, however, provide for recovery of losses due to system security failures. Failure to provide insurance against losses from security failures may require disclosure of a material uninsured risk.

Data processing insurance is a highly technical area. Policies should be chosen to cover specific areas of loss and types of data processing hazard. Areas of loss include damage to computer equipment, damage to file media and paper, damage to records, and losses due to business interruption. Types of data processing hazard include water damage from sprinkler systems, damage from high temperatures caused by malfunctioning of the air-conditioning system, and theft of data and programs from the system.

Failure of Bypass Procedures

Loss and disruption from system security failures can be reduced by the use and control of off-line bypass procedures in on-line systems. Bypass procedures are alternative methods of off-line system operation during the failure period. They permit continued operation of at least some system functions. The procedures should include controls over the accuracy and completeness of transactions handled off-line.

In an on-line system, for example, credit approval might be an automatic function provided by criteria built into the application programs. Under normal operating conditions, credit approval would be communicated to the sales department via an on-line terminal. In the event of a system failure, however, this approval would not be forthcoming. An alternative off-line procedure would be necessary to ensure that the sales department could continue to process sales orders. This procedure might include a phone call to specific individuals in the credit department. These individuals would be those authorized to grant credit approval in emergencies.

Recovery Plan

An essential element of control for recovery from system failure is a formal recovery plan. A recovery plan ensures that management has evaluated the likelihood of system security failure and has adopted those procedures necessary to minimize data and asset loss. A sound recovery plan should cover the following:

- The plan should be fully documented. All recovery tasks should be clearly spelled out. Responsibility for every task should be assigned to an individual or department.
- The plan document should be stored in multiple locations. This ensures the availability of the plan regardless of where disaster may strike. It also precludes the destruction of the plan by fire or other disaster.
- The plan should be based on a careful analysis of the impact of loss of resources. Data that are critical for continued operation of the system, for example, require plans for immediate recovery. Data that are less essential to the system can be recreated or replaced over a longer period of time.
- The plan should deal with recovery from all possible system security failures. Such failures range from simple computer operator errors to complete destruction of the computer facilities by fire or other catastrophe.
- The plan should be adequately tested to ensure that it works as intended. The recovery plan may appear to work correctly, but individuals may not understand their responsibilities, and instructions may not be clear. Emergency drills are an excellent way of determining whether the plan can be relied upon.
- The plan should be comprehensive in its coverage of system resources. Recovery procedures should be provided for computer facilities and equipment, software, data, personnel, and supplies.

Recovery Procedures

In this section we describe recovery procedures that are commonly used for five types of computer resources.

1. *Computer Facilities and Equipment.* Arrangements should be contracted for backup facilities and equipment in case disaster renders existing resources inoperative. Such arrangements should be designed to provide service up to a predetermined level for a reasonable period of time. The predetermined level of service should permit essential services to be performed; it would be too expensive to duplicate the existing level and convenience of service.

Backup arrangements can provide for the use of compatible equipment in some reasonably convenient location or provide alternative premises to set up an emergency data processing operation. Arrangements to use compatible equipment can be made with the hardware vendor, a service center, or another company. Wherever the backup equipment is located, it is advisable that essential application programs be tested periodically on the backup equipment.

By securing alternative premises, existing equipment can be relocated on these premises, or deliveries of equipment can be obtained on an emergency basis from the hardware vendor. Prompt delivery of equipment can be ensured by an emergency delivery agreement with the hardware vendor. Backup arrangements for alternative premises should cover space, light, power, communications, environment, and security. All of these factors should be adequate to provide a minimum level of service.

Regardless of the type of backup arrangement, it should be described in detail in the recovery plan. Agreements with third parties should be in contractual form.

2. *Software.* The recovery plan should ensure that backup copies of software and documentation are available in the event of an emergency. Backup copies of software should include the operating system, utilities, and application programs. Software and documentation should be updated periodically to ensure that the backup programs are equivalent to the regular production programs.

Software and documentation should be stored in a separate location. This location may be a different area within the company, or it may be space rented from an outside party. Some companies choose to locate the software near the site of backup facilities and equipment. Wherever the location, it is advisable to store the software under the same environmental and security controls that are used for the main software library.

3. *Data.* The data recovery should permit reconstruction of master files, transaction files, and source documents. Specific methods of data recovery should be based on the importance of the data, and on the cost and ease of recovery from data loss. Important data files that are used frequently should be capable of reconstruction within a short time frame, even though the cost of backup may be high. Data files that are used infrequently, and whose loss would cause little more than inconvenience to system users, could be duplicated infrequently and reconstructed over a longer time frame at lower cost. Data recovery methods should be devised for data files stored on magnetic tape or disk, and for source documents.

Magnetic Tape Files. File reconstruction is generally easy in batch-oriented systems that use magnetic tape. Batch updating of master files is accomplished by physically creating a new tape for the updated master file. The old master file and transaction file tapes are *not* destroyed in the update process. Consequently, the old master file and transaction file tapes are retained to permit recreation of the new master file. This technique is known as the grandparent-parent-child concept. It is most effective when the old master file and transaction file tapes are moved as soon as possible to off-premises storage.

The grandparent-parent-child concept can be described as follows for an accounts receivable program that updates the customer master file for new credit sales orders (see Figure 8–1). New sales orders are accumulated weekly. Prior to processing, sales orders are validated, corrected, and sorted by customer number. The tape of sorted weekly transactions is used to update the customer records on the old customer master-file tape (parent). The updated customer records are written onto the new customer master file (child). The parent master file and related transaction tapes are retained so that the child master-file tape can be recreated if necessary. Additional backup security is provided by retaining the master file and transaction tapes from the preceding week's processing. The master-file tape from the preceding week is the grandparent tape. The grandparent master file and related transaction tapes are retained until the third week of processing when another generation of master files is created.

Magnetic Disk Files. The reconstruction of disk files differs from that used for tape because the update of a disk file involves the writing of new data over old. The old data are physically erased by the update and replaced by the new data. Consequently, the grandparent-parent-child approach cannot be used. Instead it is common practice to either copy the contents of the disk file onto another disk or copy the contents onto another file medium such as tape. In both cases, it is necessary to retain all transactions since the last time the file was copied.

Figure 8–2 illustrates disk-to-disk backup for a customer master-file update run. Sales orders are entered during the day via remote terminals and stored on disk. Every night the customer master file (on disk) is updated by the day's batch of sales orders. Upon completion of the update run, the customer master file is copied onto another disk. Both the master-file copy and the day's sales order file are retained for at least one day.

The customer master file in Figure 8–2 is duplicated daily because

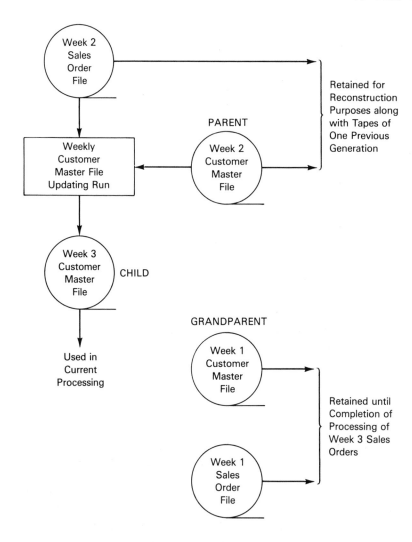

Figure 8–1.   Retention of Grandparent-Parent-Child Tapes for Customer Master-File Update Run

of the many sales transactions involved. If file duplication were less frequent, it would require extensive processing to reconstruct a master file. In some systems, however, it is sufficient to duplicate the master file weekly or biweekly.

Source Documents. Source documents should be retained at least until the related input transaction file is discarded. At that time the input

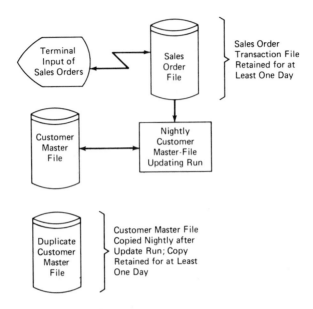

Figure 8–2. Disk-to-Disk Backup for On-Line Entry and Daily Batch Processing of Customer Master-File Update Run

transaction file is no longer needed for backup, and presumably the file's control totals have been balanced with the master file.

4. *Personnel.* The recovery plan should identify the principal individual responsible for each important duty. In addition, the plan should identify substitute personnel in the event that a disaster causes injury or loss of life.

5. *Supplies.* The recovery plan should include an inventory of the amount and location of required emergency supplies. These supplies should include all input and output forms that are required for essential applications. If customer billings are an essential application, for example, it will be necessary to provide an adequate supply of invoices and envelopes.

Understanding and Tests of Controls

If the auditors plan to assess risk at a low level on controls that ensure recovery from detected system security failures, they should include the following kinds of procedures to obtain an understanding of the internal control structure and tests of controls in their examination:

1. Visit the computer facilities and observe the type, location, and availability of hand-held and automatic fire extinguishers.
2. Examine insurance policies to ensure that all important data processing risks are covered.
3. Review bypass procedures for use during failure of on-line systems to ensure that controls over the accuracy and completeness of off-line transactions are adequate.
4. Discuss bypass procedures with selected data-entry operators to ensure that they fully understand the bypass procedures and related controls.
5. Examine the recovery plan to determine whether management has an anticipated all reasonably possible security risk and developed procedures for recovery from loss of computer resources.
6. Review the results of tests of the security plan to ensure that it does in fact minimize the possibility of data and asset loss.
7. Visit the data processing library and examine copies of backup master and transaction files to ensure that management's data recovery procedures are being followed.

SUMMARY

System security controls can protect computer facilities, equipment, programs, and data from destruction by environmental hazard, error, or abuse. System security controls are important because of the vulnerability of modern computer systems to loss of assets, the possibility of lack of compliance with legal requirements for data retention, and the creation of a possible material loss contingency in the absence of adequate controls. Controls should enhance system security, detect breaches of system security, and provide for recovery from system security failures.

Controls that enhance system security include security management, facilities security controls, library controls, and on-line access controls. The purpose of these controls is to reduce the likelihood of system security failures.

Controls that detect failures in system security include detection devices, authentication of system use, and system monitoring. Detection controls provide an opportunity to take timely action to minimize loss or damage that may result from the security failure.

Controls for recovery from system security failures are the procedures that are triggered by the detection of a security failure. They include fire extinguishment, insurance, on-line system bypass procedures, a recovery plan, and recovery procedures. These controls ensure that the recovery procedures used will minimize loss or damage from the immediate security failure and from subsequent operational problems.

APPENDIX

Lava Butte, Inc:
System Security Controls Questionnaire

Are the general controls over system security sufficient to provide reasonable assurance that damage or loss of assets or data is unlikely to occur because of failures in system security, that any failures in system security will be detected on a timely basis, and that recovery procedures will minimize loss that results from security failures?

Yes ____✔____   No _____

In assessing system security controls, the auditor should consider the following:	Contributes to Possible Reduction in Control Risk		Comments
	Yes	No	
— The utilization of controls that provide a secure system:			*no formal security management*
a. Security management		✔	*no serious hazards in Bend area. located on ground floor.*
b. Location controls	✔		*window to street. No drains or water pump.*
c. Construction controls		✔	*use magnetic stripe card for computer room door.*
d. Facilities access controls	✔		*No usage log for door files and documentation*
e. Library controls	✔		*Terminals in open office area. no key locks.*
f. Terminal access controls		✔	*Salespeople restricted to inventory inquiry*
g. Authorization controls	✔		*Password is mother's maiden name.*
h. Identification controls	✔		
i. Data communication access controls	N/A		
— Controls that detect failures in system security:			*Observed location of heat sensitive devices*
a. Fire detection devices	✔		*ultrasonic detectors in tape & disk storage room*
b. Access detection devices	✔		*Supervisors observe terminals on random basis*
c. Authentication	✔		*Closed circuit TV monitored by building guard*
d. System monitoring	✔		

In assessing system security controls, the auditor should consider the following:	Contributes to Possible Reduction in Control Risk		Comments
	Yes	No	
— Controls that ensure recovery from system security failures:			
a. Fire extinguishment	✓		*Observed placement of hand operated CO_2 extinguishers*
b. Insurance	✓		*Policy covers most dp uses*
c. Bypass procedures	N/A		
d. Recovery plan		✓	*no formal plan*
e. Facilities and equipment backup	✓		*Contract to use bank's computer on an emergency basis*
f. Software backup	✓		*Programs and data files kept in bank vault*
g. Data recovery procedures	✓		*Disk to tape backup on weekly basis*
h. Personnel backup		✓	*no considered necessary because of staff flexibility*
i. Supplies backup	✓		*Observed supplies kept in bank vault*

REVIEW QUESTIONS

8–1. What is the purpose of system security controls?

8–2. What are the causes of system security failure?

8–3. Why should the independent auditor be concerned with system security controls?

8–4. What planning and control steps should management take to ensure adequate system security?

8–5. Why is it necessary to test security procedures?

8–6. List some environmental, technological, and social hazards that should influence the decision to locate the computer facilities.

8–7. How can you reduce security risks by proper construction of the computer facilities?

8–8. Would restriction of access to the building perimeter be sufficient to restrict access to the computer facilities?

8-9. What access procedures would you recommend to help restrict access to the computer facilities?

8-10. Describe two different kinds of "key" that could be used to unlock a security door to the computer room.

8-11. What is the best alternative if a company cannot justify employing a full-time librarian for all the hours during which the computer is operating?

8-12. What duties can the librarian perform to ensure physical control over file usage and quality?

8-13. What is the purpose of a protection ring and how does it work?

8-14. Why is control over access to the computer room inadequate in an on-line system?

8-15. What is the function of an authorization scheme in an on-line system?

8-16. How should the authorization scheme relate to job description and organizational level?

8-17. What is the purpose of authorization tables and locks on data records? How do they work?

8-18. What is the relationship between authorization and identification?

8-19. Differentiate between a simple password and a complex password.

8-20. What procedures increase the effectiveness of password identification?

8-21. What additional security risk does data communication create?

8-22. Describe how fragmentation and message intermixing work.

8-23. What are the advantages of hardware versus software coding of logic for data encryption?

8-24. Compare the usefulness of heat-sensitive and smoke-sensitive devices.

8-25. Describe two ways of detecting unauthorized access.

8-26. Differentiate between authentication and identification.

8-27. What are the disadvantages of water sprinkler systems?

8-28. Should standard insurance policies be used in data processing?

8-29. Why do we need special control procedures when on-line systems are down?

8-30. What characteristics would define a *good* recovery plan?

8-31. What should be the objective in providing backup facilities and equipment?

8-32. What factors should influence the choice of specific data recovery procedures?

OBJECTIVE QUESTIONS

8-33. An auditor should determine that header labels are used on magnetic tape files to
a. Enable variable-length records to be processed

b. Assure that the correct files will be processed
c. Assure that the end-of-file procedures will be followed
d. Indicate the absence of file protection rings
e. All of the above (*IIA adapted*)

8-34. In evaluating the security of a computer installation, the auditor should consider
a. Organizational chart of the EDP department
b. Size of the computer installation and the number of programmers
c. Recommendations of the insurer
d. Size of the organization
e. Items a and c above (*IIA adapted*)

8-35. A computer master file that is the output of the most recent updating operation is referred to as the
a. Grandparent file
b. Parent file
c. Child file
d. Scratch file
e. None of the above (*IIA*)

8-36. Controls that restrict access to data communication systems include
a. Microswitches
b. Read-only switches
c. Fragmentation
d. Bypass procedures
e. Halon

CASES AND EXERCISES

8-37. In completing the Internal Control Questionnaire for Lava Butte, Inc., you discover that there is no formal management planning and control of system security. Why is security management so necessary, and what problems might you find at Lava Butte in the absence of security management?

8-38. Lava Butte's computer room is located on the ground floor of the company's administrative headquarters. The computer room is on the south side of the building, with a window facing busy Main Street. Write a memo outlining the security risk associated with the computer room location, and list your recommendations for the location and construction of new facilities.

8-39. According to the response to the Internal Control Questionnaire, Lava Butte has on-line terminals located in open office space. The terminals do not have key locks. What security risk does this pose, and what recommendations would you make to management to reduce this risk?

8-40. Lava Butte uses heat-sensitive devices in the computer room to detect fire. Do these devices provide adequate fire detection? Are you concerned when you also learn that the computer room is not equipped with either adequate drainage or a water pump?

8–41. In reviewing the Internal Control Questionnaire for Lava Butte, you notice that there is no formal recovery plan. What impact might this have on Lava Butte's disaster recovery capabilities?

8–42. Lava Butte's recovery capability for disk files is provided by weekly disk-to-tape backup. Transactions are batched daily on a removable disk pack and processed at night.

a. Draw a flowchart of the disk-to-tape backup. Include master and transaction files, and show retention dates for all files.

b. What kind of an application would warrant weekly rather than daily backup?

8–43. A UCLA electrical engineering student was charged with stealing more than $1 million of equipment from the telephone company. He accomplished this by breaching the security of the company's on-line computer system.

By posing as a journalist, he was given tours of the company's computer facilities and was given copies of all documents requested. He found other documents in trash cans outside the supplies department. The documentation included inquiry passwords for the equipment budgets and the inventory control system. On one document he found a handwritten phone number for an equipment storage location. He called this number, posed as a storage attendant, and obtained the password for ordering telephone equipment.

Armed with telephone-ordering password, it was a simple matter to order equipment. He had the equipment delivered to a remote site. He then signed the bill of lading and returned it to the central office.

His ability to make inquiries in the budget and inventory systems was put to good use. He restricted his order size to prevent each equipment storage location from exceeding its equipment budget. His knowledge of inventory levels and reorder points permitted him to order sufficient quantity to reduce inventory below the reorder point. Knowing that an order would be placed to replenish the inventory item, he was then able to contact the telephone company's purchasing agent and sell the equipment back to him.

What on-line access and other security controls might have prevented this fraud?

8–44. GROT COMPANY II. Mr. Reginald Perrin's visit to the Grot Company's computer room served the additional purpose of reviewing computer room security. His subsequent report was based on the following observations:

1. Mr. Perrin had intended to test the new sophisticated signature verification system controlling access to the computer room. He was unable to do so because the door was propped open by a portable fire extinguisher.

2. After several minutes of searching, he found one other fire extinguisher located behind a large cabinet. A few minutes of effort were sufficient to move the cabinet so that he could examine the extinguisher. It carried a label that said it had been checked in June 1979.

3. A large window was open at one end of the computer room. The window opened onto a quiet back alley. An operator explained that the window was open to help dispel the cooking odors from the company cafeteria next door.

4. The door to the library was open, so Mr. Perrin walked in. It was several minutes before the librarian noticed his presence. During that time an operator walked into the room and helped himself to two disk packs. Most of the files were on wooden racks. Several reels of magnetic tape, however, were sitting in a corner. The librarian explained that these reels were last week's backup tapes. Mr. Perrin noticed the file usage record sitting on the librarian's desk. The last entry was dated the preceding week. The file record was also sitting on the desk. Mr. Perrin selected ten files at random from the record and attempted to locate the files on the racks. He could only locate three of the files.

5. Upon returning to the computer room, he noticed a piece of tape over the read-only switch on the disk drive. The operator explained that taping the switch in the off position gave him one less thing to think about.

6. Mr. Perrin noticed several unusual items pinned to the computer room bulletin board. Included among these items were several current passwords for access to the on-line system.

For each observation, describe the control weakness, the audit implications of the weakness, and suggest alternative procedures that would provide better control.

8–45. Identify the control weaknesses and recommend controls that would correct the weakness in each of the following unrelated situations:

1. A programmer in an on-line system was fired. He was given two week's pay in lieu of notice and discharged from the company's premises immediately. He subsequently accessed the on-line system and stole proprietary programs and sensitive data.

2. A disgruntled operator entered the library storage area and removed the external labels from all magnetic tape reels. Subsequent identification of the tapes was a protracted and costly task.

3. During the accounts receivable update, the computer operator accidentally mounted the receivables master file as an output tape. There was no console error message to notify the operator of the error. The tape was completely erased during processing. Reconstruction of the tape was accomplished manually from the preceding month's customer statements and the transaction source documents for the month.

4. Fire caused extensive damage to the Corbett Company's program and data file library. When the backup tapes were retrieved from off-premises storage, it was found that extensive effort was required to replace the lost programs and files. Systems and application programs were not updated with recent changes. Application master files were found to be several processing periods old, with none of the transaction files for those periods available.

8–46. BANK HOLDING CORPORATION: Review of System Security Controls. (This case is an extension of Case 6–43. It can be completed independently of 6–43, but the reader should review the background information contained in that case.)

Ms. Johnson decided to continue her data center review by obtaining an overview of company control policies and standards dealing with recovery, restart, and general security. In particular, she wished to learn how the Data Center planned to prevent a computer failure (from disasters to brownouts), to recover from any such failure, and to ensure the security of data under all circumstances.

Initial Data Collection

The following Monday morning Ms. Johnson met with the manager of the BHC Data Center, Michael Heckman, to discuss existing documentation of control objectives and guidelines. Mr. Heckman noted that no one document summarized all the control features of the system but provided her with the main documents which dealt with control. Ms. Johnson, after looking at the mountain of documents, was glad she did not take on auditing projects like this very often. Her fifth cup of coffee gave her enough courage to start reviewing the two stacks of paper. As she proceeded, she made note of the following important points:

- Each transaction from an affiliate bank is processed by a teller through an intelligent terminal. In the case of CPU or communication interruptions the terminal itself can do limited processing. At the end of each day the computer prints transaction totals for balancing the cash drawer. A log tape of all transactions received during the day is reprocessed off-line that evening and compared to the day's on-line processing. These totals along with an updated general ledger are transmitted via the terminal to the affiliate banks each morning.
- Disaster is seen as the greatest threat of a reduction in service level and long-term interruption of business. Policy suggests that areas that deserve attention when discussing disaster include assurance of interim processing if a disaster should occur, and recovery to normal processing.
- The Data Center has set up procedures to control visitor and employee access. Specifically,

- All visitors sign in and out in a log indicating the time of day, whom they represent, and whom they are visiting.
- Visitors are issued badges and are required to wear them in plain view while on the premises.
- Access to the data processing area of BHC is restricted to authorized management and operating personnel. Access is controlled by doors activated with magnetic card readers attached on-line to a separate computer security system. Codes in the magnetic cards issued to each authorized employee designate which doors in the bank are available for access. A log is maintained of the card number and all access attempts.
- Access to the computer room is restricted to the operations staff and equipment vendors only.
- A building security guard is on duty at all times.

- The computer center has the following policy pertaining to the control of fire:

- A heat, fire, and smoke detection alarm system with sensors located in the computer facility and in the tape library has been installed at the computer center. A halon gas fire-extinguishing system is incorporated into the sensor system to put out any fire in the computer area.
- The fire alarm system is connected to an automatic power-off trip switch and to the building's staffed engineer console.
- Portable carbon dioxide fire extinguishers are readily accessible in and around the computer facility. These are periodically weighed and kept charged, and computer operators are trained to use them.

- All electrical equipment is approved by Underwriters' Laboratories (UL).
- Flammable material in or around the data processing center is removed daily to avoid potential fire hazards. Waste containers are designed to retain and smother fires.
- Paper and other combustible supplies are not stored in the computer room.
- The computer room construction material is noncombustible. Exterior computer room walls have a two-hour fire rating.
- A no-smoking rule is enforced in the computer room.
- The following measures have been taken to ensure adequate temperature and humidity for the data processing equipment:

- There are several independently controlled air-conditioning modules distributed between two independently fused power panels. The failure of any module can be compensated for by the other modules.
- All air-conditioning modules are inspected monthly when filters are changed.

— There is a backup system for pumping water to the air-conditioning system. If one motor fails, that motor will be bypassed and pumping capacity maintained by a second motor and pump. The water-softening system utilizes a dual filter to prevent clogging of water intake systems.

— A separate electrical power supply for the air-conditioning system is maintained.

• Proper maintenance policies concerning hardware help the Data Center prevent failures.

— The computer engineers perform preventive maintenance on the peripherals daily and on every Sunday they check the mainframe.

— The operations manager, in order to locate problems, reviews the engineers' weekly report of preventive and remedial maintenance.

— The operations manager also closely supervises the work being done to ensure a prompt and proper solution.

• Protective measures have been instituted by the Data Center to prevent unauthorized access to the data communication channels and unauthorized use of files.

— The identification of each terminal is hardwired. Each transaction from a terminal to the computer is identified by the terminal number, along with the window, branch, line, and affiliate number supplied by the terminal software.

— The central computer initiates all communications with the terminals, recognizing only authorized terminal identifications and requests to use the system.

— Software controls are used to ensure that affiliates use only their own data files and the application programs authorized for them.

— All files and programs are protected by frequently changed codes and passwords.

— The library of tapes is physically controlled by a librarian who maintains a record of the status of all tapes and who uses them.

— After every six uses, tape reels are cleaned and their condition certified.

— The librarian is the only person authorized to erase tapes.

— The librarian controls all files in the library and in the off-site storage location.

— All tapes which are necessary for recovery and restart are stored in a heat-resistant, fireproof, locked vault.

• Procedures which are necessary for computer operators to restart and recover from a business interruption are fully documented.

— Files are maintained and controlled by a tape library system. Each file has retention instructions printed on it.
— The locked computer center vault holds the first generation backup tapes which can be used for immediate backup. The tapes in the vault include program object tapes, transaction backup tapes, and account master files.
— Operating system backup is ensured by periodically copying the object code and related data files from the system residence device directly to tape. A copy of the source code for each application is also kept on tape.
— Each day, two copies of the daily transactions are prepared and put on tape. One tape is placed in the computer room vault and the other one is sent to an off-site storage location.
— Murphy's Supply provides off-site storage for the backup tapes. On-line and off-line month-end master files, month-to-date history, and object and source programs are sent to off-site storage twice a week and after each end-of-month processing.
— Either of the two computers can be used individually for running all on-line and off-line processing. In high-volume periods the two machines are used jointly. If hardware problems should develop in one machine, the other is available for backup.
— All peripheral equipment, which includes tape drives, disk drives, printers, and communication equipment, can be switched to either computer.
— Backup telephone lines connect the telephone center to the computer room.
— If a restart is needed, the on-line system files from the beginning of the day can be processed against the on-line transactions entered by the affiliates during the day.
— The run manual documents all necessary recovery and restart procedures for the on-line system together with their priorities.
— The tape library retains all necessary system files and transaction tapes so that the on-line processing for any of the last thirty days can be recreated.
— In the event of the destruction of files at the Data Center, the present system provides the capability to be operational with up-to-date files in twenty-four hours. To achieve this type of recovery, tapes would be removed from off-site storage and the most recent masters would be processed off-line with the one to three days of daily transactions required to recreate current masters.
— There is a twenty-page set of detailed procedures and guidelines to be followed in the case of a disaster. These procedures indicate who is to be notified, what tasks they are to perform, and in what order.

Ms. Johnson found that letters of support from suppliers of the computer center's equipment and related elements indicate that in case of a disaster, support will be offered on a timely basis. These letters are from the suppliers of business forms, the air-conditioning company, the computer manufacturer, the suppliers of the peripheral equipment, and the telephone company. Ms. Johnson considered the most important letter of support to be the one from the computer manufacturer concerning backup equipment and facilities (which she copied).

CPU INCORPORATED

PARKVIEW PLAZA
CLEVELAND, OHIO 44114

Mr. Heckman
Manager of Computer Operations
Bank Holding Company
Cleveland, Ohio 44114

Dear Mr. Heckman:

This is in response to your letter of September 10, in which you request our position in the event a disaster should destroy your computer operations center.

We will try to return you to normal operating conditions by replacing your equipment as soon as possible.

To achieve recovery from disaster, equipment can be secured from three areas:

- Production—The next unit in production which is not under a contractual agreement that would result in damages for delay in delivery.
- Company Systems—If production cannot supply needed equipment without extended delay we will examine our company's internal operations looking for a possible replacement machine.
- Demonstrator Systems—In the event of a disaster the fastest possible solution may be a demonstrator system. These systems usually are operational and have no contractual agreements affecting them.

No contractual agreement is presently in existence with any of our customers. But we pledge to do our part to help you recover from a disaster as soon as possible.

Very truly yours,

Bert Bell, Jr.
Sales Manager
CPU Incorporated

BB:tj

On Site Observations

Ms. Johnson proceeded to investigate the most important features of the computer center's control policy to see if they were being implemented properly. She felt that a physical review of the computer operations facility would be a helpful place to start to see if controls actually existed and were being followed. An appointment was set up to see that Mr. Heckman could give her a tour.

On Tuesday morning, Ms. Johnson, accompanied by Mr. Heckman, arrived at the computer facility and stopped to sign the visitor's log. Mr. Heckman insisted it was not necessary for her to sign, however, as she was with him. When they approached the computer room door, Mr. Heckman remembered that he had forgotten his magnetic card used to gain access to the room, but luck was with them and the door was unlocked. Inside the computer room Ms. Johnson saw that five operators were gathered in a group. Mr. Heckman explained that they were deciding who would run which jobs that day. She commented that the computer room seemed rather drafty, and Mr. Heckman pointed out that this was caused by opening the back door on cool days to help reduce the load placed on the air conditioners.

In the back of the computer room, where the magnetic tape drives were located, Ms. Johnson accidentally surprised an operator loading a tape and the operator dropped it. Ms. Johnson expressed concern to the operator about the possible injury to the tape. He assured her that no damage had been done and proceeded to load the tape. Ms. Johnson inquired what tape the operator was loading. The operator replied that he was to load this tape on 612 but he did not know what the tape contained. She also noticed a large computer printout proclaiming "HAPPY BIRTHDAY HARRY" hanging from a fire detector and a halon gas register. Mr. Heckman explained that the computer has a program that can create these large printouts and operators and programmers are always creating these signs when the work gets slow. "It adds a personal touch and helps boost morale," he said.

Ms. Johnson commented on how clean and well organized the computer room was and Mr. Heckman responded "we have an efficient cleaning crew that really scrubs this place clean on Sunday. There are no employees around to bother them and they do quite a job." She also discovered that Sunday is the day when technicians perform preventive maintenance on the computer.

Ms. Johnson, after assuring herself that she had seen all the computer equipment, suggested to Mr. Heckman that they go have a cup of coffee and then visit the tape library. At the coffee machine she met an old friend, Mr. John Carlson, who was Vice-President of Personnel. They got into a long conversation and decided to go out to lunch at a new restaurant across town.

Ms. Johnson got back from her luncheon date shortly before three. She was met by Mr. Heckman and was informed that if they hurried they could view Murphy's Supply picking up the tapes for off-site storage.

When they arrived at the tape library, they learned from the librarian that the pickup man from Murphy's Supply was late again. Ms. Johnson asked the librarian if the messenger was late often. She said that she was not sure because she had only been working here for about two weeks, but had been told during training that sometimes the storage representative did not show up at all. Mr. Heckman interjected that this did not happen very often.

As they waited for the messenger, Ms. Johnson noticed the large volume of tapes stacked on the desk. Mr. Heckman informed her that many of the tapes were past the date when they should be destroyed, but the librarian had been very busy lately. At that moment Mr. Roll, a programmer, walked into the library, picked up a tape, and was greeted cordially by Mr. Heckman. Ms. Johnson later learned from Mr. Heckman that Mr. Roll had been the first programmer with the company and, since his wife died five years ago, had become so devoted to his work that he rarely took a vacation.

The off-site storage man finally arrived at 3:45 P.M., complaining about a big traffic jam. He left the old storage tapes and picked up the box of tapes to be sent and briefly counted nine of them. He asked the librarian why there were not the usual ten tapes and she replied that one was temporarily misplaced. She added that the tape was probably in the bank vault, but that she was too busy to look right then.

As the day came to a close, Ms. Johnson made arrangements with Mr. Heckman to visit the off-site storage facility the following week.

A Visit to Murphy's Supply

On the following Friday, May 5, she visited Murphy's Supply, located on the outskirts of Cleveland. Ms. Johnson talked with John Murphy, the owner of the storage site. She found that all doors into the off-site storage site were locked and that the building was very hot inside. The receptionist informed her that it gets even hotter in the summer because the storage site is right next to a restaurant kitchen. Ms. Johnson asked Mr. Murphy for a list of the blank tapes that were stored at the site, and noticed that the list given her was outdated and that a more current set of tapes was actually stored there. After investigating further, she found that the latest date on tapes stored there was April 22 and that only a partial inventory list for these tapes existed. The physical storage of the tapes was in locked closets labeled only by letters. When asked if there was any fire detection device in the storage site, Mr. Murphy replied that there was none, but added that there had never been a fire in the building since it was built sixty years before.

Back at the office, Ms. Johnson concluded that even with historical tapes, adequate recovery from disaster depended on supplier support of the computer mainframe. Because of this, she asked Mr. Heckman to reconfirm the computer manufacturer's promise of support in case the mainframe were destroyed. Mr. Heckman received the following letter of reply from the manufacturer:

CPU INCORPORATED

PARKVIEW PLAZA
CLEVELAND, OHIO 44114

Mr. Heckman
Bank Holding Company
Cleveland, Ohio 44114

Dear Mr. Heckman:

We have reviewed your equipment requirements in the event of a disaster. The highest priority will be made to make the demonstrator system available to you. You must realize, however, that the demonstrator system and its configuration is different from yours. Additional equipment would have to be added to accommodate your processing. Also, demonstrator systems are changed yearly and during this transition no backup would be available.

I hope you understand our position. We reiterate the promise of our best efforts to help your company formalize and implement backup disaster procedures.

Very truly yours,

Bert Bell, Jr.
Sales Manager
CPU Incorporated

BB:tj

Questions:

- What major areas should be considered to determine the potential for loss of data or the ability to process it? Identify some controls in each of these areas.
- Evaluate the general security and recovery procedures at each of the locations visited by Ms. Johnson
- What other areas might bear investigating in connection with security and recovery procedures?

Prepared by Frederick Neumann, Richard Boland, and Jeffrey Johnson, with funding from the Touche Ross Foundation. Used and adapted with permission of the authors.)

Chapter 9
DATA CAPTURE AND BATCH DATA ENTRY CONTROLS

Learning Objectives

After completing this chapter, the reader should be able to:

1. Examine the relationship between errors, control objectives, and controls.

2. Understand the role played by the audit trail in control and audit.

3. Determine what constitutes an adequate audit trail.

4. Understand why it is important to control transactions prior to processing.

5. Identify the purposes of data capture controls, batch data preparation controls, and batch input controls.

An understanding of controls in manual accounting systems is insufficient background for the computer auditor. EDP accounting systems require a new set of application controls that matches new technology and different transaction flows. Knowledge of these computer application controls and their role in EDP accounting systems is a prerequisite to the assessment of control risk in computer systems.

Application controls are manual and automatic procedures that relate to specific EDP accounting systems such as payroll, accounts receivable, and cash disbursements. Their purpose is to ensure an acceptable level of control in each EDP accounting system. This purpose is accomplished in conjunction with the general controls described in Chapters 5 through 8. Application controls include user and EDP procedures and are located in each of the data processing functions of input, processing, and output. The specific application controls encountered will vary depending on the type of accounting system, the method of input and processing, and the stage in the transaction processing cycle.

In this chapter we focus on (1) controls methodology, which describes the impact of application controls on the auditor's assessment of control risk in EDP accounting systems; (2) the audit trail and its relationship to application controls; (3) data capture controls; and (4) batch data entry controls, including batch data preparation and batch input. The Appendix contains flowcharts and control questionnaires for data capture and entry in the payroll system at Lava Butte, Inc.

CONTROLS METHODOLOGY

Controls methodology is a description of the role that controls play in EDP accounting systems. Understanding this role is important to both management and the auditor. Management is concerned with the cost of controls and with the benefit that can be derived from their use. The auditor is concerned with the impact of controls on his or her assessment of control risk.

Controls methodology states that management or the auditor must make a series of evaluations and determinations before the usefulness of controls can be defined. This series of steps involves the following: (1) determine the likelihood of errors and irregularities and their impact on audit and business exposures; (2) set broad management objectives that specify the need for error-free processing and the avoidance of significant exposure; (3) draw up detailed system objectives that represent the conformity of individual EDP accounting systems with the general objectives; and then (4) evaluate the role that controls play in an EDP accounting system (see Figure 9–1).

In this section we describe each of these four steps and explain the

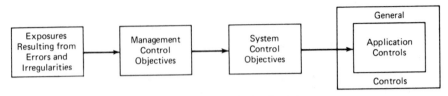

Figure 9–1. Controls Methodology

relationship between controls methodology and the organization of Chapters 9 and 10.

Exposures Resulting from Errors and Irregularities

Errors and irregularities in data processing can affect the reliability of data, the proper processing of data, the security of assets and records, the effectiveness of the organization in meeting stated objectives, and the efficiency of operations. As a result, both the independent auditors and management may be subject to unacceptable exposures.

Unreliable Data. Unreliable input data are the result of such errors as incorrect source data, incorrect translation of source data to a machine-readable medium, or loss of transaction data during the processing cycle. Uncorrected erroneous input data may result in erroneous output.

Improper Processing. Transaction data may be processed incorrectly. Data may be valued or classified or otherwise accounted for contrary to management's prescribed accounting policy. Transaction data may also be processed in violation of specific management authorizations, such as credit or inventory replenishment policies.

Loss or Destruction of Assets and Records. Errors in the system may result in the diversion of assets or records to purposes that are wasteful or unauthorized. Accounting data stored on magnetic file media could be permanently destroyed. Sensitive financial data could be obtained by unauthorized personnel or competitors.

Failure to Accomplish Organizational Objectives. Errors in accounting data or processing may interfere with the accomplishment of organizational objectives. Many organizations, for example, rely on accounting reports to provide feedback on divisional or departmental performance. Errors in these reports could reduce management's ability to evaluate performance and take appropriate corrective action. As a result, organizational effectiveness could suffer.

Operational Inefficiency. Data processing errors may affect the efficiency of operations. The data processing function itself could be affected by excessive costs, and the user departments could suffer a general waste and loss of resources.

Both the independent auditors and management could be subject to unacceptable exposure when these problems are extensive. Exposures that are of specific concern to the auditors include materially incorrect financial statements, a qualified audit opinion, violations of the rules of regulatory bodies, and violation of the 1977 Foreign and Corrupt Practices Act. Also of concern to the auditors, but primarily of concern to management, include significant loss of revenues and business opportunities, business interruption, and excessive costs of doing business.

Management Control Objectives

The reduction of data processing errors and irregularities should be an explicit policy of management. Such a policy requires a statement of objectives for the reduction of errors in EDP accounting systems to an acceptable level.

The statement of management objectives should address each of the following three elements of the control structure:

1. Control environment
2. Accounting system
3. Control procedures

The control environment pertains to the overall attitude, awareness, and actions of management toward the control structure. The attitude, awareness, and actions are indicators of the philosophy of management about the importance of control and the emphasis it is given in the entity. These philosophical issues are not unique to the audits of computer systems. They must be considered no matter what method of data processing is utilized. These issues are not discussed in the material that follows, however, because the focus is on specific EDP system control objectives that must be assessed by the auditor.

The two remaining elements of the control structure contain objectives that can be uniquely analyzed within the context of the EDP system. The accounting system must contain specific methods and records. There are specified control procedures that must be provided. These two elements of the control structure are discussed in detail in this section.

The purpose of the objectives is the reduction of errors to an acceptable level. An *acceptable level* of errors is one in which management's exposure is reduced to an immaterial or insignificant level. Failure to define this level could result in either unacceptable exposure or excessive costs of control.

System Objectives

Management's broad objectives can be translated into detailed system objectives that specify the characteristics of acceptable systems. The purpose of these detailed system objectives is to guide the systems designer in the choice of specific controls for specific systems. Table 9–1 lists the systems objectives for the management objectives. These system objectives guide the choice of controls in each accounting application system and in the data processing system as a whole.

Table 9–1. Management and System Objectives

Management Objective	System Objective
1. To provide an effective accounting system	a. *Completeness.* Input, processing, and output should be complete. No transactions, data, or processing steps should be omitted.
	b. *Validity.* The system should not process fictitious or nonexistent transactions.
	c. *Classification.* Transactions should be properly classified in the journals and properly posted to the subsidiary and general ledgers. Proper classification applies to written output as well as to secondary file storage media.
	d. *Valuation.* Data processing should result in proper calculation, recording, and summarization of transactions in conformance with prescribed accounting policies.
	e. *Timeliness.* Transactions should be captured, entered, and processed in the correct accounting period.
2. To provide effective control procedures	a. *Transaction authorization.* Transactions should be properly approved and authorized. Proper authorization applies to both input transactions and transactions that are generated automatically by the computer during processing.
	b. *Errors are detected, corrected, and resubmitted.* Transactions that are in error should be detected. The erroneous data should be corrected and the transactions resubmitted for normal input and processing.

Table 9–1. (Continued)

Management Objective	System Objective
	c. *Security of data and records.* Data and records should be secure against loss or destruction. Security should cover source documents, secondary file storage, and printed or microfilmed output.
	d. *Distribution of output.* Output should be distributed only to authorized individuals or departments.
	e. *Accuracy.* Input, processing, and output should be accurate. Erroneous data, incorrect processing, and processing of wrong records or files should be avoided.
	f. *Uniqueness.* Transactions should not be entered into the computer or processed more than once.
	g. *Reasonableness.* Processing results should fall within a range of normal system results.

Role of Controls in EDP Systems

System objectives are met by the use of application and general controls that prevent, detect, or correct errors in each phase of the transaction cycle. Application controls are specific to each accounting application, such as accounts receivable or payroll. General controls create the environment within which the application controls function.

The relationship between controls and system objectives is one of prevention, detection, or correction of errors. Prevention controls prevent the occurrence of errors. The use of passwords with on-line terminals, for example, prevents unauthorized terminal input. Detection controls are designed to detect those errors that inevitably occur despite effective prevention controls. The validation of terminal input, for example, is to detect errors in the data entered into terminals. Correction controls ensure that errors that are detected will be properly corrected and resubmitted for input and processing. The display of an error message on a terminal, for example, ensures that the operator will correct the transaction properly prior to its acceptance for processing by the computer system.

Different objectives and different controls should be emphasized to reflect the different types of error that may occur in each phase of the transaction cycle. There is a possibility, for example, of including unauthorized transactions in data capture. An objective of data capture controls, therefore, is the prevention of unauthorized transactions. Output, however, represents the results of input and processing. Very little can be done during output to prevent unauthorized transactions. The most that can be done is to review output to detect unauthorized transactions included during prior phases of the transaction cycle. Output objectives and controls should instead focus on the types of error that may occur during the output phase, such as the distribution of output to unauthorized individuals.

Controls Methodology and Chapter Organization

This chapter and Chapter 10 are organized by phase of the transaction cycle and within each phase by objective. The objectives are written in the following general form:

1. *Prevention Objective.* Assurance that the incidence of errors is sufficiently low to provide reliability, adherence to accounting policy, and protection of assets and records.
2. *Detection Objective.* Assurance that errors that do occur are detected.
3. *Correction Objective.* Assurance that errors that are detected are properly corrected and resubmitted for processing.

These three objectives are tailored in each phase of the transaction cycle to reflect the most important system objectives in that phase. This serves to tie the controls in with the system objectives in Table 9–1. For example, the detection objective for data capture emphasizes the detection of unreliable, improper, unauthorized/invalid, or lost source data. This approach reduces the redundancy that would result from treating each system objective separately. The redundancy would occur because so many controls serve multiple system objectives.

The primary purpose of this chapter and Chapter 10 is to describe application controls that meet the control objectives in each phase of the transaction cycle. The contribution of application controls to control objectives, however, is influenced by the existence and strength of general controls. General controls that have a specific influence on objectives in each phase are therefore referenced alongside the application controls.

AUDIT TRAIL

The audit trail is essential for operational control, accounting control, audit, and compliance with government regulations. The audit trail permits management to respond to operating exceptions, such as an out-of-stock inventory item. Management can use the audit trail, for example, to determine the amount on order, the expected delivery date, and the supplying vendor of the out-of-stock item. The audit trail acts as an application control because it can be used to diagnose the cause and effect of an error. Internal and external auditors make use of the audit trail as the basis for audit tests of transactions and account balances. An audit trail is required by IRS regulations when the application is used for tax as well as accounting purposes.

The *audit trail* consists of the input, processing, and output documentation and file data that permit the tracing of transaction processing. This tracing can be either from the initiation of the transaction to the results of the processing of the transaction or from the results of transaction processing back to the source of the transaction. The full scope of the audit trail with related documentation and file data is shown in Table 9–2.

The audit trail in the input phase of the transaction cycle provides evidence of the initiation, authorization, approval, and recording of trans-

Table 9–2. Audit Trail in EDP Accounting Applications

Transaction Cycle	Audit Trail
Input —Data capture —Batch data preparation —Batch input —On-line entry	Source documents Source (transaction) lists Transaction identifiers Validated transaction files on tape or disk Batch transmittal logs Batch transmittal tickets Manual error log Error suspense file on tape or disk Error listing
Processing —Data validation —Calculation —Comparison —Summarization —File updating —File maintenance —Sequencing —Inquiry —Error correction	Application program documentation Table contents Factor values Operator input data Default options Transaction listings Listing of computer-generated transactions File activity data Error suspense files Error log
Output —File content —Reports —Documents	Field data by record File balances Accounting reports Management reports Reference reports Error logs Error report Output documents

actions. The specific documentation and file data that provide this evidence depend on the method of input. Source documents, for example, will be available in a batch input system but may not be available in an on-line input system where individual transactions are entered via a terminal. Instead the auditor may have to rely on indirect evidence of on-line transactions, such as a computer-generated list of transaction input.

The audit trail must be followed through the processing phase in order to link transaction input and processing results. Processing is an internal computer function, however, and does not provide a directly visible audit trail. Consequently, the auditor must rely on following the logical sequence of processing events and identifying the data, transactions, and results linked to each event. The evidence for this includes the application program logic documentation, listings of transactions used in processing, and table and factor values used in processing.

The output of transaction processing can represent the end or the beginning of the audit trail. As the end of the audit trail, output is the final evidence that transactions have been properly recorded. As the beginning of the audit trail, the output provides the starting point for determining whether it is the result of processing valid, authorized transactions. The audit trail for output includes accounting reports, error reports, reference reports, and file balances.

DATA CAPTURE CONTROLS

Data capture is a manual procedure that covers the initiation, approval, authorization, review, and preparation of documentation for source transactions. It is generally a user department function. Data capture occurs in both batch and on-line entry systems, although the actual procedures and controls may differ. In on-line systems where the data capture function is reduced or combined with data entry, the focus of control shifts to data entry.

Data capture controls are designed to ensure the reliability and accuracy of data, *before* the data enter the computer application system. The following risks are controllable during data capture:

1. *Accounting System*
    — Valid and completed source transactions may be omitted from data capture.
    — Source data may be inaccurate.
    — Source transactions may be captured in the wrong accounting period.
    — Source data may be improperly valued or classified.
    — Source transactions may be invalid.

2. *Control Procedures*

— Valid and completed source transactions may be captured more than once.
— Errors may not be properly detected, corrected, and resubmitted.
— Source transactions may be unauthorized.
— Source transactions may not be lost.

These risks can be reduced by the use of application controls that meet the following objectives.

Prevention Objective: To ensure reliable, proper, authorized, approved, and secure source data. Application controls that can help meet this objective are user procedures manuals, source document design, prenumbering, forms security, separation of duties, sound personnel practices, identification of preparer, and evidence of approval.

User Procedures Manuals. Each application should have written procedures to encourage consistent performance of data capture responsibilities. These written procedures should include the following:

• Guidelines for document preparation, including the use of special codes
• The flow of documents both within the department and from the department to data processing
• Schedules for data capture, including batch cutoff dates
• Requirements for control over data prior to transmittal to data processing
• The scope of management review and approval of work performed
• The names of individuals authorized to review and approve documentation
• Identification of proper evidence of approval

Source Document Design. The likelihood of errors can significantly be reduced by the careful design of source documents. Source document design involves the use of special formats and preprinted data to ensure conformity of work performed to written procedures. Conformity encourages completeness, accuracy, and proper authorization. Special formats include the use of specific boxes for authorization signatures, control totals, footing and cross-footing balances, and retention dates. Preprinted data should include repetitive items such as form number and title, department responsibility, transaction code, and product number.

Prenumbering. Prenumbering of source documents ensures that each transaction will be uniquely identified. It reduces the likelihood that a transaction will be lost or omitted.

Forms Security.   Security over the forms used for source documents reduces the likelihood of unauthorized or invalid transactions. Security should include physical control over the forms as well as dual signatures for the release of forms for source document preparation.

Separation of Duties.   Separation of duties in the user department reduces the likelihood of unintentional errors. Four types of separation are useful:

- Separation of the custody of assets from the data capture function
- Separation of the authorization of transactions from the custody of related assets
- Separation of the functions of transaction authorization and source document preparation
- Separation of error correction from initiation and source document preparation

Sound Personnel Practices.   The user department should follow sound personnel practices. These should include procedures to ensure the hiring of competent personnel, the continuing evaluation of individual performance, periodic rotation of assignments, required vacations, and bonding of key personnel.

Identification of Preparer.   Identification of the person preparing transactions increases the likelihood that the separation of duties is being followed. Identification is provided by signature, initials, work number or stamp on the source document, or written department work assignments. In terminal entry systems, identification is provided by the terminal's code, terminal operator's sign-on code, and logs of physical access to the terminal.

Evidence of Approval.   There should be evidence that the transaction has been properly authorized and approved. If a source document has been prepared, an authorized signature on the document provides this evidence. Where there is no source document, review and approval may be subsequent review of a transaction source listing or by approval during data entry. An authorized signature on the source listing will be evidence of subsequent approval. If approval is given during terminal entry, there should be an approval code in the transaction record.

Detection Objective: To ensure that unreliable, improper, unauthorized, invalid, or lost source data are detected. Application controls that can help meet this objective are batch controls and user review.

Batch Controls. The preparation of batches of source documents permits the use of batch controls to discover errors. Batch controls include the following:

- A batch number identifies the batch of transactions and can be used to keep track of the receipt or transmittal of the batch.
- Limiting the number of transactions in a batch facilitates reconciliation when the batch is out of balance.
- Control totals for the number of transactions, amounts, and quantities in a batch permit subsequent discovery of loss of items or changes in data that occur during data preparation, data entry, or data processing. This is accomplished by reconciliation of source data control totals to equivalent totals included with the output that is returned upon completion of processing.
- The control totals are usually recorded manually by the user in a control log.
- The log also records the time and place of batch transmittal and receipt. Each batch should be sent to EDP or another department with a transmittal ticket attached. The transmittal ticket controls the flow of data from one department to another. The ticket usually identifies the sending and receiving parties and describes the accompanying batch (see Figure 9–2).

User Review. A manual review should be performed by the user prior to transmittal of the data. The purpose of the review is to check the source documents, transmittal tickets, and control log for completeness, accuracy, and conformity with department policy.

Correction Objective: To ensure that unreliable, improper, unauthorized, or invalid source data are, if appropriate, corrected and resubmitted for data capture. Application controls that can help meet this objective are error correction procedures and an adequate audit trail.

Error Correction Procedures. Error correction is more likely to be complete and accurate when sound procedures are followed by the user:

TO:	Batch No.
FROM:	Date
Sequence	No. in Batch
Received Documents as Described	
Signature	Date
PLEASE SIGN AND RETURN TO SENDING DEPARTMENT UPON RECEIPT	

Figure 9–2. Transmittal Ticket for Batch of Receiving Reports

- Written error correction procedures should be included in the user's procedures manual to provide guidance to personnel in understanding and correcting errors. Included should be descriptions of all commonly encountered error conditions, correction procedures for each error type, and directions for resubmitting the transaction for source document preparation.
- Resubmitted source documents should be reviewed for errors in the same way that documents are reviewed after the initial preparation.
- An entry should be made in an error log for each erroneous source document. The entry should include the batch number, transaction number, cause of error, date of occurrence, dates of correction and resubmission, and initials of user personnel. A review of the log will show that errors have been corrected and resubmitted on a timely basis.

Audit Trail.   The audit trail for data capture consists of a copy of the source documents or a listing of source transactions. The source document is either prepared manually during data capture or printed by the terminal or the computer as a byproduct of transaction processing. A source list is produced as an audit trail in systems where no source document is prepared.

Reference to source documents by the auditor requires a search of the source document file. If transactions are collected into batches during data capture, the auditor can usually find the original source documents filed by batch. The documents are organized within the batch by name, account number, or some other document characteristic. Many companies retain copies of the source documents on file. These copies are filed alphabetically by name or numerically by document number (see Figure 9–3).

RECEIVING REPORT			No. 6012
Prepared by	Date	P.O. No.	Vendor
Quantity	Units	Description	
Delivered by		Inspected by	
Shipping Weight		Approved by	

Figure 9–3.   Example of a Source Document

In some on-line systems, no source document is prepared. Instead the terminal or computer prepares a source list. The source list will identify each transaction by number and will include such audit trail information as the type of transaction, identification of the preparer and approver, terminal identification, and time and date of entry. The source list may be printed or it may be stored on a machine-readable medium such as magnetic disk or tape. The auditor must use the computer to reference source lists on disk or tape.

Understanding and Tests of Controls

The auditor should perform the following procedures to obtain an understanding of the internal control structure and tests of data capture controls:

1. Review the user department's procedures manual to determine the completeness of documentation of procedures and controls.
2. Review source document design and security to determine their effect on the incidence of errors.
3. Review the user department's organization plan to determine that no one individual performs incompatible duties.
4. Review source documents and source listings on a test basis for proper identification of preparer and evidence of approval.
5. Recompute and balance batch totals on a test basis.
6. Review reconciliations of batches on a test basis to ensure that errors were properly discovered.
7. Review the error log to ensure that errors are corrected and resubmitted on a timely basis.

BATCH DATA ENTRY CONTROLS

Batch data entry controls are controls over the initial preparation of data for computer input and the entry of the data into the computer in batch input systems.

Batch Data Preparation

Batch data preparation is an off-line process in batch input systems that assembles and prepares data for subsequent input to the computer. *Assembly of data* is the organization of transactions into batches, if not performed in data capture, and (optionally) the sequencing of the batch into master-file order. *Preparation* involves the conversion and coding of data in machine-readable form. Batch data preparation provides a major opportunity for control of errors early in the transaction cycle.

Batch data preparation creates the following risks of error:

1. *Accounting system*
   - Source data may be inaccurate.
   - Transactions may be omitted from data preparation.
   - Transactions may be improperly valued or classified as a result of conversion and coding errors.

2. *Control procedures*
   - Transactions may be converted more than once.
   - Transactions may be added.
   - Conversion and coding of data may be inaccurate.

These risks can be reduced by the use of application controls that meet the following objectives.

Prevention Objective: To ensure reliable and properly prepared batch data. The following procedures and methods can generally be used to avoid errors in the preparation of batch data: written instructions, a low error environment, a review of input data, turnaround documents, and formatting.

Written Instructions. Written instructions reduce the likelihood of error by encouraging compliance with standard procedures. Written instructions should cover the assembly of batches of data, operation of key entry devices, application of controls, and response to errors.

Low Error Environment. Management can control the incidence of errors by a conscious effort to create a low error environment. A low error environment will have some or all of the following characteristics:

- Adequately trained personnel.
- Comfortable seating, lighting, noise, temperature, humidity, and air quality.
- Replacement of old equipment that creates reliability problems.
- Installation of modern equipment that permits correction of operator errors prior to data recording. Some equipment has a buffer for temporary storage of keyed data and a CRT for visual display of the data. The data are recorded only after the operator has visually confirmed their correctness.

Review of Input Data. Data should be reviewed upon receipt for completeness and accuracy. Data that have been assembled into batches by user departments during data capture should also be reviewed for conformity with the batch data on the transmittal slip.

Turnaround Documents. Turnaround documents are output documents that double as source documents. If input data are prerecorded on the turnaround document in machine-readable form, the amount of data keying is reduced. Turnaround documents are used extensively in credit card and other receivables billing operations. The normal approach is to send the customer a monthly statement that is divided into two parts. The bottom part, for example, may contain the billing information; and the top part may contain the encoded customer account number and amount due. The customer returns the top part of the statement as a remittance advice with his or her check. All that is left for data preparation is the keying of the check amount on the remittance advice if it differs from the amount due.

Formatting. Document keyboard and screen formats ensure consistency of data keying and reduce the likelihood of errors. Document formats provide the exact number of spaces for the data. A customer number, for example, with fewer or more digits than standard would easily be detected by the key entry operator. Terminal devices use templates over the typewriter keys or screen formats to guide the operator.

Detection Objective: To ensure that unreliable and improper data preparation is detected. Application controls that can help meet this objective are batch controls, key entry validation, and key entry verification.

Batch Controls. Data preparation batch control involves establishing initial batch control over source documents or acting as an interface between the user and EDP if batch controls were established during data capture. Batch controls include initial batch assembly, computation and reconciliation of control totals, recording a batch data on batch header records, batch transmittal and route slips, and logging of batch receipt and transmittal.

• *Assembly.* Unbatched source or turnaround documents should be batched prior to key entry. Batch size should be restricted to facilitate reconciliation of out-of-balance conditions. Batch size should not be so small, however, as to increase the number of batches at the expense of efficiency. Each batch should be assigned a batch sequence number.

• *Control Totals.* Control totals should be computed as a byproduct of data preparation. Control totals are used to detect loss of documents or data items, nonprocessing of documents or data items, or errors in data preparation. This is accomplished by comparing the totals with equivalent totals prepared by the user during data capture, or with totals computed during subsequent input or computer processing. Control totals are of three types: financial totals, hash totals, and record counts:

1. *Financial totals* are summaries of field amounts for all the records in a batch that are normally computed as a result of processing. Examples include the total dollars received, inventory items requisitioned, or total dollars billed on vendor invoices.

2. *Hash totals* are summaries of field amounts for all records in the batch that are computer only for control purposes. A control total for all the customer numbers in a batch, for example, is a hash total. It can be compared with a similar total computed during processing.

3. *Record counts* are totals of the number of logical and physical records (if different) keyed during data preparation. The counts provide assurance that all logical and physical records received have been keyed. An example of where the logical and physical record counts are different is in a job-costing system where the operator keys the data from several job cards that relate to each job. The number of jobs in the batch is the logical record count, and the number of job cards in the batch is the physical record count.

- *Batch Header Record.* A batch header record can be prepared upon completion of data entry and attached to the front of the batch. The header record is a machine-readable record of the batch control totals and is used by the computer during input or processing for automatic balancing of control totals.

- *Batch Transmittal and Route Slips.* Transmittal and route slips provide visible identification and destination information. The transmittal slip includes the batch description and control totals. The route slip shows the organizational path of transaction processing.

- *Log.* A log should be maintained to show the receipt and transmittal of batches. The log normally contains the batch sequence number, job description, times of receipt and transmittal, and signatures of responsible individuals.

Key Entry Validation.   The purpose of data validation is to detect inaccurate, incomplete, inconsistent, or improper data through calculation and logical comparison. Until recently, most data validation was performed during input and processing but not during data preparation. This is because data preparation equipment had limited, if any, logic capabilities. Older-model card punch equipment, for example, calculated the check digit but did not use logic tests.

Modern data preparation equipment, however, has logic capabilities that permit logic tests as well as calculation tests. Key-to-disk equipment, for example, has logic capabilities for testing classification or code validity, character and field validity, and data reasonableness. This is in addition to the check digit and balancing of control totals.

• *Logic Tests.* The use of logic tests in data preparation depends not only on the equipment capabilities but also on the nature and importance of the input data. The following tests are available to the system designer:

- Tests of *data classification* and *transaction codes* are fairly easy. There is usually a limited set of valid codes from which the key entry operator may choose. If the key entry device stores a table of valid codes, it is a simple matter of referencing the table to determine whether a code is included in the valid set. For example, valid acquisition transactions for updating accounts payable would be limited to certain types of transactions and related codes.
- A *sign test* is used when a character or field should always be negative or positive. A payroll bonus program, for example, may calculate bonuses on the basis of seniority. The program may check for employees who have worked for three years or more, and for employees who have worked for one to three years. All other employees are assumed to have worked for less than one year and receive no bonus. If an employee with five years of service, however, is incorrectly credited with *minus* five years of service, his or her service will be classified as less than one year and this employee will receive no bonus. A sign test will prevent this type of error because the contents of the length of service field must always be positive.
- A *value test* can be used if a data field always contains a certain value. The field that always contains zero, for example, can be tested for other invalid data.
- An *alphanumeric condition test* is used for characters that should be either alphabetic or numeric. The customer account number, for example, may be numeric. The presence of an alphabetic character in the account number field will signal an error.
- A *field size test* is used when the size of the field is prespecified. An employee's social security number, for example, will always consist of nine digits. Any other number of digits will signal an error.
- A *limit test* determines whether a data value falls within certain limits. The limits represent a range of expected data values. Any item that is outside the limits is assumed to be in error. In a payroll application, for example, all employee records with more than forty-eight hours or less than zero hours of work in one week could be rejected as clearly in error.

• *Check Digit.* The check digit is a redundant digit calculated from the number in an identification field and attached to that number. That logical relationship between the number and the check digit is recalculated by a program instruction during data entry to ensure that no error has been made in keying the number. In this way, the check digit is able to catch most of the transposition and substitution errors that are common key entry errors. The check digit is frequently used to validate record identification fields such as part numbers, customer numbers, employee numbers, and bank account numbers. It is not used, however, to validate fields that contain financial data.

The check digit's ability to catch errors depends on the method of calculation, which varies according to the modulus and digit weights. The *modulus* is the base multiplier and is usually 10 or 11. The *digit weights* are position multipliers applied to each digit in the field. The order and combination of the digit weights varies but could be, say, 2, 3, 4, 5, 6, 7 or 1, 3, 5, 7, 9, 11. Following is the calculation of a check digit using modulus 11 and the weights 1, 2, 3, 1, 2, 3.

Arithmetic Operations	Calculations
1. Read the number.	6 2 3 4 7 1
2. Multiply each digit by its position digit weight.	$\times 1 \times 2 \times 3 \times 1 \times 2 \times 3$ 6 4 9 4 14 3
3. Sum the products in step 2.	40
4. Calculate the next higher multiple of the modulus.	$4 \times 11 = 44$
5. Subtract the sum from the modulus. The result is the check digit.	$44 - 40 = 4$
6. Add the check digit to the number	6 2 3 4 7 1 4

• *Balancing of Control Totals.* The data preparation equipment can be used to calculate control totals and, in some cases, to balance these automatically with previously determined totals. Alternatively, control totals can be balanced manually by the key entry supervisors.

Key Entry Verification. Key entry verification is a method for detecting operator errors in the keying of data onto disk, tape, or some other input medium. Verification is a duplicate process that requires a second operator to rekey the same set of source documents as a verifier. The verifier compares the second keying with the first keying of the data and identifies any difference for immediate or subsequent correction. Immediate correction is possible on key-to-disk or key-to-tape devices with a CRT. The incorrect transaction is displayed to the verifying operator for immediate correction.

Key verification is an expensive process. If all fields are verified, it doubles the cost of converting data to machine-readable form. One approach to reducing the cost is to verify only those fields in which an error is critical. The dollar amount of a vendor invoice may be verified, for example, but the name, address, and part description fields may not. Another approach is to reduce the number of fields that require keying and verification by the use of turnaround documents with preprinted data. Still another approach is to verify only the work of operators whose error rate is above an acceptable level. The error rate is determined by periodic sampling of an operator's work. The actual error rate is then compared with a predetermined standard error rate.

Correction Objective: To ensure that unreliable and improper data detected during data preparation are properly corrected and resubmitted. Many companies have excellent controls for the prevention and detection of errors during data preparation but fail to ensure that any errors detected are properly corrected and resubmitted. In one case, for example, a data entry supervisor was relieved of his duties. After he left the company, a search of his desk revealed six months' worth of rejected transactions that had not been corrected and resubmitted.

Proper correction and resubmission of errors in data preparation requires control of (1) errors from source and (2) keying errors during data conversion. *Errors from source* result from illegible source documents and errors in the preparation of the source documents. Source documents that are illegible or erroneous must be returned to the source department for correction. Controls that ensure that these source documents are returned to source, corrected, and resubmitted should include the following:

- A transmittal log to ensure that all errors are properly identified and transmitted to the user
- Transmittal tickets to control the movement of the erroneous source documents back to the user
- Adjustment of batch transmittal tickets and logs for the new control totals after elimination of the erroneous source documents

Errors during data conversion result from operator keying errors. How these errors are handled depends on the type of key entry system. In some modern key entry systems, operator keying errors are displayed on a CRT for immediate operator error correction. In other systems, the erroneous transactions are identified for subsequent error correction. In this latter case, it is necessary to control the errors to ensure proper correction and resubmission. Controls should include

- An error log to ensure identification and recording of keying errors, and monitoring to ensure proper correction and resubmission of errors
- The reverification of corrected transactions to ensure that they are properly corrected before returning them to their batch

Understanding and Tests of Controls

Assessment of risk at a low level on batch data preparation controls requires the performance of procedures to obtain an understanding of the internal control structure and tests of controls. These should include some or all of the following:

1. Review the procedures manual for completeness and coverage of batch procedures, operation of key entry devices, and control over errors.
2. Inquire regarding environmental measures to reduce the underlying error rate in data preparation.
3. Review the design of source and turnaround documents, and the use of formatting procedures, to determine their impact on the incidence of errors.
4. Examine outgoing batch transmittal and route slips on a test basis and reconcile to incoming transmittal and route slips, the batch log, and the error log for proper control over batches.
5. Review program logic documentation to determine the use of logic and other data validation tests for effective error detection.
6. Review procedures for verification of data to ensure that keying errors are detected.
7. Review error correction procedures to ensure that errors are properly corrected and resubmitted on a timely basis.

Batch Input

Batch input is the on-line reading of batch data from a machine-readable medium such as disk or tape into primary storage. As an on-line process, input takes place under the control of the CPU. This provides the opportunity to use a full range of programmed data validation and editing tests to ensure that data are reliable and proper prior to processing. The following risks are controllable during batch input:

1. *Accounting system*
   — Transactions may be omitted from input.
   — Input data may be inaccurate.
   — Data may be improperly valued or classified as a result of errors during reading of the data.
2. *Control procedures*
   — Transactions may be read more than once.
   — Input data may be missing.
   — Operator-entered data may be inaccurate.
   — Input data may be read incorrectly.

These risks can be reduced by the use of application controls that meet the following objectives.

Prevention Objective: To ensure reliable and proper input of batch data. Each application should have *written procedures* to guide the control clerk and the computer operators and should limit data to be entered at the computer console. Procedures to guide the control clerk include schedules for receipt of input and return of output, and control information to be logged for each batch. Procedures for the operator include parameters to be added during input and appropriate responses to error conditions.

Application programs should be written to limit the data to be entered by the operator at the computer console. Data should be limited to descriptive and identifying items, such as the date of processing or the closing date of the reporting period. Other data should not be accepted by the application programs.

Many of the general controls discussed in Chapters 5 through 8 contribute to the prevention of input errors. Relevant general controls include the use of a separate control group or clerk, sound personnel practices that ensure competent operators, standard operating procedures for computer operations, and adequate documentation of operating and application procedures. Hardware and system software controls often substitute for similar application controls.

Detection Objective: To ensure that unreliable and improper batch input is detected. Detection of errors during batch input involves batch control and input validation.

Batch Control. Batch control over input requires establishing control over batches upon arrival from data preparation and reconciling batch data upon completion of the input and validation run. Establishing control over each batch is accomplished by a review of the transmittal slip and accompanying batch data to ensure completeness and conformity with the description. The batch control totals, descriptive data, time of receipt, and reviewing clerk's initials should be entered in a control log. Control totals should be recomputed and recorded where small batches are accumulated into one larger batch. The computer usually calculates and prints control totals for the input run. These can be reconciled to the incoming batch totals by the computer or manually. Computer reconciliation should be reviewed by the control clerk. An input run transaction should also be reviewed for obvious errors.

Input Validation. Input validation has the same purpose of detection of unreliable and improper data as it had in key entry. The scope of validation tests, however, is generally greater during input because system designers can take advantage of the computer's logic capabilities. It is also possible to simplify data validation during input by using generalized data validation routines.

Validation tests covered earlier in the section on data preparation—logic tests and the check digit—are also used during batch input, along with the following additional logic tests:

• A *sequence test* can be performed after sorting of the input transactions to ensure that they are in the required sequence.

- The program can anticipate the receipt of input transactions and display or print an error message when an anticipated transaction fails to materialize. This is called the *anticipation control*. Every employee on the weekly payroll, for example, may be required to submit a time card for each working day. If there is no time card, the computer prints an error message for subsequent follow-up.
- The application program can check for invalid combinations of data. This is called the *invalid data combination test*. A customer number, for example, indicates whether the customer is a cash or charge customer. If the customer is a cash customer, and the transaction is a credit sale, the transaction will be rejected.
- Each input transaction should have a certain number of fields. The program can check to ensure that all required data fields are present (the *field presence check*).

Some computer systems use generalized program routines for the validation of input. The generalized routines provide validation logic that is common to several applications. Each individual application that uses these routines will reference a table of specific validation parameters, such as the correct number of fields, required for that application. Generalized validation routines simplify the programming of individual applications. They also encourage the validation of transactions at, or shortly after, input rather than during file update. Validation at the time of input provides more timely notification of errors and, therefore, permits the user to correct these errors while the transactions are still familiar.

Correction Objective: To ensure that unreliable and improper data detected during batch input are properly corrected and resubmitted. Error correction can be quite complex in a batch input system, creating the danger that errors will not be corrected properly, the correction will not be made at all, or the correction will be made more than once. Controls over the correction of errors are procedures to prevent these problems. These procedures include controls tailored to match error correction system design, upstream resubmission, and an adequate audit trail.

Controls to Match Error Correction System Design. There are three basic approaches to error correction system design: delay batch processing until all input transactions have been validated, continue processing using valid and rejected transactions, and process valid transactions only.

- *Delay Processing until Entire Batch Is Validated.* In some systems, it is necessary to validate all input data in the batch so that the entire batch can be processed. This requirement is common in systems with a processing cycle of a week or longer where transactions cannot possibly be delayed until the next cycle. In a monthly payroll system, for example, it would not be satisfactory to reject a payroll transaction and inform an employee that due to a data processing error he or she would not receive the regular monthly paycheck.

When all transactions in the batch must be validated in the current processing cycle, the general approach is to write the rejected transactions onto a suspense file. A printed report of the errors is sent to the user department for immediate correction. When the corrected transaction is returned, the rejected transaction is removed from the suspense file, corrected, revalidated, and added to the file of validated transactions.[1]

Control totals are normally maintained for files of both validated transactions and rejected transactions. The totals will be adjusted as transactions are corrected and transferred to the validated file.

The suspense file can be created for an individual application, or it can be common to several applications. If it is a common suspense file, it is known as a *circulating error file*. It is used in connection with generalized input data validation routines (see Figure 9–4). It has the advantage of centralizing error correction and reporting, thereby ensuring standard procedures and formats for all users. Individual users still receive separate error reports on their transactions, and control totals for valid and rejected transactions are still maintained for each application.

• *Process Validation and Rejected Transactions.* In some systems, it may be necessary to process a transaction even though it may be in error. This occurs when the processing of other transactions depends on the prior processing of the erroneous transaction. A transaction to establish a new customer account, for example, would need to be processed to establish the new record in the receivables master file. Without the new customer record, it would be impossible to process existing credit sale transactions for this customer.

In such situations, it is not feasible to delay the processing of the batch or to process the batch without the erroneous transaction. Instead the approach to error correction is to process the transaction and to attach an error notice to the erroneous data field in the master-file record. The error notice is left in the record until the correction is made.

• *Process Valid Transactions Only.* In systems where processing of the entire batch is not required, validated transactions can be processed, and rejected transactions can be returned to the user for correction. Corrected transactions can be resubmitted in the batch for the following cycle. This is common in systems that validate and process on a daily basis.

---

[1]In some systems, the entire batch of transactions is returned to the user along with a list of the rejected transactions. The user then corrects the erroneous transactions and resubmits the entire batch.

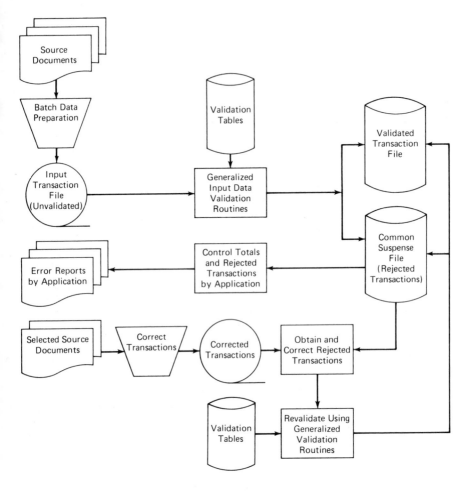

Figure 9–4.   Generalized Input Data Validation and Common Suspense File

By returning the transaction to the user, the transaction is removed from the transaction file. Control totals must be adjusted to the remaining validated transactions. An error log provides a record of transactions returned to the user.

Upstream Resubmission.   There is no guarantee that corrected transactions will be in fact be correct. The correction could have been faulty, could have been applied to the wrong field, or could have been made more than once. Consequently, it is necessary to submit all corrected transactions to the same input validation requirements used during the original input. This is called *upstream resubmission*. It ensures that the corrections are correct. Upstream resubmission is used in Figure 9–4 where corrected transactions are revalidated using the generalized validation routines.

Audit Trail. An adequate audit trail can aid in the proper correction and follow-up of rejected input transactions. The following constitutes the audit trail for batch input:

- A listing of validated input transactions for each batch with associated control totals
- A listing of rejected input transactions for each batch with associated control totals
- In lieu of a rejected transaction listing, a manually prepared error log of rejected transactions
- Transaction files on tape or disk for validated transactions and rejected transactions (suspense file)

Understanding and Tests of Controls

Assessment of risk at a low level on batch input controls requires that the auditor perform procedures to obtain an understanding of the internal control structure and tests of controls. Tests of controls require computer auditing techniques and are covered in Chapters 11 through 13. Audit procedures to obtain an understanding of the internal control structure, however, should include the following:

1. Review written procedures for control and computer operation for each application to ensure that they are likely to provide reliable handling of input transactions.
2. Review procedures for logging and adjustment of batch control totals to ensure that transactions cannot be lost, duplicated, or altered without being detected.
3. Review input validation tests to determine their adequacy in detecting errors in transactions received from data preparation, and errors that occur in the reading of input transactions.
4. Review error correction procedures to ensure that errors are properly corrected and resubmitted.
5. Review documentation and file data to determine the adequacy of the audit trail.

SUMMARY

Application controls are controls that relate to specific accounting procedures. They work together with the general controls to ensure that internal control is satisfactory. Application controls include input controls, processing controls, and output controls. Input controls for data capture, batch data preparation, and batch input have been described in this chapter. Table 9–3 summarizes these controls.

Controls over data capture include user procedures manuals, properly designed source documents, and evidence of preparation and approval. Batch controls and reviews by the user provide assurance that data capture errors will be detected. Written and complete error correction procedures and an adequate audit trail ensure that data capture errors will be corrected.

The reliability of batch data preparation is enhanced by use of written instructions, a low error environment, reviews of input data, turnaround documents, and formatting. Batch controls, validation tests, and key entry verification are used to detect source or preparation errors. Proper correction of data preparation errors can be ensured by the use of such procedures as transmittal logs and tickets.

Controls over batch input focus on the detection of errors using batch controls and validation tests. Data validation tests can be used extensively because batch input is an on-line process under program control. Correction of errors detected during batch input can be quite complex, and the specific controls required depend on how error correction is handled. Controls include a suspense file, error notices, return of transactions to source, upstream resubmission, and an adequate audit trail.

Table 9–3.   Summary of Data Capture and Batch Data Entry Controls

Step in Transaction Processing Cycle	Controls Objective		
	Prevention	Detection	Correction
Data capture	1. User procedures manual 2. Source document design 3. Prenumbering 4. Forms security 5. Separation of duties 6. Personnel practices	1. Batch controls —Batch identification numbers —Batch size control —Control totals —Control log —Transmittal ticket	1. Error corrections procedures 2. Audit trail —Source documents —Source listing —Transaction identifiers

Table 9–3.   (Continued)

Step in Transaction Processing Cycle	Controls Objective		
	Prevention	Detection	Correction
	7. Identification of preparer 8. Evidence of approval	2. User review	
Batch data preparation	1. Written instructions 2. Low error environment 3. Review of input data 4. Turnaround documents 5. Formatting	1. Batch controls —Batch assembly control —Control totals —Batch header record —Control log 2. Key entry validation —Classification tests —Code tests —Sign test —Value test —Alphanumeric condition test —Field size test —Limit test —Check digit —Balancing of control totals 3. Key entry verification	1. Audit trail —Transmittal tickets —Transmittal log —Error log 2. Reverification 3. Control total adjustment
Batch input	1. Written procedures 2. Field restriction on input data	1. Batch control —Review —Control log —Reconciliation of control totals 2. Input validation —Sequence test —Anticipation control —Invalid data combination test —Field presence check	1. Error correction procedures 2. Upstream resubmission 3. Audit trail —Manual error log —Error listing —Validated transaction files listing —Error suspense file listing

APPENDIX

Lava Butte, Inc.: Data Capture and Batch Data Entry Controls Questionnaire and Flowcharts for Weekly Payroll System

1. Do the controls over data capture appear to provide a basis for a reduction in control risk?

Yes   ✔   No _____

In answering the above question, the auditor should consider the following:

A. Do data capture controls ensure that source data are reliable, proper, authorized, and approved?

Yes   ✔   No _____

Data capture controls include:	Contributes to Possible Reduction in Control Risk		Comments
	Yes	No	
— User has adequate written procedures		✓	*No written procedures in warehouse or personnel*
— Source documents are prenumbered and designed with special formats and preprinted data		✓	*Only transmittal slips are prenumbered*
— Source documents are adequately secured	✓		
— Separation of duties in user department	✓		
— Evaluation of personnel	✓		
— Rotation of duties	✓		
— Required vacations	✓		

Data capture controls include:	Contributes to Possible Reduction in Control Risk		Comments
	Yes	No	
— Bonding	✓		
— Evidence of preparation and approval	✓		

B. Do data capture controls ensure that unreliable, improper, unauthorized, or invalid source data are detected?

Yes ____✓____   No _____

Data capture controls include:	Contributes to Possible Reduction in Control Risk		Comments
	Yes	No	
— Batch controls a. Unique batch identifying number	✓		*Prenumbered transmittal slip provides batch number*
b. Batch size limited	✓		
c. Control totals	✓		*Hash total of employee numbers; record count of time cards*
d. Batch control log	✓		*Logs maintained in payroll and personnel*
e. Batch transmittal slips	✓		
— User review of source and batch documents	✓		*Reviewed by payroll control clerk and personnell clerk*

C. Do data capture controls ensure that unreliable, improper, unauthorized, or invalid source data are properly corrected and resubmitted?

Yes ____✔____   No _____

Data capture controls include:	Contributes to Possible Reduction in Control Risk		Comments
	Yes	No	
— Error correction procedures a. Adequate written procedures		✔	Only payroll has written procedures
b. Review of corrected source documents	✔		By payroll department
c. Entry in error log	✔		By control clerk in data processing
d. Review of error log	✔		By control clerk in data processing
— Adequate audit trail for data capture	✔		

2. Do the controls over batch data preparation appear to provide a basis for a reduction in control risk?

Yes ____✔____   No _____

In answering the above question the auditor should consider the following:

A. Do batch data preparation controls ensure reliable and properly prepared batch data?

Yes ____✔____   No _____

Batch data preparation controls include:	Contributes to Possible Reduction in Control Risk		Comments
	Yes	No	
— Adequate written procedures	✓		
— Low error environment		✓	old key-to-tape equipment creates reliability problems
— Review of input data	✓		By control clerk
— Use of turnaround documents	N/A		
— Document, screen, and keyboard formats	N/A		

B. Do batch data preparation controls ensure that unreliable and improper data preparation is detected?

Yes _____✓_____   No _____

Batch data preparation controls include:	Contributes to Possible Reduction in Control Risk		Comments
	Yes	No	
— Batch controls a. Batch assembly	N/A		Sorting is done during input
b. Computation and reconciliation of control totals			
— financial totals		✓	omission not significant
— hash totals	✓		} manual reconciliation with payroll
— record counts	✓		} department totals
c. Batch header record	✓		Entered from transmittal slip as first record on tape for each batch

Batch data preparation controls include:	Contributes to Possible Reduction in Control Risk		Comments
	Yes	No	
d. Batch transmittal and route slips	✓		
e. Logging of batch receipt and transmittal	✓		*By control clerk*
—Key entry validation a. Transaction classification test			
b. Sign test			*Key-to-tape equipment*
c. Value test		✓	*has no validation capabilities*
d. Alphanumeric condition test			
e. Field size test			
f. Check digit			
g. Balancing control totals			
—Key entry verification	✓		*all fields are verified*

C. Do batch data preparation controls ensure that unreliable and improper data are properly corrected and resubmitted?

Yes _____✓_____   No _____

Batch data preparation controls include:	Contributes to Possible Reduction in Control Risk		Comments
	Yes	No	
—Controls over correction of source document errors: a. Transmittal log			*N/A*

Batch data preparation controls include:	Contributes to Possible Reduction in Control Risk		Comments
	Yes	No	
b. Transmittal slips			*Validation performed during input*
c. Adjustment of batch transmittal tickets and logs			
— Controls over correction of operator errors: a. Error log		✓	*Reverified without Logging*
b. Reverification		✓	*Error cards not reverified*

3. Do the controls over batch input appear to provide a basis for a reduction in control risk?

Yes ___✓___   No _____

In answering the above question the auditor should consider the following:

A. Do batch input controls ensure reliable and proper input of batch data?

Yes ___✓___   No _____

Batch input controls include:	Contributes to Possible Reduction in Control Risk		Comments
	Yes	No	
— Adequate written procedures	✓		
— Limited entry of data by operator	✓		*Date only*

B. Do the controls over batch input ensure that unreliable and improper batch input is detected?

Yes ____✔____   No _____

Batch input controls include:	Contributes to Possible Reduction in Control Risk		Comments
	Yes	No	
— Batch controls a. Review of batch upon receipt	✔		By control device
b. Reconciliation of batch totals	✔		By control clerk and also by payroll department
— Input validation: a. Transaction classification	✔		
b. Sign test		✔	
c. Value test		✔	
d. Alphanumeric condition test	✔		
e. Field size test		✔	Validation tests deemed adequate for likely payroll errors
f. Sequence test	✔		
g. Anticipation control	✔		
h. Invalid combination test		✔	
i. Required fields test	✔		
j. Check digit	✔		Calculated on employee number

C. Do the controls over batch input ensure that unreliable and improper data are properly corrected and resubmitted?

Yes ____✔____   No _____

Batch input controls include:	Contributes to Possible Reduction in Control Risk		Comments
	Yes	No	
— Effective error correction system design	✓		*Suspense file, all errors corrected prior to processing*
— Upstream resubmission	✓		*all error corrections are revalidated*
— Audit trail	✓		

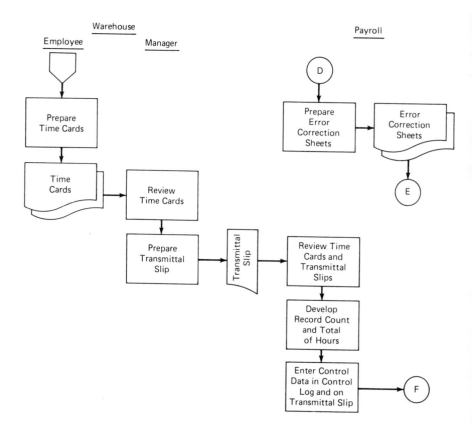

Figure A9–1.   Lava Butte, Inc. Weekly Payroll Preparation: Data Capture

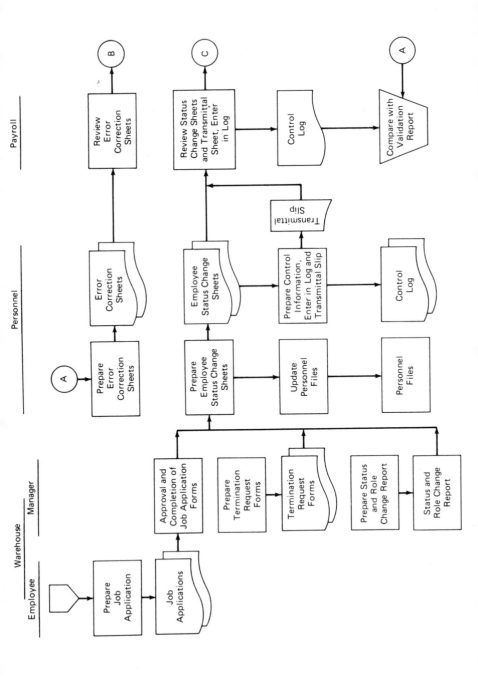

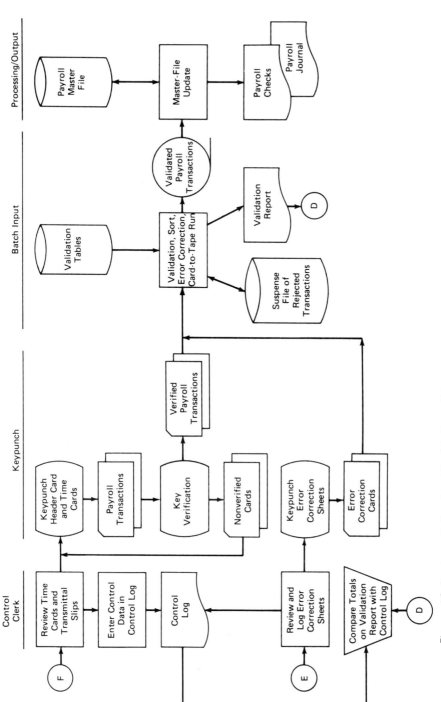

Figure A9–3. Lava Butte, Inc. Weekly Payroll Preparation: Batch Data Preparation and Batch Input

341

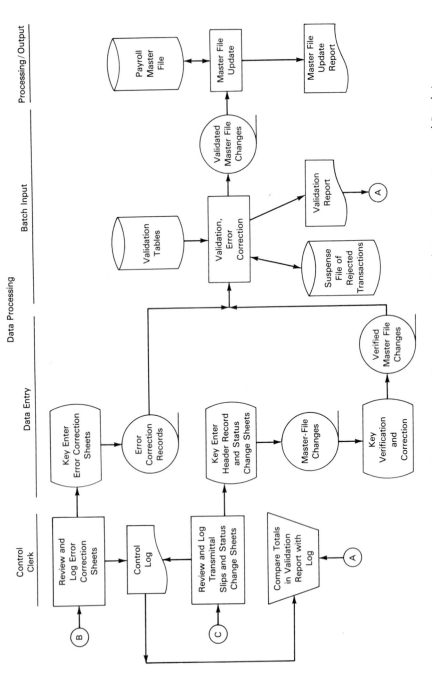

Figure A9-4. Lava Butte, Inc. Payroll: Master-File Maintenance, Batch Data Preparation, and Batch Input

342

REVIEW QUESTIONS

9-1. What is the likely impact of erroneous transaction processing?

9-2. Why should management set control objectives for accounting systems?

9-3. Define control environment, accounting system, and control procedures.

9-4. What purposes does the audit trail serve?

9-5. What constitutes an adequate audit trail?

9-6. Why must the auditor rely on more than just documentation for the audit trail?

9-7. What risks are inherent in data capture?

9-8. Identify four user procedures that should be described in a user procedures manual.

9-9. What characteristics would you include in the design of source documents to reduce the likelihood of errors?

9-10. What duties should be separated in the user department?

9-11. What should a user do to establish control over a batch of transactions?

9-12. How does the audit trail for data capture differ between batch systems and on-line systems?

9-13. What risks can arise from erroneous batch data preparation?

9-14. Distinguish between financial totals, hash totals, and record counts.

9-15. To ensure batch control, what steps are followed from receipt of source documents to transmittal of prepared transactions to data processing?

9-16. Describe the classification, code, sign, value, alphanumeric condition, and field tests.

9-17. What is the data reasonableness test?

9-18. What is key verification and how is it applied to make it effective at a reasonable cost?

9-19. How do error correction controls in batch data preparation differ in errors from source and keying errors?

9-20. What risks are inherent in batch input?

9-21. What general controls contribute to reliable and proper batch input?

9-22. How does the anticipation control work?

9-23. What are generalized validation routines?

9-24. Describe three different approaches to system design of error correction in batch input.

9-25. What is an error suspense file?

9-26. Describe the use of error notices in error correction.

9-27. What is the value of upstream resubmission?

OBJECTIVE QUESTIONS

9-28. Data fields such as social security number or vendor number are not usually added for accounting purposes. They may be added for control purposes, however, and the resulting totals are called

   a. Hash totals
   b. Record counts
   c. Financial totals
   d. Cross-footing totals

9-29. In its electronic data processing system a company might use self-checking numbers (check digits) to enable detection of which of the following errors?

   a. Assigning a valid identification code to the wrong customer
   b. Recording an invalid customer's charge account number
   c. Losing data between processing functions
   d. Processing data arranged in the wrong sequence (*AICPA*)

9-30. A customer inadvertently ordered part number 12368 rather than part number 12638. In processing this order, the error would be detected by the vendor with which of the following controls?

   a. Batch controls
   b. Key verifying
   c. Self-checking digit
   d. An internal consistency check (*AICPA*)

9-31. In the audit of a credit card operation, the internal auditor ascertained that check digits used are derived from

   a. Parity checks of internal and external EDP transmissions
   b. Application of an algorithm to identification numbers
   c. Computer programs checking for nonnumeric characters appearing in numeric fields
   d. Limit checks applied to the amount of credit available to each customer
   e. None of the above (*IIA*)

9-32. As part of an internal audit, the auditor was studying a computer flowchart which contained the logic diagram shown below. Which of the following controls is represented by this diagram?

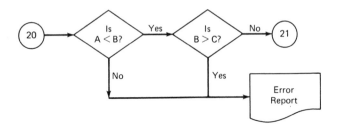

a. Field check
b. Reasonableness (limit) check
c. Control total
d. Password check
e. Numeric check (*IIA adapted*)

9–33. A customer payment recorded legibly on the remittance advice as $13.01 was entered into the computer from punched cards as $1301.00. The best control procedure would be
a. A limit test
b. A valid field test
c. Key entry verification
d. A check digit (*AICPA*)

9–34. In a batch processing system, control over the data entry of hours worked could be most efficiently established by use of
a. Dual entry
b. Batch verification
c. Hash totals
d. Sight checking (*AICPA*)

9–35. An apparent error in input data describing an inventory item received was referred back to the originating department for correction. A week later the department complained that the inventory in question was incorrect. Data processing could not easily determine whether or not the item had been processed by the computer. The best control procedure would be
a. Input edit checks
b. Missing data validity check
c. Transmittal control
d. An error log (*AICPA*)

9–36. A sales transaction document was coded with an invalid customer account code (7 digits rather than 8). The error was not detected until the updating run when it was found that there was no such account to which the transaction could be posted. The best control procedure would be
a. Parity checks
b. Key entry verification
c. A hash total check
d. A check digit (*AICPA*)

CASES AND EXERCISES

9–37. The Lava Butte case contains little information on separation of duties. Which duties should be performed by independent employees? Are there any apparent violations of the separation of payroll duties by Lava Butte?

9–38. Review the flowchart and questionnaire for the payroll system at Lava Butte and identify the items that would constitute an adequate audit trail for data capture, preparation, and input.

9–39. The Internal Control Questionnaire for Lava Butte's payroll system reveals several control weaknesses. Comment on the control implications of each of the following:

    a. Neither the warehouse nor the personnel department has written procedures.

    b. Source documents are not prenumbered.

    c. Key-to-tape equipment is old, is prone to frequent breakdowns, and lacks validation capabilities.

    d. Amount totals were not computed during data preparation.

    e. Errors were not recorded in a log.

    f. Errors were not reverified.

    g. Input validation omits the sign test, value test, field test, and invalid combination test.

9–40. The auditor completing the Control Questionnaire for Lava Butte's payroll system came to the following conclusion: Controls over data capture, data preparation, and data input provide a basis for assessment of control risk at a low level. How is this conclusion affected by the following general control weaknesses discovered previously?

    a. There is no review and approval of application systems development.

    b. Application documentation is not reviewed by management.

    c. Program changes are not restricted to systems personnel.

    d. Application program documentation is stored in an unlocked room.

    e. The systems manager is responsible for modifying systems and application programs.

    f. The operating system is not scanned and not run in a privileged mode.

    g. There is no equipment failure report and no review of equipment failures by management.

9–41. Scouse Company utilizes a cash disbursements system with off-line data preparation and weekly batch input using magnetic tape files. Describe the controls that would be appropriate in the following excerpts from the system:

    a. The accounting department receives receiving reports and bills of lading from the job site, purchase orders from the purchasing department, and vendors' invoices in the mail. An input sheet is prepared for each invoice including job number, account code to be charged, and vendor number.

    b. The input sheets are forwarded to data processing for data entry and input to the computer. Validation is performed during input, and it is company policy to return invalid transactions to the accounting department for correction and inclusion in the following week's batch.

9–42. What controls would you recommend for batch data preparation in each of the following situations? (There may be more than one control per situation.)

    a. Checks are received from customers in settlement of their account balance as shown on their monthly statement.

    b. Key entry of invoice data includes appropriate general ledger account numbers.

    c. The vendor account number consists of five numeric digits.

    d. Company policy requires that strict credit limits be set for every credit customer.

    e. Errors in the key entry of inventory part numbers can have serious implications for the operating departments.

    f. Due to a tight labor market, the turnover of data entry operators is very high.

9–43. What controls would you recommend for batch input in each of the following situations? (There may be more than one control per situation.)

    a. Invoices must be processed in sequence according to vendor number.

    b. Supervisory factory personnel are not permitted to earn overtime pay.

    c. The status of every job in the factory must be accounted for and reported weekly.

9–44. **KING COMPANY: A Centralized Cash Disbursement System**

Introduction

    King Company manufactures and distributes photocopying machines and related supplies. The Company has grown rapidly since its formation by the merger of two smaller manufacturing companies in 1963. Sales last year reached $80 million. This growth has been particularly due to a management policy emphasizing high product quality and fast, responsive customer service.

    Initially, the photocopying machines were manufactured entirely in King Company factories. The rapid growth in machine sales, however, has forced the Company to buy an increasing number of subassemblies rather than produce and assemble all the parts itself. All photocopying supplies, however, are purchased from outside vendors.

    King's four manufacturing plants and thirteen warehouses located in the midwest and western states are managed from corporate headquarters in Des Moines, Iowa. Sales are made through local sales agents who place orders with the nearest warehouse.

    To provide greater flexibility in meeting local needs, purchases of parts, subassemblies, materials, and supplies are made by the individual plants and warehouses. Each manufacturing plant purchases the raw materials and subassemblies for its own production requirements. Warehouses order machines from the factories and purchase photocopying supplies from the best local vendors. Corporate headquarters does not interfere with this decentralized purchasing function unless a plant or warehouse is not providing an adequate return on investment or shows other signs of difficulty. All cash disbursements for purchases, however, are centralized in the headquarters at Des Moines.

Processing at Purchase Location

    Purchases by manufacturing plants and warehouses are made with prenumbered purchase orders issued by a separate purchasing section. One copy of each purchase order goes to accounting which also gets and date-stamps a copy of each receiving report and all copies of the vendor's invoices. The Accounting Department accounts for purchase order numbers and matches their detail to the receiving reports and the vendor's invoices. The latter are also checked for clerical accuracy.

When all the detail is in agreement, a prenumbered disbursement voucher is prepared by Accounting summarizing the detailed information of each purchase. These disbursement vouchers, together with supporting documents, are reviewed and approved for payment by plant controllers or warehouse office managers. The vouchers, together with the supporting documents, are then turned over to the approver's secretary who holds the former, cancels the latter, and returns them to Accounting for filing. Periodically, the secretary batches the approved disbursement vouchers, attaches a transmittal slip indicating the number of vouchers in the batch, and forwards them to Des Moines for payment.

The corporate office at Des Moines distributes to each plant and warehouse a report listing the checks prepared that week, cross-referenced to the disbursement vouchers submitted. At the four manufacturing plants the controller's office compares the checks listed to a retained copy of each disbursement voucher. The warehouse accounting offices are severely understaffed and do not perform this reconciliation. Vendor statements and inquiries about unpaid bills are replied to by the purchase location if invoices have not yet been forwarded for payment. Otherwise, they are sent to Des Moines for a response.

Cash Disbursement Processing

Corporate headquarters in Des Moines processes each disbursement voucher using the combination of manual and computer data processing activities flowcharted in Figure 1 and described below:

GROUP	ACTIVITY PERFORMED
Input	Open the mail containing approved disbursement vouchers and transmittal slips from the manufacturing plants and warehouses. Make test counts of disbursement vouchers against transmittal slips and forward both for further processing.
Vendor Code	File transmittal slips. Sort disbursement vouchers alphabetically by vendor. Scan vouchers for completeness and check vendor code, name, address, and terms to Vendor Master File. Initiate changes or additions to Vendor Master File if warranted. Forward acceptable vouchers for further processing.
Batching	Scan vouchers for missing data and check calculations. Group acceptable vouchers by type, in batches of approximately 50. Forward batches to ten-key operators.

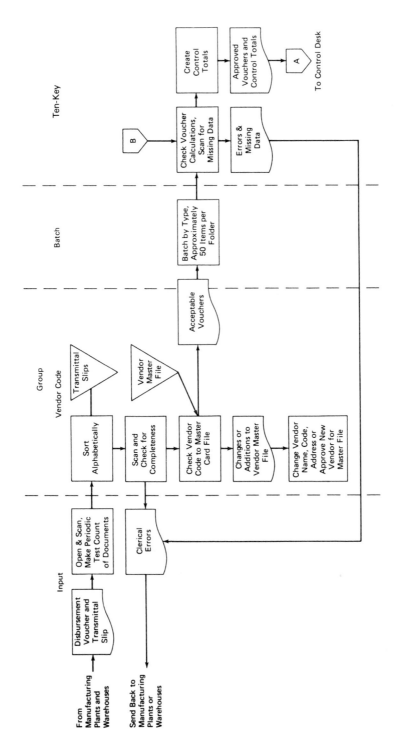

Figure 1. Manual and Computer Processing Activities: Cash Disbursements

349

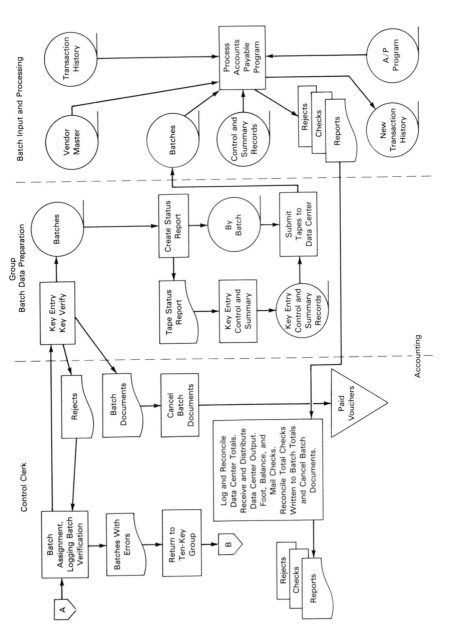

Figure 1. (Continued)

GROUP	ACTIVITY PERFORMED
Ten Key	Create batch control totals on dollars and hash totals on quantities. Forward batches and control totals for processing.
Control Desk	Scan batches for missing data and recalculate control totals. Assign control numbers to batches. Log them in with their control totals. Forward batches with control numbers and totals for further processing.
Batch Data Preparation	Key enter and key verify data. Send batched documents to Control Desk for cancellation and return to Accounting for filing. Create tape status report. Key enter control and summary records onto control tape. Forward batch tapes with control and summary record tape for processing.
Batch Input	Perform program edits for completeness and reasonableness as well as appropriate limit and validity checks. Process acceptable data against Vendor Master File and Transaction History File. Mechanically sign resulting prenumbered checks. Forward signed checks, reports, and unresolved rejects to Control Desk.
Control Desk	Log and reconcile Data Center Totals. Distribute Data Center output as appropriate. Foot, balance, and mail checks. Correct errors and otherwise resolve rejects.

Questions (omit the processing and output phases):

1. What additional information would you like to obtain before making your evaluation of the Cash Disbursement System?

2. What are the objectives of the Cash Disbursement System?

3. How are these objectives accomplished in this system and what controls are available to assist?

4. What recommendations would you make to King Company management about the control over their centralized disbursements system?

Prepared by Frederick Neumann, Richard Boland, and Jeffrey Johnson, with funding from the Touche Ross Foundation. Used and adapted with permission of the authors.)

Chapter 10
ON-LINE ENTRY, PROCESSING, AND OUTPUT CONTROLS

Learning Objectives

After completing this chapter, the reader should be able to:

1. Understand why the control of on-line entry differs from that in batch input systems.
2. Identify the purposes of processing controls and output controls.

In this chapter we focus on application controls for on-line entry, processing, and output, and we use the same methodology that we used in Chapter 9. These controls are designed to ensure that data are reliable and accurately processed. Our approach is to define for each of the three areas the risks of error, control objectives for the reduction of these risks, and application controls to meet these control objectives.

ON-LINE ENTRY CONTROLS

On-line entry is the entry of individual transactions directly into the computer via a terminal. On-line entry avoids the need for batch data preparation and requires a control approach that differs from that used in batch input. The on-line entry approach involves immediate data validation, batch control subsequent to rather than prior to entry, and heavy reliance on general on-line access controls.

On-line entry creates several risks of input error:

1. *Accounting system*
   — Transactions may not be entered into the terminal.
   — Data entered into the terminal may be inaccurate.
   — Transactions may be entered in the wrong accounting period.
   — Data entered into the terminal may be improperly valued or classified.
   — Invalid transactions may be entered into the terminal or inserted during transmission.

2. *Control procedures*
   — Transactions may be entered more than once.
   — Data entered into the terminal may be lost or changed in transmission.
   — Unauthorized transactions may be entered into the terminal or inserted during transmission.

These risks can be reduced by the use of application controls that meet the following objectives.

Prevention Objective: To ensure reliable, proper, authorized, and valid transaction entry. Application controls for on-line transaction entry are written procedures to guide the terminal operation and computer-assisted procedures to reduce the possibility of error. *Written procedures* should cover the operation of the terminal as well as application-related procedures for the referencing of files, entry of transaction and parameter data, correction of keying errors, and withdrawal of transactions with source errors. *Computer-assisted procedures* include the following:

- *Screen formats* guide terminal operators in supplying the proper data in the proper location. They ensure consistency of data entry for all terminal operators.
- *Computer dialogue* is conversation between the terminal operator and the computer. The dialogue permits the computer to instruct the terminal operator at each step in the data entry process. This ensures correctness and consistency of input.

The general controls to restrict access to on-line systems are necessary to ensure that only authorized and valid transactions are entered into the terminal. These controls are covered in Chapter 8 and include the following:

- Restriction of physical access to the terminals to ensure that only authorized operators can use terminals
- A formal authorization scheme that designates authorized system users and uses
- A method of terminal and operator identification, such as a password, to ensure that only authorized terminals and users can access the system for authorized purposes
- Protection of data by fragmentation, intermixing, and encryption to prevent unauthorized additions or changes during data transmission

Detection Objective: To ensure that unreliable and improper data entry is detected. Application controls to detect errors in on-line transaction entry include batch control and data validation tests.

Batch Control.   The effectiveness of batch control in terminal entry systems depends on whether the transactions are batched prior to entry. Batching of transactions prior to entry means that the terminal is being used as a batch input device. Batch control in this case is just as effective as in any batch input system because it is a preentry control. When transactions are entered individually, however, control totals for a batch of transactions cannot be computed prior to entry. Control totals can only be computed upon completion of data entry for the transactions actually entered during a given time period. These control totals are called postentry batch control totals. Postentry batch controls, however, cannot ensure that all transactions that should have been entered into the terminal have in fact been entered. The postentry control totals will not reveal, for example, a transaction that is lost and never received by the terminal operator.

Postentry batch control does provide limited assurance, however, that data and transactions entered into a terminal are complete, accurate, and unique. This is accomplished by the independent computation of two sets of control totals that are compared at the end of each period of data entry. One set of control totals is generated by the computer. The computer sorts transactions into logical batches for application, terminal, and terminal operator. Control totals are then generated automatically for each logical batch. The same logical batch totals are computed at the point of data entry. The computation can be performed manually by the terminal operator or automatically by an intelligent terminal. The point of entry and computer-prepared control totals are then balanced and reconciled.

An inventory control department, for example, may have two different terminals and four different operators for entry of materials receipts and requisitions. The computer keeps track of the transactions entered daily into each terminal by terminal identification codes. Transactions entered daily by each operator are distinguished by operator identification codes. Each operator manually computes daily totals for transactions entered into the terminal. Individual operator totals are then consolidated into terminal and application totals. Manually computed operator, terminal, and application totals are then balanced with the equivalent computer-generated totals.

Data Entry Validation.   Data validation of individual transactions occurs at the time of data entry and prior to acceptance of the transaction by the computer. Validation can take place at the terminal or in the computer. Terminal validation requires an intelligent terminal with logic capabilities.

The extent of data validation depends on the terminal's ability to access file data. When there is no access to file data, validation tests are usually limited to

- Classification and code validity tests
- Valid character and field tests
- Limit tests
- Check digit tests
- Data echo check tests

With the exception of the *data echo check,* all of these tests were described in Chapter 9. The data echo check provides the terminal operator with visual confirmation that the data have been properly entered and received by the computer. Data entered into the terminal are transmitted to the computer. The computer immediately transmits the data back to the terminal and displays the data on the terminal screen. The terminal operator can then visually verify that the data are correct.

Some on-line entry systems provide on-line inquiry of reference files (usually copies of the master files). Access to the data in the reference files allows three other validation tests to be used: the record confirmation check, verifying data, and the data approval test:

- The *record confirmation check* is an extension of the data echo check. Instead of simply echoing the input data back to the terminal, descriptive file data are added to the echo. The inclusion of descriptive data in the echo reduces the amount of data that needs to be keyed in by the operator and provides logically related data to confirm the correctness of the original input. A terminal operator, for example, may enter the inventory part number 013461 and the echo may read: 013461 FILE CABINETS FIVE DRAWERS.
- The inclusion of *verifying data* in the transaction involves the input of an item of reference data from the master-file record in addition to the transaction identification data. The computer identifies and reads the record in the reference file and determines that the reference data in the transaction match. Only if there is a match is the transaction accepted. The entry of the inventory part number from a receiving report for the receipt of materials, for example, may be accompanied by the related purchase order number.
- A *data approval test* can be used to determine that the transaction does not violate management policies. The amount of a credit sale, for example, can be added to the account balance in the reference file and compared with the customer's credit limit.

Correction Objective: To ensure that unreliable and improper data entry is corrected. Control of error correction of data entry is straightforward because each transaction is corrected individually. Special effort is required, however, to ensure an adequate audit trail.

Error Correction. Error correction in data entry occurs in response to a message displayed at the terminal. The message tells the operator that the transaction has failed a particular validity test.

If the error is a keying error, the operator rekeys the erroneous data element. It is usually not necessary to rekey the entire transaction. The computer or terminal will revalidate the data and accept them if they are now correct.

If the error is a source error, the operator will cancel the transaction input and return the transaction to the user. Cancellation of the transaction will exclude it from computer-calculated control totals. Return of the transaction to the user should also exclude it from manually calculated operator and terminal control totals.

Audit Trail. There is often no preentry listing of transactions in an individual transaction entry system, and there may even be no source documents. Consequently, it is essential that computer-generated audit trail data be printed or available on file. Audit trail data should include the following:

- Each transaction should be assigned a unique identifying number that will permit tracing of the transaction through processing to report and file totals.
- Transaction or source listings should be prepared for all transactions entered by an operator, through a terminal and for an application for each period of data entry. These listings are equivalent to transaction journals in a manual system. Each listing should include control totals for the batch of transactions on the list.

Understanding

Procedures for obtaining an understanding of immediate transaction entry controls for each application should include the following:

1. Review written procedures for data entry to determine whether they are clear and complete.
2. Review screen formats and computer dialogue to determine their effectiveness in reducing keying errors.
3. Review reconciliations of computer and manually prepared control totals for evidence of reliable input and proper resolution of discrepancies.
4. Review data entry validation tests to determine their effectiveness in detecting keying and source errors.
5. Review documentation and file data to determine the adequacy of the audit trail.

PROCESSING CONTROLS

Processing is an internal computer function in which operations are performed on data in accordance with program instructions. The operations performed during processing include one or more of data validation, calculation, comparison, summarization, file updating, file maintenance, sequencing, inquiry, and error correction.

These processing operations create the following risks of error:

1. *Accounting system*
   - Errors may result from incorrect calculations.
   - Errors may result from incorrect processing logic.
   - The wrong file may be used in processing.
   - The wrong record may be used in processing.
   - The operator may enter incorrect data at the computer console.
   - Incorrect table values or factors may be used in processing.
   -- The wrong default value may be used in processing.
   - Input data that are invalid may be used in processing.

— Processing may be performed with the wrong version of the program.
— Transactions that are automatically generated during processing may not follow management's stated policy.

2. *Control procedures*
— Input data that are unauthorized may be used in processing.

These risks can be reduced by the use of controls that meet the following objectives.

Prevention Objective: To ensure that processing is reliable, proper, and authorized. The controls that prevent errors in processing are general controls and input controls (but not processing controls). The general controls create an environment for processing that ensures that application logic is correct, proper, and complete; that the correct version of the application program is being used; and that the correct data files are being used. Input controls ensure that the data used in processing are reliable, proper, and authorized. Processing controls are important for the detection of errors but do not actually prevent errors in data, programs, or files.

Assurance that program logic is correct, proper, and complete is provided primarily by systems development controls, personnel practices, program change controls, library controls, access controls, and separation of duties. Systems development controls ensure that the programs are written properly in the first place. Personnel practices ensure that systems development and programming are performed by competent personnel. Program change controls ensure that all subsequent changes are proper, authorized, and fully tested. Library controls, access controls, and separation of duties reduce the opportunity for unauthorized changes to application programs.

Application programs are frequently updated, improved, corrected, or otherwise changed. In some data processing installations, these changes take place on a daily basis. Without adequate controls, it would be easy in such situations to use an old out-of-date version of a program. Controls to ensure that the current version of a program is used include program change controls, library controls, and recovery procedures. Program change controls and library controls ensure that the production program is the most recent authorized version of the program. Recovery procedures ensure that programs held for backup purposes either are the latest version or are clearly distinguished from the latest version by full program change documentation.

Data files are also changed frequently as a result of transaction processing and file maintenance. It is important that the current period's transaction file and the latest master file be used in processing. General controls that prevent the use of incorrect files are library controls, standard operating procedures, and operations documentation. Library controls include a librarian function to ensure the release of the proper files to operations, as well as physical controls over file usage, such as external and internal file labels, that protect files from physical damage during use. Standard operating procedures and operations documentation ensure that the operator reads external labels, checks console messages, and otherwise reduces the chance of using an incorrect file.

Processing will not be correct unless the input data used are reliable, proper, and authorized. Input data include transaction data, data entered by the operator at the computer console, and table or factor values. Assurance that these data are correct is provided by data capture and data entry controls.

Detection Objective: To ensure that unreliable, improper, and unauthorized processing is detected. Controls for the detection of processing errors make an important contribution to internal control even though general controls and input controls may be strong.

Strong general controls, particularly systems development and systems change controls, help ensure that a program is written properly. The complexity of systems and the vulnerability of programs to subsequent change, however, make it necessary to test that the program has performed as intended. The complexity of many systems makes it difficult to anticipate and test all possible logical alternatives or combinations of alternatives. Consequently, errors may remain in the program and may surface unexpectedly during processing. Even if the program is written or modified properly, it is still vulnerable to subsequent events that change the program's logic. Hardware or systems software errors, for example, could cause temporary changes in program logic.

Input controls can help ensure error-free input data but cannot prevent changes to input data subsequent to input or prevent the improper processing of automatic transactions. Input data may be correct when they are read into primary storage during input. Errors may be introduced, however, during subsequent writing onto secondary storage files, during merging or sequencing of the data, or during reading of the data back into primary storage for processing. Automatic transactions such as the reordering of inventory using minimum stock levels cannot be directly controlled during input. This is because the authorization is programmed and is not a specific input to the system.

For all of these reasons, it is important to have strong processing controls for the detection of errors in input data and processing logic. These processing controls include manual reviews of processing activity output, programmed validation tests to detect data errors, programmed validation tests to detect processing error, and system balancing.

Review of Processing Activity Output. Processing is an internal computer function not directly visible to the human eye. Indirect evidence of what did happen during processing, however, is provided by processing activity output. This output provides a record of the programs and input data used in processing and of transactions generated automatically during processing. Review of this output subsequent to processing can serve to detect a variety of processing and input data errors. Processing activity output includes documentation of program logic, input data, and computer-generated transactions.

- *Program.* Documentary evidence of the application program used is provided by a printout of the identification data of the program used. Program identification data should include the program number, name, and date on which it was placed in production.

- *Input Data.* Documentary evidence of the input data used in processing should include the following:

  - A transaction listing provides a record of transactions processed. The listing may be for all transactions in a batch or may be organized by transaction type, account, or other logical association.
  - Application output should include a list of table and factor values used in processing and supplementary data required to understand the use of the values in processing. An interest rate factor used in present-value calculations for a lease, for example, should be listed along with the payments, payment dates, time period of payment, and calculated results.
  - Operator data entered at the computer console or at a terminal should be printed as part of the application documentation. This provides confirmation of dates and other descriptive operator-entered items.
  - Any default option taken during processing should be included in the application output for review by the user. A *default* option is the utilization of a predefined option in situations where the transaction fails to specify a preferred option. An employee will be paid for a forty-hour week, for example, if the transaction fails to specify some other number. The default option ensures a standard processing response to transactions that do not specify a preferred option. A review by the user is necessary, however, to ensure that the default option is the intended option.

- *Computer-Generated Transactions.* Output should include a printout of all computer-generated transactions. This printout can be reviewed by the user to ensure that the transactions conform to management's stated policy. An accounts payable system, for example, might be programmed for automatic payment of payables by due date. These automatic payments could be specifically designated on the check register or printed on a special report for review by management.

Validation Tests to Detect Data Errors. Reliable and proper processing requires that the application programs process the correct data. Processing the correct data requires that the correct files be read, that the relevant record be read, and that the transaction match the master-file record. Validation tests to detect the use of wrong files, records, or transactions include file label checks, record identification tests, transaction code tests, sequence tests, and anticipation control.

• *File Label Checks.* Internal file labels should be checked to determine whether the correct file as well as the correct version of the file is being used. File label checks may be performed by the systems or application programs.

• *Record Identification Tests.* In processing a sequentially organized file, the application program will read each record in turn. To ensure that the next record is in fact the logically correct next record, the application program should check the primary field of each record for a positive identification prior to processing.

• *Transaction Code Tests.* Transaction files are often composed of different classes of transactions, each of which requires different processing. The different classes of transactions are identified by transaction codes. The transaction code of each transaction should be read by the application program so that the transaction can be directed to the relevant portion of the application program. An inventory update program, for example, may process a transaction file of inventory issues and receipts. The program checks the transaction code that identifies an issue or receipt and directs the transaction to the relevant subroutine for processing.

• *Sequence Tests.* An out-of-order file could lead to the omission of transactions or records in the processing of sequentially organized files. An out-of-order condition can result from the use of an incorrect file, a failure to sort the file, or an incorrect sorting or merging of the files. Consequently, the application program should check file sequence by comparing the primary key on each transaction or record that is read with the primary key on the preceding transaction or record. This should be done even if a sequence check was performed during data preparation or input because the files may not have been in the proper sequence subsequent to the original check.

• *Anticipation Control.* The anticipation control was described in Chapter 9 under "Batch Input." This control can also be used during processing to identify missing transactions.

Validation Tests to Detect Processing Errors. Processing errors may occur because of logic errors in the application programs or because of hardware or systems software errors. Validation tests to detect processing errors include arithmetic accuracy tests, dual field input, data reasonableness tests, data limit tests, and cross-footing tests. Tests of sign, value, alphanumeric condition, and field size are also useful for detecting processing errors (see Chapter 9).

• *Arithmetic Accuracy Tests.* Arithmetic accuracy is ensured through the use of double arithmetic, reverse multiplication, and overflow checks at critical points in the application program calculations. *Double arithmetic* is the inclusion of instructions to perform an arithmetic operation twice. Depreciation, for example, can be determined by two independent calculations. The results of the two calculations can then be compared to see if they are the same. In *reverse multiplication*, the results of multiplication are divided by the multiplier, and the result is compared with the original multiplicand. The *overflow check* identifies computations where the results contain too many digits for the assigned storage location. The check prevents the loss of significant digits by signaling an error condition and storing the overflow in a separate location.

• *Dual Field Input.* Dual field input is the entry of data into the computer twice. One calculation is made with one field, and another calculation is made with a duplicate field. The two calculations are then compared. In an accounts receivable system, for example, the customer account is debited with one field, and the control account is debited with the duplicate field. At the end of batch processing, the total of debits to individual accounts is compared with the control account total debits.

• *Data Reasonableness Tests.* Data reasonableness tests are used to detect processing results that fall outside a set of expected results. Programmed instructions compare the contents of a field in a transaction or master-file record with other information in the record or elsewhere in the master file. If the contents of the field fall outside the set of expected results, an error message is printed for subsequent review for possible error. A company producing only metal furniture, for example, can use a reasonableness check to ensure that raw materials purchases are only for materials that are used in the production of metal furniture. The part number on each purchase order is compared with the set of part numbers that appears on the bill of materials. A purchase order for one thousand square feet of plywood would trigger an error message for subsequent review.

• *Data Limit Tests.* Data limit tests detect processing results that fall outside a range of normal processing results. Program instructions compare the processing results with the predetermined limits. An inventory reorder program, for example, might compare inventory quantities with a quantity limit that would not be exceeded under normal circumstances. If the limit were exceeded, it could signal an error in the computation of the economic order quantity. This test would have been useful in the case of a company that misprogrammed its inventory reordering. Inventory reorders were automatically generated by the company's computer when inventory levels hit a maximum rather than a minimum level.

• *Cross-Footing Tests.* Cross-footing is used to test for processing errors in systems where a total amount is distributed to two or more categories. If the individual distribution categories are totaled independently, they can be cross-footed and compared with the total that is being distributed. In a payroll system, for example, the cross-footing of the net pay and various withholding totals should equal the total of gross pay.

System Balancing Controls. The balancing of control totals upon completion of processing has the same purpose it did in each of the previous stages of the transaction cycle—detection of inaccurate, incomplete, or duplicate processing. Control totals are accumulated during processing and are balanced with totals stored in a separate file or in the trailer labels of the input and master files. Control totals include inter-subsystem totals and run-to-run totals.

• *Inter-Subsystem Totals.* Financial totals from one subsystem can be compared with totals from another subsystem where processing activity or results are equivalent. An example of processing activity equivalence is the number of hours processed in the factory payroll and job-costing systems. An example of processing results equivalence is the total of accounts receivable detail and the general ledger control account balance. A difference between the amounts in either case would indicate an error.

• *Run-to-Run Totals.* Run-to-run totals are control totals for the completion of one processing run that are used as preprocessing control totals for a subsequent processing run. The totals from one processing run plus the input totals for the second processing run should equal the totals that result from the second processing run. The beginning balance in accounts receivable, for example, plus this period's debits (invoices and adjustments) and minus this period's credits (receipts, credit memos, and other adjustments) should equal the ending receivables balance.

Correction Objective: To ensure that unreliable, improper, and unauthorized processing is corrected. Correction of processing errors requires sound procedures for error correction and resubmission, an adequate audit trail for each application, and breakpoints. Normally these application controls will be sufficient to meet this objective. In the event of a disaster, however, correction will also depend on general disaster recovery procedures. It should be possible to recreate all transaction and master files, and to restart processing, without further errors or loss of data.

Error Correction and Resubmission Procedures.   There are two types of processing error and different approaches for correction and resubmission of each type. The first type of error is the one detected by processing validation tests. This type of error can be written onto a suspense file and processed after correction with the current batch. Alternatively, the transaction can be removed from the current batch and returned to the user for correction and resubmission with a later batch. The second type of error is one that is discovered subsequent to processing by manual review of processing activity output or by reconciliation of control total discrepancies. This type of error is controlled by an error log and is corrected by nondestructive update of the master file.

• *Error Corrected and Processed with Current Batch.*   The correction of errors in time for processing with the current batch is handled by writing the erroneous transactions onto a suspense file and by preparing a suspense listing. Like the input suspense file, the processing suspense file can be a unique file for a single batch or can be common to several applications. Each transaction entered into the suspense file is automatically assigned a unique serial number to facilitate subsequent correction and resubmission. A suspense listing of rejected transactions is prepared automatically for each user. The user corrects the transaction on the suspense listing and returns the listing to data processing. The correction is made by posting to the error transactions on the suspense file. The transaction is then returned to the transaction file for processing.

• *Error Removed from Current Batch.*   Erroneous transactions are removed from the current transaction file. Rejected transactions are returned to the user. The user corrects the errors and includes the corrected transactions in a subsequent batch. Details of the transmittal of the errors and return of the corrected transactions are maintained in an error log.

• *Error Discovered Subsequent to Processing.*   Errors discovered subsequent to processing have already affected the master-file balances. Use of an error log and nondestructive update ensure that the corrections to the master file are properly made.

Assurance that all errors are corrected requires that each error be entered in an error log along with all pertinent data. Pertinent data include the times of transmittal of the errors to the user, the receipt of the correction from the user, and the entry of the corrections into the computer. The control group should review the log daily to ensure that open items are not overdue.

Nondestructive update ensures that there is an adequate audit trail of the correction. *Nondestructive update* is the posting of debit and credit entries to the files to create the correct balances. The debit and credit entries are different from the original correct transaction amounts in order to offset the effect of the error. Nondestructive update can be enforced by system design that will not accept a delete command.

Audit Trail.   An audit trail for processing is a picture of the events that occurred during processing. These events occur inside the computer, invisible to the human eye, using internally stored data and program instructions. Only in the simplest systems are these events fully documented. In most systems, it is necessary to piece together the processing trail using documentation of processing activity and program logic and machine-readable file activity data.

• *Processing Activity Output.*   Processing activity output provides documentary evidence of application programs used in processing, input data used by the programs, and transactions generated automatically by the computer. Input data documentation should include transaction listings, table and factor values used, operator input data, and default options. Transaction listings are equivalent to journals in manual systems, include references to transaction or source document identification numbers, and provide batch control totals. Computer-generated transactions should be specifically identified on the transaction listings or included on a separate listing.

• *Program Documentation.*   Program documentation describes program logic used in transaction processing. It includes system and program flowcharts and source and object code listings.

• *File Activity Data.*   Transaction listings and other processing activity output may be insufficient to trace the processing trail where program logic is complex. Supplementary data, therefore, should be available within the master file for tracing purposes. Supplementary file data may be included within the master file in the following ways:

- A trailer record of transaction data is attached to each master-file ledger record. The trailer record maintains debit and credit entry amounts, date, and transaction or source document identification numbers for each transaction posted to the ledger record. This approach makes tracing a simple matter by assembling transaction data in one place. If file activity is extensive, however, it may require excessive storage space and too much time for sequential file processing.
- A variant of the trailer record approach is to include in the trailer only those transactions that have occurred since the last closing date or since the last transaction listing was produced. In both cases, the amount of data stored in the master file is reduced.
- Each master-file ledger record contains a reference identification number for the last transaction posted to the account. The reference is then traced manually to a transaction listing for a full description and a reference to the preceding transaction. The preceding transaction is then located in a prior transaction listing where its description is provided along with the reference to its preceding transaction. The auditor can follow this chain of references to develop an analysis of account activity. Analysis of file activity, however, is very time-consuming where account activity is high. Consequently, its use is often restricted to infrequent file maintenance transactions. A change of address for an accounts payable vendor, for example, may be referenced to a transaction listing where a further reference will direct the auditor to the transaction listings containing the original address.
- Each master-file ledger record contains "before-and-after looks" that provide the content of a field prior to a transaction, the transaction detail, and the content of the field after the transaction. An example of a before-and-after look for gross earnings in an employee earnings record is shown in Table 10–1.

Breakpoints. Correction of errors is facilitated by providing breakpoints in processing. *Breakpoints* are intermediate points in processing at which control data are calculated and written onto a file. Control data may include master-file financial totals, record counts indicating the number of records processed, and the number of the last instruction executed. If a processing error is discovered, it will be possible to identify the processing point at which the error occurred. The error can then be corrected, and reprocessing can commence at the prior breakpoint. It will not be necessary to reprocess the entire run.

In an accounts receivable system using magnetic tape, for example, a breakpoint was established after a certain number of master-file records had been read. The system went down about two-thirds of the way through the processing of credit sales. A careful review determined that the shutdown was caused by a momentary surge in voltage. The parent and child master files and the transaction file tapes were rewound to the breakpoint immediately preceding the shutdown. Processing was restarted at that point. A subsequent review of the control totals at the end of the run indicated that reprocessing had been error free.

Table 10–1. Before-and-After Look in Employee Earnings Record

| Employee Number | Name | Gross Earnings 7/31/X4 | Current Period Gross Earnings | | Gross Earnings 8/6/X4 |
			Reference No.	Amount	
212–72–4133	J. Smith	$11,200	2143	$1,600	$12,800

Understanding

Procedures for obtaining an understanding of transaction processing controls in each application should include the following:

1. Review application program documentation for use of validation tests to determine the likelihood that incorrect data, records or files, and mismatched transaction and master records are detected.
2. Review computer balancing of control totals and subsequent manual reconciliation of discrepancies to ensure that all differences are properly accounted for.
3. Obtain the user copy of error suspense listings and review selected and related corrections. Trace the corrected transactions to transaction listings to determine whether the transactions were properly resubmitted for processing.
4. Review manually prepared error logs to determine whether errors were properly detected, corrected, and resubmitted on a timely basis.
5. Review processing activity output, program documentation, and copies of file activity data to determine the adequacy of the audit trail.

OUTPUT CONTROLS

The output of a data processing system can be stored in machine-readable form, visually displayed on a CRT, or printed on paper or microfilm. The primary concern of output controls is printed output, although control of visual display is also important. Output in machine-readable form was covered under "Processing Controls."

Data processing output creates the following risks of error:

1. *Accounting system*
   — Output received by the user may be inaccurate or incomplete.
   — Output received by the user may be improperly classified or valued.
2. *Control procedures*
   — Output may be distributed or displayed to unauthorized individuals.

These risks can be reduced by the use of controls that meet the following objectives.

Prevention Objective: To ensure that output is not distributed or displayed to unauthorized persons. Access to output by unauthorized users creates the risk of loss of assets or vital data. Transaction documents such as checks or purchase orders could be used to divert assets to unauthorized uses. Distribution or display of output to unauthorized individuals could inadvertently override the separation of duties and create opportunities for defalcation. Sensitive report contents such as executive salaries or customer lists could be used to a company's disadvantage if they fell into the wrong hands. These risks are controlled by output-handling procedures and terminal display controls.

Output-Handling Procedures. Procedures for the distribution of output should be described in the operations documentation of each application so that all output will be distributed as authorized. The procedures should be performed by an independent control clerk or group in the data processing department. They include a distribution checklist, a distribution schedule, transmittal sheets, a distribution log, and report release forms.

• *Distribution Checklist.* A checklist should identify each item of output and the authorized recipient of each item of output. The checklist serves as a guide to the routing of output.

• *Distribution Schedule.* A distribution schedule will indicate the frequency of report preparation and distribution. It can be used by the control group to ensure that reports are distributed on a timely basis, and by the user to ensure that expected reports are received on time.

• *Transmittal Sheets.* A transmittal sheet should be attached to each copy of the output. It should identify the name of the report, the name of the individual recipient, and the department and mailing address.

• *Distribution Log.* The control group should maintain a log of all reports for each application. The log should record the destination, individual recipient, and date of distribution for each copy of output.

• *Report Release Forms.* A report release form requires that the recipient sign it to acknowledge receipt of the output. Thus, it ensures that sensitive output is delivered as intended and reminds the recipient of the need to keep the output secure.

Terminal Display Controls. The restriction of display of data to authorized users is accomplished by general on-line access controls. These access controls include physical restrictions on access to or use of terminals, authorization schemes to restrict access to data to specific individuals or departments, and controls such as passwords that enforce the authorization schemes. (These controls are described in Chapter 8.)

Detection Objective: To ensure that inaccurate or incomplete output, and the distribution of output to unauthorized users, are detected. The control group and the user should share the responsibility for the detection of errors in output or in the distribution of output. Reviews by the control group provide an independent data processing department check on the work of the operations area. Reviews and tests of output by the user department represent its acceptance of ultimate responsibility for the output of its application systems. This is an opportunity for the user department to ensure that data processing has been performed in conformance with its authorization.

Control Group Procedures. The control group should perform the following reviews and reconciliations:

- The output of each application, including processing activity output and control totals, should be reviewed for completeness and accuracy.
- Processing transaction logs should be compared with input or terminal transaction logs to ensure that the transactions processed by the system are complete and in accordance with those accepted by the system at time of entry.
- Processing control totals should be reconciled to preprocessing control totals prior to release of the output. The total amount of checks entered into the system, for example, can be compared with the total amount processed by the system.
- The distribution log should be reconciled to the distribution checklist to ensure that output has been distributed as authorized.

User Procedures. The user department should carefully review all output received and should perform whatever tests or reconciliations are necessary to ensure that output is complete and received on a timely basis. User reviews should include the following:

- Review the transmittal sheet to determine whether the output description matches the accompanying output.
- Review the distribution schedule to determine whether all reports and other documents have been received on a timely basis.
- Review the listing of transactions processed and compare it with a listing of

source transactions. This comparison provides assurance that all authorized source transactions have been processed.

- Review a listing of all computer-generated transactions to ensure that they are in accordance with the form and authorization included in the application programs.
- Review a schedule of master-file changes, including file maintenance, to determine whether the changes appear reasonable and proper.

In addition to these reviews, the user should perform tests and reconciliations of the output data:

- The user should reconcile the computer-generated batch control totals to the control totals prepared manually prior to the release of the source documents to data processing.
- The balances from detail files should be reconciled to the file control balances. The debit balances of individual customer accounts, for example, should be reconciled to the balances in accounts receivable control.
- Computer-generated balances should be reconciled, where possible, to independent physical counts of items such as cash or inventory.
- Where exact physical counts or other independently maintained totals are not available, it may still be possible to compute approximate control totals for comparison with computer-generated figures. The cost of inventory, for example, can be estimated using the gross profit method. If the computer-calculated cost of inventory is within a certain acceptable range of the estimate, it should be accepted as reasonably correct.
- The user should periodically verify that transactions that have been processed are valid and authorized. A sample of transactions should be selected from the processing transaction listing and vouched to the source documents. The sample size and items should be selected scientifically using statistical-sampling techniques. In a cash disbursements system, for example, a sample of items from the vouchers processed listing should be vouched to purchase requisitions, purchase orders, receiving reports, and vendor invoices.

Correction Objective: To ensure that errors detected in output are properly corrected and resubmitted to data processing on a timely basis. Errors detected in output by either the control group or the user should be properly corrected and resubmitted on a timely basis. Error correction and resubmission procedures and a complete audit trail should ensure that this occurs.

Error Correction and Resubmission Procedures. Error correction and resubmission procedures should include the following controls:

- Errors should be transmitted to the department designated as being responsible in the operations documentation (for the control group) and in the user documentation (for the user). As a general rule, errors originating at source should be returned to and corrected by the user departments. Errors originating in the data processing department should be returned to data processing for correction.

- Error correction and resubmission should follow written procedures in the operations and user documentation.
- Error logs should be maintained by the control group and the user departments. The error logs should be reviewed periodically to ensure that established procedures for the correction and resubmission of errors have been followed on a timely basis.
- Open items on the error logs should be aged periodically. An error aging report should be produced and used as a basis for follow-up of uncorrected errors.

Audit Trail. The output portion of the audit trail consists of computer-generated output and error documentation. Computer-generated output consists of master-file record data and file balances. It also includes printed reports for accounting, management, and reference purposes, as well as copies of printed output documents such as invoices. Error documentation includes error logs and error reports maintained by the control group.

Understanding

Procedures to obtain an understanding of output controls for each application should include the following:

1. Review operations documentation to determine whether output-handling procedures are sufficient to ensure that authorized individuals or departments will receive the proper documentation.
2. Review operations documentation to ensure that control group procedures for the review of output are likely to detect errors in the content and distribution of output.
3. Review user documentation to determine whether user procedures for the review and testing of output are likely to detect errors.
4. Review operations and user documentation to determine the adequacy of procedures for the correction and resubmission of errors.

SUMMARY

Application controls consist of on-line entry controls, processing controls, and output controls (see Table 10–2). On-line entry controls that prevent errors include written procedures for data entry, computer aids for the terminal operator, and general on-line access controls. Error detection relies on subsequent batch control and immediate data validation. The immediate validation of individual transactions is a powerful error

Table 10–2.   Summary of On-Line Entry, Processing, and Output Controls

Step in Transaction Processing Cycle	Controls Objective		
	Prevention	Detection	Correction
On-line entry	1. Written procedures 2. Screen formats 3. Computer dialogue	1. Batch control totals 2. Data entry validation: —Classification tests —Code validity tests —Valid character tests —Valid field tests —Reasonableness tests —Check digit —Echo check —Data echo check —Record confirmation check —Verifying data —Data approval tests	1. Error correction procedures 2. Audit trail —Transaction identifier —Transaction listings
Processing		1. Review of processing activity output: —Program —Input data —Computer-generated transactions 2. Validation tests to detect data errors: —File label checks —Record identification checks —Transaction code tests —Sequence tests	1. Error correction and resubmission procedures 2. Audit trail —Program documentation —Table contents —Factor values —Operator input data —Default options —Transaction listings —Computer-generated transaction listings

Table 10–2. (Continued)

Step in Transaction Processing Cycle	Controls Objective		
	Prevention	Detection	Correction
		—Anticipation control 3. Validation tests to detect processing errors —Arithmetic accuracy tests —Dual field input —Data reasonableness tests —Data limit tests —Crossfooting tests 4. System balancing controls —Inter-subsystem totals —Run-to-run totals	—File activity data —Error suspense files —Error log 3. Breakpoints
Output	1. Output-handling procedures —Distribution checklist —Distribution schedule —Transmittal sheets —Distribution log —Report release forms 2. Terminal display controls	1. Control group procedures 2. User procedures	1. Error correction and resubmission procedures 2. Audit trail —Field data by record File balances —Accounting reports —Management reports —Reference reports —Output documents —Error logs —Error reports

detection device and simplifies the process of error correction. Special care must be taken, however, so that the audit trail will be adequate in a terminal entry environment.

The prevention of errors during processing depends on adequate input and general controls. Processing controls that ensure the detection of errors during processing include reviews of processing activity output, validation tests such as file label checks and record identification tests that detect data errors, validation tests such as the limit and cross-footing tests that detect processing errors, and system balancing controls. The proper correction and resubmission of errors is ensured by sound error correction and resubmission procedures, an adequate audit trail, and processing breakpoints.

Unauthorized individuals should not have access to output, and output should be correct and complete. Controls that prevent unauthorized access to output include output-handling procedures and general terminal display controls. Controls that detect inaccurate or incomplete output, and unauthorized distributions of output, include control group procedures and user department procedures. Controls that ensure proper correction and resubmission of output errors include procedures for error correction and resubmission as well as a complete audit trail.

APPENDIX

Lava Butte, Inc.: Sales Order Entry and Batch Processing of Orders and Shipments

GENERAL DESCRIPTION

Lava Butte, Inc., utilizes three terminals in the sales department for entry of customer orders. The terminals are hardwired to the IBM 4381 located in the EDP department. Customer orders vary from 400 to 500 per day. There are approximately eight thousand active customer accounts and nine thousand inventory items. Customer orders are entered into the terminal by six clerks who alternate duties according to a sales department master schedule. The clerks also maintain the customer order tickler files.

The order entry system is an on-line input/batch processing system. Customer sales orders are validated and authorized on-line and are written onto on-line transaction files. Read-only versions of the master files are available for reference during order entry. Processing of the day's orders is performed nightly on a batch basis. All printed output is produced nightly. The order entry system described is a subsystem of a larger sales, receivables, and inventory system.

The system and its application controls are described by the following systems flowcharts and accompanying systems narratives. The numbers on the flowcharts correspond to the numbers in the system narrative.

SYSTEM NARRATIVE: SALES ORDER ENTRY

1. The terminal operator receives customer orders for order entry. The customer orders are on preprinted forms. The empty boxes on the forms are completed by the salespeople according to written instructions. Each order is completed in duplicate and forwarded to the terminal operator.

2. The terminal operator locates the transaction code on the customer order and keys it into the terminal. The computer compares the transaction code with a table of valid transaction codes. If the transaction code is one of a set of valid codes, and also represents a transaction that can be entered by the specific operator at this specific terminal, the computer will automatically display an appropriate format on the terminal screen. An invalid code causes a message to be written on the screen requesting a valid transaction code. Five repeated failures to validate a transaction code result in automatic disconnection of that terminal by the computer. Reconnection requires entry of a special code known only to the department supervisor.

3. The computer assigns a unique customer order number to each validated order. The order number provides the computer with a record of every customer order. It also provides a reference number for subsequent order follow-up. The operator manually writes the order number on both copies of the customer order.

4. The terminal operator keys in the customer number, inventory item number, order quantity, and other data. The computer echoes the data back to the terminal and displays them in the appropriate location in the screen format.

5. The customer and inventory item numbers are validated. This is accomplished by a search of the read-only copies of the receivables and inventory master files. Upon location of the matching number, the computer displays the related customer data and inventory description. The operator compares these descriptive data with the descriptions on the customer order.

6. When the customer or inventory item number cannot be validated, an error message is displayed on the screen. If the error is a keying error, the operator rekeys the number and validation is repeated.

7. Inability to correct the error results in the writing of the order onto an error suspense file. Each erroneous order is assigned a unique identifying number to ensure proper follow-up and resolution. A daily error report is produced at night and sent to the sales department supervisor the following day.

8. The two copies of the customer order are separated and filed in tickler files of the day's orders. One tickler file is organized numerically by customer number; the other, numerically by inventory item number. The tickler files are referenced by the salespeople prior to forwarding a customer order to the terminal operator. The dollar amount or quantity of any prior order for a customer or item is entered on the customer order. These data are used in the credit and inventory status checks (steps 9 and 12).

9. The credit check ensures that the order will be accommodated within the customer's established credit limits. A total is calculated of the customer's outstanding account balance, the amount of prior orders that day, and the amount of the current order. If the total does not exceed the established credit limit, authorization is granted automatically.

10. If the total computed in step 9 exceeds the established credit limits, the order is written onto a credit suspense file. A daily credit suspense report is prepared nightly from the credit suspense file. This report is sent to the credit department for review and action. A decision to authorize credit (not drawn on the flowchart) requires completion of a credit authorization form with signed approval. The authorization is keyed into the computer via a terminal in the accounting department.

11. A file is maintained on disk of the day's credit authorizations. A report is prepared from this file each night and lists all automatic credit authorizations and all specific credit department authorizations. This report is sent to the credit department as a record of all credit authorizations.

12. The inventory status check confirms the availability of an item prior to preparation on the shipping documents. The program reads the item balance from the read-only copy of the inventory master file. Any prior order for the item that day is deducted from this balance prior to comparison with the current order quantity. Orders that can be shipped immediately are written onto the day's customer order file.

13. An inadequate inventory quantity precludes completion of an order. The order is assigned a back-order number to facilitate keeping track of the unfilled order. The order is written onto a back-order file and is subsequently included on the daily back-order report.

SYSTEM NARRATIVE: BATCH PROCESSING OF ORDERS AND SHIPMENTS

14. Each transaction record is matched against a master-file record. Unmatched transaction records are written onto a processing error suspense file. Matched records are processed to update the master-file records.

15. Unmatched transactions on the processing error suspense file are printed on a daily error report. This error report is reviewed by the responsible departments, and corrections are returned to data processing for rekeying and removal from the suspense file.

16. Printed output includes the bills of lading for shipments and several reports for audit trail and management purposes. The bills of lading are forwarded to the shipping department. Reports are prepared and distributed according to the following daily checklist:

REPORT	DEPARTMENT	INDIVIDUAL
1. Input validation error report	Sales	Supervisor
	Data processing	Control Clerk
2. Credit suspense report	Credit	Credit manager
	Data processing	Control clerk
3. Credit authorization report	Credit	Credit manager
	Data processing	Control clerk
4. Back-order report	Sales	Supervisor
	Order expediting	Manager
	Data processing	Control clerk
5. Processing error report	Sales	Supervisor
	Credit	Credit manager
	Data processing	Control clerk
6. Daily orders and shipments—by customer number	Shipping	Manager
	Sales	Supervisor
	Credit	Credit manager
	Accounts receivable	Supervisor
	Data processing	Control clerk
7. Daily orders and shipments—by item number	Shipping	Manager
	Order expediting	Manager
	Data processing	Control clerk
8. Updated accounts receivable file	Accounts receivable	Supervisor
	Data processing	Control clerk
9. Updated inventory file	Inventory control	Manager
	Accounting	Assistant accountant
	Data processing	Control clerk

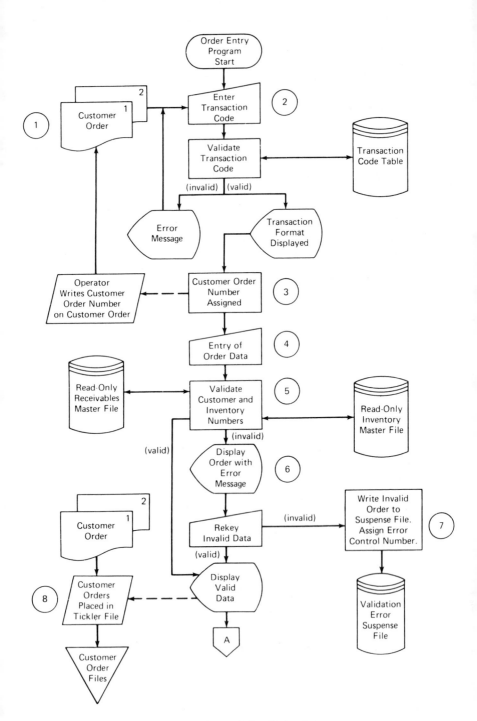

Figure A10–1.   Sales Order Entry

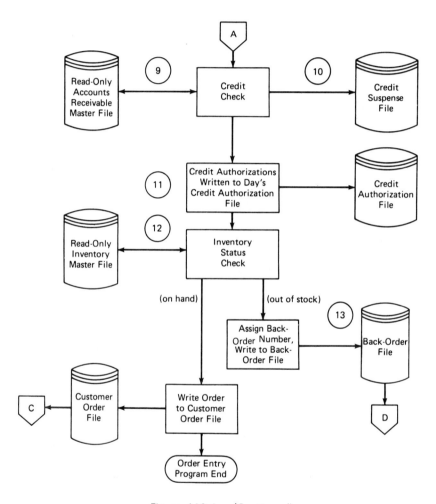

Figure A10–1. (Continued)

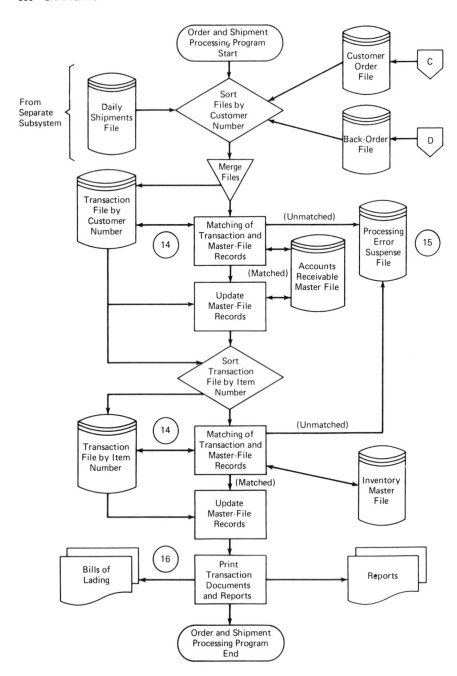

Figure A10–2. Batch Processing of Daily Sales Orders and Shipments

REVIEW QUESTIONS

10-1. What risks are inherent in on-line entry of individual transactions?

10-2. How do screen formats and computer dialogue prevent errors in on-line entry?

10-3. How does batch control work in an on-line entry system?

10-4. What is the record confirmation check and how does it differ from the data echo check?

10-5. How does data validation in on-line systems differ from that in batch input systems?

10-6. What constitutes an adequate audit trail for on-line entry when no source documents or preentry transaction listing exists?

10-7. What risks can arise from erroneous processing?

10-8. What role do general controls play in the prevention of processing errors?

10-9. Why is it important to review processing activity output?

10-10. Describe the transaction code test.

10-11. Why is the sequence test important?

10-12. Contrast the data reasonableness and data limit tests.

10-13. What kind of errors will a cross-footing test detect?

10-14. Describe the two ways of using control totals to detect errors that occur during processing.

10-15. Describe the use of double arithmetic, reverse multiplication, and overflow checks.

10-16. How does dual field input work?

10-17. Contrast the use of an error suspense file and nondestructive update in the correction of processing errors.

10-18. What constitutes audit trail evidence of transaction processing?

10-19. What risks are inherent in data processing output?

10-20. List the procedures that ensure that output will be distributed as authorized.

10-21. How is the terminal display of output restricted?

10-22. What role does the control group play in detecting output errors?

10-23. What user procedures are likely to detect any errors in output?

OBJECTIVE QUESTIONS

10-24. When erroneous data are detected by computer program controls, such data may be excluded from processing and printed on an error report. The error report should most probably be reviewed and followed up by the

    a. Supervisor of computer operations
    b. Systems analyst
    c. EDP control group
    d. Computer programmer (*AICPA*)

10–25. Data control activities in a computer department would appropriately include
    a. Reviewing error listings and maintaining error logs and reports
    b. Investigating deviations from standard procedures in data handling
    c. Supervising distribution of output
    d. Reviewing and balancing input and output
    e. All of the above (*IIA*)

10–26. The record confirmation check, the use of verifying data, and the data approval test have the following in common:
    a. They detect unreliable and improper on-line entry.
    b. They validate individual transactions at the time of data entry.
    c. They are dependent on the availability of reference data for inquiry.
    d. None of the above.
    e. All of the above.

10–27. The comparison of two independent calculations of FICA in a payroll program is known as:
    a. Data echo check
    b. Dual field input
    c. Double arithmetic
    d. Before-and-after looks
    e. Default option

10–28. In preparing the labor distribution report, the control total does not always agree with the sum of the distributions to the individual accounts because of some latent program error. This error would have been detected by one of the following controls
    a. Header label
    b. Trailer label
    c. External label
    d. Limit test
    e. Cross-footing test

10–29. The designer of a payroll system determines that no individual's paycheck can amount to more than $2,000 for a two-week period. Accordingly, she has specified that the payroll program be written to print out an error message if any payroll calculation results in a check in excess of $2,000, This type of control is called
    a. A limit or reasonableness check
    b. Default option
    c. Data validity test
    d. Sequence test

10–30. Due to an unusual program error which had never happened before, the accounts receivable updating run did not process three transactions. The error was not noted by the operator because he was busy working on a tape-drive malfunction. There were control totals for the file which were printed out. An examination of the console printout would have disclosed the error. The best control procedure would be

a. An error message requiring operator response before processing continues
b. Reconciliation of control totals by the control clerk
c. Internal audit review of the console log
d. Label checking by the next computer program (*AICPA adapted*)

10–31. A weekly payroll check was issued to an hourly employee based on ninety-eight hours worked instead of thirty-eight hours. The time card was slightly illegible and the number looked somewhat like 98. The best control procedure would be

a. A hash total
b. A code check
c. Desk checking
d. A limit test (*AICPA*)

10–32. An expense report was prepared by the computer center. One executive questioned one of the amounts and asked for the source documents that support the total. Data processing was not able to do so routinely. The best control procedure would be

a. An error listing
b. An audit trail
c. Transmittal control
d. Documentation

10–33. In identifying the controls to be tested in an on-line, real-time system, which of the following controls would not be included?

a. Passwords
b. Message controls
c. Batch controls
d. Answer-back feature on terminals
e. Test transactions (*IIA*)

10–34. Which of the following should the auditor recommend as the most economical point to correct input errors in an on-line system?

a. Input data are balanced with computer-produced control totals.
b. Output data are delivered to the user.
c. Entry of data into each field of an EDP record is completed.
d. Output data are balanced with computer-produced control totals.
e. Entry of data into each EDP record is completed. (*IIA adapted*)

10–35. Means of controlling the accuracy and completeness of data entered online into a computer include all of the following except

a. Editing and validating routines
b. Predetermined formats
c. Header labels
d. Input control totals
e. Warning and error messages (*IIA*)

CASES AND EXERCISES

10-36. Ultimate Life Insurance Company recently established a data-base management system. The company is now planning to provide its branch offices with terminals that have on-line access to the central computer facility.
Required
   a. Define a "data base."
   b. Give one fundamental advantage of a data base.
   c. Briefly describe three security steps to safeguard the data base from improper access through the terminals.
   d. Briefly describe four steps to control the completeness and accuracy of data transmitted through the terminals to the data base. (*IIA*)

10-37. The systems narratives for Lava Butte's sales order entry and batch processing of orders and shipments describe sixteen different control points. What is the purpose of each control and how does it relate to control objectives?

10-38. An audit memorandum prepared by the manager on the Lava Butte engagement listed the following weaknesses in the sales order entry and batch processing of orders and shipments systems. For each of these weaknesses, describe the type of control that is missing and explain its effect on the prevention, detection, or correction of errors. If you believe the weakness has little effect on the control objectives, explain your reasoning and identify offsetting application controls (if any exist).
   a. Customer orders are not prenumbered.
   b. There are no preentry control totals such as number of orders per salesperson and hash totals of quantities or items per customer order.
   c. No source listing of sales order entry transactions is prepared.
   d. There are no computer-prepared control totals for sales orders by terminal, salesclerk (terminal operator), and transaction code.
   e. There is no balancing of the daily customer orders file, back-order file, credit suspense file, and validation error suspense file.
   f. There are no checks of internal transaction and master-file labels by the application program.
   g. There is no balancing of transaction files and parent and child master files.
   h. The following validation tests are not used during processing:
   — Sequence test
   — Anticipation test
   — Record identification test
   — Arithmetic accuracy test
   i. Error control numbers are not assigned to processing errors.
   j. Output is not reviewed by the control clerk prior to distribution.
   k. Control of output does not include transmittal sheets, distribution log, and report release forms.

10–39. The auditor obtaining an understanding of application controls over sales order entry and batch processing at Lava Butte concludes that there is a basis for assessing risk at a low level for these controls. How is this conclusion affected by the following general control weaknesses?
  a. On-line terminals are located in open office space.
  b. There are no key locks on terminals.
  c. The terminal and computer activity logs are not reviewed.
  d. Terminal operators do not need passwords to access the system.
  e. Application program documentation is stored in an unlocked room.
  f. The operating system is not scanned and not run in a privileged mode.

10–40. Each teller at a savings and loan association is assigned a cash box and supply of money orders at the beginning of the workday. The teller is assigned a terminal work station and teller window. When the teller is relieved at various times during the day, she removes her cash box. When she returns to duty, she takes her cash box with her and may be assigned to a different terminal. The teller handles monetary transactions involving checks, cash, and money orders. Each transaction is entered into the on-line terminal at the time of teller handling. If you were the systems designer, how would you incorporate the use of batch control totals into this system? What objectives would you accomplish by doing so?

10–41. The data processing manager of I.M. Gormless, Inc., has eliminated several controls from the company's application systems in the belief that they duplicated existing controls and therefore did nothing to increase control effectiveness. Comment on his rationale in each of the following situations:
  a. He eliminated key verification when Gormless converted from a key-to-disk batch entry system to on-line terminal entry.
  b. He removed internal file labels from disk and tape files but left the external labels in place.
  c. He modified program logic to eliminate logic and validation tests during processing. He retained several logic and validation tests performed during terminal entry.
  d. He eliminated control group reviews of output after reading an internal audit report that evaluated on-line entry controls as being highly effective.

10–42. For the following situations, indicate the control or controls that would be applicable, describe how they would work, and identify the information that would be required:
  a. Payment of a medical insurance claim where only certain types of claims are reimbursable, and reimbursement can only occur after meeting an annual deductible amount of $500.
  b. Payment of overtime wages to hourly factory employees at one and one-half times their normal rate for hours in excess of 40 per week.
  c. Receipt of raw materials by a manufacturing company that uses the economic order quantity (EOQ) to determine order size.

d. Customers of mail-order company phone in orders that include catalog number, item number, quantity, customer name, and address.

10–43. ZIEGLER COSMETICS: Programmed Validation of Purchases

Introduction

Ziegler Cosmetics is a rapidly growing manufacturer of women's and men's fragrances. Its success has come from the discovery (by its founder) of a means to help perfumes, colognes, etc., retain their fragrance longer.

Computer Conversion

The rapid growth has prompted the Company's decision to put its accounting system on the computer. Cash disbursements have already been successfully converted. A flowchart of the proposed Purchasing–Accounts Payable System appears as Figure 1. The system begins with the traditional acquisition control of matching purchase orders to receiving reports and invoices. The processing of the documents will update the Accounts Payable File and produce three output tapes.

One output will be a payment tape which will be used to produce the checks, a check register, and a payment report. Processing the report tape will produce several reports including an aged listing of unmatched documents. The distribution tape is also used to produce several reports including the list of accounts to be debited. The list is subdivided between matched and unmatched documents. The latter amount will be reversed at the start of the following period.

Document Format

A standard format, which has been developed for processing each of the three major input documents, includes the following fields:

			Document		
Fields	Size	Content	PO	RR	Inv
Vendor no.	5	numeric & 1st digit nonzero	X	X	X
Purchase order no.	6	1st 3 alpha, last 3 numeric	X	X	X
Item no./name	16	alpha/numeric	X	X	X
Terms (code)	2	1st alpha, 2nd numeric	X		
Tax (code)	2	numeric	X		
Effective date	4	year (0–9), month (1–9/A–C), day (01–31)	X		
Expiration date	4	year (0–9), month (1–9/A–C), day 01–31)	X		
Freight (code)	1	A–X or blank	X	X	

			Document		
Fields	*Size*	*Content*	*PO*	*RR*	*Inv*
Unit of measure	2	01–50		X	X
Receiving report no.	7	numeric	X	X	
Shipping date	3	month (1–9/A–C), day (01–31)		X	
Quantity	6	numeric		X	X
Received date	3	month (1–9/A–C), ay (01–31)		X	
Invoice gross amount	8	numeric			X
Type of material (code)	1	1–8/A–C	X	X	X
PO type (code)	1	104	X		

The proposed programmed edit controls for each document are listed in Figures 2, 3, and 4. They are defined as follows:

Alphanumeric Condition Test	Determines that data are entered in the proper mode—alpha, numeric, alphanumeric—within designated fields of a record.
Value Test	Assures that data entries are made in fields which cannot be processed in a blank state.
Reasonableness	Tests various fields of data through comparison with other information available within the transaction or master records.
Limit Test	Tests specified amount fields against stipulated high or low limits of acceptability.
Field Validation Test	Examines characters comprising an indicative field for alphanumeric conditions, transaction subcodes, or character values using logic and arithmetic rather than tables.
Transaction Code Test	Matches the characters in a coded field to an acceptable set of values in a table. Only transactions with matching codes are acceptable.

The proposed validation controls for each document, by field, are listed in Figures 2 (purchase order), 3 (receiving report), and 4 (vendor's invoice).

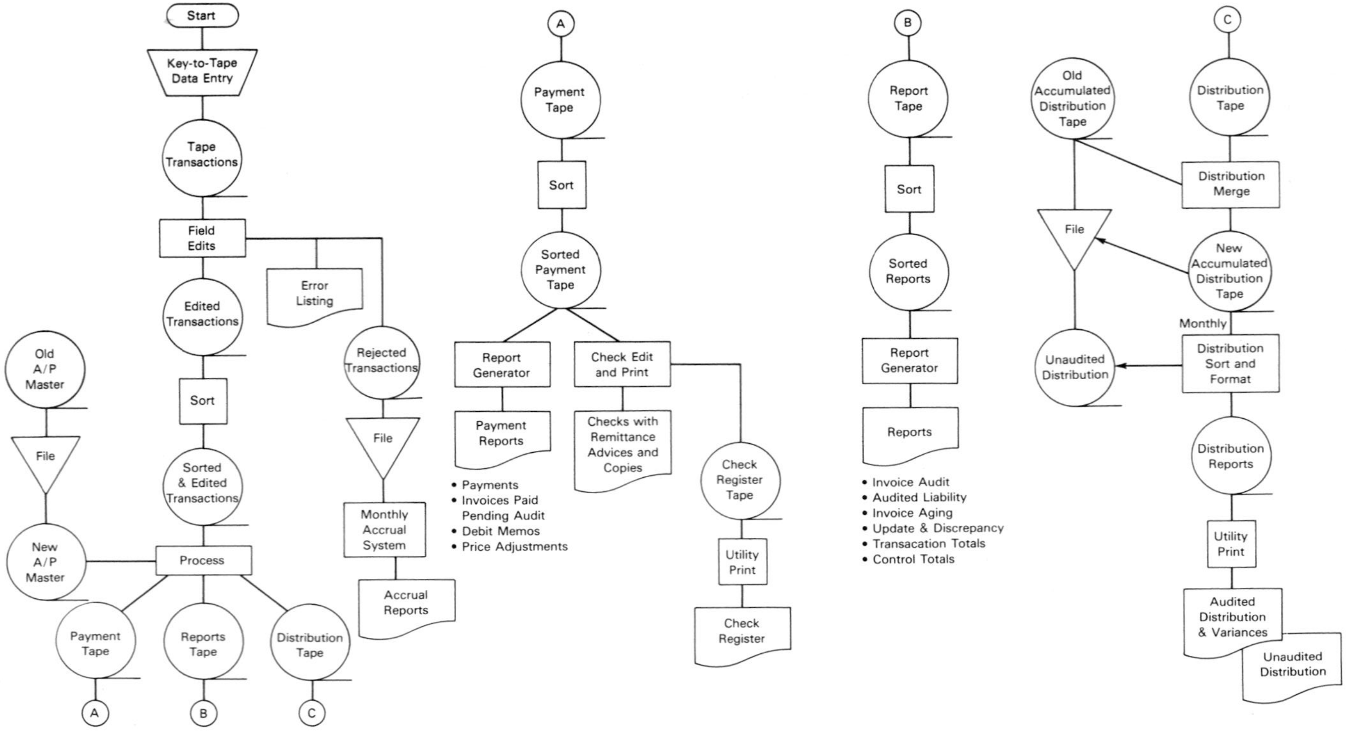

Figure 1. Purchasing–Payables–Disbursements System

Function: Purchasing — Prepared by

Activity: Purchase Order — Date

Controls

What Can Go Wrong?	Transaction Code Test	Field Validation Test	Limit Test	Reasonableness Test	Value Test	Alphanumeric Condition Test
Vendor No. (Numeric, First Position Nonzero)	X				X	X
PO No. (First 3 Characters Alpha, Rest Numeric)				X	X	X
Item No./Name (Numeric/Alpha)		X			X	X
Terms, Code (First Character Alpha, Second Numeric)		X			X	X
Tax, Code (Numeric)		X			X	X
Effective Date (4 Characters): Year, Month, Day (0-9) (1-9/A-C) (0-9)			X	X	X	X
Expiration Date (4 Characters): Year, Month, Day (0-9) (1-9/A-C) (0-9)			X	X		X
Freight, Code (A-X or Blank)		X				X
Type of Material Code (1-8/A-C)		X			X	X
Purchase Order Type, Code (1-4)		X			X	X

Figure 2.

Examination of: Acquisition System	As of:	Exam. no:	W/P no._____
Function: Material Receipt			Prepared by_____
Activity: Receiving Report			Date_____

What Can Go Wrong?	Alphanumeric Condition Test	Value Test	Reasonableness Test	Limit Test	Field Validation Test	Transaction Code Test					
Vendor No. (Numeric, First Position Nonzero)	X	X				X					
PO No. (First 3 Characters Alpha, Rest Numeric)	X	X	X								
Item No./Name (Numeric/Alpha)	X	X				X					
Unit of Measure	X	X				X					
Receiving Report No. (All Numeric)	X	X	X								
Shipping Date (Month 1-9/A-C, Day No.)	X	X		X	X						
Freight, Code (A-X or Blank)	X					X					
Quantity (Numeric)	X	X									
Received Date (Month 1-9/A-C, Day No.)	X	X		X	X						
Type of Material, Code (1-8/A-C)	X	X				X					

Controls

Figure 3.

Examination of: Acquisition System	As of:		Exam. no:		W/P no.____
Function: Accounts Payable					Prepared by____
Activity: Vendor Invoices					Date

Controls

What Can Go Wrong?	Alphanumeric Condition Test	Value Test	Reasonableness Test	Limit Test	Field Validation Test	Transaction Code Test
Vendor No. (Numeric, First Position Nonzero)	X	X			X	
PO No. (First 3 Characters Alpha, Rest Numeric)	X	X	X			
Item No./Name (Numeric/Alpha)	X	X			X	
Unit of Measure	X	X			X	
Shipping Date (Month 1-9/A-C, Day No.)	X	X	X	X		
Quantity (Numeric)	X	X				
Invoice Gross Amount (Numeric)	X		X	X		
Type of Material, Code (1-8/A-C)	X	X			X	

Figure 4.

Question:

- Evaluate the appropriateness and expected effectiveness of the proposed controls:

    —By field
    —By source document

(*Prepared by Frederick Neumann, Richard Boland, and Jeffrey Johnson, with funding from the Touche Ross Foundation. Used and adapted with permission of the authors.*)

Chapter 11
AUDITING COMPUTER PROGRAMS

Learning Objectives

After reading this chapter, the reader should be able to:

1. Identify the auditor's objectives in performing tests of controls and substantive tests on computer programs.

2. Learn how the auditor performs tests of controls and substantive tests on computer programs without processing any data through them.

3. Understand how the auditor performs tests of controls and substantive tests on computer programs by processing actual client data through them.

4. Determine how the auditor performs tests of controls and substantive tests on computer programs by processing simulated data through them.

5. Identify the techniques available to help the auditor test computer programs.

Auditing computer programs is one of the most difficult tasks facing the computer auditor. Although numerous techniques are available to aid the auditor, it is a challenge to ascertain that a computer program is processing accounting data correctly over an extended period of time. Even more of a challenge is determining whether the program being audited is the one actually used by the client.

In this chapter we discuss computerized and other techniques available to meet these challenges. The verification of processing reliability includes testing controls built into the programs and testing the arithmetical accuracy with which the program processes data. Determining whether the program being audited is the one actually used by the client includes comparing programs from one audit period to the next and making surprise visits to EDP centers to perform tests while the programs are being used.

The three main topics of this chapter are oriented toward the auditor's objectives: (1) controls testing and the computerized techniques available to help the auditor determine the reliability of controls built into a computer program; (2) substantive testing and the computerized techniques available to help the auditor perform direct tests of account balances; and (3) dual-purpose testing and the way in which the auditor can utilize computerized techniques to combine the controls and substantive testing objectives by satisfying both with a multipurpose test.

The emphasis in this chapter is on the verification of processing reliability, starting with input to the program and ending with the printing of computer output or the placing of that output on a magnetic medium such as disk or tape. (The analysis of the content of computer files, which may result from the use of computer programs, is discussed in the next chapter.)

TESTS OF CONTROLS
AND SUBSTANTIVE TESTING

Tests of Controls

Controls testing is performed as one aspect of assessing control risk. In auditing computer programs, this testing is performed primarily on the input, processing, and output application controls. Input controls are tested to ascertain that data are validated properly before entering the mainstream of processing. Such testing includes determining whether the errors detected are corrected and resubmitted. Processing controls are tested to ascertain that the accounting is performed correctly. Output controls are tested to ascertain that the results of processing reconcile to the input.

The auditor can utilize essentially three approaches in the testing of controls in a computer program. One approach does not require the processing of accounting data. In selecting this approach, the auditor decides that the audit objectives can be satisfied without processing data through a program. Alternatively, the auditor may decide that satisfying the audit objectives requires processing actual client data through a program. Actual client data are also referred to as *real* or *live* data. A third approach also processes data through a program but utilizes simulated data instead of actual client data.

Substantive Testing

Substantive testing is performed to satisfy the audit objective of the collection of evidence. Although analytical review is a component of substantive testing, our primary concern is with direct tests of account balances.

To satisfy the objective of direct tests of account balances in the auditing of computer programs, the auditor performs two types of tests: (1) determine whether computer results are arithmetically accurate, and (2) trace the flow of information through a computer program to determine whether the program classifies and posts amounts to the correct accounts or records.

These procedures in computer auditing can be illustrated by comparing them with the same two types of procedures performed in a manual system. In performing the first procedure, for example, we may perform substantive tests on invoices in a manual system by recomputing the extension of price times quantity. In a computer system, however, we ascertain that the program is correctly making that extension as it prepares invoices. In performing the second procedure, for example, we trace postings in a manual system from invoices to the sales journal to the general and subsidiary ledgers. In a computer system, however, we trace debits and credits in a similar fashion to ascertain that amounts are posted to the correct accounts. The sales journal may not exist, but we test to determine whether the computer program properly summarizes and classifies the invoices for posting to the appropriate accounts receivable and sales general and subsidiary ledger accounts.

The three approaches to compliance testing—nonprocessing of data, processing of actual data, and processing of simulated data—also apply to substantive testing of computer programs. The organization of the material that follows, therefore, is based on the same three approaches.

Controls and Substantive Testing Techniques

Nonprocessing of Data

Test of Controls. Inferences about the operating effectiveness of application controls can be made without processing any data through the computer program. Four techniques are involved in this approach: flowchart verification, program code checking, examination of job accounting and control information, and examination of printouts.

The auditor makes inferences about the operating effectiveness of application controls without processing data by examining documentation. The documentation, for this purpose, is of two types. Flowcharts and program listings depict what the program is supposed to do. Job accounting and control information and printouts depict what actually happened. With this documentation, the auditor obtains some information on what controls are supposed to exist and how they may be functioning.

The auditor may decide to use this approach because of its relatively low cost. In contrast to the other approaches, there is no cost for collecting actual data or creating simulated data, nor is there any computer cost involved in processing data. There is also relatively little cost in training an auditor to understand the techniques. Another reason for deciding to use the approach is that it may be faster than the others. Examining the documentation may take less time than collecting, running, and examining the data.

A major reason for deciding not to use this approach is the limited information obtained. The computer printouts and job accounting and control information, for example, may not depict the operation of all the application controls because relatively few errors were encountered. The auditor may also have no assurance that the documentation pertains to the program actually used by the client. Another reason for deciding not to use the approach is that although it may be relatively easy to understand the techniques, actually applying them in an audit situation may require specialized expertise in analyzing program code or job accounting and control information.

Substantive Tests. The auditor can also make inferences about the accuracy of computer processing without processing any data through the computer program. This is accomplished by examining documentation showing the logic of the program. Three of the techniques introduced earlier utilize this approach: flowchart verification, program code checking, and printout examination.

The auditor examines each type of documentation for evidence that the program logic is correct. For example, in preparing invoices, is the logic for obtaining the appropriate prices a correct one? Is the logic for obtaining quantities correct? Is the logic for extending price times quantity correct? Is the logic for calculating discounts correct? The same types of substantive tests are made in a manual system when we trace from the price list to an invoice, compare quantities shipped with those billed, and recalculate extensions and discounts. In a manual system, we ascertain whether a person is doing the job correctly. In a computer system, we ascertain whether the program is designed to do the job correctly.

The decision to perform substantive tests without processing data may be made for the same reasons as those for tests of controls.

Flowchart Verification. Flowchart verification is the preparation and analysis of a diagram depicting the flow of logic through a computer program. One purpose of this analysis is to satisfy both control structure understanding and controls testing objectives. Another purpose is to satisfy substantive testing objectives.

Flowcharts can be prepared either manually or with software available for that purpose. In deciding which method of preparation to use, the auditor must consider such factors as the relative efficiency of each, the level of detail desired, and the difficulty of establishing correspondence between the flowchart and the actual program used by the client.

Manually prepared flowcharts may require more time than computer-prepared ones but may cost less. The cost of manual preparation consists primarily of the preparer's salary. Computer preparation costs can include salaries for the auditor and EDP personnel required, plus computer time and possibly software charges.

The level of detail contained in the flowchart may aid or hinder the auditor's search for controls. With manually prepared flowcharts, the auditor can select the amount of detail he or she wants to depict, such as highlighting the application controls. Flowcharts prepared by computer programs usually just follow the program code and show all the details. On occasion the overabundance of detail may hinder the auditor's search for controls.

It may be easier to determine the correspondence between a computer-prepared flowchart and the actual program than between a manually prepared one and the program. A computer-prepared flowchart is prepared from the computer program itself. A manually-prepared flowchart is prepared from a listing of the program. The listing may not correspond to the program actually used by the client.

The objective of understanding the control structure is to determine which controls have been prescribed. Flowcharting is often performed as part of this understanding to depict the controls that are supposed to be in a computer program. Analyzing the flowchart provides the auditor with a list of these prescribed controls.

To satisfy the controls testing objective, the auditor must determine whether the controls shown in the flowchart represent functioning controls in the program actually used by the client. There are two steps to this process. First, the auditor must ascertain that the flowchart represents the program actually used by the client. One method is to ask the client for a copy of the source code, prepare a listing from the code which is then used for the flowchart, and then recompile the program provided to the auditor. The object code of the recompiled program is then compared with the object code of the production program to determine whether they are the same. Second, the auditor must trace sample transactions through the flowchart to determine whether the code as depicted will actually detect errors.

An example of the flowchart verification technique in tests of controls is checking the proper functioning of a reasonableness test. If payroll checks of over $10,000 are to be rejected, the auditor would trace through the flowchart to ascertain that the processing for all checks would have to pass through that test and that the test rejected those over $10,000.

When flowchart verification is performed as a substantive test, the objective is to determine whether the program logic to calculate an account balance is appropriate. A payroll program can be used to illustrate such substantive testing. The auditor can examine the flowchart to determine whether the logic for calculating gross pay, including overtime, is appropriate. The flowchart can also be examined to determine whether all the withholdings and deductions were included and the correct logic was used in calculating them. The flowchart should also indicate that the logic for determining net pay is correct. If the logic is correct, the amounts calculated by the program should be correct.

The auditor may decide to use flowchart verification because of its relatively low cost and because it is easy to understand. A major reason for deciding not to use the technique, however, is the difficulty of determining whether the program flowchart represents the logic of the program actually used. Just because the flowchart shows that controls function in a certain way does not necessarily mean that the actual program also functions this way. An additional reason is that although the technique is not hard to understand, flowcharting itself can be extremely complex. Preparing and understanding flowcharts for complex systems can require considerable expertise.

Program Code Checking. Program code checking consists of the review of a computer program listing line by line. Additional terms sometimes associated with this technique are *desk checking, code checking,* and *program listing verification*. One purpose of this review is to satisfy the controls testing objective by analyzing the controls built into the program. Another purpose is to satisfy substantive testing objectives. Although program code checking is usually a manual process, some aspects of the verification can be done by computer.

The auditor performing the program code checking can satisfy the controls testing objective only by inference because the actual program is not tested. As with flowchart verification, the fact that the controls appear in the program listing only implies that they are functioning. An example of the program code-checking technique is testing of a data validation input control. If customer numbers incorporate a check digit, the auditor can examine the program code analyzing the check digit to determine whether the calculations and comparisons are logically correct and are coded properly.

The objective of program code checking in substantive testing is to determine whether the instructions given to the computer will lead to correct account balances. The payroll program described above can also be used to illustrate program code checking in substantive testing. Instead of reviewing the logic of the flowchart, the auditor examines the specific instructions given to the computer to calculate gross pay, withholdings and deductions, and net pay.

The computer can be of assistance in some aspects of program code checking, such as when comparing one program with another. The auditor may have a copy of a program that has been thoroughly tested, along with another copy of the same program that the client states he or she is currently using. If these copies are on a magnetic medium, the auditor can use computer software to compare the two to determine whether they are identical programs.

The auditor may decide to use the technique of program code checking because of the cost savings involved in not having to collect and process data and the ease of understanding the concept. The auditor may decide not to use the technique because of a lack of expertise required to understand the coded programs, the time required to analyze the code of complex programs, and a lack of assurance that the code examined is for the program actually used.

Examination of Job Accounting and Control Information. The examination of job accounting and control information consists of reviewing the information printed on the console log as jobs are processed. For some sophisticated systems, this information may be stored on a console diskette or disk pack instead of being printed by the console. Depending on the system, information captured can include accounting data for billing purposes, job start and stop times, operating statistics on equipment utilization, and interruption, halt, or termination information.

The objective of reviewing the job accounting and control information in the controls testing of a computer program is to make inferences about the existence and operating effectiveness of controls. Error conditions, abnormal halts, and excessive running time, for example, may indicate that prescribed controls on input validation are not functioning. An example of an abnormal halt caused by a missing input validation would be in multiplication involving alphabetic data. If the quantity field in a price times quantity multiplication contained alphabetic information, the system would detect an error. On some systems, the job would be terminated. The abnormal halt would be indicated in the job accounting and control information. In analyzing the operation being performed and the content of the data fields at the time of the halt, the auditor would conclude from examining the input that a numeric field contained alphabetic data. This was not detected before the abnormal halt because of the missing input validation control.

The factors considered by the auditor in deciding whether to examine job accounting and control information are similar to those for other nonprocessing-of-data techniques. The auditor may decide to use the technique to avoid the costs of collecting and processing data and because of the ease of understanding the concept. The auditor may decide not to use the technique because of a lack of expertise in understanding the job accounting and control information, the time required to analyze what may be voluminus information, and the nonoccurrence of some error or control conditions of interest.

Review Printouts.   The review of computer printouts consists of the review of the output of data processing. The examination of printouts from the computer may be similar to reviews performed with a manual or mechanical system. The review may be similar because the computer may produce the same journals and ledgers available in a manual or mechanical system.

The objective of reviewing the printouts in the controls testing of a computer program is to be able to make inferences about the existence and operating effectiveness of controls. Transaction listings, journals, and ledgers, also found in manual and mechanical systems, can be examined for validity of transactions, proper account classifications, and so forth. Not available in a manual or mechanical system, however, are error listings. *Error listings* are computer-prepared analyses of the effectiveness of input controls in detecting input errors and the effectiveness of processing controls in detecting computational errors.

An example of a controls test using a computer printout would be a review of postings to subsidiary accounts receivable ledgers to ascertain if computer-monitored credit limit controls are functioning as prescribed. For each ledger selected, the auditor would ascertain the credit limit for that customer and determine whether sales were being made in excess of that limit. The auditor would also verify that credit limits were specified for each ledger selected.

The objective of printout examination in substantive testing is to determine from direct examination whether the documents, journals, and ledgers prepared by the program have been prepared correctly. Again using the payroll audit mentioned above as an example, the auditor can select a sample of payroll checks and manually recalculate the gross pay, deductions and withholdings, and net pay to determine whether the computer-processed amounts are correct.

A major reason why the auditor may decide to use the printout review technique is the relative ease of understanding the concept and applying it. Another reason is that the costs of collecting and processing data can be avoided. A major reason for deciding not to use the technique is the relative ease with which a programmer can have the computer print names or amounts that have no relationship to what is being processed internally or stored on magnetic tape or elsewhere. Another reason is that not all the errors a program is designed to detect are likely to appear on a single printout. Some errors detectable by the program may never occur.

Processing of Actual Data

Tests of Controls.   The operating effectiveness of application controls can be determined by processing actual client data through a computer program. Techniques utilizing this approach include controlled processing, controlled reprocessing, and parallel simulation. Other techniques, also used in the processing of simulated data, typically require either modifying a client's program or incorporating them into the program when initially written. These include the concurrent auditing techniques of mapping, tagging, and tracing.

The purpose of processing actual client data through a computer program is to provide the auditor with information about the effectiveness of application controls under operating conditions. The auditor can examine the input and compare the processing result with what would have happened if the controls had been functioning as designed. This approach can provide the auditor with direct confirmation that the controls function as prescribed.

The auditor may decide to perform controls tests by processing actual data for various reasons. The auditor can use data already generated by the client and does not have to create such data. Results examined by the auditor depict how the controls function in detecting errors actually occurring from normal activity. The auditor may be able to examine the process by which detected errors are corrected and resubmitted if the technique being used allows him or her to follow the error correction cycle. The decision not to perform tests of controls by processing actual data may be made for the following reasons: (1) the actual transactions selected may not trigger all of the controls—in fact, finding actual transactions to test every control may be an impossible task; (2) maintaining control over the actual data and programs to ensure the integrity of the tests may be disruptive to the client's operations; (3) the auditor may not be able to determine whether the program used in the tests is the one normally used by the client in processing transactions; and (4) the auditor needs to be fairly knowledgeable about data processing operations in order to perform or monitor the testing adequately.

Substantive Tests. The auditor can also process actual client data through a computer program to make inferences about the processing accuracy of that program. Techniques that utilize this approach for substantive testing include controlled processing, controlled reprocessing, parallel simulation, and concurrent auditing.

In processing actual client data through a computer program, the auditor's primary objective is to obtain information about the processing accuracy of that program under operating conditions. In addition to ascertaining the accuracy under normal workload conditions, the auditor can also test the program's ability to process data accurately as the load on the system varies. For example, at the authors' university a computer system provided a purely random number as output instead of the correct number when some arithmetic operations were performed while the system was under a heavy load. This did not occur under medium-to-light loads. Computer auditors should recognize that the phenomenon of deteriorating processing accuracy experienced with manual systems under heavy workloads can also apply to computer systems.

The reasons for deciding to perform substantive tests by processing actual data are the same as those for controls testing. The reasons for deciding not to process actual data in performing substantive tests on computer programs are also the same as those for controls testing.

Controlled Processing. Controlled processing means that the auditor maintains control over the processing of an actual accounting application. This can be done in the client's facility by verifying or establishing controls over input, processing or monitoring the processing of those data with the production program, and then analyzing the results to determine whether the controls functioned as prescribed. The auditor can test the validity of the production program by copying it and then comparing that copy with a previously tested and verified copy of the program.

The objective of performing controls testing with controlled processing is to determine the operating effectiveness of input, processing, and output controls. For example, the auditor can determine the effectiveness of input validation by examining input errors as they are being corrected and resubmitted. Processing controls can be tested by examining error listings and printouts. Output controls can be tested by reconciliation to input and following the distribution of output.

An accounts receivable application can be used to illustrate controlled processing. In the posting of sales and cash receipts to accounts receivable, the auditor may wish to verify or establish control totals on dollar amounts and the number of records to be processed. After processing, the auditor will reconcile the beginning and ending control total balances to the debits from sales and credits from receipts. In making this reconciliation, the auditor may have to take into account records not processed because of rejection upon input because of customer number or other errors. The auditor can follow these transactions as they move through the correction and resubmission process. The auditor can also follow the physical movement of printouts to test the distribution controls. The validity of the program used can be tested by comparing a hash total of binary digits in the program used with the equivalent total in a copy of the program that has previously been tested for authenticity.

The objective of controlled processing in substantive testing is to determine whether the computer system generates accurate processing results under actual operating conditions. The accounts receivable application can also be used to illustrate controlled processing in substantive testing. The auditor can calculate the ending balance for both the control account and a sample of subsidiary accounts by adding and subtracting debits and credits to the beginning balances. The results of actual processing are then compared with these manually computed amounts. During the processing of the application, the auditor would establish or monitor control totals on input, perform the actual computer processing or monitor such processing, and review reconciliation of the output to the input control totals.

Controlled Reprocessing.   Controlled reprocessing means that the auditor maintains control over the reprocessing of data that have previously been processed. It is similar to controlled processing except that instead of controlling the initial processing of data for an actual accounting application, data are processed a second time and the results are compared with the initial processing.

The objective of performing controls testing with controlled reprocessing is to determine the effectiveness of the input, processing, and output controls. The testing of these controls is the same as that used in controlled processing. The difference is in the timing of the tests.

The accounts receivable application that was used to illustrate controlled processing can also be used to illustrate controlled reprocessing. Instead of processing the next scheduled set of actual transactions, the auditor goes back into the past period and selects a sample of previously processed transactions. These transactions are then reprocessed with the appropriate production program. Four types of tests can then be performed. First, the auditor can compare the results with those from the initial processing to determine whether the same input will result in the same output. Second, the auditor can determine how errors were dealt with. Instead of the technique used in controlled processing—that is, following the errors as they were being corrected and resubmitted—the auditor ascertains how the errors were handled during the earlier processing. Third, the auditor can inquire as to whether the intended recipients received output from the previous processing in testing distribution controls. The disadvantage of this test is that memories fail and unintended recipients may never be found. Fourth, program validity can be tested in the same way as in controlled processing by comparing hash totals of the production program with the equivalent totals of a control program.

The objective of performing substantive testing with controlled reprocessing is to determine whether the computer system can accurately reproduce the results previously obtained. The accounts receivable example discussed above can be used to illustrate the application of this technique. Instead of having to compute the ending balances, the auditor will already have them from the preceding processing run. The auditor should, however, verify that the balances are accurate by manually posting the debit and credit transactions to the beginning balances for the samples selected. After reprocessing the master and transactions files, the results are compared with the initial verified processing results.

The reasons to be considered in deciding whether to use the controlled reprocessing technique include those pertaining to the processing of actual data. An additional reason is that the auditor may be able to minimize disruption to the client's operations because the previously processed transactions can be reprocessed at the client's and auditor's convenience. A major reason for deciding not to use controlled reprocessing is that the client may retain the transaction files and master files for only a short period of time after processing as needed for backup. It may be impossible to obtain files for reprocessing.

Parallel Simulation. Parallel simulation is the construction of a processing system for an accounting application and the processing of actual data through both the client's program and the auditor's program. The results of the parallel processing are then compared either manually or with a computer, as shown in Figure 11–1.

The objective of performing controls testing with parallel simulation is to test the input, processing, and output controls by comparing

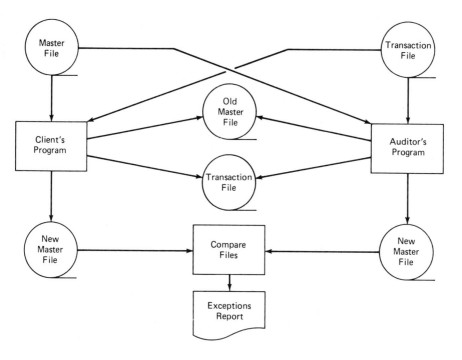

Figure 11–1. Parallel Simulation

the results from two independent programs. If the auditor is satisfied that his or her program contains all the appropriate controls, the results from that program should be the same as the client's. Any differences may suggest weaknesses in controls in the client's program.

An hourly payroll program can be used to illustrate parallel simulation. Payroll programs multiply hours by rates, calculate withholdings and deductions, and compute net pay. The auditor can develop a general-purpose payroll application that can be used with various clients. For each client, the auditor modifies the program for input and master-file formats, input validation tests, limit and reasonableness tests, and various changes in deductions and withholdings. The output from parallel processing through the auditor's and client's payroll programs is then analyzed for differences.

The objective of performing substantive testing with parallel simulation is to determine the accuracy of processing by the client's program by comparing the results with those of a program that the auditor has previously determined is functioning correctly. Again using accounts receivable as an illustration, the auditor processes the master and transactions files through the parallel program. The auditor then uses the computer system to compare the results from each program for each subsidiary ledger and the control account.

A major reason why the auditor may decide to use parallel simulation is that it eliminates some of the tediousness associated with analyzing large volumes of data manually. As a result, the auditor may be able to do a more thorough job in less time. Another reason is that the auditor may not be quite so dependent on client personnel, programs, and facilities, and, therefore, his or her evaluation may be more objective.

A major reason for deciding not to use parallel simulation is that the cost of developing the software can be high. To reduce this cost, the auditor may test only one aspect of a program, such as FICA deductions and accumulations. Another reason for not using the technique is that the processing results analyzed by the auditor may be the fictitious creation of a programmer and may have no relationship to the actual processing being performed. In the auditor's absence, the program may be manipulated to produce different results.

Concurrent Auditing. Concurrent auditing means that while the system is performing application processing, the auditor will be conducting audit tests of that processing. Names associated with concurrent auditing include *auditing concurrently with processing, continuous processing,* and *continuous auditing by exception.*

Concurrent auditing is an advanced technique used to audit programs by tracing the flow of transactions through the programs. Names associated with these techniques of tracing transactions through programs are *mapping, tagging,* and *tracing.* These techniques analyze transactions as they pass selected processing points. Their use requires that the programs incorporate program logic designed specifically for the auditor. The techniques can be classified into those that analyze all transactions and those that analyze only selected transactions.

A decision to analyze all transactions that pass by specific processing points requires that the auditor make an additional decision as to whether the focus of the tests will be on the transactions or the program logic. A decision to focus on transactions means that code is inserted into the program which will display on a CRT and/or list on a printer information on every transaction that passes a particular processing point. An acronym associated with this technique is SCARF, for *System Control Audit Review File.*

This technique of code insertion could be used, for example, to monitor a real-time order entry system. For all orders or for orders over a certain amount, such as $25,000, the program could print the customer name, amount of order, credit limit, amount currently receivable, and amount back-ordered.

The auditor's decision to use the technique should be based on the benefits and costs in the particular audit circumstance. The usefulness of this technique is its ability to monitor controls on a real-time basis as each transaction occurs and passes by specific processing points. In the illustration, for example, the auditor could monitor all sales to determine whether sales were being approved by the system for customers whose credit limits had been exceeded. The auditor may decide not to use this technique, however, for two reasons: (1) the costs may exceed the benefits—information about customers exceeding credit limits, for example, can be obtained by sampling accounts receivable files instead of testing every transaction; and (2) the auditor must be fairly knowledgeable about the system to ensure that the code is inserted at the proper point and obtains the correct information.

The focus of the transaction tests can also be on program logic. This technique requires that code be inserted into the program to indicate on a printer or CRT the logic paths either taken or not taken by transactions processed through the system. Names associated with this technique include *mapping, missed branch indicator* (e.g., COMBI, for *CObol Missed Branch Indicator*), *control monitors*, and *logic supervisors*.

The COMBI technique could be used, for example, in the audit of an accounts payable system. The COMBI technique sets a flag for every branch taken upon execution of an *"IF"* statement in a program. After processing transactions controlled by the auditor through the accounts payable system, COMBI will list all those paths not taken. The auditor would then examine the program to determine whether this resulted from a particular type of transaction that was not processed or from a fraud or an error in the processing logic.

The logic analysis technique is particularly useful when the auditor wants to examine the processing logic in a high-risk program. Accounts payable programs, for example, are often considered high risk because the programs often automatically issue checks to vendors on payment dates. The technique will reveal all the situations in which a check can be issued automatically. The auditor may decide not to use this technique, however, for three reasons: (1) insertion of the logic analysis code may introduce processing errors into the program; (2) the technique requires considerable programming expertise; and (3) the code introduces significant overhead into the program and will slow it down.

A decision to analyze selected transactions that pass by specific processing points requires that two things be done: (1) each transaction selected for analysis must be tagged in some way; and (2) code must be inserted into the program that will display on a CRT and/or list on a printer information on the transactions that are selected by tagging and pass the specified processing points. Names associated with this technique are *audit indicator* and *snapshot*.

The technique could be used, for example, to monitor a real-time order entry system. For a sample of orders originating from a salesperson or territory, or for a particular product, extra characters would be appended to the transaction record on data entry. When these records passed by specified processing points in the system, such as input validation and updating of the accounts receivable master record, the program could print the customer name, number, item ordered, quantity, salesperson, and sales territory.

This technique is useful because of its ability to trace the flow of selected transactions through the system on a real-time basis. Instead of all sales transactions, the auditor may be interested only in those occurring on a specific date. In the illustration, for example, the auditor could determine whether all selected transactions were properly recorded in the accounts receivable master file in order to satisfy valuation and cutoff objectives. The auditor may decide not to use this technique, however, for some of the same reasons cited earlier for other advanced techniques: Insertion of the code may introduce processing errors into the program; the technique requires considerable programming expertise; and the code introduces significant overhead into the program and will slow it down. An additional disadvantage unique to this technique is that insertion of the tag on the transaction records may also introduce errors into the system.

Processing of Simulated Data

Tests of Controls. The operating effectiveness of application controls can be determined by processing simulated client data through a computer program. Techniques for processing simulated client data include test records and the integrated test facility (ITF).

Processing simulated client data through a computer program provides the auditor with information about the effectiveness of application controls under simulated operating conditions. As with the processing of actual data, the auditor compares the processing results with what would have happened if the controls had been functioning as designed. In contrast to the processing of actual data, the auditor has to create a transaction record to confirm that a specific control is functioning as prescribed.

A major reason why the auditor may decide to perform controls testing with simulated data is that the auditor can substantially reduce the number of records that have to be processed. If actual data were being used, numerous records would have to be assembled to test the various controls built into a program. With simulated data, the auditor can design a single record to test several controls. For example, a single record could be used to test for character validation on each field by entering alphanumeric data where all fields should be numeric. It would be unusual to find an actual transaction where every field contained a validation error.

The auditor may also decide to use simulated data because it permits the auditor to test every control. With actual data, it may be impossible to find a transaction that violates a particular input or processing control. A major reason why the auditor may decide not to use simulated data is the difficulty sometimes experienced in creating the records. The more complex the program, the more difficult this creation becomes. The difficulty can be mitigated by a structured approach to test data creation. The decision tables discussion in Chapter 3 can be a very efficient technique for generating the records manually. (Exercises at the end of this chapter illustrate this technique.) Computer software, called *test data generators*, is available to generate the test information automatically.

The auditor may also decide not to use simulated records because only those conditions known to exist can be tested. Code of which the auditor is unaware will not be tested because test records will not be prepared for that code. An additional reason for deciding not to use the approach is that the auditor may have difficulty in ascertaining that the program being tested is the one actually used by the client.

Substantive Tests.   The auditor can also make inferences about the processing accuracy of a computer program by processing simulated data through that program. The two techniques of test records and the integrated test facility (ITF) can be used for substantive testing.

The objective of using simulated data to perform substantive testing on a computer program is to determine the accuracy of processing under simulated conditions. If the computer achieves the correct results using test data, the auditor can infer that the computer is processing accurately under actual operating conditions.

The factors to be considered in deciding whether to perform substantive tests by processing simulated data are the same as those for controls testing. With simulated data, the auditor can specifically test each arithmetic calculation or account classification in which he or she has an interest. On the other hand, it may be difficult to create the test records, and only those calculations and classifications known to exist can be tested.

Test Records.   Test records and test data are simulated transactions created by the auditor. The auditor conducts the testing of the client's program by processing these simulated transactions through that program. The data processing results are then compared with what should have been the results. These predetermined results are typically generated manually and are entered on a workpaper called a *control worksheet* (see Chapter 3, Table 3–4). The test record process is illustrated in Figure 11–2.

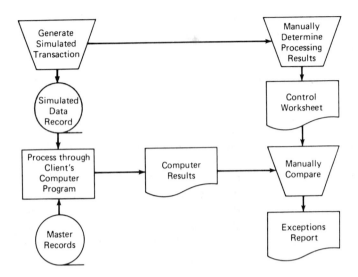

Figure 11–2. Test Record Approach

The objective of performing controls testing with test records is to examine those input, processing, and output controls, or combinations of controls, in which the auditor has an interest. By simulating the data, the auditor can structure the approach very precisely to ensure that no significant audit controls have been overlooked.

An order entry program can be used to illustrate the test record approach. To check the operation of the check digit control on customer numbers, the auditor creates a record with an incorrect check digit. Another record may be created to place an order in excess of credit limits if such limits are under program control and not specific to individual customers. Another simulated record may contain nonnumeric data in the numeric fields for customer number, part numbers, quantities, and so forth. If the input validation controls are functioning, the auditor would expect error messages for the intentionally erroneous data.

The objective of performing substantive testing with test records is to determine the accuracy of that computer processing for which a test record is submitted. In an order entry program, for example, the auditor can submit test records containing simulated customer numbers, part numbers, and quantities. The computer will determine the appropriate price and extend price times quantity. The auditor can then manually ascertain that the appropriate price was used and that the extension was correct.

Integrated Test Facility. Integrated test facility (ITF) is a technique whereby the auditor creates simulated transactions, intermixes the transactions with a client's actual transactions, waits for the processing of the intermixed transactions, and then analyzes the processing of the simulated transactions. The simulated transactions contain a special code so that they can be segregated and eliminated from the system at a future date. Other terms used to describe the ITF approach are *minicompany, dummy company, extended test data,* and *auditor's central office.*

The objective of performing controls testing with ITF is to test input, processing, and output controls using simulated data but under actual operating conditions. It is referred to as the *extended test data* approach because it uses the basic concept of the test data technique but extends it by integrating simulated data with actual data.

The order entry program discussed previously can also be used to illustrate the ITF technique. Instead of entering the test records in isolation with the program being dedicated to testing, these same records are entered along with actual transactions. Each simulated transaction, however, has a unique code, such as department 99, to permit it to be identified and eliminated from the system later. The auditor performs the same input validation tests as before, but instead of an error listing for only those records, the errors are listed among those for actual transactions. Some auditors go so far as to have merchandise ordered by the simulated transactions actually shipped and billed to test as many controls in the sales and collection cycle as possible.

The objective of performing substantive testing with ITF is to determine whether specific arithmetic calculations and classifications selected by the auditor for testing are processing data correctly under actual operating conditions. In an order entry program, for example, the auditor will create simulated sales orders, intermix the simulated orders with actual orders, wait for the mixture to be processed by the program, and then analyze the results. For the simulated orders, the auditor will determine whether the prices, extensions, and discounts are correct.

The major reason why the auditor may decide to use the ITF technique is that it gives some assurance that the program being tested is the one actually used by the client. This assurance is best achieved if the simulated transactions are submitted randomly throughout the year.

There are two major reasons why the auditor may decide not to use the ITF technique. One reason is that is is relatively easy to write code that will treat the simulated transactions differently from actual transactions. In some companies, the code identifier for the simulated transactions is common knowledge or can easily be obtained by a skilled programmer. The other reason is that errors can be produced in the actual transactions when the simulated transactions are introduced or eliminated from the system. The simulated transactions, for example, may be entered improperly into the account of an actual customer. In addition, the reversing entry to eliminate the simulated sale may be classified incorrectly. The auditor must exercise considerable care to avoid disastrous interruptions to the client's business.

DUAL-PURPOSE TESTING

Dual-purpose testing is a combination of tests of controls and substantive testing. The computer-auditing techniques presented in this chapter, and discussed under separate controls and substantive testing objectives, will normally be used in dual-purpose tests to accomplish both objectives simultaneously. In performing these dual-purpose tests, however, auditors must be aware of the assumption they are making and not lose sight of the objective they are trying to achieve.

Controls testing and substantive testing are dealt with separately in the auditing literature because they relate to separate aspects of the audit. The nature, extent, and timing of substantive tests depend on the auditor's conclusions regarding the operating effectiveness of the control structure. These conclusions and subsequent substantive tests are a result of the evaluation of controls tests on that system. The techniques for performing controls and substantive tests in computer auditing are discussed separately to emphasize these separate objectives.

In the real world, however, the auditor combines these tests into dual-purpose tests. With the sales invoices in hand, or a computer program loaded into a system and all files on a tape or disk drive, it is more efficient to perform all the tests at once instead of having to go through the same process several times.

In using the test records technique, for example, the auditor will create records to test input, processing, and output controls. Records will also be created to test the accuracy of processing. These records will be combined and processed through the computer program. The auditor will analyze the results in terms of both the effectiveness of controls and the accuracy of processing.

In performing the tests simultaneously, the auditor must make some assumption about the effectiveness of the control structure. The substantive testing is performed based on an evaluation of the effectiveness of controls. By explicitly recognizing the effectiveness level expected, the auditor is in a better position to determine the extent of additional substantive testing necessary if those expectations are not fulfilled.

In performing the tests simultaneously, the auditor should not forget that two objectives are being satisfied. With one test it is not uncommon to concentrate on just controls or just processing accuracy, ignore the other aspect, or at least fail to give it the attention it deserves. To satisfy the separate aspects of the audit, the auditor should keep the objectives separated just as we have intentionally done for emphasis in this book.

SUMMARY

The auditor can perform both tests of controls and substantive tests on a computer program to ascertain that it is processing accounting data correctly. Controls testing is performed to determine whether the application controls are operating effectively. Substantive testing is performed to satisfy the objective of direct tests of account balances. These tests include those for arithmetic accuracy and proper account classifications. Controls and substantive tests are typically combined into dual-purpose tests.

Controls tests on computer programs can be performed with three approaches: (1) not to process any data through the program, (2) to process actual client data through the program, and (3) to process simulated data through the program. The first approach, called the nonprocessing of data, includes the techniques of flowchart verification, program code checking, examination of job accounting and control information, and examination of printouts. The second approach includes the techniques of controlled processing, controlled reprocessing, parallel simulation, and concurrent auditing. The third approach includes the techniques of test records and integrated test facility. The auditor must consider various factors in order to decide which of these techniques to use.

The approaches and techniques described for controls testing, with the exception of examining job accounting and control information, can also be used for substantive testing. Instead of testing for controls, the auditor tests for arithmetic accuracy and proper account classification.

Dual-purpose tests, combining controls and substantive tests, are performed to increase the audit's efficiency. The substantive testing portion is designed with an assumption as to the effectiveness of the controls, which cannot be verified until the results of the controls testing portion are obtained. In performing dual-purpose tests, the auditor must be aware that controls testing and substantive testing have separate objectives.

REVIEW QUESTIONS

11–1. Why does the auditor concentrate on application controls in testing computer programs?

11–2. What are the three approaches to testing computer programs? Under what computer system operating conditions would the auditor select each one?

11–3. What techniques are available for testing computer programs without processing any data through the program? Describe each one. Under what conditions is the auditor likely to select each one?

11–4. What factors must the auditor consider in deciding whether to test computer programs without processing any data through them?

11–5. What techniques are available for testing computer programs by processing actual client data through the program? Describe each one. Under what conditions is the auditor likely to select each one?

11–6. What factors must the auditor consider in deciding whether to test computer programs by processing actual client data through them?

11–7. What techniques are available for testing computer programs by processing simulated data through them? Describe each one. Under what conditions is the auditor likely to select each one?

11–8. What factors must the auditor consider in deciding whether to test programs by processing simulated data through them?

11–9. The auditor of complex computer systems may decide to focus on a technique that traces the flow of transactions through the application program. For each of the following approaches, describe how the testing would be performed:
   a. The auditor decides to trace all transactions flowing through the program.
   b. The auditor decides to trace selected transactions flowing through the program.

11–10. On what type of tests is the auditor likely to concentrate in performing substantive tests on computer programs?

11–11. How do the nonprocessing of data, processing of actual data, and processing of simulated data approaches used in substantive testing differ from those used in controls testing?

11–12. What assumption is implicit in designing a dual-purpose test of a computer system?

OBJECTIVE QUESTIONS

11–13. In connection with his examination of financial statements a CPA may use duplicate programs which he controls to process a client's current data. This procedure may be an acceptable alternative to
   a. Examining a sample of source documents
   b. Reviewing controls over data processing
   c. Reviewing data processing flowcharts
   d. Using a test data deck with client programs (AICPA)

11–14. The night operator understood more about programming than anyone realized. Working through the console, he made a change in the payroll program to alter the rate of pay for an accomplice in an operating department. The fraud was discovered accidentally after it had been going on for several months. The best control procedure would be
   a. A review of the console log for unauthorized intervention
   b. Payroll review and distribution controls outside of data processing

c. Audit trail use of payroll journal output
d. Control total review (*AICPA*)

11-15. Which of the following is not a problem associated with the use of test records for computer audit purposes?

    a. Auditing through the computer is more difficult than auditing around the computer.
    b. It is difficult to design test records that incorporate all potential variations and transactions.
    c. Test data may be commingled with live data causing operating problems for the client.
    d. The program with which the test data are processed differs from the one used in actual operations. (*AICPA*)

11-16. Parallel simulation programs used by the auditor for testing computations

    a. Must simulate all functions of the production computer application system
    b. Cannot be developed with the aid of generalized audit software
    c. Can use live data or test data
    d. Do not require advanced EDP knowledge by the auditor
    e. None of the above (*IIA*)

11-17. The technique of computer program comparison can be used by the auditor to

    a. Verify that the computer program performs a required function
    b. Test the efficiency of the computer program codings
    c. Disclose unauthorized changes in the computer program coding
    d. Determine that the data produced by the computer program are reliable
    e. All of the above (*IIA*)

11-18. An auditor used a computer audit program to process all financial transactions for the accounting period to construct the general ledger independently

    a. Examining a statistical sample of source documents
    b. Evaluating controls over the master file for the general ledger
    c. Manually tracing postings to and footing the accounts
    d. All of the above
    e. Items a and c above (*IIA*)

CASES AND EXERCISES

11-19. You are involved in the audit of accounts receivable, which represent a significant portion of the assets of a large retail corporation. Your audit plan requires the use of the computer, but you encounter the reactions described below:

    1. The computer operations manager says that all time on the computer is scheduled for the foreseeable future and that it is not feasible to perform the work for the auditor.

2. The computer scheduling manager suggests that your computer program be cataloged into the computer program library (on disk storage) to be run when computer time becomes available.

3. You are refused admission to the computer room.

4. The systems manager tells you that it will take too much time to adapt the computer audit program to the EDP operating system; the computer installation programmer will write the program needed for the audit.

Required:
For each of the four situations described, state the action the auditor should take to proceed with the accounts receivable audit. (*IIA*)

11–20. Controlled processing and controlled reprocessing are two techniques for auditing computer programs using actual client data. Discuss the conditions that are likely to exist at a client's EDP operations that will lead the auditor to select each method.

11–21. Computer programs can be audited by reviewing the printouts resulting from the processing of those programs. Discuss the similarities and differences of printout review in auditing computer programs with the more general concept of auditing around the computer.

11–22. A major problem in testing computer programs is the difficulty in ascertaining that the program being tested is the one actually used by the client. For each of the following techniques, describe how the auditor may be able to ensure that the tested program is the production program:
   a. Flowchart verification
   b. Program code checking
   c. Review of job accounting and control information
   d. Review printouts
   e. Controlled processing
   f. Controlled reprocessing
   g. Parallel simulation
   h. Concurrent auditing
   i. Test records
   j. Integrated test facility

11–23. The Deadwood Gold Company payroll for miners is maintained on a computer. These miners are paid based on hours worked, with overtime paid at double the regular time rate. Deductions and withholdings include those for federal and state income taxes, social security, state industrial accident insurance, union dues, and medical insurance. In addition, Deadwood Gold Company pays federal and state unemployment insurance.

The time cards are reviewed and approved by a foreman and then forwarded to the payroll department. In the payroll department a clerk creates a disk transaction file by typing social security numbers and hours worked on a CRT. Another clerk then verifies that file by retyping the information. A program compares the original contents of the transaction file with the information keyed in on verification. After errors are corrected, another program then processes the payroll and prepares payroll checks, earnings statements, and a payroll journal showing gross pay, deductions, withholdings, and net pay by employee. This program also updates the master file by calculating the revised year-to-date information.

You have been told that although the program was thoroughly tested before being put into production, errors sometimes occur when the payroll is run. These errors have included miscalculations of gross earnings, deductions, and withholdings. On further investigation you find that the errors seem to occur most frequently during periods of heavy workload for the staff and computer. You also know that the computer operates in a multiprogramming environment.

Focusing on the payroll programs, and excluding the computer files:

1. What should be your controls testing objectives and what controls tests are you likely to perform?
2. What should be your substantive testing objectives and what substantive tests are you likely to perform?
3. Which computer-auditing approaches and techniques are you likely to utilize in the performance of your controls and substantive testing? Why? What additional information do you need before making a final decision?

11-24. Each of the following independent situations is encountered by an auditor in conjunction with the audit of a computerized accounting system. For each situation in the audit of programs, excluding the computer files, discuss:
   a. Which computer-auditing approach is likely to be utilized? Why?
   b. Which computer-auditing technique is likely to be utilized? Why?
   c. What additional information does the auditor need in order to make a final decision?

Situation 1:
Sharon Youngblood, CPA, has recently opened her own office after working for Stick and Stone, CPAs, for five years. Ms. Youngblood is a competent auditor but has had limited experience in computer auditing. Her major client has just installed a computer for the processing of payroll, accounts receivable, inventory, and accounts payable. The application programs, acquired from a software vendor, are well documented and provide transactions listings, journals, and general ledgers.

Situation 2:
Sam Hotblood, CPA, has been involved in all types of computer auditing over the past ten years. He has just been assigned to the audit of a major

client who installed an accounts payable system during the past year. This system automatically prepares checks to vendors as the invoices become due.

Situation 3:
Sally Trueblood, CPA, is a computer-auditing specialist with an international CPA firm. One of her clients has an order entry system that is accessible by terminal from multiple sales offices. This system provides on-line responses to sales personnel inquiries regarding the quantity on hand of items in inventory. Sales orders entered by terminal, however, are accumulated in a transaction file during the day for batch processing at night.

11-25. A payroll program flowchart is shown in Chapter 3, Figure 3-7. You have decided to audit this program using the test record technique. You have also decided that the most efficient and effective method for creating the test records is by using a decision logic table (DLT). Dual-purpose testing seems to be appropriate here, so you have decided to combine your controls and substantive testing. Discuss or perform the following:

a. Why does dual-purpose testing seem to be appropriate? What assumptions are you making with regard to the results of your tests before you even start? What will you do if these assumptions are not correct?

b. What are your controls testing objectives? What are your substantive testing objectives?

c. Prepare a DLT for your dual-purpose tests assuming that the transaction record appears as shown and that the fields are tested for data entry errors as indicated. The program tests each field in the order indicated and within each field for data entry errors in the order indicated. As soon as an error is detected, that record is rejected and an error message printed stating the reason.

Field Position	Description	Data Entry Errors Edited*
1–6	Employee number	1,2,3,4
7–10	Payroll date	1,2,3,7
11–12	Hours worked	1,2,3,6
13–16	Pay rate	1,2,3,6
17–20	Department code	1,2,3,5,8
21–23	Branch code	1,2,3,5,8

*Data entry error codes:
1 Blanks
2 Sign
3 Alphanumeric
4 Sequence
5 Logical (branches 1 to 5 have departments 1 to 59; branches 6 to 10 have departments 60 to 99)
6 Limit (must be less than or equal to 50 hours for hours field and $15 per hour for pay field)
7 Date (must be 1st or 15th)
8 Code values (department codes range from 1 to 99; branches from 1 to 10)

For the substantive portion of the dual-purpose test, assume that the following four data records will be submitted:

	Hours	Rate of Pay
1	10	$ 5.00
2	20	$ 7.50
3	30	10.00
4	40	15.00

d. How will you use the DLT to create your test records? What technique will you use to determine whether the results generated by the computer program upon processing of your test records are accurate and reliable? Illustrate this technique and state any assumptions you make.

11–26. An inventory program is illustrated in Chapter 3, Problem 3–36. You have decided to audit this program using the test record technique. You have also decided that the most efficient and effective method for creating the test records is by using a decision logic table (DLT). Dual-purpose testing seems to be appropriate here, so you have decided to combine your controls and substantive testing. Discuss or perform the following:

a. Why does dual-purpose testing seem to be appropriate? What assumptions are you making with regard to the results of your tests before you even start? What will you do if these assumptions are not correct?

b. What are your controls testing objectives? What are your substantive testing objectives?

c. Prepare a DLT for your dual-purpose tests assuming that the transaction record appears as shown and that the fields are tested for data entry errors as indicated. The program tests each field in the order indicated and within each field for data entry errors in the order indicated. As soon as a data entry error is detected, that record is rejected and an error message printed stating the reason. The hash totals and document counts control totals are calculated by the computer for all transaction records, excluding those rejected because of data entry errors or unmatched transactions.

Field Position	Description	Data Entry Errors Edited*	Other Controls†
1–6	Part number	1,3,5	1,3
7–10	Transaction date	1,3,7	
11	Transaction code‡	1,3,8	2
12–14	Unit-of-measure code	1,3,5	
15–19	Quantity change	1,2,3,6	1
20–24	Cost per unit	1,2,3,	

*Data entry error codes:
1 Blanks
2 Sign

(continued)

3 Alphanumeric
4 Sequence
5 Logical (unit of measure code 1 for part numbers starting with 1, 2 for part numbers starting with 2)
6 Limit (quantities for part numbers starting with 1 cannot exceed 999 units; quantities for part numbers starting with 2 cannot exceed 99 units)
7 Date (0001 to 0366)
8 Code values

†Other control codes:
1 Hash totals
2 Documents counts (issues and receipts transactions are counted separately)
3 Unmatched transaction

‡1 for receipt, 2 for issue

Note: Computer-generated controls for codes 1 and 2 are manually compared with manually calculated controls submitted as batch control totals with transaction records.

Assume 222222 is a part number with no corresponding master-file record. For the substantive portion of the test, assume the following data records will be submitted:

	Part Number	Transaction Code	Unit of Measure Code	Quantity Change	Cost per Unit
1	123456	1	1	100	$ 1.00
2	123457	2	1	200	2.00
3	223456	1	2	10	10.00
4	223457	2	2	20	20.00

    d. How will you use the DLT to create your test records? What technique will you use to determine that the results generated by the computer program upon processing of your test records are accurate and reliable? Illustrate this technique and state any assumptions you make.

Chapter 12
AUDITING COMPUTER FILES AND DATA BASES

Learning Objectives

After reading this chapter, the reader should be able to:

1. Review the auditor's objectives for performing tests of controls and substantive tests on computer files or data bases.

2. Determine how the auditor performs tests of controls and substantive tests on computer files or data bases without processing any file or data-base data.

3. Learn how the auditor performs tests of controls and substantive tests on computer files or data bases by processing actual file or data-base data.

4. Understand how the auditor performs tests of controls and substantive tests on computer files or data bases by processing simulated file or data-base data.

5. Identify the techniques available to help the auditor test computer files or data bases.

The task of auditing computer files or data bases[1] can range from easy to difficult. It is relatively easy if the file produced by the computer is printed and similar in appearance to the same file produced in a manual system—the auditor may be able to use the same procedures used in a manual system. It is relatively difficult if the same file is on machine-readable storage because (1) the contents of the records or data elements[2] may be changed as the transactions are being processed, and (2) the auditor needs a computer and a program to read the file.

In this chapter we discuss computerized and other techniques available for verifying the contents of files produced by computer programs. These files, resulting from the output of computer programs, can include printouts on paper, magnetic tape files, and disk files. The verification of the contents of files does not include an analysis of the computer process for putting data into the files. Data are put into files by programs, and the auditing of that computer process was discussed in the preceding chapter.

As in the preceding chapter, this chapter is oriented toward the auditor's objectives: controls testing, substantive testing, and dual-purpose testing. For each of these objectives, we discuss computerized and other techniques used in conjunction with computer files.

The emphasis in the auditing of computer files is on substantive testing objectives. Although we discuss both controls and substantive testing objectives in this chapter, the auditor is concerned primarily with direct tests of account balances. These tests are a type of substantive test.

TESTS OF CONTROLS
AND SUBSTANTIVE TESTING

Tests of Controls

Computerized and other techniques that aid the auditor in the assessment of control risk are oriented toward two aspects of control: controls over access to the files, and compliance of the contents of the files with control and procedural requirements. Evidence of controls over access to the files includes, for example, locked doors on the computer center and an inability to obtain information from a file through a terminal without entering a correct password. Contents of files provide evidence of compliance with control requirements, such as fields showing customer credit limits. They also provide evidence of compliance with procedural re-

---

[1]The term "computer files," when used subsequently by the authors, also is intended to include "data bases."

[2]The terms "records" and "file data," when used subsequently by the authors, also are intended to include "data elements" of a data base.

quirements, such as proper authorization, account classification, and the recording of entries in the proper time period. The auditor can utilize three approaches in controls testing of the contents of computer files. The nonprocessing-of-file-data approach can be used if the files are in a storage medium, such as paper, that allows the auditor to inspect them visually. Controls can also be tested by processing actual client files or processing simulated files when the auditor cannot visually inspect them. (Some of the techniques pertaining to these three approaches were introduced in Chapter 11 and will, therefore, be discussed less extensively than the others.)

Substantive Testing

Substantive testing is performed to satisfy the audit objective of the collection of evidence. Although substantive testing includes both analytical procedures and direct tests of transactions and balances, our primary concern in computer auditing is with direct tests.

Computerized and other techniques that aid the auditor in the substantive testing of computer files are oriented toward various procedures for direct tests of transactions and balances. These procedures can include tests for omitted amounts (such as understated accounts payable), valuation tests (such as arithmetic errors in extending inventory), tests for classification errors (such as charges to repairs and maintenance that should be capitalized), tests for time period recording errors (such as an incorrect purchases cutoff), and tests for footing and reconciliation errors (such as accounts receivable subsidiary records that do not sum to the control account total).

The three approaches of nonprocessing of file data, processing of actual file data, and processing of simulated file data utilized by computer auditors in the controls testing of computer files are also used in substantive testing.

Controls and Substantive Testing Techniques

Nonprocessing of File Data

Tests of Controls. Inferences about the existence and operating effectiveness of the two aspects of control pertaining to computer files can be made without processing file data through an EDP system. Two techniques that utilize this approach are discussed here: testing access controls and examining file printouts.

The two aspects of control that can be tested without processing file data are file access controls and the compliance of the contents of paper files with accounting requirements. The auditor can test for the effectiveness of file access controls by trying to read, change the contents of, or copy the contents of files without using the appropriate passwords. No data are processed because access to the files should be restricted to prevent processing. The auditor can visually examine the contents of paper files for compliance with requirements, such as credit limits for each customer.

The reasons why the auditor may decide to perform controls testing of computer files without processing the contents of the files through an EDP system include the relatively low cost, the consumption of less time than that necessary in other approaches, and the ease of understanding the concepts. The reasons why the auditor may decide not to use the approach include the lack of assurance that the controls exist or function under all operating conditions, the lack of assurance that the controls or files tested actually exist and are not just bogus copies for the auditor to work on, and the difficulty of understanding some of the more complex file access control techniques.

Substantive Tests. Direct tests of transactions and balances can also be made without processing file data through an EDP system. This is accomplished by examination of file printouts.

The auditor considers various factors in deciding whether to use printouts in the substantive testing of computer files. Reasons for deciding to use printouts include the relatively low cost, consumption of less time than other approaches, and ease of understanding the concepts. A reason for deciding not to use them is the lack of assurance that the printouts represent the contents of actual files.

File Access Control Testing. File access control testing means that the auditor attempts to determine whether the controls preventing unauthorized additions to files, changes to files, or deletions from files are functioning as prescribed. File access controls pertain to master files and transaction files used in application processing, as well as files containing the system and application programs and software.

The auditor's objective in testing file access controls is to determine whether an unauthorized user can get access to the files to add, modify, or delete information. If the files are stored off-line, the auditor may be concerned about their physical accessibility. If the files are stored on-line, the auditor may be concerned about their accessibility through the computer systems.

A payroll system application can be used to illustrate both physical and computer accessibility. If the payroll master file is stored off-line on magnetic tape or disk, the auditor will determine whether the files are locked in a storage cabinet or vault requiring librarian permission for their removal. If the master file is stored on-line on magnetic disk, the auditor may attempt to access the file through a computer terminal without the appropriate password. The auditor may also review the job accounting and control information on the computer console to see if the unauthorized attempt was recorded.

Printout Examination. Printouts of file contents are reviewed for evidence of compliance with controls. This examination of file output in printed form is very similar, for example, to reviewing accounts receivable subsidiary ledgers produced by a manual or mechanical system.

The auditor's objectives in reviewing the contents of files printed by the computer include testing for proper authorization, proper account classifications, and proper time periods. *Proper authorization* refers to examining the controls included in the files, such as customer credit limits used in processing orders. *Proper account classifications* refer to examining whether the chart of accounts has been followed in posting amounts to accounts. *Proper time periods* refer to examining for sales cutoffs and purchases cutoffs.

The sales and collections cycle can be used to illustrate the performance of tests of controls on printed files. By examining accounts receivable subsidiary ledgers, the auditor can perform all three types of controls tests mentioned above. The auditor reviews the ledgers to ascertain that credit limits are shown for each customer. By tracing from debit entries to the supporting invoices and shipping documents, the auditor determines whether sales entries were recorded in the proper time period and for the correct customer. By tracing from credit entries to the supporting remittance advices, bank deposit slips, and bank statements, the auditor determines whether cash receipts entries were recorded in the proper time period and for the correct customer.

Printout examination can also be used for the substantive testing of the content of computer files. The objective of such testing is to collect evidence on omitted amounts, valuation, classification, and so forth. An example of such an examination is a search for amounts omitted from the accounts payable master file. The auditor can trace a sample of vendors' invoices to a payables listing to determine whether they are properly posted for the correct amount.

Processing of Actual File Data

Tests of Controls. The operating effectiveness of controls can be determined by processing actual file data. Techniques discussed in this section using this approach include custom-designed programs and generalized audit software. Data-base management system (DSMS) software can also be used for controls testing with actual data-base data. Such testing is similar to using generalized audit software.

Processing actual file data provides the auditor with information about the effectiveness of controls from evidence that exists in production files. This evidence can demonstrate that controls pertaining to proper authorization, account classifications, and time period recordings are operating effectively.

The reason why the auditor may decide to perform controls tests by processing actual file data is that the evidence collected is based on actual operating conditions. Another reason is that the auditor can use file data already generated by the client and does not have to create such data.

The auditor may decide not to perform controls tests by processing actual file data for the following reasons: (1) the client's operations may be disrupted because the files must be placed under the auditor's physical control to ensure their integrity—it may be necessary to deny the client access to the files during the audit of their contents or while copying the contents into a working file for subsequent examination; (2) the file data analyzed may not include evidence of all the controls in which the auditor is interested; (3) the auditor may not be able to determine whether the file being tested is the one actually used by the client in processing; (4) the auditor must be fairly knowledgeable about data processing operations so that the tests can be performed or monitored adequately; and (5) the auditor may be concerned about inadvertently damaging or destroying the file.

Substantive Tests. The auditor can also process actual file data in order to perform substantive testing. This approach to substantive testing is used both for direct tests of transactions and account balances and for analytical procedures. Three techniques for direct tests of transactions and account balances include utility programs, custom-designed programs, and generalized audit software. We also describe regression analysis and other special-purpose programs that are used for analytical procedures and some types of direct tests.

The purpose of processing actual file data is to obtain evidence about the processing accuracy of the system from information that exists in production or operating files. Evidence about such accuracy includes tests for omitted amounts, valuation, classification, cutoffs, and footing of subsidiary ledgers and reconciliation to control accounts.

The reasons why the auditor may decide to perform substantive testing by processing actual file data are the same reasons as for controls testing. The auditor may also decide not to perform substantive testing by processing actual file data for the same reasons as for tests of controls.

Utility Programs. Utility programs are programs used for general purposes, such as sorting data files and moving file data from one device or storage medium to another. Utility programs are typically supplied by a vendor to aid in utilizing the equipment, but the programs can be developed by users or software houses.

The auditor's objective in using utility programs is to move, sort, prepare, or otherwise manipulate file data in the process of performing substantive tests on them. Such programs are used to

- Copy disk files to tape, tape files to tape, and so forth, for further processing of the copy
- Print the contents of a file in its entirety, or print only balances over a certain amount
- Sort files into specific sequences, such as alphabetical or numerical
- Print file labels

Utility programs, for example, can be used in the audit of a perpetual inventory system file. A utility program can be used to transfer the contents of the file maintained on disk to tape. Another utility program can then be used to print the entire contents of the tape file. This frees the disk file for ongoing processing.

In addition to the reasons discussed earlier regarding the processing of actual file data, the auditor may decide to use utility programs for the following reasons. These programs are usually readily available because vendors generally supply them with almost all systems. If the auditor obtains a copy of a program directly from a vendor, he or she can be fairly certain that the utility program will function as anticipated. For some applications, such as copying a file from one device to another or printing the contents of a file, utility programs may be faster and easier to use than other software such as generalized audit software.

The reasons why the auditor may decide not to use utility programs include those discussed earlier for processing actual data. An additional reason is that utility programs are written for programmers and computer operators and may be difficult for the auditor to understand and use.

Custom-Designed Programs. Custom-designed programs are programs written for specific audit tasks. These programs are also referred to as *special-purpose programs*. The auditor's objective in using custom-designed programs for controls testing of computer files is to allow him or her to perform tests that may not otherwise be possible. The client may have a unique computer or operating system, for example, for which no other available programs can be adapted. Custom-designed programs are written by auditors, by EDP personnel employed by the client, and by software houses specializing in computer programming.

The acquisition and payment cycle for inventory can be used to illustrate controls testing with custom-designed programs. The auditor may wish to test which purchases and payments have been recorded in the proper time period for a system for which no other audit software is available. To perform this test, the auditor writes a program to print a list of transactions recorded in inventory and accounts payable master files for three days before and after a year-end cutoff date. The auditor then examines receiving reports for acquisitions and vouchers, bank statements, and vendors' invoices for disbursements to determine whether the transactions were recorded on the computer files in the correct time period.

Custom-designed computer programs may also be used for substantive testing. For example, on a system for which no other audit software is available, the auditor can use a custom-designed program to prepare confirmation requests for all accounts payable with zero balances in a search for omitted amounts.

The auditor may decide to use custom-designed programs because he or she may be able to perform testing not otherwise possible. When new, sophisticated, and complex systems are involved, the auditor may be forced to use such programs.

The auditor may decide not to use custom-designed programs because writing or buying such programs can be expensive; long lead times are often necessary in designing and writing them; and the programs are inflexible and can rarely be modified for use with any other client.

Generalized Audit Software. Generalized audit software consists of a program or set of programs that the auditor uses to perform testing on computer files. Such programs are typically written by computer-auditing specialists within an audit firm or acquired from a software house or other audit firm.

One purpose of using generalized audit software is to enable the auditor to perform controls testing on computer files efficiently. It is more efficient to have a single set of programs that will run on the computer systems of numerous clients and accomplish numerous audit tasks than to have a separate set of programs for each client or task. For controls testing computer files, these tasks can include the following:

- Sample selection—calculate the size of the sample to be pulled given the desired confidence or reliability levels and the precision. The software then selects the sample by using random selection or systematic selection techniques.
- Analysis—print dates of selected transactions for cutoff tests or print selected postings to an account for classification tests, such as all entries to repairs and maintenance of over $200.

- Examination of files for quality—list all accounts receivable missing credit limit information.

A second purpose of using generalized audit software is to increase the auditor's efficiency in performing substantive testing on computer files. For substantive testing of computer files, these tasks can include the following:

- Sample selection—calculate the size of the sample to be pulled given the desired confidence or reliability levels and the precision. The software can then select the sample by using random selection or systematic selection techniques.
- Analysis—recompute depreciation or the aging of accounts receivable.
- Duplicate data comparison—compare the pay rates in the payroll master file with those used in the payroll transaction file.
- Footings and extensions—foot the accounts receivable subsidiary ledgers and compare the total with the control account. Extend inventory prices and quantities.
- Audit data comparison—compare quantities in the perpetual inventory records with machine-readable totals from inventory test counts.
- Confirmations—print confirmations for accounts receivable or accounts payable.
- Examination of files for quality—list accounts receivable with balances in excess of the credit limit.

The auditor instructs the generalized audit software to perform these tasks by responding to screen prompts on a computer monitor or by coding information on worksheets or specification sheets. These coded worksheets are read by an optical character or mark sense reader and then interpreted by the software to create a set of instructions used by the computer in analyzing the data file.

Controls testing of accounts receivable file data can be used to illustrate the generalized audit software technique. The auditor must establish objectives, design the test, instruct the software, process the file data, and act on the output.

- Establish the objectives
  - Randomly select 200 accounts, based on specified tolerable error and confidence level.
  - Print all invoices dated up to three days before December 31 cutoff date for sales test.
  - List all accounts missing credit limit information.
- Design the test
  - Specify the data file to be used for the test and obtain a file layout. The accounts receivable master-file layout is shown in Table 12–1.

Table 12–1. Accounts Receivable Master File

Description	Field Number	Location
Customer number	1	1–10
Customer name	2	11–30
Street address	3	31–50
City and state	4	51–70
Zip code	5	71–77
Credit limit	6	78–82
Last paid invoice		
Number	7	83–87
Date	8	88–93
Amount	9	94–99
Unpaid invoice 1		
Number	10	100–104
Date	11	105–110
Amount	12	111–116
Unpaid invoice 2		
Number	13	117–121
Date	14	122–127
Amount	15	128–133
Unpaid invoice 3		
Number	16	134–138
Date	17	139–144
Amount	18	145–150
Unpaid invoice 4		
Number	19	151–155
Date	20	156–161
Amount	21	162–167
Unpaid invoice 5		
Number	22	168–172
Date	23	173–178
Amount	24	179–184
Unpaid invoice 6		
Number	25	185–189
Date	26	190–195
Amount	27	196–201
Unapplied payment 1		
Date	28	202–207
Amount	29	208–213
Unapplied payment 2		
Date	30	214–219
Amount	31	220–225
Amount due	32	226–232
Back-order 1		
Date	33	233–238
Purchase order number	34	239–245
Amount	35	246–251
Back-order 2		
Date	36	252–257
Purchase order number	37	258–264
Amount	38	265–270
Trailer record code	39	271–275

- — Identify the fields and their locations in the file. For credit limit test, field number 6. For the cutoff test, last paid and unpaid invoice date fields numbers 8, 11, 14, 17, 20, 23, and 26.
- — Specify the report formats. For the credit limit test, print customer number and name. For the cutoff test, print customer number and name, and for each invoice selected, print number, date, and amount of invoice.

- Instruct the software

  - — Code the generalized audit software worksheets or enter information on computer monitor.
  - — Submit worksheets, if used, to optical character or mark sense reader to select audit program options.
  - — Submit client's data files and audit program to computer for processing.

- Process the file data

  - — Most generalized audit software functions in two stages by first extracting the necessary information from the client's file and then analyzing the extracted information. The extracted information is typically placed in a work file, and all further processing is performed on that file. To avoid inadvertent changes or destruction, no further processing is performed on the client's files.

- Act on the output

  - — For invoices dated up to three days before the cutoff date, examine shipping documents.
  - — For accounts missing credit limit information, review each account with the credit manager.

The auditor may decide to use generalized audit software for several reasons. The auditor (1) does not need the level of EDP expertise and special training required for some of the other techniques, such as writing custom-designed programs; (2) may be able to service a wide variety of clients without preparing a special program for each task; (3) may be able to maintain better control of the testing without having to rely on the client's personnel and programs; and (4) may, therefore, be more independent of the client's personnel.

The auditor may decide not to use generalized audit software because (1) developing or acquiring such software is expensive; (2) writing the software for relatively uncommon computer systems is also expensive; and (3) such software is typically designed for use only with sequential file structures.

Regression Analysis Programs and Other Special-Purpose Programs. In addition to the techniques discussed above for direct tests of transactions and balances, special-purpose programs are available for performing analytical procedures and some types of direct tests. These special-purpose programs include regression analysis, financial statement consolidation programs, and other analytical programs available with microcomputers, through time sharing, and elsewhere.

The objective of performing substantive testing with special-purpose programs is to enhance the auditor's analytical abilities and remove some of the tediousness of such analysis. Regression analysis provides information about relationships among data that are difficult to see visually or are not apparent from simple trend or ratio analysis. Multiple regression performed manually is prohibitively time-consuming. Multiple regression, as well as the other analyses described below, can be performed more efficiently by a computer.

The techniques and tasks that special-purpose programs can perform, examples of each, and their unique advantages and disadvantages include the following:

- Regression analysis—Regression analysis can be used to analyze established patterns among variables and then detect unusual fluctuations. If inventory is usually within some range as a percentage of sales or cost of sales, for example, significant fluctuations outside that range may be the result of cutoff errors. In some cases, the regression programs may be able to use the historical information in the client's data files to perform the analysis. In other cases, the auditor may have to abstract the data from the files and convert them to the format necessary for processing. Advantages of regression analysis include the ability to perform common statistical tests to determine the significance of fluctuations, the interactive nature of many programs which allows the auditor to experiment with relationships, and the speed with which the analysis is usually performed and available. Disadvantages include the difficulty of understanding the statistical technique and its limitations, and understanding of a specific regression analysis program.
- Financial statement consolidation—Computer programs can be used to perform or verify the consolidation of financial statements from information contained in client data files. Such programs, for example, can detect out-of-balance conditions on initial entry of the data, perform the consolidation calculations using auditor-supplied elimination entries or rules, and then print the consolidated statements. The advantages of such programs include the ability to redo the consolidation rapidly if there are last-minute adjustments, consolidate statements from different charts of accounts, and provide a complete audit trail.
- Other analytical programs—Other analytical programs can be used to analyze information in client data files. Analyses include calculation or verification of amortization on loans, depreciation, price-level supplemental information, lease capitalizations, and earnings-per-share calculations. These programs may function on the client's computer processing information from actual data files or may require conversion of the data to another format for processing on a microcomputer or time-sharing system. Advantages include speed of calculation or recalculation, accuracy, and comprehensive documentation usually supplied by the program. Disadvantages include the difficulty of understanding how to process the data with the program that

operates on the client's system or files, or understanding the requirements of microcomputer or time-sharing systems.

Processing of Simulated File Data

Tests of Controls. Processing simulated file data provides the auditor with information about the operating effectiveness of controls from evidence that exists in simulated files. Techniques discussed in this section using this approach include test records and the integrated test facility (ITF).

The objective of performing controls testing on computer files using simulated data is similar to testing computer programs with simulated data. The objective is similar because evidence as to the effectiveness of some controls programmed into the computer can be found by testing either the program or the file. An input validation control, for example, can be tested in two ways. First, the auditor can submit simulated data to the program to determine whether erroneous transactions, such as those containing invalid characters, are rejected by the program and printed on an error listing. Second, the file can be tested by printing the contents of records that would be posted with the erroneous data if not rejected on input. The second test may be necessary because in some applications the erroneous data have appeared on an error report but have still ended up being posted to records.

The objective of performing tests of controls on files can be contrasted with testing programs because the files may contain evidence of controls that do not exist in the application program. Such evidence, for example, may pertain to user controls outside the EDP department. Controls outside the EDP department, but evidenced by data in a computer file, include the same controls tested using actual data: proper authorization, account classifications, and time period.

One reason why the auditor may decide to perform controls tests on files with simulated data is that he or she may be able to reduce substantially the number of records that have to be processed as contrasted with the processing of actual data. Another reason is that every control of interest to the auditor can be tested specifically. The auditor may decide not to test with simulated data because it may be difficult to create the test files needed. Furthermore, only those conditions known to exist can be tested.

Substantive Tests. The auditor can also process simulated file data in substantive testing of computer files in order to determine the processing accuracy of the system. The evidence provided by tests of computer files using simulated data extends beyond the evidence gained by similar tests on computer programs. Tests on programs and files provide evidence on the accuracy of the processing logic of the programs. This is accomplished in the testing of files by examining the results of program processing posted to the files. The testing of files, however, also provides evidence on the accuracy of system processing performed outside the computer. Such processing includes tasks performed manually in a user department.

In an accounts payable application, for example, the user can determine the appropriate payment date for each invoice by examining the invoice and following appropriate written instructions. The auditor reviews the correctness of the payment dates by examining a listing of the payment dates from the accounts payable master file.

The specific type of tests of interest to the auditor in the substantive testing of computer files includes tests for omitted amounts, valuation, classification, proper time period recording, and subsidiary record footing and reconciliation. Although similar to controls testing files using simulated data, substantive testing does not concentrate on the existence and reliability of controls but on arithmetic and processing accuracy. The tests may be the same, but the objectives are different.

The reasons why the auditor may decide to use or not use simulated data in the substantive testing of files are similar to those for the testing of controls.

Test Records. Test records are simulated transactions that the auditor creates and processes with the client's system. Manually prepared, predetermined results are then compared with the processing results. The purpose of these comparisons is to enable the auditor to test those controls in which he or she has an interest.

The test record approach for the testing of controls can be illustrated with an order entry system. Proper authorization of credit requires that each customer record contain a credit limit. The auditor can generate the source document used to place credit limit information in customer files and can follow that simulation through the system to the simulated file to see if the appropriate field eventually receives the information. The account classification control requires that transaction coding be performed correctly in the user departments. The auditor can generate a simulated transaction and follow it through the system to determine whether it ends up in the appropriate computer files. Proper time period recording can be tested in a similar fashion. The auditor creates simulated transactions on each side of the cutoff to determine whether the information eventually ending up in the computer file reflects that cutoff.

The test records technique can also be used in substantive testing. Examples of the use of this technique include tests for the following:

- Omitted amounts—create transaction and master files by simulating the source documents necessary for such creation. Analyze the contents of the files after creation to determine whether all accounts and transactions were processed through both the manual and the computer phase of the system without omitting any amounts, accounts, or transactions.
- Valuation—simulate sales orders and examine the resulting accounts receivable balances on computer files to determine whether the processing, including manual pricing and extensions for sales invoices, was performed correctly.
- Classification—simulate various expense transactions and examine the resulting general ledger account balances on computer files to determine whether the manual account coding and subsequent processing were performed correctly.
- Proper time period recording—simulate inventory receipt transactions before and after a cutoff date to determine whether the resulting perpetual inventory balances on computer files are correct.
- Subsidiary records footing and reconciliation—simulate an accounts receivable master file and source documents for payments transactions. After the source documents have been converted to machine-readable form and the master file has been updated, foot and reconcile the master file to determine the accuracy of the updating.

Integrated Test Facility. Integrated test facility (ITF) is a technique whereby the auditor submits simulated transactions to be processed by a client's computer system intermixed with the client's actual transactions. It is an extension of the test record approach that mixes actual and simulated transactions instead of keeping them separate.

The objective of auditing with ITF is to test the reliability and accuracy of processing using simulated data but under actual operating conditions. Files created and updated under system load conditions may contain sporadic errors, such as invalid field contents, not encountered under the light loads of other testing conditions.

The order entry example for test records is also relevant for ITF. Instead of submitting only test records for processing, however, the test records are submitted along with actual transactions.

DUAL-PURPOSE TESTING

The computer-auditing techniques presented in this chapter, and discussed under separate controls and substantive testing objectives, are typically used in dual-purpose tests to accomplish both objectives simultaneously. As in any dual-purpose tests, auditors must be aware of the assumption they are making regarding the interrelationship of controls and substantive tests. They must also be careful not to lost sight of the objectives they are trying to achieve.

Dual-purpose tests accomplish both the controls testing objective and the substantive testing objective simultaneously. In using generalized audit software to examine accounts receivable records, for example, the auditor typically accomplishes several tasks. A controls testing objective is satisfied by determining whether credit limit information exists in the appropriate field. Substantive testing objectives are satisfied by recalculating the aging of accounts receivable, footing the subsidiary records, and so forth.

The assumption that auditors make in performing dual-purpose testing is that they will conclude that a specific operating effectiveness level exists to support the extent of substantive testing performed. To avoid implicitly assuming a reliability level that is too high or too low, this operating effectiveness level must be determined before testing starts. If the assumed effectiveness level is too high, the auditor will undertest and fail to meet the substantive testing objective. If the assumed effectiveness level is too low, the substantive testing may be in excess of that necessary.

Auditors must not lose sight of the dual objectives—controls and substantive—that they are trying to achieve in performing dual-purpose testing. In using generalized audit software, for example, the auditor must determine what data will be needed for both types of tests in specifying the content of the working file. If this is not done, and data for only one type of test are specified, a second file will have to be created or the first one redone, wasting time and resources.

SUMMARY

The auditor can perform both controls testing and substantive testing on computer files to ascertain that the EDP system is processing accounting data correctly. Controls testing is performed to determine the existence and operating effectiveness of controls evidenced by computer output into files. The objectives of substantive testing are satisfied by performing direct tests of transactions and balances and analytical procedures. Controls and substantive tests are typically combined into dual-purpose tests.

Controls tests on computer files can be performed with three approaches: without processing any file data, processing actual file data, and processing simulated file data. The first approach, nonprocessing of file data, includes the techniques of testing access controls and examining file printouts. The second approach includes custom-designed programs and generalized audit software. The third approach includes test records and the integrated test facility.

Substantive tests on computer files can also be performed with the three approaches used in controls testing. For substantive testing, the nonprocessing-of-file-data approach includes the techniques of examining file printouts. The processing-of-actual-file-data approach for performing substantive tests on transactions and account balances includes the techniques of using utility programs, custom-designed programs, and generalized audit software. Techniques for performing analytical procedures substantive tests using the same approach include regression analysis and other special-purpose programs. The approach involving simulated file data includes techniques using test records and the integrated test facility.

Dual-purpose tests, combining controls and substantive tests, are performed to increase the audit's efficiency. Auditors should be aware of the assumption made regarding the interrelationship of controls and substantive tests when performing dual-purpose testing. Auditors should also pay particular attention to the objectives they are attempting to achieve.

REVIEW QUESTIONS

12-1. What types of controls tests can be performed on computer files? Are these tests related to general controls or application controls?

12-2. What are the three approaches to testing computer files? Under what computer system operating conditions would the auditor select each one?

12-3. What techniques are available for testing computer files without processing any file data? Describe each one. Under what conditions is the auditor likely to select each one?

12-4. What factors must the auditor consider in deciding whether to test computer files without processing any file data?

12-5. What techniques are available for testing computer files by processing actual file data? Describe each one. Under what conditions is the auditor likely to select each one?

12-6. What factors must the auditor consider in deciding whether to test computer files by processing actual file data?

12-7. What techniques are available for testing computer files by processing simulated file data? Describe each one. Under what conditions is the auditor likely to select each one?

12-8. What factors must the auditor consider in deciding whether to test computer files by processing simulated file data?

12-9. On what types of tests is the auditor likely to concentrate in performing substantive tests of transactions and account balances on computer files?

12–10. How do the nonprocessing of file data, processing of actual file data, and processing of simulated file data approaches in substantive testing of transactions and account balances differ from those used in controls testing?

12–11. What techniques are available for performing analytical procedures substantive tests on computer files? Describe each one.

12–12. Discuss how the DBMS may become both the target and the tool of the auditor in the audit of files of advanced computer systems.

OBJECTIVE QUESTIONS

12–13. An auditor obtains a magnetic tape that contains the dollar amounts of all client inventory items by style number. The information on the tape is in no particular sequence. The auditor can best ascertain that no consigned merchandise is included on the tape by using a computer program that
   a. Statistically selects samples of all amounts
   b. Excludes all amounts for items with particular style numbers that indicate consigned merchandise
   c. Mathematically calculates the extension of each style quantity by the unit price
   d. Prints on paper the information that is on the magnetic tape (*AICPA*)

12–14. Auditors often make use of computer programs that perform routine processing functions such as sorting and merging. These programs are made available by electronic data processing companies and others and are specifically referred to as
   a. User programs
   b. Compiler programs
   c. Supervisory programs
   d. Utility programs (*AICPA*)

12–15. The primary purpose of a generalized computer audit program is to allow the auditor to
   a. Use the client's employees to perform routine audit checks of the electronic data processing records that otherwise would be done by the auditor's staff accountants
   b. Test the logic of computer programs used in the client's electronic data processing systems
   c. Select larger samples from the client's electronic data processing records than would otherwise be selected without the generalized program
   d. Independently process client electronic data processing records (*AICPA*)

12–16. An auditor can use a generalized computer audit program to verify the accuracy of
   a. Data processing controls

    b. Accounting estimates

    c. Totals and subtotals

    d. Account classifications *(AICPA)*

12–17. The purpose of using generalized computer programs is to test and analyze a client's computer

    a. System

    b. Equipment

    c. Records

    d. Processing logic *(AICPA)*

12–18. An auditor would be least likely to use a generalized computer audit program for which of the following tasks?

    a. Selecting and printing accounts receivable confirmations

    b. Listing accounts receivable confirmation exceptions for examination

    c. Comparing accounts receivable subsidiary files to the general ledger

    d. Investigating exceptions to accounts receivable confirmations *(AICPA)*

12–19. In auditing a data-base management system, which of the following should the auditor expect to find?

    a. The same data elements in two or more files

    b. A data dictionary/directory

    c. All storage of data on computer tapes

    d. Each data element used on one computer run only

    e. None of the above *(IIA adapted)*

CASES AND EXERCISES

12–20. A CPA's client, Boos & Baumkirchner, Inc., is a medium-sized manufacturer of products for the leisure-time activities market (camping equipment, scuba gear, bows and arrows, and so on). During the past year, a computer system was installed, and inventory records of finished goods and parts were converted to computer processing. The inventory master file was maintained on a disk. Each record of the file contains the following information:

- Item or part number
- Description
- Size
- Unit of measure code
- Quantity on hand
- Cost per unit
- Total value of inventory on hand at cost
- Date of last sale or usage
- Quantity used or sold this year
- Economic order quantity
- Code number of major vendor
- Code number of secondary vendor

In preparation for year-end inventory the client had two identical sets of preprinted inventory count cards. One set is for the client's inventory counts and the other is for the CPA's use to make audit test counts. The following information has been printed on the cards:

- Item or part number
- Description
- Size
- Unit of measure code

In taking the year-end inventory, the client's personnel will write the actual counted quantity on the face of each card. When all counts are complete, the counted quantity will be read by an optical character reader. The cards will be processed against the disk file, and quantity-on-hand figures will be adjusted to reflect the actual count. A computer listing will be prepared to show any missing inventory count cards and all quantity adjustments of more than $100 in value. These items will be investigated by client personnel, and all required adjustments will be made. When adjustments have been completed, the final year-end balances will be computed and posted to the general ledger.

The CPA has available a general-purpose computer audit software package that will run on the client's computer and can process both card and disk files.

Required:
a. In general and without regard to the facts above, discuss the nature of general-purpose computer audit software packages and list the various types of uses of such packages.
b. List and describe at least five ways a general-purpose computer audit software package can be used to assist in all aspects of the audit of the inventory of Boos & Baumkirchner, Inc. (For example, the package can be used to read the disk inventory master file and to list items and parts with a high unit cost or total value. Such items can be included in the test counts and increase the dollar coverage of the audit verification.) (*AICPA*)

12–21. Roger Peters, CPA, has examined the financial statements of Solt Manufacturing Company for several years and is making preliminary plans for the audit for the year ended June 30, 19X4. During this examination Mr. Peters plans to use a set of generalized computer audit programs. Solt's EDP manager has agreed to prepare special tapes of data from company records for the CPA's use with the generalized program.

The following information is applicable to Mr. Peter's examination of Solt's accounts payable and related procedures (see Figure 1):

1. The formats of pertinent tapes.
2. The following monthly runs are prepared:
   a. Cash disbursements by check number
   b. Outstanding payables

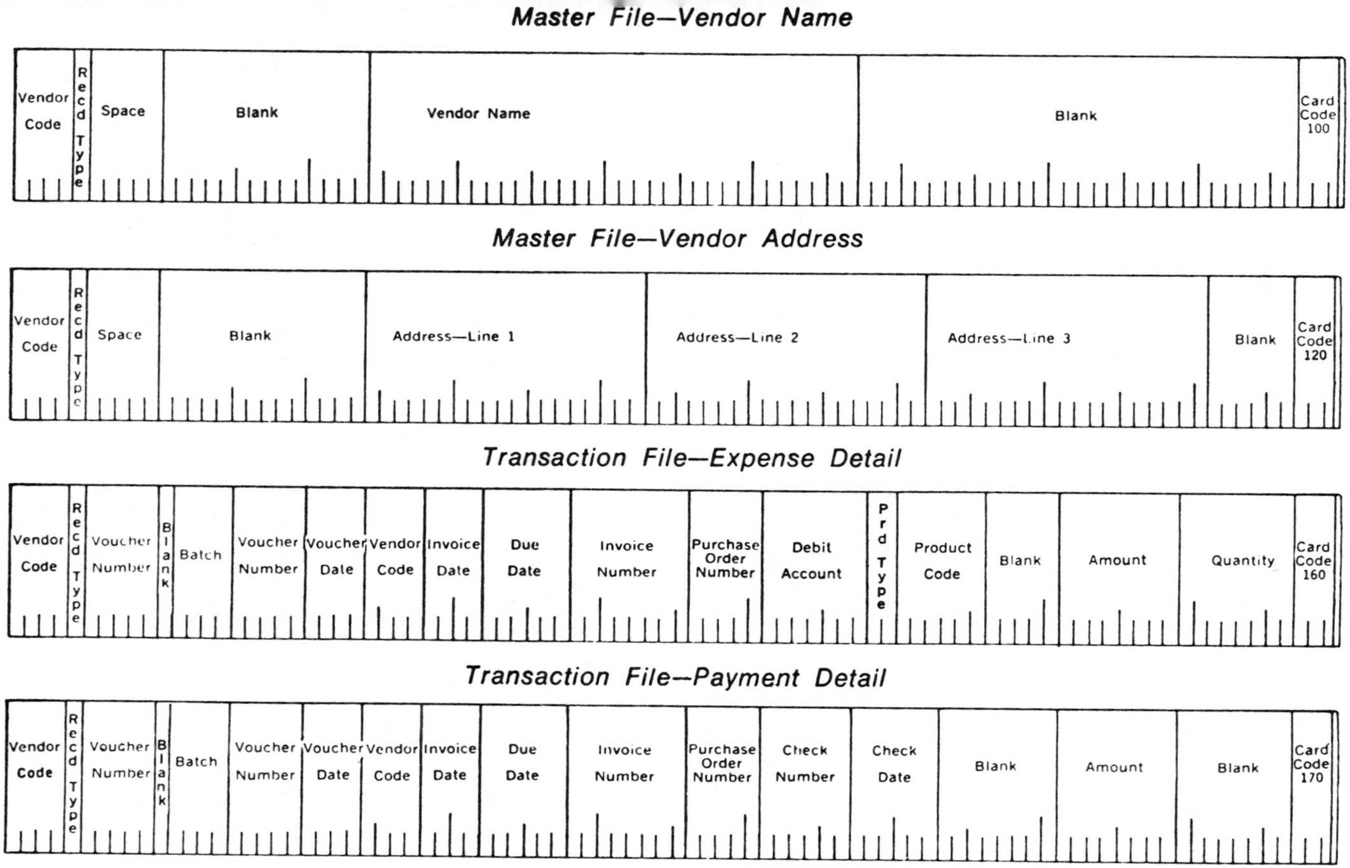

Master File—Vendor Name

| Vendor Code | Record Type | Space | Blank | Vendor Name | Blank | Card Code 100 |

Master File—Vendor Address

| Vendor Code | Record Type | Space | Blank | Address—Line 1 | Address—Line 2 | Address—Line 3 | Blank | Card Code 120 |

Transaction File—Expense Detail

| Vendor Code | Record Type | Voucher Number | Batch | Voucher Number | Voucher Date | Vendor Code | Invoice Date | Due Date | Invoice Number | Purchase Order Number | Debit Account | Product Type | Product Code | Blank | Amount | Quantity | Card Code 160 |

Transaction File—Payment Detail

| Vendor Code | Record Type | Voucher Number | Batch | Voucher Number | Voucher Date | Vendor Code | Invoice Date | Due Date | Invoice Number | Purchase Order Number | Check Number | Check Date | Blank | Amount | Blank | Card Code 170 |

Figure 1.

    c. Purchase journals arranged (1) by account charged and (2) by vendor

3. Vouchers and supporting invoices, receiving reports, and purchase order copies are filed by vendor code. Purchase orders and checks are filed numerically.

4. Company records are maintained on magnetic tapes. All tapes are stored in a restricted area within the computer room.

Required:

a. Describe the controls that the CPA should maintain over

    (1) Preparing the special tape

    (2) Processing the special tape with the generalized computer audit programs

b. Prepare a schedule for the EDP manager outlining the data that should be included on the special tape for the CPA's examination of accounts payable and related procedures. This schedule should show the

    (1) Client tape from which the items should be extracted

    (2) Name of the item of data (*ACIPA*)

12–22. An auditor is conducting an examination of the financial statements of a wholesale cosmetic distributor with an inventory consisting of thousands of individual items. The distributor keeps its inventory in its own distribution center and in two public warehouses. An inventory computer file is maintained on a computer disk and at the end of each business day the file is updated. Each record of the inventory file contains the following data:

- Item number
- Location of item
- Description of item
- Quantity on hand
- Cost per item
- Date of last purchase
- Date of last sale
- Quantity sold during year

The auditor is planning to observe the distributor's physical count of inventories as of a given date. The auditor will have available a computer tape of the data on the inventory file on the date of the physical count and a general-purpose computer software package.

Required:

The auditor is planning to perform basic inventory auditing procedures. Identify the basic inventory auditing procedures and describe how the use of the general-purpose software package and the tape of the inventory file data might be helpful to the auditor in performing such auditing procedures.

Organize your answers as follows:

Basic Inventory Auditing Procedure	How General-Purpose Computer Software Package and Tape of the Inventory File Data Might Be Helpful
1. Observe the physical count, making and recording test counts where applicable.	Determining which items are to be test counted by selecting a random sample of a representative number of items from the inventory file as of the date of the physical count. *(AICPA)*

12–23. In your audit of the accounts receivable file for Lava Butte, Inc., you plan to use generalized audit software. The format of the accounts receivable master file is shown in Table 12–1. Discuss the types of substantive tests that you might be able to make on the computer files.

12–24. The payroll files of Deadwood Gold Company, introduced in Chapter 11, must also be audited. These files consist of the transaction files and the master files.

The transaction files are created in the payroll department on diskettes from information on the time cards. For each employee, a clerk enters a social security number, pay rates, and hours worked.

The master files are created in the data processing department on magnetic tape from information on the diskettes and old master files. For each employee, the master-file record contains the following information:

- Name
- Address
- Social security number
- Pay rate
- Number of exemptions
- Voluntary deductions for each pay period, such as union dues or fair share, medical insurance, United Way, and U.S. savings bonds
- Year-to-date cumulative totals for gross earnings, federal and state income taxes withheld, social security withheld, state industrial accident insurance withheld, and voluntary deductions.

Focusing on the computer files, and excluding the payroll programs:

1. What should be your controls testing objectives and what controls tests are you likely to perform?
2. What should be your substantive testing objectives and what substantive tests are you likely to perform?
3. Which computer-auditing approaches and techniques are you likely to utilize in the performance of your controls and substan-

tive testing? Why? What additional information do you need before making a final decision?

12-25. Each of the following independent situations is encountered by an auditor in conjunction with the audit of a computerized accounting system. For each situation in the audit of computer files, excluding the computer programs, discuss:
  a. Which computer-auditing approach is likely to be utilized? Why?
  b. Which computer-auditing technique is likely to be utilized? Why?
  c. What additional information does the auditor need in order to make a final decision?

Situation 1:
Sharon Youngblood's client, introduced in Chapter 11, maintains on tape the master files for the payroll, accounts receivable, inventory, and accounts payable applications. The computer system is an IBM 370/125. The application programs and files do not contain any unusual processing routines or record formats.

Situation 2:
Sam Hotblood's client, introduced in Chapter 11, processes the accounts payable application on a disk-based system. All transaction and master files are maintained on disks. The computer is a one-of-a-kind Computem 100, acquired at a liquidation sale.

Situation 3:
Sally Trueblood's client, introduced in Chapter 11, processes the order entry application on an IBM 370/145. Disk transaction files are used to accumulate the sales orders. Master files are also maintained on disk.

Chapter 13
AUDITING
COMPUTER PROCESSING:
GENERAL CONCEPTS

Learning Objectives

After completing this chapter, the reader should be able to:

1. Understand how the nonprocessing-of-data approach integrates parts of the computer processing system.

2. Identify the conditions necessary for the nonprocessing-of-data approach in auditing computer processing systems.

3. Identify elections and options available to the auditor using the nonprocessing-of-data approach and understand how they affect the course of the audit.

4. Determine how the auditor integrates the testing of a computer processing system by combining separate tests into an overall evaluation.

5. Understand how the auditor integrates the testing of a computer processing system by combining the testing of programs and files into a single test.

6. Discover how the auditor integrates the testing of a computer processing system by combining mixtures of controls and substantive tests on both programs and files into multiple tests.

The computer auditor must usually make two comprehensive evaluations for each computer processing system application: (1) an overall evaluation, based on controls tests, of whether the controls for the computer system application are operating effectively; and (2) an overall evaluation, based on substantive tests, of whether the system is processing data accurately.

In this chapter we discuss the audit of an accounting application (1) as an integration of information from various parts of the computer processing system and (2) as an integration of the results of various types of tests. These concepts are illustrated with numerous examples throughout the chapter and a comprehensive Lava Butte, Inc., case in the Appendix.

Integration of Parts of System. The auditor can integrate information from various parts of the computer system by ignoring the separate existence of those parts. Instead of testing programs and files separately, the system is treated as an integrated unit or single entity. In this view of the system, often referred to as the *black-box approach*, the computer is regarded as receiving input, processing it, and producing output. The auditor concentrates on the examination of input and output.

Integration of Types of Tests. The auditor can integrate information from various types of tests. Separate tests on programs and files can be integrated as well as separate tests on user, general, and application controls. The integration can also result from a single test of both programs and files, or from multiple tests combining mixtures of tests on programs and files.

The emphasis in this chapter is on the integration of information into overall evaluations of computer system applications in contrast to the separate evaluations of the programs and files in the two preceding chapters. This is necessary for several reasons. First, a separate evaluation that a program is functioning properly does not mean that the files created by the program contain the correct information. They may be modified intentionally or by accident with a different program. Second, a separate evaluation that a file contains the correct information does not mean that the programs that use that file function properly. Errors introduced into the files may have been corrected, whereas the programs that caused the errors may still be incorrect. Third, the auditor may have elected to rely on user controls and test neither programs nor files stored on a magnetic medium. An overall evaluation of computer systems processing in this case will integrate the information from parts of the computer processing system, such as reconciling the input to the computer to the output from it.

INTEGRATION OF PARTS
OF THE COMPUTER PROCESSING SYSTEM:
NONPROCESSING OF DATA

The auditor can make inferences about the existence and operating effectiveness of controls for the computer system and the accuracy of processing through it without processing any data through the system. Auditing computer systems without processing any data through the system is often referred to as auditing around the computer. *In this approach, the auditor may assess a low level of risk on controls external to EDP called user controls. The auditor does not assess a low level of risk on EDP controls.*

Assessing a low level of risk on user controls serves to integrate the parts of the computer system. The auditor is not concerned with the functional parts of the system such as input, processing, and output. The concern is with reconciling what goes into the system with what comes out. The computer is treated as an integrated unit.

Our discussion of auditing without processing data comprises four segments: (1) the conditions that must exist so that the auditor can use the technique; (2) controls testing, including the objectives the auditor will satisfy when using the technique and examples of performing tests of controls without processing data; (3) a brief discussion of substantive testing using the approach; and (4) the factors the auditor must consider in deciding whether to use the approach.

Conditions Necessary for Using the Approach

In order to perform tests without processing data, the auditor must be able to (1) locate copies of the source documents for the transactions and accounting reports resulting from the transactions, (2) read the source documents and accounting reports without the aid of a computer, and (3) trace transactions from the source documents to the accounting reports and from the reports back to the source.

The source documents and accounting reports must be filed in such a manner that the auditor can locate them. It may be impossible to trace from receiving reports into an inventory file if the only copy of the report is attached to vendors' invoices filed alphabetically with no cross-reference listing available. The auditor would also not be able to audit around the computer when the printouts of general ledger postings for the months that the auditor has selected for testing are missing because someone misfiled them.

Source documents and accounting reports must be available in a readable form so that the auditor can audit without processing data. An example of a readable source document is a sales order prepared on paper by a salesperson. If phone orders are entered directly into visual display units, however, with no hard copy available, the auditor has no source document to read. An example of readable output would be a detailed listing of accounts receivable subsidiary ledgers showing names, beginning balances, debits and credits, and ending balances. If the content of subsidiary ledgers, however, is available only on magnetic tape or disk, the auditor cannot read the output without the help of the computer.

The auditor must be able to trace transactions from source documents to output, and vice versa. To perform such tracing, the output must be listed in sufficient detail. A general ledger listing of account balances only with no detail on individual debits and credits, or no transactions file from which they were obtained, may prevent the auditor from tracing.

Tests of Controls

Objectives

The controls testing objective of determining operating effectiveness can be satisfied by using the technique of nonprocessing of data. After obtaining an understanding of the internal control structure, the auditor using the nonprocessing-of-data approach may elect to take one of two alternative courses of action: assess a low level of risk on controls external to EDP *after* evaluating the strengths and weaknesses of EDP controls; or assess a low level of risk on controls external to EDP *before* evaluating the strengths and weaknesses of EDP controls. With either of these elections, the auditor must determine whether the assessment of a low level of risk on controls external to EDP is justified.

Understanding the Internal Control Structure. The computer auditor's decision regarding the assessment of risk on EDP controls requires the completion of an understanding of the internal control structure. This understanding is normally completed before the auditor can decide which course of action to follow, or whether controls tests will even be performed.

One course of action *may* lead to the design of controls tests. This will happen if the auditor concludes that strengths exist in the controls systems. To design the tests of controls and then perform them, the auditor cannot audit around the computer. Tests on programs and files will be necessary. Such testing is not of interest to us in this section on auditing without processing data.

A second course of action *may not* lead to the design of EDP controls test. This may be true because of two elections available to the auditor. First, the auditor may forgo controls testing *after* assessing the perceived strengths and weaknesses of the EDP controls. Second, the auditor may also decide to forgo controls testing *before* assessing the perceived strengths and weaknesses. Each of these elections of interest to the auditor using the nonprocessing-of-data approach will be discussed in turn.

Election to Evaluate the EDP Controls. The auditor may elect to forgo controls testing *after* assessing the strengths and weaknesses in the EDP control system. This election to disregard the EDP controls may be made irrespective of whether the controls are weak or adequate. The auditor's objectives after making such an election will depend on the circumstances and reasons for the election.

If the auditor determines that the EDP controls are weak, the auditor will have to adopt as his or her objective the evaluation of user controls or the performance of substantive tests, or both. If the user controls are perceived as being strong and the auditor decides to test them, controls testing will be followed by substantive testing. If the user controls are perceived as being weak, or the auditor decides not to test strong controls, the auditor will proceed directly to substantive testing.

If the auditor determines that the EDP controls are adequate, but still decides not to assess a low level of risk on them, this will lead to various courses of action depending on the reason for the decision. One reason not to assess a low level of risk on adequate EDP controls is that the effort required to complete the controls testing exceeds the reduction in effort that would be achieved by such a low level of risk assessment. The auditor can follow two different courses of action in this situation: either proceed directly to performing substantive tests or examine user controls.

Another reason not to assess a low level of risk on adequate EDP controls is that they are redundant because other control procedures are in existence. In this case, the auditor will perform tests on these other controls, controls maintained by the users. The auditor will design and perform substantive tests after the operating effectiveness of user controls has been evaluated.

Election Not to Evaluate EDP Controls. The other election that the auditor can make is to decide not to assess a low level of risk on EDP controls *before* evaluating their perceived strengths and weaknesses. This election can be made *regardless* of whether the EDP controls are adequate or weak. One reason for making this election is because of an assessment of risk on user controls. By electing to assess a low level of risk on user controls initially, the auditor avoids the process of having to determine whether EDP controls are adequate or weak. This may result in a considerable savings in audit effort. If weaknesses later come to the auditor's attention, however, their effect on the financial statements must be evaluated.

Reliance on Controls External to EDP.   Controls external to EDP can be assessed at a low level of risk only if two requirements are satisfied.[1] First, there must be adequate controls external to EDP. This is a subjective determination based on segregation of functions within the user department and the controls maintained by the users. Second, there must be no incompatible assignments of processing functions within the computer. *Incompatible assignments* are those functions normally segregated in a manual system, such as execution and recording or recording and custody. For example, if the computer can authorize and execute checks as well as record the checks, EDP personnel can embezzle funds by modifying the program and having the computer write checks to them. The auditor may be forced to examine EDP controls, such as program change controls, that prevent such unauthorized changes.

The first objective if the auditor elects to assess a low level of risk on controls external to EDP will be to perform testing of these user controls. The auditor will test for incompatibility of assignments within the user department and the functioning of controls reconciling input to the computer and output from it. The second objective will be to perform substantive tests based on the evaluation of the operating effectiveness of user controls.

Examples

Testing of user controls can be described by the following accounts receivable example. Before sending payments, sales, and miscellaneous debits and credits to data entry for conversion to machine-readable form, the accounts receivable personnel generate such control totals as the following:

- Financial totals on the dollar amount of debits and credits, including calculating the new accounts receivable control account total after processing
- Document or record counts on the total number of transactions to be processed and the total number of accounts receivable subsidiary ledgers to be updated

After processing, the accounts receivable personnel reconcile the new control total balance to the beginning balance, determine that the total dollar amounts of debits and credits agree with the total generated before

---

[1]These criteria are based on material presented by Deloitte, Haskins, and Sells at an *AUDITSCOPE* seminar held in Hyannis, Massachusetts, August 5–8, 1980.

processing, and ensure that the number of transactions and subsidiary ledgers updated agree with the control totals. In testing of these user controls, the auditor would ascertain that the reconciliations and verifications were actually being made and would test a sample of them.

A payroll application provides another example. A payroll department calculates the gross payroll, estimates the withholdings and deductions, and estimates the net payroll within some range as financial control totals. It also generates a record count control total for the number of payroll checks to be prepared. After the payroll has been prepared by the computer, the payroll department compares the computer-calculated amounts and number of checks printed with the manually prepared control totals. In the testing of these user controls, the auditor would again ascertain whether the comparisons were actually being performed and would test a sample of them to ensure that they were being performed properly.

Substantive Testing

Substantive tests will be performed regardless of whether a low level of risk is placed on EDP controls, user controls, or a combination. The level of risk placed on these controls, however, will determine the extent of testing. If these controls are perceived to be weak, the auditor may proceed directly to substantive testing without performing controls tests. In such a situation, substantive testing will be extensive. If the controls are strong, as determined by controls testing, the auditor may be able to reduce the amount of substantive testing that would otherwise be performed.

The performance of substantive tests on computer systems without processing any data through the system involves examining computer printouts and source documents. The auditor can trace from the computer printouts to the source documents or from the source documents to the printouts. For example, a computer printout of accounts receivable can be examined for omission of a payment on account. An entry to the sales account can be examined for correct valuation based on correct extension of the proper price and quantity by the computer program. Debits to the repairs and maintenance account can be vouched to the source documents for proper classification.

Factors to Be Considered in Deciding
Whether to Use the Approach

The auditor may decide to use the approach of testing without processing data because of its relatively low cost, ease of understanding, and ease of application. If the client's information system maintains the necessary source documents and detailed output, auditing around the computer can be an efficient, effective, and acceptable approach.

There are several reasons why the auditor may decide not to use the approach of testing without processing data. First, the auditor may lack assurance that the computer output is an accurate representation of the processing performed. Second, the amounts printed by the computer may be fraudulent. For example, the total for the accounts receivable control account may not agree with the sum of the subsidiary ledgers. Manually footing several thousand ledgers may not be feasible. Third, fraud that should be detected by other controls may not be detected because of other adjustments or transfers made in the system. Fourth, the ease with which the computer can be instructed to calculate one thing and print another introduces a high level of risk to auditing without processing data. Testing without processing data is an option available to the auditor, but one that we feel should be avoided whenever possible.

INTEGRATION OF TYPES OF TESTS

Separate Tests, Single Tests, and Multiple Tests

The auditor can integrate information from various types of tests to determine, on an overall basis, whether the controls for the computer system application are operating effectively and whether the system is processing data accurately. The various types of tests that are the subject of this integration are:

1. The *separate* tests on each program in a series of programs for a single application can be combined into an overall evaluation for all programs for that application.
2. The *separate* tests on each file used in or resulting from the processing for a single application can be combined into an overall evaluation for all files used in that application.
3. The *separate* tests on programs and files can be combined into an overall evaluation.
4. The testing of programs and files can be combined into a *single* test. This single test may enable the auditor to perform (a) a controls test of both programs and files at the same time, (b) a substantive test of both programs and files at the same time, and (c) a dual-purpose test of both programs and files at the same time.
5. *Multiple* tests can combine mixtures of controls and substantive tests on both programs and files into an overall evaluation of the system.
6. The *separate tests* performed on user, general, and application controls can be combined into an overall evaluation.

Series of Programs. The auditor may need to determine the overall processing reliability and accuracy of a series of programs for an application. This integration of information from a series of programs can be illustrated by a payroll application.

This payroll application is assumed to have three major programs: (1) a *maintenance program*, which processes additions, deletions, and other changes, such as exemptions for the payroll master file; (2) an *update program*, which calculates gross payroll, withholdings, and deductions, along with the year-to-date totals, and prints the payroll checks and journals; and (3) a *report program*, which prepares quarterly and annual payroll reports for union, pension, profit-sharing, and government purposes.

After testing each of these programs separately, the auditor must make an overall evaluation as to whether the payroll system is providing reliable and accurate information. If one of these three programs is not reliable and accurate, additional testing may have to be performed on various components of the payroll system. The update program, for example, may be calculating income tax withholdings incorrectly for some employees and correctly for others. This may be traced to a problem in the maintenance program where records adjacent to those being added or deleted are also modified. This may lead to additional testing of change controls for program modifications and payroll reports for materiality of monetary errors. The auditor may conclude that the problem existed for a single processing run and that the overall system is reliable. However, the auditor may also conclude that numerous control weaknesses exist and that additional substantive testing is necessary to determine the extent of monetary error.

Multiple Files. The information from separate tests on multiple files used by a single application must also be integrated. An order entry application can be used to illustrate this integration of information.

The order entry application accesses two separate files to determine whether a sales order should be processed. An accounts receivable master file and an inventory back-order file are accessed to determine whether the sum of the new order, amount to be due for back orders, and amounts currently receivable exceed the customer's credit limits.

After performing tests on each of these files separately, the auditor must make an overall evaluation of whether the sales order application is accepting customer orders within established credit limits. If one of these files contains inaccurate information, additional testing may have to be performed on other components of the sales and collection cycle. The inventory back-order file, for example, may contain incorrect information. This may lead to additional testing regarding accounts receivable valuation. To determine whether the receivables are properly valued, the auditor may examine subsequent period receipts to determine the collectibility of receivables. The auditor may conclude that no customers have exceeded their credit limit, or that customers who did exceed their credit limit have paid promptly anyway. However, the auditor may also conclude that the allowance for doubtful accounts must be materially increased.

Programs and Files. Three different types of tests provide information that must be integrated by the auditor into an overall evaluation of the reliability and accuracy of programs and files used in an accounting application. As mentioned earlier, these consist of separate tests, single tests, and multiple tests on programs and files. The single and multiple tests are discussed later in this chapter under "Processing of Actual Data," "Processing of Simulated Data," and "Dual-Purpose Testing."

Two issues must be addressed in the integration of information from the separate testing of programs and files. One issue occurs when the programs work properly, but the files still contain incorrect data. The other issue occurs when the files are correct even though the programs contain errors.

A file may contain incorrect data, even though a program tested by the auditor that updates that file works properly, because the file is subsequently changed by another program. The payroll illustration introduced earlier can be used to describe this situation.

The update program in the payroll illustration may be calculating the payroll and year-to-date information correctly, but the auditor discovers that the master-file year-to-date totals are still incorrect. The auditor may trace this problem to a program *not* tested (in this illustration) because of a determination that no changes were made to the program since the last audit when it was found to be reliable. This program is the maintenance program that is changing year-to-date values on records adjacent to those that are being added or deleted. The auditor will proceed as before to determine the extent of the problem, the overall reliability of the application, and the amount of monetary error.

A file may also be correct even though a program used to update it contains errors. The maintenance program for the payroll illustration can also be used to describe this situation. The errors caused by the faulty program, for example, may be detected and corrected, but the maintenance program is never modified to eliminate the problem. The auditor will again have to determine why the changes have not been made, whether there is a problem in the internal control structure, and whether the application is generally reliable.

User, General, and Application Controls. The auditor must decide whether to assess a low level of risk on the internal control structure and reduce substantive testing by integrating information from a combination of tests on user, general, and application controls. The decision to assess a low level of risk on a combination of these controls may result from a determination, for example, that the general controls are strong and that weak application controls are compensated for by strong user controls. The payroll illustration can again be used here.

The auditor evaluates general controls pertaining to the client's inventory, accounts receivable, accounts payable, and payroll applications and concludes that they have a low level of control risk. In evaluating the application controls for payroll, the auditor determines that data capture, data entry, and output controls are strong, but that processing controls are nonexistent. Specifically, there are no limit tests in the processing of payroll to detect latent errors resulting in exorbitant payroll checks, and there are no cross-footing tests to determine whether the totals of net pay, withholdings, and deductions sum to total gross pay. The auditor also determines, however, that the payroll department manually scans paychecks for unreasonable amounts and manually cross-foots the computer-prepared payroll journal. This user control is tested and evaluated as operating effectively. The auditor concludes that this user control compensates for the nonexistent processing control and that the combination of user, general, and applicable controls is operating effectively.

Processing of Actual Data

A computer system can be tested for compliance with controls and accuracy of results by processing actual data through the programs and files. Processing actual client data through a computer system provides the auditor with information about the operating effectiveness of application controls in programs and files and the accuracy of processing under actual operating conditions. To determine whether the controls function as prescribed and the results are accurate, the auditor can compare actual processing results with what should have happened.

Instead of concentrating on testing pertaining to just programs or just files, the emphasis in auditing systems in on selecting a combination of techniques to determine the overall operating effectiveness of controls and processing accuracy for the entire application. Techniques include controlled processing, controlled reprocessing, parallel simulation, custom-designed programs, and generalized audit software. (See Chapter 11 for a complete description of these techniques and the reasons why one technique may be selected over another.)

In auditing computer systems, a combination of techniques should be selected so that the techniques complement each other. Techniques that test different controls or processing results complement each other.

Techniques that test the same controls or processing results in the same way do not complement each other. Table 13–1 lists combinations that may be complementary for testing a system. Illustrations of some of them for performing controls tests and substantive tests follow.

Controls Testing Illustrations

The first combination of controlled processing and a custom-designed program can be illustrated by an accounts receivable application. Using controlled processing, the auditor can test for proper functioning of input and output controls. The auditor can ascertain that input errors detected were corrected and resubmitted, that output was reconciled to input, and that distribution of output was to authorized personnel. Using a custom-designed computer program, the auditor can analyze the accounts receivable subsidiary ledgers to ascertain that the credit limit field in each account contains a certain amount and that the balance due does not exceed that credit limit.

A combination of parallel simulation and a custom-designed program can be illustrated by a payroll application. Using parallel simulation, the auditor can process a payroll using both the client's and the auditor's system. The output tapes used for printing checks and earnings statements are then compared for differences. Using the custom-designed computer program, the auditor compares the pay rates on the transaction file used in processing the payroll with the pay rates on the master file.

Generalized audit software can be used instead of a custom-designed program in the examples above. The generalized audit software can analyze the accounts receivable subsidiary ledgers to determine compliance with the credit limit control. In the payroll example, generalized audit software can compare the pay rates in the transaction file with those in the master file.

Generalized audit software can also be used to test program controls. Software suitable for such a purpose has the ability to process transactions—for an order entry application for example—and reject input that

Table 13–1. Combinations of Techniques for Testing

Technique for Testing Controls in	
Programs	*Files*
1. Controlled processing	1. Custom-designed program
2. Controlled reprocessing	2. Generalized audit software
3. Parallel simulation	3. Custom-designed program
4. Custom-designed program	4. Generalized audit software
5. Generalized audit software	5. Custom-designed program

is invalid because of erroneous transaction codes, missing data, character checks, and so forth. These rejections can then be compared with rejections from the actual program input controls. If the rejections are logged on tape or disk, a custom-designed program can be used to compare the two files of rejections.

Substantive Testing Illustrations

The second mixture of controlled reprocessing and generalized audit software can be illustrated by an accounts receivable application. Using controlled reprocessing, the auditor can process accounts receivable payment transactions. Using generalized audit software, the auditor can then foot the subsidiary ledgers to see if the sum agrees with the balance in the control account.

A mixture of a custom-designed program and generalized audit software can be illustrated by a payroll application. Using a custom-designed program, the auditor can process a payroll. Using generalized audit software, the auditor can foot all the balances for gross earnings, deductions, and withholdings in each employee's year-to-date record and compare the total with the balances in the control accounts.

Reasons for Deciding to Use a Mixture

Effectiveness and efficiency are two reasons why an auditor may decide to use a mixture of techniques, rather than a single technique, in performing controls and substantive tests on a computer processing system. First, the auditor may be able to test *all* the controls in an application only by using a mixture. The available generalized audit software, for example, may have the ability to test for evidence of controls in files but not programs. A custom-designed program may be necessary for the latter. Second, a mixture of techniques may be less expensive. The available generalized audit software, for example, may have the ability to test for accuracy of processing results in programs. To do so, however, may require twice as much time to set up and process as a custom-designed program.

Processing of Simulated Data

The operating effectiveness of application controls and the accuracy of processing results can be determined by processing simulated client data through the computer system. Processing such data through a computer system provides the auditor with information about the effectiveness of application controls and the accuracy of processing results under simulated operating conditions. After creating each record and processing the records through the system, the auditor compares the processing results with what would have happened if the controls had been functioning as designed and the results had been accurate.

Techniques available to the auditor for the performance of tests using simulated data include test records and the integrated test facility. (See Chapter 11 for a complete description of these techniques and the reasons why one may be selected over the other.)

Controls Testing Illustration

Simulated transactions can be used, for example, to test the controls in an accounts receivable application. Master and transaction files are created using simulated transactions. Program controls on input can be examined as these files are being created by determining whether erroneous transactions are detected and rejected. File controls can be tested by determining whether access to files is restricted to specific types of programs, transactions, or inquiries. The contents of the file can also be tested for the existence of controls such as credit limits. Instead of using the simulated transactions to test just programs or just files, the integration occurs by extending the procedure to test both.

Substantive Testing Illustration

Simulated transactions can be used, for example, to test the processing accuracy of a sales order system. The simulated orders can be processed against the inventory and accounts receivable files, and those files can be checked for correct balances as part of the valuation objective. The simulated transactions posted to the various sales accounts by product number can be tested for proper account classifications.

Dual-Purpose Testing

Dual-purpose testing is a combination of controls testing and substantive testing. The computer-auditing techniques presented in this chapter, and discussed under separate controls and substantive testing objectives, are normally used in dual-purpose tests to accomplish both objectives simultaneously. In auditing computer systems, the auditor also combines techniques to audit both programs and files.

Dual-purpose tests accomplish both the controls testing objectives and the substantive testing objectives simultaneously. For example, in auditing computer programs, parallel simulation can be used to test input controls for compliance with requirements and also to perform substantive tests in comparing the account balances produced by each of the computer systems. In auditing computer files, generalized audit software can be used to examine a particular field, such as credit limits for accounts receivable, to satisfy a controls testing objective. The software can also be used to foot the accounts receivable subsidiary ledgers in performing substantive tests.

In performing dual-purpose tests on computer systems, the auditor is likely to combine techniques used to test both files and programs separately. In the preceding example, parallel simulation and generalized audit software are used to test programs and files separately. In that example, two different techniques are used to perform the controls tests and substantive tests, whereas one technique each is used for testing programs and files. Combining these techniques in auditing the computer system is illustrated by the matrix in Table 13–2.

In performing dual-purpose testing, the auditor assumes that the results attained on completing the controls testing will agree with his or her preliminary assessment of control risk as to the operating effectiveness of the control system. The extent of substantive testing performed as part of the dual-purpose testing is based on that assumption. If the internal control structure is not operating as effectively as anticipated, the auditor may have to increase the extent of substantive testing.

In performing combinations of tests, auditors should not lose sight of the objectives they are trying to achieve. The auditor may find it relatively easy to become enamored of the techniques and the process of computer auditing and forget that specific controls and substantive testing objectives must be satisfied. This is a danger whenever dual-purpose testing is performed, but it is even more so in computer auditing because the techniques and process are more complex. The complexities of the techniques and process may overwhelm the complexities of the audit.

SUMMARY

The auditor must integrate information from various parts of the computer system or from various types of tests in order to make a comprehensive evaluation of the operating effectiveness of controls and processing accuracy of the system. The integration of information from various parts of the computer system can be done by using the approach of nonprocessing of data. The integration of information from various types of tests can

Table 13–2. Combining Techniques for Dual-Purpose Testing of Computer Systems

	Program Tests	File Tests
Controls Tests	Parallel simulation	Generalized audit software
Substantive Tests	Parallel simulation	Generalized audit software

be done by using the approaches of processing actual data and processing simulated data.

The nonprocessing-of-data approach can be used only if several conditions are satisfied. When using this approach, the auditor has numerous elections to make and options available within those elections. In addition to the conditions necessary in order to use the approach, the auditor must consider several factors in deciding whether to use it.

A comprehensive evaluation of system operating effectiveness and accuracy can be made by integrating information from various tests using the processing-of-actual-data approach. Techniques available include controlled processing, controlled reprocessing, parallel simulation, custom-designed programs, and generalized audit software. The most efficient and effective means of testing using this approach may be to use mixtures of these techniques.

The processing-of-simulated-data approach can also be utilized to make a comprehensive evaluation of system operating effectiveness and accuracy. Techniques available include test records and ITF.

Dual-purpose tests, combining controls and substantive tests, are performed to increase the audit's efficiency. The substantive testing portion is designed with an assumption as to the effectiveness of the controls, which cannot be verified until the results of the controls testing portion are obtained. In performing dual-purpose tests, the auditor must be aware that controls testing and substantive testing have separate objectives.

APPENDIX

Lava Butte, Inc.: Auditing Computer Processing in a Complex System Environment

Some EDP auditors wake up from a nightmare in which they were auditing a complex computer system. Their fear is in not knowing how to audit such a system. Their nightmare system operates in real time with a data-base management system (DBMS). It includes a large mainframe computer for real-time processing plus numerous minicomputers in a distributed data processing (DDP) network. The DDP computers perform some processing tasks on their own and, for other tasks, serve as remote job entry (RJE) terminals for data input and printing of output from the mainframe computers.

In this Appendix we discuss the control and audit of a complex EDP system. To illustrate this discussion, we use a single complex system like the one in the auditor's nightmare so that we can focus on analyzing the control structure and audit procedures for such systems. We will not discuss the auditing of simpler systems that lack some of the characteristics of the illustrative system. Simpler systems can be analyzed by eliminating those characteristics of the control structure of these systems that do not apply. Controls tests would then be performed on the remaining controls. This approach is illustrated in the case studies.

This Appendix is divided into three major sections: (1) the complex system that serves as the basis for analysis, (2) the distinguishing characteristics of the control structure for the specified system, and (3) the audit of such a system.

The emphasis in this Appendix is on the unique problems, controls, and audit approaches for complex systems. The controls and audit approaches that are also used for less complex systems and have been discussed previously will be mentioned only briefly here.

COMPLEX SYSTEM ILLUSTRATION

The design of the complex system that is the subject of this analysis is depicted in Figure A13–1. The distinguishing characteristics of this system are its hardware and software components. To a lesser degree, such a system can also be distinguished by the procedures followed in its operation and the personnel performing these procedures.

Hardware

The hardware for the system consists of equipment at a central location and at decentralized locations. The mainframe computer with peripheral equipment is installed at the central location. The decentralized locations contain various types of equipment.

At the central location, the mainframe computer has a memory storage capability of several megabytes. In addition to the mainframe computer, the central location contains the following peripheral equipment:

- Numerous disk drives with controllers for storing the operating system, application programs, and data
- Numerous tape drives with controllers for logging transactions processed in real time, for batch processing of master and transaction files for various accounting applications, and for batch processing of historical data for sales and various other analyses
- Several high-speed printers
- Multiplexor and selector channel data communication control units
- Various key-to-tape and key-to-disk data preparation devices

The decentralized locations include two major types of equipment—terminals and minicomputers. The following types of terminal equipment are found at some of these locations:

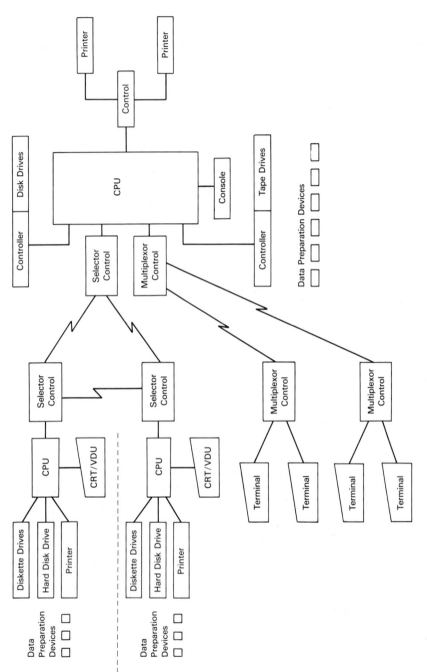

Figure A13–1. Illustration of Complex EDP System

- Typewriter keyboards
- Cathode-ray tube (CRT)/visual display unit (VDU) terminals
- Multiplexor control units enabling the terminals to communicate with each other and with the mainframe computer

Minicomputer configurations at some of the decentralized locations include the following:

- CPU with up to two megabytes storage capacity
- Diskettes and hard disk drives with up to forty million bytes of on-line storage capacity
- CRT/VDU consoles
- Medium-speed printers
- Various key-to-disk data preparation devices
- Selector channel control units enabling all minicomputers to communicate with each other and with the mainframe computer

Software

Operating Systems

The operating system on the mainframe computer provides the following support and/or resources:

- Multiprogramming
- Data communication
- Resource allocation of processor time, memory, secondary storage, and channels on a priority basis
- Compilers for several languages
- Utilities

The operating systems on the DDP computers provide the following support and/or resources:

- Data communication
- Resource allocation of processor time, memory, secondary storage, and channels
- Interpreters for BASIC
- Compilers for BASIC
- Utilities

Applications

Accounting applications processed on the mainframe computer include the following:

- *Real-time (immediate) processing of sales, purchases, and inventory changes using DBMS*

  1. Order entry/sales
     - Approval of order based on customer credit limits, amounts currently receivable, and accounts from back-order file
     - Preparation of pick slips on terminals in warehouses stating locations of system components
     - Preparation of packing slips; bills of lading, including calculation of freight and handling charges; and address labels on terminals in shipping area

  2. Billing/accounts receivable
     - Preparation of invoice ready for mailing to customer
     - Updating of accounts receivable records

  3. Purchasing
     - Preparation of purchase order to restock inventory if level has fallen below reorder point

  4. Inventory
     - Updating of perpetual inventory records

The DBMS provides for linkages among the following:
- Accounts receivable file and back-order file by customer
- Inventory file and back-order file by product
- Inventory of all products supplied by the same vendor
- Inventory of all components for an assembled product
- Multiple-address locations for the same customer

- *Batch processing of*

  1. Accounts payable payments to vendors
  2. Payroll
  3. General ledger, other than those acounts updated on a real-time basis

Accounting applications on the DDP systems include the following:

- *Distributed data entry*—payroll information for batch processing on the mainframe computer is entered through the minicomputers. Data are stored on disk and automatically transferred at night to the central site where the payroll checks are printed.
- *Distributed decentralized processing*—parts inventory processing is performed by each minicomputer installed at a regional parts distributor. Processing associated with the parts inventory performed at each decentralized site on a batch basis includes (1) order entry/sales, (2) billing/accounts receivable, (3) purchasing, and (4) inventory update.
- *Distributed centralized processing*—all fixed-asset accounting for the entire organization is batch-processed on one of the minicomputers. For this pur-

pose, fixed-asset additions, deletions, and other information are transmitted to it by the other minicomputer and the mainframe computer.

• *Distributed data with a central data base*—accounts payable payments to vendors for parts. Checks to parts vendors located in the geographic area of the distributor are drawn on banks in that area. The central computer maintains the data base for these vendors, including such information as name, address, identification number, history of purchases, purchase order numbers, and amounts due and payment dates by invoice. On the date a check is to be prepared, the central computer transfers the necessary information to the diskette of the appropriate minicompter. Checks are then printed and mailed from the minicomputer site.

The terminals—typewriters and CRT/VDU—are used for order entry.

Procedures and Personnel

The procedures and personnel associated with a complex system are both similar to and different from those with other simpler systems. They are similar because both types of systems require procedures pertaining to application controls for data capture, data entry, data processing, and output like those discussed previously. They are also similar because both types of systems require the skills of systems analysts, programmers, and operators, as discussed previously.

The differences between the two systems occur in three areas: (1) procedures pertaining to the environment for general controls, (2) procedures pertaining to application controls for real-time processing, and (3) the addition of a data-base administrator.

Changes in procedures pertaining to the environment for general controls and to application controls for real-time processing are discussed in the next section. (The data-base administrator and functions performed by that individual are discussed in Chapter 2.)

CONTROLS IN A COMPLEX SYSTEM ENVIRONMENT

The internal control structure for a complex system has the same objectives as any other data processing system: to prevent, detect, and correct errors. The controls discussed in previous chapters still apply in achieving these objectives.

There are two major differences in the internal control structure for complex systems. One difference is that certain controls are emphasized in order to compensate for some of the weaknesses inherent in such a structure. The other difference relates to the requirement for additional controls. In this section we discuss both of these differences.

Our discussion of the control structure for complex systems is divided into general controls and application controls. *General controls* are further broken down into organization controls, personnel practices, and standard operating procedures; systems development and documentation; hardware and systems software; and systems security. *Application controls* are discussed in the context of data capture and entry, data processing, and output.

General Controls

Organization Controls, Personnel Practices, and Standard Operating Procedures

Organization Controls. Organization controls pertain primarily to the segregation of functions. We attempt to maintain a separation of those who initiate transactions from the EDP personnel involved in recording the transactions. We also attempt to separate the EDP function of programming from that of operating the computer. The data-base administrator enhances control and at the same time presents an organizational control problem. With advanced systems, we may end up with the best and worst of function segregation.

The best of function segregation is associated with centralized processing on the mainframe computer. This occurs in two ways. First, individuals initiating sales order transactions at the terminals are physically separated from the mainframe computer where the recording of these transactions takes place. Second, with large systems we normally have no problem in maintaining a separation of the functions of programmers and computer operators because of the many people involved.

The worst of function segregation is also associated with centralized processing on the mainframe computer. For example, we combine the functions of initiating transactions as well as recording them in the accounts payable application for electronic systems. This program automatically prepares checks on the due dates of vendor invoices. The program also records information by updating vendor files. A programmer could take advantage of this functional aggregation by writing a routine to have the program issue checks to the programmer. The recording of the check could be hidden in an account not likely to be audited. This program should be tested thoroughly and changes to it tightly controlled to prevent embezzlement.

In addition, the worst of function segregation is associated with the DDP minicomputers. At these decentralized sites, we are likely to find that individuals with both programming and operator skills have access to the computer. The parts inventory processing will be highly susceptible to fraud, for example, because the operators skilled in programming may be able to steal parts and hide the theft by changing the contents of transaction or master files. (Compensating controls that may be appropriate for the lack of segregation of functions at these sites are discussed in Chapter 14.)

The worst of function segregation may also be encountered with the position of data-base administrator. This position is usually established to enhance control but may have exactly the opposite effect. The position is used as a preventive control by having the administrator monitor additions, deletions, and changes to the data base. The power to monitor, however, may also provide the administrator with the tools to override established controls. The administrator, for example, may be able to add to, delete from, or change the data base undetected by anyone else because the administrator is the final control for such activity.

The function segregation problems introduced with the data-base administrator position can be mitigated in various ways. One way is to maintain logs of the administrator's requests for access to the data base; programs in object or source code, utility programs, and documentation. The auditor would then examine the log for unauthorized activity. Another way is to rotate individuals fulfilling the role of administrator. An administrator in the position for a relatively short period of time is less likely to perpetrate a fraud. In addition, by training several people for the position, others are more likely to detect fraudulent activities of the current position holder. Finally, each person holding the position should be carefully evaluated as to competence and trustworthiness and then bonded.

Personnel Practices.   Personnel practices pertaining to the selection, promotion, and termination of employees in organizations with complex system designs are usually good. The training and supervision of employees in such organizations are also usually good. These personnel practices are good because large organizations typically devote the necessary resources to their design and implementation.

Good personnel practices generally result in competent employees. In such an environment, the EDP auditor may anticipate a low error rate, such as few data entry errors. This can be confirmed through testing input controls. The auditor may then conclude, therefore, that reliance can be placed on that aspect of the internal control structure.

Standard Operating Procedures.   Complex systems can also exemplify the best and worst of standard operating procedures. The best will be found at the central site and the worst at the DDP sites.

Operating procedures found at the central site may include operating schedules for computer processing and enforced vacation schedules. The former may help detect the use of the computer for unauthorized purposes. The latter often result in uncovering problems while someone is on vacation.

Operating schedules and enforced vacation schedules are no less important at the DDP site but may not be enforced there as rigidly. This lack of enforcement can be attributed to both the type of equipment used at such sites and the personnel employed there.

Operating schedules may not be used at the DDP sites for the following reasons:

- The equipment is used only a few hours each day and is readily accessible without scheduling.
- No logs are printed by the system for subsequent comparison with scheduled time and length of use.
- Only one or two people are trained in the use of the equipment, and whenever they have time, they perform the required processing.

Vacation schedules may not be enforced at the DDP sites because no one is available to replace the operator if only a single individual is trained on the equipment. Even if on vacation, that person may be expected to come in and run a particular job.

Additional problems pertaining to operating procedures may arise at the DDP sites because of the operator's ability to determine the following:

- Which controls to implement or enforce on applications processed at the site
- What editing to perform on applications processed at the site
- Which transactions are to be included in each batch of input for both on-site and off-site processing
- Which verification procedures will be performed on output resulting from both on-site and off-site processing
- When input will be submitted for both on-site and off-site processing

Systems Development and Documentation Controls

Three aspects of system development should be emphasized in the complex system environment: programming and design standards, user participation in design, and the library function.

Programming and design standards should be emphasized in the complex system environment. Without development conventions, several problems may arise. There may be a proliferation of programs that fail to meet the organization's needs. Programs that are developed may also be difficult to maintain because they contain unusual approaches to specifying input, processing, or output. Good programs may even be turned into disasters with unauthorized or poorly conceived changes.

User participation in the design of programs for advanced systems will help ensure that the programs meet the needs of the users. In addition, with user and internal audit participation, it is more likely that adequate controls will be designed into the system from the beginning. With complex systems, it is almost impossible to incorporate controls after they have reached production status.

The library function is becoming increasingly important in complex systems for two reasons. First, because of the complexity of these systems, the prevention of unauthorized changes is crucial. A programmer's unauthorized attempt at a minor fix in one program, for example, may cause processing errors in other interrelated programs. Second, in the DDP environment where there is distribution of processing, numerous copies of the same program exist. It is difficult to control and maintain all of these copies. The parts inventory processing, for example, is distributed. Each system requires a copy of the program. Any changes must be incorporated into each system. Monitoring all of this activity through the library function is difficult but essential.

Adequate documentation is as much a requirement in complex systems as it is in any other type of system. The discussion in previous chapters regarding this control area is also appropriate here.

Hardware and Systems Software Controls

Vendor-supplied hardware and systems software controls in complex systems can also range from the best to the worst. The best controls will again be associated with the central system and the worst with the DDP systems.

The large central system will contain numerous hardware and systems software controls. Hardware controls will include parity checking and other electronic diagnostic features to ensure the integrity of processing (see Chapter 7). Systems software controls will include boundary protection for multiprogramming, internal file labels and file checking, and other controls (see Chapter 7).

The DDP systems are likely to be distinguished by their lack of hardware and systems software controls. Electronic diagnostic circuitry that can detect and/or correct hardware malfunctions may be missing. File checking and other software controls may be nonexistent.

Systems Security Controls

Systems security controls are typically emphasized in complex systems because these systems, operating in real time, are vital to the continued operational functioning of the organization. Some organizations, for example, are almost paralyzed when their real-time systems go down. The following often receive greater attention: (1) the librarian function, (2) file backup, and (3) power supply. In addition, in a DBMS environment, additional control problems arise in the areas of (4) defining and maintaining linkages among files in the data base, and (5) concurrent updating of the same data record by two different processes at the same time.

Other problems encountered in a DBMS environment, in addition to the five mentioned above, are discussed later under "Application Controls."

Librarian Function. In complex systems, several components of the librarian functions are emphasized: control over utilities, control over production program access, control over master copies of DDP distributed processing programs, multiple passwords for system access, and multiple levels for program and file access.

System modification utilities are always a problem because of their ability to modify programs or file content. Similar utilities associated with complex systems are even more of a problem because of their advanced capabilities. SUPERZAP, for example, can be used to change programs without leaving a trace. These utilities should be placed in a restricted library, perhaps accessible only when two people with completely separate passwords work together.

Production program access can be a significant problem with the DDP systems because of the difficulty of providing source program integrity. To prevent operators at any of the DDP sites from making unauthorized changes to the parts inventory distributed processing program, for example, these programs could be distributed only in object code format.

Control over the master copies of the parts inventory distributed decentralized processing program is another major problem. The master copies of this program are likely to be kept at the central site. Access to this program should also require the joint efforts of two people.

Multiple passwords for system access in complex systems may be an effective means of preventing unauthorized access to programs or files. Multiple passwords would require that each terminal or DDP system have a hardware identifier and that each operator also have an identifier. If the terminal or DDP system were not authorized to process a particular type of transaction, or the operator were not authorized for that transaction, the system would not allow any further activity. In addition, a log on magnetic tape should be maintained to record all system access, both unauthorized and authorized, for subsequent analysis.

A control closely related to multiple passwords is multiple levels for programs or file access. With this control, one level would provide only for the reading of programs or files. Another level providing for both reading and writing would be available only to those authorized to change programs and files.

File Backup. File backup is likely to be more of a problem at the DDP sites than at the central site. At the central site, we would anticipate the grandparent-parent-child approach to processing with magnetic tape. For the real-time system, we would anticipate that one or more magnetic tape drives would be devoted to logging transactions to provide for system recovery in case of failure. Periodically the disk files should be backed up by copying their contents to another disk or magnetic tape. Some organizations do this monthly, or even weekly.

The DDP sites are likely to create a more severe file backup problem. There are no magnetic tapes attached to these systems. Transactions cannot be logged on tape, therefore, nor can the diskettes be backed up with tape. At these sites, backup may be done by copying the one diskette's contents to another diskette. These diskettes could also be backed up by copying their contents on the magnetic tapes at the central site.

Power Supply. Complex systems operating in real time should have protected power supplies. Power failures, or even voltage surges, with such systems can create horrendous problems of file reconstruction or system restart. Protection devices include voltage regulators and standby generators.

Defining and Maintaining DBMS Linkages. Access to information in DBMS records is provided by defining linkages among these records. Such a linkage, for example, ties together information in the back-order file with information in the current accounts receivable file for each customer in the illustrative system. Destruction of this linkage may make it impossible to fill customer orders on back-ordered merchandise. Therefore a DBMS requires a control that will prevent application programs from destroying or changing these linkages.

Concurrent Updating. Concurrent updating occurs when two different processes attempt to access and update a data record at the same time. The order in which the updates take place may lead to entirely different results. An inventory receipt followed by an issue may result in the orderly processing of a customer's order. An issue followed by a receipt may result first in an out-of-stock situation, partial fulfillment of a customer's order, and preparation of a rush purchase order. The subsequent receipt may not result in completion of the sale and cancellation of the purchase order. Therefore a DBMS requires a control that determines which activity has priority on a concurrent updating.

Application Controls

Application controls include those for data capture, entry, and processing. These controls are primarily used to prevent errors from occurring or to detect those errors that do occur. Application controls also include output controls. Output controls primarily detect those errors that have occurred during the processing cycle. They also prevent fraud and embezzlement by restricting the distribution of output to authorized parties.

Application controls appropriate for the described system are discussed in Chapters 9 and 10. The data capture and batch data entry controls in Chapter 9 apply primarily to the DDP systems. The on-line entry, processing, and output controls in Chapter 10 apply to both the DDP systems and the central computer system. The reader is referred to those chapters for a discussion of those controls.

A new emphasis for application controls should be considered for the real-time processing portion of the system. Controls for the prevention of errors are still important, but the focus of control in the real-time processing environment is on the detection and correction of those errors that do occur.

Control for the detection and correction of errors is especially important for the files. With real-time updating of files, the contents are changed as each transaction is being entered into the system. Errors that get by the prevention controls must be detected and corrected to keep the files from deteriorating. Large numbers of undetected and uncorrected errors would eventually render the files worthless.

A control technique typically used in the real-time environment for the detection and correction of errors is to log all transactions entering the system. This transaction log can serve several purposes:

- Record attempts to access the system with illegal passwords for follow-up by the auditors
- Serve as the basis for generating document counts, financial totals, and hash totals by transaction for audit trail and the tracing of transactions by the auditors
- Provide backup for reconstructing the files if a system crash or some other problem occurs
- Record errors detected on data input for subsequent analysis by auditors as to type and frequency

Chapter 10 discusses additional controls for the prevention, detection, and correction of errors. The on-line entry, processing, and output controls discussed there can also be used in this environment.

AUDITING THE COMPLEX SYSTEM

The auditor of complex computer systems must assess control risk and collect sufficient competent evidential matter to form the basis for an opinion. Controls tests are performed in assessing control risk, and substantive tests are performed in collecting evidence to issue an opinion.

Tests of Controls

The auditor of complex computer systems must evaluate the operating effectiveness of both general and application controls. (See Chapter 4 for a discussion of the approach.)

General Controls

The assessment of risk for general controls may lead either (1) to the assessment of risk for application controls or (2) directly to the performance of substantive tests. Strong general controls will lead to the former; weak general controls will lead to the latter.

Controls tests performed on general controls in complex computer systems have two characteristics. First, as with other computer systems, they tend to be manual procedures. Second, the auditor may tend to focus on some controls because of the specific configuration of the system. These two characteristics are illustrated in the following discussion.

The assessment of risk for organization controls, personnel practices, and standard operating procedures requires that the auditor physically observe who is doing *what* and *when* and that the auditor manually review organization charts, manuals, and schedules. The lack of segregation of functions resulting from one person serving as both a user and an operator of the system is especially acute at the DDP sites. Excellent controls over diskettes containing programs and files, and passwords restricting the operator from unauthorized changes to diskettes, can compensate for the lack of function segregation.

Systems development and documentation controls can be tested by manually evaluating the procedures followed in designing, implementing, and changing application programs, as well as the documentation of the entire process. Again, at the DDP sites there is an especially acute problem regarding control over program changes. The fixed-asset accounting and parts inventory programs, for example, should be compared periodically with master copies controlled by the auditor.

Hardware and systems software controls may be minimal or nonexistent on the DDP systems. Testing of these controls and those on the central system to determine their availability and operating effectiveness consists of manually reviewing vendor-supplied literature and preventive maintenance schedules. Weak controls necessitate substantive testing to determine the reliability and accuracy of processing by the computer. Systems security controls are evaluated by manually reviewing restrictions on access to programs, including the DBMS, the files, and the computer itself, and by manually reviewing file backup and reconstruction procedures. The multiple locations of the DDP systems mean that the auditor's task is complicated somewhat, but the procedures are essentially the same. The auditor can emphasize surprise audits at the DDP sites to determine what is going on under actual operating conditions. The auditor encountering weak controls on restriction of access to the system may have to increase substantive testing substantially. Weak file backup, reconstruction procedures, or lack of protection on communication lines may not necessitate increased substantive testing, but at the very least they should be brought to management's attention.

Application Controls

The testing of application controls in complex computer systems is essentially a synthesis of material presented previously. The approaches of nonprocessing of data, processing of actual data, and processing of simulated data are all applicable. The controls testing of each of the applications listed in the illustration earlier in this chapter is included as a case study at the end of the chapter.

Substantive Tests

The substantive testing of complex computer systems is also a synthesis of material presented previously. This testing of each of the illustrated applications is also included as a case study at the end of the chapter.

REVIEW QUESTIONS

13–1. How does the testing of computer systems differ from the testing of computer programs and computer files?

13–2. In the auditing of computer systems, on which type of application controls is the auditor likely to concentrate in testing computer programs and computer files?

13–3. What technique is the auditor likely to select in controls testing using the approaches of nonprocessing of data, processing of actual data, and processing of simulated data? Under what conditions is the auditor likely to select each approach?

13–4. What objectives can the auditor satisfy in auditing around the computer?

13-5. What conditions must exist in order for the auditor to be able to audit around the computer?

13-6. What elections and options are available to the auditor in auditing computer systems using the nonprocessing-of-data approach? Why is the auditor likely to select each election or option?

13-7. The auditor may have to integrate information from several types of tests in arriving at an overall evaluation of the reliability and processing accuracy of a single accounting application. Explain what is meant by integrating information from tests performed on
   a. A series of programs
   b. Multiple files
   c. Programs and files
   d. A combination of user, general, and application controls

13-8. Using the approaches of processing actual data and processing simulated data, which mix of techniques is the auditor likely to use in controls testing? Why?

13-9. In the auditing of computer systems, which substantive test is the auditor likely to concentrate on in testing computer programs and computer files?

13-10. What techniques is the auditor likely to select in substantive testing using the approaches of nonprocessing of data, processing of actual data, and processing of simulated data? Under what conditions is the auditor likely to select each approach?

13-11. Using the approaches of processing actual data and processing simulated data, which mix of techniques is the auditor likely to use in substantive testing? Why?

OBJECTIVE QUESTIONS

13-12. Which of the following client electronic data processing (EDP) systems generally can be audited without examining or directly testing the EDP computer programs of the system?
   a. A system that performs relatively uncomplicated processes and produces detailed output
   b. A system that affects a number of essential master files and produces a limited output
   c. A system that updates a few essential master files and produces no printed output other than final balances
   d. A system that performs relatively complicated processing and produces very little detailed output (*AICPA*)

13-13. Data Corporation has just completely computerized its billing and accounts receivable record keeping. You want to make maximum use of the new computer in your audit of Data Corporation. Which of the following audit techniques could not be performed through a computer program?

a. Tracing audited cash receipts to accounts receivable credits
b. Selecting on a random number basis accounts to be confirmed
c. Examining sales invoices for completeness, consistency between different items, valid conditions, and reasonable amounts
d. Resolving differences reported by customers on confirmation requests (AICPA)

13-14. Which of the following combinations of techniques would least likely be used for controls testing the programs and files for an accounts receivable application?
a. Generalized audit software and controlled processing
b. Test records and custom-design programs
c. Integrated test facility and test records
d. Controlled reprocessing and custom-design programs

13-15. Which of the following conditions is not necessary for auditing around the computer?
a. Source documents are filed chronologically.
b. Printouts show the detail for debits and credits to the repairs and maintenance account.
c. Printouts from the computer are reconciled daily to the beginning balances.
d. Transactions listings and journals are prepared as part of the audit trail.

13-16. In making an overall evaluation of a computer system to determine whether data are being processed reliably and accurately, the auditor must integrate information from various types of tests. Which of the following types of tests is likely to result in the most difficult integration problem?
a. Separate tests on each program in a payroll application consisting of maintenance, update, and report preparation programs
b. Separate tests on files in an order entry system accessing an accounts receivable master file and an inventory back-order file
c. Separate tests on the programs and files for an accounts payable application which automatically issues checks to vendors on payment due dates
d. Separate tests on user, general, and application controls for a fixed-asset accounting application whose sole function is to print a list of office equipment by room number from a deck of punched cards

CASES AND EXERCISES

13-17. In preparing for the dual-purpose testing to be performed on the acquisition and payment cycle, the junior auditor prepared the following matrix. The matrix was to demonstrate to the supervisor the mix of techniques the junior planned to use.

	Program Testing	File Testing
Controls Testing	Test records	Custom-designed program
Substantive Testing	Controlled reprocessing	Generalized audit software

Considering the dual-purpose and computer systems objectives, what do you think the supervisor's reaction will be?

13–18. In the past, the records to be evaluated in an audit have been printed reports, listings, documents, and written papers, all of which are visible output. However, in fully computerized systems which employ daily updating of transaction files, output and files are frequently in machine-readable form such as tapes or disks. Thus, they often present the auditor with an opportunity to use the computer in performing an audit.

Required:
  a. Discuss how the computer can be used to aid the auditor in examining accounts receivable in such a fully computerized system.
  b. Discuss how the computer can be used to aid the auditor in examining the programs used in processing accounts receivable in such a system.
  c. Discuss how the auditor would be likely to perform dual-purpose tests and utilize a mix of computerized techniques in examining such a system. (*AICPA adapted*)

13–19. A summary of the control risk assessment process was given in Chapter 4 and illustrated in Figure 4–2. In this chapter we elaborated on that process by introducing some additional procedures not included in that summary. Prepare a flowchart that revises Figure 4–2 by incorporating the additional procedures introduced in this chapter.

13–20. Your company has procured a number of minicomputers for use in a distributed processing network. One of these has been installed in the stores department for a "distributed computing" application. The stores department has the responsibility for disbursing stock items and for maintaining stores records. In your audit you find, among other things, that a competent employee, trained in computer applications, receives the requisitions for stores, reviews them for completeness and for the propriety of approvals, disburses the stock, maintains the records, operates the computer, and authorizes adjustments to the total amounts of stock accumulated by the computer.

When you discuss the applicable controls with the department manager, you are told that the minicomputer is assigned exclusively to that department and that it therefore does not require the same types of controls applicable to the large computer systems.

Required:
Comment on the manager's contentions, discussing briefly five types of control that would apply to this minicomputer application. (*IIA adapted*)

13-21. George Beemster, CPA, is examining the financial statements of Louisville Sales Corporation, which recently installed an off-line electronic computer. The following comments have been extracted from Mr. Beemster's notes on computer operations and the processing and control of shipping notices and customer invoices:

To minimize inconvenience Louisville converted with minimal change its existing data processing system. The computer company supervised the conversion and has provided training to all computer department employees in systems design, operations, and programming.

Each computer run is assigned to a specific employee, who is responsible for making program changes, running the program, and answering questions. This procedure has the advantage of eliminating the need for records of computer operations because each employee is responsible for his or her own computer runs.

At least one computer department employee remains in the computer room during office hours, and only computer department employees have keys to the computer room.

System documentation consists of those materials furnished by the computer company—a set of record formats and program listings. These and the tape library are kept in a corner of the computer department.

The company considered the desirability of programmed controls but decided to retain the manual controls from its existing system.

Company products are shipped directly from public warehouses which forward shipping notices to general accounting. There a billing clerk enters the price of the item and accounts for the numerical sequence of shipping notices from each warehouse. The billing clerk also prepares daily adding machine tapes ("control tapes") of the units shipped and the unit prices.

Shipping notices and control tapes are forwarded to the computer department for data entry and processing. Extensions are made on the computer. Output consists of invoices (in six copies) and a daily sales register. The daily sales register shows the aggregate totals of units shipped and unit prices which the computer operator compares to the control tapes.

All copies of the invoice are returned to the billing clerk. The clerk mails three copies to the customer, forwards one copy to the warehouse, maintains one copy in a numerical file, and retains one copy in an open invoice file that serves as a detailed accounts receivable record.

Required:
Describe weaknesses in internal control over information and data flows and the procedures for processing shipping notices and customer in-

voices and recommend improvements in these controls and processing procedures. Organize your answer sheets as follows:

Weaknesses	Recommended Improvements

(AICPA adapted)

13-22. TOOL-ALL MANUFACTURING: Computerized Payroll System

Introduction

Ted Mason, a junior auditor for a regional CPA firm, was assigned to the job of reviewing the computerized payroll system of a medium-sized client, Tool-All Manufacturing. Ted was to review the systems and procedures of Tool-All's data processing department to establish the reliability of computer-generated payroll data.

Tool-All Manufacturing produces metric tools for both commercial and industrial use. The firm consists of a factory in Waterloo, Iowa, where the tools are made and a warehouse, where they are stored for sale to wholesalers. The company's information processing facility has an IBM 4381 with both disk and tape drives.

Ted defined the scope of his payroll application review at the basic information gathering stage to include:

1. Identify the various types of input transactions related to payroll and review the controls thereon.
2. Review the controls over the processing of payroll information.
3. Review the various payroll reports to determine if they are effectively used and properly controlled.

Results of the Review

Through the use of a questionnaire, supplemented by other inquiries and observations, Ted gathered information about the input, processing, and output of the payroll application, together with the applicable controls. He summarized his findings in the following memo written for the work papers.

Memo Re: EDP Payroll Processing

Company Procedures

The payroll department accumulates the hours reported by factory and warehouse, applies appropriate pay rates, and forwards the results to the EDP Department where pay is calculated and payroll checks are prepared simultaneously with a payroll register and other reports listed below. Checks are protectograph signed in the EDP Department and distributed to the departments by the general manager's secretary.

Factory personnel are hired and terminated by the factory manager in coordination with the personnel department. The payroll department adds and removes personnel from the payroll master file based on notices received from the personnel department. Changes in pay rates are similarly processed. Factory personnel submit their clock-punched time cards to their department heads at the end of each week, for review and initialing and forwarding to the payroll department. Factory personnel are paid a week later.

Warehouse personnel are hired by the warehouse manager in coordination with the personnel department. The warehouse personnel report their hours to their department head daily, who prepares a time summary report by individual and forwards it to the payroll department at the end of each week. The employees are paid every other week, on an hourly basis, for two standard forty-hour weeks plus or minus any adjustment from the previous two-week period for overtime, time-off, and so on. The payments are staggered so that half the employees are paid at the end of any one week.

The payroll department receives the following reports from the EDP department for each payroll:

- The payroll checks/vouchers (approximately 2,000–2,500 per week) for distribution to employees
- A weekly payroll-distribution report for making the accounting expense entry and determining the amount to deposit in a payroll imprest bank account
- An account distribution report for supplementing the weekly payroll-distribution report
- A payroll register of each individual's pay, for reference
- A weekly year-to-date earnings trial balance for verifying that year-to-date earnings and accumulations are in balance each week
- A weekly year-to-date deductions trial balance for verifying that year-to-date deduction accumulations are in balance each week
- An employee payroll master listing (microfiche), providing all records on the Employee Payroll Master File, for reference

A simplified flowchart of the payroll system is included as Figure 1.

Findings

- The programs and procedures used to process various payroll applications lack adequate documentation. The programs were written by persons no longer with the company. These systems lack current flowcharts and user and operator manuals. This complicates the maintenance process.
- Unused payroll checks/vouchers held in the vault by the payroll department are forwarded weekly to the data processing department for

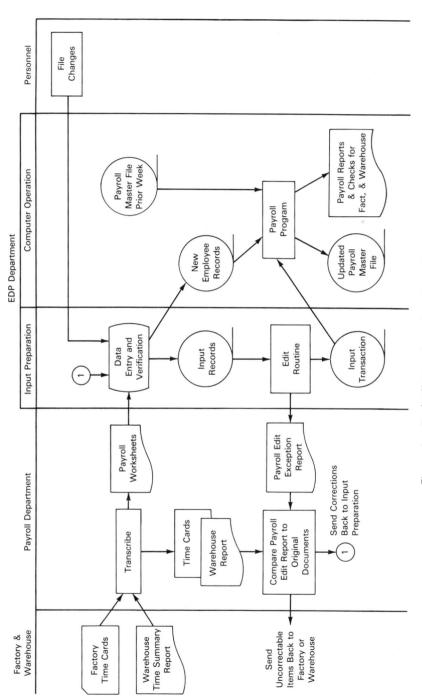

Figure 1. Tool-All Manufacturing: Payroll System

481

preparation of the payrolls. Although the checks/vouchers are logged out, there is no verification that all checks/vouchers are returned or accounted for after processing is completed.

- No batch control or transmittal documents are attached to input information for new employees, file maintenance, checks issued, or hours worked.

- Since the payroll department initiates changes to the master file based on information from various sources, a direct, postreview function—by someone independent of the payroll department—would be reasonable. For example, a listing of changes to the master file for new employees and for file maintenance could be provided to the factory manager and warehouse manager for postreview.

- The payroll system generates several erroneous reports because of an error in program logic. The payroll department must now manually recalculate or redetermine this information on a regular basis.

- In some cases, the edits performed by input preparation are not adequate to detect material errors. For example, no limit checks are performed in the field reporting overtime hours worked. Failure to check the social security number field for blanks results in an error in processing, when encountered, that uses up valuable processing time.

Question:
- What other information would you like to have in order to evaluate Ted's review of the payroll processing system and why would you like to have it?

[*Prepared by Frederick Neumann, Richard Boland, and Jeffrey Johnson, with funding from the Touche Ross Foundation. Used and adapted with permission of the authors.*]

13–23. THOMPSON PUBLISHING COMPANY: Publication Sales and Unearned Subscription Revenue

Introduction
All sorts of potential problems occurred to Bob Hiergel as he pondered the news that Thompson Publishing had just completed a conversion to a computer without letting him know in advance. Thompson was Bob's biggest client as an audit manager with the firm of Hammel & Son. Bob hoped the conversion had gone well, for there were a couple of systems that were pretty important to proper income determination and the audit, such as the one for subscriptions unearned and earned.

Thompson Publishing Company has its home office and main production facilities in New York City, with branch sales offices throughout the United States and Canada. It is a well-managed firm that has increased in size continuously since its beginning in 1936. In the last few years, it has grown especially rapidly, reaching the present annual sales volume of $137 million. Thompson publishes industrial trade journals and directories containing product, market, and technological information. Sales are largely on a subscription basis with the average paid subscription running about two years. Thompson Publishing defers the revenue from all subscription sales as unearned until issues are published and mailed. At that time, the appropriate amount of revenue is transferred from the "Unearned Subscription Revenue" account to the income statement account,"Revenue from Subscriptions."

The Old and New Systems

The old system, on unit-record equipment, had been time-comsuming but it did the job and was not difficult to audit. The data flow has been easy to follow (Figure 2), with a report produced daily, cumulative to weekly, cumulative to monthly (Figure 3), listing individual sales by publication.

This report provided the list of individual new subscriptions (additions to unearned revenue) for the month and the total amount to be transferred to earned revenue as the result of that month's publications. The unearned revenue was stored by invoice by month for up to twenty-six months (the longest subscription term) though it was shown by month for only the current calendar year. Only the current month's additions were detailed by invoice. Prior subscriptions were reported as single line accumulated totals. Nevertheless, there was little or no difficulty in tracing additions to and transfers from unearned subscription revenue.

Bob called his client and they sent over a flowchart of the new process (Figure 4). The edit checks have been retained. Daily errors are reported, corrected, and reinserted as previously. Even though postings are still made daily (now onto magnetic tape), only monthly reports are produced. There is a report on net additions to unearned subscription revenue for the month (Figure 5) and a report of the amount of unearned revenue to be transferred to income as earned that month. Both of these reports provide only totals for each publication. The computerized files maintain running totals of the dollar amount to be credited as revenue for each type of subscription for the next thirty-six months. Only the total dollar amount for each month is stored, not the details of actual subscriptions comprising those totals. The general ledger is still kept by hand and posted from these two reports for the respective entries.

Questions:

- For both unearned and earned subscription revenue, describe the changes probably caused by the conversion to the computer with regard to
  - Audit objectives
  - Audit procedures

(Prepared by Frederick Neumann, Richard Boland, and Jeffrey Johnson, with funding from the Touche Ross Foundation. Used and adapted with permission of the authors.)

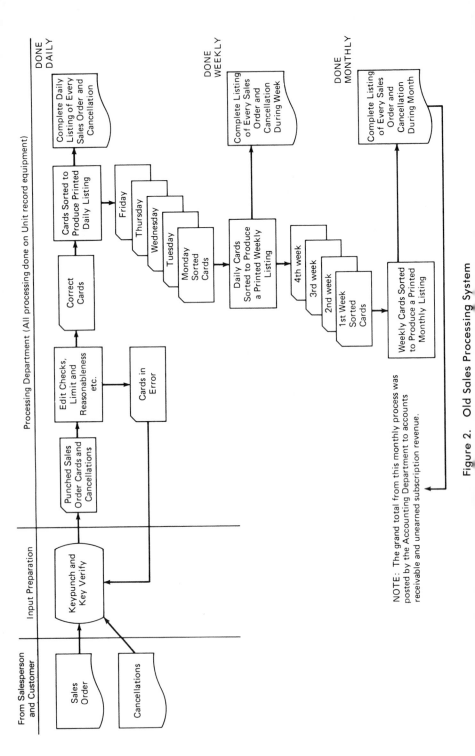

Figure 2. Old Sales Processing System

484

Thompson Publishing Company
Example of Daily, Weekly or Monthly Report (Produced During June 19X4)

| Publication | Invoice Number | Effective Date | Expiration Date | Salesperson Code | Territory Code | New or Renewal | 1st Year Sales | | | | | | | | 2nd Year | 3rd Year | 4th Year | Total Unearned |
							June	July	Aug	Sept	Oct	Dec					
81-32	43																
87-32	97																
88-32	138																
89-32	905																

Figure 3.

485

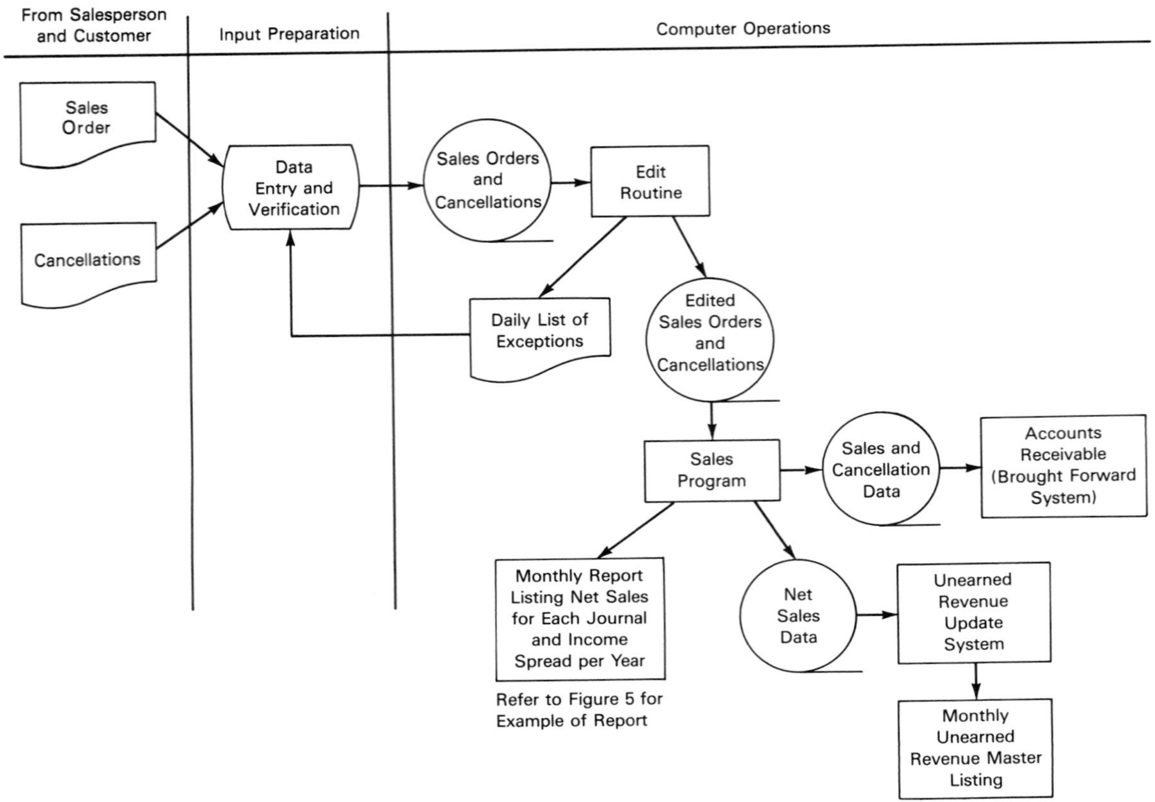

Figure 4. New Computerized Sales Processing System

486

Thompson Publishing Company and
Deferred Income & Net Sales Journal
For October 19X4

Technical Journal	Current month total sales	Deferred income by year				Monthly addition to total deferred
		First year sales	Second year sales	Third year sales	Fourth year sales	
74–32	X X X	X X	X	X	X	
91–87						
15–43						
27–39						
Totals for Month	XXXXXXXXXX	XXXX	XXX	XXX	XX	XXXX

Note: This report is printed only once a month. It usually takes only one computer page. It shows only net orders by each publication. It does not show the detail of every order placed during month as the former reports did.

Figure 5.

13-24. The following applications are processed on the system illustrated in the chapter:

Real-time processing using DBMS on central computer
  Order entry/sales
  Billing/accounts receivable
  Purchasing
  Inventory
Batch processing on central computer
  Accounts payable
  Payroll
  General ledger
DDP systems
  Fixed-asset accounting
  Parts inventory processing
    Order entry/sales
    Billing/accounts receivable
    Purchasing
    Inventory update

Required:
For each of the applications and each type of testing, discuss the following:

a. Which approach the auditor is likely to use
  (1) Auditing without processing data
  (2) Auditing using actual client data
  (3) Auditing using simulated data
b. Why the auditor is likely to select the approach specified
c. What manual or computerized techniques are likely to be used
d. Why the auditor is likely to select the techniques specified

Organize your answer as follows:

Part I. Controls Testing

	Audit of Program(s)		*Audit of File(s)*	
Application	*Approach and Reason(s)*	*Technique(s) and Reason(s)*	*Approach and Reason(s)*	*Technique(s) and Reason(s)*

Part II. Substantive Testing

	Audit of Program(s)		*Audit of File(s)*	
Application	*Approach and Reason(s)*	*Technique(s) and Reason(s)*	*Approach and Reason(s)*	*Technique(s) and Reason(s)*

13-25. The system illustrated in this chapter utilizes a DBMS. A data-base administrator is responsible for maintaining the integrity of the data base. Discuss the audit procedures you are likely to perform during the assessment of control risk pertaining specifically to the DBMS and the database administrator.

13-26. (*The following case is used with permission. Copyright © 1977 by the American Institute of Certified Public Accountants, Inc.*)

Ultimate Corporation is in the business of processing and formulating liquid chemicals. Inventories of raw chemicals are maintained in large vats. These vats are equipped with a sensing device which signals Ultimate's computer system, called UAS (Ultimate Advanced System), when the inventory level falls below the reorder point.

UAS then analyzes the future inventory requirements and economic order quantities to determine the amount to be ordered from one of Ultimate's four major vendors. UAS can connect itself by data communication facilities to each of the four vendors' computers. This capability is used to query the vendors' computers to determine the availability and best price for each item to be ordered.

The actual order is transmitted to the selected vendor computer from UAS by data communication and is given a common order/shipping number. No traditional purchase order document is prepared.

The vendor's computer then processes the order for delivery. Liquid chemicals are delivered through a direct pipeline connecting the vendor to Ultimate. Ultimate has a sensing device on this pipeline which meters the amount of chemical received and transmits that directly to UAS.

When Ultimate has received the ordered amount, UAS then communicates directly to its bank's computer. Payment for the chemicals received is made by an electronic fund transfer system (EFTS) from Ultimate's bank account to the vendor's bank account. The vendor's computer acknowledges receipt of payment directly to Ultimate's computer. No traditional check evidences this payment.

Ultimate Corporation obviously presents some unique and interesting auditing problems. A number of events have taken place during this transaction cycle. None of these events has been evidenced by any form of traditional documents as we know them. There are no purchase orders, receiving reports, vendor invoices, canceled checks, accounts payable, or other documents or transactions, either internal or external. The integrity of Ultimate's processing is dependent upon the effectiveness of controls in very advanced EDP systems.

Specifically, the problems facing the auditor of Ultimate's financial statements are these:

1. Absence of available independent evidence supporting transactions
2. Lack of a clear audit trail
3. Lack of evidence of authorization for transactions
4. The need to place heavy reliance upon the internal control struc-

ture, such as those control procedures over authorization and recording of transactions

5. The need to understand the flow of information through the processing cycle and its relationship to controls
6. The need to test the controls being relied upon
7. The need for auditor's hardware or software to be incorporated into this system

Required:
Discuss how the Ultimate Corporation EDP system could be audited.

13-27. Equivocal Savings and Loan Association utilizes an advanced design system for the processing of teller transactions (see Figure 6). Information about these transactions and internal controls established over them is presented below. For each paragraph, discuss the strengths and weaknesses of the internal control structure. Organize your answer as follows:

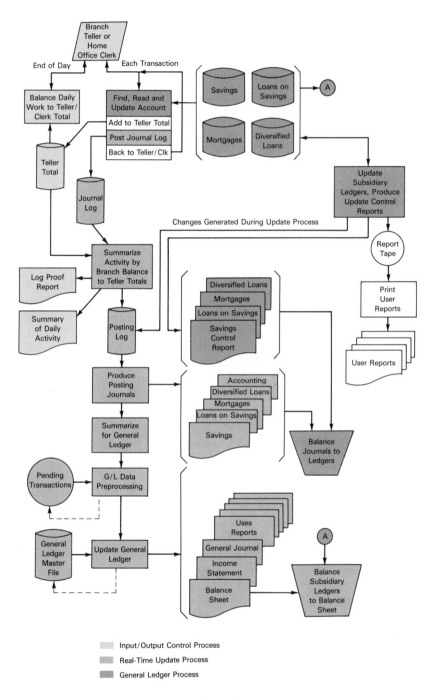

Figure 6.

Paragraph Number	Strengths	Weaknesses
Teller Transactions:		
1. At the beginning of each day, every individual teller inputs her confidential teller identification through the teller terminal. The host computer back at the home office will look up the identification in a computer table. If the identification code is found in the table, the terminal is accepted by the computer.		
2. Each teller has a cash box and a supply of money orders at her work station. The computer system maintains an "electronic cash box" in which, like her real cash box, the teller has a beginning balance in the morning and an ending balance at night. The balance in the real cash box and the balance in the computer file are expected to be the same.		
3. Every monetary transaction, whether check, cash, or money order, is entered through the terminal for processing. The system updates the customer file, records the transaction on a transaction file for subsequent posting to the general ledger, and records the transaction as an addition to or a reduction from the cash balance in the "electronic cash box."		
4. If a teller leaves her work station during the day, she is supposed to disassign her terminal to prevent unauthorized use.		
5. Two tellers usually use the same terminal. The terminal is equipped with an "A" key for one teller and a "B" key for the other.		
6. Certain types of transactions, such as correcting balances of savings accounts, require supervisory approval. The supervisor approves the transaction, the teller writes an explanation in the supervisor's log book, and the supervisor then inserts her magnetic card key into the terminal. The terminal accepts the transaction, and the host computer records the use of the supervisor's key.		

Paragraph Number	Strengths	Weaknesses
7. At the end of each day, every teller balances her real cash box to her electronic cash box. Any differences are entered through the terminal and recorded in the electronic cash box. The next working day, the ending balance will become the beginning balance and the teller cycle will start over again.		
8. After all the tellers have balanced and all the branches are closed, the teller files are balanced to the transaction files.		
Daily Control Processing:		
9. After all the tellers have balanced their cash boxes, the branches are closed for the day. At the same time, all the home office departments with computer terminals end their day's work. After all the branches and terminals sign off from the host computer, the home office computer operators terminate the on-line programs and go into their daily off-line update processing.		
10. The savings daily accrual program computes the daily interest earned on each individual account. The daily interest is added to the preceding day's balance, and this new balance will be carried forward into the next day. The interest is not posted to the general ledger savings account until the end of the month.		
11. The changes that occurred during the day as a result of deposits and withdrawals are added up and compared with the debits and credits in the transaction file. The amounts must balance.		
12. The debits and credits in the transaction file are summarized by type of savings plan and branch, and the totals are posted to the general ledger. The total of the individual account balances is balanced to the total of the general ledger controlling account.		
13. The accounting staff prepares an estimate of how much interest should		

(Continued)

Paragraph Number	Strengths	Weaknesses

be accrued each day. The accrual program reports the amount accrued to the computer operators. If the accrual is not within tolerances, the operators stop all further processing and notify management.

14. The control processing takes place in the evening. The following morning the accounting staff reconciles and balances all major accounts to the daily transactions reports. All journal entries are vouched to source documents and proper authorization is noted.

Transaction Posting:

15. The teller inputs a transaction code that calls an application program, such as for posting a deposit or withdrawal.

16. The teller then inputs the customer's account number. Savings account numbers start with the digit "10." Edit routines will compare the first two digits with the name of the application program. If the program that has been called is not a savings program, the transaction is rejected and an error message is sent to the teller.

17. The teller functions are divided into basic categories, such as deposits, withdrawals, and corrections. A separate and distinct key is provided on the teller terminal keyboard for each function. Depressing a function key calls in another program edit which tests for the compatibility of the transaction code with the function that has been selected. If the function and transaction code are incompatible, the transaction is rejected and an error message is sent to the teller. As an example, a withdrawal transaction code combined with a deposit function key will be rejected.

18. After the transaction has passed the various edit tests, the transaction is processed. The on-line program first calls in the file access program, and it in turn finds the customer account

Paragraph Number	Strengths	Weaknesses
and passes the desired data elements to the application program. The application program processes the transaction but does not yet write the results back to the customer file.		
19. The on-line program also calls for the teller file access program, and it in turn then finds the teller's "electronic cash box" and passes the desired running balance to the application program. The application program processes the transaction but does not yet write the results back to the teller file.		
20. The on-line program also calls for the transaction file access program, and it in turn accepts the transaction for posting. Only then are the new data written on the customer file, teller cash box file, and transaction file.		
21. The on-line program then recognizes that the transaction has been successfully posted and becomes available for the next transaction.		

Chapter 14
AUDITING COMPUTER PROCESSING: USER-CONTROLLED SYSTEMS

Learning Objectives

After completing this chapter, the reader should be able to:

1. Determine the control and audit problems associated with the unique hardware, software, procedures, and personnel characteristics of user-controlled systems.

2. Identify the distinguishing characteristics of the general controls environment for user-controlled systems.

3. Identify the distinguishing characteristics of the applications controls environment for user-controlled systems.

4. Discover what is unique about the performance of tests of controls with user-controlled systems.

5. Discover what is unique about the performance of substantive tests with user-controlled systems.

No matter where the auditor practices, it is no longer possible to ignore computers, computer controls, or computer auditing in user-controlled systems. Auditors who practice in small towns and previously thought that computers were a big-city phenomenon are now being inundated by requests from small clients for assistance with their control and auditing problems. User-controlled systems are being installed in the remote mountain and desert areas of Oregon and other states. These installations are being made in such client organizations as small hospitals and medical clinics, sawmills, cattle ranches, and wheat ranches. Auditors who practice in small firms in big cities and previously thought that computers were a problem only for the Big 8 firms are also being inundated by requests for assistance. In these big cities, user-controlled systems are being installed in service stations, convenience grocery stores, doctor and dental offices, and other small organizations.

User-controlled systems can be defined as those where an information user, such as the accounting department, controls the hardware, software, and operating procedures. These systems are typically small systems such as minicomputers and microcomputers. A service station operator, for example, may process his payroll on his own microcomputer. These systems also include, however, larger computer systems. An IBM System 36 is an example of a large and powerful computer with small space requirements. These systems are often placed in a corner of the room occupied by the accounting department, with access available to all members of the department.

The control and audit problems of small computers in the user-controlled environment differ from those of larger systems. In this chapter we discuss (1) the control and audit problems caused by user-controlled systems, (2) the controls that need to be emphasized in these systems, and (3) the audit approaches that are different in these systems.

The emphasis in this chapter is on the *combination* of control and audit techniques that is unique in the user-controlled systems environment. This uniqueness does not derive from different controls and audit techniques. It derives instead from various controls and techniques encountered elsewhere that typically occur as a "package" with these computer systems.

CONTROL AND AUDIT PROBLEMS IN USER-CONTROLLED SYSTEMS

User-controlled systems are more than just small versions of large systems. User-controlled systems differ from large systems because of hardware, software, procedures, and personnel characteristics. Our discussion of control and audit problems in these systems relates to these four major differences in characteristics.

Hardware

Control and audit problems in user-controlled systems arise because the small size and accessibility of the hardware may lead the auditor to ask, Is the computer being tested the one that is actually used by the client in production processing? This question applies to the entire system as well as the individual components. With larger systems, for example, the auditor may ask, Are the programs and files being tested the ones that are used in actual processing? The hardware itself is rarely an issue. With small systems, however, the hardware also becomes an issue. A different computer or circuit board may be used for production processing.

The size and accessibility of small computers make the entire system easily transportable. The user can provide the auditor with one system for testing and use a different one for data processing. The "auditor's computer" may be stored in a back room and simply switched with the production system on the auditor's arrival.

The system's components may also be switched prior to the auditor's testing of the system. One electronic circuit board may be used for data processing, and another circuit board may be installed only when the auditor is around.

Software

Control and audit problems can result from the particular characteristics of software in the small computers of user-controlled systems. These problems relate to operating systems and application programs.

Operating Systems

The operating systems of small computers may lead to control and audit problems because of the use of interpreters instead of compilers. Unauthorized changes to programs are easier to make with interpreters than with compilers. Such changes are often facilitated in the small systems environment because of ready accessibility to the computer.

Interpreters cause control and audit problems because of the ease with which programs can be changed without detection. Each time the program is run, the interpreter converts each line of code in the program to machine language as it is needed for processing. The user, therefore, has the opportunity to modify the program each time it is run. After processing, the program can be changed back to its original state. There may be no way to detect what has happened because such systems normally do not have console logs providing printouts of such activity.

Systems using compilers make it much more difficult to make unauthorized changes to programs. On systems using compilers, programs are written in source code, converted to machine language (object code) by the compiler prior to production processing, and the machine-language version of the program is stored and used for application processing. It is almost impossible to modify programs available only in a machine-language version. Restricting access to the source code is, therefore, a good control for preventing unauthorized program modification for systems with compilers.

Application Programs

Control and audit problems associated with the application programs of small computer systems arise because of user control of both hardware and application software. These problems are in addition to the problems created by the use of operating system interpreters.

The user in a compiler environment with access to the source code can make unauthorized program changes. The user can change the source code, recompile it, and use the modified object code for processing. The auditor, however, may be provided with an unmodified version for testing and be unaware of the changes in the production program.

Procedures

The procedures and work flow for processing transactions in user-controlled computer systems may create control and audit problems. These problems may be caused by the concentration of duties and elimination of source documents.

The concentration of duties in the hands of one person increases the opportunities for creating unauthorized transactions or making unauthorized changes to transactions and files. In many small systems, for example, one person may

- Initiate or authorize transactions
- Prepare batch control totals
- Enter transactions into the computer
- Verify that the transaction totals calculated by the computer agree with the manually prepared batch control totals
- Correct errors

User-controlled computer systems using on-line data entry also create control and audit problems because source documents may be eliminated. Orders received by phone, for example, may be entered directly into the computer through a visual display unit or console. In such an environment, controls for data capture and data entry may not exist. Furthermore, there may not be any audit trail.

Personnel

A control and audit problem caused by personnel in user-controlled computer systems is that the user can make all the important decisions regarding which controls to establish or enforce. These decisions can include the following:

- Determining what controls are to be used for data processing
- Specifying the editing that will take place on input of data to the system
- Deciding how the transactions will be batched for processing
- Reconciling computer output control totals to those calculated on input
- Scheduling when the data processing is to be done

If the user does not make these decisions initially, he or she can often override those made by someone else. The auditor may find it difficult to determine which controls existed at any specific point in time.

CONTROLS IN A USER-CONTROLLED SYSTEMS ENVIRONMENT

The control and audit problems associated with the small computers of user-controlled systems create a control structure that differs from that of larger systems. Therefore certain controls should be emphasized in order to compensate for these control and audit problems.

In this section we describe the controls that are most useful in overcoming small system control and audit problems: general controls and application controls. *General controls* for small computer systems can be further broken down into organization controls, personnel practices, and standard operating procedures; systems development and documentation controls; hardware and systems software controls; and systems security controls. *Application controls* for these systems are discussed in the context of data capture and entry, data processing, and output.

The objectives of the control structure are the same in a small computer system as they are in any manual, mechanical, or computer system. Simply stated, errors should be prevented from happening. If they do occur, they should be detected and corrected. The controls discussed in previous chapters still apply to the achievement of these objectives.

General Controls

Organization Controls, Personnel Practices, and Standard Operating Procedures

Organization Controls. Organization controls pertain primarily to the segregation of functions. We attempt to maintain a separation of the users who initiate transactions from the EDP personnel involved in recording the transactions. We also attempt to separate the EDP function of programming from that of operating the computer. With user-controlled systems this may be impossible. A single person may perform all of these activities.

One approach to the problem of segregation of functions is to limit the concentration of functions within a single individual. An attempt can be made to separate, at a minimum, the initiation, record keeping, and custody functions. For example, if one person uses the minicomputer to prepare checks, another person should be responsible for initiating payroll preparation by submitting time cards and the diskette containing the payroll master and payroll program when it is time for processing. Still another person should have custody of unused payroll checks and supply them as needed for processing.

Another approach is to maintain very close supervision of people operating the system to compensate for the missing segregation. Such supervision could include having a manager make periodic surprise observations of anyone operating the computer.

Personnel Practices. In the user-controlled computer system environment, where one or two individuals may be responsible for the processing of all accounting data, competent and honest people are extremely important. Personnel practices pertain to the selection, promotion, and termination of employees. Errors and defalcations can be prevented, to some extent, by hiring capable and honest employees at the outset. Promotions should go to those employees demonstrating competence and honesty. Employees not demonstrating competence and honesty should be terminated.

Standard Operating Procedures. Several operating procedures should be emphasized in the user-controlled computer system environment. First, employees should be properly trained and supervised. With so few persons involved in the small system environment, it is important that each one know how to do his or her job. Second, operating schedules should be prepared for computer processing and reviewed regularly to ensure that they are being followed. This procedure can detect the use of the computer for unauthorized purposes. Third, the policy for taking vacations should be enforced. In addition to uncovering problems while someone is on vacation, such a policy provides for cross-training additional individuals in operating the system. This can also be valuable in case of absence due to illness or other personal problems.

Systems Development and Documentation Controls

Two aspects of systems design and change controls should be emphasized in user-controlled systems: (1) controls over the acquisition of and changes to software, and (2) controls relating to adequate documentation.

In a small computer environment of user-controlled systems, the software is typically supplied by a vendor. The only input the buyer may have is in selecting among alternative systems. There may be no opportunity for incorporating specific features or controls of interest to the buyer into the software. The primary control, then, may be on the initial selection of the software.

The selection of software should be based on an established set of criteria for desired features and controls. The features will be based on the functions the buyer wants the software to perform. The controls incorporated into the software can be evaluated based on a checklist developed from the materials presented in Part III of this text.

If the buyer feels inadequate in selecting among alternative software packages, third-party review may be an appropriate control. The third party—a CPA or other consultant—can assist in the evaluation process and perhaps counteract some of the buyer's biases.

Once acquired, changes to software also need to be controlled. One technique is to prohibit all changes unless made by a vendor in response to a specific request through a purchase order. Another technique is to have all changes reviewed and tested by a third-party consultant. Still another technique is to require that all changes made by in-house personnel after appropriate approvals be reviewed and tested by another employee.

Adequate documentation is always a problem area. Without it, the auditor may not be able to determine exactly what processing is done by a particular application or what controls exist. In the user-controlled system environment, documentation is normally supplied by the software vendor. The problem is that it is often inadequate. Input, processing, and edit features may not be properly described for application programs. Controls may not be mentioned or may be poorly explained.

One approach to ensuring that adequate documentation exists is to have someone outside EDP be responsible for it. This person should be responsible for maintaining the documentation library, evaluating each manual received by comparing its contents with a checklist of desired coverage, and occasionally testing the adequacy of the documentation by attempting to process a particular application by using it.

Hardware and Systems Software Controls

The distinguishing characteristic of hardware and systems software controls in the small computer environment of user-controlled systems is the lack of them. Many of the controls taken for granted in larger systems simply do not exist in the smaller systems. A major problem in the hardware control area for small computer systems is the lack of error detection electronics. Parity checking incorporated into larger systems, for example, is often not available in smaller systems. There is no assurance, therefore, that the integrity of the data will be maintained as they are being moved within the system.

System software controls often missing on the smaller systems include machine utilization logs and file checking. With no machine utilization logs, for example, there is no machine-maintained information available on console activity. There is no record of who used the computer, for what, or when. One way to overcome this deficiency is to enforce manual maintenance of usage logs that are then reviewed by the auditor.

If the computer does not perform file checking internally, the wrong file may be mounted and not detected by the system. A payroll master file, for example, could be destroyed by being used as a scratch file. This deficiency can be partially overcome by enforcing the use of external labels and requiring that operators check them. Unfortunately, mistakes can still be made.

The problems sometimes encountered in the area of hardware and systems software controls can be avoided by emphasizing the systems development control area. Systems should not be acquired or developed if they lack the necessary hardware and software controls.

Systems Security Controls

Systems security controls need to be emphasized with user-controlled systems because of the potential for user changes to the hardware, software, and procedures. Systems security controls to be emphasized include access to programs and files, access to the computer, and file backup and reconstruction.

Access to Programs and Files. Access to programs and files is a control problem in the user-controlled systems environment because of the few individuals involved. One person who performs all the functions in processing accounting data, with unrestricted access to programs and files, can modify their contents to perform or disguise a defalcation.

One approach to controlling access to programs and files in a user-controlled systems environment is to have a part-time librarian. This person could be a receptionist or secretary outside the accounting or EDP area. With such a control, the librarian checks out diskettes of programs and files only as scheduled for processing and ascertains that they are returned at the end of the period needed for processing.

Utility programs that are provided by the vendor and can change programs and data in files without leaving an audit trail must be tightly controlled by the librarian. Requests for diskettes containing these programs should require written approval from a manager before their release. As an alternative, or in addition, access to the programs on a diskette should be by a supervisor only, using a special password.

Another approach to using passwords for controlling access to files is to have one password for inquiry and another for updates. Salespeople inquiring as to the quantity on hand of a particular inventory item, for example, would use one password. A different password would be required for processing the inventory file to record issues and receipts.

A similar approach for controlling access to programs is to have one set of passwords provide only for the reading of programs. Any changes to a program would then require a different password, perhaps only given to a supervisor.

A particular problem with controlling access to programs occurs when the system operates in interpreter mode. In such a situation, the source code can be changed for a specific defalcation and then changed back again without the auditor's knowledge. The password approach to security discussed above may be one means of preventing such unauthorized changes. Another approach is to have all production programs stored on the system in object code if such a facility is available. Changes are much more difficult to make in object code.

Unauthorized changes to programs can also be hindered if sensitive programs, such as payroll, are omitted from the menu listing. Some systems provide for selected menu deletions. Without having the specific name of the program as provided by the menu listing, it cannot be accessed.

Another control over the menus is to link them to specific passwords. A password, for example, would provide the user with a menu in the area of inventory but not payroll processing.

Displaying menus on the screen for only a limited period of time provides another control. This time constraint serves two purposes: (1) someone cannot sit and ponder over what program he or she wants if attempting to make an unauthorized change (this is especially effective if a menu can be called up a limited number of times over a specific period—say, three times in thirty minutes); (2) if a menu is on a screen for a limited time, it is more difficult for people walking by to obtain unauthorized information.

Access to the Computer. Unauthorized changes to programs and files can be controlled by restricting access to the computer itself. Two approaches are available for restricting access. The obvious approach to restricting access to the computer is to lock it up in a room by itself. Anyone needing the computer for processing would then have to go through a formal procedure to get access to the system. Once on the system, such an approach will not prevent unauthorized changes. Each person operating the system, however, would be expected to be on the system for a specific period of time to perform a specific task. A supervisor could check periodically to ascertain what was being done.

An alternative approach to locking up the computer is to have it in the open in as conspicuous a place as possible. It should not be in the corner, but in the middle of the room so that everyone can see who is on the system and doing what. The operator may find it more difficult to deviate from standard processing procedures and perform a defalcation with several people watching.

Some user-controlled computer systems have multiple-terminal work stations. (See Chapters 9, 10, and 13 for a discussion of the controls that may be suitable in such situations.)

File Backup and Reconstruction. File backup and reconstruction in the small computer environment of user-controlled systems is characterized by the differences in hardware. Traditional procedures will not work. New procedures are required.

The differences in hardware include the absence of magnetic tape in most systems and the manner in which the diskette read/write head functions when compared with that in large systems. Many small systems use diskettes exclusively. Magnetic tape capability may not be available. Cassette tapes on some systems have such slow data transfer rates that they are not suitable for backup.

Diskettes will lose data because they wear out—the diskette read/write head on many small systems rides directly on the diskette, much like a phonograph needle rides on a record. On larger systems, in contrast, the head floats 20 to 100 microinches above the surface of the disk. With the head floating above the disk, the disk does not wear out. The diskette does wear out, however, because the head touches it. As a result, many diskettes have an operating life of only forty hours or so.

Traditional backup procedures are embodied in the grandparent-parent-child concept where processing is on magnetic tape. If the "child" tape is damaged, files can be reconstructed by going back to the "parent" tape and reprocessing.

New procedures are required with small systems because of the absence of magnetic tape and the limited life of the diskettes. It may be difficult, if not impossible, to keep track of the usage of each diskette.

Backup may, therefore, have to be performed on a periodic basis regardless of diskette usage. In some organizations, for example, all diskettes are copied *every morning* before any processing takes place. File reconstruction, if damage occurs, then has to go back only to that morning with a minimal loss of time and effort.

Application Controls

The application controls discussed below under data capture and entry, data processing, and output are not *individually* unique to user-controlled systems. They are all encountered on other types of computer systems. What makes them unique in this environment is that the *combination* of controls discussed below is often encountered as a "package." Our discussion focuses on a typical control environment for user-controlled systems.

Data Capture and Entry

Data capture and entry controls help ensure that the appropriate data are entered correctly into the computer system. Typical data capture and entry controls in the small computer environment of user-controlled systems include screen controls—formatting, prompting, and editing; reconciliation of debits to credits on input; and generation and reconciliation of control totals.

Screen Controls—Formatting, Prompting, and Editing. Several types of screen controls may be encountered on small computer systems.

Screen formats are used to control the information that the operator supplies to the system. The screen format reduces errors in data entry by providing the operator with a framework within which to enter the data. Formats on larger systems differ from those on small systems. Larger systems are often source document oriented, whereas small systems are journal oriented.

Formats on a large microcomputer system usually involve the display of a document on the screen. The operator is required to enter names, addresses, part numbers, or amounts on the lines or in the spaces provided on the screen.

Formats on a small microcomputer often display account titles from a journal on the screen. The operator then enters the dollar amounts or a zero for each account shown.

Screen prompting is closely associated with formatting. Prompting is used to control the order in which the operator supplies the information. The format may be a display of all the information needed, for example, while a blinking line, frame, or cursor will prompt the first entry of data. The first entry of data could be the name of a customer. Once the customer's name has been entered, the system will prompt the entry of the amount of the sale and then other data in proper order until all the required information has been supplied.

Screen editing can be used to control, character by character, the information submitted to the system. The user, for example, may be prompted to enter a customer name onto the format of a sales order. If only alphabetic characters are allowed, the screen editor will display an error message to the user as soon as a numeric character is entered.

Reconciliation of Debits to Credits on Input.   If the system requires that the total of the debits must equal the total of the credits for each transaction before input is accepted by the system for processing, out-of-balance conditions can be avoided. The operator is forced to enter a complete transaction and not eliminate some component of it.

Generation and Reconciliation of Control Totals.   There are three aspects to the generation and reconciliation of control totals: The operator or user must manually calculate these totals; the computer must be programmed to calculate a similar total; and the two totals must be reconciled. Control totals serve as data capture and entry controls to the extent that they detect erroneous data or prevent them from being processed. They also serve, however, as output controls by detecting the generation of erroneous output.

Control totals include document or record counts, hash totals, and financial totals. All or some of them should be calculated by the user or operator for each application. In an accounts receivable update, for example, the operator or user should calculate the number of accounts receivable records to be updated (document or record count) and the total dollar change in the control account (financial total).

The computer program should count the number of records processed and the net change in the control account as the accounts receivable update is being performed. At the completion of processing, these totals should be displayed and printed on a summary report.

The user or operator should compare the computer-prepared control totals with the manually calculated totals. Any differences should be accounted for and noted on the computer-printed summary report.

Data Processing

Data processing controls suitable for the small computers of user-controlled systems are the same as those encountered in large systems. These include limit or reasonableness tests and cross-footing tests. As with large computer systems, these controls replace the type of visual checking that is done in manual systems to detect unreasonable processing results. (See Chapter 10 for a complete discussion of processing controls.)

In the small computer systems environment, there are usually few options available when it comes to processing controls. The controls are those provided by the vendor in vendor-supplied software. The selection of controls is thus determined by the selection of the software. The emphasis, then, should be on software selection. The vendor should be asked to state specifically which controls are incorporated into the software. In many cases, unfortunately, small computer system application programs do not come with controls. The buyer should avoid such programs.

The small computer system user can request the inclusion of processing controls in application programs created by the user's staff. The user can also request the inclusion of specific controls in custom-designed programs acquired from a software vendor.

Output

In the small computer environment of user-controlled systems the user generally has the responsibility for the maintenance of output controls. In such an environment, the user should verify the reasonableness of the output and reconcile it to input as appropriate. In addition, the user should verify the number of copies of each report prepared by the computer and the distribution of those reports.

Reasonableness Tests. Reasonableness tests on small computer systems can be done in various ways. One test involves daily summaries of transactions by type of total debits or of total credits for specific journals, accounts, or ledgers. A review of such totals on a daily basis may indicate problems because of unusual activity. Another test consists of a reasonableness comparison of accounting activity with some other base. In an order entry system, for example, a reasonableness test is a comparison of the number of phone calls received with the number of input transactions. An additional test could be the preparation of exception reports for high-value transactions.

User Reconciliations. A user reconciliation requires that the user compare the computer output with some control, such as document or record counts, hash totals, or financial totals. A proprietor, for example, can easily compare the number of payroll checks to be signed with the number of employees working for the firm.

Distribution Controls. The distribution of output is usually easier to control in a small computer systems environment than in a large systems environment. The reason is that in a small systems environment, all the recipients of output are usually personally known to each other. It is relatively easy to determine whether someone should receive copies of payroll reports or accounts receivable listings.

AUDITING USER-CONTROLLED COMPUTER SYSTEMS

The objectives the auditor pursues in the audit of user-controlled systems do not differ from those pursued in the audit of other systems whether they be manual, mechanical, or large computers. The auditor must still assess control risk and collect sufficient competent evidential matter to form the basis for an opinion.

In this selection we discuss the controls and substantive tests performed by the auditor in auditing the small computers of the user-controlled systems environment. The emphasis is on the differences in procedures the auditor of small systems is likely to follow compared with those followed in large systems.

Tests of Controls

The auditor of user-controlled computer systems must evaluate the operating effectiveness of both general and application controls. (See Chapter 4 for a discussion of the approach.)

General Controls

The assessment of general controls risk may lead either (1) to assessing application controls risk or (2) directly to the performance of substantive tests. Strong general controls will lead to the former, and weak general controls will lead to the latter, as discussed previously. The latter course is often followed with user-controlled computer systems because the general controls are weak.

Tests of controls performed on general controls in user-controlled systems have two characteristics. First, as with other computer systems, they tend to be manual procedures. Second, in contrast to audits of larger computer systems, the auditor may tend to focus on controls that may compensate for weaknesses. These two characteristics are illustrated in the following discussion.

The evaluation of organization controls, personnel practices, and standard operating procedures requires that the auditor physically observe who is doing what and when, and that the auditor manually review organization charts, manuals, and schedules. In some user-controlled systems, a person serving as a combination operator and programmer still provides for some control if that person is independent of the user. The auditor should focus on the segregation of functions between the user and the programmer-operator. Excellent controls over diskettes containing programs and files, passwords restricting the operator from unauthorized changes to diskettes, and user controls over input and output may compensate for the lack of EDP function segregation. If the programmer-operator is also the user, however, the auditor may not be able to assess a low level of control risk for general controls and may be forced to focus on substantive testing.

Systems development and documentation controls can be tested by manually evaluating the procedures followed in selecting vendor-supplied software. The lack of segregation of functions within EDP over systems development and changes can be compensated by outside review of all system designs and changes. This outside review can be conducted by software consultants or the auditors.

Hardware and systems software controls may be minimal or nonexistent on the small computers of user-controlled systems. Testing of these controls to determine their availability and effectiveness consists of reviewing vendor-supplied literature and preventive maintenance schedules, as discussed previously. Weak controls necessitate substantive testing to determine the reliability and accuracy of processing by the computer.

Systems security controls are evaluated by manually reviewing restrictions on access to programs, files, and the computer itself, and by reviewing file backup and reconstruction procedures. The auditor encountering weak controls on restricting access to the system may substantially have to increase substantive testing. Weak file backup and reconstruction procedures may not necessitate increased substantive testing, but at the very least they should be brought to management's attention.

Application Controls

The testing of application controls in the small computers of user-controlled systems is very similar to the testing of such controls in large computer systems. The difference is in computerized techniques that may not be available.

The testing of small computer systems is similar to the testing of large systems in that the three approaches of nonprocessing of data, processing of actual data, and processing of simulated data are all applicable. (See Chapters 11, 12, and 13 for a discussion of these approaches and the reasons why the auditor may decide to use one of them.)

The availability of computerized techniques is perhaps the main difference between auditing small computer systems and auditing large computer systems. Techniques available to the auditor for both types of systems include controlled processing, controlled reprocessing, parallel simulation, test records, integrated test facility, utility programs, custom-designed programs, and special-purpose programs (see Chapters 11, 12, and 13).

A computerized technique often unavailable to the auditor in performing tests on application controls for small computer systems is generalized audit software. Such software is usually written for a specific computer system, sometimes for only selected configurations of that system. The proliferation of dissimilar small computer systems makes it difficult to justify the cost of developing generalized audit software for each system.

The absence of generalized audit software for small computer systems means that the auditor will often rely heavily on utility programs supplied by the vendor. These programs can be used for inquiry into the contents of files and printing reports.

Substantive Tests

Substantive testing in the audit of the small computers of user-controlled systems is relatively more extensive than in the audit of larger systems because control risk in the former is usually higher. The scope of testing may be broader as the auditor examines a greater diversity of accounts and transactions than would be necessary if control risk were lower. The depth of testing may be greater as the auditor examines more transactions of the same type or sends out more confirmation requests than would be necessary if control risk were lower.

The approaches available to the auditor for performing substantive tests on small computer systems are the same as those for large systems. The approaches of nonprocessing of data, processing of actual data, and processing of simulated data are all applicable.

Computerized techniques available to the auditor for performing substantive tests on small computer systems are also the same as those for large systems. These techniques include controlled processing, controlled reprocessing, parallel simulation, test records, integrated test facility, utility programs, custom-designed programs, special-purpose programs, and generalized audit software, if available.

The auditor of small computer systems may rely heavily on utility programs for substantive testing because of the usual unavailability of generalized audit software. Depending on the vendor, the auditor may be able to use utility programs for inquiring into the contents of files, printing file contents, sorting file contents, adding amounts in files, comparing the contents of two files, selecting and printing items meeting some specified criteria, and counting the number of records in a file.

SUMMARY

The small computers of user-controlled systems have unique hardware, software, procedures, and personnel characteristics that distinguish them from large systems. Various problems in control and audit are associated with these characteristics. Hardware size and accessibility make transportability a control and audit problem because the auditor may not be certain that the computer the client uses is the one being tested. Operating system software for many small computers is unique because programs that run in interpreter mode are easy to modify without detection. Control and audit problems occur with application program software for small computers because of user control of the software. Procedures associated with small systems are unique because one person often performs all transaction processing functions. A distinguishing characteristic of personnel in small computer systems is that the user may make all the important decisions regarding which controls to establish and enforce.

The objectives of the internal control structure remain the same with a small computer as they are with any other processing system— prevent, detect, and correct errors. The difference in the small computer system's control environment is the emphasis placed on various controls. The emphasis changes in order to compensate for some of the weaknesses inherent in the control environment for small systems.

In the general controls area, the auditor is likely to focus on the lack of segregation of functions; policies for reviewing and acquiring application software; documentation; the lack of vendor-supplied hardware and software controls; and program, file, and computer access.

In the application controls area, the auditor is likely to focus on controls over data capture and entry, and output. Data capture and entry control procedures receiving scrutiny will include screen controls, reconciliation of debits with credits on input, and generation and reconciliation of control totals. Output controls rely on users. Users will be involved with reasonableness tests, reconciliations, and distribution of output.

The tests of controls and substantive testing of small computer systems is similar to the testing of large systems. The objectives and many of the procedures are the same. Differences occur in the emphasis on various controls, as mentioned above, and the availability of software that will aid the auditor. Generalized audit software is often unavailable. Vendor-supplied utility programs are used extensively.

REVIEW QUESTIONS

14-1. The small computers of user-controlled systems have unique hardware, software, procedures, and personnal characteristics. For each of these four categories, discuss what is unique about small systems and how this uniqueness contributes to problems in the control and audit of such systems.

14-2. There are numerous weaknesses inherent in the general controls environment for user-controlled systems. For each of the following, discuss one potential weakness:
   a. Organization controls
   b. Personnel practices
   c. Standard operating procedures
   d. Systems development
   e. Documentation
   f. Hardware and systems software controls
   g. Program, file, and computer access
   h. File backup and reconstruction

14-3. Application controls include those pertaining to data capture and entry. Discuss the control procedures that may be appropriate in a user-controlled computer system environment to ensure that data are entered correctly into the system.

14-4. Processing controls are a type of application control. Discuss the similarities and differences of these controls in the small computer of the user-controlled systems environment as contrasted to a large systems environment.

14-5. Is there anything unique about output controls in a user-controlled systems environment? Discuss.

14-6. In testing general controls in user-controlled systems, the manual procedures performed by the auditor are likely to focus on controls that may compensate for weaknesses. For each of the following, discuss (1) the procedures likely to be used by the auditor and (2) the compensating controls on which the auditor is likely to focus:
   a. Organization controls, personnel practices, and standard operating procedures
   b. Systems development and documentation controls
   c. Hardware and systems software controls
   d. Systems security controls

14-7. Describe how the substantive testing of small computers in the user-controlled systems environment is likely to differ from such testing of large systems. Why is there a difference?

14-8. Utility programs are used more extensively than generalized audit software in the audit of small computer systems. Why? How are utility programs used for performing the following:
   a. Tests of controls
   b. Substantive tests

OBJECTIVE QUESTIONS[1]

14-9. User-controlled systems are characterized by all of the following except
   a. Lack of segregation of functions between the EDP department and users
   b. Limited knowledge of EDP by data processing supervisor
   c. Segregation of computer from user department
   d. Lack of segregation of functions within EDP

14-10. All of the following characteristics are found in the small computers of user-controlled system environments except
   a. Utility programs are used extensively to enter and change data
   b. Terminals are used for transaction data entry, inquiry, and other interactive functions
   c. Internally developed application software is used extensively rather than purchased software packages
   d. User documentation may be limited or nonexistent

14-11. Utilities supplied by the vendor with small computer systems may be able to perform all of the following functions except
   a. Calculate the number of records in an input file
   b. Update sequential, indexed sequential, and direct-access files
   c. Perform logic tests (e.g., equal to, greater than, or less than or equal to tests) to select subsidiary ledgers from an accounts receivable file
   d. Convert source language statements into machine-executable form

14-12. A small computer system uses BASIC and operates in interpreter mode only. A utility program supplied by the vendor allows users to add, change, or delete programs or records in a file without leaving an audit trail. Which of the following techniques would be inappropriate for preventing unauthorized use of this utility?
   a. Create a separate library for the utility and restrict access to the library
   b. Remove the enter and update modules from the utility and allow changes to files through application programs only
   c. Remove the utility from the system except when needed to perform authorized functions
   d. Maintain object programs in libraries separate from source programs

14-13. An auditor of small computer systems is least likely to use which of the following computer-auditing techniques?
   a. Generalized audit software
   b. Special-purpose programs
   c. Custom-designed programs
   d. ITF

---

[1]The first three questions in this section have been adapted from AICPA, *Audit and Control Considerations in a Minicomputer or Small Business Computer Environment* 1981, pp. 1, 18–24.

CASES AND EXERCISES

14-14. If there are weaknesses in general controls, such as controls over changes to production programs, then certain techniques, such as using test data and reviewing program logic, may not yield reliable audit information. Discuss why this is so and how this affects the nature, timing, and extent of subsequent audit procedures.[2]

14-15. The auditor may encounter organizations with one or more minicomputers in each major department or division. Discuss how the characteristics of the general and applications controls environment presented in this chapter apply when the processing performed by any one of these minicomputers is independent of that performed by another minicomputer.

14-16. Some minicomputers are exclusively used to convert source transactions into machine-readable form. The storage media containing input transactions are generally used by another computer to process and update application master files. Discuss how the characteristics of the general and applications controls environment presented in this chapter apply in this situation.

14-17. Some vendors of small business systems stress that an advantage of their system is its ability to handle mixed-mode input. *Mixed-mode input* means that transactions can be processed as they occur. A payment on accounts receivable, for example, can be followed by a vendor payment, which can be followed by an inventory update. Discuss the problems the auditor is likely to encounter in such an environment that can be attributed to the mixed-mode input feature.

14-18. At a weekly meeting of your business club, one of your clients excitedly told you of his recent acquisition of a microcomputer for general ledger accounting. Your client was particularly pleased with the hiring of a young man to handle all the processing on the system. This young man not only knows how to program in BASIC, Pascal, and some other languages but has been a home computer hobbyist for years. During the hiring interview, he had proudly displayed several computer circuit boards which he had constructed at home. Your client is convinced that this young man will be able to resolve every problem that could possibly develop with the new system.

Required:

a. Discuss the control and audit problems you are likely to encounter with your client's system.

b. What controls should you recommend that your client implement for the system?

c. What tests are you going to perform on the controls you have recommended?

---

[2]This exercise has been adapted from AICPA, *Audit and Control,* p. 1.

    d. What substantive tests are you going to perform to minimize the audit risks associated with the new system?

14–19. A client recently acquired by your firm has asked for an assessment of control risk for their accounting system. During a discussion over lunch to review your client's request in greater detail, you obtained general information about the system. You found out that the client utilized five microcomputers to perform the payroll processing in each of five different departments. Each computer is physically located in its respective department where the processing is performed and paychecks are distributed.

Required:
    a. Describe how you would determine whether you have one control structure to evaluate or five separate control structures.
    b. Discuss the general control strengths you are likely to encounter during an evaluation of your client's accounting system.
    c. Discuss the general control weaknesses you are likely to encounter in the evaluation of your client's system.

Chapter 15
AUDITING COMPUTER PROCESSING: THIRD-PARTY SYSTEMS

Learning Objectives

After completing this chapter, the reader should be able to:

1. Determine the unique hardware, software, procedures, and personnel characteristics of third-party systems.

2. Identify the distinguishing characteristics of the general controls environment for third-party systems.

3. Identify the distinguishing characteristics of the application controls environment for third-party systems.

4. Discover what is unique about the performance of tests of controls with third-party systems.

5. Determine what is unique about the performance of substantive tests with third-party systems.

Auditors may have to evaluate the processing reliability of third-party systems regardless of whether their clients also have in-house systems. Clients with in-house systems may utilize third-party systems because of the processing capabilities of these systems. These capabilities may include more storage capacity than available in-house, an accounting application available only through the third-party system (e.g., patient billing by hospitals and clinics to insurance companies), and on-line real-time processing where the in-house system is batch (e.g., on-line savings account deposit and withdrawal system for a savings and loan). Clients without in-house systems may prefer third-party processing because it is more efficient. This efficiency may result from avoiding the costs of an EDP staff, avoiding the costs of software development, and avoiding the costs of hardware, site preparation, and occupancy.

Third-party processing can be defined as those situations where the processing of accounting data by an application program is done by an entity other than the auditor or client. Such processing is usually done at a location other than the client's premises and is referred to as *off-site processing*. In some situations, such as under a facilities management contract, the computer may remain at the client's site, but a separate legal entity operates it. Third-party processors include organizations referred to as *service bureaus* or *centers*. Service bureaus may provide batch or on-line real-time processing. Third-party processors also include *time-sharing organizations* that may also provide both batch and on-line real-time services. The distinction between the two will be explained in the following section.

Our discussion of the control and audit of third-party systems is divided into three main segments: (1) the characteristics of a third-party system in terms of hardware, software, procedures, and personnel; (2) the control environment for third-party systems; and (3) tests of controls and substantive testing in the audit of third-party systems.

The emphasis in this chapter is on what is unique in the control and audit of third-party systems. This uniqueness includes problems caused by these systems, controls that need to be stressed in these systems, and audit approaches that are different in these systems.

THIRD-PARTY SYSTEM CHARACTERISTICS

The distinctions between service bureaus and time-sharing organizations are no longer as sharp as they once were. These distinctions, and the similarities between the two types of operations, are discussed in the following subsections under "Hardware," "Software," "Procedures," and "Personnel."

Hardware

Differences in hardware have historically been one of the major characteristics separating service bureaus from time-sharing firms. These differences are disappearing because both types of organizations are increasingly offering the same types of services.

Service bureaus often established themselves by providing a large batch processing system to numerous clients. Source documents were typically transported to the facility by car, truck, or plane and were converted to machine-readable form at the service center. After processing, the checks, ledgers, and other output were transported back to the client.

Service bureaus today, in addition to functioning as described above, provide various types of services utilizing teleprocessing techniques. Clients often install small computer systems that serve as remote job entry stations to the service bureau system. Source documents are converted to machine-readable form on the client's premises and stored in a diskette on the small system. At scheduled times, sometimes automatically in the middle of the night, the data are transmitted to the service bureau and processed, and the output is transmitted back to the small system and stored in a diskette on it. At the client's convenience, the output is then printed by the small system.

Service bureaus today can also be connected to terminals in the client's facility and provide on-line real-time processing. Hospitals, for example, often utilize such an approach for patient admission, patient billing, and so forth. Another major application is in banks and savings and loan associations for processing savings account deposits and withdrawals.

Time-sharing systems established themselves by providing access to large teleprocessing systems through typewriter-type terminals. These terminals were used for low-volume data input and output—for example, in general ledger applications where journal totals were entered on the terminal, the system posted the amounts to the general ledger and then printed a balance sheet and income statement on the terminal. Other applications included the calculating of depreciation and the preparing of loan amortization schedules. In each case, the printing of output started on the terminal as soon as the last line of input was submitted.

Time-sharing systems today, in addition to functioning as described above, provide services similar to those initially offered by service bureaus. Large volumes of input data can be submitted in source document or machine-readable form via mail or parcel delivery service. Even data input via terminal in the client's office can be submitted for deferred processing in batch mode at night, with the results printed out the next day or whenever desired on the client's terminal.

Software

Software includes both operating systems and application programs. The software of third-party systems is not unique except as to locus of control. Operating systems are controlled by the third-party processor. Application programs may be controlled by the user or the third-party processor.

Operating Systems.   Operating systems for third-party processors function in both batch and real-time modes. (These systems have already been discussed in detail, and no additional characteristics need be mentioned here.)

Application Programs.   Application programs available through third-party systems are unique for two reasons: the diversity of sources for the programs, and the auditor's inaccessibility to program listings for some of them.

Application programs used in third-party processing are available from three sources. First, the user can write and supply programs to be processed on the third-party system. Second, the user can acquire programs from an independent software vendor to be processed on the third-party system. Third, the third-party processor can write and make programs available to systems users.

Listings of programs written by third-party processors and accessible to systems users may not be available to auditors. These programs are often considered to be proprietary and can be tested only by processing data through them.

Procedures

The procedures for third-party processing are unique because the work flow physically leaves the user's premises and passes to a separate legal entity. The work flow may leave the premises in the form of source documents or electronic pulses. Problems encountered with the former are more severe than those encountered with the latter.

Source documents leaving the user's premises create problems because of the potential loss of data. This is particularly acute in banks where all checks, for example, may be photocopied before leaving the premises. When the source documents must be transported to a separate facility, stringent controls are usually enforced. Control totals may be established on the number of documents and dollar amounts involved, for example.

Information on source documents that leaves in the form of electronic pulses does not create as severe a problem as that created when the documents themselves leave, but there are still problems. While being transmitted, data can be lost, added to, or changed. These data transmission problems may be unintentional because of equipment problems or intentional as the result of a defalcation. Control totals are still needed to ensure the integrity of the data.

Personnel

A distinguishing characteristic of personnel in third-party processing is that the data processing persons involved are usually the employees of a separate legal entity. This may not be true, however, if the user is simply renting block time from a service bureau.

Personnel employed by the third-party processor are hired, trained, promoted, supervised, and terminated by the third party. The auditor may not have access to the personnel records, and documentation of personnel practices, to determine the quality of personnel as in the case of an in-house audit.

Users that rent block time from a service bureau supply their own personnel. They may even provide their own programs and supplies. Such an arrangement is similar to on-site processing, and, therefore, the control and audit considerations in this chapter do not apply.

CONTROLS IN A THIRD-PARTY
SYSTEM ENVIRONMENT

The objectives of the control structure to prevent, detect, and correct errors also apply to third-party systems. The difference in the control structure of third-party systems is the inapplicability of some controls and the emphasis placed on others.

Our discussion of the control structure for third-party systems is divided into general control characteristics and application control characteristics.

General Controls

Organization Controls, Personnel Practices,
and Standard Operating Procedures

Organization Controls.   Organization controls pertain primarily to the segregation of functions. The separation of users who initiate transactions from the EDP personnel involved in recording the transactions is automatically provided by the third-party approach. The separation of the EDP function of programming from that of operating the computer may be difficult for the auditor to ascertain. This latter separation, however, may not be as important in the third-party environment.

The separation of users from EDP personnel provided by the third-party approach may reduce the possibility of the deliberate manipulation of records. Users without access to the computer programs and files will not be able to change the contents of either.

The auditor's inability to determine whether there is a separation of programming from operations in the third-party system environment may not be as important as when the system is in-house. The reason is that being able to change programs and files may not be sufficient to perpetrate a fraud for someone unfamiliar with the user's business practices or without access to other accounting information and documents.

Personnel Practices. The auditor may be unable to determine the personnel practices of the third-party processor as to the hiring, training, promoting, supervising, and terminating of personnel. The auditor may be able to ascertain the reliability of the individuals as a component of the control system only by testing the output from the system.

Standard Operating Procedures. Two different sets of standard operating procedures must be evaluated by the auditor in the third-party system environment. One set will be provided by the third-party vendor to establish procedures for submitting data, processing these data, and receiving output. The other set will be developed by the user for collecting and controlling data up to the point where they are submitted to the third-party processor and for controlling and distributing output received from the processor.

Standard operating procedures specified by the vendor will include the following:

- Schedules for submission of data
- Schedules for receipt of output
- Transmittal controls for submitted data, such as (1) document or record counts, (2) financial totals, and (3) hash totals
- Error correction and resubmission procedures

These procedures will usually be monitored and enforced by the vendor to facilitate processing by the vendor. The auditor's task is to determine what the procedures are, ascertain whether they provide sufficient safeguards over the integrity of the data, and evaluate the degree to which they are enforced by the vendor.

Standard operating procedures developed by the user include those pertaining to data capture, data entry, and output. These procedures will be discussed later under "Application Controls." Other procedures that should be enforced by the user and evaluated by the auditor are the following:

- Proper training and supervision of people involved in data capture, data entry, output reconciliation, and output distribution
- Mandatory vacations for people involved in data processing activities

Systems Development and Documentation Controls

Two aspects of systems design and change controls should be emphasized: (1) controls over the development of, acquisition of, and changes to software, and (2) controls relating to adequate documentation.

Software in a third-party system environment can be developed by the user or acquired from a software vendor, or it may be available from the third-party vendor while using the system. Software developed and maintained by the user should be subject to all the controls discussed in Chapter 6. Controls on software acquired from vendors—both software houses and third-party processors—include those on acquisition and subsequent changes.

There may be no opportunity for incorporating specific features or controls of interest to the user into software acquired from vendors. The only influence the buyer may have is in selecting among alternative systems. The primary control, then, may be on the initial selection of the software.

The selection of software should be based on an established set of criteria for desired features and controls. The features will be based on the functions the user wants the software to perform. The controls incorporated into the software can be evaluated based on a checklist developed from the materials presented in Part III of this text.

If the user feels inadequate in selecting among alternative software packages, review by a consultant may be an appropriate control. The consultant—a CPA or an EDP specialist—can assist in the evaluation process and perhaps counteract some of the user's biases.

Once acquired, changes to software must also be controlled. One technique is to prohibit all changes unless made by a vendor in response to a specific request through a purchase order. Another technique is to have all changes reviewed and tested by an EDP consultant. Still another technique is to have the vendor send a list of all changes to software to an independent reviewer, either a consultant or a supervisor employed by the user.

Adequate documentation is always a problem area. Without it, the auditor may not be able to determine exactly what processing is done by a particular application or what controls exist. Documentation supplied by the software vendor may be inadequate. Input, processing, and edit features may not be properly described for application programs. Controls may not be mentioned or may be poorly explained.

One approach to ensuring that adequate documentation exists for programs supplied by vendors is to refuse payment for a portion or all of the fee for software and/or processing until the documentation has been received. This assumes, of course, that provision for the documentation is included in the contract with the vendor.

Another approach to ensuring that adequate documentation exists, whether it is to be developed internally or supplied by a vendor, is to have someone outside of EDP be responsible for it. This person could maintain the documentation library, evaluate each manual by comparing its contents with a checklist of desired coverage, and occasionally test the adequacy of the documentation by attempting to process a particular application by using it.

Hardware and Systems Software Controls

Hardware and systems software controls provide assurance that the processing is reliable and accurate. Third-party processors want reliable and accurate processing. If it is not or if their systems cause problems for the users, they will not be able to stay in business. The desire to stay in business may be the only assurance the auditor has as to the existence and reliability of hardware and systems software controls.

The auditor's inability to obtain this assurance may be caused by lack of cooperation on the part of the vendor; lack of controls in the vendor's system; multiple systems used by the vendor, each with a slightly different set of controls, and the difficulty of determining whether a specific system is always used for the same application; and lack of information on hardware or software controls in the system.

A lack of assurance as to the existence and reliability of hardware and software controls might require that substantive testing be more extensive than would otherwise be necessary.

Systems Security Controls

Systems security controls can, to some extent, offset the exposures encountered in the third-party processing environment. Systems security exposures in this environment include loss of documents in transit, access to proprietary programs, access to customers and other sensitive file information, and file backup and reconstruction.

Loss of Documents in Transit.   The loss of source documents in transit to and from a service bureau may result in the inability to collect receivables or pay vendors and the dissemination of sensitive business information, such as customer lists. Control procedures include preventing such losses or reconstructing the missing data.

Loss of documents in transit can be prevented by utilizing the services of professional couriers. Such couriers utilize procedures, equipment, and personnel to ensure the safety of document transportation.

The data contained in documents lost in transit can be reconstructed by photocopying the documents before they leave the premises. Banks typically utilize this approach.

Access to Proprietary Programs.   Some users of third-party systems develop their own programs at considerable cost and do not want these programs to fall into the hands of competitors or software vendors. Access to such programs can be controlled either by the user or through control procedures implemented by the third-party processor.

The user can control access to proprietary programs by delivering them to the third-party processor when needed, observing the processing and deletion of a copy of the program from memory, and then returning with the program.

Proprietary programs can be controlled by the third-party processor by establishing additional procedures to obtain copies of the program from the library. Examples of additional procedures include a supervisor's signature to check out a disk pack or magnetic tape containing the program, or a password entered by a supervisor to access a program resident on the system.

Access to Customer and Other Sensitive File Information.   Separation of the EDP facility from the user's premises may prevent the user's employees from having access to files, but a greater concern may be the prying eyes of the EDP facility's employees. Customer lists and payroll records are examples of information that users would rather not have readily accessible to the EDP staff or visitors passing through the facility.

Third-party processors are generally aware of their user's needs for confidentiality. They usually require that tapes, disk packs, listings, and other output not be left lying around for anyone walking through the premises to see or to pick up. Users and auditors should ascertain what procedures are prescribed and should ask for a tour of the facility so that they can determine whether these procedures are being enforced.

Customer, payroll, and other sensitive information can be coded. Instead of supplying names for payroll processing, for example, social security numbers would be used on input. Printouts containing names could be controlled by having the output run into a locked receptacle accessible only by a supervisor.

In extreme situations, the entire processing cycle can be controlled by the user. The user would deliver the input to the EDP facility, observe the processing, and then take all files and printouts on completion.

File Backup and Reconstruction.   File backup and reconstruction can be a significant concern to the user because master files are retained by the third-party processor. Procedures used by the third-party processor for file backup and reconstruction should be ascertained before entering into a service contract. In addition, these contracts should specify ownership and accessibility to these files by the user.

Procedures used by the third-party processor for file backup and reconstruction will depend on the system used. Tape systems should employ the grandparent-parent-child concept with off-site storage of the grandparent. Disk systems should provide for periodic dumping of disk files to a backup disk or a tape file. (File backup and reconstruction procedures are discussed in more detail in Chapter 8.)

Contracts not specifying ownership and accessibility of files retained by third-party processors may result in disaster for the users. One of the authors of this book is aware of a company that was forced into bankruptcy because a third-party processor refused to release accounts receivable master-file information.

Application Controls

Data Capture

Data capture in the third-party processor environment is no different from data capture in in-house systems. The differences start with procedures employed after data capture.

Data capture procedures and controls are no different in third-party processor systems because the user's employees must collect the same information using the same process they would for a similar in-house system. The source documents or information needed for on-line data entry will be the same. Authorization policies to initiate transactions will be the same. (These procedures and controls are discussed in detail in Chapter 9.)

Data Entry

Data entry in the third-party processor environment is different from data entry in the in-house systems because of the emphasis placed on controls for the detection of errors. This emphasis can be attributed to source documents leaving the user's premises and to the third-party processor's obligation to ensure the quality of processing.

The transporting of source documents to and from the third-party processor for data entry is controlled by photocopying these documents and establishing control totals over them. Photocopying as a control, as mentioned earlier, is typically used by banks. Control totals used include document or record counts, financial totals, and hash totals.

Third-party processors typically require data entry controls to ensure the quality of processing. By establishing good controls on input, they are able to minimize processing problems and provide accurate output. For service bureaus, these controls are usually the batch control totals described above. For time-sharing systems, the controls are usually transaction listings generated at the user's terminal accompanied by a request for verification before processing starts.

Data Processing

The emphasis placed on data processing controls may differ depending on whether the application program is developed by the user, is acquired from a software vendor, or is made available by using the system. Programs developed by the user can include all those controls deemed important by the user. These controls will be specified and incorporated into the system during the design and development phase.

Processing controls for application programs that are acquired from a software vendor or made available by using the system may be an issue only when initially acquiring the software or service. The scope of these controls must be evaluated at the time of software or service selection by comparing them with a checklist of desired controls. Software or services not meeting minimum standards should be rejected from further consideration.

Output

In the third-party processor environment, the reconciliation of output to input will often be performed by both the third-party processor and the user. The user, however, normally has sole responsibility for the distribution of the output.

The third-party processor will often reconcile the output to the input before transporting or transmitting the processing results to the user. This is done by the third-party processor for quality control purposes to eliminate or reduce complaints from the user. The reconciliation performed by the processor will be done with control totals submitted by the user and perhaps others calculated by the processor on data entry. If the user, for example, does not provide a document count, the processor can compute one. For batch systems, these reconciliations can be performed manually. For on-line systems, the reconciliations can be performed under program control.

The user can perform additional reconciliation upon receipt of the output from the processor. These reconciliations can be the same ones performed previously by the processor or additional ones used solely by the user. The user, for example, can use hash totals on social security numbers in a payroll application not used by the processor.

Upon receipt of output from the third-party processor, the user has the responsibility for controlling distribution. (These controls are the same as those for in-house systems discussed in Chapter 10.)

AUDITING THIRD-PARTY SYSTEMS

There are several unique aspects to the auditing of third-party systems: These third-party systems are separate legal entities; they have numerous clients and may resent dealing with the auditors of each one; and the emphasis in such audits is often on user controls. Following a review of these aspects, we discuss tests of controls and substantive testing in the third-party system environment.

The fact that third-party systems are separate legal entities means that the auditor may be denied access to the facility. Unless provided for in the contract with the user, some processors refuse to cooperate with the auditor. In such a situation, the auditor may have to treat the system as a "black box" and audit around it. With such an approach, the auditor may place heavy reliance on user controls. If these controls are weak, substantive testing may be substantial.

The fact that third-party processors have numerous clients and may resent dealing with the auditors of each one may lead to a different approach than that described above. Third-party processors who prefer to cooperate in the audit of their clients may request that their operations be audited by a single CPA firm and that the work papers and results be made available to all inquiring client auditors. This is often the case, for example, when the processor serves a single industry, such as commercial banks or savings and loan associations.

The fact that the emphasis in the audit of third-party processors is often on user controls is a result of the difficulties mentioned above. The result of such emphasis is the establishment of an adequate audit trail up to the point of data entry and an ability to pick up that trail in the output from the processor. To accomplish this, the processor may be required to provide detailed transaction listings, journals, subsidiary and general ledgers, and financial statement reports. Without this information and the audit trail it provides, the auditor may have to perform substantial substantive testing.

Tests of Controls

The auditor of third-party systems performs tests of controls as part of the assessment of control risk. The emphasis in the discussion of the testing of general and application controls that follows is on those procedures unique to the third-party system environment.

General Controls

The testing of general controls in the third-party processor environment is similar to such testing in the in-house systems if the auditor has access to the information needed or to the work papers of other auditors who have performed the tests. If not, the auditor will evaluate user controls or proceed directly to substantive testing.

The assessment of general controls risk, when performed, may lead either (1) to an assessment of application controls risk or (2) directly to the performance of substantive tests. Strong general controls will lead to the former, and weak general controls will lead to the latter, as discussed previously.

Tests on general controls are characterized by their manual approach. The procedures ranging from physically observing the segregation of functions of EDP personnel to evaluating file backup and reconstruction plans are performed manually. (The procedures discussed in Chapters 5 through 8 are equally appropriate here.)

Application Controls

The testing of application controls in third-party computer systems will occur only if the auditor concludes that the general controls are operating effectively. To reach such a conclusion, one of two events will have occurred. The auditor either will have access to the facilities of a cooperative processor or will have reviewed the work papers of another auditor with such access.

The auditor who has access to the facilities of a cooperative processor will proceed with the testing of application controls in a manner similar to that for in-house systems. The auditing will be similar because the approaches of nonprocessing of data, processing of actual data, and processing of simulated data are all applicable. The computerized techniques described in Chapters 11, 12, and 13 are also applicable. They include controlled processing, controlled reprocessing, mapping, tagging and tracing, concurrent processing, parallel simulation, test records, integrated test facility, utility programs, generalized audit software, custom-designed programs, and special-purpose programs.

Auditors who rely on the work papers of other auditors for their assessment of general controls risk can also rely on these work papers for their evaluation of application controls risk. If they conclude that the controls are operating effectively based on this evaluation, they will proceed to substantive testing restricted to some extent because of that effectiveness. They will also proceed to substantive testing if they conclude that the controls are not effective. In this case, however, they would not restrict the extent of their testing.

Auditors who rely on the work papers of other auditors for their assessment of general controls, but not for their assessment of application controls, will test those controls using the approaches and techniques discussed above. Limited accessibility to the processor's facilities, however, will result in some modifications.

Auditors denied access to the computer facility for the testing of application controls may consequently not be able to use some of the computerized techniques. This may occur where the technique requires hands-on processing. These techniques include the use of utility programs, generalized audit software, custom-designed programs, and special-purpose programs in an off-line, batch processing environment. With on-line access, even in a batch processing environment, the auditor will be able to load and process these programs through remote job entry or other data entry terminals.

Substantive Tests

Substantive testing is performed to collect evidence to form a basis for an opinion on the financial statements. The emphasis in the following discussion is on those procedures that are unique in the third-party system environment.

Substantive testing in the audit of third-party systems is often more extensive than that in the audit of in-house systems because of the auditor's inability to assess general and application controls risk at a low level. The scope of testing may be broader as the auditor examines a greater diversity of accounts and transactions than would be necessary if controls were effective. The depth of testing may be greater as the auditor examines more transactions of the same types or sends out more confirmation requests than would be necessary if controls were effective.

The approaches available to the auditor for performing substantive tests on third-party systems are the same as those for in-house systems. The approaches of nonprocessing of data, processing of actual data, and processing of simulated data are all applicable.

Computerized techniques available to the auditor for performing substantive tests on third-party systems are also the same as those for in-house systems. These techniques include controlled processing, controlled reprocessing, mapping, tagging and tracing, concurrent processing, parallel simulation, test records, integrated test facility, utility programs, custom-designed programs, special-purpose programs, and generalized audit software. The last four, as mentioned previously, may not be suitable in an access-restricted, off-line, batch processing environment.

A major concern of the user and the auditor in the third-party environment may be that the contents of master files are being retained by the processor and are, therefore, not under the user's control. In such cases, the user and/or the auditor may request a periodic dumping of this file for testing on an interim basis.

SUMMARY

Third-party systems include services provided by service bureaus and time-sharing firms. These organizations have hardware, software, procedural, and personnel characteristics that distinguish them from in-house systems. The sharp distinction formerly made between the two types of systems is slowly disappearing as they tend toward offering the same types of services.

Service bureaus established themselves by offering large batch processing systems. Documents were transported to and from them by motor vehicle. Time-sharing systems established themselves by providing access to large teleprocessing systems through typewriter-type terminals. Today both types of organizations offer similar services, and, therefore, their hardware characteristics are also similar. These characteristics include large mainframe computers, high-speed printers, large-capacity magnetic tape and disk equipment, and teleprocessing capability through remote job entry, visual display, and other types of terminals.

Operating system software used by third-party processors is the same as that used by in-house systems. Application program software includes that developed by the users and that acquired from software vendors, as well as programs written by the third-party processor and available only to system users.

Procedures associated with third-party processors are unique because the work flow physically leaves the user's premises and passes to a separate legal entity. The work flow may leave the premises in the form of source documents or electronic pulses.

A distinguishing characteristic of personnel in third-party processing is that the data processing persons involved are usually the employees of a separate legal entity. This may not be true, however, if the user is simply renting block time.

The objectives of the control structure to prevent, detect, and correct errors are the same in the third-party processor environment as in any other. These objectives are achieved through general and application controls.

Unique characteristics of the general controls environment for third-party processors include the following:

- Separation of users from EDP personnel
- Inability of the auditor to determine the personnel practices of the third-party processor
- Standard operating procedures specified by the third-party processor for submission of input and receipt of output
- Incorporation of controls into vendor-supplied software only through the software selection process
- Ability to control changes in vendor-supplied software through the purchase order process

- Provision of adequate vendor-supplied documentation through the software selection and acceptance process
- Inability to determine the existence or reliability of hardware and operating system software vendor-supplied controls
- Potential for loss of documents in transit
- Access to user proprietary programs
- Access to customer and other sensitive information
- File backup and reconstruction procedures

Unique characteristics of the application controls environment include the following:

- Emphasis on data entry controls by the third-party processor to ensure quality of processing
- Ability to incorporate processing controls into vendor-supplied software only through the program selection process
- Performance of output reconciliation to input by both third-party processor and user

There are several unique aspects to the auditing of third-party systems: These processors are separate legal entities; they have numerous clients and may resent dealing with the auditors of each one; and the emphasis in such audits is often on user controls. As separate legal entities, the processors may deny access to their facilities and force the auditor to "audit around" them. A cooperative processor with numerous clients and auditors may request that a single firm perform the audit and make the work papers available to all other auditors. The emphasis on user controls may result in the provision of an adequate audit trail up to the point of data entry and again on output through detailed transaction listings, journals, subsidiary and general ledgers, and financial statement reports.

The performance of tests of controls and substantive tests in the audit of third-party systems is similar to that in in-house systems. The same audit approaches and computerized techniques may be appropriate. An exception may be techniques requiring hands-on processing where access to the facility is denied. These techniques include the use of utility programs, generalized audit software, custom-designed programs, and special-purpose programs in an off-line, batch processing environment.

REVIEW QUESTIONS

15–1. Third-party computer systems have unique hardware, software, procedures, and personnel characteristics. For each of these four categories, discuss what is unique about these systems.

15-2. There are numerous strengths and weaknesses inherent in the general controls environment for third-party systems. For each of the following, state whether the environment results in a potential strength or weakness. Discuss why.
   a. Organization controls
   b. Personnel practices
   c. Standard operating procedures
   d. Systems development
   e. Documentation
   f. Hardware and systems software controls
   g. Program, file, and computer access
   h. File backup and reconstruction

15-3. Application controls include those pertaining to data entry. Discuss the control procedures that may be appropriate in the third-party processor environment to ensure that data are entered correctly into the system.

15-4. Processing controls are a type of application control. Discuss what is unique about processing controls in the third-party system environment.

15-5. Discuss whether there is anything unique about output controls in the third-party system environment.

15-6. Describe how the testing of controls in third-party systems is likely to differ from such testing of in-house systems. Why is there a difference?

15-7. Describe how the substantive testing of third-party systems is likely to differ from such testing of in-house systems. Why is there a difference?

OBJECTIVE QUESTIONS

15-8. The strongest control characteristic of third-party systems is usually
   a. Separation of the functions of programming and computer operator
   b. Separation of the functions of data capture and data entry
   c. Separation of the functions of data entry and output reconciliation
   d. Separation of the functions of user and EDP personnel

15-9. Third-party systems are characterized by
   a. Batch data entry and processing
   b. On-line data entry and batch processing
   c. On-line real-time processing
   d. All of the above

15-10. The most difficult application programs for the auditor of third-party systems to audit are likely to be those
   a. Written by the third-party processor and available only to system users
   b. Written by the user
   c. Acquired by the user from a software vendor
   d. Supplied by the hardware vendor

15–11. Auditors of third-party systems are least likely to utilize which of the following computerized techniques?
   a. Controlled processing
   b. Generalized audit software
   c. ITF
   d. Parallel simulation

15–12. In the third-party systems environment, the strongest application controls are likely to be found in the area of
   a. Data capture
   b. Data entry
   c. Processing
   d. Output

CASES AND EXERCISES

15–13. In the third-party system environment, it may be impossible for the auditor to assess general controls risk. In this situation, two courses of action are available. The auditor may proceed directly to the performance of substantive tests, or first to the assessment of user controls risk and then to the performance of substantive tests. Discuss how the assessment of user controls risk in a third-party system environment is likely to differ from the assessment of such controls risk with an in-house system that has weak general controls.

15–14. Third-party processors with teleprocessing capability may provide for data entry either through visual display units operating interactively or through remote job entry stations operating in batch mode. Discuss how the data entry controls are likely to differ between these two types of data entry devices.

15–15. Third-party processors often write application programs and make them available through their system only to users of it. Source code listings are not available because of the proprietary nature of such programs. Describe how an auditor might audit such a program created for an on-line real-time patient-admitting and billing system for a hospital.

15–16. One firm of auditors is sometimes requested by a third-party processor to audit its operation and make the auditors' work papers available to other auditors whose clients use its services. What procedures are the auditors of the users likely to follow in the conduct of their audit?

15–17. An auditor of a user of a third-party system has concluded that auditing around the system is not feasible. The auditor has decided that the auditing objectives can be satisfied only by auditing through the system. The third-party processor, however, has denied the auditor access to the computer site. Discuss
   a. Why the auditor has probably concluded that auditing around the system is not feasible
   b. How the auditor denied access to the computer site will be able to audit through the computer

15-18. The auditor of third-party systems encounters differences in hardware, software, procedures, and personnel compared with other types of systems. These differences create exposures—audit risks and audit difficulties—not found in these other systems. For each of the four major distinguishing characteristics of third-party systems, discuss these exposures.

15-19. Mr. Egg was rehired by a previous employer to "straighten out the accounting system" he had left some time before. Promised a handsome salary and percentage of the profits, Mr. Egg accepted the offer. But once back on the job, he became disgruntled with all the fighting going on. He began to think that the company was not living up to its promise of sharing profits. Mr. Egg decided to take the situation into his own hands.

Realizing that the company used very complicated accounting and purchasing techniques and was never extensively audited, Mr. Egg figured it would be easy to obtain the profits to which he was entitled. To do this, he invented several dummy companies as customers and vendors and set up bank accounts for these firms. Sales and receivables were recorded at less than the amounts actually billed to customers. On receipt of the payment, the difference was transferred to the dummy customer as a credit and paid out by check. Purchases and liabilities were recorded at more than the amounts actually owed to vendors. On payment of the liability, a check was issued to the dummy vendor for the difference. The scheme became too complicated to be done by hand, so Mr. Egg wrote a computer program to handle the details. All he had to do was provide the data. This computing service was provided by a computer service bureau operated by Mr. Egg as a sideline.

The only thing that threatened Mr. Egg's scheme was the audit. But Mr. Egg took care of that problem by befriending the auditors and making them rely on him to provide financial data collected in the audit. More-intensive auditor participation was precluded by deliberately limiting the engagements the auditors were hired to perform.

This went on for six years, and in all that time, poor old Mr. Egg never took a vacation. In the last two years of the embezzlement, he netted $250,000 per year!

Required:
What controls would have made such an embezzlement more difficult to perpetrate? How could the company have detected such defalcations at any time in the six years during which they took place?

15-20. AC Company is a computer service bureau in a midwestern city. Its major rival for business in the area is D. B. Cooper and Company. On January 15, at 7:23:05, the terminal log at AC Company blurted out a line of type indicating that one of AC's customers was requesting some computer time. Nothing unusual. On the following line was printed a request for the printing of 515 records, dutifully performed by the computer. Next a command was recorded indicating that 489 lines of data be printed out at the customer's terminal. And finally, a command to read 110 records from the customer site terminal was logged—but this time the computer only recorded one second of CPU time and showed that seven more lines had been printed out at the customer's site. The last entry recorded an abort command by the customer. Still nothing particularly unusual.

The problem was that the customer the computer thought it was communicating with was not the real customer at all—it was the head programmer at D. B. Cooper and Company, a Mr. Ferret.

It seemed that Mr. Ferret was trying to get some secret information out of AC's computer. To do this, all he had to do was call up AC's computer on the phone (he knew the unlisted number because he had formerly worked for a customer of AC). The two-digit site code and the account number required to link up with the AC computer were the same numbers needed at D. B. Cooper by the customer Mr. Ferret fictitiously used to gain access to AC's computer (this same customer, of course, had used the services of both companies and had insisted that the same numbers be assigned by both).

Once Mr. Ferret had gotten on the AC computer, he requested that the program he was looking for be printed at his terminal. The only problem was that the computer printed the program at the AC site instead. Once Mr. Ferret realized what had happened, he asked the AC computer to print the special program at Mr. Ferret's site, which it did, and he then tried to get the computer to discard the records already printed. All he could do was make an unauthorized command and hope the abortion of the session would accomplish the same end. Needless to say, it did not.

Required:
What controls were missing in this case and allowed this theft?

15-21.   MIDWEST MUNICIPAL DATA CENTER: Program Maintenance Documentation

Introduction
Midwest Municipal Data Center provides data processing services to four municipalities in the Chicago area. It was created and is jointly owned by these municipalities because none, alone, has sufficient data processing needs to justify acquiring a computer of its own.

The two major services offered to the municipalities by the service center are a utility billing application and a payroll application. The utility billing system was designed to perform the billing and statistical reporting functions for any type of utility. It is composed of about twenty programs, ranging from input validation to creating billing address labels. MMDC is a small organization employing but five people. (Figure 1 is an organization chart.)

Audit Arrangements
Last year, the Board of Directors of MMDC decided that an audit should be conducted of the service center, primarily for two reasons: (1) Though the service center is a distinct and separate entity, it plays an important part in each municipality's data processing and accounting control system, and (2) the auditor of each municipality wishes to rely on a review

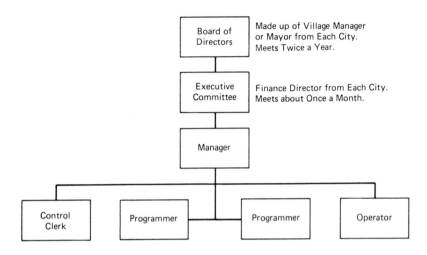

Figure 1.

of the controls maintained and services performed by the service center in determining the scope of the separate examinations.

No previous audit had been conducted of MMDC although a public accounting firm had participated in setting up the service center and currently audited one of the owner municipalities. They were invited to consider auditing MMDC. They responded to the request with the following proposal, which could be converted to an engagement letter by acceptance.

Gentlemen:

We are pleased to have this opportunity to propose financial and EDP audits for Midwest Municipal Data Center. Our experience with and interest in this area will provide MMDC with effective and efficient audits over the increasingly important services it provides.

The financial audit will be planned to provide an unqualified opinion of the financial position of Midwest Municipal Data Center as of December 31. The EDP audit will be performed in accordance with the guidelines for audits of service center produced records as set by the American Institute of Certified Public Accountants. The objectives of the EDP audit will be to support and complement the present financial audits of the customers served by MMDC and to assist MMDC management. Accordingly, concentration will be focused on evaluating and testing controls within the data center. Controls over the individual applications will continue to be reviewed by the auditors for the individual municipalities.

The data center controls covered will include those surrounding data and program files, computer operations, program documentation and maintenance, and disaster recovery. We will also comment on information privacy, as various state and federal legislation currently under consideration on this subject may have an impact on data center operations within the next two years.

The results of this engagement will include:

1. The audit opinion or comments regarding the financial position of Mid-west Municipal Data Center as of December 31.

2. EDP Audit report in accordance with the AICPA guidelines.

3. Management letter suggesting, where appropriate, areas for improvement.

Our total fees for these initial audits will not exceed $_____.

The audits will begin within two weeks of the acceptance of this proposal and should be completed within a period of three weeks. We have previously discussed with you our qualifications and experience in the areas of government and EDP auditing. We will be pleased to discuss any of these matters with you at your convenience.

Yours very truly,

As the result of the acceptance of this letter, a financial audit was performed and separate EDP audits of the payroll and the utility billing applications were completed by the auditor. After the audit of the payroll application, the auditors sent the following letter to the Board of Directors of MMDC.

Gentlemen:

We have reviewed and tested, to the extent we consider necessary, data center controls for Midwest Municipal Data Center. The controls reviewed included those surrounding data and program files, computer operations, disaster recovery, and program maintenance and documentation. These controls are described in the MMDC User Procedures Manual and Standards and Procedures Manual which are available to all users. The documentation and operations of the *payroll application* were tested during June. Our review and tests were limited to activities performed at the data center and did not include consideration of procedures performed by customers of the data center.

Certain limitations in controls are inherent for operations the size of MMDC. Controls realized through segregation of responsibilities are not practical on a continuous basis due to the small size of the organization. This emphasizes the importance of application controls performed by the users, as described in the User Manual. Also, the exclusive use of disks for processing efficiency at a low cost excludes the retention of extensive backup copies of files for recovery in case of disaster.

Our observations indicate a high degree of competence in data center personnel—their understanding of their responsibilities and their knowledge of the hardware and application software. Techniques used to document program modifcations are particularly effective for program maintenance and review. (Underscore added for purposes of this case. It was not present in the original letter.)

Recommendations for improved control are limited to formalizing data corrections that are presently phoned in by municipal clerks in emergencies. Due to the limited time available, changes may have to be communicated by phone. However, additional steps should be taken to highlight these transactions on transaction listings and error reports to allow the user to exercise appropriate control. As operations expand and economics permit, organization changes should be made to segregate programming, operating, and library activities.

The attached supplemental report includes a brief description of the system, the documentation, the organizational controls, security, and backup. It includes a description of the scope of our review and of the tests performed during our review.

The Utility Billing Application was purchased by MMDC. The package was designed to perform billing and statistical reporting for any type of utility and is used by MMDC for billing and reporting for MMDC customers. For two years now, MMDC personnel have made a significant effort to document fully the Utility Billing Application and to maintain the complete history of modifications to the system. Resulting documentation and maintenance procedures are extremely well done. (Underscore added for purposes of this case. It was not present in the original letter.) Our review of the documentation as it related to actual production programs and to operations uncovered no significant differences.

One important control desirable in a data center, such as at MMDC, related to segregation of responsibilities. Such a plan of organization, providing appropriate segregation of duties, assures that the functions of authorizing and processing transactions and of maintaining custody of assets are effectively separated. Thus, with complete segregation, programmers would not have access to "live" data files and computer operators would not have the capability of modifying data or master files during operations. Because of its size and budget MMDC cannot assure complete or adequate segregation of duties. For instance, normal workloads require only a single operator for the MMDC staff. However, during peak periods, vacations, emergencies, etc., the programmers and the MMDC manager often participate and operate the computer. Given the size of the organization, such sharing of responsibilities is realistic even though it results in a lack of segregation of responsibility. Such lack of organizational segregation emphasizes the importance of customer control of data input and output.

An additional factor noted during our review was the cost and inconvenience of making backup copies of master files. MMDC uses disk files for normal processing operations and for backup. However, tape files would be more effective and efficient for creating security and backup copies of master files. Because of budget considerations MMDC has elected not to purchase tape files. While present revenue levels may not warrant incurring the additional cost to achieve easier and more convenient backup processing, as volume increases tape facilities for backup should be considered.

In our opinion the Utility Billing Application of the Midwest Municipal Data Center during the time of our review conformed with the appropriate systems descriptions. Because of the lack of organizational segregation noted above, the user controls are of significant importance. Because our review and tests were limited to the Utility Billing Application and related procedures performed by the Midwest Municipal Data Center and did not extend to other procedures performed by MMDC, we express no opinion on the adequacy of internal accounting controls as they apply to either a specific customer of MMDC or to MMDC itself.

This report is intended solely for distribution to auditors of customers served by Midwest Municipal Data Center. Distribution to other parties is not authorized.

Yours very truly,

Question:

In each letter to the Board of Directors of MMDC, the auditor commented favorably upon the documentation of program modifications (underscored for reference purposes). Directly following, below, are excerpts from the auditor's work papers describing MMDC's procedures in this regard. You are to evaluate the writeup and the evaluation of the system to determine whether the auditor's praise was warranted in all respects.

System Documentation

For the past two years, a concerted effort has been made to document the system and to maintain a history of modifications on the system.

The system documentation contains the following information:

- System Design Overview with corresponding system flowcharts showing all existing programs and input/output files used.
- Program narratives, in many cases very brief, detailing the purpose of the program, its inputs and outputs, major functions of the program, and any controls included to show the major logic decisions within the program.
- Program flowcharts are included for all programs which have been written in-house, to supplement the system.
- Layouts and field descriptions for all disk and report files.

Program changes are received on a "Request for Systems Service— Request for Change" (Figure 2). When received, the request is given a

MIDWEST MUNICIPAL DATA CENTER
REQUEST FOR SYSTEMS SERVICE

System Request No.

_____

Date _____

Submitted by: _____   Date: _____

NATURE OF REQUEST:

☐ New System   ☐ Change in Current System   ☐ Current System Problem

Description of Request:

Received _____   Initial review to be completed by _____
     mgr.

Proposed Resolution:

Implemented by Date _____   Date _____
                                                Mgr.

Action Taken:

Date _____

Figure 2.

sequential control number and logged on a master control sheet for the system. After the modification has been reviewed to determine its validity and need, it is placed on the "Master Systems Service Request Log" (Figure 3).

When the request is implemented, an entry is made on the "Program Control Form" (Figure 4) to update the program maintenance history and a "Program Modification Sheet" (Figure 5) is created. The Program Modification Sheet is assigned a number which consists of the program number (first four digits) and a sequentially assigned change number (fifth and sixth digits). The Program Modification Sheet describes the change and indicates all the steps which are necessary to incorporate the modifications.

The computer instructions coded to implement the changes within the computer program itself are tagged with the program modification number which was initially assigned (Figure 6).

When the change has been tested and placed in production, the completion date is posted to Master Systems Service Request Log (Figure 3) and to the Program Control Form (Figure 4) and Program Modification Sheets (Figure 5) which are then filed.

With this type of control placed upon modifications, it is possible to trace a change in the system from its origin all the way to the actual program instructions necessary to implement the changes within the system.

An important aspect in using this approach to program modifications is its ability to self-document the system. It is very time-consuming and many times impractical to change the original program specification for all new modifications made. Using the modification procedure described eliminates the need to change the original specifications except in the case where the actual purpose and/or function of the program has been significantly modified.

A sampling of the system and program documentation as it relates to the actual production programs uncovered no significant differences.[1] (*Prepared by Frederick Neumann, Richard Boland, and Jeffrey Johnson, with funding from the Touche Ross Foundation. Used and adapted with permission of the authors.*)

---

[1]Note the addition of the controls test which verifies that the prescribed procedures are being followed.

MIDWEST MUNICIPAL DATA CENTER

Master

SYSTEMS SERVICE REQUEST LOG

Request	Description	Submitted by	Date Submitted	Scheduled Completion Date	Actual Completion Date	Comments

Figure 3.

PROGRAM/MODULE MAINTENANCE CONTROL FORM Page _____ of _____

Project No. _____

ID/TITLE _____

Organization _____

System _____

User Rep. _____

Prepared by _____

Reviewed by _____

Date _____

Phase _____

PROGRAMMING SPECIFICATIONS

Description of Program/Module:

Programming hour estimate _____ Date required _____ Language _____

Specifications completed by _____ Date _____

Specifications approved by _____ Date _____

PROGRAMMING ASSIGNMENT

Program/Module assigned to: _____ Scheduled Completion Date _____

Assigned by _____ Date _____

Comments

CERTIFICATION

Program/Module written by	Date	Documentation completed by	Date
Program/Module quality assurance by	Date	Project acceptance by	Date

MAINTENANCE HISTORY

No.	Prob/Request Cont. Sht. No.	Changed by	Date	No.	Prob/Request Cont. Sht. No.	Changed by	Date
1				7.			
2.				8.			
3.				9.			
4.				10.			
5.				11.			
6.				12.			

Figure 4.

PROGRAM MODIFICATION

Program Changed _____   Modification No. _____

New Name _____   System _____

CHANGES REQUIRED

ITEM	PERFORMED BY	DATE COMPLETED	ITEM	PERFORMED BY	DATE COMPLETED
☐ System Summary	_____	_____	☐ Good Test Run	_____	_____
☐ Run Write-Up	_____	_____	☐ Cntrl. & Balanc.	_____	_____
☐ Program Listing	_____	_____	☐ Oprt. Instrctn.	_____	_____
☐ Logic Flowcharts	_____	_____	☐ User Manual	_____	_____
☐ Input Specs.	_____	_____	☐ _____	_____	_____
☐ Record Layouts	_____	_____	☐ _____	_____	_____
☐ Report Layouts	_____	_____	☐ _____	_____	_____

REASON FOR CHANGE

DESCRIPTION OF CHANGE

COMMENTS

Changed by_____   Date_____

Figure 5.

REMARKS	PAGE/LINE OLD	NEW	CATE GORY	REFERENCE	CODE OPERATION	LOCATION OPERANDS	LENGTH	DP TYPE	VALUE/COMMENTS
DEL.	300020		C*OVERLAY4	{ENTR}	VFIELDCHGZ,DELETESUB,.NEWNAME.				
OMIT	330020		C		OMIT				ᵦ
DEL.	330020		C*OVERLAY7	{ENTR}	HOURLY				
ADD.	330035		C*		{NOTE}THIS ROUTINE ALSO HANDLES PAY CODE 3.				P05008
NET.	330050		C*		{---->GO TO PC1E. IF NOT 0, THIS IS FLOATING				P05008
DEL.	330050		C*		{---->GO TO PC1E-OVERLAY8. IF NOT 0, THIS IS FLOATING				
RET.	330070		C*		{PROC}COMPUTE REG 2 AND REG 3 EARNINGS.				P05008
DEL.	330070		C*		{PROC}COMPUTE SHIFT2 SHIFT3 EARNINGS.				
OMIT	340010		C		OMIT				
DEL.	340010		C*OVERLAY8	{ENTR}	HOURLY1, PC1E.				ᵦ
ADD.	340055		C*TAG		{PROC}DETERMINE EARNINGS THAT ARE SUBJECT TO PENSION.				P05008
ADD.	340613		C		COMPLE	'3',PENSFL2-NETSUB	* PENSION - OTHER2 IS NOT			P05008
RET.	340614		C		ADD	SAVEREG,PENEARNMTD	*THIS IS FOR IMRF			P05005
DEL.	340614		C		ADD	SAVEREG,PENEARNMTD	* PENSION - OTHER2 IS NOT			P05005
ADD.	342400		C		BR	$02				P05008
OMIT	350020		C		OMIT				ᵦ
DEL.	350020		C*OVERLAY9	{ENTR}					
OMIT	360020		C		OMIT				ᵦ
DEL.	360020		C*OVERLAY10	{ENTR}					
OMIT	370020		C		OMIT				ᵦ
DEL.	370020		C*OVERLAY11	{ENTR}	INCENTPAY COMMIS.				
OMIT	370050		C		OMIT	370070				ᵦ
DEL.	370050		C*COMMIS	{ENTR}					
DEL.	370060		C*		{PROC}COMPUTE EARNINGS - COMMISSION WITH DRAW				
DEL.	370070		C*		{GOTO}NETSUB*OVERLAY 0 - MAIN PROGRAM				
OMIT	360020		C		OMIT				ᵦ

Chapter 16
AUDITING
COMPUTER PROCESSING:
EXPERT SYSTEMS

Learning Objectives

After completing this chapter, the reader should be able to:

1. Learn what is an expert system and how to describe its basic components.

2. Determine some of the common information organization techniques for expert systems.

3. Learn about some of the common inference searching techniques used in expert systems.

4. Identify some of the ways in which expert systems are used as a tool of the auditor.

5. Determine some of the unique characteristics of the expert system control structure.

6. Understand how tests of controls and substantive tests are performed on expert systems.

Many auditors are familiar with expert systems as tools in the performance of the audit. As tools, expert systems help, for example, in the evaluation of loan collateral. Computer auditors are finding, however, that expert systems are more frequently becoming the target of the audit. They are becoming the target of the audit as these systems take over more and more of the routine processing of accounting data, such as credit approval or order entry.

Expert systems can be defined in a simple manner as computer programs that employ unique programming techniques to provide users with prepackaged expertise in a particular field. A more complex definition is provided in the next section.

Our discussion of expert systems is divided into three main segments: (1) the basic concepts and terminology of expert systems; (2) how expert systems are used as a tool by the auditor to assist in the audit process; and (3) the auditing of expert systems as the target of the audit like other computer programs.

The emphasis in this chapter is on those aspects of expert systems that are unique in contrast to other computer programs. This uniqueness includes, for example, problems in determining the reasonableness of output from expert systems. It does not include most general controls which are similar for all computers.

BASIC CONCEPTS AND TERMINOLOGY OF EXPERT SYSTEMS

Basic Concepts

A more complex definition of an expert system than that provided in the introduction is that

> . . . an expert system is one that has expert rules and avoids blind search, performs well, reasons by manipulating symbols, grasps fundamental domain principles, and has complete weaker reasoning methods to fall back on when expert rules fail and to use in producing explanations. It deals with difficult problems in a complex domain, can take a problem description in lay terms and convert it to an internal representation appropriate for processing with its expert rules, and it can reason about its own knowledge (or lack thereof), especially to reconstruct inference paths rationally for explanation and self-justification. An expert system works on (generally at least) one of these types of tasks: interpretation, diagnosis, prediction, instruction, monitoring, planning, and design.[1]

---

[1]Brachman, et al., "What Are Expert Systems?," in *Building Expert Systems*, Hayes-Roth et al., Eds. (Reading, Mass.: Addison-Wesley, 1983), p. 50.

The two basic components of the expert system are its *knowledge base* and its *inference engine*. The *knowledge base* contains rules, facts, and information used in formulating a solution, solving problems, and helping users reach their goals. The knowledge base is similar to the files and data bases discussed previously because it contains information used in processing. It is different because the incorporation of rules in it is like putting part of the computer program in the master file.

The other basic component of the expert system is the *inference engine*. The inference engine is a computer program that contains the analytical framework for generating and explaining advice to the user. It combines the user's answers to questions with the rules in the knowledge base in order to produce the advice the user needs to solve a problem or reach a goal. In performing this task it can evaluate user's answers to questions, generate additional questions as required, and conclude, based on rules that are satisfied, what the final conclusions or recommendations are.

Other components found in expert systems include the user interface and an explanation facility. The *user interface* provides the communication between the inference engine and the system user. The inference engine uses the user interface to conversationally ask the user for facts about the rules in the knowledge base, deliver its conclusions, and—in conjunction with the explanation facility—explain the system's reasoning. The *explanation facility* helps the user understand why certain questions are asked or why specific conclusions are reached. The system may do this by listing the steps followed by the system in reaching its conclusion or by explaining the reason for asking a particular question during dialogue with the user.

Expert systems are used for many different purposes in a number of fields. Several of these purposes are illustrated in Figure 16–1, along with a description of the problems addressed and examples of applications.

Terminology

The computer auditor starting to work with expert systems will encounter a plethora of new terms. Our introduction to many of them is organized within the categories of information organization techniques, inference searching techniques, and expert systems personnel.

Information Organization Techniques. Three techniques used to organize information in the knowledge base include if-then rules, framing, and semantic networks. The components of *if-then rules* include a declaration, condition, and an action. Expert systems using the rule representation scheme are sometimes called *production systems*. The following is an example of an if-then rule approach to organizing information:

Purpose	Problem Addressed	Examples
Interpretation	Inferring situation descriptions from sensor data	Leading economic indicators describing condition of an average family
Prediction	Inferring likely consequences of given situations	Investment portfolio outcome on a given purchase or sale
Diagnosis	Inferring system malfunctions from observables	Traditional audit risk scoring systems
Design	Configuring objects under constraints	Audit testwork planning; DEC computer configuration system
Planning	Designing actions	Manufacturing resource planning
Monitoring	Comparing observations to plan vulnerabilities	Foreign exchange what-if; bankruptcy forecasting; audit operational monitor
Debugging	Prescribing remedies for malfunctions	Circuit diagnostic aids; IBM YES monitor, COBOL productivity tools
Repair	Executing a plan to administer a prescribed remedy	Circuit design tool
Instruction	Diagnosing, debugging, and repairing student behavior	Computer-based training
Control	Interpreting, predicting, repairing, and monitoring system behaviors	Military command, communications, and control

From *Building Expert Systems*, p. 14.

Figure 16–1. Categories of Expert Systems

Declaration:	Petty cash is an asset account.
Condition and action:	If asset is negative, then audit.

The problem with the if-then approach is that from an auditor's standpoint the real world is not binary enough. There may be asset accounts, for example, that do not have negative balances that should be audited.

Framing organizes information around expected events. A frame is a group of attributes that describes a given object. The following diagram illustrates this approach to specifying the petty cash relationship—petty cash is an asset which appears in the balance sheet.

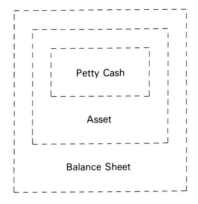

Semantic networks are another approach to organizing information. These networks focus on objects and their relationships. The following is an example of how a semantic network would specify the petty cash relationship.

Petty cash	
is an account of	Relationship
asset account	

Inference Searching Techniques.   Inference searching techniques refer to how and the order in which the inference engine will use the knowledge data in the knowledge base. There are many techniques available for this purpose including forward chaining, backward chaining, and various search strategies.

Forward chaining develops solutions from facts. It is based on inductive reasoning. The following is an example of forward chaining.

If the RISK SCORE rises in month 1,
Do the audit in month 2.

Forward Chaining

Fact:	RISK SCORE is up
Fact:	Today is in month 2
Action:	Do audit

Backward chaining begins with the results and moves backwards. It is based on deductive reasoning. The following is an example of backward chaining.

Backward Chaining

IF

| | Prior audit is bad |
| and | Reports are late |

THEN

	Call manager
	Audit in three months
IF	
	Audit was qualified or unsatisfactory

THEN

	Prior audit was bad
IF	
	Reports are not here
and	Due date was at least five days ago

THEN

| | Reports are late |

Searching strategies involve describing a desired solution as a goal and the set of possible steps leading from initial conditions to the goal as a search space. A search is conducted through the space of possible solutions for ones that satisfy the goal. Techniques used include depth-first search, breadth-first search, and heuristic search. *Depth-first search* follows a single path to its end, reaches a conclusion, and then follows another single path if appropriate. *Breadth-first search* simultaneously examines all paths starting with the first step for each one then moving to the second step for each one. *Heuristic search* employs rules of thumb to help solve problems by reducing the search space. These searching strategies can be illustrated as follows.

Path 1	*Path 2*	*Path 3*
IF test of details risk is greater than 50 percent AND IF account balance has changed since last audit THEN audit account	IF account balance exceeds 10 percent of net income AND IF account balance has changed since last audit THEN audit account	IF account balance has not changed since last audit
		PHOTOCOPY work paper and DO NOT audit account

The depth-first search technique would first go through path 1, then path 2, and finally path 3. The breadth-first technique would go through all three paths simultaneously. The heuristic technique might first check path 3 and avoid looking at paths 1 and 2 entirely if the account balance has not changed.

Expert Systems Personnel. Among the new terms the computer auditor must contend with in working with expert systems are those identifying various personnel. They include the domain expert and the knowledge engineer. The *domain expert* is the person who is recognized as having the knowledge and know-how necessary to solve a particular type or class of problem. The burden of uncovering and formalizing the domain expert's knowledge falls on the shoulders of the knowledge engineer. The *knowledge engineer* defines the problem to be solved, discovers the basic concepts involved through an extended series of interactions with the domain expert, and loads the information with related rules into the knowledge base.

EXPERT SYSTEMS AS A TOOL OF THE AUDITOR

Many expert systems have been developed to aid the auditor in performing the audit. Such systems are referred to as tools of the auditor. These systems will be discussed under the three topics of planning the audit, audit testing, and issuing the financial statements. A summary is provided in Figure 16–2.

Planning the Audit

Three of the activities typically undertaken by the auditor during the planning phase of the audit are (1) evaluating audit risk, (2) specifying audit materiality, and (3) performing analytic procedures. Expert systems have been developed to help the auditor perform all three of these activities.

One of the components of audit risk specified during the planning phase of the audit is control risk. An expert system called ICES focuses on a preliminary assessment of control risk for sales and accounts receivable transactions.

The materiality judgments made during the planning phase of the audit are the subject of another expert system. AUDITPLANNER was developed to help in this analysis.

Analytic procedures are performed during the planning phase to identify accounts that may be problem areas requiring audit attention. An expert system is also available to assist in this evaluation.

Figure 16–2. Examples of Expert Systems as Audit Tools

Task Performed	Expert System	Developer
Planning the audit		
Audit risk	ICES	Grudnitski
Materiality	AUDITPLANNER	Steinbart
Analytic review	?	Braun, Chandler
Audit Testing		
Controls testing, general	TICOM	Bailey et al.
Controls testing, EDP	EDP-EXPERT	Hansen
Controls testing, revenue	INTERNAL-CONTROL-ANALYZER	Gal
Controls testing, disbursements	ARISC	Meservy
Tests of details, bad debt allowance	AUDITOR	Dungan
Tests of details, loan loss reserve	CFILE, LOAN PROBE	Willingham, Peat Marwick
Issuance of Financial Statements		
Going concern	GC-X	Biggs, Selfridge
	AOD	Dillard, Mutcher
Report checklist	CheckGaap	Pattenden

Note: For more information about these systems see N. A. D. Connell, "Expert Systems in Accountancy: A Review of Some Recent Applications," *Accounting and Business Research,* Vol. 17, No. 67, pp. 221–233, 1987.

Audit Testing

The term *audit testing* is used to refer to two types of activities performed by the auditor during this fieldwork phase: (1) evaluating the control structure by performing tests of controls and related activities to assess control risk, and (2) tests of details of transactions and account balances.

Expert systems exist for evaluating the control structure in general and for specifically evaluating two major transaction cycles. One expert system for evaluating the control structure in general is called TICOM. It assists the auditor in identifying potential weaknesses by building a model of the flow of documents and control procedures. Another expert system for evaluating the control structure is EDP-EXPERT. This system focuses on the reliability of supervisory, input, processing, and output controls.

The two major transaction cycles that have been the subject of expert systems development are the revenue and collection cycle and the acquisition and payment cycle. A model called INTERNAL-CONTROL-ANALYZER was developed for examining the control structure in the revenue cycle. ARISC focuses on understanding and evaluating the control structure for purchasing, accounts payable, and cash disbursements.

The expert systems developed to aid in the tests of details phase of the audit focus on the valuation of receivables in the revenue and collection cycle. A model called AUDITOR aids in investigating the allowance for bad debts in hospital audits. Another model called CFILE, or LOAN PROBE, is used to analyze the reasonableness of loan loss reserves in bank audits.

Issuance of Financial Statements

Two types of expert systems have been developed to aid the auditor during the final phase of the audit when financial statements are issued. One type helps determine the opinion to be issued by assisting in making "going concern" judgments. GC-X and AOD are examples of these systems.

A second type of expert system provides the auditor with a checklist to ensure that the audit report complies with all reporting requirements. This system is called CheckGaap.

EXPERT SYSTEMS AS A TARGET OF THE AUDIT

Expert systems become the target of the audit when they are involved in processing significant accounting transactions. They may also become the target of the audit when they are involved in the processing of significant information used by the auditor in the conduct of the audit. Some examples of these types of expert systems will be followed by a discussion of control structure issues and of audit testing to determine the accuracy and reliability of the system.

Expert Systems Processing of Accounting Information

Expert systems used in the processing of accounting information are of two types: (1) systems that directly affect the balances reported in financial statements because they are involved in the processing of significant accounting transactions, and (2) systems that indirectly affect the balances reported in financial statements because they provide the auditor with information about the reasonableness of that reported information.

The revenue and collection cycle has benefitted the most from expert systems used in the processing of significant accounting transactions. Expert systems are available in the areas of sales approval and accounts receivable valuation. One example of sales approval is an insurance company underwriting system that assists in determining whether insurance policies should be issued and for what premium rate. Another sales approval system is used to determine whether customers should be allowed to charge particular types of purchases on their credit cards. A third system is used by commercial banks in making lending decisions. Accounts receivable valuation expert systems are used to determine the amounts in the allowance for bad debts or loan loss reserve.

The revenue and collection cycle has also been the primary beneficiary of expert systems used to provide information to the auditor about the reasonableness of reported information. This information is generated by expert systems that perform financial forecasting. These forecasted results can be used by auditors in performing analytic procedures when actual results are compared with the forecast. Auditors are also often asked to perform a review of the financial forecast itself. In performing this review they may have to investigate not only the basic assumptions going into the model but also the reasonableness of the expert system model.

Expert Systems Control Structure

The computer auditor focusing on the expert system as the target of the audit will examine general and application controls as discussed previously for all computer systems. For most general controls the auditor will not change the approach to the audit just because an expert system is involved. This is not true for systems development and documentation controls where several additional issues may have to be raised. All of the application controls discussed previously are also applicable for the expert system. The change in audit approach for application controls is the emphasis placed on some of them.

General Controls.   General controls minimally affected by expert systems technology include: (1) organization controls, personnel practices, and standard operating procedures; (2) hardware and systems software controls; and (3) system security controls. These three categories of controls are discussed in detail in Chapters 5, 7, and 8, respectively.

Organization controls such as segregation of functions, personnel practices such as periodic evaluation of people, and standard operating procedures such as scheduling when the system is to be used for specific processing tasks are generally independent of the type of processing performed. An exception might be segregation of functions which becomes more difficult the smaller the system. Processing by an expert system, however, has an insignificant affect on these controls.

Hardware and systems software controls are built into the system by the vendor. The auditor of expert systems must examine these vendor-supplied controls just as with any other computer system. The types of controls likely to be encountered and the approach to auditing them do not differ significantly just because an expert system is involved.

System security controls are just as important for expert systems as they are for any computer system and the auditor's approach to them will be the same. Password protection for access to the knowledge base and inference engine, for example, will provide security similar to that for the data base and program execution of other systems.

Expert systems have their greatest impact on the general control of systems development and documentation. This is so because of the complexity of expert systems development and the ongoing nature of such development. The complexity of the expert system makes it difficult to determine if the system is actually doing what it is supposed to do. The ongoing nature of development means that documentation will often lag far behind actual system status.

The computer auditor's attention will likely be focused on three major areas in assessing the systems development and documentation general control: (1) expertise of the team developing the system, (2) testing of the system, and (3) documentation of the system. The more expert the team and the more thorough the testing, the more likely the system functions as anticipated. The better the documentation, the easier it will be to determine if the system is functioning reliably and accurately and to monitor subsequent changes in the system.

The auditor assessing the expertise of the team developing the system will be concerned with two major issues. These issues are the experience of the project team and the qualifications of the experts.

The most important general control for expert systems is that of system testing. Tests performed in validating the expert system are also probably the most difficult area for the computer auditor to evaluate, especially for highly complex systems with many rules where some decision paths may not even be known to the developers or auditor as the system learns from its past mistakes and autonomously modifies its knowledge base. The following issues need to be addressed as to the reliability of tests of the expert system:

1. Have the expert system results been tested and compared against a human expert?
2. Have the expert system results been tested and compared against other models, if available?
3. Do the users believe in the results?
4. Is instability detected with minor changes?
5. Will the system explain why it reaches the conclusions that it does?

6. Are several test cases with known results processed through the system?
7. Are changes in the system subjected to the original tests?[2]

The general control of adequate documentation is almost always a problem with computer systems. It is a much larger problem when expert systems are involved because, by their very nature, these systems are constantly being modified and expanded to handle more and more complex tasks. It is highly unlikely that the computer auditor will find completed documentation that describes the current status of the system. The best that the auditor can hope for is that the documentation does not lag too far behind system development. A compensating control may be an expert system that self-documents explaining in great detail every step of every decision that it makes.

Application Controls.   The application controls of input, processing, and output discussed previously for other computer systems are also applicable for expert systems. The difference is that with expert systems some of them are more important than for other systems.

Several controls for validating input have been discussed previously. One that deserves special consideration when expert systems are involved is a reasonableness test. When it may be difficult to ascertain the reasonableness of output from the system because of its complexity, it is even more important to determine that the data being submitted are appropriate. Calculations are made by LOAN PROBE, for example, when data are submitted to the system to determine if the data correspond with other information previously submitted such as balance-sheet ratios.

Processing controls are another very important application control in expert systems. Limit and reasonableness tests can be incorporated into both the knowledge base and the inference engine to determine that intermediate processing results are appropriate. The user is asked by LOAN PROBE, for example, whether an intermediate result or decision by the expert system seems appropriate.

The output control that is as important for expert systems as it is for the user-controlled systems discussed previously is the output reasonableness test. As with user-controlled systems, the user becomes an important compensating control in determining if the final results produced by the expert system make sense. This may be difficult to determine in a complex system. With such a system, the explanation facility may be

---

[2] For an excellent discussion of expert system validation, see Daniel G. O'Leary, "Validation of Expert Systems—With Applications to Auditing and Accounting Expert Systems," *Decision Sciences*, Summer 1987, pp. 468–486.

crucial in helping the user understand the decision process leading up to the final results.

Audit Testing

The auditor of expert systems will conduct tests of controls and substantive tests to determine the reliability and accuracy of processing as with other computer systems. This testing will include a mixture of manual and computerized techniques.

The testing of general controls usually involves manual procedures, as discussed previously. The systems development and documentation controls described in detail above can be tested by visually examining information about the expertise of the development team, tests performed by the team to validate the system before putting it into production, and documentation prepared to explain the operation of the system.

Testing of the application controls will almost always require a computerized technique. The input, processing, and output controls described in detail above can best be tested by examining the actual processing of data by the expert system. Computerized techniques appropriate for the testing of controls are presented in Figure 16-3.

Substantive testing focuses on the detection of monetary errors in transactions, amounts, or account balances resulting from expert systems processing. It may be possible for the auditor to determine manually what the result should be and compare that with the output from the expert system. This may be especially true for simple systems, but perhaps not for complex ones. For complex systems, the auditor may have to use one of the computerized techniques presented in Figure 16-3.

Figure 16-3. Computerized Techniques for Performing Audit Tests on Expert Systems

Technique	Example
Controlled processing	Monitoring of input to and output from the system as it is being used
Controlled reprocessing	Resubmission of previously solved problem to determine if same conclusion is reached
Parallel simulation	Submission of problem and data to another model or expert system to determine if same conclusion is reached
Test records	Submission of data with known conclusion to determine if expert system reaches same conclusion

Note: Additional information about the computerized techniques presented above can be found in Chapters 11 and 12.

SUMMARY

Expert systems are computer programs that employ unique programming techniques to provide users with prepackaged expertise in a particular field. Their two basic components are the knowledge base and the inference engine. Additional components are the user interface and the explanation facility.

The terminology encountered with expert systems can be organized under the categories of information organization techniques, inference searching techniques, and expert systems personnel. Information organization techniques include if-then rules, framing, and semantic networks. Inference searching techniques include forward chaining, backward chaining, and the searching strategies of depth-first search, breadth-first search, and heuristic search. Expert systems personnel include the domain expert and the knowledge engineer.

Expert systems are used as tools of the auditor in the areas of planning the audit, audit testing, and issuing the financial statements. In the planning phase of the audit, expert systems aid in evaluating audit risk, specifying audit materiality, and performing analytic procedures. These systems are used in audit testing by aiding in the evaluation of the control structure and by performing tests of details. The systems are used in conjunction with the issuance of the financial statements by aiding in determining the type of opinion to issue and by leading the auditor through a checklist to determine that all reporting requirements have been satisfied.

Expert systems are the target of the audit when they are involved in processing significant accounting information. This has primarily occurred in the revenue and collection cycle. As the target of the audit, expert systems are subject to control structure evaluation and substantive tests for monetary errors in processing.

Differences in the control structure of expert systems as contrasted to other computer systems occur in the areas of both general controls and application controls. Expert systems have their greatest impact on the general control of systems development and documentation. The computer auditor's attention will likely be focused on three major areas in assessing this control: (1) expertise of the team developing the system, (2) testing of the system, and (3) documentation of the system. The focus of attention in assessing control risk for input, processing, and output application controls will be on reasonableness tests.

The audit testing of expert systems will involve manual and computerized techniques. Manual techniques will usually be used in evaluating general controls. Computerized techniques will be used in evaluating application controls and in performing substantive tests of details. Appropriate computerized techniques include controlled processing, controlled reprocessing, parallel simulation, and test records.

REVIEW QUESTIONS

16-1. Define an expert system. What are its two basic components? What are two other components of an expert system?

16-2. List and describe the common information organization techniques for expert systems.

16-3. List and describe the common inference searching techniques for expert systems.

16-4. What is a domain expert? What is a knowledge engineer?

16-5. Describe some of the ways in which expert systems can aid in audit planning.

16-6. Describe some of the ways in which expert systems can aid in audit testing by evaluating the control structure. By performing tests of details.

16-7. How are expert systems used in conjunction with the issuance of the financial statements?

16-8. Under what circumstances do expert systems become the target of the audit?

16-9. Why do expert systems have their greatest impact on the general control of systems development and documentation? What specific issues is the computer auditor likely to raise in evaluating the systems development and documentation control?

16-10. How is the computer auditor's evaluation of application controls affected by expert systems? What is the likely focus of the auditor's attention in evaluating these controls?

16-11. Which controls will most likely be tested by the computer auditor using manual techniques? Using computerized techniques?

16-12. List and describe the computerized techniques most likely to be used in performing tests of controls and tests of details.

OBJECTIVE QUESTIONS

16-13. The _____ is a computer program that contains the analytical framework for generating and explaining advice to the user.
a. Knowledge base
b. Inference engine
c. User interface
d. Explanation facility

16-14. Traditional audit risk scoring systems infer malfunctions from observables. This is an example of which category of expert system?
a. Interpretation
b. Prediction
c. Diagnosis
d. Monitoring

16–15. The information organization technique that organizes information around expected events is called _____. This technique uses a group of attributes to describe a given object.
   a. If-then rules
   b. Production system
   c. Framing
   d. Semantic network

16–16. The inference searching technique that develops solutions from facts and is based on inductive reasoning is called
   a. Forward chaining
   b. Backward chaining
   c. Heuristic searching
   d. Breadth-first searching

16–17. The _____ is the person who is recognized as having the knowledge and know-how necessary to solve a particular type or class of problem.
   a. Domain expert
   b. Knowledge engineer
   c. Domain engineer
   d. Knowledge expert

CASES AND EXERCISES

16–18. Several ways in which expert systems can be used as a tool of the auditor are described in the chapter. List and describe some additional applications for expert systems as tools of the auditor, not mentioned in the chapter, that may be areas for future development.

16–19. The revenue and collection cycle has received the most attention in the development of expert systems. Why do you believe this is so? Which cycles do you believe are most likely to receive the attention of expert systems developers in the future? Which do you believe are the least likely to receive their attention?

16–20. The greatest impact of expert systems on the control structure is on the general control of systems development and documentation. Describe how expert systems might affect the control structure for the other general controls.

16–21. Controlled processing, controlled reprocessing, parallel simulation, and test records are described as the most appropriate computerized techniques for the audit testing of expert systems. Discuss why each of the following computerized techniques are not included in this list:
   a. Integrated test facility
   b. Custom-designed programs
   c. Generalized audit software
   d. Utility programs

16–22. One of the inference searching techniques that an auditor of expert systems is likely to encounter is backward chaining. Using the following for purposes of discussion, describe how you would audit the expert system.

Backward Chaining

IF	
	Prior audit is bad
and	Reports are late
THEN	
	Call manager
	Audit in three months
IF	
	Audit was qualified or unsatisfactory
THEN	
	Prior audit was bad
IF	
	Reports are not here
and	Due date was at least five days ago
THEN	
	Reports are late

16-23. Various searching strategies are available as inference searching techniques for expert systems. Using the paths shown below for purposes of discussion, how would you:

a. Determine whether the system is using a depth-first, breadth-first, or heuristic search technique?

b. Audit the expert system incorporating the technique?

Path 1	Path 2	Path 3
IF test of details risk is greater than 50 percent AND IF account balance has changed since last audit THEN audit account	IF account balance exceeds 10 percent of net income AND IF account balance has changed since last audit THEN audit account	IF account balance has not changed since last audit PHOTOCOPY work paper and DO NOT audit account

INDEX

Access controls
    computer facilities, 270–271
    customer file information, 525–526
    data communication, 277–279
    files, 424–425
    on-line, 273
    programs and files, 505
    proprietary programs, 525
Accountability function, 147
Accounting controls, 17–18, 119–122 (see also Controls)
Accounting department, 12
Acoustic couplers (see Modems)
Address, 28
    change, 252
    validity, 243
Algorithm, 277
Alphanumeric condition test, 321
American Accounting Association (AAA), 108
American Institute of Certified Public Accountants (AICPA), 2, 206, 208
Analog computers, 22
Analytical tools, 75–105
Annotation symbol, flowcharting, 81
Anticipation control, 326, 361
Application controls, 18, 472, 506–509 (see also Controls)
    definition of, 305
    expert systems, 556–559

Application controls (Contd.)
    methodology, 305–310
    user-controlled systems, 510–511
Application program error check, 245
Application programming, 153
Application software, data processing system, 31
Applications
    computers, 9–10, 22
    third-party systems, 520
Arithmetic accuracy tests, 362
Arithmetic and logic unit, 29
Arithmetic code, 26–27
Artificial intelligence (AI), 7
Assembler programs, 8, 33, 247
Assembly language, 32
Assembly of data, 317
Asynchronous mode, 56
Audit
    flowchart, 77
    indicator, 407
    significance, system security controls, 266–267
    software, 428–431
    testing, 554–555, 559
Audit trail
    for batch input, 329
    for data capture, 316–317
    definition of, 5–6, 117–118, 310–312
    and flowcharts, 77

Audit trail (*Contd.*)
  for on-line entry, 356–357
  for output, 371
  for processing, 365
Auditing
  around the computer, 13–14, 127–129, 447, 452
  changes in approach to, 13–15
  computer, 110–111
  computer files and data bases, 421–444
  concepts, 106–142
  concurrently with processing, 130
  conventions, 195
  definition of, 108
  and EDP, 1–19
  the phases of processing, 130–131
  skills, 15–17
  standards, 2–3, 15, 17
  through the computer, 14–15, 128–129
  with the computer, 14, 128–129
Auditing, computer processing
  expert systems, 547–563
  general concepts, 445–495
  third-party systems, 518–546
  user-controlled systems, 496–516
Auditing, computer programs, 393–420
  controls and substantive testing techniques, 395–411
  dual-purpose testing, 412
  tests of controls, 394–395
Auditing process
  assessing control risk, 109, 111–123
  effect of computer on, 110–111
  internal control, 109
Auditor's control office, 411
Authentication, 280–282
Authorization
  controls, 274–275
  function, 146–147
  tables, 275
Automatic error diagnosis, 241–242
Automatic retry, 241

Background checks, 162
Backup, 471, 505–506
  computer facilities and equipment, 285
  magnetic disk files, 286

Backup (*Contd.*)
  software, 285
  source document, 287–288
Backward chaining, 552
Balancing of control totals, 322
BASIC (Beginners All-purpose Symbolic Instruction Code), 32
Batch control, 319–320, 325
Batch control, on-line entry, 354–355
Batch data entry controls, summary, 330–331
Batch data preparation, 317
Batch header record, 320
Batch input, 324–325
Batch input, controls to match error correction system design, 326–328
Batch input/batch processing, 46–48
Batch logs, 320
Batch transmittal and route slips, 320
Baud rate, 54
Beams, 280
Binary coding methods, 26–28
Binary system, 25–26
Bit (binary digit), 25
Black box approach, 446
Block diagrams, 82
Blocks, records, 41, 43
Boundary protection, 243, 249
Breadth-first search, 552–553
Breakpoints, 366
Buffering, 24
Business data processing, 22
Bypass procedures, 283–284
Byte, 25

Cameras, 281
Carbon dioxide fire extinguisher systems, 283
Cathode-ray tube (CRT), 23
Central Processing Unit (CPU), 23, 28–30
Chaining, 551–552
Channel, communication, 54
  full-duplex, 57
  half-duplex, 57
  simplex, 57
Channels, input/output
  multiplexor, 24
  selector, 24
Character code, 26–27

Character validity, 243
Check digit, 321–322
Circulating error file, 327
COBOL (Common Business Oriented Language), 32
Code checking, 398
Code conversion, 24
Coding, 26–28, 35, 192–195
COMBI (COBOL Missed Branch Indicator), 407
Communication channels (see Channels, communication)
Communication control unit (CCU), 55
Compiler program, 33
Compilers, 8, 247
Computation, 22
Computer access, 505
Computer-assisted procedures, on-line entry, 353–354
Computer auditors, 126–132
Computer dialogue, 354
Computer files and data bases
    controls and substantive testing techniques, 423–435
    dual purpose testing, 435
    substantive testing, 423
    tests of controls, 422–423
Computer graphics terminals, 52
Computer output microfilm (COM), 23
Computer processing
    general concepts
        integration of parts, nonprocessing of data, 446, 447–452
        integration of types of tests, 446, 452–459
    third-party systems
        auditing, 528–530
        characteristics, 518–521
        controls, 521–528
    user-controlled systems
        auditing, 509–512
        control and audit problems, 497–500
        controls, 500–509
Computers
    analog, 22
    applications, 9–10, 22
    and changes in auditing, 13–15
    and changes in hardware, 3–8
    changes in location of, 11–13
    and changes in software, 8–11

Computers (Contd.)
    data-base management systems, 10–11
    definition of, 22
    digital, 22
    effect on accounting control, 115–126
    equipment, 22–25
    first-generation, 5
    languages, 8–9
    micro-, 7–8
    mini-, 7–8
    multiprogramming, 6
    operating systems, 10
    operation of, 25–30
    overview of, 21–30
    problems with, 4–8
    role in testing, 126–132
    second and third generation, 6
    and service bureaus, 13
    storage, 37–45
    subsequent generations, 6–8
    and time sharing, 13
Concentrators, 54–55
Concurrent auditing, 406–408
Concurrent updating, 471
Console logs, 166
Construction controls, 269–270
Continuing professional education (CPE), 162
Continuous auditing by exception, 406
Continuous processing, 406
Control
    and auditing process, 109
    environment, 13
    and file updating, 35
    group procedures, output, 369–370
    monitors, 407
    procedures, 113–114
    and risk assessment, 109, 111–123
    structure, 112–114
    totals, 507
    unit, 28–29
    worksheet, 409
Controlled processing and reprocessing, 402–404
Controls
    accounting, 17–18
    application, 118–119, 305–310
    applications, for user-controlled systems, 506–509
    audit trail, 310–312

Controls (*Contd.*)
 batch data entry, 317–330
 complex systems, 466–468
 data capture and data entry, 304–351
 data processing, 507–508
 documentation, 468–469
 EDP, 119–122
 environmental, 244
 expert systems, 556–559
 general, 118–119, 122–123
 hardware and software, 469
 hardware and systems software, 232–263
 magnetic tape, 43–44
 methodology, 305–310
 on-line entry, 353–357, 372–373
 output, 367–371, 372–373
 positive attitude toward, 164
 processing, 357–367, 372–373
 program change, 203–206
 responsibility for, 158–160
 standard operating procedures, 144, 165–167
 system documentation, 206–215
 system security, 264–303
 systems development, 186–206, 468–469
 systems development and documentation, 185–231
 user, 17–18, 119–122
 user-controlled systems, 501–505
Controls, organization, 143–184, 466–467
 assignment of responsibilities, 150–151
 control function, 151–152
 division of knowledge, 157–158
 responsibility, 158–160
 segregation of EDP and user functions, 145–146
 segregation of functions within EDP department, 149–150
 segregation of incompatible functions, 146–149
 separation of duties, 152–154
 size, 154–156
 understanding and test of, 160–161
Controls, personnel practices, 144
 attitudes, 164–165
 formalization, 164
 hiring and evaluation, 161–163
 scheduling, 165
 understanding and testing of, 165

Controls, testing, 122–123
 batch data entry, 323, 329
 data capture, 317
 hardware, 245–247
 organization, 148–149, 158, 160–161, 165, 167
 software, 254–256
 system security, 278–279, 281–282, 288
 systems development, 192, 196, 197, 198, 200, 201, 203, 206
Conventions, flowcharts, 77, 78, 82–88, 193–195
Conversion
 control, 201
 data, 35
Cradle-to-grave flowchart testing, 82
Cross-footing tests, 363
Cross-reference listings, 214
Cryptoboxes, 278
Custom-designed programs, 427–428, 431–433
Cylinders, 44–45

Data
 approval test, 356
 base, 10–11, 39, 60
 calculation, 35
 capture, 33–34
 classification test, 321
 coding, 35
 collection terminals, 53
 comparison, 35–36
 conversion, 35
 dictionary, 61–62
 echo check, 355
 entry
  definition of, 35
  on-line, 355–356
  terminals, 51
 limit tests, 363
 live, 395
 nonprocessing of, 396–401, 423–425
 preparation, batch, 34–35
 preparation equipment, 24–25
 processing, third-party systems, 527
 real, 395
 reasonableness tests, 362
 records locks, 275
 recovery, 244, 285–286

Data (*Contd.*)
   representation, 25–26
   review, 318
   schema, 62
   set, 54
   structures, 38, 62–63
   summarization, 36
   validation, 35, 320
   value, 38
   verification, 356
Data-base administrator, 60
Data-base management system
      (DBMS), 10–11, 60–61, 247
Data capture controls
   approval, 314
   audit trail, 316–317
   batch, 315
   error correction procedures, 316
   forms security, 34
   identification, 314
   personnel practices, 314
   prenumbering, 313
   separation of duties, 314
   source document design, 313
   summary, 330–331
   user review, 315
   users procedure manuals, 313
Data communication, 50
   access control, 277–279
   concepts, 55–57
   devices, 51–55
   errors, 236–237
Data descriptive language (DDL), 60
Data manipulation language (DML),
      60
Data processing system
   functions, 33–37
   output function, 36–37
   overview, 30–37
Debugging, 195
Decision logic tables (DLT), 88–97
Decison tree conventions, 192–195
Default option, 360
Demodulation, 53
Depth-first search, 552–553
Desk checking, 398
Detection devices, 279–280
Digital computers, 22
Disk drive, 236
Disk pack, 44
Diskettes, 44, 58, 505
Display terminals, 51–52
Distortion, 237

Distributed data entry, 66
Distributed data processing, 63–66,
      67
Distributed networks, 64–65
Distributed storage, 66
Distribution
   checklist, 368
   controls, 508–509
   log, 368
   schedule, 368
Document flowchart, 77
Documentation
   controls, 212–213, 468–469, 523–
      525
   definition of, 206–208
   operations, 210–211
   problem definition, 208–209
   program, 209–210
   software aids to, 213–214
   systems, 209
   user, 211–212
Domain expert, 553
Double arithmetic, 362
Double parity bit, 238–240
Dual field input, 362
Dual operation, 241
Dual-purpose testing, 125–126, 412,
      435–436, 458–459
Dual read, 240
Dummy company, 411
Duplicate process check, 240–241

Echo check, 241
EDP
   and auditing, 1–19
   concepts, 20–74
   controls, accounting, 17–18, 119–
      122
   controls, user, 17–18
   personnel, 150–151
   technicians, 16–17
Electronic dichotomy, 26
Encryption, 250, 257
Environmental controls, 244
Equipment
   check, 241–242
   failure, 235–236, 243–244
Errors
   acceptable level of, 307–308
   correction code, 36, 240, 356–357
   detection, correction, and resub-
      mission, 145–146

Errors (*Contd.*)
  during data conversion, 323
  listings, 400–401
  reports, 37
  from source, 323
Evaluations, personnel, 162–163
Exception reports, 37
Execution function, 147
Executive programs (*see* Operating
  systems)
Expert systems, 7
  audit testing, 559
  as auditor's tool, 553–555
  basic concepts and terminology,
    548–552
  control structure, 556–559
  as part of the audit, 555–559
Extended Binary Coded Decimal Interchange Code (EBCDIC), 26
Extended test data, 411
External labels, 272
External references, 249

Facilities security controls, 268–271
Fading, 237
Fetching, 29
Fidelity bonds, 162
Field
  definition of, 38
  presence check, 326
  size test, 321
File access control testing, 424–425
File
  backup, 471, 505–506
  control standards, 166
  definition of, 39
  description generators, 214
  labels, 43, 251–252, 361
  maintenance, 36
  protection, 251–252
  protection ring, 44
  reconstruction, 505–506
  storage media, 42–45
  updating, 36
File organization
  direct, 40–41
  indexed sequential, 41
  list, 41–42
  sequential, 39–40
Financial totals, 320
Fire detection devices, 279–280
Fire extinguishing, 282–283

Flat file structure, 62
Floppy disks, 44, 59–60
Flowchart
  packages, 214
  verification, 397–398
Flowcharting
  advantages, 76–77
  conventions, 77, 78, 82–88, 193
  program, 82–88
  systems, 77–82
  testing, 77–78, 81–82, 88
Foreign and Corrupt Practices Act of
  1977, 267, 307
Formatting, 319
FORTRAN (Formula Translator), 32
Forward chaining, 551
Fragmentation, 277
Framing, 550
Full-duplex channel, 57
Functions
  accountability, 147
  authorization, 146–147
  data processing system, 33–37
  execution, 147
  librarian, 153
  segregation of (*see* Controls)

GANNT Chart, 192–193
Generalized audit software, 428–431
Generally accepted auditing stan-
  dards (GAAS), 2
Graph plotters, 23
Grid charts, 97–98

Half-duplex channel, 57
Halon gas fire extinguisher systems,
  283
Hard disks, 44
Hardware, 3–8
  data processing system, 30
  small computer systems, 58–59
  third-party systems, 519
  user-controlled systems, 498
Hardware controls, 233–247, 469
  expert systems, 556–558
  third-party systems, 523–524
  user-controlled systems, 503
Hardwiring, 254
Hash totals, 320
Heat-sensitive devices, 279–280
Heuristic search, 552–553

Hexadecimal code, 26–27
Hiring
  background checks, 162
  fidelity bonds, 162
  tests, 162
Horizontal parity bit, 239
Housekeeping, 166

Identification controls, 275–277
If-then rules, 549–551
Incompatible assignments, 450
Inference searching techniques, 551
Information systems group, 12
Input
  data processing systems, 45–51
  devices, 23
  function, data processing system, 33
  validation, 325
Input/output
  channels, 24
  devices, 23–24
Inquiry, 36
Installation and change control, 253
Insurance coverage, 283
Integrated test facility (ITF), 408–412, 435
Integration
  of parts, nonprocessing of data, 447–452
  of types of tests, 446, 452–459
Intelligent terminal, 48, 58
Intersubsystem totals, 363
Interactive computing, 52
Intermediate records, 5–6
Internal control flowchart, 77
Internal header and trailer labels, 272
Internal storage, 5
Interpreters, 59
Invalid data combination test, 326

Job control routines, 195
Job documentation, 212–213
Job-run procedures, 166

Key, 39
Key entry validation, 320–323
Key, special, 273, 275
Keyboard/printers, 53
Knowledge engineer, 553

Languages
  computer, 8–9
  programming, 32–33
Layout charts, 97
Librarian package, software, 214
Librarians, 504
Library controls, system security, 271–273
Library function, 153, 469, 470–471
Library program
  control reports, 250–251
  software, 249–251
Limit tests, 321, 507–508
Line printers, 23
Linkage editing, 249
Live data, 395
Local area network (LAN), 64
Location controls, 269
Log, 320, 368
  activity analysis and maintenance, 252
  computer usage, 281
  console, 166
  systems software changes, 253
Logic
  diagrams, 82
  supervisors, 407
  tests, 321
Longitudinal parity bit, 239
Low error environment, 318

Machine language, 8, 32
Machine operation and performance, 166
Macro instruction, 33
Magnetic disk, 23, 44–45, 286
Magnetic ink character readers, 23
Magnetic tape, 42–44, 272–273, 286
Magnetic tape drives, 23, 236, 241–242
Maintenance, hardware, 245
Management and accounting reports, 37
Management objectives, 307–308
Manual systems, 3–4, 164
Mapping, 406
Master files, 39
Mechanical systems, 4
Media controls, 243
Memo file (see Reference data file)
Memory clear, 252
Menus, 59

Message intermixing, 277
Methodology, controls (*see* Controls)
Microcomputers, 7–8, 58
Microfilm, 23
Microphones, 280
Microswitches, 280
Minicompany, 411
Minicomputers, 7–8, 57
Missed branch indicator, 407
Modems, 53–54
Modulation, 53, 55–56
Monitoring, 281
Monitors (*see* Operating systems)
Multiple files, 453–454
Multiple terminals, 505
Multiple tests, 452
Multiplexor channels, 24
Multiplexors, 54–55
Multiprogramming, 6, 49–50
Multipurpose terminals, 51–52

National Bureau of Standards (NBS),
    277
Networks
    distributed, 64–65
    hybrid, 65
    ring, 65
    star, 64
    structure, 63
Noise, 237
Nondestructive update, 365
Nonprivileged instructions, 253–254

Object code, 8
Object program, 33
Objectives, management and sys-
    tem, 307–309
Off-line storage symbol, flowchart-
    ing, 81
Off-site processing (*see* Third-party
    processing)
On-line access controls, 273
On-line entry, 353–357
On-line input/batch processing, 48–
    50
On-line input/real-time processing,
    50–51
On/off page connectors, flowchart-
    ing, 80–81
Operand, 29
Operating systems, 10, 249–250, 520

Operation
    code, 29
    program error check, 245
    validity, 242
Operational controls, 243–245
Operations documentation, 210–211
Optical character recognition, 23
Optical mark recognition, 23
Organization controls (*see also* Con-
    trols)
    expert systems, 556–558
    third-party systems, 521–522
    user-controlled systems, 501
Output
    controls, 367–371, 508–509 (*see
        also* Controls)
    devices, 23
    error correction and resubmission
        procedures, 370–371
    function, data processing system,
        36–37
    handling procedures, 368
    third-party systems, 527–528
Overflow check, 362

Packed decimal, 26
Parallel
    simulation, 404–406
    tests, 199
Parity bit, 26–27
Passwords, 250, 252, 276, 504
Periodic evaluations, 162–163
Periodic reports, 37
Personnel
    career paths, 163–164
    data processing system, 31–32
    evaluations, 162–163
    expert systems, 553
    formalization of practices, 164
    hiring, 162–163
    position descriptions, 150–151
    practices, 467, 501, 556–558
    scheduling, 163
    third-party systems, 521, 522
    time records, 166
Physiology, in identification, 275
Pilot tests, 199
PL/1 (Programming Language 1), 32
Point-of-sale terminals, 52
Position descriptions (*see* Personnel)
Postentry batch control, 354–355

Postimplementation review, 201–202

Power
  protection, 244
  supply, 471

Preparation, data, 35 (*see also* Batch data preparation)

Preventive maintenance, 245

Primary storage unit, 28

Printer, 236

Printout examination, 399–401, 425

Privileged mode, 253–254

Problem definition documentation, 208

Procedures, data processing system, 31

Process control, 22

Processing, 357–367
  actual data, 455–457
  actual file data, 425–433
  continuous, 406
  controlled, 402–403
  controls, 508
  error correction and resubmission procedures, 364
  function, data processing systems, 35
  simulated data, 408–412, 433–435, 457–458
  use of expert systems in, 555–556

Production systems, 549–551

Program
  documentation, 213, 209–210
  flowchart, 77, 82–88
  listing reports, 250, 251
  listing verification, 398, 425
  listings, 33
  protection, 249–251
  tests, 199

Program changes
  controls, 203–204
  developing, 204–205
  implementing, 205–206
  planning, 204

Program code
  checking, 398–399
  formatting systems, 214

Programming
  conventions, 193–195
  languages, 32–33

Programs
  compiler, 33
  custom, 427–428

Programs (*Contd.*)
  machine language, 8
  object, 33
  source, 33
  subroutine, 33
  utility, 427

Project management, 192–193

Proper account classifications, 425

Proper authorization, 425

Proper time periods, 425

Protective rings, 272–273

Punched cards, 23

Query language, 60

Radar detectors, 280

Read after write operation, 241

Read or write error routine, 248

Read/write head, 44

Real data, 395

Real-time systems, 7, 15

Reasonableness tests, 507–508

Reconciliation of debits to credits on input, 507

Record-only switch, 273

Records
  confirmation check, 356
  contents, 320
  definition of, 38
  identification tests, 361
  intermediate, 5–6
  length check, 248
  organization, 39

Recovery
  plan, 284
  procedures, 244, 284–288

Redundant character check, 237–240

Reference
  data file, 49
  reports, 37

Regression analysis programs, 431–433

Remote terminals, 51–53

Report release forms, 368

Reports, 37

Reverse multiplication, 362

RPG (Report Program Generator), 32

Run-to-run totals, 363

Sample-of-one flowchart testing, 82
SCARF (System Control Audit Review File), 406–407
Scheduling, 165
Screen
 controls, 506–507
 editing, 507
 formats, 354
 formatting, 506–507
Searching strategies, 552–553
Secondary storage, 23
Security (*see also* Systems security controls)
 management, 267–268
 procedures, 167
 protection, 252
Segregation of duties, 253 (*see also* Controls)
Selector channels, 24, 55
Self-protection, 253–254
Semantic networks, 551
Separate tests, 452, 454–455
Sequence tests, 325, 361
Sequencing, 36
Service bureaus, 13 (*see also* Third-party processing)
Sign test, 321
Simplex channel, 57
Simulated data processing, 408–412
Single parity bit, 238–240
Single tests, 452
Smoke-sensitive detection devices, 280
Snapshots, 195, 407
Software, 8–11, 33
 aids, 213–214
 backup, 285
 controls, 469 (*see also* Systems software)
 data processing system, 31
 generalized audit, 428–431
 small computer systems, 58–59
 system controls, expert systems, 556–558
 third-party systems, 520
 user-controlled systems, 498–499
Source code, 8
Source code listing report, 250–251
Source document, 287–288
Source program, 33
Source statement change summary report, 250

Special-purpose programs (*see* Custom-designed programs)
Sprinkler systems, 283
Standard operating procedures
 general concepts, 467–468
 organization controls, 166–167
 third-party systems, 520–521, 522–523
 user-controlled systems, 501–502
Standards
 auditing, 2–3, 15, 17
 documentation, 207–208
 programming, 193–195
Storage, 5, 23, 37–45
 device check, 248
 protection, 243 (*see also* Program protection)
String tests, 199
Structure
 flat file, 62
 network, 63
 tree, 62
Subroutine programs, 33
Substantial tests, 110, 111, 123–125
Substantive testing
 auditing around the computer, 451–452
 computer files and data bases, 423
 computer programs, 395
 expert systems, 559
 third-party systems, 530
 user-controlled systems, 511–512
Supervision, 166–167
SUPERZAP, 251, 253, 470
Suspense file, 327
Symbols, flowcharts, 80–81
Synchronous mode, 56
Systems
 analysis, 153
 balancing controls, 363
 complexity cross-reference, 254–255
 development and documentation (*see* Controls)
 documentation, 212–213
 expert, 7
 flowchart, 77
 implementation, 189–192
 modification program control, 251, 253
 monitoring, 281
 objectives, 308–309
 planning, 189–192

Systems (*Contd.*)
  procedure manual, 164, 210–211
  programming, 153
  real-time, 7, 15
  testing, 199
  utilities, 153
Systems development, 186–187,
      189–192
  auditor's role in, 187–188
  controls, 468–469
  conversion control, 201
  documentation controls, user-con-
      trolled systems, 503
  final approval, 200
  management, user, and auditor re-
      view and approval, 197–198
  methodology, 189–192
  postimplementation review, 201–
      203
  program change controls, 203–206
  programming conventions and
      procedures, 193–196
  project management, 192–193
  systems testing, 199–200
  test of controls, 192, 201, 206
  third-party systems, 523–524
  user, accounting, and audit partici-
      pation, 196–197
System security controls, 469–470
  audit significance of, 266–267
  definition of, 265
  expert systems, 556–558
  facilities, 268–271
  for failure detection, 279–282
  for failure recovery, 282–289
  library, 271–273
  on-line access, 273–279
  security management, 267–268
  user controlled systems, 503–508
Systems software controls, 469
  file protection, 251–252
  handling errors, 248–249
  program protection, 249–251
  security protection, 252
  self-protection, 253–254
  system complexity cross-refer-
      ences, 254–255

Tagging, 195, 406, 407
Tape (*see also* Magnetic tape)
  density, 42
  marks, 43

Technicians, EDP, 16–17
Teleprocessing, 7
Terminal symbol, flowcharting, 80
Terminals
  authorized, 274
  computer graphics, 52
  data collection, 53
  data entry, 51
  display, 51–52
  display controls, 369
  identification, 275
  intelligent, 48, 52
  keyboard/printers, 53
  multipurpose, 51–52
  physical security of, 273
  point-of-sale, 52
  private, 274
  remote, 51–53
  touch-tone devices, 52–53
Test data generators, 409
Test records, 409, 434–435
Testing
  access controls, 424–425
  computer programs, 395
  controls, 148–149, 158, 160–161,
      165, 167
  decision logic tables, 94–97
  dual-purpose, 125–126, 412, 435–
      436, 458–459
  expert systems, 559
  flowcharts, 77–78, 81–82, 88
  substantial, 110, 111, 123–125
  system, 199
Tests of controls
  auditing around the computer,
      448–451
  computer programs, 394–395
  third-party systems, 528–530
Theoretical flow of data, 209
Third-party systems
  characteristics, 518–521
  controls, 521–528
  auditing, 528–530
Time records, 166
Time sharing, 13 (*see also* Third-
      party systems)
Touch-tone devices, 52–53
Tracing, 406
Tracks, 44–45
Transaction
  code, 321, 361
  documents, 37
  input, 45–46

Transaction (*Contd.*)
  log, 49, 473
  processing, 46
Transmission mode, 56–57
Transmittal sheets, 368
Tree structure, 62
Turnaround documents, 318–319

Ultrasonic detectors, 280
Unit record equipment (*see* Mechanical systems)
Universal Product Code (UPC), 52
Upstream resubmission, 328–329
User
  controls, 119–121
  documentation, 211–212
  identification, 275
  procedures, output, 369
  reconciliations, 508
User-controlled systems, 497
  application controls, 510–511
  auditing, 509–512

User-controlled systems (*Contd.*)
  control and audit problems in, 497–500
  controls in, 500–509
  substantive tests, 511–512
  tests of controls, 509–510
Users, authorized, 274–275
Utilities, 60, 247
Utility
  programs, 427
  scan, 253

Valid action, 242–243
Validity check, 242–243
Value test, 321
Verifying data, 356
Vertical parity bit, 239
Visual display terminals (VDTs), 23

Walkthrough flowchart test, 82
Wide area network (WAN), 64
Written procedures, 318, 324, 353